UNDERSTANDING and TEACHING PRIMARY GEOGRAPHY

Sara Miller McCune founded SAGE Publishing in 1965 to support the dissemination of usable knowledge and educate a global community. SAGE publishes more than 1000 journals and over 800 new books each year, spanning a wide range of subject areas. Our growing selection of library products includes archives, data, case studies and video. SAGE remains majority owned by our founder and after her lifetime will become owned by a charitable trust that secures the company's continued independence.

Los Angeles | London | New Delhi | Singapore | Washington DC | Melbourne

UNDERSTANDING and TEACHING PRIMARY GEOGRAPHY

2ND EDITION

SIMON CATLING

TESSA WILLY

⑤SAGE

Los Angeles | London | New Delhi
Singapore | Washington DC | Melbourne

Los Angeles | London | New Delhi
Singapore | Washington DC

SAGE Publications Ltd
1 Oliver's Yard
55 City Road
London EC1Y 1SP

SAGE Publications Inc.
2455 Teller Road
Thousand Oaks, California 91320

SAGE Publications India Pvt Ltd
B 1/I 1 Mohan Cooperative Industrial Area
Mathura Road
New Delhi 110 044

SAGE Publications Asia-Pacific Pte Ltd
3 Church Street
#10-04 Samsung Hub
Singapore 049483

Editor: Amy Thornton
Copy Editor: Diana Chambers
Proof reader: Clare Weaver
Senior Project Editor: Chris Marke
Marketing Manager: Lorna Patkai
Cover design: Wendy Scott
Typeset by: C&M Digitals (P) Ltd, Chennai, India
Printed and bound in the UK

First published in 2009 by Learning Matters Ltd
Second edition published in 2018
© Simon Catling and Tessa Willy

Library of Congress Control Number 2018939030

British Library Cataloguing in Publication Data

ISBN 978-1-5264-0838-9
ISBN 978-1-5264-0839-6 (pbk)

At SAGE we take sustainability seriously. Most of our products are printed in the UK using responsibly sourced papers and
boards. When we print overseas we ensure sustainable papers are used as measured by the PREPS grading system.
We undertake an annual audit to monitor our sustainability.

CONTENTS

About the authors   vii

Acknowledgements   ix

Introduction   x

Part 1 Understanding Primary Geography   **1**

1 Geography in primary schools   3

2 Valuing geography: the importance and nature of geography   30

3 Children's geographies: experience, awareness and understanding   55

4 Understanding geographical enquiry   103

5 Exploring places: key ideas in understanding places   126

6 Understanding the environment: aspects of physical,
   human and environmental geography   148

7 Exploring sustainability: environmental impact,
   sustainability and sustainable schools   195

8 Geography and social justice: citizenship,
   equity and controversial issues   219

9 Experiencing and visualising geography: fieldwork,
   photographs, artefacts and maps   247

Part 2 Exploring Geography Teaching and Curriculum   291

10 In the beginning: geographical learning in the early years   293

11 Investigating the school and its grounds   316

12 Exploring locally, regionally and nationally   339

13 Exploring global dimensions and places elsewhere in the world 378

14 Planning primary geography teaching   422

15 Assessing geographical learning   456

16 Developing learning in primary geography education   484

Appendix 1 Examples of primary geography
curriculum requirements and guidance internationally   509
Appendix 2 Examples of geographically-informed
children's picture story books   514
References   518
Index   565

ABOUT THE AUTHORS

Simon Catling taught in several primary schools in London, including holding a deputy headship, before moving to Oxford Brookes University, where he was latterly Professor of Primary Education and tutor in primary geography in the School of Education. Widely experienced in primary teaching and teacher education, he held roles as Dean of Education and Assistant Dean for programmes and research development. In 1992–3 Simon was President of the Geographical Association in the UK. He has written more than 280 publications on geographical education for teachers, children, student teachers and researchers, presented at national and international conferences, contributed to developments in primary geography, and run many teachers' continuing professional development courses during his career. His interests include younger children's geographies, the nature of geography, primary geography textbooks and information books, citizenship and social justice, and children's voice in primary geography. Between 2008 and 2012 he was Honorary Secretary of the International Geographical Union Commission on Geographical Education and has been a long-standing member of its UK Committee. Though Simon retired formally from his university post in 2012, he remains actively involved in geography education, including being a member of the Geographical Association's Early Years and Primary Committee and of the Geography Education Research Collective (GEReCo). He has contributed to England's national curriculum geography developments since the 1980s. In 2015 he edited *Research and Debate in Primary Geography* (Routledge) and in 2017 edited *Reflections on Primary Geography* (Register of Research in Primary Geography). Simon was awarded the title of Professor Emeritus in 2012 and was awarded Honorary Membership of the Geographical Association in 2017.

Tessa Willy has been Associate Professor, School Director of Teacher Education at Kingston University, since early 2018. She spent the first years of her career as both a primary school teacher in a variety of different settings across the UK and a secondary school geography teacher in the UK as well as in Malawi. Moving into higher education, she worked as senior lecturer in primary geography at the University of Roehampton, where she developed an outdoor environmental area with colleagues and students that has been used as a model in initial teacher education and continuing professional development for teachers. Tessa became the Programme Leader for the PGCE Primary course at the University of Roehampton from 2010 to 2012 before joining the UCL Institute of Education, London. From 2012, she was tutor in primary geography initial teacher education and also focused on the school direct programme and university school partnership. Her areas of particular interest are in issues around the ethics of geography, notably climate change, sustainability, social justice and global citizenship. Tessa has been a member of the Editorial Board of the Geographical Association's journal *Primary Geography* and has edited several issues.

Dedication

This edition of *Understanding and Teaching Primary Geography* is dedicated to the participants in the Charney Manor Primary Geography Conferences for their joy, compassion, knowledge, thoughtfulness and contributions to primary geography research, practice and thinking over many years. We have appreciated so much all that they have given.

We also dedicate this edition to our families and friends with love and our deepest thanks for their support in this venture.

ACKNOWLEDGEMENTS

We wish to acknowledge the contribution of John Butler to the development of this second edition of *Understanding and Teaching Primary Geography*. He was a valuable co-author when we revised the original edition (2009) of *Teaching Primary Geography* for Australian primary schools in 2013, as *Teaching Primary Geography for Australian Schools*. We have made use of much that we learned from him.

We wish also to thank the many colleagues who have attended the Charney Manor Primary Geography Conferences in Charney Bassett, Oxfordshire, since 1995, who unwittingly have contributed more than they will ever know to the thinking behind the first and this second edition of *Understanding and Teaching Primary Geography*.

We are very grateful to the range of schools that have been visited and from which we have gained much knowledge, understanding and experience during our careers.

Our grateful thanks go to Amy Thornton and colleagues at SAGE/Learning Matters for their support, patience and help during the preparation of this edition.

Simon Catling and Tessa Willy

INTRODUCTION

Geography is fundamental in everybody's experience – the daily experiences of every adult and every child, wherever they are in the world. Geography concerns how we understand and use places, the spatial and environmental experiences of our daily lives, and our information about and connections with places elsewhere in the world. It concerns, for instance, where and how we live, how we feed ourselves, the journeys we make and the connections we have with places and other people. Geography explores, investigates, examines, analyses, extrapolates from, seeks to understand and explain, and is concerned to develop our appreciation of the world, its places, environments and as a whole. It examines the ways in which we live on and make use of what our planet offers, where this happens and why it occurs where it does, how we inhabit and change places, the Earth's natural and human resources and processes, our impact on the Earth and the variety of ways it affects us. We do this at a range of scales from our neighbourhood to the wider region, nationally and globally. Geography investigates the opportunities, benefits, challenges, dangers, constraints, awe and fascination our world provides. It is our home, as humans, that we share with a multitude of other living creatures and plants, and with which we are utterly interdependent. It is important that we think carefully about this, understand our world and act responsibly.

Understanding and Teaching Primary Geography provides an introduction to geography for those teaching and intending to teach in primary and elementary education. It explores aspects of the subject and examines the teaching of geography with younger children. By 'younger children' we mean children aged from 3/4 to 11/12 years of age. This book draws on a wide range of sources from within the geography discipline, from geography education and from children's studies, as well as from yet other sources. These communities intertwine in the context of children's geographies, a theme that underpins our perspective and approach. The book is about the knowledge, curriculum, teaching and learning of geography for children in pre-school and school settings.

For us, its authors, geography is an essential subject for all children at every age. Its teaching needs to draw on how children make sense of the world for themselves, and it has to enable them to make greater sense of and take them into new experiences of and perspectives on places, environments and the Earth, and its peoples and the processes involved. Geography is a school subject that has evident links with its academic discipline, and both are concerned to enable children to become increasingly aware of their own places as well as with those of others as yet beyond their experience and appreciation. The purpose of *Understanding and Teaching Primary Geography* is to support teaching children from their earliest years at school to enable them to know about and understand the world better, and to appreciate it for what it truly is: our home, a fragile blue planet, of which we must take great care and which during their lifetimes is facing many changes and challenges, not least to do with our uses of its land, its climate, its oceans and our interdependence on each other. This book provides knowledge and guidance about the geography that might be included in children's curricula and how it might be taught as children undertake the first part of their journey through school systems.

Geography is included in some form in almost every nation's primary or elementary school curriculum. In some countries it is a named individual subject, but in most nations it is a subject within the social studies area of the curriculum. In a few cases it is intertwined with the science curriculum. Where geography is listed as a distinct curriculum subject, it may be taught as a separate subject, but in many nations it is linked with other subjects in a cross-subject or integrated primary school curriculum. Depending on the country, geography may appear in the curriculum for 5-year-olds or children may not be taught it formally until they are 8, 9 or 10 years old. In a few cases, pre-school curricula initiate aspects of geographical learning for very young children, although they do not identify the subject. *Understanding and Teaching Primary Geography* has been written to support geography teaching in all these contexts during children's earliest educational years and through their primary schooling. Its purpose is to encourage and foster well-grounded geographical understanding for children through high-quality planning, teaching and learning in and of geography for children from 3/4 to 11/12 years old.

Understanding and Teaching Primary Geography is based in developing your subject understanding and teaching capability in geography. It examines and promotes ways in which these two key dimensions underpin teaching geography to support primary age children's progress in learning geography. To provide the best teaching for learning for children, you need a secure understanding of the nature of geography, what is important in its curriculum, how its teaching may be planned and undertaken, a range of approaches through which children's geographical learning can be addressed and assessed, and the variety of resources that can be used. This book explores these aspects of geography teaching.

Understanding and Teaching Primary Geography is organised in two parts with 16 chapters. The first half of the book discusses what geography is, aspects of the subject and children's geographical experience. In the second half, the focus moves on to particular aspects of and approaches to geography teaching, planning and assessment. In Part 1, *Understanding Primary Geography*, Chapter 1 outlines the situation and state of primary geography and identifies some of the current influences on its future for children and schools. Chapter 2 examines geography as a subject and considers its role and value for us all. Understanding and appreciating its centrality to our lives is vital for our futures. Chapter 3 examines the variety of children's geographical experience, emphasising that children bring geographical awareness and engagement into the classroom throughout their early years and primary schooling. Chapter 4 explores geographical enquiry, while Chapters 5, 6, 7 and 8 focus in greater detail at the ideas of place, physical, human and environmental geography, sustainability and environmental impact, and geography and social justice and citizenship. These are considered separately here, but are brought together in later chapters which provide a scale-based approach to developing geographical understanding. Chapter 9 considers fieldwork, photographs and map work as core skills in geography teaching and learning.

In Part 2, *Exploring Geography Teaching and Curriculum*, Chapter 10 introduces the teaching and learning of geography in the pre-school or early years, which sets some of the foundations for children's later geographical learning and understanding. Chapters 11, 12 and 13 explore three developing spatial contexts for geography teaching and learning. They connect studies of place, environment and sustainability from the familiar locales to the world. They emphasise that each of these scales – the local, the regional, the national and the global – can and should be aspects of children's geography curriculum across their schooling, drawing on the concept of a spiral, rather than linear, geography curriculum. Chapters 14 and 15 provide advice about the planning, progression and assessment of geography teaching and learning. Chapter 16 draws together several aspects of children's geographical learning, offers a basis for constructing the primary geography curriculum, and concludes on matters related to researching primary geography in classrooms and schools.

Throughout the book you will find, at different points, examples of geography teaching and learning from across the primary age range, references to relevant research and guidance, and suggestions for geography topics and teaching approaches. Other elements include several information boxes, and practical and reflective tasks throughout the chapters.

In many parts of the world, national professional standards for teachers have been developed. *Understanding and Teaching Primary Geography* is intended to support and enhance your professional practice. The two parts of the book will help you develop your understanding, capability and achievements as primary teachers, whether you are preparing to become a teacher, are in your early years in teaching or are an experienced early childhood or primary teacher. To be able to foster and extend primary children's learning and development, you need to develop and maintain your knowledge and practice in teaching geography, just as you would wish to do in your other subjects and your cross-subject teaching. It will be useful for you to have access to your local and/or national geography curriculum requirements for pre-school children and for primary education as you use this book, so that you can make connections between the advice offered here and your local or national geography curriculum. A valuable way to further your understanding of geography is to make use of the resources on the wide range of geography-based and related websites about the subject and its teaching and learning, and about the extensive variety of topics that make up geographical studies. Some sources are given at the end of each chapter.

Whether already you enjoy geography and have studied it in some depth or you come to it wishing to be inspired about its relevance and value for early years and primary children, we hope that you will find that *Understanding and Teaching Primary Geography* opens your eyes to a fuller sense of what geography is about, how it builds on and deepens children's inherent geographical awareness, interest and understanding, and how you can contribute confidently, effectively and excitingly to their learning. We wish you an enjoyable journey in your teaching, reading and learning.

Simon Catling and Tessa Willy

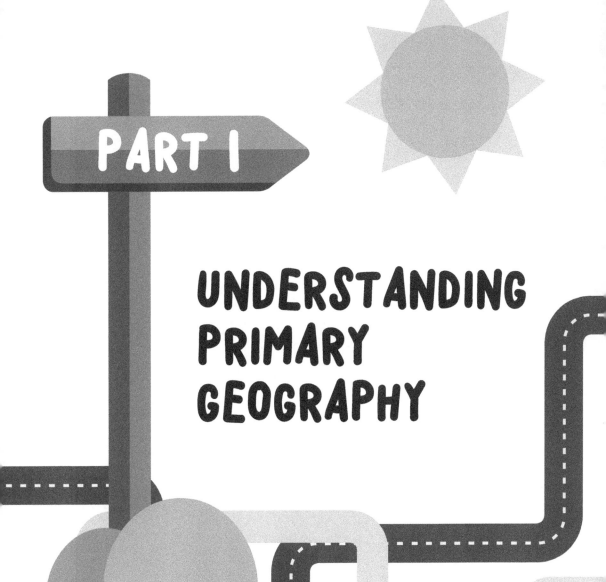

PART 1

UNDERSTANDING PRIMARY GEOGRAPHY

CHAPTER 1

GEOGRAPHY IN PRIMARY SCHOOLS

 Chapter objectives

This chapter enables you to:

- develop an understanding of the situation of geography in primary schools;
- recognise some of the challenges and opportunities for primary geography;
- become aware of how primary geography's teaching and learning can be of high quality and enjoyed;
- reflect on your own experiences in learning geography;
- appreciate various contexts and influences affecting primary geography.

Introduction

Geography is 'the world discipline'.

(Bonnett, 2013, p. 7)

Geography is a fascinating, invigorating, inspiring and exciting subject to teach and learn (IGU-CGE, 2016). Understanding geography makes a difference to ourselves and others (Catling, 2012b). It is fundamental to our appreciation of and knowledge about the world in which we live, including our daily interactions and through the ways the world impacts on us, whether the causes are nearby or occur far away (Dorling and Lee, 2016). Geography studies the world as our home, from the local to the whole planet, and people's lives, activities and events across it; it examines what happens in the natural, physical environment, in human society and the interactions and impacts between the two. It concerns places, what they are, where they are, what happens, how they change, what the effects are – and above all, *why* and *where* and *what next?* It is descriptive, analytic and predictive. Geography investigates causes, influences, consequences, changes and short- and long-term impacts in our environments. It seeks to understand locations, distributions, patterns and processes to help us make sense of the world and to enable us to improve our decisions about what we do that will affect our planet both in our neighbourhood and globally.

The International Geographical Union Commission on Geographical Education's *International Charter on Geographical Education* (IGU-CGE, 2016, pp. 4–5) expresses the nature, importance and significance of geography for all of us at all ages in the following words.

> *Whether it is through appreciating the beauty of the Earth, the immense power of Earth-shaping forces or the often ingenious ways in which people create their living in different environments and circumstances, studying geography helps people to understand and appreciate how places and landscapes are formed, how people and environments interact, the consequences that arise from our everyday spatial decisions, and Earth's diverse and interconnected mosaic of cultures and societies.*

> *Geography is therefore a vital subject and resource for 21st century citizens living in a tightly interconnected world. It enables us to face questions of what it means to live sustainably in this world. Geographically educated individuals understand human relationships and their responsibilities to both the natural environment and to others. Geographical education helps people to learn how to exist harmoniously with all living species.*

> *Geographical investigation both satisfies and nourishes curiosity. Geographical perspectives help deepen understanding of many contemporary challenges such as climate change, food scarcity, energy choices, overexploitation of natural resources and urbanisation. Teaching geography serves several vital*

educational goals. Building on people's own experiences, learning geography helps them to formulate questions, develop their intellectual skills and respond to issues affecting their lives. It introduces them not only to key 21st century skills but also to distinctive investigative tools such as maps, fieldwork and the use of powerful digital communication technologies such as Geographic Information Systems (GIS).

Geographers investigate the Earth's human and physical environments and within these explore what different places, areas and peoples have in common as well as the diversity of our world. Geography is interested in similarities and regularities, looking for patterns to explain what is distributed where, what happens and why, and it is stimulated by differences, what these are, where they occur, why they arise, and how they give us value – just think of the many different places, environments and communities you have been in and are involved with. Difference is a relational concept for geography (Martin, 2012). This means that in order to understand or appreciate similarities and differences we need to be able to relate features, lives, cultures, events and activities to others. What geography recognises is that the consistencies and the variety across our planet and its peoples and ecology are what provide such rich environments for our lives and for exploration and investigation. Relational understanding is vital for informative and transformative geographical learning. It is this that is fascinating and provides such stimulating opportunities for living and learning for us all.

From their earliest years children experience the world about them and begin to build an understanding of it. We have all done this. Both in their local neighbourhood and community and through their encounters with the wider world, each child's 'personal geography' amazes, enthralls and engages them from their first years – the constant encountering of the 'new' and the revisiting of familiar sites that fascinate, entice, or just provide what is wanted at particular times – because of the opportunities and the relational comparisons encountered. As we grow, explore for ourselves and encounter through many sources the 'wider world' – a little further locally or different places altogether, through television, the Internet, stories and travel – we discover the possibilities, the *affordances*, that places offer: We interrelate these and we make use of them in myriad ways. Geography is an aspect of our lives whether we realise and recognise it or not. It is always part of us and always affects us, from the places we love, to the food we eat, to where we want to go and how we feel about the concerns and issues that affect different environments, ourselves and everyone else. Geography is an amazing, essential and fundamental subject.

Throughout this book we provide a variety of insights into ways in which the teaching and learning of geography in primary schools can develop children's geographical awareness, understanding, knowledge, interest and enthusiasm. We begin by considering geography's situation in primary schools and what makes for stimulating and enjoyable teaching and learning.

The chapter concludes by noting that various initiatives and interests provide opportunities for geography's role and development. Some of these are generated by geography educators; others have arisen from emergent and preferred teaching practices, opportunities for development and government policies and priorities in different parts of the world.

Geography in the primary curriculum

Geography appears in one form or another at some point in the primary school curriculum in almost all countries. In some nations it is a named single subject, as in England and Ireland (Catling, 2013a; DES/NCCA, 1999; DfE, 2013; Pike, 2015). In very many countries geography is contained within a humanities and/or social sciences curriculum area, as in Australia, New Zealand and South Africa (Australian Curriculum, 2015; Lane, 2015; Maude, 2014; NZC, 2014; Wilmot and Irwin, 2015; Wassermann, 2017) or included in a social studies curriculum, as in Scotland, the USA, South Korea, Singapore, China, Brazil, Japan, Turkey and Oman, to name just a few (Al-Nofli, 2013; Bednarz et al., 2014; Boyle-Baise and Zevin, 2014; Chang, 2014; Education Scotland, 2009; Halvorsen, 2013; Incekara, 2010; Lastória and Papadimitriou, 2012; Lee and Butt, 2014; Morgan, 2014a; Murayama, 2015; Shimura, 2015; Singapore Ministry of Education, 2012; Xuan et al., 2015; Yoshida, 2015, 2017). It may be linked with one other subject, often history or science, as in Chile, Finland and Germany (Salinas-Silva et al., 2015; Schmeinck, 2017; Tani, 2014). While in many countries geography may not appear in the primary curriculum until children are seven or nine years old, in some it is part of children's curriculum from age five or is initiated in their pre-school years, as in England (DfE, 2017). This presents a very mixed picture of geography in primary school curricula across the world. As an illustration of the variation in geography's curriculum provision in just one nation, in the UK geography appears differently in its four constituent jurisdictions: a named subject in England; an element in the humanities area of learning in Wales; in the social studies grouping in Scotland; and in Northern Ireland in 'The World Around Us' curriculum area (DfE, 2013; Donaldson, 2015; Education Scotland, 2009; CCEA, 2007). What is important to note, though, is that in each of the four UK contexts geography is an element of children's primary education.

Although geography is an element in primary curricula, there is little evidence around the world about the quality of its teaching. It is acknowledged in the USA, for example, that little is understood about how geography is taught, the contexts in which it is taught successfully, what children do and learn, and what understanding of geography teaching and learning elementary school teachers have (Battersby et al., 2013). This has been recognised similarly as a concern in Australia (Erabus International, 2008). More research is certainly required into the nature, extent and quality of primary geography teaching globally (Catling, 2013b). However, there is one country that has a long, but irregular, history of evaluating the quality of geography teaching in primary schools from the 1960s to the present. That country is England. It is worthwhile drawing on the evidence that has been gathered by school inspectors in recent years about good quality teaching and what some of the concerns are.

Characteristics of good quality geography teaching

Well-taught geography is stimulating and enjoyable, uses a variety of approaches to teaching, engages the children through topical matters and issues of interest that often relate to their experience, challenges their thinking, introduces them to new themes and ideas, and holds high expectations of them. These three scenarios for topics illustrate aspects of and approaches to primary geography that have been used in primary classes.

> Children examine local planning issues and put forward development plans of their own.

> The initiation and use of links with schools elsewhere, nationally and in other countries, involves children in exchanging local information and gaining insight into each other's lives and communities.

> Investigating topical events when they occur (perhaps even suspending the current topic of study) – e.g. the earthquakes in New Zealand and Italy in 2016, cyclones affecting Queensland, Australia, and the Philippines in 2017, and the East African famine of 2017 – enables children to explore the natural processes involved, their impacts on people, and the responses locally and elsewhere to them.

A vital motivating factor for primary children is gathering material at first hand, using learning outside the classroom. This involves undertaking fieldwork in the school grounds, in the local area and further afield. The first quotation in the box below reinforces this approach and its value. Equally motivating is exchanging information with children elsewhere about their own localities. Children are fascinated and energised by investigating topical and dramatic events and issues, such as earthquakes, dramatic weather events and planning developments and disputes. Such investigations involve undertaking geographical enquiries and engage children in active learning. These practical approaches are indicated in the fourth quotation in the box, which notes children working independently, taking their own lines of investigation within a common topic. The second and third examples reinforce that there are alternative approaches that can be used to examine issues and investigate other places with primary children. The development of positive attitudes to learning in geography is evident.

Examples from England's school geography inspectors' perspectives on stimulating primary geography

During the first half of the autumn term, work in geography for [a class of 5–6-year-old] pupils was based on fieldwork in the local environment. They explored the human and physical features in and around the school and local area. Work on aerial photographs, Google Earth and digital photography determined which features were most common. They studied the advantages and disadvantages of human and physical features, discussed which were most prominent and whether it was better to live in an area with more human or more physical features. The unit culminated in the pupils selecting and improving a derelict local shop which formed the focus of their fieldwork The fieldwork and the subsequent activities provided opportunities to explore environmental issues such as recycling, sustainability and graffiti and gave pupils the opportunity to learn about individual actions on the local area as well as the global community.

(Ofsted, 2011, p. 42)

In the last few years, more pupils had joined the school from different countries. [For a class of 6–7-year-olds] it was decided to study life in a Turkish village, as a child had recently arrived from there. The pupils interviewed her and used photographs, maps, atlases, weather forecast and clothes effectively to explore similarities and differences between their own locality and a locality in Turkey. The pupils had very specific knowledge and understanding. They were enthusiastic, interested and respectful of differences. They were also able to recognise that they had changed some of their views about Turkish weather, lifestyle and religion.

(Ofsted, 2011, p. 46)

[8–9-year-olds] pupils used drama to consider the impact of loggers and tourists on the native population of the Brazilian rainforest. Small groups of pupils presented their cameos and others listened carefully to the viewpoints.

(Ofsted, 2011, p. 46)

[A class of 10–11-year-olds], as part of the 'Blue Planet Unit' which focused on water and rivers, pupils were given the opportunity for self-directed learning, although the teacher provided an outline of the task. This set out clearly what pupils should do and ensured that it had a suitable geographical focus. The pupils were given about six weeks to complete the project.

This was done mainly in their own time, but if they finished work in lessons they were allowed to work on their project in school. The pupils were allowed in discussion with the teacher, to choose the area to research and report upon and the style in which they would produce the work. Examples seen included:

- *a standard report of European rivers including computer-generated data and descriptions and explanations related to the differing characteristics of these rivers*
- *a standard report on a single river*
- *a large poster display of the River Thames from source to mouth including details of flooding and river management*
- *a report on the River Danube which included a contour model of the centre of Budapest*
- *A DVD and note cards of a simple experiment made at home to produce a hydro-electric power machine and a written report setting out the advantages and disadvantages of hydro-electricity.*

The pupils spoke very enthusiastically about their projects and had very good understanding about their chosen topics. They really appreciated the freedom to decide what they wanted to learn within the framework given.

(Ofsted, 2011, pp. 15–16)

These examples illustrate several characteristics of high-quality primary geography teaching identified from England's primary school inspection reports (Bell, 2005; Catling, 2004a, 2013c; Iwaskow, 2013). These are that:

1. Geography teaching must be *purposeful*. This means that the children know and appreciate the point of what they are studying, recognise its relevance and value, and have their curiosity whetted and engaged.
2. Their geographical studies need to be *problem* oriented. Children are not to be limited to information gathering and description, but must be involved in investigating, analysing, evaluating and proposing possible, even most likely (if not always preferred), solutions.
3. Their geographical learning should be undertaken using a *geographical enquiry* approach. This involves children in asking, selecting and

structuring questions, working out how to investigate them, undertaking investigations using a variety of sources, and in drawing conclusions based on evidence and rigorous thinking.

4. Children undertake their geographical studies *cooperatively*. This should involve them in contributing independently pursued studies of a chosen problem or issue to a common topic, in which the focus is on learning with and through each other in paired and larger team investigations outdoors and in class.

5. Children's geographical enquiries must involve *active engagement with the world*. This may be through fieldwork locally or further away, involve investigations of topical issues, or by engaging with experts and invited visitors to school from whom they seek information, insight and understanding.

6. Children are stimulated by *engagement with good quality resources*. Such resources will be the stimulus of the outdoor environment, and opportunities to use photographs, maps, leaflets, postcards, rocks, newspapers, artefacts, news websites, resource packs, and the many other sources that can be drawn on, including through the Web. Along with high-quality geography teaching, informative resources can be the catalyst that makes the difference between satisfactory learning and high achievement by children.

Geography curriculum making

A further feature of the ways in which good and better quality teachers teach geography is their use of *curriculum making*. Curriculum making describes a 'liberated' approach to planning a geography topic that may last a half or a full school term (Catling, 2013c). The word *liberated* describes how teachers feel about and view their responsibility for planning their curriculum; it refers to teachers feeling re-energised to make decisions about what to include and how to organise their geography teaching, whether in a single subject or a cross-curricular context. Curriculum making endorses primary teachers to reclaim their *agency* in determining and managing their teaching – that is, they have control in their classroom decision-making. Underpinning this practice are several other features of good quality teaching. These concern their attitudes and organisational responsibility. The essential attitude of curriculum makers is that they are confident in themselves as teachers and as curriculum organisers and managers. They are equally confident in their children as learners and engage them actively in developing the class geography curriculum. This means that while the particular geography topics, and their sequencing, may be school plan or year group directed, the particulars in a topic's study are not closely structured but developed by the teacher with the children's involvement. To enable this approach to be effective requires that primary teachers are committed to maintaining their professional development to enhance their subject and pedagogic understanding in geography (as well as in the other subjects they teach).

In making decisions about their geography curriculum, its topics and the approaches to study, teachers as curriculum makers recognise, draw on and engage their children's geographical experiences and awareness to develop their understanding, and in so doing help their children to enhance and extend what they already know, through engagement with new geographical knowledge and considerations. By involving children in developing their geography topics, these teachers ensure they construct their medium-term plans so as to take opportunities that arise during a topic. They are clear in their intentions and sense of direction. Their mapping out of a topic enables them to adapt content and approaches to develop children's geographical learning as the topic develops. These teachers make very effective use of their range of teaching skills and look to ways to extend and enhance these. Curriculum makers are open-minded but also rigorous, using discussion and debate through active dialogue to challenge children's ideas and proposals for lines of study, to question children's ways of working and the decisions they make about evidence and proposals, and to engage them in self and shared evaluation of their learning. This is reflected in the GA's primary geography quality mark awards in England and Wales (Owens, 2013) and in high-quality primary geography in Ireland (Pike, 2016).

These characteristics are supported by other findings (Catling, 2015a, 2017a) from an examination of high-quality teaching and learning identified by school inspectors across the humanities subjects (geography, history and religious education) in UK primary schools. This refers to the very best humanities teaching and learning found only in some five to ten per cent of primary schools. From an analysis of inspection reports, it was evident that teachers' subject knowledge was influential, particularly in terms of their appreciation of their pedagogic content knowledge, that is, their understanding of the geography they were teaching and their effective decisions about their approaches to its teaching. This analysis noted teachers' involvement of their children in identifying good lines of enquiry, the high expectations they hold of their children, and how they recognise and help children develop their understanding into new areas and more deeply. At the heart of this are the ways teachers convey enthusiasm for the subjects they teach and how they draw the relevance of what is studied to the children's attention. In such ways teachers develop children's geographical engagement, interests and deep learning (Eaude, 2018).

Reflective task

Consider some teaching of geography that you have seen in a pre-school or a primary school, whether taught in cross-curricular studies or as a separate subject. In pre-school this may have included looking at some aspects of local life and the area nearby.

Which *characteristics* of good quality geography teaching are you able to recall?

If the lesson was not of good quality, what would you want to improve? Consider how one or more of the *characteristics* in this section might be used to make such improvements. Why have you selected those ones?

Which *characteristics* you would like to apply to and develop in your own teaching of geography?

Geography in primary schools: limitations and opportunities

We have a very limited understanding of the state of geography teaching, learning and curriculum in primary schools around the world because there are few recent sources of evidence that provide a picture of the range and quality of geography in children's primary education. In the USA there is negligible evidence about geography's teaching during social studies lessons (Battersby, 2013; Boyle-Baise and Zevin, 2014; Segall and Helfenbein, 2008), just as little is known in Northern Ireland (Greenwood, 2013). Evidence about practices in primary school geography is important because it provides insight into those aspects of geography that are taught, how well taught the subject is and how children engage with it. The most informative reports that we have are found chiefly in school inspection reports in three of the UK's jurisdictions: England, Scotland and Northern Ireland (Education Scotland, 2013; ETI, 2014; Iwaskow, 2013; Ofsted, 2008a, 2011). In addition, there is limited evidence from Australia (Erebus International, 2008; Catling *et al.*, 2013). We need to be aware, though, that this evidence is not directly up to date; the need remains to seek the latest reports on the quality of and concerns about primary geography. There have been various studies of primary teachers' perspectives on their teaching of geography, and these provide some insight into the subject's teaching but they do not give independent insights into classroom practices (Bent *et al.*, 2017; Pike, 2015; Salinas-Silva *et al.*, 2015; Shimura, 2015; Wilmot and Irwin, 2015; Xuan *et al.*, 2015). There have also been reviews of teachers' geographical knowledge (Catling, 2014b; Catling and Morley, 2013; Lee, 2018) and of geography in England's initial teacher education (Catling, 2017b). What emerges from school inspectors' reports is that much geography teaching is modest in its practices and accomplishments, and that there is a sizeable flipside to the characteristics of good quality primary geography identified above. These findings suggest concerns about the state of primary geography but indicate also directions for its development to increase the amount of good quality early years and primary geography teaching.

Constraints affecting primary geography teaching

Where geography is not well provided for or taught well, the concerns raised have been as follows.

- Too often geographical studies receive too little teaching time in primary classes with the result that teaching is often ineffective: children study superficially rather than in depth.
- Geography is much more frequently taught in an integrated or cross-curricular context, in which often it tends to be given only a minor role and not be readily identified by the teacher to the children or well thought through by themselves.
- Such an integrated or cross-curricular approach fails frequently to provide a clear focus on the key ideas, knowledge and skills of geography, resulting in weak geography and ineffective geographical learning.
- A core impediment for many teachers is their lack of or weak geographical knowledge and understanding, which inhibits their capacity to plan their geography curriculum and teaching satisfactorily, since they do not appreciate the key ideas and skills of geography and find it hard, even where they are aware of these, to apply them in the geography topics and content they teach, with resulting incoherence.
- This reflects the low status and priority given to geography in too many primary schools and classes, which weakens the opportunities for geographical learning.
- Geography teaching may often not engage children's interest – and even where its topics may do, children remain unaware that there is geography in what they are studying.
- Children's personal geographies and the everyday geographies that affect them are drawn on only to a limited extent where they are recognised at all: children can remain disconnected from their studies.
- The application of geographical enquiry and investigation is lacking in much geography teaching, which tends to focus on using limited information sources to provide descriptive accounts of what is read about or seen in pictures used in a topic, in which stereotypes and misunderstanding can be reinforced.

- Geography topics have been focused too heavily on studies of places, environmental concerns and skills, with too little emphasis given to physical and human geography.
- Geographical studies can be overshadowed by a focus on literacy and numeracy in a geography topic rather than be properly focused on geographical understanding and learning.
- Opportunities for geographical fieldwork and outdoor learning are very limited, if used, and may be constrained by school leadership decisions as much as by teachers' lack of experience, interest or determination.
- In too much primary geography teaching, teachers either rely too heavily on closely structured published resources, from worksheets to textbooks, which they follow unquestioningly and do not adapt to their children's context and needs, or they simply use web-found sources which they do not question and for which they set simple comprehension questions, indicating that they do not have the skills to plan their own topics or engage children in geographical analysis, evaluation and thinking in an effective way.
- Many children develop little deep understanding in their geographical learning because of a lack of progression across a year, or between years, in the topics they study, often only repeating skills or information they have met and used before, with the result that their learning is frequently superficial.
- Assessment is under-played, with records noting little more than the geography topics covered by children, resulting in negligible reference to children's learning of and progression in understanding key geographical ideas, content knowledge and skills: this inhibits planning for progression in their learning.

While many primary teachers may teach geography just about adequately, they lack the self-belief and confidence to teach the subject effectively, finding it hard to challenge, stretch and excite their children about geography, inhibiting what children can achieve: this relates to their limited subject understanding. A contributing factor is that very many primary teachers lack any or have very limited initial or in-service education in geography and its teaching, resulting in too many teachers not having the opportunities to develop their knowledge and skills to teach geography adequately. This lets their children down, who have an entitlement in most parts of the world to good and high-quality geography teaching.

Approaches to improve primary geography teaching

Although this is a challenging scenario, in many primary schools there are teachers whose approaches to teaching geography benefit and enhance children's geographical learning. They aim for and often achieve the high-quality characteristics noted in the previous section. Their approaches include the following.

- Valuing and enjoying teaching geography, fostered by drawing particularly on their colleagues who are passionate about the subject and its learning, and communicating this to their children.
- Ensuring they and their colleagues are well-informed about the nature and content of geography and that they can maintain their subject understanding of and extend their capabilities in its teaching through consistent personal professional development, particularly in school.
- Making adequate provision of time for geography teaching in the curriculum, whether as a single subject or integrated in cross-curricular topics, and where this happens for geography to be identified and visible to the children and to take its fair share as a lead subject in topics.
- Planning geography topics to ensure a balance between the different aspects of geography, including its study of locations and places, its physical and human aspects, concern and care for the environment, and the skills to use and understand maps and to engage in fieldwork.
- Planning topics that involve the development of children's geographical understanding, knowledge and skills both within a topic and between a class's topics across a year to provide for children's progression in geographical learning.
- Rebalancing planning from overly teacher-directed and led topics to a greater involvement of children in developing lines of investigation and approaches within topics, and perhaps at times to suggest geographical topics for study themselves.
- Recasting approaches to teaching to involve more fully or entirely in a geography topic an enquiry approach that requires the children to identify and select questions, to seek evidence to respond to these, to evaluate this, and to draw conclusions and perhaps make recommendations.
- Using fieldwork and outdoor learning consistently to motivate children and to extend and enhance geography teaching and learning.
- Incorporating problem-solving and thinking skills approaches in geography planning and teaching, which engage children in critical questioning and reflection on their geographical enquiries and learning.
- Broadening and using a wide variety of teaching approaches and activities to enhance geographical learning.
- Making greater and more varied use of digital and other technologies and websites to engage and involve children in geographical learning.
- Involving children in practical projects, particularly of local interest and value, and which might contribute to the community, and to take up opportunities provided by a range of topical events and activities around the world.

- Ensuring that children can connect with and appreciate their geographical topics and studies as relevant to their lives, experiences and futures, understanding why what they study matters.
- Accessing good quality and current geographical resources, used thoughtfully and critically.
- Providing thoughtful formative and summative assessments of the children's work in geography, which involves making good use of focused and rigorous questioning and encouraging children's self-assessment of their learning and next steps in learning, and recording simply and clearly children's achievements, needs and progress in their geographical learning.

Enjoying geography teaching and learning

Enjoyment is the birthright of every child (DfES, 2003, p. 3). For many, the purpose of a primary curriculum is to develop children's sense of wonder and curiosity about and respect and care for places, people, cultures and environments throughout the world. These aims allow teachers to develop their curriculum in creative, imaginative and stimulating ways, resulting in many classes in enriched learning experiences for children. Geography is very well placed to realise this, affording many opportunities for children to be active participants in their learning through its rich and diverse subject matter and engaging its enquiry-based approach. To enjoy their learning, children need to be excited and inspired by what they do, necessitating a creative and flexible approach to teaching. Geography offers all this and, to enable it, provides highly relevant and inspiring subject matter (Pike, 2016).

When asked what they remember about geography at primary school, people tend to recall a diverse set of experiences, ranging from colouring maps to eating sandwiches in the rain on a beach during an excursion. When asked what the truly enjoyable and memorable learning experiences that they had were, responses, if offered at all, invariably refer to being outside and carrying out one form or another of experiential, interactive fieldwork, usually connected to an enquiry of some kind which had obvious purpose and relevance. People talk about how this stimulated their enjoyment of the countryside, generated an interest that led to work in planning or opened their eyes to how we pollute but can look after our streets and urban places. Alongside the content of their fieldtrip, pleasure in being out of the classroom in the environment clearly was stimulating.

Geography teaching that informs, stimulates and motivates children, and which really involves them in their learning, is at the heart of enjoyable learning, as the approaches in the box above illustrate. What is essential is to make the geographical experiences you provide purposeful, meaningful and relevant to the children and, equally important, enjoyable. If the children enjoy the activities, they will be engaged and committed to them and effective geographical learning will take place as a matter of course (Reynolds, 2014).

Creating enjoyable geography learning and teaching involves a range of skills and processes, and a commitment to having and applying an open and creative mind (Mackintosh, 2007; Pike, 2016; Scoffham, 2017b). It necessitates flexibility and a willingness to take risks and make mistakes occasionally and to learn with the children. It is about giving children permission and creating opportunities for them to find their own enquiry path, and to explore and discover issues and situations that are real and relevant for them. It involves, inevitably, using a range of appropriate resources from the sophisticated, such as geographic information systems (GIS), to the basic, such as some string and pieces of paper to show an unfolding journey in a story book, and developing motivating and inspiring ideas in a creative and open-minded way. And it requires understanding the geography you teach in ways to which your children relate and from which they gain insight.

In the classroom

Getting into geography with a bear hunt

The classic and hugely popular picture story book, *We're Going on a Bear Hunt* (Rosen and Oxenbury, 1989), has been a stunning stimulus for geography teaching. Children in a class of 4–6-year-olds were entranced with the *swishy, swoshy grass* and the *splashy, sploshy water*, subliminally learning about direction and developing their geographical vocabulary as they practised acting out going *over, under, into* and *through* all sorts of exciting natural features: rivers, mud, caves, forests and snowstorms. Making a 3D model map of the area travelled through in the story enhanced the learning opportunities for one group as the children navigated their way around the increasingly familiar landforms and natural features. For another group, props, including a map, binoculars and a compass, provided the stimulus for planning a 'journey' in the playground using questions such as 'Where are we going?', 'Which way do we go?' and 'How do we know it's the right way?' To assess their understanding and recall of the story, as well as developing their spatial awareness, these children painted picture maps of the bear hunt, identifying and depicting individual features and their locations. Encouraging children to talk about their map as they created it, using prompt questions, such as 'What' is that feature?', 'Which way do you go?', 'What is it like there?', and, more openly, 'Tell me about your map', involved them in describing and explaining what they knew and understood.

Reflective task

Think back to your geography classes at school. Did you enjoy geography? What has stayed with you about its teaching and what you learned? Why is this? Would you have wanted it to be different or to be even better?

Can you recall your geographical learning from your primary school? What do you remember? Did you realise that you were taught geography? Why do you think this is so?

As a primary teacher, you will teach geography. How do you feel about this and why? What would help you to teach geography well? What would provide the children with memorable learning experiences? Make brief notes for your future reference of your views.

Initiatives in education

Appreciating geography teaching in primary schools requires awareness and understanding of the changes in and evolution of the primary curriculum, as well as of other matters affecting primary schools and younger children's education. Here we outline some influences that are directly relevant to primary geography. It is essential to keep alert to developments in the curriculum and schooling, whether government or locally initiated, and to consider how they might and can affect geography teaching and children's geographical learning in primary schools. Some of these initiatives concern how we might consider the purpose of primary education, while others focus directly on geography education and may, if not immediately, have an impact on geography in the primary curriculum. The first influence we note concerns what many governments now see as centrally important – that is, setting the context for school learning – or, to put it alternatively, providing aims and purposes for education. We discuss, second, the matter of geographical knowledge before noting matters of government, state or local geography curriculum guidance. These are followed by reference to several other educational matters. Several are developed in later chapters.

Contexts for learning

Countries around the world set children's school lives and learning in wider educational and social contexts by specifying the national intended aims and outcomes for children's schooling. For instance, one approach has been to set goals for children to develop towards during their schooling.

In Australia these goals have been identified as: successful learners, confident and creative individuals, and active and informed citizens (MCEETYA, 2008, pp. 8–9). You might seek out such statements in your own country. Many of the points that were made about these three areas are reflected in other countries' intentions for schooling in society, and in debates about primary education (Alexander, 2010). In view of what has been presented in this chapter, it is pertinent to dwell on this aspect of educational intentions and to say something about each one.

A key element in becoming a *successful learner* is that children play an active role in their learning, develop their abilities to think logically with increasing depth of understanding, to gather and evaluate evidence thoughtfully, applying disciplinary knowledge, and to be resourceful and innovative in problem-solving approaches and tasks. Children should make consistent use of their developing numeracy and literacy skills, alongside applying digital technologies across their studies, not least to analyse, evaluate and communicate their learning effectively. They should develop the ability to work independently as well as alongside others collaboratively in teams. Important in their learning is being motivated by what they do in school in order to achieve their potential. A core purpose in this is to enable children to make sense of the world and to understand and appreciate how things have come to work as they do and be as they are. Not just this last point but clearly all the others contribute to primary children's high-quality geographical learning, resonating with the points made about good geography teaching and learning.

To become *confident and creative individuals* children need to be self-aware, to build their self-identity and to have self-worth, to believe in and be confident in themselves. Their physical and mental health are as important as their emotional, spiritual and cognitive well-being, and these are engendered through optimism about the future, evolving a set of personal values that include respect for others and empathy, and their sense of living satisfying lives. This includes becoming aware of, understanding and considering the challenges in the world and exploring possible mitigations and resolutions. Building the confidence to be enterprising and resilient, to be creative and take opportunities, and to develop decision-making skills and take responsibility for their actions are important qualities for children to develop. Each of these can support and be enhanced through primary children's geographical learning.

By being *active and informed citizens*, children appreciate the value of diversity in their local, national and international communities, and act with ethical integrity. They will hold to the values of democracy, the rule of law, justice and equality, and have respect for all people and for natural and social environments. As developing responsible local and global citizens, they will act for the common good, to sustain and improve society and the natural and human created world. Geographical learning plays a central and fundamentally important role in fostering such citizenship.

Various aspects of these three aims and goals for education underpin and are explored and illustrated in the rest of this book.

Debating knowledge for the primary geography curriculum

Teaching geography has always involved developing primary children's knowledge of the subject; it would be pointless if it did not do so. Across the years the prioritised content of primary school geography has evolved universally, if not contemporaneously, and to emphasise similar content. In the first part of the twentieth century there was an emphasis on regional geography, with children introduced to information about the continents and a selection of nations around the world, as well as some aspects of local geography. By the middle of the century in a number of countries there had been a shift in emphasis to investigations in local environments and studies of particular aspects of the physical and natural world in other places, in some nations using a sequentially concentric approach across year groups from the local to the global in geography. However, some felt that world knowledge – for instance, of continents, oceans and countries – had become less important. Towards the end of the twentieth century and into the twenty-first century, moves were made to rebalance these different aspects of the subject. It was appreciated that children needed to develop a factual base of information about the world, to appreciate the importance of maps and atlases in studying and finding out about the world, to develop their understanding of places and of aspects of human and physical geography, and to appreciate such core concepts in geography as location, scale, place, spatial distribution and connections, and environmental processes and diversity, as well as undertake fieldwork investigations locally and further afield. In different ways these aspects of subject information, key areas of content and the core ideas in geography were written into curriculum guidelines in countries like England, Australia, the USA and South Africa (ACARA, 2011; DBE, 2011; Halvorsen, 2013; DfE, 2013; Heffron and Downes, 2012).

Debates about the nature and importance of subject knowledge and the school curriculum are nothing new. They have always considered what ought to be taught and have focused on concerns about which aspects of a subject's matter should be prioritised and emphasised in teaching and learning (Winter, 2011). The debate engages with what is meant by 'knowledge' in the context of the school curriculum. To what extent is it about the factual information which children should 'know'? Does a focus on 'information' sideline other ideas about curriculum knowledge that should be discussed? Does curriculum knowledge cover the main areas of content a subject should cover, such as urbanism, agribusiness and climate change effects in geography, or is it about deeper subject ideas, such as location, scale, place, spatial processes and environmental management, or does it encompass both? This debate has been given impetus by educational sociologists who are interested in knowledge specialisation and what is termed 'powerful knowledge' (Young, 2008; Young and Muller, 2016). The phase 'the knowledge turn' (Lambert, 2014) has been coined to encapsulate this move into a renewed debate about the nature of school knowledge. In particular, it has been taken up in geography education (Butt, 2017; Firth, 2011, 2012, 2018; Lambert, 2018; Maude, 2016, 2017, 2018; Morgan, 2014b; Young *et al.*, 2014), although it is not an uncontested or unproblematic focus (Catling, 2014a; Maude, 2017; Uhlenwinkel, 2017).

The notion of 'powerful knowledge' refers to 'the language, norms and ways of thinking' such as the core ideas and conceptual understanding of school subjects like geography (Butt, 2017, p. 17). It is recognised that subjects such as geography are not static but evolve and have historical antecedents. They are sanctioned by their academic communities who provide a sense of and limits to what counts as knowledge in the subject (Morgan, 2014b). In England, 'powerful knowledge' has been of interest particularly in the geography education community, where debates about what is 'powerful' about and within geography are linked to examining what should be included in the school geography curriculum (Dolan, 2019). To an extent, this concerns justification of the subject as much as internal debates about what should be the focus of geography education in primary and secondary schooling.

In primary geography there has been limited debate about the idea of knowledge and what conceptions of knowledge should underpin, or provide the content for, the geography curriculum (Dolan, 2019). One approach to the debate has been to argue that children bring into school their own powerful geographical knowledge from their experience and that this is important in enabling the development of their geographical understanding in the primary curriculum (Catling and Martin, 2011). Where governments, or others, attempt to define what might be the 'essential knowledge' that children should develop through schooling, it has been suggested that a clear distinction needs to be drawn between 'inert knowledge', meaning factual information, and 'applied knowledge' which focuses on understanding geographical *patterns, relations and generalisations* which build on previous experience and new encounters to *enable us to make sense of the world in new ways* (Scoffham, 2011, p. 126). Applied knowledge is argued to be 'powerful knowledge' and proposes that children's evolving understanding of a subject like geography must be built around its key 'big ideas' and main concepts and aspects of study (GA, 2009; Martin, 2013a; Young *et al.*, 2014). This is not to say that factual information is unimportant; indeed, encountering and knowing factual information in the context of geographical aspects such as river studies, earthquakes and volcanoes, tourism and trade is very helpful in enabling understanding of these areas of the subject and the underpinning of ideas such as scale, environmental processes and place, which provide coherence to geography. To investigate and examine them without information and examples would create a fruitless geography education.

Discussion of the knowledge that primary children should learn in their geographical studies is important and will continue; it is never concluded. It is being usefully developed in geography around the idea that what is important is not so much the teasing out of the key ideas or areas of content, let alone the relevant information, as to how such knowledge can help primary and secondary age children (Maude, 2016, 2017, 2018) apply their geographical knowledge to understand the world. This realigned focus within the notion of 'powerful knowledge' may be more helpful for thinking about the knowledge that matters in primary geography. Maude proposes five types of knowledge that he considers powerful for geographical learners of all ages. These are summarised as follows.

- Knowledge that provides children with 'new ways of thinking about the world', helping them to engage with geographical ideas such as, place, environment and interconnections during their investigations and build their understanding of geographical aspects such as, weather, energy, city, country and resource.
- Knowledge that provides children with powerful ways to analyse, explain and understand the world, using geography's analytic and explanatory concepts, such as spatial distribution and environmental processes, to help children apply what they learn to begin to make geographical generalisations, such as that trade occurs between people and companies at local and international levels.
- Knowledge that gives children some power over their own knowledge, in that importantly it encourages them to question, evaluate and critique what they come across and learn about the world.
- Knowledge that enables children to follow and participate in debates on significant local, national and global issues, fostering their opportunities for an increasingly full engagement in conversations and consultations as citizens.
- Knowledge about the world, which builds on, deepens and takes them beyond their personal knowledge to stimulate their curiosity about elsewhere and foster their sense of wonder at the world, helping them see their own and others' connections and interdependence.

Maude is arguing that it is not the particular knowledge in the subject that makes its knowledge powerful, but that it is what you do with what you learn and understand. It is about applying knowledge, and it concerns taking a creative and critical stance in gaining and using it. This links with a much bigger debate about the purpose of primary education (Alexander, 2010) and, indeed, the role of geography in primary schooling. It connects with the section above on contexts for learning.

Reflective task

Reflecting on the sections on 'Contexts for learning' and 'Debating knowledge for the primary geography curriculum', consider these two questions and the subsequent request.

- What types of knowledge do you think it is important for primary children to understand through their geographical studies?
- How will this knowledge help them become successful and creative learners?

Suggest three ways in which you would want children to undertake their studies in geography and explain why you have selected these.

National requirements for geography in the primary curriculum

National frameworks or guidance set out what governments want children to learn through the curriculum. In some countries the primary school curriculum may be set by the state or locally. You need to be aware of such requirements or if there is none, and it is a matter for the school to decide. It is important, therefore, that you find out about the national or local curriculum requirements or guidance for geography in primary education. Examples of national curricula and guidance websites are listed in Appendix 1.

Some governments require all or only state-financed primary schools to include geography as a named subject in their curriculum, such as in England (DfE, 2013; Lambert and Hopkin, 2014). Other countries specify a curriculum area such as social studies or social sciences for inclusion in primary children's school curriculum. Geography will be found, if included, in a social studies/sciences curriculum area, although which aspects of geography are listed may be briefer than in a single subject specification. Indeed, the social studies/sciences curriculum may include a number of subjects, such as history, economics, civics and sociology, alongside geography, or it may be organised around a variety of themes, such as those put forward by the National Council for Social Studies in the USA, which include 'people, places and environments', 'global connections' and 'production, distribution and consumption', all of which involve geographical studies (Brophy *et al.*, 2013; NCSS, 2010), although these may or may not have taken account of the geography standards set out separately by geography educators for the states and schools in the USA to use to guide geography curriculum construction (Heffron and Downs, 2012). The geography standards in the USA provide greater detail than the geography national curriculum for schools in England. In whichever national context, it is important to know what is specified and whether this must be taught or is for guidance, although guidance from national or state education departments might imply core consideration for a primary school's curriculum.

Furthermore, it is important that you seek out advice about understanding and teaching primary geography. Some local and national governments provide these, but they will be supplied by national associations of geography teachers. As an example, in the UK the Geographical Association promotes geographical education at all levels. It recognises the importance of primary geography, particularly through the professional development provision on its website and through its publications. Its manifesto, *A Different View* (GA, 2009), affirms geography's place in the school curriculum, argues for its value, emphasises links with children's experience and of learning in the real world out of the classroom, focuses on the world today and about alternative futures, and is inspirational in illustrating the power of geography in our lives. The various geographical and geography education societies in the USA make the point in their joint booklet, *Why Geography is Important* (Adams, 2012), that geography really does matter in our lives. This publication argues that geography helps us to understand and appreciate a range of matters, including globalisation, diversity, location, uses of geospatial technologies, energy, climate change, environmental hazards, resource management, infrastructure, employment and national and international security. It concludes by giving geography a personal context, stating that *geographic knowledge is fundamental to reaching our personal and societal goals, and in attaining a higher quality of life* (Adams, 2012, p. 15).

There may well be national and commercial texts and websites that provide advice about teaching geography with primary children. These may provide topics and structures for different year groups or refer simply to the primary stage of schooling, leaving you to make decisions relevant to your school and class. They can guide you to relevant resources and provide lesson outlines and/or suggested teaching approaches, including links with other subjects. You can complement national advice by searching internationally for further advice – for instance, from global and national organisations that are engaged in charitable and commercial international and global activities. Some are listed at the end of this chapter.

Pre-school or early years learning

Pre-school, or early years, provision for children focuses on a number of aspects of early childhood. These include developing their social skills and lives, initiating their awareness of the capabilities and skills involved in school learning and providing a stimulating and well-provided indoor and outside environment in which their learning may take place through play, story telling and reading and organised engaging activities and provided resources. Early education is underpinned by a set of values to foster positive ways in which children can live their lives. For example, in Australia, these values include the creation of a mutually respectful and responsible society and an equality-based future for all that is mutually caring and empowering (DEEWR, 2009, 2010). They can lead to the development of the following outcomes for pre-school education.

- Holding a strong sense of identity.
- Being connected to and contributing to their world.
- Having a strong sense of well-being.
- Being effective communicators.
- Being confident and involved learners.

Such statements of values and outcomes about pre-school children 'being, becoming and belonging' as people in society promote a perspective that applies across societies, nations and education in early childhood. Elements of geographical understanding and appreciation support learning in all these outcomes, although the second may appear to have the most obvious subject connections. In England (DfE, 2017) and Wales (Welsh Government, 2015) in the UK, the statutory frameworks for 3–5-year-olds' learning include 'Understanding the world' and 'Knowledge and understanding of the world', which contain geographical elements about the children's own local area and its features, similarities and differences with other places, directions and maps, and changes in the environment. Through such experiences to help children begin to develop their awareness and understanding of the world, they are initiated into aspects of geographical experience and learning, even though geography may never, of course, be mentioned directly. For such young children geography is an implicit aspect of their lives and inevitably part of their learning.

Sustainable schools initiatives

Increasingly, schools around the world are engaged in sustainable initiatives. Sustainability education is intended to help children understand the need to care for and manage the natural and human created environment, as well as to support schools and their communities to become sustainable. This can be for people and families as much as for the places where they live. It involves also developing a global awareness and perspective. Many primary schools have developed whole-school approaches, often linked with the geography and science curriculum to help children learn through real-life learning experiences. Sustainability initiatives have also been used by governments to improve schools' resource and facilities management. These include the water, waste, energy, products and materials used within the school, as well as landscape design. Sustainability is a key aspect of geography, and there are good examples of ways in which primary schools and teachers have used practical approaches to stimulate children's creativity to identify practical ways that sustainability can be improved and demonstrated within the school and communities. Geography contributes strongly to these.

Fostering citizenship

Geography has a long history of considering ways in which it engages with citizenship linked, for instance, with children's evolving identity, their activities in and connections to local and more distant communities, and their consideration of, respect for and interactions with others (Stoltman, 1990). This means that geography is particularly suitable for developing citizenship understanding and involvement with primary children. In considering how people relate as citizens to their localities and to activities that directly affect places, geography examines people's environmental attitudes and behaviour, and explores the results of their decisions that affect places (Boyle-Baise and Zevin, 2014). However, citizenship is broader than its environmental interests. It is more than local; it is global as well. Citizenship recognises and appreciates that children are growing up in diverse local, national and global communities. Children begin in geography to learn respect for diversity and difference, as well as to seek what is shared and common between peoples and communities. As a subject it can help children develop their sense of belonging and their identity, which are often linked to place and communities. Primary children can begin to recognise that others may hold different perspectives and views from their own, and learn to discuss and respect these, even if they disagree.

Learning outside the classroom

Outdoor education is popular and well developed in many parts of the world, although it is neglected in others. The UK, the USA and Australia are generally recognised as international leaders in outdoor education and related fields such as nature tourism. This has come to be thought more important for schools to take up since in their home lives increasing numbers of children spend less time outside (Louv, 2005; Pickering, 2017). Primary school outdoor education includes such activities as fieldtrips, museum visits and time spent away from school for a couple of days or for up to a week or more. Such activities are important for geographical and environmental education, alongside history and science education. The importance for geographical learning and teaching lies in the opportunities that fieldwork provides as a highly motivating and engaging approach to learning and understanding geography.

Developing children's general capabilities and skills

Internationally, the view is that all subjects must contribute to teaching the general capabilities and skills children need to enhance their learning. Indeed, general capabilities and skills are essential in all subjects, because all subjects make use of them in various ways. Such capabilities and skills are:

- literacy capability;
- numeracy skills and competence;
- information and communication technology (ICT) skills and application;
- critical and creative thinking;
- personal and social capability;
- ethical behaviour in relation to oneself and others;
- intercultural understanding.

Developing these capabilities and skills should be through the context of the specific ideas, skills and content of the subject. This applies for geography whether as a stand-alone subject or within social studies/sciences.

Practical task

Select one of general capabilities and skills. Identify a number of aspects of that capability and skill, consulting sources if you need to do so.

Have a particular age group of primary children in mind.

How do you think you could develop your chosen capability and skill through geography teaching?

List some activities and approaches in geography that you think will help your group of primary children to develop that capability and skill.

Key points

This chapter has:

- noted the opportunities and challenges for geographical learning and teaching in primary schools;
- illustrated the enjoyment that can come through and from geographical learning;
- identified a number of developments, initiatives and priorities that influence or affect geography in primary schools.

Moving on

Keep abreast of the curriculum initiatives by government and other agencies and organisations concerning developments in primary geography. Look out for reports in the press. Make a note of geography curriculum developments and changes. Use your own and other nations' websites to help you. Several are listed in Appendix 1.

Further reading

Many books, chapters, journal articles and websites will help you to develop your understanding and appreciation of primary geography and its teaching. The following texts debate, stimulate interest in and provide ideas for teaching and learning geography with early years and primary age children.

Brophy, J, Alleman, J and Halvorsen, A-L (2013) *Powerful Social Studies for Elementary Students* (3rd edn). Belmont, CA: Wadsworth Cengage Learning.

Catling, S (2011) Children's Geographies in the Primary School, in Butt, G (ed.) *Geography, Education and the Future*. London: Continuum, pp. 15–29.

Catling, S (ed.) (2015b) *Research and Debate in Primary Geography*. Abingdon: Routledge.

Dolan A (2019) *Powerful Primary Geography: A toolkit for 21st century learning*. Abingdon: Routledge.

Geographical Association (2009) *A Different View: A Manifesto from the Geographical Association*. Sheffield: Geographical Association. Available at: www.geography.org.uk/adifferentview

Gersmehl, P (2014) *Teaching Geography* (3rd edn). New York: The Guildford Press.

Marsh, C and Hart, C (2011) *Teaching the Social Sciences and Humanities in the Australian Curriculum*. (6th edn) Melbourne: Pearson.

Martin, F (2006) *Teaching Geography in Primary Schools: Learning How to Live in the World*. Cambridge: Chris Kington Publishing.

Maude, A (2018) Geography and powerful knowledge: A contribution to the debate. *International Research in Geographical and Environmental Education*, 27(2), pp. 179-190.

Palmer, J and Birch, J (2004) *Geography in the Early Years*. London: RoutledgeFalmer.

Reynolds, R (2014) *Teaching Humanities and the Social Sciences in the Primary School* (3rd edn). South Melbourne: Oxford University Press.

Scoffham, S (ed.) (2010) *Primary Geography Handbook*. Sheffield: Geographical Association.

Scoffham, S (ed.) (2017b) *Teaching Geography Creatively* (2nd edn). Abingdon: Routledge.

See the magazine *Primary Geography,* published by the UK's Geographical Association (GA) three times a year, available to primary school members of the GA (see the GA website).

Useful websites

Association of Geography Teachers of Ireland: http://agti.ie/

Australian Geography Teachers' Association (AGTA) – GeogSpace: www.agta.asn.au

Canadian Council for Geographic Education: www.cangeoeducation.ca

Geographical Association: Early Years and Primary Area (UK): www.geography.org. uk/eyprimary

Geography for Kids: www.kids-world-travel-guide.com/geography-for-kids.html

Geography Teachers Association of Singapore: https://gtasg.wordpress.com/

National Council for Geographic Education (USA): http://ncge.org/; www.natgeo kids.com/uk/category/discover/geography/

National Council for the Social studies (USA): www.socialstudies.org/

National Geographic Society (USA): www.nationalgeographic.com/

Social Sciences online (New Zealand): http://ssol.tki.org.nz/

South African Geography Teachers Association: http://sagta.org.za

CHAPTER 2

VALUING GEOGRAPHY

The importance and nature of geography

 Chapter objectives

This chapter enables you to:

- appreciate what geography is about and why it is relevant to us all, including primary age children;
- become aware of the key ideas that are important in understanding geography and what it studies;
- recognise and give examples of geography in everyday life from your own experience;
- consider geographical thinking, living geographies, topicality and geography, and geographical significance;
- appreciate the aims of and focus for geography in early childhood and primary education for children from 3 to 11/12 years of age;
- make links to your national, local and school geography curriculum requirements and/or guidance.

Introduction

This chapter considers what geography is about in order to develop your understanding of the subject. It shows how you are already involved in geography, explores geography and its 'big ideas', and considers geographical thinking and significance. It examines ways in which geography helps us understand topical events and issues in our world, outlines the contribution geography makes to children's learning about the world, and indicates what might be some aspects of geography that pre-school children can explore, and the range and topics in geography that 5/6 to 11/12-year-old children can be introduced to during their schooling. It will be helpful for you to have available your national, local and/or school geography curriculum requirements or guidance for pre-school and primary school children.

Whether we recognise it or not, geography is very much part of our daily lives. We begin by considering this.

Everyday geographical encounters

Geography is such a commonplace aspect of daily life that generally we overlook it because our use of the environment, our connections with people and places, the goods that we consume, and the decisions we make about how we go about our daily business are so obvious and mundane that we scarcely take notice of them, until something untoward happens. Daily life is largely habitual and might be termed 'routine geography'.

Our 'routine' geography seems invisible, like much else we take for granted, until brought to our attention (Dorling and Lee, 2016; Moran, 2008; Perkins and Thorns, 2012). Yet, this *everyday geography* (Martin, 2006a) is not habitual for young children; it is novel, fascinating, wondrous and important. We need to be conscious of it. It is the 'stuff' of geography for pre-school and primary age children, easily dismissed as parochial – yet it is exactly the opposite. From our earliest years we are constantly interconnected with our local and wider world. Consider these two scenarios.

A bite to eat

At lunchtime you head for a café. You fancy a salad and tea. You add rice to your mixed salad. You collect a bottle of water from the cooler. You head to the drinks counter to buy fair trade tea. You add a chocolate bar and pay the Romanian cashier, find a seat and chat with friends, of whom one is Kenyan.

(Continued)

(Continued)

What is the everyday geography? A commercial outlet; produce on sale, delivered by truck from a wholesaler; you are unsure where the food originates, since there are few clues on the labels; some state it is locally sourced, while other unseasonal ingredients must come from abroad or be hot-housed; yet other goods carry a national Fair Trade label; electrical energy used to cool the salad bar and refrigerators and provide light; manufactured, recyclable, containers; tap and bottled water; waste food disposal; migrant workers; and friends. Just to have this lunch you are linked to many other people, activities and places.

E-news time

You get home and turn on your smart device to check the news stream. First up is a report on major flooding in northern New Zealand, the actions taken by residents and shopkeepers, the initial impact on streets and towns, and expected further flooding and flood damage. Next you note the state of a refugee camp in the Middle East and the concerns about water, food, hygiene and shelter as well as children's education; these are illustrated by ground and aerial photographs and maps. A local update covers the city council's decision about your shopping centre redevelopment, which sounds positive since it will increase your shopping choices. You switch to your social media contacts and check the latest postings from a friend travelling in South America.

What is the everyday geography? Communicating global information into our living rooms; how a natural phenomenon looks and is responded to as a natural hazard; how political conflict impacts on people and creates population movement and relocation; who decides about change at a local scale; what redevelopment is and what impact it might have on whom; the use of maps and film to communicate images of places and the lives and activities of people there, about which you have concerns; a friend's travel in and reports about places you have not yet visited in other parts of the world. Current and topical events and social communications affect us directly or indirectly whether locally or in or from a distant part of the world.

These scenes are commonplace geography, reflecting situations, events and activities that are part of people's everyday lives and the diet of news media. Martin's notion of 'ethnogeography', or everyday geographies, describes them (Martin, 2006a, 2006b, 2008).

Ethnogeography reflects the view that all learners are geographers because they all live in the world. They all negotiate and interact with a variety of land-scapes (human and natural) on a daily basis {.} They will have built up a knowledge base about the world, near and far, through a range of direct and indirect experiences. What they don't perhaps recognise is that this knowledge is useful geographical knowledge and a point from which deeper conceptual understanding can be developed.

(Martin, 2006b, p. 180)

Everyday and personal geographies matter. They are the context and ingre-dients of our daily decisions about what we do, how and why we do it, our understandings of the world, and of our feelings and views. It is not just our own daily geographies that matter, but also those of people around the world. Hurricane damage to banana crops in the Caribbean not only cuts the income of the farmers, but it also raises the price in our supermarkets. We pay more or do not buy them, with consequences to the supplier and the supply chain.

 Practical task

What is your everyday geography? Make notes about two or three con-texts in the style of the scenarios given. Try to identify as many everyday geography connections as you can. You might consider the following.

- Your journeys to the shops, work or out for an evening.
- Your digital phone, tablet or other smart device use.
- Where you live and what that place means to you.
- Your uses of energy, water and waste disposal.
- Travelling and visiting places nationally and abroad, wherever in the world.
- How you treat places and the environment, such as through care and recycling.

What is geography?

Bonnett (2008, p. 121) describes geography as a fundamental fascination, as an exploration and about giving order and meaning to the world. Geography helps us make sense of the planet we live on and discover all we can to understand our 'home' (Matthews and Herbert, 2008; Martin, 2005; Holt-Jensen, 2018; de Blij, 2012; Boyle-Baise and Zevin, 2014;

Dorling and Lee, 2016). It is a wide-ranging discipline, providing structure to what we observe and find out, through investigation, analysing and structuring information and the use of our imagination. We order the myriad information about the world we encounter to appreciate what is vital about the natural and human processes that create, modify, adapt and influence what goes on – whether earthquake occurrences and their impact; where and how our food is grown, manufactured and reaches us; or how and why various goods are made and what value they have for us and the people who made them. We use logic and imagination to decide how to organise the information so that we can explain it and make sense of what other places and environments are like, perhaps through pictures or words, and what it may be like to live in those places, developing our appreciation of how people live and what effects change may have on them.

Geography is a creative discipline (Catling, 2015c; Hawkins, 2017; Scoffham, 2017b); it is not, simplistically, only about facts about the world. Of course, without information there can be no creativity. It was information mapped about the location globally of volcanoes and earthquake events that led, with other evidence, to the theory of plate tectonics, the notion that it is the interconnected movement of massive plates riding the crust of the Earth that causes volcanic eruptions and earthquakes, be these in the Caribbean, Italy or China. This explanation initiated the idea of 'continental drift' to describe and explain the movement of the continents across the globe over hundreds of million of years. It helps explain how the Earth is an active, dynamic planet (Thomas and Goudie, 2000; Holden, 2011; McGuire, 2012; Stewart, 2018).

Research into how people use their local environment to go about their daily business provided the information to understand that we hold all sorts of knowledge about places cognitively and that we use our 'mental maps' to work creatively for us. This research has investigated how we find our way about, and how we use that information for shopping, leisure and other activities. This is encapsulated in the theory of mental mapping to explain our behaviour in familiar and novel environments, providing insight into how children and adults understand and make use of places. Without the information and the capacity to think innovatively there would not be such an interesting and insightful way to account for these phenomena (Downs and Stea, 1977; Kitchen and Freundschuh, 2000; Amedeo et al., 2009), nor to understand and account for the importance and roles of spatial knowledge and thinking in our lives (National Research Council, 2006; Plumert and Spencer, 2007; Montello et al., 2014; Ness et al., 2017). The spatial dimension and dynamic in geography is argued to be one of geography's central ideas, if not its core concept. It is certainly important, as we notice when we think about it in our daily lives and in helping us to piece together and understand the world about us (Brooks, 2017; Stewart, 2018).

The 'big ideas': key concepts in geography

Central to understanding geography's way of thinking are a number of 'big ideas' or key concepts. While different geographers debate their importance or how they might best be described, they serve modern geography well in helping to understand how the world works, what we do in and to it, and what the effects of natural and human actions are and might be. Figure 2.1 states geography's key concepts and core method of enquiry.

Geography's key concepts need some explanation. At one level they are all obvious ideas, concepts of which we have some everyday understanding. In geography, that 'everyday' understanding is useful, but they have more specific meanings within geography of which we must be aware (Lambert and Morgan, 2010).

Place

Places are physical entities – the city, town or village where we live – and can be as small as a room in our home or the local area where our home is sited, the size of the national region, which includes our home town, or as large as our country or continent. Places are identifiable through their location and extent, their features and boundaries, and their land- and

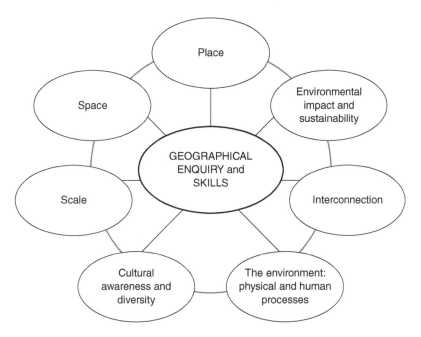

Figure 2.1   Geography's 'big ideas' or key concepts (modified from North, 2008a)

urbanscapes and cultures. They have physical and human characteristics that we can represent in words, pictures and maps, and through art forms, music and drama. Places are unique, be they neighbourhoods or national parks, but their essential characteristics may be similar to those of other 'like' places, such as other seaside resorts, agricultural villages, industrial estates or national parks. Places are dynamic, in which small or major changes result from human decisions and actions, such as changed shop use and as in conflicts over developments, or can be generated by the effects of natural hazards and people's responses to them, such as earthquakes, hurricanes and floods. Their characters are influenced in these ways by human and natural processes (de Blij, 2009; Cresswell, 2015).

Places enable us to develop a sense of belonging, whether to a country (being Brazilian), a region (being a 'Northerner') or locally, which support our sense of identity and give meaning to our lives. Each of us develops images of places from our direct and indirect encounters with them. From personal experience we develop our perceptions of and feelings and viewpoints about places. In this way we develop a sense of place, how we connect and identify with (or disconnect from) places familiar to us, such as home and our favourite places (or places we avoid). Places are real and they exist in our images of them, arising from our experience. Different people hold very different ideas and have very different feelings about the same places (Holloway and Hubbard, 2001). These perspectives make places fascinating and underline the concept of place as central to geography.

Space

For geographers, one understanding of space concerns where features, sites and places are located. Geographers examine the distribution of features and consider the patterns they show to see how and why they create networks and of what sort these are. Studying spatial layout explores the interactions between features and places and how they affect each other. Geographers are particularly interested in the natural, social, economic and political processes that help to explain distributions and networks. Such processes may be fluid rather than fixed (Massey, 2005), as may be their outcomes over time. Spatial locations, distributions, patterns and processes result from natural processes and events, and from human decisions and activities that create the structures we see or that we perceive to be there. In looking at spatial processes, geographers investigate what may be causing changes and impacts, such as shifts in weather and climatic patterns, perhaps making some places drier and others more humid, or the creation of new road or air transport networks and faster broadband links, and how these are altering and shortening travel and communication 'distance'.

Scale

Geographers study features, places and environments at a range of scales from the immediate (a room or floor layout), to the local neighbourhood and community, to the regional, national, continental and global (Herod, 2011). Scale affects what happens in places, what we observe and the way we see things. Depending on who is looking, we may see scale differently; a place that a young child perceives to be large may seem to be a small place to an adult very familiar with it.

At local, regional and global scales we see distributions and patterns in different contexts (Sheppard and McMaster, 2004). This enables us to identify relationships and to make generalisations that can be very different from one scale to another. Thus, while we would use a road atlas or website to examine the route to take across the country, we will want to look at the detail of the road network locally to get to a particular address, which using GPS for navigation enables, enlarging or reducing scale appropriately. Digitally based mapping enables us readily to move between different scales related to our needs. Observing weather movements and patterns at different scales helps weather forecasters to predict how the weather will change and what we can expect nationally and locally. This can help them to see causes and effects for different regions in a country and help us to prepare, for example, for a hot and sunny or stormy weekend.

Interconnection

Interconnection concerns the interrelationships we have at different scales between places, features, events and people. It includes the connections between people in their local community and its facilities and services, as well as the global trade links that encourage, for instance, coffee to be grown in various places and traded for others to drink around the world (Massey, 2005; Dorling and Lee, 2016). Interconnection exhibits our interdependence locally and globally. Interconnections are significant in our lives and are major influences on places and their characteristics through such activities as sales and goods delivery to our homes. The connections we have and use include digital communications that may be local or to other parts of the world, railway and shipping networks to transport people and goods, and family links where people have migrated from one place to another whether for work or as refugees. Interconnections are essential in the generation of and our access to and uses of electricity and other sources of energy supply. Interconnections occur in the natural world within the processes at work, such as in ecological systems and the water cycle. Interconnectivity is both natural and people generated and managed in our physical and social environments.

The environment: physical and human processes

Environments have been created through the actions and events in and the interconnections between different aspects of our world: its geology – the rocks beneath our feet; its atmosphere – our climates and weather; its hydrology systems – river and oceanic processes, the water cycle; the biosphere – plants and living creatures; and human activities and changes – agriculture and urban development. From the Earth we source raw materials such as water, minerals and food. The Earth holds, absorbs or recycles our waste. Different environments fascinate and inspire us, in wild, rural and urban places, providing for pleasure and relaxation, but equally they can challenge and concern us as in volcanic environs, along coasts as sea levels rise, in urban slums and at decayed industrial sites.

Environmental processes encompass these natural or physical world processes, such as our daily weather and climatic systems and characteristics, the changes created by river and sea floods, and the types and outcomes of volcanic eruptions and earthquakes (Anderson *et al.*, 2007; Holden, 2011, 2012). Human processes examine contexts and activities such as the manufacture of goods, transport and travel, the types and development of settlements, nations and states, our planning for and responses to natural hazards, and how we change our physical environments. They examine how decisions are made, how people respond and the consequences of change, socially, economically, politically and environmentally (Jones, 2011; Cloke *et al.*, 2014). Understanding such processes and the changes created helps explain the locations, distributions and patterns we see in places and the environment at different scales and their interconnections, which allow us at times to make predictions.

The world is dynamic and constantly changing. Change is key to understanding the natures and results of the actions and effects of environmental processes over space and time in our planet's physical and human environments, through their interconnections and interactions (Castree *et al.*, 2009). Change occurs at different scales from local improvements to people migrating within and between nations as a result of conflicts. It can be for better or for worse for people and the natural environment. Change does not occur evenly nor have the same impact on places. An increase in rainfall can be helpful where it ameliorates long-term dry conditions, but equally it can lead to flooding and be damaging for agriculture elsewhere by creating over-wet conditions for crops. Change can help or hinder the sustainability of places. Studying physical and human process and people–environment relationships helps us understand this.

Environmental impact and sustainability

Environmental impact examines the interactions within and between natural and human environments, focused on people's effect on each other and the environment, and the natural environment's impact on itself and people (Goudie, 2013; Huggett, 2003). This connects with human and physical processes but emphasises the effect rather than the processes at work and causing change. It considers how people perceive, make use of and adapt to or adapt the environment, and examines their values and views to understand how and why people do what they do in environments. It takes into account what natural and human factors may have an impact, be these population changes, climate movements, the introduction of newer technologies or changes in the economy of a place or region. It recognises both benefits and hazards, and considers how people prepare to respond whether by taking preventative measures such as building flood defences or through mitigating actions by encouraging new industries and services as others decline in an area.

Sustainability concerns natural environments, communities and economies (Moseley *et al.*, 2014; Robertson, 2017). It examines environmental quality, looking at how and why places are managed and damaged or improved, the provision and distribution of goods and wealth, and their effect, matters of cultural continuity and change, and issues of social justice concerning access to goods and services, where and why this is and with what effect. There is evident overlap with environmental impact studies, but the emphasis lies in ways to maintain or rehabilitate and restore the environment to sustain life and lives. One aspect is to find ways to sustain and even improve good environments, while its concern is also to tackle what causes unsustainability in places, essentially how people damage, exploit and degrade environments in rural and urban areas, and to look at ways in which to bring such places 'back to life'. This involves considering economic, social, cultural and political causes, and ways to address these challenges.

Environmental impact and sustainability together consider the future, how things might change, what we would want such changes to be and what may be the preferred but most probable outcomes. Central to the idea of environmental impact and sustainability is 'stewardship' of the environment, to ensure that it is passed on to future generations in a better state than it is held by the current generation. This brings to the fore the question of environmental justice in the contexts of social and natural environments and their interplay with each other. For example, how we respond to the causes and effects of climate change or highly extractive fishing or open-cast mining can be considered in terms of just dealings, the justice of what is undertaken where and with what effect, and the mitigations of impacts on people and the natural world. It builds on the notion that we borrow the world from our children and we have a responsibility to care for it as we use it, not to exploit and denude their future.

Cultural awareness and diversity

The world is diverse, with a wonderful range of environments and an exhilarating variety of peoples who have created their communities through beliefs, social structures and norms, varied ways of living, relationships with those outside their culture, and how they see themselves. Geographies are imbued with the contexts of cultures (Anderson, 2010). Cultures influence the varied ways in which similar and different environments are perceived, modified, adapted to and used by people, communities, commercial companies and nations. Cultural interests and variations can be seen through the variety of shops and commercial areas in cities reflecting different interests and styles, through population balances in communities and through social activities and celebrations. It is important to appreciate the concepts of similarity and difference in the context of culture. These two notions, like commonality and diversity, are important in geography and can be unintentionally linked to perceptions about 'others', those whose lives and living may not be like 'our own', be this in relation to poverty and wealth, landscapes, architecture, social activities or food preferences. Yet our societies are inherently diverse and differing, and we cannot know ourselves without knowing others. Building on Martin's (2012) argument, culture involves relational awareness and understanding since we cannot appreciate cultural norms and values, variations, similarities and differences other than through comparison. Comparisons open up possibilities and opportunities for understanding – for example, identity and belonging, people's senses of place and ecological and environmental values – and for recognising that there are varied ways in which we can interact in and support diversity in our social and physical environments (Horton and Kraftl, 2014). Geography helps us to recognise, appreciate and value such diversity as fundamental to our being and living, and to see the significance of its inclusivity within our own and others' societies.

Cultural awareness is the starting point for intercultural understanding and for appreciation of the diversity of people and their lives around the world. It concerns ourselves as much as anyone else, and explores ideas such as identity, our sense of ourselves and our communities at various scales, and our appreciation and valuing of others elsewhere, even those not even known. Geographers consider how our communities and nations function and work in relation to cultural influences and examine international relations and their impacts.

Geographical investigations

The development of geography's big ideas or key concepts has been enabled and supported through the subject's key methods of investigation in the real world and by examining data and other information gathered about it in numbers and words, through mapping or by photography, and aerial, satellite and digital imaging. Central in this is geographical enquiry supported by the key skills that geography uses.

Geographical enquiry and skills

Geographers gather information through many and varied investigations, known as geographical enquiries (Roberts, 2013). Physical geographers almost always use scientific processes of investigation. Some human geographers use similar approaches when studying large-scale phenomena such as populations, and gathering and analysing statistical data to look for explanations. Other human geographers, perhaps exploring aspects of neighbourhood geographies, may use more qualitative approaches where they are trying to find out what people think and feel, how people are affected by changes or what people might want undertaken to improve an area. Inevitably, geographers will engage in fieldwork, working in the real world to gather the data they need, using a variety of techniques from land use mapping and interviews to traffic counts and time-lapse photography to air pollution lichen studies, river flow measurement and chemical weathering analysis. A wide variety of techniques and tools are used in geographical studies.

Geographical enquiries involve working through the stages of an investigation, from observations, questions and directions of study about a concern or problem to analysing data and identifying possible solutions. Geographers decide how best to gather and record relevant information, how to analyse and evaluate it, how to assess the benefit of what has been found, and how most effectively to communicate it through articles and books, the press and television, and in conference presentations.

Geography uses a variety of skills or literacies. Graphicate literacies are as essential as textual literacies. The term 'graphicacy' encompasses the visual skills geographers and others use to gather, interpret and explain evidence (Balchin and Coleman, 1965). It includes using and making maps and photographs and visual observation, as well as skills in reading and understanding, and making sketches, diagrams, charts and graphs, and in annotating maps, photographs and drawings, be these on paper or in digital forms. Geography also uses literary documents such as reports and government policies. To facilitate these and to enhance numeracy skills and work with virtual and dynamic models, computer software and related technological skills are used to aid weather recording, traffic counts, chemical analysis and much more. Such literacies are essential to investigations in geography and to communicate its ideas to a wide variety of audiences.

Thinking geographically

The reason for developing primary children's awareness and understanding of key geographical concepts and skills is to foster their capability in thinking geographically. It is not simple and straightforward to state what geographical thinking looks like, but various attempts to identify its meaning exist (Morgan, 2013; Catling, 2015a; Örbring, 2017; Lambert, 2017; Brooks *et al.*, 2017). Perhaps the most helpful outline is: '*An essential educational outcome of learning geography is to be able to apply knowledge and conceptual understanding to new settings: that is, to 'think geographically' about the changing world*' (GA, 2009, p. 9). Here, the word 'knowledge' seems to refer to the topics of geography, such as settlements, river studies and trade and agriculture. Geography uses the key concepts outlined above – of the human and physical processes involved, the different scales at which they can be appreciated, the interconnections involved, the spatial locations, distributions and patterns identified, the places where they occur and the environmental impacts that are noted, as well as their sustainability and cultural awareness and diversity – to understand these topics. The use of geography's key concepts and its enquiry mode provide insights into, appreciation of, explanations for and, possibly, predictions about how we understand the world at a range of scales and in different contexts. Geographical thinking is the capability to transfer our understanding from one topic or context and scale to another to note the processes and interconnections that would normally be missed without geographical insight (Jackson, 2006; GEG, 2013; GA, 2012).

This means that while younger primary children might examine their local environment by investigating local features and considering why selected features are where they are located, older children might look at the patterns among selected features, such as housing and shops, which they then apply in looking at another area through maps and photographs and, perhaps, fieldwork. They might then apply their understanding of these ideas of place, space and physical and human processes to investigate weather features, processes and patterns locally and nationally. It will be a matter of encouraging them to understand the key concepts and to apply them in new studies. This provides the power in geographical thinking and, indeed, to geographical knowledge, that power residing in the ways geography not only helps us to understand the world but also to think through what impacts we have on our planet and each other, and how we respond to these to ensure our sustainable future. Geographical knowledge enables geographical thinking (Brooks *et al.*, 2017).

Practical task

The café in 'A bite to eat' above illustrates several geographical 'big ideas' or key concepts. It is a distinctive type of place with particular features and layout. The goods and the person serving at the till indicate local or wider world interconnections, and the products on sale are the result of the physical and human processes of farming, commerce and transport. There are diversity and cultural dimensions. Recycling and energy use link with sustainability and the environmental impact of people's actions.

Use the 'E-news' scenario at the start of the chapter or write a similar scenario of your own. Make a chart with two columns, listing the scenario in the left-hand column. In the right-hand column note which of the key concepts are most appropriate to help understand the situation outlined in that scenario. Give your reasons for why you selected them.

The role of geography

Geography is a living and topical discipline. Its content is not just the stuff of the everyday, such as shop locations, countryside tourism and parking issues; it is also about matters that have wider regional, national and global impacts, such as access to food, water, energy and hygiene, and about the effects of climate change. It is important, therefore, to appreciate what makes something geographically significant. This is where the value and importance of geography lies.

Living geography

The term 'living geography' extends the idea of everyday geographies noted earlier. It draws on and focuses geography's key concepts (Owens and North, 2008; Mitchell, 2009). It emphasises developing the context of children's geographical awareness and engagement to enhance their knowledge and understanding beyond what they already encounter. It builds from children's daily experiences but takes them into 'new areas of the world' to develop and deepen their geographical thinking. Living geography's characteristics include:

- focusing on but beyond people's everyday geographies – children's and adults';
- examining what is relevant to and affects people, daily and longer term, directly and indirectly;

- being interested locally but set in and connected to the wider world context at a range of scales (regional, national, international, global) to broaden children's understanding of the world by applying geographical concepts and enquiry;
- investigating environmental processes, changing environments and the impacts of change on people, places and environments;
- developing critical awareness and understanding of sustainability;
- encouraging children's curiosity about and enquiries into the world;
- exploring current times and being future-oriented, looking at what is and could, should and might occur;
- involving creative and critical responses to everyday matters and issues.

Living geography is active and pertinent. It is about 'being alive' to the world as it is. It focuses on what is topical and significant for us, and what has daily meaning and impact in our lives. It introduces us to geography's key concepts through this liveliness and immediacy.

Topicality

Geography examines topical matters and concerns to provide insight into our own and the wider world. Geographical topicality can be at the level of the personal and everyday, about the weather or travel to work; about local matters and concerns, such as street closures to create pedestrian zones and play streets in residential areas; or about national to global actions and events that affect us directly or indirectly, such as the effect of government decisions to increase airport facilities and the debate about carbon impacts on global climate change. The events, people and places reported and commented on in the local and national news provide us with our daily sense of the world, perhaps about such matters as vehicle-polluted streets and the number of surveillance cameras in our towns. Using and understanding topical reports keeps us informed. However, important topical matters may pass all too quickly through the 'news', providing a short-term and superficial perspective. To that extent what we understand as topical is determined for us, at local, national and international scales.

Topicality cannot be considered uncritically. We must question the particular information, perceptions and understandings of the world we take from the news and why and how these topical events are put before us (de Blij, 2012). While topical issues bring geography alive, we should be concerned about the images of places and peoples that are portrayed and wonder what is excluded or unconsidered. We should use topicality to evaluate our own perceptions and understanding of the world. For example, what do we really know and presume about people's lives in the countries south of the Sahara in Africa? How does the 'newsworthy' focus on deprivation and hardship create single rather than multiple perspectives on these millions of people? When we hear about a redevelopment in our neighbourhood, how do we react? Do we look for the range of arguments, hear the variety of points of view put forward, and consider what might be for the better beyond our own interests? We may support or challenge this change, but is it through emotional reaction or considered thought?

Geography's interest in the topical provides opportunities to investigate the topic and the ways information is communicated, who makes the decisions, and how we think about and respond, or not – the 'stuff' of critically effective environmental citizenship (Dower and Williams, 2002; Hicks and Holden, 2007; Joubert, 2009; Hayward, 2012; Kraftl *et al.*, 2012). Geography gives us clarity and keeps us informed. It alerts us to our preferences, biases and prejudices, providing opportunities to reconsider.

Geographical significance

To gain the most from geographical studies, we need to appreciate what is significant to study. Geographical significance concerns understanding what is most appropriate to focus on in geography and to whom and at what scale matters are significant. No geographical features, places or events are in themselves significant. Significance is an attribute that individuals or groups ascribe to such geographical phenomena and events. In terms of what is topical, it would seem that a particular event and place, such as Cyclone Debbie, which hit Queensland in Australia in early 2017, and Hurricane Maria, which devastated much of Puerto Rico in the Caribbean during late 2017, were given significance by the media. It reported them because of the destruction caused to these places, through floods and very high winds, and the consequent disruption to people's lives; they were devastating for those who lived through them and were ascribed significance by the governments of Australia and the USA because of the damage caused to these places. For geographers, these events were globally significant because they illustrate key geographical concepts, including place, environmental impact and sustainability, physical and human processes, scale, and cultural awareness and diversity. Other matters are significant regionally or locally. In a national park in South Africa a planning application might generate local debate because it is about encroachment and the loss of a conserved natural environment in a sensitive area. Nationally, it may be considered of geographical significance because of its connections with the place, environmental impact and sustainability, physical and human processes, international connections and scale. Geographers would examine how these concepts help understand what is happening, might happen and the effect in such situations.

Questions about features, places, environments and events and/or changes in them
1. How and why are place and location significant?   o Why is this location worth considering? What does it say about the role of location?
2. How, why and to what extent is the scale significant?   o At what scale is it? Is it significant at local, national or global scales? What makes the scale important to note?
3. How and why does it have meaning for people? How might it be revealing through its representation of how individuals and groups of people think about a place or event?   o How does it contribute to personal or collective perceptions, meanings, images and representations of places and environments? Is the meaning significant locally and/or more widely? What different meanings do different people (including from the past) attach to it?
4. How does it help understand the way natural environmental systems and places are created and function, shaped and change, and why this happens?   o How do functions and change help us identify patterns in the world and the processes at work creating and changing them? Why do places and environments develop the characteristics they have?
5. What types and levels of impact does it have on people, places and environments, and why?   o How does it change the physical and/or human environment? What effect is there on people's lives and activities, indeed, on their perceptions of places and environments? What actions and changes does it lead to?

Table 2.1   Questions to use in considering geographical significance (adapted from Catling and Taylor, 2006, p. 37; Taylor and Catling, 2006, p. 124)

We must consider carefully what makes an aspect of the social or physical environment significant and worthy of geographical study. The questions in Table 2.1 can be used to consider the geographical significance of a place or event.

We make daily decisions about where we will shop, meet friends or spend our holiday. Local and national politicians decide about housing developments, aid to support people caught up in disaster events and areas, and trade agreements and subsidies. These decisions may affect us as much as our own personal decisions. They interweave our everyday geographies, are our 'living geographies', and are matters of environmental topicality that we know to be significant, although we don't always recognise them as aspects of geographical studies. Our holiday decisions and plans to expand an airport are geographically significant because they affect others, not just ourselves. Geographical significance is not simply about 'us'; it concerns everyone it impacts on, whether it makes the news media or not.

Reflective task

List examples of some ways in which geography plays an active role in your life. Describe what you consider geography to be about. Draw on what you have read above and state in a few sentences your idea of geography and its relevance to your life.

Now write down, similarly, in a few sentences how geography is relevant to children's lives and why it should be part of their primary education.

Geography in children's primary education

The years in primary school from ages 5/6 to 11/12 years old should provide a vital grounding for children's geographical learning and understanding. Indeed, incipient geographical awareness may well have been initiated in pre-school through studies related to 'knowing about the world' for 3- to 5/6-year-olds. Geography, as an element in many social studies and humanities curricula as well as a stand-alone subject, has much to offer. It has a long history in many countries (Meyer *et al.*, 1992; Head *et al.*, 1996; Walford, 2001; Halvorsen, 2013), including within studies of the environment and society (Gilbert and Hooper, 2011; Marsh and Hart, 2011; Reynolds, 2014). Its concern has been to develop children's geographical awareness, knowledge and understanding, their capability to make investigations and use its skill set, positive attitudes to the subject and their values about the human and natural world. These might suitably be summed up for primary geography – indeed for geography education generally – as about stimulating, fostering and developing children's

- interest in the world around them: their local surroundings and the variety of the Earth's places and its human and physical characteristics;
- sense of curiosity and wonder about, and their respect for people, cultures, places and environments across the world;
- well-grounded geographical knowledge of their own locality, their country, their continent and the world;
- capacity to think geographically, using geography's key concepts and substantive knowledge of geography's topics of study;
- effective, critically aware and creative use of geographical enquiry to investigate geographical topics;
- informed concern for the nature and quality of the natural and human environment and future;

- engagement as responsible and active geographically informed citizens, able to contribute to a just, resilient and sustainable world, socially, environmentally and economically.

There are direct links to the key concepts in geography. The study of places, not least their own, is central, as is understanding physical and human processes, alongside environmental impact and sustainability. Fundamentally, these aims for geographical education are focused on values and attitudes, to be underpinned by knowledge about the world and understanding of the ways in which it works. The attitudes of interest in their surroundings and a sense of wonder are aligned with the values of concern about the quality of the environment and the future and their sense of responsibility for care. That these attitudes and values apply to all children from the youngest to the oldest children emphasises that geographical education intends to look to the present and the future and to their personal role and involvement. Geography is not described as a subject separate from children but as a perspective on the world in which they are integral players. These attitudes and values identify a sense of living geography in which children's everyday geographies play a central role, but which also requires consideration about the significant geographies for study among their own and topical interests. Geography, from their earliest years, is about enhancing children's understanding by involving them in looking anew at their own places and experiences as well as about taking them beyond where they are at any given time – that is, about growing and engaging their sense of the world.

The aims for geography and its key concepts provide a basis, engaged with everyday and living geographies, for stating the main themes to be developed through primary geography. These must support children's everyday geographical learning. The purpose of primary geography is to:

- help children be inquisitive about, make sense of, put into context and develop further their own experience in the world – their everyday geographies;
- introduce children to the excitement of and extend their awareness, knowledge and appreciation of peoples, cultures, places and environments in the wider world;
- develop their sense of wonder, their understanding and their critical questioning of what places and environments are like, why they are like they are, how and why they are changing, what processes and patterns shape them, and what impacts there are or might be and why;
- foster children's critical interest in and valuing of the environment and of the Earth as their home, and help them understand why a sustainable approach to the future is vital though contested;
- encourage children to be thoughtful as global citizens about the impression or 'footprint' they leave on places and the environment, and about

making decisions which affect their lives and the lives of others, including those they will never know;

- develop children's spatial awareness and understanding of distributions, patterns and networks, and of the representations of places and the environment, through such skills as map work, using photographs and making sketches, and through their studies of places and environments;
- engage them in geographical enquiries about place and environmental matters and issues, and about the wider world;
- foster their fascination with places through fieldwork and the use of new technologies in and beyond the school grounds and the local area;
- stimulate and develop their locational knowledge and understanding about the world.

The reasons for geography's value in children's education rarely remain static over time. In England, the reasons for studying geography were revised from the 2000 statement of 'importance' (DfEE/QCA, 1999) to the 2014 statement of 'purpose' (DfE, 2013). These two statements are set out in the box below. The revision between 2000 and 2014 reflected changed government priorities for the subject in the school curriculum. These statements applied across the school geography curriculum for 5- to 14-year-olds.

England's shifting statements from the 'importance' to the 'purpose' of geography

2000: The importance of geography

Geography provokes and answers questions about the natural and human worlds, using different scales of enquiry to view them from different perspectives. It develops knowledge of different places and environments throughout the world, an understanding of maps and a range of investigative and problem-solving skills both inside and outside the classroom. As such, it prepares pupils for adult life and employment. Geography is a focus within the curriculum for understanding and resolving issues about the environment and sustainable development. It is also an important link between the natural and social sciences. As pupils study geography they encounter different societies and cultures. This helps them realise how nations rely on each other. It can inspire them to think about their own place in the world, their values and their

(Continued)

(Continued)

rights and responsibilities to other people and the environment (DfEE/QCA, 1999, p.14).

2014: Purpose of study

A high-quality geography education should inspire in pupils curiosity and fascination about the world and its people that will remain with them for the rest of their lives. Teaching should equip pupils with knowledge about diverse places, peoples, resources and natural and human environments, together with a deep understanding of the Earth's key physical and human processes. As pupils progress, their growing knowledge about the world should help them to deepen their understanding of the interactions between physical and human processes, and of the formation and use of landscapes and environments. Geographical knowledge, understanding and skills provide the frameworks and approaches that explain how the Earth's features at different scales are shaped, interconnected and change over time (DfE, 2013, p. 214).

Source: Taken from DfEE/QCA, 1999; DfE, 2013

Practical task

Re-read the government statements of curriculum aims for school geography that applied in England from 2000 and 2014.

Which aims for geography do you consider to be shared between and which are distinct to each statement? If you have found similarities and differences, can you give any reasons for the changes made between the 2000 and 2014 statements? Note what you found and your ideas about reasons why.

Now examine the (primary) geography requirements or guidance document for your country, state or regional education authority, or school. What are the aims or purposes given for geography education for primary school children? Do you agree with them? Would you amend them and, if so, to what? If, for some reason, there is no 'aims' statement, try to write the purpose of the geography curriculum you are examining.

The focus for primary children's geographical learning

Studying places emphasises developing pre-school and primary children's initial understanding of the idea of place through the study of small-scale places such as their immediate environment and own locality. They should also begin to investigate other similar sized localities, through setting these in their wider local, regional and national context, and learning where in the world they are, encouraging awareness of Earth's size and space. In this way ideas about scale are introduced, as is the notion of interconnection. Cultural awareness and diversity, and the physical and human processes creating and changing places are important to children's developing idea of the characteristics of places. There are opportunities for children to develop a 'sense of place' and to explore their perceptions and images of places, as well as their identity with places and communities, and to consider environmental impact and sustainability.

Physical and human processes create and change the environment. Beginning to understand them helps children to appreciate the interconnections and relationships between these processes. Environmental impact and sustainability focus on how people intentionally and unintentionally affect their environments, how they might manage, repair and care for the world, how and why decisions are made that affect the environment and people's lives for better or worse, and our own and other people's personal feelings for and responses to the environment. Pre-school and primary age children can consider how they may help to manage the environment sustainably, looking at their classroom, the school grounds and the local area, considering decisions to make and their own engagement and participation. Scale and interconnections should be used to develop understanding, through local, regional, national and global examples.

Examining space is concerned with location and the distribution of features and events, and with recognising and explaining patterns in places and the environment. The interconnections between and scale of features and phenomena are an inevitable part of the understanding of spatial patterns in the environment, as are the developing ideas of closeness and distance. This helps to understand the interdependence of people, communities and places. Pre-school children can be introduced to some local connections while primary children will develop these ideas at increasing scales and in various contexts.

Geographical enquiry develops children's questioning and investigative skills and their capabilities in undertaking enquiries from inception to presentation. Enquiry involves children in checking and noting different interpretations of evidence and in recongising differing points of view about problems and issues. Geographical skills emphasise the development of vocabulary, observational skills, using and understanding globes and maps, undertaking fieldwork while learning to use a variety of techniques and

resources, and employing a range of other sources of primary and secondary evidence including via digital technologies. It introduces children to
decision-making skills. In pre-school, children can be encouraged to question and to talk about and refer to simple maps, while primary children can
develop their language and skill sets across their geographical studies.

There is breadth to geography across the pre-school and primary years.
For the youngest children this should begin with their immediate environment in the nursery school, its outdoor area and the streets beyond. For
primary school children it covers the school grounds, the local neighbourhood the school serves and other localities and regions nationally, and in
other countries and continents. In such studies children will build up some
national and global locational knowledge about their locality, their country,
the continents and globally. Various themes can be examined across the
years, from local to global scales, including our communities, weather, climate change, the uses of resources, recycling, sustainability, trade, rivers
and coasts, access to energy and water and their effect on the landscape,
and the impact of digital technologies on communication and people's
interconnections with each other. Places, environments and issues should
be studied in a range of contexts and at various of scales. Fieldwork should
be undertaken throughout the primary years.

These requirements for the breadth of children's learning underline that
the key geographical concepts are central to primary geography. Place,
space, human and physical processes, environment and sustainability, and
cultural awareness and diversity are interwoven by scale and interconnections. These aspects of the geography curriculum are examined further in
later chapters. You might wish to compare and connect them with your
national or local primary geography curriculum requirements or guidance.

 Key points

This chapter has:

- argued that geography is a core aspect of our lives;
- introduced the idea of everyday geographies;
- provided examples of geographies in and impinging on our lives;
- introduced geography's key concepts;
- referred to geographical thinking;
- developed the ideas of living geographies, topical geography and
  geographical significance;
- considered the purpose of geography in the primary curriculum.

Moving on

Develop your understanding of everyday geography. Follow local, national and international news online or through television bulletins or newspapers. Notice when and how news reports refer to or are provided from different places, the aspects of the places, and the environmental impact and sustainability matters they refer to and the range of scales involved. Use these and the other geographical concepts to reflect on the ways in which you interact with the world and how it affects your day-to-day life.

Further reading

To discover more about geography, the following books are informative and accessible introductions to the discipline of geography:

Armitage, S (2017) *Approaches to Learning and Teaching Geography: A toolkit for international teachers*. Cambridge: Cambridge University Press.

Bonnett, A (2008) *What is Geography?* London: Sage.

de Blij, H (2012) *Why Geography Matters More Than Ever*. Oxford: Oxford University Press.

Dorling, D and Lee, K (2016) *Ideas in Profile: Geography*. London: Profile Books.

Holloway, L and Hubbard, P (2001) *People and Place: The Extraordinary Geographies of Everyday Life*. Harlow: Prentice Hall.

Holt-Jensen, A (2018) *Geography: History and Concepts*. London: Sage.

Matthews, J and Herbert, D (2008) *Geography: A Very Short Introduction*. Oxford: Oxford University Press.

The following books provide valuable introductions to primary geography:

Halocha, J (2012) *The Primary Teacher's Guide to Geography*. Witney: Scholastic/Book End.

Martin, F (2006) *Teaching Geography in Primary Schools: Learning How to Live in the World*. Cambridge: Chris Kington.

Reynolds, R (2014) *Teaching Humanities and Social Sciences in the Primary School*. South Melbourne: Oxford University Press.

Scoffham, S (ed.) (2010) *Primary Geography Handbook*. Sheffield: Geographical Association.

Scoffham, S and Owens, P (2017) *Teaching Primary Geography*. London: Bloomsbury.

To read the requirements for your pre-school or early years learning guidance and those for your primary education geography curriculum requirements or guidance, you need to access the relevant national, state, local authority or school documents.

Useful websites

Association of Geography Teachers of Ireland: http://agti.ie/
Australian Geography Teachers' Association (AGTA) – GeogSpace: www.agta.asn.au
Australians Need Geography: www.science.org.au/natcoms/nc-geography/documents/nc-geography-australians-need.pdf
Canadian Council for Geographic Education: www.cangeoeducation.ca
Geographical Association: www.geography.org.uk
Geography Teachers Association of Singapore: https://gtasg.wordpress.com/
National Council for Geographic Education (USA): http://ncge.org/
National Council for the Social studies (USA): www.socialstudies.org/
Social Sciences online (New Zealand): http://ssol.tki.org.nz/
South African Geography Teachers Association: http://sagta.org.za

CHAPTER 3

CHILDREN'S GEOGRAPHIES

Experience, awareness and understanding

 Chapter objectives

This chapter enables you to:

- explain that children have a range of geographical experience that develops their awareness, knowledge and understanding of the world around them and more widely;
- appreciate that children's geographical experience is always changing and developing;
- recognise that children hold views, ideas and values in relation to the nearby and wider world, about places and the environment;
- realise that adult geographies affect them.

Introduction

This chapter focuses on children's place-based and environmental experiences, their awareness and understanding of the world through direct and indirect experience and sources, and their values and perspectives about their world. It develops your understanding of what are termed 'children's geographies'. This encompasses children's personal geographies and geographies not of children's making but those that affect their lives directly and indirectly. It concerns children's experience of their lived or everyday geographies, as well as their awareness of distant places encountered only through secondary sources and their virtual and imagined 'worlds'. It includes their environmental understanding, interests and concerns. It refers also to children's experience in a hazardous world. In effect, it makes the point that children bring geographical knowledge and understanding from their everyday lives to the classroom and that this should be valued, given credibility and used throughout their studies, as well as be challenged, enhanced and extended (Catling and Martin, 2011).

Current understanding of children's geographies has developed from observation-based studies in psychology 'laboratories' to real-world studies of children's activities and behaviours in and uses of real places and environments. Recognising children as active members of society, studies have sought primary age children's 'voices' about their views and concerns. Within geography, sociology, psychology and environmental education there has been much research into children's environmental and place experience and knowledge. Throughout this chapter many texts have been drawn on that complement the studies referred to in this chapter. They provide the overview for the perspectives that follow (Ataöv and Haider, 2006; Cele, 2006; Christensen and James, 2000; Christensen and O'Brien, 2003; Christensen *et al.*, 2018; Fog Olwig and Gulløv, 2004; Foley and Leverett, 2011; Fraser *et al.*, 2004; Freeman and Tranter, 2011; Greene and Hogan, 2005; Hackett *et al.*, 2015; Hallett and Prout, 2003; Higgins and Freeman, 2013; Hörschelmann and van Blerk, 2012; Jones, 2009; Kraftl *et al.*, 2012; Kreutz, 2015; Lewis *et al.*, 2004; Lolichen, 2007; McLeod, 2008; Murnaghan and Shillington, 2016; Scourfield *et al.*, 2006; Smith, 1995; Somerville and Green, 2015; Spencer and Blades, 2006; Tudge, 2008; Veale and Donà, 2014; Waller, 2006; Yarwood and Tyrrell, 2012). Several of these and a number of informative journals are listed for follow-up reading at the end of this chapter.

We begin with some consideration of pre-school children's geographies before looking more widely at children across the primary age range.

The youngest children pre-school

Children enter school with an embryonic geographical background (Catling, 2006b; Cooper, 2004a; Matthews, 1992; Palmer and Birch, 2004; Stea *et al.*, 2001; Martin and Owens, 2010). Within home and play centre environments children play together or alone with toys and other equipment inside and in the garden or the outdoor area, possibly 'explore' a little, watch some television and computer software, and talk. Children are taken out and make journeys because parents or siblings go shopping, visit places and meet relatives and friends. Through such experiences the youngest children begin to develop a number of facets of their personal or everyday geographies (Bilton, 2010; Bilton *et al.*, 2017; Catling, 2003, 2006a; Garrick, 2009; Knight, 2013b; Palmer and Birch, 2004). Bilton *et al.* (2017) make the point that we underestimate what children under and over the age of three have the capability to learn – and they learn quickly. School and other outdoor play areas and sites for visits can be challenging, with aspects of adventure and risk (bearing in mind real safety issues) in the range of activities in which young children become involved (Knight, 2011b), something with which their parents and/or carers are not always happy given the understandable desire to keep their children safe (Little, 2015). Forest school sites, parks, woodlands, and stream and riversides, as quasi-natural environments can provide enticing and exciting opportunities for young children to explore ordered and nature-based features, places and environments, places and environments, taking them beyond what for many are their built and urbanised homes and streets.

Young children's awareness of the local and wider environment

Very young children learn the layout and location of features and items in their home. Children notice landmarks, routes and directions when out walking or in a bus or car. From as early as 2–3 years old they build a sense of the places they encounter and familiarity with those to which they are often taken. Evidence suggests that while they find it hard to communicate their awareness, they can retrace some routes even after their first experience. Many 3–4-year-olds can say what activities like shopping are about and know of places elsewhere, naming or describing some characteristics of those they like or do not like. This awareness draws on being in places, their travel experience, what they have heard through the family, and from stories and television. Their experience and knowledge are partial and may at times be less than accurate.

 Research summary

Pre-school children's emergent environmentalism

A cross-cultural international study led by Palmer into 4-year-old children's 'emergent environmentalism' identified that young children

(Continued)

(Continued)

construct conceptions about people, places and environments from an early age. Children could associate trees with forests, explain that melting snow makes water and talk about not throwing away items but recycling them. Within these embryonic environmental and scientific understandings young children clearly have considerable gaps in their knowledge and understanding, and certainly have naive ideas, although some might be the result of unintentionally misinformed adult stories (Palmer and Birch, 2004; Palmer and Suggate, 2004; Palmer *et al.*, 1996).

Outdoor experience and play has long been valued in engaging children with the environment (Tovey, 2007; Bilton, 2010; White, 2014). Children are introduced to and encounter vicariously many scales of place, as already indicated. At their own level in play spaces, pre-school children use play areas for physically active and quiet play depending on their mood and interest, so provision of a varied environment is essential. One aspect in such play is children's 'secret places', such as dens, they have created. In an investigation of nursery children's secret play, Dixon and Day (2004) found that 4–5-year-olds were already developing their own sense of their place and were able confidently to show they were beginning to understand uses of space and to note position, as well as indicate knowledge of the natural environment. Young children were able to make use of constructed and natural spaces as dens, which they regarded as their own private and meaningful places as sites they felt they 'owned' and shared as they chose. They are already intimating awareness of adult supervision and making use of the environment to create an element of resistance and even transgression (Moore, 2015), stretching the bounds of what 'seems' to be allowed. Alongside this, pre-school children exhibited some understanding of risk in their play area behaviours, although they are not usually fully aware of what injury might result from risky play, such as when climbing or using monkey bars (Little and Wyver, 2010). Not just the site but the affordances offered by place are adopted by young children to meet their own interests. Pre-school children have preferences for their play spaces and exercise choices where there is a good range of play areas (Holmes and Procaccino, 2009). For instance, in more spacious 'natural' nursery play areas young children seem to concentrate for longer on activities than in commodified, equipment-based areas, perhaps because 'natural' areas afford more room for imaginative play (Luchs and Fikus, 2013). It seems that young children will note the affordances a pre-school setting offers them and will use what is offered variously as well as those aspects that suit their preferences.

Young children and feature and place representations

From their first naming of objects, children build a vocabulary about various everyday features, such as home, street, tree. This enables them to talk about places and environments as well as about journeys and basic directions. Verbal representations are supplemented by the capacity to begin to use visual/graphic images. When children of 4–5 years are introduced to large-scale aerial photographs and clear plans/maps of particular large-scale places, many can use these to identify and locate features in these places as well as to undertake some rudimentary navigation (Plester *et al.*, 2006; Kim *et al.*, 2012). Pre-school children certainly find the largest scale of aerial photographs (at 1:500, 1:1,250 and 1:2,500 scales) to be most readily 'legible', and they can recognise that they are not maps, although they may not be able to say that they are photographs taken from overhead looking directly down. This indicates that pre-school children can begin to use such representations and that their spatial representational awareness and skills are already developing. They can identify features such as buildings, routeways and open spaces using their everyday vocabulary. Research also notes that young children can begin to make some sense of the satellite images on Google Earth (Danby *et al.*, 2016), again using large-scale views. Success in identifying features in the environment, such as rivers and streets, was strongest when pre-school children were working collaboratively.

Young children live in a strongly visual world, in stories, media and the environment. When they begin to 'play' with crayons and paper, they begin to depict activities, people, events and places, perhaps their play toys, a room, a game or a journey, perhaps 'peopled', often through what we as adults describe as 'scribbles'. Their doodles and early drawings will need explanation, but young children depict features and where they are in 'pictures' of places, which in time become recognisable. This is the beginning of learning to represent for themselves. Consider, for instance, how young children you know draw their homes and those of other people. Children also see many representations in their environment – for instance, on street signs. As symbolic forms they can mean little to pre-school children, and they do not often find it easy to interpret them without help (Ljung-Djarf *et al.*, 2015). However, pre-school children appear to understand more readily some icons, such as for waste bins.

Young children's environmental and 'other' place values

Many young children are aware about waste and its disposal in bins, and some are beginning to understand about recycling (Palmer and Birch, 2004). Even our youngest children appear to be developing a sense of concern for our world – for example, the need to protect natural features such as trees and flowers – just as they appear through their expressions and verbal responses to develop a sense of 'wonder' about the environment, particularly natural places where they can wander freely and safely (Jørgensen, 2016). Their experiences and learning foster consciousness about the natural environment and its features, driven by curiosity and emotional engagement, and provide the basis for pre-school children's emergent environmental viewpoints, values and attitudes. These can lead to children considering what to do when they identify a concern they have in their nursery environment. Caiman and Lundegård (2014) note four stages where young children work together to resolve a concern: recognising there is a problem because they can 'foresee' negative outcomes; negotiating options to resolve the problem; negotiating a solution and taking action; and achieving their aim to resolve the concern. Important in this is what we might call team or co-operative working. This shows the possibility in their own environment for young children to have agency in dealing with a concern they recognise at their own scale.

Wiegand (1992) reported that young children have positive and negative views about people and places that they have no information about, assimilated from home life, play with peers and stories they hear. We must listen carefully to what young children say and be ready to address ideas they express, which are partial, misconceived, inaccurate or negative to help them build a sound and affirmative foundation for future place, cultural and environmental learning. As Dolan (2013) notes, the use of picture stories read to and with pre-school children, as well as viewed by themselves, can be informative and helpful. Such picture stories can bring matters of inequity and social justice in different places around the world to children's thoughtful attention. Indeed, nursery children's sense of the nature and diversity of places beyond their direct experience is often developed through picture story books, which need, therefore, to be carefully selected. Such stories act as introductions to the world, to elsewhere and to others, and can have lasting impacts. Where children might connect negative images with these stories, this needs discussion to open their minds to the value of differences and diversity, and to draw out similarities and connections.

Imagining 'being in places and events'

Young children's play is a vital element in their learning about the environment, whether it is through outdoor play (Tovey, 2007; Bilton, 2010; White, 2014; Bilton *et al.*, 2017) or involves play with toys, through stories and imagination (Catling, 2006b). In an outdoor setting, as much as in a wild or other safe area for exploration, imagination provides young children with opportunities to engage with places and 'make them their own'. This is supported by the role of stories such as *We're Going on a Bear Hunt* (Rosen and Oxenbury, 1989) and *The World Came to my Place Today* (Readman and Roberts, 2002) to encounter and make familiar environmental and locational language in naming features and places, and using positional, directional and scale-based vocabulary and discussion. Toy play and home or shop corners provide opportunities for children to re-create experiences they may have had or witnessed. Guided and open play provide ways for children to imagine and act out people, place and 'environmental' events in large and small spaces creatively using their imagination and props.

Reflective task

Why is it important that teachers are aware of and ensure they draw on, extend and challenge, as necessary, young children's developing place and environmental understanding and any alternative conceptions they may exhibit? List what you think are the most important aspects of pre-school children's geographies for early years teachers to engage with.

Children's perspectives on school grounds

The common, shared place and environment in all children's and teachers' experience is the school itself. School is as much a place of children's geographical and environmental experience as is their local area. Research into children's experience of school as a place has proved informative (Catling, 2005c; Devine, 2003; Freeman and Tranter, 2011; Garrick, 2009; Holt, 2007; Johnson, 2013; Lucas and Dyment, 2010; Titman, 1994).

Children have strong views about the nature and quality of their school grounds. Where these are expanses of asphalt and grass with little variety, grounds are seen to be uninviting and 'boring'. Where there is variety in the features, with colour, with planted and wild areas, providing natural habitats as well as play spaces, they are regarded as 'cheerful' and interesting environments. Playgrounds offer opportunities for children to make use of them as they can, particularly for play but also for learning (Freeman and Tranter, 2011). Titman (1994) identified playgrounds as vital places for children, but that how they use and value them varies dependent on the child and their social context in the school. Observations of children's play in school grounds has noted that while some children enjoy playing in 'green' or more naturalistic areas, others make consistent use of 'sport' areas, such as the tarmac or concrete area for more robust and 'sporting' activities

(Lucas and Dyment, 2010). These choices seem to relate to pleasure in games play (all-weather areas) and to perceived safer places that also offer opportunities for more social activities (natural sites). The latter sites, where there may be rough ground, grass, and even small hillocks and 'hidden' spaces, provide options for children's play and engagement with each other, from conversations to den building and the use of natural materials as imagined artefacts for role and imaginative social play (Johnson, 2013). While school grounds can offer 'natural' or rather 'concrete' places to play, it remains very much the case that children will make of them what they can and in doing so develop their sense of place and understanding of the affordances of school grounds.

      Research summary

Children with disabilities in primary environments

Holt's (2007) study of the socio-spatial reproduction of disability in English primary school playgrounds highlights ways in which others affect children's personal geographies. When friendship groups play shared playground games, children who are not liked or with physical, learning or emotional disabilities may find themselves excluded from such uses of the playground space and even restricted to marginal areas in the playground. Teachers can affect these children's environmental experiences by excluding them from parts of the playground or the playground itself because of problematic behaviour, or for personal safety and health reasons. Children in such contexts find themselves on the margins of their school environment. It seems that this marginalisation in the environment is an unintended side-effect of decisions about who is viewed as able to behave sensibly in playgrounds and who is not. Children learn from such socio-spatial practices to include and exclude others in their wider society, assimilating perspectives, for instance, that 'other' or stigmatise those who are disabled in some way, which they then reproduce in their treatment of others during adolescence and adulthood. Where there are inclusive approaches, the reverse can be the case.

Stephens *et al.* (2017) found marginalisation to be a feature of their Canadian study of accessibility around school for a small sample of older primary age children with disabilities who used a mobility device. Most children had difficulty navigating toilets independently, perhaps because of inadequate space or heavy doors, creating obstacles in their toilet use and a need for support. Moving around buildings and going in and out of them could be problematic because of entrances, heavy doors, steps or a lack of lifts. Children noted that school buildings could appear accessible in their 'public' areas, but this was not consistently the case around buildings. Children often felt excluded at playtimes as non-participants in play activities and during games lessons when they might sit out activities. The lack of or a failure to ensure a fully inclusive approach by many schools was noted.

Children perceive that often adults do not value playgrounds or children's play in them, exhibited through adult lack of interest, care and concern for quality grounds and play areas (Devine, 2003). There seems to be little recognition of the school's classrooms, building and grounds as environments in their own rights (Dudek, 2005) as well as being enticing and exciting places for learning. Research with children about their school play areas indicates that what they want bears little relation to what adults consider children want, which include more varied and challenging play areas with natural and constructed features, a point made by children in a Canberra primary school as much as elsewhere (Freeman and Tranter, 2011). Many playgrounds remain unexciting and quite barren places, though increasingly schools are providing more varied environments, including green spaces and quiet areas. Children have limited faith in adults' understanding of their own preferences, interests and needs. They want diverse playground settings, including 'naturalistic' spaces where they can play in stimulating ways, such as 'wild' spaces and materials they can use to build (Powell, 2007; Tranter and Malone, 2004), supporting their connections with the natural world. Since school grounds are supervised spaces, children's play can be constrained by teachers' risk concerns (Chancellor, 2013), which children recognise, and children can feel frustrated by what they perceive to be over-protective rules and constraints. This can be the case where schools have become more inclusive of children with mobility difficulties, including wheelchair users, but this is not always so (Stephens *et al.*, 2017) if primary schools have been slow to adapt their environments to the needs of all their children.

Where organisations help improve school grounds, children enjoy more varied environments around the year through a variety of activities – quiet and personal, social, rowdy play, small group and large group games, etc. In some schools this has been the ethos, where a strong curriculum focus works alongside a playtime focus in using the school grounds (Jeffrey and Woods, 2003; Rowe and Humphries, 2012). Perhaps the real issue is involvement and trust, evident where varied school grounds are available and used fully, as well as in schemes involving children outside schools in various parts of the world (Adams and Ingham, 1998; Bellamy, 2003; Freeman and Tranter, 2011). Providing inclusively for all children's interests and needs in an enabling way remains an approach to be fully adopted.

Reflective task

Consider your own playground experience or, if you have the opportunity, spend time in a school playground and observe what occurs there.

How would you describe your own and other children's personal geographies of the playground?

What do you notice about children's use of the playground space, with whom they use it, what for and what their demeanour is? Ask the children and reflect on how their explanation is like or differs from your own. What does this tell you about children's personal geographies?

Children's evolving direct experience of places

Children's daily experiences in places provide many opportunities to develop their knowledge and understanding of places and environments, or what has been described as their *ethno-geographies* (Martin, 2006a, 2008; Catling and Martin, 2011; also see Chapter 2). Primary children's ethno-geographies develop, as has been indicated above, from their earliest years, and they bring this range of experience and understanding into school. Inevitably, their daily geographies develop and evolve as they grow and mature through childhood. Analysis and reviews of this research point out clearly that children's experience in the environment is essential to their appreciation of places and environments and to developing their spatial skills through mobility in using places. Through their experience in places children develop their sense of place.

There is a rich research background to this area of children's lives and this section draws on various of these studies (Blundell, 2016; Catling, 2003, 2005b, 2006b; Cele, 2006; Chawla, 1992; Christensen and O'Brien, 2003; Christensen *et al.*, 2018; Cregan and Cuthbert, 2014; Fog Olwig and Gulløv, 2003; Foley and Leverett, 2011; Freeman and Tranter, 2011; Griffiths, 2013; Hackett *et al.*, 2015; Higgins and Freeman, 2013; Hörschelman and van Blerk, 2012; Katz, 2004; Matthews, 1992; Murnaghan and Shillington, 2016; Nairn and Kraftl, 2016; Pike, 2008; Spencer and Blades, 2006; Valentine, 2004).

Learning about places

Day (2007) argues that adults and children conceive the world differently. For children, the world is new and their learning to come to terms with it involves making use of it in non-adult ways. Walls are for climbing and are restrictions to be overcome; the street and open spaces are for meeting and chatting; the shopping centre is for keeping warm and safe when there is nothing much else to do. Many places are fresh, novel and enticing – exciting to make use of and to be in. Opportunities to explore locally, including their streets and open spaces, help children to get to know an area, to make it familiar and to develop understandings of how they might be able to use it for their own interests in play and meeting friends – that is, to identify and exploit its affordances where they felt safe to do so, while recognising the restrictions that local places, traffic and adult 'cultures' put on place use (Blundell, 2016; Carroll et al., 2012; Papageorgiou et al., 2016). Such realisations by children are cross-national and present in children whose lives are spent in rural places as much as in urban environments (Matthews, 1995; Matthews et al., 2000; Nairn and Kraftl, 2016).

International studies surveying over 30,000 mid-age and older primary children's satisfaction with their lives found that a large majority of 8- to 12-year-olds reported that they were relatively satisfied with their localities – for instance, with outdoor areas and the community they inhabited, although there were clear minorities who were not content with their neighbourhoods (Jacobs Foundation, 2015, 2016), particularly if they perceived their place to lack facilities they would like and felt it to be unattractive (Avriel-Avni et al., 2010). Most 8-year-olds tended to be happier with their neighbourhoods, their places to play and local safety than did 10- and 12-year-old children. These findings identified that there was a range of satisfaction in each nation in the survey and that there were clear variations across the countries and continents (Dinsman and Rees, 2014). In any community children have mixed feelings about their own neighbourhoods. Christensen et al. (2015) noted children's preferences for play spaces, but they found too that children were sensitive to sites and areas in neighbourhoods in terms of safe and what they regarded as unsafe places. Spaces where older children 'hung out' and areas with which younger children were unfamiliar were to be avoided, while they regarded sites close to home as safer. However, a 'bad' place for one child might be a 'good' place to another and what one group of children might wish to do at a site might be complained about by another group or by adults, indicating that senses and uses of place are contested, indeed conflicted (Massey, 2005).

Place learning emerges from undertaking errands but is most strongly fostered through 'free exploration', outside adult control, enabling children to learn for themselves about places. This grows with experience, with children initially developing their experience as 'accompanied explorers', extending this through 'supervised exploration' and later becoming 'independent explorers' (Ba, 2009; Catling, 2011). Freedom of movement leads children to extend their 'home range', enables their wayfinding skills, and develops their competence in and styles of representation of features, nature and spatial form of the familiar environment, as mental representations and in descriptions, models and maps. The greater children's mobility in their neighbourhood and extended environments, the more they develop their spatial awareness and representations, their environmental knowledge and their social uses of urban and/or rural spaces (Ahmadi, 2011; Freeman and Tranter, 2011; Pike, 2011). Inevitably, as parents give children greater freedom to explore, this appears related to age – yet it seems that experience, whether at earlier or later ages, is the key developmental factor.

Children's local knowledge

Place learning is about developing local and locational knowledge. Children's locality knowledge depends in part on the constraints they place or have placed on their exploration (Ahmadi, 2011; Ba, 2009; Bowles, 2004a; Cullingford, 1999, 2007; Fog Olwid and Guløv, 2003; Freeman and Tranter, 2011; Matthews, 1992; Rissotto and Giuliani, 2006; Valentine, 2004). Their knowledge focuses on what is distinctive for them. Play spaces are important, both formal playgrounds and games areas, and patches of grounds they designate as meeting places and 'games' places (Min and Lees, 2006; Pike, 2008, 2011). Other places include the sites of particular familiar shops and places to eat. Their 'home range' in or beyond a neighbourhood – often more limited in cities – extends environmental awareness, if only in passing. This 'neighbourhood learning' provides an insight into the range of elements in a neighbourhood that children identify, which include features and areas as well as social activities and interactions (Lehman-Frisch et al., 2012). Between them, children bring a variety of knowledge of the school's catchment to share: personal geography becomes community geography. Such overlapping and cumulative children's everyday geographies provide information that includes the following:

- shops, shopping streets, shopping centres;
- businesses and commerce;
- parks, play areas and other open spaces;
- homes and gardens;
- places of worship, libraries, health centres, etc.;
- waterways and bridges;

Research summary

Children's neighbourhood knowledge

Lehmann-Frisch and colleagues (Lehman-Frisch *et al.* 2012) used children's drawings to investigate 9- and 10-year-old children's knowledge and representations of their Parisian neighbourhood. They found a wide variation in the detail of content and the areas shown in the children's drawings, but they learnt much more about children's experience and perceptions through interviews. They summarise their findings about neighbourhood knowledge as follows:

> *Where some [children] might insist on the properly urban dimensions of the neighbourhood (density, architectural characteristics), others concentrate on the natural elements (parks, vegetation and animals). Several children associate the notion of neighbourhood not with the landscapes but with the activities and people who liven it up on a daily basis. But the drawings do not demonstrate the variable scope of the neighbourhood according to the children. Only the interviews allow access to the contrasting expanse of the territory, from the apartment building to an area of several blocks. These differentiations can sometimes be explained along the lines of class, gender, family situation or the children's personal history. However, our study reveals that, in this socially diverse gentrified neighbourhood, these traditional lines are sometimes blurred {.}*
>
> *{.} on the whole, the neighbourhood is for them a territory based primarily around the home, the school and the park. They are deeply fond of them and their fondness rests upon a functional, social and physical judgment. In other words, the neighbourhood is made up of what they see, of what they do, what they feel and the people they meet. And it is this combination of different methods, visual and oral, which enables us to comprehend the complexity of the child's relationship with the urban space.*
>
> (Lehman-Frisch *et al.* 2012, p. 33)

- roads, traffic, paths and railways.

Children also bring their use, interests, feelings about and nuanced sense of place to school and class. The range of knowledge among a primary school class of children will vary, dependent on where in a school's catchment area they live and on their freedom to travel. It will also be varied because of the length of time children have been resident and whether they walk with family, friends or alone, or are transported to school. While those born in or who have lived long in a particular community may know it more widely and in greater detail, those who have recently migrated into the neighbourhood may well centre their sense of the community around their home (Harrington, 2016). It takes time to get to know a locality, and among any group of children there is likely to be a wide range of knowledge and experience of an area.

Sites of personal importance, place attachment and sense of place

Children's place learning provides opportunities to see the possibilities or limitations in using sites for their own interests, the site's functionality or 'affordance' (Kytta, 2004, 2006; Min and Lee, 2006). The place affordances – the benefits and opportunities available – that children most value concern sites where they can play, meet and spend time with friends (Blundell, 2016; Cele, 2006; Henshall and Lacey, 2007; Pike, 2011; Else, 2009; Tanner, 2010; Hayward, 2012). Such valued places are complemented by places that are purely functional, such as particular shops in which to spend pocket money. Specific sites may be valued for their accessibility, because they are 'safer' from adult surveillance, they are interesting spaces or appropriate for particular activities. Other sites may be avoided because of traffic, older children or other potential interferences. Children personalise sites such as dens, and 'desecration' is keenly felt when adults or rival children invade children's personal places. Their capacity to make use of places fosters their place attachment, the feeling of being comfortable and 'at home' in a particular place, which has meaning, value and happiness for us (Catling, 2009a; Chawla, 1992; Tanner, 2009). This may be countered or weak where children have concerns for their personal safety in a neighbourhood (Witten and Carroll, 2016).

Children's involvement with communities and place(s) is a factor in developing their sense of belonging, an element in their sense of place. Particularly it concerns the places they inhabit (Foley and Leverett, 2011), and for the large majority these are city spaces (Hörschelmann and van Blerk, 2012; Christensen et al., 2018). For many indigenous peoples, including Australians, Americans, Canadians and many others around the world, the home site, neighbourhood and wider area and region are vital components of personal identity (Gerber and Robertson, 2008; Sarra, 2011; Winkler, 2012). For many children this sense of belonging engages and encompasses their sense of ethnicity, homeland and nationality (Scourfield at al., 2006; Barrett and Buchanan-Barrow, 2005; Barrett, 2007). Local experience, awareness and understanding have wider implications than simply about local knowledge and an enjoyment or dislike for particular sites – it is deeply important in children's development of self and self-esteem.

Research summary

Children's understanding of the local area

In her research into 8- and 11-year-olds' views of their local urban environments in Sweden and the UK, Cele (2006) used creative and interactive ways to involve the children. They annotated maps, walked a self-chosen route using them, and were interviewed about the area using photographs they took and drawings they made. The results provided a rich insight into how the children used their environment: what mattered to them; favourite places and places disliked or thought dangerous; how they enjoyed parks and green spaces as much as street spaces, and how their uses of them changed with the seasons; outdoor, unsupervised play was important to them and often related to what they found; they had fears and concerns about areas of their neighbourhood; they held views and expressed emotions about how places were treated by adults and adolescents; they noticed people and events; they might vary their choices of routes linked to friends or mood; and they were aware of environmental issues such as traffic. The children demonstrated evident knowledge of their environment, well-developed spatial capabilities in the environment and the capacity to make use of the environment for their own interests, linked to play and socialising with friends.

Neighbourhoods are ambiguous places, sites of pleasure as well as threat (Cullingford, 2007; Nair and Kraftl, 2016). Children's sense of place is based in the physical environment but constructed around the social environment and their feelings for places, alongside their desire to play in the environment. It evolves from their sense of the affordance of places, and is closely linked to their place attachment. It enables their 'enchantment' with the spaces they are in as they engage with them (Pyyry, 2017). While being outside may be intentional and planned, the activities that create enchantment are almost always unintended and of the moment. Children's engagement with place and attachment to it may be fleeting as much as it can be extended and deep. They do not reflect attractiveness but focuses on interest to and for them. Waste ground can be attractive while a manicured playground may be uninviting. Senses of place can be positive, negative or ambivalent. Their home locale may be 'their place', but they may also be positive about a 'holiday' place, reflecting time there and escape from adult oversight.

Children in 'natural' places

Concern about children's outdoor experience has been highlighted strongly by Louv (2005) who argued that a particular aspect of children's experience that was diminishing was their experience of nature and natural environments. This is not a new argument and it continues (Nabhan and Trimble, 1994; Kahn and Kellert, 2002; Brown and Patte, 2013). While there is a widely held view that children are outdoors in 'natural' sites less frequently than in the past and need to be more so (Rupprecht et al., 2016), recent evidence from a national survey in England indicates that while almost 90 per cent visited natural environment sites during the previous year, some 70 per cent of children do so at least weekly with a third doing so several times a week (Natural England, 2016). The critique that children lack the engagement with nature that previous generations had may not be as clear-cut today as protagonists imply, but it has led, importantly, to a strong case being made to develop this aspect of experience for and with children (Faber Taylor and Kuo, 2006; Kahn, 1999; Sobel, 2008, 2011; Wilson, 2012). Certainly, it seems that experience in 'natural' places, from gardens to parks to wild areas (which may be vacant or wasteland – informal green spaces), most usually in their local area, has been and continues to be important to children's well-being across the primary age range. Increasingly for children across the world, living in urban areas, 'natural' spaces and places are publicly provided spaces, such as parks, or unintended sites, such as vacant land, in which nature is present in plants and creatures.

For urban children, 'natural' environments, where many children play given the opportunity, have been created or modified by adults at times in very structured and even cosmetic ways, as can be seen in very many parks and play areas. However, these environments offer play spaces and playgrounds for children where they encounter and engage with nature. Gardens, recreation grounds, parks and other accessible, perhaps unintended, open spaces can be found in or near very many neighbourhoods in cities, while in rural areas field edges, fallow fields, woods and paths can be sites for exploration and play. The challenge has been that access to such environments has declined (Louv, 2005; Wilson, 2012), because green spaces have been and are being built over, and health and safety concerns are used to constrain children's more adventurous play activities, particularly if overseen. Yet the arguments continue to be made that children's experience in the 'natural' environment is vital to their general development, health, well-being and enjoyment of life as well as to building understanding and appreciation of the natural world that is our planet (Freeman et al., 2015), and that a range of forms of play, social interaction and agency in activity choice help children make the most of 'natural' sites (Änggård, 2016). A study of primary age non-national migrant children found that exploration and sensory play in natural spaces helped their confidence and settling down in a new environment as well as engaging their interest in nature in such places (Hordyck et al., 2015), experiences which may help any child begin to settle who moves home to a new location.

Today more than half the world's population lives in urban environments. In very many Western countries this is well over three-quarters of the national population. Experience of a truly natural or nature-strong environment is declining. Most families and schools provide children with experiences of nature in created and modified 'natural' sites, be these a local park or play area, in school grounds or through occasional days out to the countryside, a national park or the beach. In studies with 6-12 and 9-11 year-olds, as might be expected, children living in urban environments were found to have less experience with nature than children living in rural areas, though city children were adept at seeking out 'natural' sites (Collado et al., 2016; Freeman et al., 2015, 2016). Primary children recognise and appreciate the value of natural places for play and leisure, and as they grow they are increasingly aware of difference between nature and human created aspects of their environment. Their developing vocabulary encompasses a wide range of named features such as rivers and lakes, flora such as trees and various plants, and fauna including birds, animals and insects by their upper primary years. Primary children understand the idea of and hold images of nature familiar and unfamiliar (Rios and Menezes, 2017). Children respond aesthetically to nature, contrasting 'beautiful' nature with 'ugly' buildings, for instance. Reactions to human impacts on nature begin to emerge with younger primary children. Rural children have greater engagement with nature than urban children, indicating that place of residence is an influential factor. For urban children this depends on the availability and accessibility of 'natural' habitats in highly built-up areas where gardens and very close-by green spaces will tend to be those most frequently used (Freeman et al., 2015). But not all children are comfortable with nature and 'natural' environments and some may act thoughtlessly and detrimentally in relation to fauna and flora, perhaps acting 'naturally' in damaging plants and killing insects (Malone, 2016a, 2016b).

Opportunities to investigate, explore and play in natural places, such as through Forest School activities, have positive impacts on children's perceptions of, engagement with and care for nature (Brown and Patte, 2013; Knight, 2013a, 2016; Austin et al., 2016; Rios and Menezes, 2017). Another approach to tackling this concern has been the growth in the school garden movement, where children are encouraged to grow edible and aesthetic plants and tend them throughout the year (Gaylie, 2009, 2011; Lockie, 2007; Williams and Brown, 2012; Woodhouse, 2017). As with young children's play in pre-school outdoor spaces, it is evident that children enjoy playing in natural and 'natured' spaces, which provide affordances for the use of natural materials in such activities as den building, imaginative creation of places and learning about the natural world (Bilton, 2011; Garrick, 2009; Freeman and Tranter, 2011).

Reflective task

What conclusions do you draw from the summary of research information above about primary children's experiences of and views about their environments?

Mobility for place exploration

Primary school age children's independent travel mobility to school and about their neighbourhood is usually on foot but may be by bicycle. It is largely influenced by adults, their parents, and it is much less likely that younger primary children will be allowed out of the home for independent journey-making; unsurprisingly, independent travel increases with age but may be influenced by cultural as well as environmental factors (Giuseppina et al., 2017). Indeed, younger primary children almost always travel locally accompanied by a parent or another adult or older sibling to a playground, shops or friends' homes, and distance to travel within a neighbourhood is rarely limited (Timperio et al., 2004). A fair degree of travel for a high minority of children is by car or other vehicle (Carver et al., 2013), quite possibly more so in rural areas in Western societies. For children, as much as for their parents, volume and speed of traffic and parked vehicles create a sense of 'unsafe' roads (Panter et al., 2010; Villanueva et al., 2014), though where parents perceived walkability in a neighbourhood to be reasonably safe, children from around ages 8 to 9 years were granted greater licence (Moghtaderi et al., 2013; Villanueva et al., 2014). In the main, adults restrict the area range of children in independent travel related to their (adult) perceptions of the local area (Giuseppina et al., 2017). Travel distance is likely to be constrained to up to half a kilometre from home whether for travel to school or to visit play areas (Schoeppe et al., 2016), though some parents give greater freedom to roam while others are more restrictive, and boys are granted a little more licence than girls (Villanueva et al., 2014). There are national variations, with parents in some European countries more usually allowing independent travel distances of up to and beyond one kilometre from home, though research does not indicate why this is. Such a distance maintains children's travel within the neighbourhood area and may be deemed helpful in supporting a growing sense of independence and maturity among older primary children and in fostering children's wayfinding and neighbourhood learning, such as for local shopping, and spatial skills.

Children's perspectives about local independent mobility appear more positive than their parents'. For instance, where parents may view an area as subject to dangerous traffic, their children may hold a more positive view in relation to safe road crossing and travel to local venues (Timperio *et al.*, 2004). Older primary children tend to remain within what they perceive to be a safe range from home, often indicated by significant 'geographical' boundaries such as major roads, rivers or canals and railway lines (Loebach and Gilliland, 2016). Distance is also a factor for children, particularly if the journey to school is far (Carver *et al.*, 2013). Children who have much experience of independent mobility tend to know their way around the neighbourhood and make use of safe routes through alleyways, low traffic streets and other pathways. Local travel also appears to relate to friendship networks locally, which encourage friends to meet or visit each others' homes, though where such networks are restricted children tend to travel less and less far. What independent mobility does seem to allow children to do is to construct their awareness of the urbanscape or rural area and to build a sense of place and belonging (Bourke, 2017). Indeed, this would seem to be supported particularly where children visited a number and variety of destinations, quite possibly regularly (Loebach and Gilliland, 2016). Journeying supports the development of children's place and environmental knowledge, over time deepening their understanding of places as not just physical, but also as social and active landscapes, not least because such journey-making may be undertaken with a friend or friends. Local mobility is important in enabling children's daily geographies and in fostering their sense of control in their lives and, thus, agency (Giuseppina *et al.*, 2017).

Environmental spatial understanding

Very young children readily learn their capacity for movement and begin to grasp the spatial layout of features in a room or floor layout important to them, such as at home. Initial ideas about the wider spatial connections between places emerge through experience of journeys and travel in the local neighbourhood, with very early ideas about distance initiated through such experiences. Young children construct mentally the spatial layouts of familiar environments and build skills to begin to navigate places as they develop experience of them (Bell, 2006; Newcombe and Huttenlocher, 2000; Spencer *et al.*, 1989; Uttal and Tan, 2000; Wiegand, 2006). This capacity to develop and use wayfinding skills and area layout is usually referred to as *mental mapping* or *cognitive mapping*. Key to the development of such mental maps, as has been implied, is a child's independent mobility, being able to go out, to do errands or simply to explore places on their own or with friends to learn their way around, making sense of the spatial and feature nature of their world.

There is sound evidence that younger children are able to recognise features on and understand and make use of the spatial representations of aerial photographs and maps (Kim *et al.*, 2012; Wiegand, 2006). Studies with children using vertical aerial photographs of familiar environments (Plester *et al.*, 2006) show that children can use them in problem-solving activities in their familiar environments. This provides a basis for examining and deriving information from aerial photographs and maps of other similar neighbourhood scale places (Kim *et al.*, 2012; Klonari, 2013). Map learning is a gradual process that involves appreciating the development of maps as spatial representations through their symbols alongside skills such as relating and aligning the map to the environment, understanding its scale and appreciating the use of more abstract aspects such as direction and coordinates (Wiegand, 2006). Children are able to relate maps to a familiar environment but at younger ages do not always pay attention to the particulars of a site (Kastens and Liben, 2010), a skill that develops with experience and maturity. Studies of children's use of street and other medium-scale maps to follow routes reinforce that map-reading skills traversing a locality increase generally with age (Hemmer *et al.*, 2013). Of importance is the capability of children to orient themselves as they make a journey in the environment using a standard medium-scale paper map. This can be challenging for many young primary children, but appears within the capability of older primary children whose competence seems to be enhanced somewhat if they can use a map-based mobile digital navigation device (Hergan, 2018; Hergan and Umek, 2017). The essential need in both contexts is for children to relate attentively their map to their surroundings as they make their journey, for there can be a tendency to turn too soon when using a paper map, while they may walk too far before turning using a mobile device even though the mobile navigator constantly orients the map to the direction children are going. It seems that children enjoy using paper maps as well as mobile devices.

Representing a familiar route, such as the way to school, 4–6-year-olds will draw topological representations that connect the start and finish, but rarely note permanent features along 'the way'. By age 7–8 or so, children are beginning to show the type of route and include features, giving a clearer sense of a map. As they get older their maps become increasingly map-like and spatially accurate and begin to include conventional elements, such as a key (Thommen *et al.*, 2010). By ages 10–11 years old, children appear to have developed a level of spatial representation by which they can record recognisably their mental map of a familiar route. Younger primary children's map-like drawings of familiar areas are often pictorial in style but spatially informed. They improve in detail and quality with environmental experience and age (Todd, 2009; Thommen *et al.*, 2010; Lehman-Frisch *et al.*, 2012) and may well use plan views and symbols as their knowledge and understanding of formal, published maps develops (Mackett *et al.*, 2007; Wiegand, 2006). Children will only develop consistent cartographic formality through the use of published maps, which introduce conventions such as symbols and keys, grid references, compass points and scale. This can occur at home or in school. Using maps in the environment is vital in their learning.

Constraints on children's environmental exploration

Children's well-being is a charged notion, not solely about opportunities but also about care and safety across a range of domains, including environmental experience (Bradshaw and Mayhew, 2003; Guldberg, 2009; Layard and Dunn, 2009). Increasingly, limits are placed on children's free exploration of their locality, be it urban or rural (Christensen *et al.*, 2018). There are various reasons for this. What is evident is that children's experience of their localities is changing, some of this allied to increased access for more families to personal car transport, with children walking less (Hillman and Adams, 1992; Prezza, 2007), and in part to an adult-driven risk-averse approach to childhood outdoor experience (Gill, 2007; Guldberg, 2009; Layard and Dunn, 2009; Blundell, 2016). But it should be noted that some children's perceptions of bullying in neighbourhoods and perceived or real sense of change and encroachment by urbanism and migrants affects how they feel about being out in their own localities or in urban centres (Hayward, 2012), particularly in inner city areas (Weir *et al.*, 2006). Parents have become more concerned about children's road safety given ever-increasing traffic on roads, reflected in part through decreasing cycling (Cele, 2006), though road accidents involving children have declined (Carver et al., 2008; Cele, 2006; Cullingford, 2007; Else, 2009; Guldberg, 2009; Henshall and Lacey, 2007; Johansson, 2006; Katz, 2005; Mackett *et al.*, 2007; Madge and Barker, 2007; Thomas and Thompson, 2004).

The nature of residential environments has an effect, illustrated by evidence that urban parents have a greater concern for older primary children going out where they live along connected roads, while those inhabiting blocks of flats and cul-de-sacs seem to give their children greater autonomy to be outside close by their home (Veitch *et al.*, 2006). Linked to this is concern that communities no longer look out for children, with parents feeling they need to keep their children under surveillance. Urban children find themselves more bounded and rule bound, and having greater adult supervision when going out, while rural children seem more able to negotiate a greater extent of movement freedom (MacDougall *et al.*, 2009). Play spaces have become more confined and 'commodified' (Layard and Dunn, 2009; McKendrick *et al.*, 2000) and children and parents have safety concerns where they are not well maintained and there is evident pollution and graffiti (Veitch *et al.*, 2006; Baylina *et al.*, 2016). Fewer wasteland and 'wild areas' are left in which to play, although these are valued by children as play spaces. Children do not decry what adventure playgrounds offer, but their security and structures inhibit the opportunities for children to create personalised and imagined places that untended areas provide. As mitigation, for example, in northern Europe forest schools, an approach to outdoor learning that allows young children to explore and investigate the natural environment independently but in a well-supervised context, is one of a number of formal approaches trying to counteract this situation (Knight, 2013b, 2011b; Williams-Siegfredsen, 2017).

Yet lack of outdoor experience and roaming is not as restricted for many children in some parts of the world as the research noted here infers. Hayward (2012) reports a study in New Zealand that indicates that older primary children appear to continue to have access to the local area. This varies between groups and it does have an effect. Those who live in high-income localities appear to see their environments in terms of the activities they are engaged in, often highly structured through timed extra-curricular learning linked with sport, music or additional subject tuition, though reference was made to beaches or shopping centres. Children from low- to middle-income areas had a well-developed sense of the social interaction and of community environmental networks, which were more important to mention than the physical spaces. Rural children, on the other hand, presented a richer sense of the physical environment resulting from wider home ranges, and they connected activities with sites and features more evidently.

While there is some evidence that children are beginning to feel more included and listened to (Madge, 2006), there remains a continuing sense of impotence in their communities (Moss and Petrie, 2002; Hayward, 2012). Children are not always viewed favourably in the environment. They can find themselves viewed as 'out of place' if not accompanied by an adult (Valentine, 2004; Freeman and Tranter, 2011). They can be seen to be at odds with the norms of adult uses of places if they transgress by loitering too long or kicking a football about too noisily. Yet they notice that if older adults gather and chat at the shops or on the street corner this is appropriate. What concerns children is adults' unwillingness often to listen. The social distancing of adults from children in shared community places such as streets can create an atmosphere where children are unwittingly pressed to use liminal, or marginal, spaces (Nieuwenhuys, 2003). Children know when they are not wanted in places and not infrequently will seek out the places that adults pass by or miss to avoid their gaze and authority. This may explain why in some central urban public spaces children have absented themselves.

While these changes in children's place experience seem negative in Western societies, this is less so in other societies where children seem to retain greater freedoms and are more positively seen and valued when out and about (Chawla, 2002; Katz, 2004).

Teachers' knowledge of the school's locality

Many teachers do not live in the localities in which they teach and, as a result, know the area less well (Bowles, 2004b). Travelling in and out of a locality using specific routes limits what is noticed and appreciated about the school's neighbourhood. An inevitable result is that many teachers find themselves disadvantaged by not knowing the area in which the children live, not simply because they are uninformed of the features, layout and social life of the area, but because they have no awareness or sense of place of their own to which to relate their children's perspectives on their area. Such a mismatch can inhibit confidence in developing effective geographical studies in a locality, in taking children into the streets for fieldwork, and in appreciating the experience that the children can and do bring into class. Where teachers explore their school's locality, they feel more confident and can draw on children's knowledge, feelings and perspectives more fully, involving them in local enquiries more effectively.

Practical task

You may know the area around where you live well. Draw a sketch map. Mark on it the features you recall. Make notes on it about which features, services and sites you value, which you avoid, and indicate the areas you do not know. Now do the same exercise for the area around the last school that you spent some time at. What are the differences between your two sketch maps? Why is this? What action can you take?

Reflective task

In a previous Reflective task (p.64) you observed, and perhaps discussed with children, their experience and perceptions of the school playground. But you too have such experience. What do you recall of your own primary school playground and playtime experiences? What did you do? Where did you most like playing in the playground? What was positive and what negative? Why? If you have supervised playtimes, consider your experiences. What do you enjoy and find frustrating about playtime supervision? What knowledge do you gain when outside with the children? Why?

Children's awareness of the wider world

Younger children's geographies include awareness and ideas about the wider world, of their homeland and of peoples and countries. Their awareness develops early, reflecting experience from various sources, including family, friends and peers, television programmes, and stories set in other places and cultures, such as *The Day of Ahmed's Secret* (Heide and Gilliland, 1997), *Kenju's Forest* (Morimoto, 1992) or *Gregory Cool* (Binch, 1994), or stories that are set in distant and 'home' places and cultures, such as *Mirror* (Baker, 2010) and *Azzi in Between* (Garland, 2012). Television and films are a source of knowledge of places that is not always accurate, but for many children travel experience can be helpful (Scoffham, 2017a). It seems that new technologies are influencing increasing numbers of older primary age children through their access to the Internet and through texting, social sites and email. These sources inform children's ideas about and attitudes to people and places beyond their direct experience, positively and critically (Cullingford, 2000, 2007; Barrett, 2007). Children's knowledge and values develop more through informal than through directed attention, although the latter can occur linked to holidays, e-friends and some school homework.

Knowing where global places are

As noted earlier, children's first mental maps develop from their earliest years evolving through their experiences based on travel around and exploring their familiar and local places. Primary school children seem also to develop a wider frame of mental mapping, which incorporates their perceptions, maturing knowledge and understandings (and misunderstandings) of the *whereness* of places in the world beyond their experience. It is sometimes thought that early years and primary age children are unaware about the rest of the world – and, indeed, it can be argued that they know comparatively little about it – but this presumes that they do not encounter information about what is where through informal learning, from family and friends, and from various media, including information and story books, and via television news and other programmes, and from the World Wide Web and social media. Our problem is that this is a little researched area and that we know almost nothing about children's learning about their whereness outside school.

Very young children develop a rudimentary awareness of the Earth as a globe, but have little idea of countries and where they are. By 11 years old, many UK children have an idea of the shape and overall layout of the continents on the globe and can locate some countries within them (Wiegand, 2006). Seeing and using globes, world and national maps must be a factor here. Wiegand's research notes that very young children hear about places around the world, and he posits that their knowledge of places increases with age and may well be influenced by news reports about particular places, which may be frequently or prominently reported on. Where children live appears also to be an influence in world map drawing, perhaps related to the global maps they see, with

European children placing the Atlantic Ocean and Europe/Africa in the centre of their maps, while Australian children place the Pacific Ocean centrally. Wiegand proposed a five-stage development for primary age children with the youngest producing world maps that showed discretely separate and bounded countries and continents scattered across a page, while middle primary children began to provide some order towards the correct parts of the world, linking some countries and continents, although still placing them discretely. The oldest primary children provided maps that appeared more correct and conventional, though not always accurate, particularly in terms of the relative size of countries and continents (Wiegand, 2006). The research by Lowes (2008) in the USA reinforces this. Inevitably, though, their world maps are partial and there occur inaccuracies in juxtaposing places. There are very many parts of the world of which children know little if anything, a point to recognise but not be surprised about. What seemed to emerge across the primary years was that children developed a sense of 'class inclusion' – the Russian dolls effect. Their ideas developed from countries and continents being entirely separate entities to realising that countries are, in very many cases, within continents. Indeed, older primary children largely recognise that major cities and physical features are within countries, indicating that they have grasped the idea of 'nested hierarchies'. There seems no doubt that this learning results from exposure to national and world maps.

We need to remain wary about the extent of primary children's world knowledge, including knowing where their home nation is in the world. For example, in a study in the UK some 20 per cent of 6- to 14-year- olds could not locate England on a world map, and only about two-thirds knew the location of Wales and Scotland accurately (Mischiefpr, 2006). In their study comparing Swedish and Australian primary children's knowledge of places, Reynolds and Vinterek (2016) found consistency with previous research. They noted that for young children, 'nearby' countries to their own were more likely to be known, although media influence means that they were aware of nations such as the USA. They identified that in their later primary years children's world knowledge grew rapidly, and that they developed attitudes and preferences as this occurred, affected by the influences already noted. However, it was found that the children's increased knowledge of countries tended to remain in the same parts of the world. The Swedish children's knowledge of European nations increased, as did the Australian's knowledge of Asia, particularly its eastern nations. However, the historical links between Australia and the UK meant that Australian children also were aware of the UK. Even so, nearby international knowledge can be limited – for example, the Australian children were less knowledgeable about the countries of Oceania. It is clear that where children live in the world is a significant influence of their locational knowledge of nations.

Research summary

Children's locational knowledge

In 1968, a study in Sweden identified elementary school children's level of knowledge of place locations in Europe and the world. This research included 9- to 12-year-olds. In 2013, the research was repeated in the same schools (Hennerdal, 2016) and comparisons were made between the generations involved. Both studies involved matching listed geographic names (lists that included distracters as well as the correct names) to marked locations on the maps. The names to locate on the world map included continents and oceans. Both studies found that there were clear variations between children, that girls scored slightly higher than boys, and that while 9–10-year-olds in 2013 performed a little better than their counterparts in 1968, results were similar for 11–12-year-olds, although slightly poorer for boys in 2013. Overall, children could better locate continents and oceans in 2013 than in 1968. However, their knowledge of geographic sites (such as of countries, regions, islands and seas) in Europe was weaker. Overall, it was noted that gender did not make a difference in locational knowledge and that this distinction found in earlier studies was fading. Children who had travelled outside Sweden performed better than students who had not, which was also the case for those who followed national and international news at least weekly. There may be a link here to socioeconomic background. It was noted that playing computer games which used maps had no noticeable effect on locational knowledge. Overall, the 2013 study provided some evidence that older primary age children knew more geographical locations than their predecessors in 1968, the earlier primary children appearing more knowledgeable about features in Europe. The conclusions were that place knowledge learning has not improved or declined across the decades, but it was appreciated that children had different 'knowledge' acquired in a different society in 2013 than in 1968. The researcher commented that the study provided no argument for restoring learning 'old-fashioned' geographic knowledge to the curriculum.

Children's images of the world

Evidence suggests that travel helps develop children's ideas about distant places (Wiegand, 1992; Schmeinck, 2006). For most children, these are holidays and they provide only a particular type of experience of other parts of the world (Barrett, 2007). Images of places visited may well be partial and even misconceived. Contact with people in other places via email and the Web both illustrate this and may help to challenge misconceptions (Holloway and Valentine, 2003). One challenge emerging from this study is that children can conflate information about other distant areas of the world – for instance, English children at times transpose information about New Zealand and Australia, the former considered hot and sunny because it is in 'the south' near to Australia. By exchanging information about their lives, the places they live, what they do and like, among much else, older primary children can begin to recognise that children elsewhere are not unlike themselves. Utall and Tan (2000) noted that children's environmental experiences and understanding may become increasingly mediated through virtual experiences of other places – cyber-geographies – leading to shifts in children's global mental maps, something that social media may be influencing with older primary children but which lacks research.

Primary children have positive and critical views about countries other than their own. In the Sweden–Australia comparative study (Reynolds and Vinterek, 2016), it was found that some nations are popular because of family and tourism links and others because of media influences, particularly the USA. Perceived climate, internationally recognised monuments and proximity to the home country were also children's reasons for liking a country. Causes of a country's unpopularity appeared to be linked to negative information about that country, as well as dislikes about such matters as its clothing, food and language. Some countries could be liked and disliked in similar measure by different children, such as the USA. All too often, children encounter largely negative images of particular parts of the world, leading to negative stereotypical views of countries in continents such as Africa and Asia. Family connections with another country do not necessarily mitigate this (Holden, 2004). Where such misconceptions go unchallenged, children's ideas may remain heavily inaccurate. Some evidence suggests that children's positive images of places can become less strong with more information, though negative images may be made more positive because children become better informed (Barrett, 2007; Wiegand, 1992, 1993; Reynolds and Vinterek, 2016).

Across nations there are migrant inhabitants born overseas, many of whom have children born locally. The existence of a diverse, multicultural population gives education a crucial role in challenging and breaking down stereotypes and negative perceptions and attitudes. Geography has an essential role to play here. For instance, children can learn from other members of their class whose cultural backgrounds differ from their own, and teachers can use vicarious means to present realistic and accurate images of differing cultures, while helping children to see the value in difference and diversity as well as understand the similarities and commonalties of each others' lives. Indeed, this is something in which all children can engage in every classroom, however much appearances may seem very similar.

As individuals in their families, differences and diversity are common heritage for all children.

A sense of national identity

Studies of children's ideas about their own nation and identity and of people of other nations (Barrett, 2007; Barrett *et al.*, 2006; Holden, 2004) suggest that children's knowledge of their own country is variable (Barrett, 2007; Catling, 2009b; Throssell, 2015; Scoffham, 2017a). Research has indicated that primary age children have some difficulty in understanding the notion of a 'country' (Scoffham, 2017a), having a stronger sense of their ascribed local town or city initially – their identification with a place (Scourfield *et al.*, 2006) – only appreciating the idea of the 'nested hierarchy' relationships at around the ages of 10–12. Broadly, primary children seem to develop an attachment to and identify with their home nation, giving it positive ratings and taking pride in it even where the level and nature of their knowledge about their country may be limited, although from a young age they may have become aware of the head of state and the national flag (Barrett, 2007; Barrett *et al.*, 2006; Throssell, 2015). Children in several nations develop a high sense of national identity very early in life, while others come to this in adolescence. Research in Europe has noted that children in many European countries think of themselves both nationally and also as European, although children – for instance, in the UK – are less inclined to have a sense of a European dimension to their identity. British children seem less well informed (Holden, 2004), indeed muddled, to the extent of believing that areas of the UK are abroad and that some places abroad are in the UK. For many European children, this dual sense of identity links to national political attitudes to 'being European' and an emphasis in their school education on Europe in geography, history and citizenship studies. Schmeinck identified that when children shared information with each other about their countries, they recognised commonalities and similarities, and appear more positive about others (Schmeinck, 2013; Schmeinck *et al.*, 2010).

This may indicate that children in any particular country hold stereotypes about their own nation's people as well as of others (Throssell, 2015; Scoffham, 2017a); they may have a very limited set of associations, perhaps linked to animals and quite negative ideas about the lives of people. An Australian study of 11–12-year-olds' views about 'being an Australian' identified stereotypical perspectives, such as the wearing of a corked Akubra hat and jeans with a checked shirt or being on the beach, while these same children also noted that most Australians were 'not like that' (Barrett, 2007). In effect, this study indicated that children develop from a young age a generalised sense of 'our' people and nationality while also recognising that it is just that, a characterisation, not what we are as individuals. A national sense of identity is important, and it seems an essential element in that identification is empathy with the cultures both of other nationals who live elsewhere and of those who have migrated to live in your country and area. Such thinking and feeling is to be encouraged from children's earliest years.

Of course, life is not always pleasant for primary age children. Cregan and Cuthbert (2014) note that in many parts of the world nationalistic politics and civil war and cross-national conflict have horrendous effects on children's lives. They note that over the centuries some children (along with their parents) can seem 'surplus' to national needs, perhaps because of their families' activities, by being in 'the wrong place at the wrong time' or the result of cultural attitudes and norms at a particular time. This, as they illustrate, can be the case in democratic states, with the state not perceiving some children as nationals in the sense of requiring protection, care and a good upbringing.

Research summary

Children's understanding of nation

Throssell (2015) examined the idea of national understanding with two groups of 8-year-olds in France and England, using interviews undertaken twice with each child. She identified four key findings. The core finding was that the children identified themselves as belonging to a nation, seeing themselves as members of national groups. Their birth was vitally important, whether in terms of birthplace or through family connections. This connects with their 'origins' and their authenticity. Second, their 'in-group' sense of national identity was consolidated by recognising those not national as 'others' or belonging to an 'out-group'. White ethnicity was a stronger element in this in France than in England. Third, the children declared a strong affective sense of *attachment, affection and love for their country* (p. 346). They valued their country and were defensive of it. The sense of nation was about 'we', as nationals being together. Fourth, the children largely had a sense of national politics and of key politicians, although in England children from working-class backgrounds were less aware and knowledgeable. The children were aware of power as domination in various forms, linked to national leadership such as the president and the queen. They recognised other nations, particularly the USA's domination internationally. Throssell's overarching conclusion is that *although the national context does have some impact on the way children learn about nations and belonging to nations, what we are observing here is the impact of an international ideology normalizing national belonging* (2015, p. 348).

Reflective task

How did you develop your own sense of national identity? Did it emerge slowly or did you realise at a given point what it is? Is it important to you? Why is this? Indeed, do you think there is an easily identifiable national identity for your nation? Does this strike you as reasonable or do you consider it to be somewhat of a stereotype, perhaps an unhelpful one?

How does your sense of your nationality reflect a view of other nationalities? How do you think this might be the case for children? How might you use geography to examine stereotypical and negative images of other nationalities and parts of the world?

Children in the wider world

We have concentrated on points that relate to children's personal geographies in local and distant places and environments. We now turn to geographies that affect children (Catling, 2003). For children, place and environment are not simply about their personal geographies. They are also about the way the world affects them – geographies that impact on children.

Whether rural or urban, suburban or inner city, island or wilderness locations, the places in which children live and the facilities, activities and access available to them impact on their opportunities and choices. For some, life is very positive. For others, poverty, lack of access to clean water and sanitation impact their families (Liebel, 2004; Minujin and Nandy, 2012; Cregan and Cuthbert, 2014; UNICEF, 2005); and being the victim of a natural disaster is the reality (Bellamy, 2004). Such issues directly affect more than half of the world's children. Poverty has negative welfare effects, with children perhaps needing to work to support their families (Liebel, 2004; Minujin and Nandy, 2012; Cregan and Cuthbert, 2014; UNICEF, 2005; Weston, 2005), with impacts on health and welfare (Ansell, 2017; Brocklehurst, 2006; Mapp, 2011), and through such life-shifting effects as migration (Ensor and Gozdziak, 2010; Ní Laoire et al., 2011; Ní Laoire and White, 2017; Waters, 2008) and press-ganging as child soldiers (Singer, 2006; Harker and Hörschelmann, 2017). Poverty, migration, welfare and well-being concerns are all aspects of many children's lives in many nations, such as in the UK (Bradshaw and Mayhew, 2005; Vleminckx and Smeeding, 2003; Ansell and Klocher, 2016). They impact on children through their access to play, to resources and services, to healthy diets and family support. These national and international issues are not 'distant' from children, but either the reality for them or infiltrating their lives through local experience, the news media and aid appeals. We might consider that life in the Western world is relatively comfortable, but this not only hides issues of poverty and its impact in our midst; it can numb us to the lives of the majority of the world's children, only noticing them when their situation reaches extremes and hits our screen for a few minutes or for a few days. Children's personal geographies around the world are incredibly varied and not to be based on the assumptions that we make as part of our lives (Katz, 2004; Minujin and Nandy, 2012).

Children and migration

We live in a mobile world, physically as well as digitally (Ansell, 2017; Veale and Donà, 2014). People and families move homes, some within a local area or a city, while others move to different parts of a country and between countries. Many children have experience of migration because they have moved home, taken to a new place because of the work their parents and carers do or because a safer or larger home is needed, or driven to move because they have been forced to relocate by circumstances beyond their control, such as war. Migration can be local and cross-national. It can be for very positive reasons or can be the result of a natural disaster or human factors. It may be to a more pleasant and engaging place, perhaps a 'nicer' neighbourhood, or to a poorer environment, such as a family hostel or a refugee encampment. Generally, we think of migration as caused by economic factors or because it is forced on people willingly or unwillingly, perhaps through war. Stories abound of family and children's migrations and its causes, positively and negatively, about loss and survival (Alabed, 2017).

It is likely that many children in a primary class will have experience of moving home, normally a decision made for them by parents or carers. Simply moving home can be exciting, providing the opportunity to explore a new place, to make use of new facilities and to make new friends. Moving home may be traumatic for some children whose friendship networks are disrupted or lost and who find it less easy to settle into a new locality and primary school. The 'new' can be stimulating and enjoyable or dislocating and uncomfortable. Different children experience moving home differently; some take it in their stride; others find it hard to adjust. However, the concept of 'home' is important to children both on the move and at arrival. This can reflect the cultural centrality of home (Zhang, 2015; Tyrrell and Kallis, 2017) and children's agency. To almost everyone, home is our locus of being, the place where we feel most comfortable and secure (Fox, 2016).

Globally, some 50 million children – that is, people aged under 18 years old – have been uprooted and found refuge within or beyond their own countries (UNICEF, 2016), with two-thirds living outside their country of birth. Home has been disrupted. Almost 28 million children have become refugees because of violence and conflict entering their lives. UNICEF estimates that one in every 200 children is a child refugee. Most primary school aged children journey with their families, but even quite young children have been found travelling alone, possibly having been sent by their family or because there is no one to look after them (Ansell, 2017; Huijsmans, 2017). Such children are extremely vulnerable (Ensor and Gozdziak, 2010). Three-fifths of child migrants live in Asia and Africa, remaining in or in a country nearby their home nation. Probably less than 20 per cent travel across continents to reach countries in North America and Europe, and to a much lesser degree South America and Australia. We need to remember, though, that the very large majority of younger migrant children live where they do now with their families because of parental decisions to migrate, positively seeking a better life especially for their children's best interests (Tyrrell and Kallis, 2017). A key experience of international travel is the crossing of borders and understanding what they represent about demarcation, being received and being in somewhere new (Spyrou and Christou, 2014). Young children experience such bordering or barrier crossing through migration and perceive that borders can be enabling as much as imposing, separating and inhibiting. They can be welcomed or made to feel different and foreign.

An important element for child migrants is maintaining their sense of national identity even while they may gradually be acquiring a familiarity with and affinity for the country in which they now reside – that is, creating a sense of belonging. Such primary age children may develop a sense of the global world because of family ties to their past homeland and may retain ties with family members in other nations (Farmer, 2017). Indeed, this will continue to be so for many children born to migrated parents where links remain with other parts of the world, though it does not mean that children may have visited their family's nation of origin (Tyrrell and Kallis, 2017). Here, children can be the catalysts for connecting people and places, making use through digital technologies of social media to maintain communications and shared lives. For younger migrant children, their 'new' location's school is an important site for their socialisation, since meeting others, building friendships and learning about their 'new' home locality helps to develop their sense of belonging and place, although this can be inhibited by parents' concerns for road safety, accessing play areas and knowing one's way around, as well as by home cultures, values and attitudes. This is not by any means straightforward for younger children where ethnic segregation, rather than inclusion and diversity, may be the case in some neighbourhoods and even schools (Sime, 2017), which can lead to the 'othering' of minority migrant populations as 'foreign' by some in the majority community

(Bhabha, 2014). To build a sense of togetherness, even 'integration' requires host and migrant children, as much as adults, to build relationships, create a sense of security and encourage local attachment (Ní Laoire et al., 2011). Migration and settlement are geographical factors that affect children's lives.

Children and natural hazards

The physical environment can appear benign and unproblematic until a natural disaster strikes. In fact, the environment is rather more hazardous than we tend to assume, as climate change impacts illustrate (Lee, 2013). The range of natural hazards includes earthquakes, tsunamis, volcanic eruptions, landslides, forest fires, hurricanes and cyclones, tornadoes, lightning and thunderstorms, flooding and drought. These have very different causes and can have equally varied impacts on the places and lives they affect, including the lives of children (Bhandari, 2014). Many millions of families live in vulnerable locations, with the consequent impact on children when disaster strikes. Climate change seems to be driving an increasing number of extreme weather events affecting not only parts of the world where cyclones and tornadoes have consistently occurred, as in the Philippines, but bringing more damaging winds and rain to places, such as in the southern USA, where people felt relatively safe, with the impact of increased flooding and wind damage (Goudie, 2013; IPCC, 2015). Likewise, a changing climate can create short- and long-term drought conditions affecting agriculture and livelihoods, as in Ethiopia and Sudan, as well as leading to devastating forest fires, which occurred in Portugal and California, USA, during 2017. Such events most certainly impinge on children's lives and there is a strong desire to prepare and support them for and in such events (Bullock et al., 2011; Gordon et al., 1999; Ronan and Johnston, 2005; Ronan and Towers, 2014; Smawfield, 2013; Walker, 2012; Zubenko and Capozzoli, 2002).

Children hear about various disaster-relief efforts, perhaps investigating events such as the 2016 Italian earthquake, and the 2017 Australian cyclone and Colombian mudslide and their flood damage after-effects. Children in school or their community may even raise relief funds. They give generously (or encourage their parents to do so) to relief charities such as Save the Children, Children in Need or Oxfam and many others to help people in their own country and around the world. Here, the geographies of the Earth's natural forces and of survival and rebuilding, the geographies of water access and cleanliness, of poverty and wealth distribution, and the geographies of aid and generosity impact on children. Children learn that it is *an imperfect world*, an unequal world (Cullingford, 2007, p. 31; Layard and Dunn, 2009). But globally, and at times in their own worlds or nearby, children are directly affected by, for instance, earthquakes, hurricanes, flooding or the collapse of buildings. Increasingly, they learn of such disasters through personal and family experiences, near or far, and can voice their concerns about causes and effects – for instance, in relation to flooding (Walker *et al.*, 2012). As in other contexts, the impact of natural catastrophic events or human-induced disasters affects their welfare and they need to be supported to understand how such events occur, what their impact is and how they may be prepared for them, even in terms of how they can act communally for their neighbours and neighbourhood in and after such events (Bullock *et al.*, 2011; Gordon *et al.*, 1999; La Greca *et al.*, 2002; Saylor, 2010). The impact of climate changes variably across the world may well require that children are included in developing disaster management and mitigation, and are not simply the focus of rescue and rehoming (Catling, 2014a).

Research into children's understanding of the nature and causes of the range of environmental hazards is limited. Nonetheless, a review of a range of regional and national studies identifies several significant children's perspectives (Catling, 2014a). Older primary age children have some basic understanding about various natural disasters and climate change and their effects, although this can for some be misinformed and simplistic. More importantly, they tend to understand disasters affectively – that is, in terms of danger, fearfulness and destruction (King and Tarrant, 2013). They may well be aware of how a damaging event may affect their future lives (Jonsson *et al.*, 2012). Where children have personal experience of a disaster, such as when an earthquake severely damaged Canterbury, New Zealand, in 2011 (Freeman *et al.*, 2015a), they are well aware of the impacts of such natural events and appreciate the need to move from a damaged home, why their daily lives and those of others are disrupted, and how physical changes have occurred locally. They not only want to know why the event happened, but what advice to follow and to give others. In other words, they desire agency, not to be treated as bystanders or passive recipients. Primary children recognise that natural disasters and a changing climate have negative effects. They wish to be better informed, in part because this will help them to participate knowledgeably in and to contribute to being prepared for the risks involved when emergencies arise, as indeed children are at school and at home in some hazardous parts of the world. Children view their education as one source that can support their increased ability to cope in such circumstances. It would seem now to be a global need, not confined to particular regions of the world and should be inclusive of all primary age children, not just as a curriculum matter but practically – for instance, in preparing for the possible local effects of climate change such as greater rainfall and increases in flooding (Chew Hung, 2014; Kagawa and Selby, 2010; Shepardson *et al.*, 2017).

Increasingly, children 'visit' abroad

Alongside their real travel to other places, children see and encounter many places elsewhere in the world through television and, perhaps, the Internet. Many of these are places in North America, Australia, east and southern Asia, the Pacific Ocean, Western Europe and other scenic sites around the world, either famed for their landscapes or particular landmarks and urban features or where they are settings for action dramas or documentaries. But they are mediated places, accessible only through adults' eyes, the creators of books, websites, documentaries and films. Places and environments are often the backdrop and may well be only subliminally 'noticed' rather than recognised as other 'realities' to the home environment, though, as noted above, children appear to gain some sense of other places and nations through media representations. The geographies of adults' and children's holidays – and there is increasing evidence that children contribute to decisions about holiday destinations (Carr, 2011; Schänzel *et al.*, 2012) – and the geographies propounded by visual media affect children's perceptions of places and sights around the world. This indicates that children's wider experience of the world is selected and selective, constrained and edited through media experience, their travel activities and destinations, by adults and, perhaps, inadvertently, by themselves through their developing preferences. Place and environmental experience reaches children in these contexts unconsciously rather than intentionally. Today's globalised and digitally accessible world makes some parts of the world seem just around the corner from our living rooms, while other places remain determinedly far away or, quite possibly, hidden. Technologies are providing new opportunities about which we still know little of the impact on children's geographies (Catling, 2008; Glaser, 2007; de Block and Buckingham, 2007). Exploring conscious and unconscious personal geographies is important.

Children as a market

The focus of advertising at particular times of the day on television indicates the ways in which adults view and exploit children as economic opportunities (Bakan, 2011; Beder, 2009; Gunter and Furnham, 1998; Hawkins, 2017; Kenway and Bullen, 2001; Marshall, 2010). The debate about the location of sweet counters in supermarkets (the geography of sales influence), the concern about the healthiness and quality of home diets and school meals, and the longer standing concerns about the manufacture of a range of goods using cheap labour in less costly parts of the world, where children can be a vital part of the labour force, are all elements of economic geographies that impact on primary age children. In this respect, children have been commercialised as a key market by corporations, from clothes and toys to the food and entertainment industries (Mitchell and Reid-Walsh, 2002; Steinberg and Kincheloe, 2004). This influences what children purchase and the way they organise their spaces, such as their bedroom, to emphasise their interests. Television influences their perception of places through the programmes and films they watch. As they grow, primary children become increasingly economically aware and autonomous (Webley, 2005) and have agency through their spending power. Their interests affect the ways in which shops select the goods they sell and the way they lay out the sales floor. Children's economic strength has an impact on the geographies that affect them.

The idea of child as consumer is questioned, since there is much in children's lives, when they attend places such as hospitals and surgeries, schools, shops and events, where they may be considered to *be consumed*, being effectively at the behest and requirements of various services (Hawkins, 2017). This has the effect of constructing aspects of children's geographies through the visits they make regularly during young childhood to clinics, the shopping trips on which they are taken during which they are confronted by goods aimed subliminally at them, and in the television programmes they watch that others control, not only their parents but also the programme schedulers. This is a geography of direct effect, if hidden from children, intended to influence them and to an extent direct their futures to particular sources and facilities. From a young age there are determined efforts to construct and constrain children's options and choices in a consumerist world, where they are drawn unknowingly into a market-based and market-led society.

Practical task

Follow news reports for a week, noting when children are involved or affected by what happens in particular places. Consider news items where children go unmentioned but in which they are likely to be affected. Reflect on what these situations might say about these children's personal geographies and how being aware of them might affect our view of the wider world. What are the implications for teaching geography?

Children's imagined geographies

There is limited geographically and environmentally oriented research into children's imagined geographies, both as imagined and in virtual contexts. These are aspects of personal geographies in that they concern how we create the world, not only as perceptions of real places, but also as imaginary places created for us or created by ourselves for personal interests.

Children's imagined places

Our imagined places are part of our 'private worlds'. Imagination is clearly stimulated in a variety of ways, not least through participation in and observation of real-world experience, but also through the stories children are told and read from an early age, and through the opportunities to play and imagine and act through scenarios. The picture storybook, *Roxaboxen* (McLerran and Cooney, 1991), based on and in a real childhood and place, captures something of this. Illustrating the way in which a group of younger children acted out the life and activities in a stone and box model of their community, it connects children's perceptions of life there and illustrates how their personal geographies form the basis for imaginative activities. These occur daily in nursery indoor and outdoor areas, in the home corner and in the playground.

For some children, imaginary worlds go deeper. They create and develop their own small- or large-scale places, from neighbourhoods to islands, countries and continents, imaginatively (Cohen and MacKeith, 1991). Such personal imagined geographies often remain among the friends who invent and inhabit these worlds. While published authors indicate their inventiveness in creating places and lives within them, it seems that many more people create 'worlds of their own', particularly in their younger childhood. Likewise, picture story books and novels for younger children support their growing awareness of the environment and places, providing informed and informative images in artwork and words of landscapes, urban areas, islands and much more (Carroll, 2011; Comber, 2016; Cutter-Mackenzie *et al.*, 2011; Gamble, 2013; Salisbury and Styles, 2012). There are many children's stories that provide these opportunities, as illustrated in Appendix 2. They can be stories based in particular real or imagined places, about journeys, concerning migration, on shopping and play, in relation to urban change or care for the environment, and concerning development and cultures (Dolan, 2014). It is evident that children's geographies encompass not just the real-world but imagined worlds that draw on and adapt personal experiences and perceptions.

Imaginary realism: places in films

Children's television and film viewing is often directed by their interest in drama and related programmes. An aspect of children's personal geographies that is under-researched is what they understand about the places that are the settings of the 'movie' stories. Filmed stories are depicted in a variety of ways in soap operas, television drama and full-screen films. Animated films have long been favourites of younger children. They depict a variety of environments and habitats for people and wildlife. Whitley (2012) examined ways in which Disney animated films depict the 'idea of nature' and a sense of ecology. Disney films portray a variety of environments from the tropics to the American wilderness, as well as ocean environments, European forests and the urban settlements of some fairy tales. What Whitley detects is their potential to raise questions about how we perceive and treat our natural environments, the role and issues around conservation and the meaning of nature. Watching such films may have an effect on how children perceive places and the environment, but this is an aspect of their personal geographies of which we know little.

Understanding places in virtual games

There is limited research into primary age children's ideas about virtual worlds as places (Burke and Marsh, 2013; Marsh, 2010; Merchant, 2016; Merchant *et al.*, 2013). It is an area of increasing interest but is yet really to take a geographical turn. Children's play in virtual worlds impacts on them in several ways (Webber and Dixon, 2007), particularly in terms of engaging their interest, giving them access to worldlike environments, and enabling them potentially to have agency in such places. There are concerns about how adults might wish to control such experiences (Aitken, 2001; Webber and Dixon, 2007) and about the time that children spend interacting in their virtual realities, but there are negligible studies yet of how playing in virtual worlds engages and fosters children's geographies. Interest lies largely in social dimensions and friendships or solitariness, the nature of such games, children's imaginations, in-school and out-of-school uses, and the effects on children's literacy and outdoor play.

One detailed study of younger children's social engagement and interaction within the virtual game, *Adventure Rock* (Jackson *et al.*, 2008; Jackson, 2013), provides some insight. This virtual world is a 3-D spatial island environment that allows players to be supported by a friendly avatar – a connection to many younger children's 'having' an imaginary friend. Children select a variety of activities and use 'creative studios' to play games, use other children's inputs, create drawings and other features themselves, or tackle mysteries. It is a virtual online space in which children can move around, have an effect on the world and benefit from social interaction (Jackson *et al.*, 2008). Analysis of children's play in *Adventure* Rock identified eight types of player (Jackson, 2013), three of whom seem to be engaged in different geographical dimensions (Catling, 2008). Others have overlapping geographical interests, including the following.

- Explorer-investigators: interested in 'being' outdoors, undertaking journeys, tackling quests and mysteries.
- Life-system builders: wanting to populate the area, add new elements to the environment, create new lands.
- Power users: focused on how the virtual world worked, spent time exploring, developed considerable understanding of the environment's geography.
- Self-stampers: had an interest in making a home base, gave themselves an identity in the game.
- Fighters: took a destructive approach to the environment focusing on power and its effect.
- Collector-consumers: interested in the economic system, wanting shops and consumerism, they accumulated value.

That children see the virtual world in relation to their different interests is not surprising. What is noticeable is the link beyond personal and social interests to environmental interests, where some want to know about this place not simply to use it, but also to enjoy the exploration of and journeys in it or to improve it as a place to be. This links with an informal geographical awareness, where some children create mental maps and others have a sense of its future by taking responsibility for caring for the virtual world. Such virtual environments, while imagined, overlap with the various aspects of real worlds and may enable children to apply and explore their personal geographies through imagined places.

From a geographical perspective, the value of virtual worlds appears to be that children create their mental maps and images of this 'world' as they explore in order to understand the place it is. It seems that:

- children learn to know where they are and can orientate themselves within it and apply their growing spatial awareness for journeys and explorations;
- these worlds engage children in social environments not simply physical spaces;
- they have some control to manipulate elements in the world's environment;
- they have responsibility to care for things.

(Jackson *et al.*, 2008)

Similar views are emerging from other studies, which have involved pre-school as well as primary age children, of similar sorts of worlds to *Adventure Rock*, which may include stylistic environmental features, such as mountains, forests and snow, as in *Club Penguin* and *Minecraft*, but which may also include various local features such as sandpits, dens, school playgrounds, houses and shopping malls, as well as involve some limited use of maps (Carrington, 2013; Marsh, 2010; Marsh *et al.*, 2016). The object of a shopping environment is consumption, which is a key feature in one form or other of many virtual world games, reinforcing child users as learning to be consumers while becoming consumed by commerce (Hawkins, 2017). While we know little about quite what is being learnt through children's activities and play in virtual worlds, it would seem reasonable to suggest that they may well learn something about the environment and social activity, and aspects of citizenship and civic engagement, although this might be incidental rather than intended (Lim and Clark, 2010; Merchant, 2016). Play for children in virtual worlds is motivating and engaging. It may well support children's spatial and environmental learning and development, alongside the social and other aspects that are the focus of almost all current research. There remains a real need to investigate the geographical dimensions in children's virtual world use.

The area of virtual worlds is a contested one, not least because of some of the concerns about the amount of time spent online, including in playing in virtual world environments (Willett, 2017), and because of some of the commercial interests at play for digital gaming companies (Ruckenstein, 2013). It introduces the question of whether children might be able to make best use of a virtual world if they lack experience in the real world through outdoor exploration, making journeys, going shopping, using places and play.

 Reflective task

We often ask children to write stories set in places, though we concentrate little on these as places and events, just as we rarely discuss the quasi-realistic and virtual worlds they see in drama and computer games.

Why do you think this is? Why might this be an area for research in children's geographies in future? Why might it be useful for teaching geography?

Children's environmental concerns and participation

A sense of environmental quality

Concern for the physical and social environment matters to primary age children. Children's moral attitudes to environmental care develop and can be fostered from their earliest years (Cutter-Mackenzie *et al.*, 2014). While children will continue to have much to learn about environmental, scientific and geographical matters during their childhood, they develop interests in and concerns to look after creatures, the way places are maintained, and how changes happen and may be thoughtfully developed (Littledyke, 2002). Positive attitudes may also be influenced in the early years by reading picture story books linked with teaching positive environmental messages (Hsiao and Shih, 2016). However, there is not necessarily a positive relationship between environmental knowledge and environmental attitudes; the latter may precede the former and alternatively the former does not necessarily lead to the latter (Malandrakis and Chtzakis, 2014).

Children are concerned about the quality of the environment and its future (Alexander and Hargreaves, 2007; Dooley, 2010; Hicks, 2002; Jonsson *et al.* 2012). They are aware of the links between poverty and degraded environments and the issues of resource access for less fortunate members of societies (Cullingford, 2000; Layard and Dunn, 2009). They recognise the efforts people make to care for and improve the environment or the lack of such determination (Chawla, 2002; O'Brien, 2003). Children are concerned about pollution and rubbish issues (Çoban *et al.*, 2011), derelict buildings and land, global climate change, and local concerns such as safety perceptions, rubbish, traffic problems and graffiti (Thomas and Thompson, 2004). Pollution research with older primary children indicates that they tend to focus on dirt, odour, waste, and their immediate and obvious local effects (Rodriguez *et al.*, 2015). They know about safe and unsafe places to play, and they value well-cared for sites. However, children's attitudes can be contradictory, recognising car exhaust fumes as unhealthy, while not desiring personally to reduce car use or not always using accessible litter bins themselves, though they wish that other people did.

Research summary

Children's environmental views

In inner and outer areas of London and a comparison new town, older primary children were asked what they thought of their environment, about unsafe areas and about its amenities (O'Brien, 2003). Homes were favoured places by inner London children, but leisure and shopping centres were more favoured places by outer London and the new-town children. For many across the three localities, places are drab and poorly looked after or too controlled. Of most concern to children were dingy and dark spaces in and around buildings. For outer London and new-town children, parks and woods could be unsafe places, while for inner London children the street was seen to be as unsafe as walkways

(Continued)

(Continued)

and stairwells. Children disliked graffiti and unkempt and poorly maintained streets. They saw maintenance as a key aspect of environmental improvement. Most important for them was that open spaces and play areas should be considerably improved. While there was evidence that more inner city children are staying indoors or near home, there was a strong desire by the children to be out and about more in places where they could play. They were concerned at the loss of unstructured and less regulated and supervised play spaces. What children seem to want is space in the public environment for their own use – not an easy request when parents want security for their children wherever they may be in a more risk-averse world.

Children notice that there is limited effective political action at local, national and international levels to address such human and environmental issues, although they want them tackled. While children wish to see a future world that reflects how they would like it to be, they are not unrealistic in considering what it might become but can be positive as well as fearful of how it may turn out (Jonsson *et al.*, 2012). Children are relatively optimistic about the future when they become involved in community improvement projects and school-based eco-initiatives linked to sustainability (Alexander and Hargreaves, 2007; Beunderman *et al.*, 2007; Hicks, 2002; Steuer *et al.*, 2006). Such opportunities and development work with children can begin in the early years (Cutter-Mackenzie *et al.*, 2014; Davis, 2015) and continue through their education (Lee, 2013; Catling, 2014a).

Children's active involvement

Increasingly, there seems to be more effort to listen to children, though not always effectively (Cox *et al.*, 2010; Gibson and Haynes, 2009; Hayward, 2012; Percy-Smith and Thomas, 2010; West, 2007). Instances of children's active involvement in environmental improvement remain limited (Adams and Ingham, 1998; Hart, 1997; O'Brien, 2003; Reid *et al.*, 2008; Spencer and Blades, 2006), some focused in school and others community based, usually around play spaces (Chawla and Malone, 2003). Too often, involvement is tokenistic, but not always. Crucially, when children are involved, they are positive about ways to contribute as well as to learn (Catling, 2014a).

Several features characterise children's genuine involvement in school-based or local participatory activities (Hart, 1997; Katsenou *et al.*, 2013; Olle, 2002; Titman, 1994). An important element is that children are encouraged and supported to know about and become familiar with possible actions they might take, the purpose and value of which they understand. The environmentally aware and care-oriented culture, in or out of school, in which this occurs is highly influential, since it provides for positive learning. Children tackle improvement in a realistic way, state clearly what they want to have and offer ideas for improvements that are straightforward. In the context of improving school grounds' quality they are not that interested in commercial equipment but want grounds that are varied, more natural in appearance and that offer challenges. They wish to see greater variety in resources for playtime activities, recognising the range of interests among their peers. In this and the wider context, children are happy to work with adults, recognising the skills, knowledge and so forth that adults bring (Freeman and Tranter, 2011). Children may become involved in local and community issues, such as stream and river cleaning, water reduction in times of scarcity or energy-saving schemes. While often children learn about, rather than act to change, environmental concerns, there seem to be many who are becoming more critically aware and who wish to participate in actions for improvement and their own futures (Catling, 2014a; Hedefalk *et al.*, 2015) For children, participation is not about taking over the task but working with people. Not unusually, when they work on improvements they become involved in maintaining them.

This is a personal geography that is active and engaged. It is a committed geography. Alexander and Hargreaves (2007) found that where children are involved, they feel they provide a positive input at a level at which they can act. The case is that children's involvement encourages a sense of ownership – for instance, of their play places (Mayall, 2008). It appears to be a small contribution to school and community improvement, but it initiates active engagement in environmental improvement and sustainability. In doing this, it is argued that primary age children develop their 'environmental identity', the sense that their notion of 'self' involves them in *being for* the environment and acting accordingly. It is about more than an attitude to the environment; rather, it concerns behaviours that are environmentally sensitive, considerate and interested (Green *et al.*, 2016). While it may be that children's experience of and in nature is strongly supportive in developing their environmental identity, it is important to recognise that, since increasingly children live in urban environments, such a positive sense of the self can develop in urban contexts where it concerns the social and physical environment.

Children's ideas about geography

By or towards the end of their primary education years, it would seem that almost all 11-year-old children have an idea of what geography is about (Catling, 2001b; Pike, 2006, 2013; Senyurt, 2014), although a few muddle it with other subjects such as history. Their awareness of geography appears to reflect not so much the timetabling of geography as when geography is highlighted for them as a subject or in cross-curricular studies. Many views about geography are reflected in these two statements by 11-year-olds:

> *Geography is to do with maps. Sometimes we draw maps and draw a key for them and we learn about different places. The type of book we use is an atlas.*

> *Geography is about countries and places in the world. We use maps to help us understand. Geography tells us all different things, like what soil is in that area we are studying, as well as how many people live there, and what is the most popular job. We do geography because it helps us to understand our world. If we did not have geography we would not know where we are.*

Among a sample of children in England, the dominant association of primary school geography was with map work: map skills and using maps to find out about places and for following or creating routes (Catling, 2004b). Children also identified geography as developing their awareness and understanding of the world and countries. This connected with references to knowing what places are like and what happens in them. These ideas indicate a traditional, indeed a public, sense of geography as being about the world and maps, which is not unlike that held by prospective primary teachers (Catling, 2017b). Local studies were mentioned by only a third of children and under a tenth mentioned environmental matters and issues. Local studies are widely taught and include some of the best geography teaching in England (Ofsted, 1999, 2008a, 2011), but few children referred to fieldwork, which in other contexts they have noted they do too infrequently (Alexander and Hargreaves, 2007). In a later English study Kitchen (2013) investigated 11–12-year-olds' ideas about geography in England, finding that place was a key aspect of their sense of the subject, along with culture, maps, and weather and climate. However, she noted some confusion about their understanding of 'the world', children having a superficial and very general notion of it. She found that children seemed somewhat hazy about subject 'boundaries'. Kitchen also found that children's broad definition of geography was well set by the age of 12.

In an Irish study, Pike (2006) identified a more balanced focus with physical features, including mountains, rivers and weather, heavily mentioned alongside countries, the world, people and places. Maps were important to a sizeable minority of children. She repeated her study in 2012/13 finding broadly similar results, although there was an increase in reference to geography being about environmental processes (Pike, 2013). She also found, as Catling (2004b) had, that reference to geographical enquiry was low, while local geographical study and fieldwork received rather more mentions. Turkish 10–11-year-olds emphasised physical geography, particularly landforms, and noted strongly study of their own country, regional geography and other countries, as well as the role of maps in geography (Senyurt, 2014). Two-fifths of children also associated geography with history. Research in the Netherlands (Jan Bent *et al.*, 2014) noted that Dutch 11–12-year-olds connected geography with knowledge about the world, of other cultures and of the physical environment and weather, as well as with maps and fieldwork. Al-Nofli (2010) found similar results from his study in Oman of 12-year-old children, where they associated geography largely with countries, landforms, weather and maps. A few children noted lifestyles and natural disasters. These reasonably consistent notions of geography held by children at the end of their primary phase of schooling in a range of countries were noted by the researchers to have obvious links with national geography curriculum requirements, whether taught in social studies or geography subject contexts.

Children's attitudes to geography were mixed, with Pike (2013, 2016) noting that across the ten years of her research they were finding the subject more interesting, with this linked to more active approaches to their teaching and learning. Nonetheless, children, even in the same class, could hold different views about the subject and about the way they worked. This echoed Al-Nolfli's (2010) study but more strongly, with children concerned about more didactic approaches and not necessarily being comfortable with Internet-based activities. Kitchen (2013) noted that teachers' choices of activities had a key effect in geography lessons, with group teaching the most positively enjoyed by children. They liked variety in their activities too. What children found much less engaging, according to Jan Bent *et al.* (2014) was too great an emphasis on comprehension-type exercises and using worksheets. This impacted on their motivation, and they too desired more active approaches, such as problem-oriented contexts for study, but high-quality textbooks could be appreciated (Pike, 2013).

 Practical task

You have read and considered the ideas about geography in Chapter 2 and the perspectives on children's geographies in this chapter. Write a summary for yourself of what you understand geography to be and how this relates to your understanding of children's geographies.

What emerges from this range of research is that throughout their schooling, early years and primary children bring a wide range of geographical experience and background to their classrooms. This involves deep personal knowledge and understanding as well as gaps and limitations to what they appear to know. In many classrooms there is much that can be drawn on, and in good teaching and learning this is enabled. But for too many children their experience and sense of geography in school is disconnected from their personal, everyday geographies – geographies that encompass not only their familiar and local experiences, but also their awareness and engagement with the wider world, as well as with their interests in the world near and far. It seems almost that some practices in primary geography create discontinuity between the geographies in and of children's own lives, and of what and how they study geography (Catling, 2005c). This might account for the 'boring' sense of primary geography for some children (Catling *et al.*, 2007; Robinson and Fielding, 2007). Many children, though, are clearly excited and engaged by their geographical studies, where their teachers take into account their experience and perspectives, and in which they are actively engaged and included. It is not surprising to find that children have critical and negative views of geography when their role is largely passive through teachers' over-reliance on structured geography units and worksheets (Ofsted, 2004, 2005, 2008a, 2011). This is important to address.

Ensuring that geography has greater relevance and connection with children's lived experience appears to encourage geographical learning to come naturally. By taking children's perspectives and experience into account and involving them to a greater extent in the planning of topics and approaches to learning, as well as being actively engaged in their learning, provides positive effects (Catling and Martin, 2011; Stanley *et al.*, 2005; Pike, 2016).

    Key points

This chapter has:

- explained that children's geographies are significant to and for children;
- noted that their personal geographies are multifaceted and multi-layered, encompassing environmental knowledge, sense of place and place attachment, and spatial awareness;
- considered that their personal geographies encompass their life in school but more so outside school;
- identified factors that are constraining and changing children's experience in the environment, linked to safety, travel and access;
- explored children's ideas about the world beyond their direct experience and their engagement with imaginative and virtual worlds, which may be changing their geographies;

- noted that locally and across the world, geography affects children, whether directly through natural hazards and human events or indirectly in relation to encountering such events through the media;
- noted that while children are concerned about environmental problems, they value and benefit from involvement in environmental activities;
- considered that children develop a sense of geography and develop attitudes to their studies in school that may or may not make helpful connections with their personal geographies.

Moving on

Select from one or more of the aspects of children's geographies outlined in this chapter and follow up by reading one or more of the references to extend and deepen your understanding of that area.

Further reading

There are many books and articles about children's place and environmental experience and learning. Several publications have drawn together interesting research or provided overviews. A sample is given here.

Ansell, N (2017) *Children, Youth and Development*. London: Routledge.

Blundell, D (2016) *Rethinking Children's Spaces and Places*. London: Bloomsbury.

Christensen, P, Hadfield-Hill, S, Horton, J and Kraftl, P (2018) *Children Living in Sustainable Built Environments*, Abingdon: Routledge.

Day, C (2007) *Environment and Children*. London: Elsevier/Architectural Press.

Dolan, A (2014) *You, Me and Diversity*. London: UCL Institute of Education.

Foley, P and Leverett, S (eds) (2011) *Children and Young People's Spaces*. Basingstoke: Palgrave Macmillan.

Freeman, C and Tranter, P (2011) *Children & their Urban Environment: Changing Worlds*. London: Earthscan.

Griffiths, J (2013) *Kith: The Riddle of the Childscape*. London: Hamish Hamilton.

Hayward, S (2012) *Children, Citizenship and Environment*. London: Routledge.

Higgins, N and Freeman, C (eds) (2013) *Childhoods: Growing up in Aotearoa New Zealand*. Otago: Otago University Press.

Tovey, H (2007) *Playing Outdoors: Spaces and Places, Risk and Challenge*. Maidenhead: McGraw Hill.

Wiegand, P (2006) *Learning and Teaching with Maps*. London: Routledge.

Wilson, R (2012) *Nature and Young Children*. Abingdon: Routledge.

Useful research journals to consult for articles about children's geographies and geographical learning include:

Children's Geographies, Taylor & Francis: www.tandfonline.com/loi/cchg20

Children, Youth and Environments, University of Cincinnati: http://cech.uc.edu/centers/arlitt/children-youth-and-environment.html

Environmental Education Research, Taylor & Francis: www.tandfonline.com/toc/ceer20

Geographical Education, Australian Geography Teachers' Association: www.agta.asn.au/htm_files/journal/index.htm

The Geography Teacher: www.myncge.bravesites.com/the-geography-teacher

Journal of Geography, National Council for Geographic Education: www.ncg.org/journal-of-geography

International Research in Geographical and Environmental Education, Taylor & Francis: www.tandfonline.com/toc/rgee20

Primary Geography, Geographical Association: www.geography.org.uk/primary geography

Research in Geographic Education, Gilbert Grosvenor Center, Texas State University: www.rge.grosvenor.txstate.edu

Review of International Research in Geographical Education Online (RIGEO), an open-access journal: www.rigeo.org

Useful websites

The Geographical Association: www.geography.org.uk

GeogSpace – AGTA: www.agta.asn.au

CHAPTER 4

UNDERSTANDING GEOGRAPHICAL ENQUIRY

 Chapter objectives

This chapter enables you to:

- understand the importance of using enquiry as an effective model for teaching and learning in geography;
- understand there are various approaches to developing children's enquiry-based skills and how to structure effective enquiries;
- recognise how enquiry can feed into the studies of places and environmental impact and sustainability;
- be able to make connections between geographical and philosophical enquiry.

Introduction

Enquiry is a fascinating and most effective way of investigating the world. It taps into children's unbounded curiosity and excitement about all that is around them. It is an active and dynamic ingredient in children's learning and understanding of the world. Enquiry is about engaging children actively in their own learning and, in so doing, developing them as self-motivated, independent learners. Geographical enquiry provides the opportunity to engage primary children's inquisitiveness and question-asking, and their desire, challenge and thirst for knowledge about their own world, about the wider world that they encounter and about which they develop informal information, understandings and misunderstandings, alongside attitudes and values. It provides children with the opportunities to consider, question, examine, share, develop and extend the knowledge and understanding they bring into school and class (Halocha, 2007; Pickford *et al.*, 2013; Pike, 2016). The focus of geographical enquiries in primary education is on real-life matters and issues that have relevance and meaning to children. Enquiry is a valuable route into tackling the alternative conceptions, misunderstandings, stereotypes, partiality, bias and prejudice that children pick up in daily life while learning about and being involved with people, places and the environment (Pickford *et al.*, 2013).

Across the world, enquiry is advocated as a key method for teaching and learning primary geography (Carter, 1998; Maxim, 2006; Scoffham, 2010; Pickford *et al.*, 2013; Taylor *et al.*, 2012; Reynolds, 2014; Pike, 2016; Kidman and Casinader, 2017). Enquiry is promoted as an approach that engages children with geographical thinking and develops their understanding of the subject. In summary, enquiry – the approach is used in history teaching, and is akin to investigative learning in science education – begins with a topic, question, problem or concern, moves on to collecting data and other information, sorting and analysing this, interpreting what is learnt, evaluating how informative it is, coming to conclusions and, possibly, making proposals for action, before evaluating how well undertaken and useful the enquiry was and what has been learnt from it both geographically and to apply in future enquiries. The scale of geographical enquiries can range from a local matter to an international and global topic. An enquiry might be undertaken individually or by a team.

The argument for teaching geography through an enquiry approach has a history (Bartlett and Cox, 1982; HMI, 1986; Naish *et al.*, 1987; Pike, 2016; Kidman and Casinader, 2017), but it has not always been taken up in primary classrooms. One autobiographical retrospective on experience in learning geography in primary school reflected what seems to be more widely felt, that children of all ages had very limited experience in enquiry in geography, whether in a subject or social studies context (Kidman, 2012). Indeed, often geography was taught through a transmission approach, frequently using worksheets or copying from books. This raised the question as to whether enquiry has been developed meaningfully and as widely in geography (and other subjects) learning (Kidman and Casinader, 2017; Grant *et al.*, 2017), as has been advocated in countries such as the UK, Australia and the USA. Since it is the approach that geographers use to develop geographical knowledge and understanding, and given that it is closely associated with children's curiosity and engagement in learning and how they gain much of their experience, it is appropriate to focus on geographical enquiry at this point, then move to consider aspects of subject content.

What is enquiry?

Lindfors (1999, p. 93) argued that 'No inquiry was ever born in a vacuum'. We enquire because we want to extend what we know, sensing that there is more to know. Through questioning and investigating we show we want to go beyond what we already know. A useful summary of geographical enquiry states that:

> *enquiry is the process of finding out answers to questions. At its simplest, it involves encouraging children to ask questions and search for answers, based on what they might already know from data sources. As their skills develop, children can move to a more rigorous form of enquiry involving the development of testing of hypotheses.*

> (NCC, 1993, p. 27)

Enquiry helps children learn about the world through:

- observing, questioning and planning an investigation;
- collecting, recording and representing information and data;
- analysing, interpreting and evaluating what has been found out;
- drawing conclusions and communicating these;
- reflecting on and making use of what has been learned.

In doing so, enquiry requires critical thinking about what is being investigated, considering and proposing solutions or ways forward where it is appropriate to do so, and reflecting on the values and attitudes involved. By its nature enquiry involves the enquirer. It is an active, not passive, approach to learning. As Martin states, enquiry necessitates that *Children are actively engaged in the creation of personal and shared meanings about the world, rather than being passive recipients of knowledge that has been created or selected by the teacher* (Martin, 2006c, p. 9). She argues that children must be both physically and mentally active when engaged in enquiry.

It is essential that they are not just doing the activities, but are intellectually and emotionally stimulated by and engaged in them (Martin, 2006c). To achieve this, children need to be able to generate thoughtful, effective and stimulating questions, which will encourage them to explore the complexities of the world about them, start to make links between geographical concepts and begin to recognise the patterns and processes that exist.

Halocha (2007) argues that enquiry is generated not only by questions, but can be stimulated by and emerge from children's discussions and debates, from reading, from close observation and from fieldwork activities and other outdoor learning. Building on Lindors's (1999) argument, Halocha reiterates that children's motivation comes from recognising and appreciating what they know and wanting to go beyond it. It is not that primary children want to stay within their current understanding but rather that this stimulates them to seek fuller and deeper understanding, to extend their knowledge, to encounter other views and values, and to become better and more widely informed, a purpose that Roberts (2013) sees as key to geographical enquiry. Hence there is often excitement in engaging with this approach to geographical learning, where children bring their own informal, even not fully realised, geographical awareness and knowledge into encounters with both geography's (the subject's) perspectives and the real world. The two intertwine to foster learning (Catling and Martin, 2011), and this can have spin-offs for the teacher in terms of subject understanding and appreciation, and through recognising, making fuller use of and enhancing children's natural enquiry stance.

Enquiry is embedded in robust pedagogical theory. Roberts (2013) states that, in the context of social constructivism, children learn most effectively not directly from teacher to pupil, but by making sense of the world for themselves. This focuses on the difference between what they are able to do themselves and what they can do when supported by others. Through supported enquiry, children learn within but are enabled to move beyond their zone of proximal development (ZPD), the point of distinction between what they are able to do for themselves and what they can do when supported by others fostering their achievement and progression. Vygotsky (1962) advocated the teacher's crucial role in supporting children's learning (Roberts, 2013; Halocha, 2007), arguing that whenever children worked within their ZPD they would need a teacher, facilitator or mentor to help them to achieve higher levels of thinking. The word 'scaffolding' has come to represent what he meant by light but well-directed assistance and building up children's knowledge and understanding (Wood et al., 1976). What is essential are the interactions in which children and adults engage so that children's thinking is guided, promoted and enhanced (Webster et al., 1996). However, scaffolding is about rather more than teachers' assistance; it involves teachers in playing a collaborative role with children and is the crucial link between the teacher and child (Webster et al., 1996).

The teacher has a vital role to play in developing effective enquiry learning, to support and guide the children's own learning from the initiation of their questions to researching and analysing their findings, and coming up with reasoned and meaningful conclusions.

Geographical enquiry in school geography

School inspectors have argued that in England, *Geographical enquiry encourages questioning, investigation and critical thinking about issues affecting the world and people's lives, now and in the future* (Ofsted, 2008a, p. 31). There is good evidence that in a number of situations enquiry can be particularly advantageous, such as:

- in developing observation and investigative skills when working out of the classroom, particularly for pre-school and primary age children;
- when employing increasingly complex questions to develop children's geographical understanding and thinking;
- where the children are involved in generating an enquiry through their own questions because it is relevant and meaningful to them and their lives;
- when children are involved in real-world enquiries, linked to their own environment, involving engaging fieldwork, analysing and using the results, such as to run a 'public enquiry' where they work collaboratively, and express their own feelings, attitudes and views;
- when children are inquisitive about topics novel to, even geographically distant from, them but which fascinate them;
- being provided with opportunities to articulate their preferred future for a development and to have their say in determining what places should look like;
- using enquiry skills to investigate what is not always immediately obvious and so look for the interconnections between seemingly disparate issues to link them together to gain a more holistic and coherent understanding. This has the bonus of stimulating their curiosity and encouraging them to find out more.

In England, school inspectors identified constraints in developing children's experience and skills in using geographical enquiries where they are limited in the scope of their enquiry, and set predetermined questions and too-prescriptive boundaries, often to make it logistically more straightforward for the teacher or linked to the school's over-structured geography curriculum units (Ofsted, 2008a, 2011). A further criticism is that many teachers lack awareness of the range of skills to use in enquiry learning and are reluctant to interconnect them, preferring to employ them in isolation perhaps because they lack confidence in their own and the children's capabilities. This situation is not unusual across countries.

Developing geographical enquiry

Traditional approaches

Traditional place and environmental enquiry has been focused on five key questions, used by teachers to provide structure, sequence and stimulus for children's investigations (Storm, 1989, p.4). These have been:

- What is this place like?
- Why is this place as it is?
- How is this place connected to other places?
- How is this place changing?
- How would it feel to live in this place?

These questions have served their purpose well, although concerns have been raised about their use to guide pre-constructed geographical enquiries, such as through 'off-the-shelf' lesson structured geography topics, used when teachers lack effective time for subject and cross-curricular planning, or when provided for head teachers who want to know in too much detail, almost day-to-day, what it is intended the children will learn and how this will be achieved. In such planning, children's questions are minimised and may well be predetermined. Other concerns include the limited ways in which geographical questions have been used by less confident teachers – for instance, when asking why a place is like it is, and focusing on the natural and built environment while excluding exploration of people's lives and the social, cultural, political and economic aspects of communities that stimulate children's interest just as much, if not more so. Rowley (2006) noted similar limitations when considering *what it may feel like to live in* a particular place, a focus that requires considerable information for it to be answered in an insightful and empathetic way. Rigidly used, or tackled simplistically, such questions have tended to create a 'straitjacketed' approach with less confident teachers who do not encourage their children to propose and pursue their own questions.

Shaping geographical enquiries

If we want to initiate innovative, problem-solving enquiries, we need to broaden the base and move beyond these *deductive* styles of questions and enquiries, which promote description and limited analysis, to the more evaluative and empathic enquiries found in *inductive* enquiry approaches. The tendency has been to be overly descriptive with younger (primary) children and more analytic with older (secondary) students, but this needs to be superseded by a balanced approach adopted across all ages. Children are never too young to start thinking about why things happen, or to offer their ideas about what might or should happen in future.

Rowley (2006) argued that enquiry provides opportunities to develop more considered and creative investigations into our environment and that we should use them to develop a greater sense of awe and wonder in children's learning as well as to provide our children with ways of looking, thinking and problem solving with greater ethical awareness. He acknowledges that although enquiry is one of the most advantageous and effective forms of learning, it is also one of the most complex and demanding (Halocha, 2007; Kidman and Casinader, 2017). It asks much of the teachers who use it, particularly when enquiries are initiated by children's curiosity, and planning the work cannot be prepared for and undertaken in a formulaic way – that is, enquiry cannot be firmly controlled, although it can be managed. Such 'unknown territory' can be uncomfortable, with the possibility of the unexpected emerging. This may cause teacher anxiety when curriculum planning, a situation some teachers find challenging to engage in with their children, or, when they do take it up, try to control and become didactic, using carefully prepared questions leading to known and safe answers. Such a teacher-dominated approach constrains children's ownership of their learning, and fails to develop the crucial skills of problem solving. It inhibits children's creative and principled investigations and responses to some of the complex and intricate problems facing us, although we know that children can work effectively when carrying out small-scale, local enquiries, and in beginning to see how possible solutions can be considered and applied to the bigger picture (Ofsted, 2008a, 2011; Pickford *et al.*, 2013; Pike, 2016).

Structured geographical enquiries have most consistently been used to find out about places and environmental concerns – what Rowley (2006) describes as *what we learn* – and has been an effective approach – *how we do it* – that supports information-oriented learning. Such an approach has inhibited children's engagement with what matters to them and with real-world problems and issues, where they might have opportunities to make proposals or even take action – in other words, to be involved in creating realistic 'outcomes', enabling them to gain a sense of greater responsibility, becoming more active participants in their own futures. This connects directly with children's everyday geographies in their places and the wider world, and with providing opportunities to examine environmental impact and ways to live more sustainably and equitably within their environment. This requires developments in the approach to geographical enquiry, which are illustrated in Table 4.1. An example of this enquiry approach in practice is shown in Table 4.2.

By its nature, the approach to enquiry in Table 4.1 is open-ended and fairly unbounded. It is essential that the geography is rigorously retained and the overall enquiry maintains a clear purpose as to why it is being carried out, its focus and what the desired objectives are to be. An issue-based enquiry requires real and meaningful input from the children. It involves them in thinking about and discussing the issue and devising their own questions, as Table 4.2 promotes. It requires them to structure their enquiry and encourages them to think in creative and empathetic ways, so developing their values and attitudes alongside their knowledge of the issue. They may then begin to see how they can take some responsibility in what is happening and propose possible solutions. This allows them to think about and possibly affect what their 'preferred' rather than just the 'probable' solution might be (Hicks, 2007). They follow a clear sequence in their approach to undertaking their enquiry, as outlined in Figure 4.1, which provides the structured enquiry framework that encourages children to develop and agree their question(s), to investigate collaboratively, draw conclusions and come to their own justified views.

In undertaking their enquiry, children will work sequentially through six stages of an enquiry.

1. Identify and agree the focus and purpose of the enquiry.
2. Raise questions through team and individual discussion and observation.
3. Plan the enquiry, how to set about it and collect information.
4. Process the information that has been gathered, interpret it and draw conclusions.
5. Consider and make possible proposals and communicate their findings.
6. Evaluate what has been learnt from undertaking the enquiry.

Raising awareness Children consider an issue that is relevant and pertinent to them and which has meaning for them. They ask questions to find out more about it and develop a structure and plan for their enquiry.
Investigating Children research their questions using primary and secondary sources to find out information and answers to their self-generated questions. They draw up and communicate their findings.
Raising concern/taking action Children articulate feelings, attitudes and values about what they have found out and begin to want to take responsibility and, possibly, action in order to change or improve something they have identified.

Table 4.1 An enquiry sequence about a place or geographical issue (adapted from Morris, n.d.)

Raising awareness
Children raise concerns about parking and about dropping off and collecting children outside their school, following some near-accidents. They generate questions, plan their enquiry and begin to investigate the issue.

Investigating
Children research their questions using observations, fieldwork and interviews to find out information and gather responses. They invite into school and interview the local councillor, the head teacher, parents, nearby residents and a local authority planner. They survey parking before, during and at the end of the school day, as well as nearby streets and other sites locally to see the parking problem and consider possible solutions. They analyse and draw conclusions about what they have found out.

Raising concern/taking action
Children weigh up the information they have gathered and the different arguments and viewpoints. They realise that they can make some proposals to put to the school governors, the local councillor and the planning authority. They create a display in the school entrance foyer and write to the local council and planning authority, who they invite in along with parents. Later they place their display in the local library.

Outcome
As a result of their local action and community interests generated by the children, the council installed a road crossing in the place suggested by the children, marked the road outside school as a non-parking zone, identified a short-term parking site and placed visible notices discouraging dropping off and picking up children. When these decisions were made and the changes occurred, the children felt that they had contributed to these decisions and the outcome

Table 4.2   An example of an enquiry sequence about a parking issue affecting their school

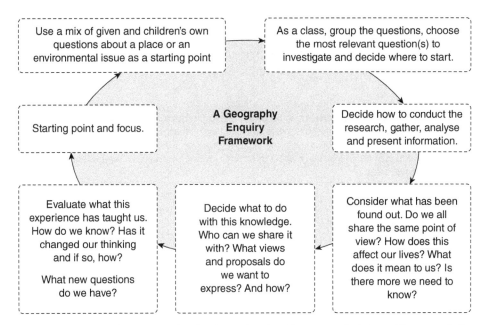

Figure 4.1   An enquiry sequence for planning and undertaking an enquiry (adapted from a curriculum-making framework created by P Owens and W North for *The Action Plan for Geography*, Geographical Association, 2006–11)

Geographical enquiry can be used in a variety of different ways and with a range of different concerns. It can be applied to local contexts as well as to investigations that are based on using secondary sources.

- Geographical topics exploring, for instance, water and rivers, the local weather, how we feel about the place where we live, and identifying changes that are taking place in different places which we compare.
- Environmental impact and sustainability problems, such as how to relieve parking congestion, ways to improve a particular area, access to places for everyone.
- Controversial issues, such as the impact of pollution, decision making about a change in land use, conflicting views about climate change.
- What a place might be like, the lives of people living there, the local businesses and activities.

Building children's skills in using geographical enquiry

The example in Table 4.2 draws on children's geographies – more specifically, the geographies that can directly affect children: change and impact in their local area. There is another dimension in their geographies to utilise: their curiosity and interest in finding out, but this needs to be initiated and honed. Developing children's skills in undertaking geographical enquiries requires that they are inducted during their primary school years into enquiry approaches, during which they take on greater agency and control of the enquiries they undertake. The approach outlined in Table 4.3 offers a structured development for this: the 'three Es' approach. This structure initiates the process of geographical investigation in which questions are

Enabling enquiry: Children are inducted into an enquiry approach, drawing on their sense of exploration and inquisitiveness. While structured by the teacher to enable young children to develop a sense of focus and for ordering their enquiries, it should enable children to put forward their own questions, which they begin to investigate systematically to identify their own responses.
Enhancing enquiry: The role of the teacher is to encourage children to take an increasing level of responsibility for identifying the questions to investigate, within a disciplined framework. The teacher challenges the children's questions and approaches, to focus them consistently on matters of geographical relevance, in relation to places, the environment and environmental spatial understanding.
Empowering enquiry: Children are encouraged to take direct responsibility for identifying, refining, using and evaluating their enquiry questions and process. This is not only about children structuring the way they work to an increasing extent, but also about them selecting their approaches and methods and identifying with their teacher their needs, to be able to achieve the challenge they set themselves. Their teacher continues to act as a critical mentor.

Table 4.3   The 'three Es' enquiry structure (source: Catling, 2003)

raised and selected by the children, and their teacher takes the role of the facilitator for the ensuing discussion, an approach consistent with that advocated in Philosophy for Children, and, with the children, for co-planning, organising and carrying out their enquiry. The next classroom example illustrates how one class undertook such an enquiry. Using enquiry in geography should encourage children to look at places and environmental interests and concerns from more than one angle and share and reflect on these, as this class did.

In the classroom

A local enquiry-based study

A class of 8–9-year-olds began a study of their local area with a group and then class discussions about what they knew about it, what they thought about it and how they felt about it. It became clear that they had a wide range of knowledge of the area between them, that they related differently to it and that they had differing views about the state of the area. Drawing out their ideas and questions, the teacher encouraged the children to work in four teams, each one focusing on a different perception of the locality and each one producing its own report. The four subtopics were:

- What is good about our place?
- A clean neighbourhood?
- What can we do here?
- What do we like here?

A variety of investigations developed. Opportunities for fieldwork were organised and many of the children were able to draw on their local knowledge and to follow up lines of enquiry outside school. Fieldwork and other investigations involved interviews with family, friends and other local people; taking and analysing locatable photographs of places liked and thought 'scruffy'; mapping local shops and other useful services; and sketching particular features and views. The children were encouraged to be creative in preparing their reports. The teams drew on items such as leaflets and posters that they had come across for inspiration.

One team produced a brochure to attract people to the area and emphasised what a good place it is to live in. Another provided a 'clean

(Continued)

(Continued)

up our neighbourhood' poster with photographs of unkempt sites and advice on what to do. The third team made a presentation of their own and other children's favourite places using maps and photographs to show the sites. The fourth team produced a map leaflet to show what services were available and where they were. The outcome of the enquiries was insightful in that it provided four differing but overlapping perspectives on the children's geographies of the area. The children's favourite sites did not mesh with the views of a range of adults and younger people on what was good about the locality, although there was some overlap with other people's ideas of what was scruffy about the area, such as the waste ground, and about how the area was valued (Catling, 2015c, p.195).

The 'three Es' structure to geographical enquiry is a focused approach to the development of children's geographical thinking. The challenge is that it requires an open-minded approach by the teacher, which involves believing in and trusting the children and increasing their level of responsibility as they gain experience and confidence in themselves and from their teacher. Roberts (2013) argues that some teachers find it difficult to release control and instead maintain their authority and control over an enquiry, which raises the question as to whether what they do really is geographical enquiry. She responds by promoting a way for teachers to build confidence in engaging with their children's ideas and learning through using more structured and supportive approaches, which increasingly involve the children, as indicated in Table 4.4. While in the 'closed' approach the teacher firmly directs the children through their investigation, the looser 'framed' approach allows the teacher to offer structure and guidance while making some use of children's contributions. The 'negotiated' approach provides for genuine mutual engagement between the teacher and the children. In the latter approach, the children's ideas come to the fore. There is clear overlap in approaches between the 'three Es' progression, and the 'framed' and 'negotiated' approaches. In both approaches the central need is for you, the teacher, to learn – even if it is gradually – to increase the children's levels of agency and control as you develop your confidence. What emerges through 'empowering enquiry' and 'negotiated enquiry' is that children can and do take real responsibility for their geographical learning.

The increasingly 'open' approach in geographical enquiry learning is developed mutually by children and their teacher, involving discussion, debate, critique and arriving at agreement. Such an 'empowering' approach requires primary teachers to ask pertinent questions, seek clear justifications

	Closed enquiry	Framed enquiry	Negotiated enquiry
Key idea	Teacher is the subject, teaching and learning authority	Teacher provides access for children to subject, processes and skills	Mutually interested focus, priorities and relevance: children and teacher
Teacher's role	Teacher applies geographical knowledge and skills, and determines the study	Teacher uses subject knowledge to structure methods and expectations, integrating some of the children's ideas	Teacher supports, negotiates and scaffolds children's geographical learning
Children's role	Children accept the teacher's control and direction, are diligent, and working is routine	Children work within the teacher's frame, providing some questions, to develop investigations and use skills	Children discuss the purpose and methods with the teacher, taking co-responsibility for the framework
Key concepts	Based on given geography subject authority, uses correct process to give the 'right' answers	Teacher provides children with access to geographical concepts, content, methods and skills for investigation	For and during investigation, focus critically on pertinent geographical ideas, methods and skills
Content	Teacher maintains tight control, determining the study's subject content and approach	Teacher manages study through a structured framework, controls most tasks and sets explicit criteria	The teacher and children discuss and agree the focus, content, questions and approach
Methods	Expository style, routine working, using prepared closed tasks (e.g. worksheets, exercises), teacher assessed	Some didactic teaching and discussion, individual and group work, set tasks, may include problems, findings discussed, is teacher assessed	Class and teams plan and undertake investigation, make presentations, co-evaluation, the teacher taking stance as 'critical friend'

Table 4.4   Children's participation in geographical enquiry (based on Roberts, 2013, p. 31, and Pike, 2016, p. 20)

and demand rigour in the ways children plan investigations, undertake enquiries and draw conclusions. Teachers retain evident responsibility for children's learning, applying their role as a 'critical friend' in which the focus is to ensure and enhance children's learning about geographical enquiry and about geography (Pike, 2016). This is key to the 'three Es' approach, just as in the framework advocated by Pickford *et al.* (2013), whose approach is based on a *focused, framed and facilitated* continuum in which the process moves from teacher initiated and structured enquiry to an approach that is child initiated and structured. They argue that teachers must facilitate this progression across children's humanities studies because the development of enquiry capability is not something children can undertake *on occasion* but should underpin and be in constant use in teaching geography (and in history and most other subjects). For them, *enquiry learning puts the learner at the centre of an active learning process* (Pickford *et al.*, 2013, p. 95). It is an approach that aligns teaching and learning closely, for by using enquiry, *the teacher also becomes a learner by finding out more about the learner and the process of enquiry learning* (p. 95). Geographical enquiry is a mutual process for teachers and children, as Pike (2016) reinforces.

Reflective task

Think of an enquiry that you could do or have done with children and consider how it might enable, enhance and empower children's enquiry skills and ultimately their geographical understanding. Relate this to the approaches illustrated in Tables 4.1, 4.2, 4.3, 4.4.

Philosophy for children

Geographical enquiry is about asking and examining questions and, importantly, getting children to ask and investigate their own questions concerning places, spaces and the environment. This motivates them to seek their answers, for rarely do we ask a question to which we are not interested in finding the answer. Often, though, we are asked questions that we are not terribly interested in investigating. Child-generated questions are the most effective and inspiring, and are being given increasing attention and consideration. Enquiry is also about debating matters that concern us, about which we are curious or that challenge us, whether locally oriented or about global matters such as climate change.

One approach encouraging children to ask questions, examine concerns and issues, and discuss what they raise is that promoted by the Philosophy for Children (P4C) movement (Gregory *et al.*, 2017). It is based on questions and open-minded enquiry. P4C encourages children to reason and to be reasoned with, asking and discussing questions about very real issues in a safe, critically enquiring environment (Haynes, 2008; Gaut and Gaut, 2012; Anderson, 2016) (see the SAPERE website). P4C was developed to encourage children to become more 'reasonable', rigorous and thoughtful through asking 'Socratic' questions on the path to the ultimate educational goal of practical wisdom and good judgement (Lipman, 2003). Using approaches adapted from social constructivism, P4C emphasises that we learn to think just as we learn to speak. Its approach is based on the notion of 'communities of enquiry' in which teachers and children work together to cultivate understanding not only about the material world but also about their personal and ethical world. It is an enquiry-based approach. This development and refining of enquiry skills enables, enhances and empowers children's enquiries (Haynes, 2008) and can be a stimulating and effective starting point for geographical enquiries (Rowley and Lewis, 2003). P4C aims to develop and improve children's thinking skills, encouraging them to engage in the thinking process and to go beyond simple information retrieval to gaining insight and understanding through analysis and reflection. This can lead to positive action being suggested and even taken in the light of understanding, reinforcing children's capacity to take greater responsibility and participate in creating their preferred futures. The resonance with the approach to and process of geographical enquiry is clear.

In the classroom

Using P4C enquiry

P4C can be used to stimulate debate about real-world geographical issues, such as climate change. P4C sessions are initiated by a stimulus to generate children's questions. This approach is used from pre-school through primary schooling.

A photograph of two polar bears atop a melting iceberg was placed in front of 9–10-year-old children sitting in a circle. They were asked to come up with questions about the picture that could be discussed. Open-ended questions such as 'Why can't they be on a bigger piece of ice?' rather than closed questions, such as 'Where are the polar bears?' were encouraged to involve the children in thinking around the wider issues and understanding the 'big' questions. The children wrote their questions on paper and put them on the floor. They voted on the one that interested them the most. They spent 30 minutes discussing and answering the question. Not only did this encourage them to generate further meaningful questions, but it also initiated real consideration of the myriad issues around concepts such as climate change and the geographical reasons and implications of it. It enabled different perspectives to be put forward and these and factual and fanciful information to be challenged and debated.

Practical task

Visit the Philosophy with Children (PWC) forum on their website (http://childrenthinking.co.uk/) and, if appropriate, contribute your views and ideas, perhaps raised from reading about philosophy, enquiry and thinking skills in the context of geographical enquiry. You might follow up by visiting the Open Spaces for Dialogue and Enquiry website (www.osdemeth odology.org.uk) to explore further concepts around enquiry and questioning.

de Bono's techniques for questioning and analysing issues

Many primary schools use the techniques described by de Bono in his many publications (de Bono, 1982, 1985). He is well-known for his promotion of lateral thinking (de Bono, 1977), a creative approach to problem solving and issues or simply an approach to looking at a concern from new directions, quite often a real need in relation to geographical and environmental challenges. The two most commonly used of de Bono's approaches are the 'Six Thinking Hats' and 'PMI'.

The Six Thinking Hats technique (de Bono, 1985) helps children focus more clearly on their thinking about an issue or enquiry. Each member of a group is given a different 'thinking hat'. The white hat focuses just on information and facts. The yellow hat is positive and optimistic. The black hat acts in judgement. The red hat concentrates on feelings and intuition. The green hat is creative. The blue hat manages the process. Children apply their 'hat' role to the matter under discussion, perhaps about an environmental concern.

In the 'PMI' technique, P stands for 'plus', M for 'minus', and I for 'interesting'. It suggests that in working on an issue or decision, during a brainstorming process the enquirer makes three lists of possible answers (de Bono, 1982). The first list (P) is of positive consequences, the second (M) notes negative consequences, the third (I) lists interesting factors. The working out of a decision can then proceed from a summation of these lists. It can provide an insightful way to explore what is being learnt about a place, the natural environment or a sustainability issue.

Reflective task

Consider how you might involve either the 'thinking hats' approach or the 'PMI' technique to the approaches to geographical enquiry outlined in either Table 4.1 or 4.3, or to the example of children's enquiry in

> Table 4.2. At what point would you use the technique? How would you organise the children in teams to use it? What sorts of questions and perspectives, knowledge, views or values would you anticipate they might come up with?

Broadening children's enquiry horizons

Expanding children's geographical enquiry horizons depends on encouraging them to ask their own questions, as much as expanding the questions that we ask them. To prompt children and to develop their questioning, we, as teachers, have a responsibility to challenge their questioning to higher levels. In this set of questions the *italicised questions* are those that encourage and allow children to move on in their understanding and to developing greater insight and deeper understanding and examine their feelings, attitudes and views.

- What is it?
- Where is it?
- What is it like?
- *How did it come to be like this and why?*
- How is it changing and *why?*
- *How and why might it change and what are the alternative possibilities?*
- *What different viewpoints and opinions are there and why?*
- *What impact is change having and why?*
- *What should happen next and why?*
- What do I think/feel/do about this and *why?*
- *How is it similar to/different from other examples and why?*

These questions help us to think about what are useful or effective geographical questions. The following criteria can help us focus on encouraging children to articulate good questions, whatever their age. Some examples are provided in Table 4.5.

- It stimulates and motivates – you want to investigate and answer it.
- It is challenging – not straightforward to answer.
- It will be about a concern or an issue, not just provide information.
- It is about why, not just what.
- It involves analytic and creative thinking skills alongside values.
- It produces informative and interesting (and perhaps, realistic) responses – not always solutions.
- It encourages proposals for action and possibly their follow up.

How can we waste less in our classroom?
Where is the best place in school?
Can we organise the school canteen/cafeteria in a more attractive way?
Where would we locate a pond in the school grounds?
How can we make the school grounds and building fully accessible for a wheelchair user?
Why can't we play on the grass all year round?

Table 4.5   Effective geographical enquiry questions based in a school environment

At its core, geographical enquiry is about facilitating children to be:

- *connected:* children's geographical enquiries have relevance for and are of interest to them;
- *involved:* children are actively engaged in their geographical learning and feel valued as participants in the process of their learning;
- *aware:* children are able to internalise meaning from their geographical enquiries, connecting with their senses, feelings and thoughts;
- *motivated:* the geographical topics and the styles of teaching are stimulating and engaging, involving a variety of teaching and learning strategies and activities;
- *challenged:* children are challenged to think and, so, to apply, adapt and develop their geographical understanding, knowledge, values and skills in continuing and new enquiries;
- *geographers:* while using a variety of methods and tasks, the approaches to teaching and learning about places and environments are through geographical skills, knowledge and understanding;
- *citizens:* children are enabled to develop and express their views and ideas through the enquiries they undertake, including being able to promote and even act on their considered judgements and proposals.

 Practical task

Drawing on the examples in Table 4.5, try to write four or five useful geographical questions of your own. Base them on the local area where you live. Select one and write a plan to outline how you would set out to investigate your question.

Progression in developing geographical enquiry

As has been indicated, developing progression in children's geographical enquiries is important to enabling them to take increasing responsibility, becoming more focused and skilful in asking questions and analysing the data they collect, and in collating their findings and presenting these in more critically thoughtful ways. While progress in understanding and undertaking enquiries can be encouraged within particular geographical topics, there is the need to develop progress in enquiry learning across topics and the school years (Pickford *et al.*, 2013). One way to consider enquiry progression is outlined in Table 4.6, which indicates the ways in which various elements of enquiry might be enhanced across the school years. It begins with young children's questioning in their pre-school settings, the starting point for 'enabling' enquiry, and moves through age phases as older primary children become more experienced, thoughtful, challenged and 'empowered' in their decision-making, planning and execution of their enquiries.

An important challenge for early years and primary geography is to plan for progression. Much of the advice about developing geographical enquiry concerns the enquiry process and creating, constructing and structuring enquiries within topics (Halocha, 2007; Roberts, 2013; Pike, 2016; Biddulph *et al.*, 2015; Jones, 2017; Kidman and Casinader, 2017). Dinkele (2010) suggests there are a number of parameters to consider, which can be applied within an enquiry and across enquiries through a year and across years. These are:

- the focus of an enquiry and subsequent enquiries;
- how pupil involvement is developed within and across enquiries;
- how the skills needed are enhanced in and across enquiries;
- what variety of resources are used and the demands they make on children;
- extending the range of viewpoints or perspectives across enquiries.

During their schooling the levels of expectations and rigour can be raised, as the children might move from more descriptive to more critically focused enquiries. The process of developing children's investigations within an enquiry might well follow a pattern that involves engaging awareness of the topic of study, question raising about what to investigate, collecting and recording the information gathered and analysing it, drawing conclusions from what is found, considering what to communicate and how, and evaluating and reflecting on what has been learnt and how the next enquiry might be improved. Enquiry topics might begin with an issue or a problem. They might examine a matter that is relatively benign or controversial. A key role for the teacher will be to involve the children from the start to generate their engagement in a 'need to know' about the topic of study (Barlow, 2017).

What is important to creating progress from topic to topic and across the primary years of schooling essentially concerns two matters. One is the way in which teachers raise expectations and the challenges and demands in each enquiry, pertinent to the children. The second is how children's evaluations, reflections and identification of what they have learnt in each

Initiating 3/4–5/6 year olds	Enabling 5/6–7/8 year olds	Enhancing 7/8–9/10 year olds	Empowering 9/10–11/12 year olds
Talk about **observations** of features in the immediate environment and in photographs.	Make observations about features and activities in the local environment and in secondary sources.	Give **reasons** for some observations about places and the environment from direct experience and secondary sources.	**Explain** reasons for making observations about places and the environment from direct experience and secondary sources.
Ask questions about what they see around them locally and in pictures to find out information.	Ask questions about features, activities, places and environmental topics.	Begin to suggest **geographical questions**, [such as: why are there more vehicles using this street?].	Ask suitable geographical questions for investigation, such as 'where would a new shop best be situated?', being critically thoughtful of the purpose and relevance of their questions.
Respond to questions about features and activities in the environment and pictures.	Respond to questions about features, activities, places and environmental topics.	Respond to **geographical questions** – for instance, why might we find shops grouped together in towns?	Respond to geographical questions – for example, about the relationships within river processes – giving reasons for responses.
Talk about how they find out information.	Discuss what they might do to carry out an investigation or enquiry.	Offer own ideas for **planning a geographical enquiry** – for example, for a fieldwork investigation – and discuss why and how these might be undertaken.	**Plan a geographical enquiry** – for instance, about a particular locality – bearing in mind the steps involved and identifying their intentions while suggesting a particular pathway for investigation.
Sometimes **collect and record** observations and information.	Collect and record evidence about their questions.	Collect and record relevant evidence – for example, through a survey.	Collect, sift and record appropriate evidence, being thoughtful of its relevance and value.
Talk about what they have observed about the place or environment.	**Use evidence** to **describe** what there is or what happens in a place or environment.	Begin to **analyse** evidence and **describe their findings**.	**Critically analyse** and **evaluate evidence** to **draw conclusions** about the enquiry topic and questions.

Initiating 3/4–5/6 year olds	Enabling 5/6–7/8 year olds	Enhancing 7/8–9/10 year olds	Empowering 9/10–11/12 year olds
Talk about what they think and feel about the place or environment.	Express and listen to each others' *views* on features and activities in the environment and places.	Identify and express clearly their own views about geographical topics. Begin to recognise that others hold views about features, activities, places and the environment.	Identify and explain the *various viewpoints* held by different people about places, the environment, problems, concerns and issues. Begin to appreciate the arguments put forward for different perspectives and that different people may hold opposing views sincerely.
Develop *vocabulary* to describe features and activities in places and the environment.	Extend vocabulary to describe features and activities in places and the environment. Begin to use appropriate *geographical vocabulary.*	Make efforts to use appropriate geographical vocabulary consistently, adding to their geographical vocabulary.	Use appropriate geographical vocabulary consistently, including the use of technical geographical terms in investigations and fieldwork.
Talk to others about what they have seen and found out about features, activities, places and the environment.	*Communicate findings* in one or more ways about features, activities, places and environments.	Communicate findings for an audience and appropriate to the investigation.	Communicate findings in ways appropriate to the topic of the enquiry and relevant to an audience. Reflect on strengths and shortcomings of the enquiry.
Talk about what they liked or did not like about observing and finding out.	Discuss what they have learnt from their enquiries and how they liked doing each one.	*Evaluate* the outcome(s) of enquiries and investigations and what they have learnt about undertaking an enquiry.	Evaluate and reflect upon the outcome(s) of each of their enquiries and investigations, considering the skills, knowledge and understanding that they gained and what has been learnt about undertaking enquiries to apply in their next geographical enquiry.

Table 4.6 Progression in geographical enquiry across early years and primary schooling (developed from Catling, 2010b, p. 82)

enquiry leads to their setting out their next steps collectively and individually, guided and advised by their teacher, to develop their enquiry skills and techniques further, as well as to raise their own expectations about what they need to understand more fully. While in many senses it is a rough guide only, the progression sequence in Table 4.6 sets in train in the earliest years' experiences that harness children's natural curiosity and desire to know and learn to initiate enquiry learning, enabling them in the first years of schooling to contribute to geographical enquiries. This is built on during the middle and upper primary years through encouraging children to enhance their approaches, skills and techniques in undertaking enquiries with the target to empower them to take a lead role, and to be more thoughtful and critically aware in doing so. As Pickford *et al.* (2013) make clear, this approach fundamentally involves the teacher increasingly *actively prompting and challenging children's questions and chosen approaches* (p. 125) as well as the topics, issues and problems that children might wish to pursue. The role of critical mentor is vital in this process, as noted in Table 4.3.

 Key points

This chapter has:

- considered what is meant by the term 'enquiry' and outlined its role and potential in teaching geography in the primary curriculum;
- explored the rationale for the practice of enquiry, demonstrating why it is a very effective way of developing children's geographical understanding;
- considered traditional enquiry questions and processes, and introduced more contemporary foci for developing and delivering enquiry, encouraging children's greater participation and involvement, taking into account their own geographies;
- considered the role and potential of pursuing enquiry in greater depth and with broader outcomes through asking more open questions and involving initiatives such as Philosophy for Children.

Moving on

You might follow up the last practical task by carrying out your enquiry to build up a picture and an understanding of your immediate locality, and to consider how enquiry helps us to understand our environment, develop a sense of place and recognise local issues.

Further reading

The following publications contain useful sections on and examples of geographical enquiries.

Halocha, J (2012) *The Primary Teacher's Guide to Geography*. Witney: Scholastic/Book End.

Martin, F (2006) *Teaching Geography in Primary Schools*. Cambridge: Chris Kington.

Pickford, T, Garner, W and Jackson, E (2013) *Primary Humanities: Learning through Enquiry*. London: Sage.

Pike, S (2016) *Learning Primary Geography: Ideas and inspirations from classrooms*. Abingdon: Routledge.

Reynolds, R (2014) *Teaching Humanities and Social Sciences in the Primary School*. South Melbourne: Oxford University Press.

Roberts, M (2013) *Geography through Enquiry*. Sheffield: Geographical Association.

Rowley, C (2006) Are There Different Types of Geographical Enquiry? In Cooper, H, Rowley, C and Asquith, S (eds) *Geography 3–11: A Guide for Teachers*. London: David Fulton.

Rowley, C and Lewis, L (2003) *Thinking on the Edge*. Morecambe: Living Earth.

Scoffham, S (ed.) (2010) *Primary Geography Handbook*. Sheffield: Geographical Association.

Examples of geographical inquiries are published regularly in *Primary Geographer*.

Useful websites

de Bono: Six Thinking Hats: www.debonogroup.com/six_thinking_hats.php
Geographical Association: www.geography.org.uk
GeogSpace (AGTA): www.agta.asn.au
Open Spaces for Dialogue and Inquiry: www.osdemethodology.org.uk
Philosophy for Children (P4C): www.p4c.com
Philosophy with Children (PWC): www.childrenthinking.co.uk

CHAPTER 5

EXPLORING PLACES

Key ideas in understanding places

 Chapter objectives

This chapter enables you to:

- appreciate the idea of place as a core geographical concept;
- be aware that place is a vital component in your own experience;
- explain why the study of places is a vital aspect in primary geography;
- consider the range of places to include in primary children's geography curriculum;
- recognise the value of developing children's mental maps of locational knowledge from local to world scales.

Introduction

Place, one of the big ideas, or core concepts, of geography was introduced in Chapter 2. We use the word 'place' variously in geography, such
as objects being in their place; a city open space as a place to meet; your
place of study or work; and 'no place like home'. These uses of place
refer to position, site and to the nature of places. Children's experience
of and in their own locality – their place – is a key element of their childhood; their knowledge of and ideas about places develop through their
varied experiences. This indicates other notions of place in our list. Places
hold meanings for us (Martin, 2006c; Cresswell, 2015). Their meanings
encompass how and why we feel about and appreciate our familiar surroundings or the new places we visit; how and why we observe and
understand places, both familiar and new; and how and why we use
places as we do. These interacting notions of 'place' lie at the core of
everyday geographies. Place is a complex, developed and potent idea
geographically (Cresswell, 2015; de Blij, 2009). Places can be personal
and public, of varied size and scale, and real and imagined. This chapter
examines these aspects of place, what might be taught about places and
the development of children's locational knowledge. These are explored
further in later chapters.

Meeting places

Childhood places are important to us. We remember particular aspects of
the places where we lived during our primary and teenage years. From our
earliest years places play a key part in our childhood everyday geographies. They help create our initial impressions of the outside world. They
are where we played, the places we used, and how we felt about them
remains with us. Such places may be small courtyard or garden-size areas
or cover a few streets, an area of countryside or a park. We recall people
and features that were important to us. Family and friends are an important
factor here, influencing us through taking us out on visits or shopping,
their experiences and their perceptions, and by giving us permission to
run errands and make journeys, allowing the possibility for exploring more
widely. We construct our understanding of places and our images of place
through our interactions with them, from our direct experiences. The
places we know most about are those closest to us, emotionally and as
physical sites.

In her novel *Blackberry Wine*, Joanna Harris (2001) describes percep-
tively a child's sense of place, using her authorial licence to explore in some
depth the meaning of a place to the central character, Jay.

Joe lived on Fog Hill Lane, one of a row of uneven terraces backing onto the railway half a mile from the station. Jay had already been there twice before, leaving his bike in a stand of bushes and climbing up the banking to reach the railway bridge. On the far side there were fields reaching down to the river, and beyond that lay the opencast mine, the sound of machinery a distant drone on the wind. For a couple of miles an old canal ran almost parallel to the railway, and there the stagnant air was green with flies and hot with the scent of ash and greenery. A bridle path ran between the canal and the railway, overhung with tree branches. Nether Edge to the townspeople, it was almost always deserted. That was why it first attracted him. He bought a packet of cigarettes and a copy of the Eagle from the station newspaper stand and cycled down towards the canal. Then, leaving his bike concealed in the undergrowth, he walked along the canal path, pushing his way through great drifts of ripe willowherb and sending clouds of white seeds into the air. When he reached the old lock, he sat down on the stones and smoked as he watched the railway, occasionally counting the coal trucks as they passed, or making faces at the passenger trains as they clattered to their distant, envied destinations. He threw stones into the clotted canal. A few times he walked all the way to the river and made dams with turf and the accumulated garbage it had brought with it: car tyres, branches, railway sleepers and once a whole mattress with the springs poking out of the ticking. That was really how it began; the place got a hold on him somehow. Perhaps it was because it was a secret place, an old, forbidden place. Jay began to explore; there were mysterious raised concrete-and-metal cylinders, which Joe later identified as capped pitheads and which gave out resonant breathing sounds if you went close. A flooded mineshaft, an abandoned coal truck, the remains of a barge. It was an ugly, perhaps dangerous place, but it was a place of great sadness, too, and it attracted him in a way that he could neither combat nor understand. His parents would have been horrified at his going there, and that, too, contributed to its appeal. So he explored; here an ash pit filled with ancient shards of crockery, there a spill of exotic, discarded treasures – bundles of comics and magazines, as yet unspoiled by rain; the hulk of a car, an old Ford Galaxie, a small elder tree growing out of its roof like a novelty aerial; a dead television. Living alongside the railway, Joe once told him, is like living on a beach; the tide brings new jetsam every day. At first he hated it. He couldn't imagine why he went there at all. He would set out with the intention of taking a quite different route and still find himself in Nether Edge, between the railway and the canal, the sound of distant machinery droning in his ears and the whitish summer sky pushing down on top of his head like a hot cap. A lonely, derelict place. But his, nonetheless. Throughout all that long, strange summer, his. Or so he assumed.

(Harris, 2001, pp. 27–8)

A key feature of primary geography is helping children to articulate and extend their awareness, knowledge, understanding and feelings about their own places through their studies and explorations, accompanied and sometimes not. It focuses on developing their appreciation of their own places, providing opportunities to express critical insights and positive perspectives to understand their place's present as well as to consider its future.

Exploring place

There are places that are part of our daily lives, and places we may visit. Being in and experiencing places provides the strongest sense of place, but words and pictures can present an idea of how places may look, be and feel. Texts can describe and provide insight. Pictures provide information about and views of places that cannot fully be captured in words. Both provide, in their different ways, understanding and senses of meaning about places. The description below is of an area in the old town, or medina, of Tunis, in Tunisia, north Africa. It comes from a tourist guidebook to the city, and provides information about and insights into the medina. A souk is a market, which may be in a building or a square or composed, as here, of narrow streets and alleyways, some covered and some open. Images 5.1 and 5.2 illustrate two features noted in the guide.

The Medina (Old Town)

*The **medina** of Tunis is probably the easiest to navigate in all of North Africa. At all the main gates you'll find a large map with all the streets clearly named, and there are small orange signposts pointing the way to the principal sights. The souks have their share of the usual hustlers, so be wary of anyone offering to show you a view, a museum or a special exhibition. These inevitably lead to carpet shops.*

*The free standing archway of the **Bab el Bahr** – also called the **Porte de France** (built 1848), on the Place de la Victoire – marks the entrance to the medina. It was once continuous with the thick medina walls, and stood on the shore of the lake of Tunis (the Arabic name translates as 'Sea Gate') before the French built their own new town on reclaimed land. Walk through the Porte de France and then take the left hand of the two narrow alleys facing you.*

*This is the rue **Jemaa ez Zitouna**, the medina's main street, and it is lined with tiny craft shops and souvenir stalls. As you merge with the crowds that shuffle slowly up hill you will find yourself immersed in a world of heady sensations. Fragrant incense and exotic perfumes compete with the mouth watering smell of roasting mutton and the aroma of freshly ground coffee. The tap tap of silversmiths' hammers and the scuff of sandaled feet on smooth paving stones almost drown out the muezzin's call to prayer from a minaret. The bright reds, blues and golds of flowing kaftans flash in the dappled interplay of sunshine and shade, and then the street disappears into a dark tunnel to emerge at the steps below the door to the Zitouna Mosque.*

(Wilson, 2009, pp. 30–1)

Image 5.1   The Porte de France, a gateway into the medina in Tunis

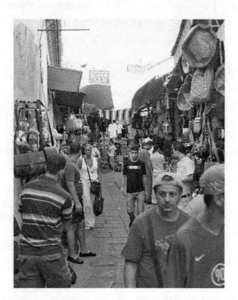

Image 5.2   Inside the souk

Reflective task

The examples give focus on localities, small-scale places: an extent of waste ground, the ancient city centre.

   What do they convey to you about the idea of place? Note the idea(s) of place that they stimulate for you.

Practical task

Select a novel, children's book or a tourist guide that describes an urban or rural neighbourhood or use photographs of somewhere you have been. What do you think the author or photographer (yourself?) is trying to convey about the place by writing about it and/or using photographs to show it? Now write about a place that you know well. How would you describe it to bring it alive?

In the classroom

Using a picture story to explore place

A teacher introduced her class of 5–6-year-olds to Belonging *(alternatively titled* Home, *Baker, 2004), a textless picture story showing the view of a street from a window. Previously, they had explored the neighbourhood around their urban school. Their teacher used* Belonging *to encourage them to think about local changes that might have taken place. Using the book's pictures, she asked the children to look carefully for changes they could see. The children quickly became adept at this. She took them through the story again, guiding them to think about how the place appeared across the pictures as time passed, encouraging them to see the whole picture rather than its particular features. They discussed how it changed. They went through the story a third time, now from the back, discussing why the changes happened and saying what they thought about them. She encouraged them to say how they felt about the place as it changed. What did they like or not like? What would they have changed and how? How would they feel if they were part of a family living there? She helped them recognise what was happening to this place, and their beginnings of an appreciation of what it might be like to live, or at least visit, there. She encouraged the children to discuss further what they knew about their own area from their personal experience and the observational fieldwork they had undertaken. Did they know about any changes? Some children brought in information from home about changes locally. She linked this with what they felt about living in their area, how they used it and what meaning it had for them.*

(Catling, 2015c, pp. 195–6)

Practical task

You might want to explore how places change and develop over a longer period of time and the impacts that change has. Another picture storybook, for children aged between 8 and 11 years old, is *My Place* (Wheatley and Rawlins, 2008). It presents in text, pictures and maps the evolution of a locality over two hundred years, beginning in 1788. See if you can obtain a copy.

What types of change does *My Place* show? Who is affected, why and in which ways at different times? What has happened to the locality during this time? What do the people who live there do? How have they caused or affected changes?

Look out for picture storybooks and novels for primary age children that tell you about local places. Collect a few that you consider to be good books to share with children, which can help them consider, think about and discuss what places are like, how they develop, what concerns or issues change or the lack of change raises, and what they feel about places. Some picture storybooks are suggested in Appendix 2 under Places.

What is place?

Geographers study the nature of 'place' by examining people's uses of and affects on places and how people perceive and understand places (Matthews and Herbert, 2008; Dovey, 2010; Cresswell, 2015). There are four important aspects to the idea of *place*.

- Where places are: the location of places.
- What places are like: the nature of places.
- What places mean to us: the meaning of places.
- What patterns and networks there are in places: place and space relationships.

Locating places

Everywhere is somewhere. Location is centrally important in geography. It helps to know, understand and appreciate where places are, to find them, to refer to them and – because this can be shared information – to anticipate that when we refer to particular places – countries, cities, mountains, resorts – others may know roughly where they are or be able to find out.

We collect and record locational information to help us, in street maps, and national and global atlases. We use satellite-sourced websites such as Google Earth, Google Maps and others to locate and view our place and other places. Increasingly, car drivers, even walkers, use global positioning systems (GPS) to check where exactly they are and their own or alternative routes. We have used GPS in ships and aeroplanes for many years. While the earliest 'GPS' was the dead reckoning and local knowledge skills employed by sailors, the development of latitude and longitude to locate places uniquely on the ocean and around coasts (with the technology later to do so very accurately) enabled ships to move precisely over the oceans and helped geographers and cartographers to state locations and make maps accurately. It is all about a core geographical question:

• Where is this place?

The sense of where is only the starting point for place studies. A place's location is important, but the place or feature itself is the reason for wanting to know.

The nature of places

Through the study of place, we try to describe what places are like, and explain why physical and human features, such as lakes and towns, are where they are. Place studies focus on what the features are like, how they came to be as they are today, what continues to influence changes to them, and what impact such development might have on people, and the built and natural environment in the future. Geographers ask about the character of places and their connections with and to other places.

• What is this place like?
• Why is this place here and like this?
• What use do people make of this place and why?
• How is this place linked to and interdependent with other places and why?
• How is this place changing and what causes this?
• What impacts will changes have here and elsewhere and why might this be?
• What is the future for this place and why?

The focus of study here is on the human and physical, or natural, features and processes that create, characterise and change places. Places are dynamic, whether developments occur with some speed – a new housing estate or shopping centre in two to three years – or over many millions of years, as in the evolution of mountains and coastlines. Change may be dramatic and have major impacts, as with Hurricane Sandy severely damaging many places and communities from the Caribbean to the north-east USA in 2012, the horrendous earthquakes in Christchurch, New Zealand, in 2011 and in Italy in 2016, and the tsunami that caused devastation and much loss of life in north-east Japan in 2011. Changes can be commonplace, such as new shops or in-fill housing developments. Places are cultural creations, the result of human activities (Dovey, 2010), like Istanbul or Shanghai, or named from a sense of 'awe and wonder' at the natural environment, such as Uluru in central Australia with its deep meanings for the Aboriginal peoples or the aptly named Death Valley in the USA. A key aspect of places is what they might become, what possible and likely futures they have. Geographers examine the impact of changes in and on places, as well as on their future development, their preferred or probable futures.

Scale provides vital insights about places. Places encompass areas of differing sizes and complexity, from small localities to large regions covering a sizeable part of the globe, and, indeed, the Earth itself. We may focus on the minutiae of the school playground, a shopping street or neighbourhood or study the relationships within a county or country, or even a large cross-national political region such as the European Union.

The meaning of places

We see places through two lenses: as real places and as imagined places. Our experience and knowledge of places is inevitably limited and partial, providing an image of these places. Our involvement in places creates a sense of that place which is personal. Yet much that we know of places through experience or via secondary sources is shared; we discuss traffic problems in the high street, and we know the shops we talk about. Many places of which we are aware we have encountered at second hand from a variety of sources: family, friends, TV news, websites, tourist brochures, novels and films. We create some of our knowledge and understanding of the reality of places from the images of place that others provide. We deal with multiple perspectives of the same place to create our own view. These 'place views' are partial and 'situated'. Place is not a simple objective notion but a matter of personal and collective meaning and interpretation.

Studying place concerns how localities have meaning for people. We all have sense(s) of place, the feelings about and appreciations of the places with which we associate particularly: places we feel at home in, places we love returning to, places we feel are 'our' places, just as there are places we avoid, find unattractive or even scary. Geographers examine people's relationships with and to places and they are interested in why we have these relationships.

- What is it like to live in this place?
- How involved do you feel in this place?
- What does this place mean to you?
- What is your reaction to change here?

- What do you want this place to be in the future?
- What do you want to see happen here?

Geography examines our knowledge and understanding of places and our emotional attachment to places. It explores how our identity interrelates with the places that have meaning for us. It examines why this is and what results from our views. It is concerned with our senses of belonging and well-being (Atkinson *et al.*, 2012). Particular interest lies in the ways that the decisions we make might affect places, daily and long term, their present and their future, as well as impact on our own and others' lives. In this context, geography explores our values, interests and preferences.

Much of our understanding of places draws from our perceptions and images of places, our geographical imagination: how we organise our knowledge of places and imagine what they might be like from that understanding. We also imagine fictional places. Imaginary places are part of our experience, whether through television drama, novels, comics or poetry. We use our knowledge and perceptions of places to construct the appearance and sense of place we have before us. We may carry such creative images of places with us for many years from our favourite places and stories.

Place and space

Geographers study the spatial aspects of the Earth's surface, locally and globally, and try to understand and explain space. Places can be thought of as 'bounded space', a territory such as a neighbourhood or country (Matthews and Herbert, 2008) in space. Space encompasses the idea of location, where places are and the relationships between locations, which links to such concepts as distance and scale. Geographers study spatial relationships in and between places, such as the locations and network of the leisure activities of children within a community or road, rail and air networks that connect places across countries and continents. They are interested in explaining the spatial patterns they find in human activities and natural phenomena, such as the reasons why there is a relationship between pick-your-own farms, road access and urban areas. They look at the physical and human processes at work in the environment and develop notions such as location theory to explain why activities and developments – for instance, schooling and shopping centres – appear where they do. Plate tectonics offers insight into the occurrence and patterns of earthquake and volcanic activities. This enables geographers to make predictions and proposals about natural and human activities. Geographers use a range of questions for doing this, such as the following.

- Where do these features or events occur?
- Is there a relationship between these features or events?

- Can patterns be discerned, what are they, and how can they be explained?
- What processes are at work causing these relationships and patterns?
- Can the patterns and processes be predicted and/or replicated or prevented?
- How can we adapt or use such processes for the benefit of people?
- What are the reasons for and the consequences of these patterns and processes, beneficial or otherwise?

The interest in spatial relationships, patterns and processes lies in how we understand and can foresee events. For example, the study of weather patterns and processes enables us to forecast the weather. Researching the best location for a new hypermarket or leisure centre might provide best access to the most people with least disturbance to the area in which it is to be sited. This is important because it concerns developing our awareness, knowledge and understanding of how the world works in order that as members of our communities and nations we might use these physical and social processes to improve the places we inhabit, use and enjoy.

Reflective task

Read your notes about the concept of place. Consider how what you have written reflects the ideas about place expressed in this section. Add new points that have struck you about the idea of place. Identify and note why your ideas have developed.

Teaching about places

Why teach about places?

Studying places helps children understand and appreciate the location, nature and meaning of places and the importance of space. It gives them insight into how places work, what characteristics they have, their layouts and how they are used, what they mean to the children, and what it is or may be like for different people to live in and visit them. It draws on their personal experiences and understanding of places, at first hand or through indirect sources. Studying places expands their horizons from their places into the wider world. Their experience of picture stories, novels and drama helps develop their awareness and sense of place.

There are strong arguments for teaching about places implicit in the points made above and in Chapter 3. These draw on children's everyday geographies, their personal experiences in their environment and of the wider world through first- or second-hand encounters, perceptions and meaning. There are reasons that draw on the ways in which geographers explore, examine and understand places and people's activities in and meanings about them. Studying places provides opportunities for children to:

- use and develop their natural curiosity about, wonder at and fascination for places;
- examine and clarify their existing experience and awareness of places;
- develop their existing knowledge and understanding of their own and other places;
- develop their appreciation of their own and others' perceptions of their and other places, of why these places have meaning for and are important to those who live there;
- develop spatial awareness from the local towards a global scale;
- recognise their interdependence in their community, region and nation, and with the rest of the world;
- build a global perspective from their local perspective, and use this reciprocally to deepen their appreciation and understanding of the local;
- build positive attitudes towards other peoples, nearby and elsewhere, including those they will never encounter;
- value diversity in peoples, cultures and places;
- combat ignorance and bias, to challenge stereotyping and prejudice, and to raise their awareness of the partiality of and limits to our understanding of people and places, locally and far away;
- explore and develop ideas and skills, and extend their place vocabulary and language;
- develop and extend their awareness, knowledge and understanding of places beyond their current experience to help them have a broader, fuller and deeper appreciation of the world and its people.

Places to explore in primary geography at different scales

A variety of places should be studied during the early and primary years, including the school and its grounds, the local area, the wider region, your country, and other places at different scales nationally and in other parts of the world. It is important to ensure that places are not studied in isolation, but are linked into their regional and national context, that their global location is identified, and that connections to nearby countries and within their continent are noted, gradually helping to develop increasingly their sense of relationships, distance and scale.

School building and grounds

The school and its grounds are a shared aspect of children's lives. This small-scale place, whether of extensive or limited grounds and with one or more buildings, offers opportunities to examine its features and activities, and the views and feelings of children and staff, among much else, inside and outdoors. Chapters 11 with 7, 9 and 10 develop these and other approaches.

The school's local area and neighbourhood

The locality of the school is usually the area where most children live. It is the children's local area and is important in and to their lives. Whether an urban or rural environment, there is much to study locally. Fieldwork is an important way into local study (Tanner and Whittle, 2015). Approaches to studying the local area are considered in Chapters 9 and 12.

Extending to national regions and your country

Investigating aspects of the wider region in which you live and/or, perhaps, another area of your country provides opportunities for children to gain an idea of a larger area nationally, in which also they can explore another locality of similar size to their own, to be able to make comparisons. Chapter 12 refers to the study of wider regions and other localities, which should draw on much the same approaches as in the local area, though you might be using secondary rather than direct or primary resources. It refers also to finding out more about your own country.

Places and countries beyond your own

It is important that younger children develop some understanding of other places elsewhere in the world. Such studies best focus on similar-sized localities and national regions to enable helpful comparisons. Recognising and appreciating the diversity across the world can be fostered through studying a locality in a similar type of country or a nation that may be economically challenging for many of its people, where similarities can be noted and contrasts considered. Such studies must be set in regional, national and global contexts. Some resources for and approaches to teaching are outlined in Chapter 13.

About the world

Pre-school children can encounter the world through play with soft and inflatable globes. We can develop their knowledge of continents, oceans and the Earth's key features from early on and build up their ideas about the world as our home and its variety of natural features and environments, human sites and activities, such as cities and trade, and countries through primary geography curriculum (Owens, 2011; Scoffham and Owens, 2017). Chapter 13 provides approaches to undertaking this, supported by Chapter 9.

Outside the classroom

Using fieldwork to identify local issues for an enquiry

A teacher of a class of 10–11-year-olds decided that fieldwork in the local area should be more than just observing and recording what is there. She wanted her children to use their observations to suggest issues that were relevant to their particular area. In this way they would see a purpose for the fieldwork, and would be encouraged to do their own thinking about what they saw. The site of the fieldwork was deliberately limited to an area very close to the school, because their teacher wanted the children to visit it at least twice. The first visit involved observations, mapping, recording of numbers of cars and pedestrians in certain locations, and most importantly looking out for issues, problems, difficulties and situations that could be improved. These were discussed in the classroom, and then through class decision, a plan was made for another visit into the same area to investigate the chosen concerns. This meant that children were aware of the purpose of their study, and had discussed their fieldwork techniques, as well as ways to present and communicate the results. The second visit involved gathering more focused data, using cameras, close observation, and mapping distributions and patterns of activities to provide evidence relevant to the enquiry.

Locational knowledge: where in the world?

The public perception of geography seems to be that it is about knowing where places are, though we know that it concerns much more than this limited vision. Yet, knowledge of location is important: being about where features, places and environments are and where events happen in the world. Maps appear regularly in the media to locate places, to provide a sense of their relationship to our country. Having an awareness of the whereabouts of the continents and oceans, and of significant places and features in the world in our mental map helps us appreciate where events occur when they are mentioned. Of course, we could look up places in an atlas or on our smart phone each time we hear the news, but this is not always convenient. Knowing basic world knowledge – having it at our fingertips, as it were – is important, because what happens nearby or far away might affect each of us directly or indirectly, and being able to make quick sense of this helps us maintain a balanced perspective.

In her children's novel, *The Travels of Oggy*, Ann Lawrence (1973) describes both his travels and his learning about the world from the local to the global. Oggy is a hedgehog whose human family moves home, but they leave him behind in the garden. He determines to find them but has only heard that they have moved to 'the country'. During his journey he encounters many other creatures who help him learn about his urban London locality and the countryside, as well as about Britain, where the story is set. He encounters a wide variety of places and weather, including a storm, following which he finds himself beside a large lake, which he thinks is the sea – of which he has heard, an error of inexperience. He meets a petrel who tells Oggy that there is not just 'the country' (*countryside*) but that there are many countries (*nations*) – and all over the world. These ideas puzzle Oggy considerably. Wilson, the petrel, tries to explain it as follows.

> *'Right, let's start here,' said Wilson. 'This country's England, right?'*
>
> *Oggy scratched and thought; he had never heard it put like that before, but if the petrel said so, he supposed it must be. He nodded and Wilson continued: 'And you know that England is surrounded by the Sea, right?'*
>
> *Again Oggy nodded.*
>
> *'Well, there's lots of other countries across the Sea – hundreds and thousands of miles of sea between them.'*
>
> *Oggy thought deeply about this. Hampstead Heath surrounded by London, surrounded by the country with roads and canals and other towns in it, and surrounded by the Sea – but now the Sea was not just a margin of blue round the green Country, it was a vast expanse of blue, dotted all over with many green countries.*

Wilson had already mentioned that New Zealand is his home and that it is 'on the other side of the world', which really threw Oggy. The conversation continued.

> *'But what about this other side business?' he asked, when he had digested the idea.*
>
> *'Well, the other side of the world,' said the petrel, evidently puzzled. 'You know – Down Under, the An-tip-o-des.' He brought out the last word slowly and with relish.*
>
> *'The Aunty whats?' said Oggy blankly.*
>
> *'It's Latin or Greek or something for the opposite side of the earth to what you happen to be on when you say it,' Wilson explained. 'Hey!' he added, as if*

something had just occurred to him. 'You do know that the World is round, don't you?'

Oggy simply gaped. 'Round?' he repeated. He had not felt so completely ignorant for a long time.

'Yes round – like a ball, see? England – that's here – is right on the opposite side of the ball to New Zealand, where I come from.'

(Lawrence, 1973, pp. 113–14)

And so this story of Oggy's journey continues. The story ends happily for Oggy; but it is what he has learnt about his home country and something of the world, with ideas about what it is like and what there is across it that helps him to develop a mental sense of the shape and nature of the Earth. It describes the initial development, albeit not very fully, of his *mental map* of the world. Mental maps are the images we 'carry in our heads' which help us to find our way about in everyday life (local mental maps) and to recall as need be our sense of a rough outline of the shape of our country and the world (national and global mental maps). They develop through experience, exploring locally, and from incidental and formal learning, using atlases and globes, such as about countries, continents and the world (Catling, 2017c).

In studying places children build up their mental maps of their locality and other places they encounter through developing their *locational knowledge* (Catling, 2002, 2013, 2017c). This describes locating where places are in the neighbourhood and the wider region, nationally and in the world. It requires introducing children to globes and maps of the world, continents and countries, which supports their growing spatial awareness of the world. It is important in primary geography to:

- enable children to identify and learn where significant places are;
- help children understand why having locational knowledge is useful;
- encourage children to find places on globes, atlases and maps, using appropriate mapping skills, when they hear about them or are studying them, so that they construct their personal set of locational knowledge – their mental maps – about the world.

Table 5.1 provides a 'rough guide' to initiating, developing and extending pre-school and primary age children's locational knowledge understanding, taking account of their increasing local experience, of wider and national regions, and continentally and globally. It indicates a sequence to help this geographical learning. With appropriate and good support, children can begin to develop their mental maps locally and of the world from before they start school.

Scales and contexts of locational knowledge		
Classroom and school grounds	Local area to wider region	Nationally to globally
Initiating locational knowledge (to encourage in pre-school and early primary education: c. 3/4 to 6/7-year-olds)		
• Learning to find their way around the pre- and school areas indoors and outside. • Becoming familiar with where particular features, areas and resources are inside and outside. • Using photographs to find features inside and outside and talk about what is near them. • Developing vocabulary to refer to relative directions and name features and locations.	• Visiting specific sites locally to be able to say what it is and name what is there, and what is next to features and facilities. • Observing and talking about and sequencing features and areas passed. • Building a sense of direction about the way home and to some familiar places.	• Playing with a soft globe among play toys and learning it is named the Earth and World. • Handling an inflatable globe and talking about what can be seen, encountering the notions of land and sea, and beginning to name key features, such as continents.
Developing locational knowledge (to develop during early to middle primary education: c. 5/6 to 8/9-year-olds)		
• Saying where features are and what they are next/near to in their classroom, using appropriate vocabulary. • Following and giving relative directions in their classroom from different locations to others. • Following directions and routes to named locations in the school and grounds. • Naming and talking about what can be seen on a large-scale aerial photograph of the school grounds, outside and in class. • Using outside and in class simple (picture) maps and plans of the room and grounds to identify features and locate them. • Pointing out the direction of particular features in class and the grounds.	• Naming various familiar features and areas in the local area and being able to say what is nearby and how to reach them. • Being introduced to a large-scale aerial photograph and a map of the local area, and discussing what can be seen. • Making and talking about a model of the local area and locating various features on it, including photographs of key features. • Using a (legible) local street map to locate streets and indicate routes. • Being aware, from their travels, of places that are outside the neighbourhood and even beyond the wider local area, and being able to name features there and give some idea of where else they are near.	• Becoming familiar with a variety of globes, inflatable and on stands, knowing they are models of the Earth. • Being able to name and locate the Earth's continents and oceans. • Beginning to recognise the shape of their country and becoming aware of key features, such as the capital city, and where they live, linked to some nearby urban and/or rural centres. • Beginning to recognise the shape of their continent and where their country lies within it. • Becoming aware of photographs of the Earth from space and the areas they show, related to a globe view. • Making use of atlases, wall maps, table maps and other resources to identify the continents and oceans and their own country.

	Scales and contexts of locational knowledge		
Classroom and school grounds	**Local area to wider region**	**Nationally to globally**
• Developing confidence in using relative location vocabulary, and being introduced to the four compass points. • Beginning to use alpha-numeric grid references on class and school grounds maps.	• Beginning to use alpha-numeric grid references on some maps of the local area.	• Becoming aware that there are and naming some significant physical features on the Earth's surface and that other countries and cities exist. • Beginning to use alpha-numeric grid references on atlas maps.

Extending locational knowledge (to enhance knowledge in older primary age children: c. 7/8 to 11/12-year-olds)

• Being able to talk familiarly about the features, layout, locations of and directions and routes in their classroom, school building(s) and grounds. • Using appropriate vocabulary to describe features, locations and routes, using both relative directional and locational language and the eight compass points. • Being able to use alpha-numeric and 4- and 6-figure grid references on maps of their class and school site.	• Being familiar with aerial photographs and a variety of maps of different scales and types of their neighbourhood and local area. • Being able to identify and describe features, locations and routes with which they are familiar, and on maps relative to other features and sites locally. • Becoming familiar with maps of the wider region in which they live and being able to identify features, locations and routes and build a sense of key places in relation to each other. • Being able to use relative locational and directional vocabulary and the eight compass points. • Using alpha-numeric and 4- and 6-figure grid references on maps of the local area and wider region.	• Being familiar with globes and atlases so as easily to find their way around them to locate places and features, and to know the locations and directions of and between key places and features. • Developing their understanding of the symbols and keys used on globes and atlas maps, including what they do and do not show. • Being able to relate satellite and space photographs of the Earth to the globe and atlas maps, and talk about their similarities and differences. • Being familiar with a range of countries, cities, islands, mountains and rivers across the world and where they are. • Being aware of the Earth's rotation and tilt and their relationship with day and night and seasons. • Being introduced to the nature and role of latitude and longitude to describe location, and to key lines of latitude such as the Equator, the tropics and polar circles and the prime meridian as a line of longitude, as well as to the international date line and the existence of time zones.

Table 5.1 A suggested sequence for developing primary children's local to global locational knowledge

In the classroom

The class of 7–8-year-olds always had access to a globe and a world map. Periodically, the children were challenged to find and locate places to remind them where places they know are and to encourage them to locate 'new' places, taken from the news and children's interests. They had become familiar with the continents and oceans, and have drawn up their own set of interesting places, which are marked on a world wall map. They use P4C circle time occasionally to debate whether to add or remove places on their map. They have a street map on the wall with their homes and other places they consider significant marked. Many have developed the habit of finding places in atlases and of bringing in obscure places for other children to locate. This reinforces and extends their emerging mental maps of their place and of the wider world.

Outside the classroom

Exploring the Earth's rotation

For a class of 10–11-year-olds, the globe became more of a 'living object' when their teacher explained how it could be 'oriented' to align with the Earth in space. This idea was introduced on a day when the sun was bright. The globe was taken into the sunshine and placed so that their country was exactly at the top of the globe, and the North Pole on the globe was pointing North. Oriented this way, the Earth was aligned as a model in relation to the sun at that particular time of day. The children saw clearly that their part of the world was in sunlight, and the (faint) shadow lines of dawn and sunset. That the areas near to the North or South Poles have very long or very short days, depending on the time of year, was discussed. When their teacher placed toothpicks in Blu Tack on to various locations, the different lengths of shadows were seen. Over the year, the globe was taken outside at different times of the day and in different seasons, helping the children to appreciate over time the contrasts between times of the day and seasons. It helped the children to understand the Earth's rotation and that it was dusk, night or dawn in other places on the Earth when it was midday where the children were.

To be able to help children most effectively as teachers, we need to have reasonable good mental maps of the local area of our school, of the wider region it is in, and of the world. We may well have built up our mental map of the world through our school and incidental learning, and as a result of travel to places in other countries and continents. We may be less familiar with the neighbourhood of the school and of the region it lies in. We can help ourselves to develop our local mental map by walking the local area and taking different routes through it when we drive or cycle to school, so we know what is there and our way around. This will also enhance our sense of place about the area in which we teach and in which the children live. There is no better way to develop the children's and our own mental maps than through undertaking a local study with the class and using aspects of the local area in the other geography topics we include in their curriculum. Localities, of course, should not be seen as isolated but within the wider context of the places they are linked to in various ways; this will help children to develop their 'regional' mental map. When coming across other places we should ensure that children know where in the world they are. Large-scale local maps, street atlases, road atlases, atlases and globes will all be invaluable resources in helping children to develop their locational knowledge.

Further aspects of map and atlas development are included in Chapters 9 and 13. These concern map skills, the use of atlases and knowledge of places.

 Reflective task

Consider where you know in the world. Which well-known and significant places can you locate in your own *mental maps* of your own country and of the world? Can you just turn to the appropriate page in an atlas? When would you need to use the Contents page and the Index to look something up, and why do so?

Listen to a local or national news broadcast, or read the news section in a daily newspaper or on a news website. How many of the places mentioned do you know the location of? Why do you know them or why do you not? Have an atlas available so that you can find their locations.

Is it important that you have 'in your head' a mental map of key places? If so, which places would they be? Why those places? Would they be the same as one of your friends? Compare them to see the similarities and differences. How can you improve your personal mental map of the world?

Key points

This chapter has:

- examined places in terms of their location, their nature, and their meanings and place as intertwined with space;
- noted that places are physical entities, perceived and imagined;
- considered the interrelationship of our experience of places and place as a central idea in geography;
- considered the value for children of developing locational knowledge and mental maps at different scales;
- provided reasons for studying places and outlined a variety of places to include in children's primary geography.

Moving on

Choose a particular place you know. Google its name to find websites associated with it. What information and images are provided about this place? Which aspects of place are covered and which are not? Since it is a place you know, what can you add to the information, particularly about the meanings attached by you and others to this place? How would you help someone unfamiliar with this place see it as you do?

Further reading

The following are informative and accessible introductions to studies of place.

Cresswell, T (2015) *Place: An Introduction.* Chichester: Wiley-Blackwell.

Matthews, J and Herbert, D (2008), *Geography: A Very Short Introduction.* Oxford: Oxford University Press.

The following will help you develop your understanding and appreciation of place studies in primary geography and provide stimulating ideas for teaching younger children about place.

Catling, S (2015) Creative Primary Geography. In Wilson, A (ed.) *Creativity in Primary Education.* London: Sage.

Halocha, J (2012) *The Primary Teacher's Guide to Geography.* Witney: Scholastic/ Book End.

Martin, F (2006) *Teaching Geography in Primary Schools: Learning How to Live in the World.* Cambridge: Chris Kington.

Owens, P (2011) *Little Blue Planet: Investigating Spaceship Earth*. Sheffield: Geographical Association.

Palmer, J and Birch, J (2004) *Geography in the Early Years*. London: RoutledgeFalmer.

Pike, S (2016) *Learning Primary Geography: Ideas and inspirations from classrooms*. Abingdon: Routledge.

Scoffham, S (ed.) (2010) *Primary Geography Handbook*. Sheffield: Geographical Association.

Scoffham, S (ed.) (2017) *Teaching Geography Creatively*. London: Routledge.

Scoffham, S and Owens, P (2017) *Teaching Primary Geography*. London: Bloomsbury.

Read the magazine: *Primary Geographer*

Useful websites

Geographical Association: www.geography.org.uk

Geography for Kids: www.kids.com/geography-for-kids

GeogSpace (AGTA): www.agta.asn.au

National Geographic for Kids: www.natgeokids.com

National Geographic Society: www.nationalgeographic.com

Oxfam Education: www.oxfam.org.uk/education

Spatial Worlds blog site: www.spatialworlds.blogspot.co.uk

CHAPTER 6

UNDERSTANDING THE ENVIRONMENT

Aspects of physical, human and environmental geography

 Chapter objectives

This chapter enables you to:

- identify and understand the different foci of physical geography and human geography;
- appreciate that physical and human geography are inextricably connected and interdependent, being brought together in environmental geography;
- become aware that the geological time in which we live is being termed the Anthropocene, because human activities are influencing major changes in our physical environment;
- recognise various opportunities to teach aspects of physical, human and environmental geography.

Introduction

Geography covers a wide range of matters and topics affecting our places, lives and planet. These are as diverse as the eruption of volcanoes, how rivers affect the landscape, the reasons why countries trade with each other, and people's access to shops and other facilities and services in communities. Studying this wide range of the natural and human environment has necessitated categorisation within geography, resulting in the demarcation of core aspects for investigative, descriptive and explanatory purposes. Three of these core aspects are *physical geography, human geography* and *environmental geography*. These aspects of geography have a long history – for instance, when regional geography was a dominant approach in school geography in the first half of the twentieth century, regions were discussed in terms of their physical geography, including rivers, lakes, plains, mountains, valleys, ecology and geology, and their human geography, such as types of industry, products, trade, settlements, commerce and ways of life. However, they were rarely considered in terms of environmental geography – for instance, how people have changed the landscape over time, human impact on climate, extracting resources, deforestation and pollution. Understanding physical, human and environmental geography is important to understand our planet, our lives and their incontrovertible interrelationships. This is the focus of this chapter, but we begin by noting briefly the geological context in which we live.

Living in a geological epoch

The interrelationship between the physical environment and human activities is argued to have become much greater in recent centuries. It is contended that humans have had such an impact on the natural environment that we should have a new name for the current geological time in which we live and that this name should be the *Anthropocene* (Hamilton *et al.*, 2015; Goudie and Viles, 2016; Bonneuil and Fressoz, 2017). The term 'Anthropocene' is being used to identify a 'new' geological epoch (Schwägerl, 2014; McNeill and Engelke, 2014). Its purpose is to reinforce just how significant humans have become in affecting the physical environment of the Earth. We have done this, it is argued, through our actions, such as deforestation, energy extraction and generation, mobility and travel, urbanisation and industrial practices (Goudie, 2013; Holden, 2012; Whitehead, 2014; Goudie and Viles, 2016; Kress and Stine, 2017). Such developments have led to changes in our vegetation, land cover, oceans, atmosphere and climate, and weather systems and patterns. One impact is described in the term 'climate change' and debated in relation to the warming of the Earth's atmospheric and ocean temperatures

(Maslin, 2014). This is having the effect of heating our planet at a much faster rate than has hitherto happened, hence the use of the phrase 'global warming' (Maslin, 2014). The Earth's climate has constantly changed; the difference today is that it is happening, in geological terms, very quickly, and that it appears already to be affecting our environments and lives very seriously through such events as higher temperatures and increased and heavier rainfall, resulting in such effects as the increased frequency and severity of storms, flooding, drought and wildfires (Core Writing Team *et al.*, 2015).

Geological eras

In its 4.6 or so billion-year existence, the Earth has developed through many geological eras, periods and epochs. Geological *eras* describe the major and very long periods of time in the evolution of the Earth's surface. Geological *periods* are subdivisions of geological eras, and are subdivided into geological *epochs*. The geological chart in Table 6.1 provides a timeline of the geological eras, periods and the epochs since the Pre-Cambrian *eon* some 550 million years ago. Evidence about the evolution of the Earth comes through many sources, including surface geology, rock and ice core samples, and plant and animal fossils (Zalasiewicz, 2016; Thomson, 2005). Until now, we have been described as living in the *Holocene* epoch, which has lasted for the last 11,700 years; it is a subdivision of the Quarternary period in the Cenozoic era and began following the last Ice Age (Woodward, 2014). Across geological time, the processes that have affected the Earth include atmospheric, climatic and weather systems and conditions affecting temperature, humidity and rainfall, activity within and beneath the Earth's crust producing earthquakes, volcanic activity and plate tectonic movements, and the effect of water on land and by seas and oceans leading to erosion and deposition, together with the impact of ice through glaciers and ice sheets, and the effects of cold and warm ocean currents and of wind. In its very nature the Earth is a dynamic planet (Redfern, 2003; Zalasiewicz, 2016).

It is only for the past three million or so years that humans have evolved and spread to inhabit the Earth, which places our appearance about half-way through the Pliocene epoch. If we think of the world's 4.6 billion years of existence as equivalent to just one year, Neanderthals would have appeared on the last day of the year at around 23.00 hours. Civilisation would have appeared at around five to midnight that day, with the beginning of our calendar at year 0 CE (Common Era) at around 23.58 and 43 seconds. Modern humans are recently evolved inhabitants of our planet, and we have already had a major impact on it. How we understand it and the effects we are having are what physical, human and environmental

Eon	Era	Period	Epoch	Estimated years before present
Phanerozoic	Cenozoic	Quarternary	Anthropocene	c. 200 years (?)
			Holocene	11,700
			Pleistocene	1.8 million
		Neogene	Pliocene	5.33 million
			Miocene	23 million
		Paleogene	Oligocene	34 million
			Eocene	56 million
			Paleocene	66 million
	Mesozoic	Cretaceous	Upper	101 million
			Lower	145 million
		Jurassic	Upper	164 million
			Middle	174 million
			Lower	201 million
		Triassic	Upper	237 million
			Middle	247 million
			Lower	252 million
	Paleozoic	Permian	Lopingian	256 million
			Guadalupian	273 million
			Cisuralian	299 million
		Carboniferous	Pennsylvanian	323 million
			Mississippian	259 million
		Devonian	Upper	372 million
			Middle	393 million
			Lower	419 million
		Silurian	Pridoli	423 million
			Ludlow	427 million
			Wenlock	433 million
			Llandovery	444 million
		Ordovician	Upper	458 million
			Middle	470 million
			Lower	485 million
		Cambrian	Furongian	497 million
			Series 3	509 million
			Series 2	521 million
			Terreneuvian	541 million

(Continued)

Table 6.1   (Continued)

Eon	Era	Period	Epoch	Estimated years before present
Precambrian Proterozoic	Neo- proterozoic	Ediacaran		635 million
		Cryogenian		720 million
		Tonian		1 billion
	Meso- proterozoic	Stenian		1.2 billion
		Actasian		1.4 billion
		Calymmian		1.6 billion
	Paleo- proterozoic	Staherian		1.8 billion
		Orosirian		2.1 billion
		Rhyacian		2.3 billion
		Siderian		2.5 billion
Archean	Neo-archean			2.8 billion
	Meso-archean			3.2 billion
	Paleo-archean			3.6 billion
	Eoarchean			4 billion
Hadean				*c.* 4.6 billion

Table 6.1   The geological time scale (ICS, 2016: International Chronostratigraphic Chart)

geography investigate, describe and analyse. They are important to appreciate and understand the sustainability of our planet, our environments and our actions in and on it, as well as how we might mitigate these.

What does it mean?

The Anthropocene

The *Anthropocene* is the name proposed for a new geological period – the one in which we live now (Crutzen and Stoermer, 2000). The name 'Anthropocene' has been proposed to describe the recent period of time in which human activities have had a significant global impact on the Earth's surface, its continents and oceans, as well as on its systems and processes. These are interrelated, and impact in one area affects the others, such as through climate and ocean circulations.

The term 'Anthropocene' has not yet been officially approved, but the recommendation has been made to the International Geological Congress (IGC) to describe the current epoch. The term was used by scientists initially in the 1960s and 1980s informally. It was put forward formally to identify and define the new geological time in which we live in 2000 by Crutzen, who regarded the impact of humankind to be so great as to justify the naming of a new geological epoch (Crutzen and Stoermer, 2000). This epoch is argued to have become strongly evident since the mid twentieth century, although its origins may go back to the start of the nineteenth or the mid-eighteenth centuries' industrial developments or further back to the development of agriculture (Lenton, 2016).

The impact of human activities in altering the Earth's atmosphere and surface cover are said to have created a new geological epoch which is distinct from the Holocene epoch. However, there is not universal agreement that the planet has moved into this new epoch; it is a contested and controversial idea (Schwägerl, 2014; Whitehead, 2014; Hamilton et al., 2015; Goudie and Viles, 2016; Ellis, 2018). Nonetheless, it is an important and interesting idea which, if agreed by the IGC, places the lives of today's children in a new geological epoch, of which at least they should begin to become aware.

Geologically, the Earth builds up rock strata that inform us about earlier eras, periods and epochs. What might inform geologists, in millions of years' time, about the Anthropocene? Perhaps there will be indications of deforestation and of agriculture, urbanism, industrial activities and waste disposal? Could there even be intermittent evidence of the existence of plastic in the ancient ocean, sea and riverbeds, and on earlier landforms? What might geologists conclude about an epoch named 'the Anthropocene'?

The box above provides a brief outline of the Anthropocene. The idea of a new geological epoch demonstrates the dynamic nature of our world in terms of its physical, human and environmental geography. We live on a constantly changing planet at local and global scales. It is important that we appreciate that our world is in a continuous state of flux in order to fully understand it. Realising this helps us to resist the temptation to perceive our living 'snapshot' of the Earth as it is now as if this is how it has always been. What we see and experience today is, simply, how the dynamic Earth is at this specific time. Change continues to occur, albeit slowly, during our lives, but nonetheless it is happening. Our role is to help primary age children to begin to become aware of and start to understand that the world today is the result of continual change through the Earth's processes in the past, across many millions of years. This will initiate children's understanding of how these processes have shaped the Earth, and how our activities in the past 200 years or so have influenced the Earth and, crucially, how they will continue to affect our world. Inevitably, this raises questions about how we ought and need to live in order to take account of and even mitigate our impacts. Helping children to understand the timescale involved introduces the idea of 'deep time' – that is, time across geological periods and the Earth's existence (Lenton, 2016). This is a very challenging idea which primary children find hard to grasp, although it is rarely taught in primary schools, with limited awareness developed informally out of school. Nonetheless, it can be initiated by drawing children in through their fascination with dinosaurs.

    Research summary

Geological time: deep time

The term 'deep time' refers to the Earth's several billion-year timeline of existence (Wormald, 2017). It is the pivotal concept of geological time, covering Earth's past since its inception (Trend, 2009). This sense of time is a challenge to understand.

Trend (1998) investigated 177 10–11-year-olds' understanding of geological or 'deep' time. Using a variety of tasks – including card sorts, sequencing, writing questions about geological specimens and a picture, and undertaking a quiz – he found that these children:

- categorised events in geological time as either 'less ancient' or 'extremely ancient';
- did not associate, in terms of time, the first volcanoes and rocks with the formation of the Earth and sun;
- are confused about and disagree over the relative timing of the Ice Age.

Nam *et al.* (2016) found that 9–12-year-olds identified three 'time zones' for geological events: close to the formation of Earth (the moon's and Earth's atmosphere formation), an intermediate period (when plants and creatures evolved), and near the present (encompassing human history). Cultural influences would seem to be important – for example, in traditionally oral societies, this sequence reflects long-standing creation chronologies. Most children noted that dinosaurs appeared before mammals, which appeared before humans, but they also held alternative conceptions about how the atmosphere and continents developed.

Trend (2001) found in another study that primary school teachers conceived geological time in terms of 'less ancient', 'moderately ancient' and 'extremely ancient'. They seem not to consider that deep time and geological periods were of much help in interpreting geological specimens. He noted that a lack of understanding about geological time could be an issue for teaching about geological time and suggested that to help primary children understand deep time they needed to learn about past Earth events and the geological time framework together. Children need to order geological events and periods, their learning scaffolded by their teachers who engage them in scientific reasoning (Nam *et al.*, 2016).

In the classroom

Exploring dinosaurs and geological time

Primary age children are fascinated by dinosaurs (Norman, 2017). There are many resources provided for them to learn about and investigate the geological periods in which dinosaurs lived.

A teacher used this interest with her class of 7–8-year-olds to help the children become aware of geological time. She initiated their study by working from children's stories that use 'dinosaurs' anthropomorphically to find out about the variety of dinosaurs and about the environments in which they lived. She provided a range of books and video material about dinosaurs for the children to refer to. This led to examining how we know about dinosaurs and to investigating the role that fossils play in helping us learn about the geological past.

To help the children become aware of the geological timescale, she placed around the classroom walls a geological 'time chart' to show something of what we know about the age of the Earth. She introduced this timeline by asking the children to imagine the Earth as the age of a 46-year-old person – equivalent to the Earth's age of 4.6 billion years – in which each Earth year represents 100 million years, although she was unsure how meaningful this was to the children at that stage of their topic (British Geological Survey, www.bgs.ac.uk/discoveringGeology/time/timeline/teachers_notes.html). The children used various

(Continued)

(Continued)

sources to populate their geological timeline, identifying how long ago it was that dinosaurs existed, for how long they 'ruled the Earth' and when they died out. They added other fossil pictures and names for older and more recent geological times. They began to get their tongues around the names of periods, eras and epochs, as well as of different dinosaurs, and began to talk about how old the Earth is, which this timeline approach helped the children begin to realise. The idea of 'a very long time ago' had a 'wow' impact.

The purpose of this topic was to begin to help the children realise that dinosaurs had existed (were not story characters or fantastical), understand more about them and understand that they were not contemporary with humans. It gave the children an introduction to the idea of 'deep time' – that is, the geological time scale. It helped them to appreciate the reality of dinosaurs and to have some idea that the Earth is very, very old and that we humans are very recent inhabitants of our planet.

Thematic geography

Physical and human geography, and more recently environmental geography, have been referred to as the thematic approach to geography. The idea has been that they take what we might call a cross-section approach to studying the environment, in balance with studies of what places are like whether at a local, regional, national or continental scale. A focus on weather or commerce around the world, rather than weather or commerce in just one particular place, would be to take a thematic approach in geography.

Physical and human geography

Physical geography includes the Earth's natural features and processes, such as weathering, glacial and coastal systems. *Human geography* helps us understand the processes and outcomes of human activities across the world, such as building settlements and undertaking agriculture. We can differentiate further within these two aspects of geography. Physical geography is usually thought of as the *hard science* side of the subject, and includes areas of study such as geomorphology, oceanography and climatology; these are often called 'earth sciences' (Holden, 2011, 2012; Lenton, 2016).

Human geography, which tends to be classified as a *social science*, examines areas covering, for instance, cultural, political, economic and population geography (Jones, 2017; Cloke *et al.*, 2014). Topics with physical and human geography are noted in Figure 6.1.

Physical and human geography appear all around us and are important in our daily lives. The natural world provides us with a wide range of resources that provide the raw materials for bricks, stone, concrete, tiles, wood and glass for buildings, as well as the sources of the metals, plastics and energy from which we manufacture materials and generate electricity. Our mobile phones depend for their materials on the natural environment, but they are also the result of human ingenuity, from design to component manufacture and to sales, supported by the sites of aerials to enable us to keep in touch with each other and with the variety of websites we access. Understanding how our food is grown, the nature and quality of the soil, what optimal agricultural conditions are for different crops and animal husbandry, how food is processed before it reaches us and then the energy we use for cooking, require and integrate many aspects of physical and human geography in describing and explaining what happens, why and with what effect for ourselves and others. Physical and human geographies are key to understanding our everyday lives, just as much as in helping us know about and appreciating the nature, events and activities of the wider world. These two interrelated aspects of geography matter a great deal to us all.

Environmental geography

Geographers have always recognised that physical and human geography are inextricably linked and highly dependent upon one another in a dynamic and constantly evolving way. They effect, change and impact on each other continuously and so, within geography, cannot realistically be seen separately, although research on particular topics may give this impression. This interface has been termed *environmental geography* (Castree *et al.*, 2009), and at times an holistic or unified approach in geography, to describe both the processes and the impact of each aspect on the other (Matthews and Herbert, 2004, 2008). This is indicated in Figure 6.1. Topics that might be included in environmental geography include climate change and deforestation as well as land reclamation and conservation.

An understanding of environmental geography is crucial if we are to appreciate the complexity of the interrelationship of human geography and physical geography and how we can live in a sustainable way on the Earth. While it is important to understand the specific processes in physical and human geography, we also need to help children appreciate the interplay between them, and how that impacts on people's lives and the physical environment in which we live. This can be exemplified through two examples.

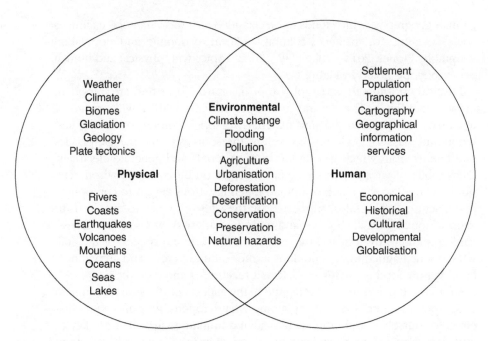

Figure 6.1   Aspects of physical and human geography and their interface with environmental geography

When building a dam to create a reservoir to provide water for settlements, it is crucial to understand the local geology and geomorphology in order to select the best valley site. In the case of a dam built in Andalucía in Spain, the engineers did not appreciate that they were building a dam in a limestone environment and could not understand why it never filled up. The water appeared as a waterfall where the rock type changed over 10km away and the dam became a white elephant and could never be used – it remains there today. Understanding the local geology is fundamental, just as it is essential to know that building a dam directly affects those who live and use the land in the chosen valley site, who will need to be moved out, as well as those who live downstream from the reservoir. It will be essential to do everything to mitigate negative impacts.

The increasing demand for food across the world creates the need to deforest land – for instance, in the Amazon basin in Brazil, to create land for grazing or arable crops. However, in areas of thin or 'weak' soil this can easily lead to rapid environmental degradation, which makes the land uneconomic within a few years. This results in more virgin forest being cleared and the process continues, destroying large swathes of previously lush, naturally appropriate vegetation. The 'Dust Bowl' in the USA is a prime example of inappropriate farming methods aligned with low rainfall, creating loose and easily wind-blown soil, leading to an infertile and damaged landscape and the loss of livelihoods.

These two examples illustrate the importance of appreciating environmental geography. Without that understanding, alongside the knowledge to make sound decisions or to develop potential solutions to avoid such eventualities, we will continue to make environmental mistakes and not take the best actions when making use of the natural world or the environments we have already modified.

In the classroom

Drowning the valley

A class of 9–10-year-olds had spent several lessons developing their understanding of life in an agricultural community in an upland steep-sided valley. They had found out about the lives of the local farmers and the village community, what work was done on the farms, the village shop and post office, and other services available. They had used local maps and photographs and had got 'to know' the area, which was far from their urban primary school. Just over half-way through the term's study, their teacher invited the children to take on the role of someone who lived in the community and to decide where they lived and what they did. The children responded enthusiastically and developed their understanding of their characters, including using role play. They remained aware that this was a role-play scenario and that they were taking on 'imagined' roles in the community.

In the context of this role play, a letter was delivered to the classroom by their headteacher. It was written to the village council to inform them that their valley had been proposed as the site of a new dam to provide electric power and water recreation for the region. When the letter was read out there was pandemonium, the children protesting in role that this was grossly unfair and could not be allowed to happen. Taking up their roles, most of the children researched what building a dam would involve and investigated the landscape and geology of the area. They developed arguments for and against this proposal, as might be found in any community. At the same time, one group of children was taken out of their community roles to role play the local officials and the electricity board planners; they had to develop the case for constructing the dam.

There was a time-frame for the different 'sides' to create their arguments, which included use of geography and literacy lessons, and had links with citizenship and social and moral education. Three weeks later,

(Continued)

(Continued)

a 'mock' public enquiry was held, chaired by the school's chair of governors with the headteacher and one other governor as the panel members who would make the decision. In their roles, the children gave their evidence and made their cases in favour of and against the construction of the dam and of the reservoir. Over lunchtime, the planning enquiry panel deliberated and then reported their decision. They concluded that the local community had made an effective case and dismissed the plan for the dam and reservoir. There was much excitement and disappointment, since all the children had entered into their roles with full commitment, although they knew that it was not a real situation. Even so, they had each to be helped to come out of role. During the afternoon and the following morning, time was spent by the teacher and children discussing what it had been like to play their roles and to make their arguments, as well as how they felt about the outcome. This helped the children to begin to understand aspects of the environmental geography, how a public enquiry meeting might work, the role of people's feelings alongside their knowledge and viewpoints, and that the outcome brought satisfaction and disappointment to different people involved. It proved to be an insightful and informative approach to a controversial (if contrived but realistic) issue. It was a valued and memorable approach to teaching and learning geography.

Sequencing learning in physical, human and environmental geography

It is important to introduce primary children to physical, human and environmental geography, but it can only be achieved by including aspects of the three themes in their geographical studies. This will enable children over time to begin to recognise the focus in geography of each theme. It can done by focusing on different topics in each theme from the early years – for instance, children can be introduced through play-based activities in their pre-school setting with the sand tray, growing plants and 'buying' items in the setting or class shop. Through their primary years children should experience a range of aspects of physical, human and environmental geography.

Table 6.2 outlines a sequence of selected aspects of physical, human and environmental geography that children might study, identifying an age-phase during which these might be the focus of studies. Inevitably, it must be a matter for each teacher and school to judge when in the curriculum what is suggested might be most suitable. What Table 6.2 identifies is the need to develop children's experience and understanding progressively.

Children pre-5 years old
Pre-school children would not differentiate between physical and human geography and should be encouraged to explore an holistic view of the world around them, observing and describing features in their local environment, exploring things outside such as puddles, different surfaces, trees and pebbles, and investigating changes in the shape of the environment such as slopes. They should observe and feel built features such as walls and windows, notice types of shops and play areas, and explore some of the things that people do for work and leisure.

Children will enjoy the opportunities to explore phenomena such as the effect of wind on bubbles and streamers. They will develop their vocabulary by using terms such as shop, apartment, home, town, village, road, and so on. They can discuss weather, means of transport and their food likes and dislikes. |

Children aged 5/6–7/8 years old		
Physical geography	**Environmental geography**	**Human geography**
Develop children's awareness of a variety of physical features in the environment locally and through photographs, stories and vocabulary, such as stream, river, beach, cliff, coast, wood and forest, hill, mountain, sea, ocean, soil, slope, valley, plants, animals, rain, sun, cloud, wind.

Study of weather and seasons, with simple weather records.

Become aware of hot and cold places on Earth. | Introduce children to connections between physical and human geography and how one can affect the other. Examples include how flooding might affect homes close to a river or how cutting down trees destroys the habitat of plants, animals and insects.

Consider how environments change and can be cared for. | Enable children to develop their vocabulary and initial knowledge of the built environment and human activities. Encourage vocabulary development, such as street, city, town, village, factory, farm, house, apartment block, office, port, harbour, store, park.

Investigate a range of these in the local environment and come across others through picture stories, information books and web sources. |

Children aged 6/7–8/9 years old		
Physical geography	**Environmental geography**	**Human geography**
Develop children's knowledge and understanding of the natural environment.

Examine landscape features such as slopes and extend awareness of particular natural features such as rivers, mountains and lakes.

Study volcanoes and earthquakes and look at patterns over the Earth.

Introduce natural processes such as the water cycle.

Develop awareness of different climates and seasons.

Develop knowledge of some key physical features nationally. | Continue to develop children's awareness and understanding of the interrelationships and interactions between the natural environment and human activities, how processes and events in each affect both.

Explore examples of how people have changed environments, such as cutting forests down to create farmland, and consider beneficial and damaging effects.

Examine examples of ways to look after and sustain environments. | Build on children's knowledge and understanding of features created by human activity.

Introduce different types of settlements, look at patterns of shops and transport and idea of land use.

Consider where goods are bought and come from to introduce ideas about trade.

Investigate a natural resource, such as water or food, and consider where it is found or grown, why it is important for us, how it is provided for people and how people use it. |

(Continued)

Table 6.2   (Continued)

Children aged 8/9–11/12 years old		
Physical geography	**Environmental geography**	**Human geography**
Continue to extend and deepen children's knowledge and understanding of natural features and environments. Develop the idea of climate zones, biomes and vegetation belts, looking at their patterns across the world and the processes creating them. Study ways in which a climate may affect the weather in particular places. Develop knowledge of a selection of physical features in your country and around the world.	Deepen children's understanding of the interrelationships between physical and human geography through enquiries into matters such as the 'lifestyle' dilemma of buying out-of-season fresh fruit and flowers in our superstores daily, the cost in 'food' miles in rapid and timely transportation, and the effect on the livelihood of those working to supply these cash crops. Investigate why people choose to live close to an active volcano despite the threat that it will erupt, and people's attitudes to wind farm energy provision and development. Consider how natural, rural and urban environments can be managed and improved sustainably.	Continue to deepen and extend children's knowledge and understanding of human-created features and activities, including a range of types of settlement and land use, and the reasons for them being located where they are. Examine a specific focus on selected economic activities such as local trading patterns. Find out about one or more natural resources that we use, such as minerals, water and wind: why they are important for us, where they are distributed, how we obtain them and the processes involved, what they are used to produce, how we access and use them. Examples can be electrical energy, computers or toys.

Table 6.2   A suggested sequence of selected aspects of physical, human and environmental geography to include in primary geography

Topics in physical, human and environmental geography

Teaching children about these three geographical themes is fundamental for geographical learning. Children need to develop their understanding of this geographical bedrock as a key dimension enabling them to grasp the subject's core complex concepts and the issues it investigates. As has been argued in Chapter 4, this is most effectively done through an enquiry approach and by always encouraging primary children to be curious and exploratory about their own local area and immediate environment, as well as the wider world beyond their experience. Through investigating their local physical, human and environmental geography, children begin to appreciate concepts to apply in other contexts and at other scales. This helps them to develop their understanding of the variety and complexity of the world in which they live.

In their studies in physical, human and environmental geography, children should be encouraged to formulate enquiry questions to investigate. For example, in looking at topics on earthquakes and volcanoes, rivers, where a commodity like chocolate is produced, fair trade or water, the sorts of geographical questions (in children's own language) that might emerge include the following.

- Where do these features, goods, activities or events occur?
- Are there aspects in common about these features, goods, activities or events?
- Can patterns be discerned, and, if so, what are they?
- How can such patterns be explained?
- What processes are at work to cause and create the features, goods, activities or events?
- What are the reasons for and the consequences of these processes, beneficial or otherwise?
- What should be looked for to see whether particular patterns are repeated?
- Can the events in the processes be predicted and/or replicated or prevented?
- How can we adapt or use such processes for the benefit of people, and how might we respond if they are potentially damaging?

By taking this approach, we can begin to build children's understanding of the processes that create, for instance, the spatial locations, distributions, patterns and relationships in the world around us. We can introduce them to the systems that are at work in the physical and human environment, and the interactions between them, to enable them to begin to appreciate the role and usefulness of making predictions about natural events, and of considering the impacts of people's proposals, priorities and decisions as they affect the natural and human worlds locally and more widely.

Topics in physical geography

The natural, physical environment, like all aspects of the Earth, is dynamic and subject to constant and at times unpredictable change. Physical geography is the study of the features of the natural environment and of the processes that create, shape and sustain or change and even destroy those features, whether speedily or slowly and incrementally. It is, therefore, for example not just about 'rivers' but about the processes that form the unique characteristics of any river such as its terrain and features, and the processes of erosion, transportation and deposition – and human interference – that shape it (Middleton, 2012). Similarly, we study the weather and the processes that create the patterns that we witness day to day, and their causes such as changes in air pressure, evaporation, condensation, and so forth (Dunlop, 2017).

There are many aspects of physical geography that we can study. Several are outlined here which seem particularly pertinent to introduce to primary children for investigation.

Weather

Weather studies concern what weather is, the myriad forms that it can take, its causes and effects (Dunlop, 2017). This is most effectively covered by local area investigations where children can take part in observing and monitoring their local weather. They can take daily temperature and rainfall readings using simple weather-monitoring equipment and can see how the weather changes over a week, month, a term or the year. They can monitor different areas in the playground and begin to consider the reasons for the variations in their findings. They can be encouraged to do this at home as well to see if there are any differences between home and school, and they can consider why there might be, so considering the impact of microclimates and variations even over small distances. National and international weather reports can be monitored to see how the weather differs from place to place, and why that might be dependent on whether sites are on the coast or inland, at low level or in hilly or mountainous areas, affected by prevailing winds, and so forth, perhaps introducing older primary children to ideas about the effect of latitude, altitude, and national and continental location (Dolan, 2019).

Seasons

Studying seasons might be a topic which comes and goes across the year, so that different seasons are investigated. This might be a focus for a week during different seasons with the youngest children. With older primary children, the focus might be to consider the types, sequence and extent of seasons, and how these relate to the movement of the Earth in our solar system. The variations in temperature, rainfall, wind direction and length of daylight that seasons bring across the year can be examined, and how these relate to different types of weather. Using secondary sources, investigations can be made of different types and lengths of seasons in different parts of the world, from tropical through temperate to polar regions.

Rivers and coasts

River and coast studies examine what they are and the differences between them, the processes that form them, the features and vocabulary associated with them, and erosion and deposition along rivers and coasts. Your class might visit and investigate a local stream, river or coastal site. Encourage children to find out about a stream or river's shape, its width and depth, how fast it flows, what the water quality is

Image 6.1 Children modelling river erosion

and how it looks, whether it is clean or polluted, where its source and mouth are, and whether it has tributaries and what these are. You might use a sand tray to make a model of part of the course of a river through a landscape to follow this up or, if you cannot undertake fieldwork at a stream or river, to introduce children to aspects of rivers (Image 6.1). You can help older primary children examine and discuss the features of a river basin using a diagram such as that in Image 6.2, supplemented by photographs and information texts. On a visit to the coast – or using photographs, video material and information texts – examine what the shoreline is like, the effect of the sea on the shore, the idea of tides and their causes, the sand or soil and rocks or pebbles along the shore, and how the sea affects them. Similar investigations can be made along lake shores.

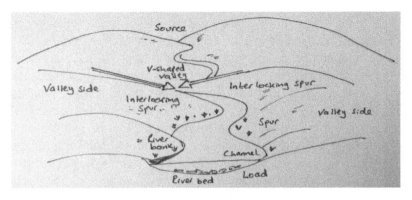

Image 6.2 The features of a river basin

Research summary

Children's understanding of rivers

Galani and Rokka (2014) investigated two groups of 10–11-year-old urban Greek children's representations of rivers, following a teaching unit. A 'control group' used the age-specific geography textbook material naming the parts of a river alongside an unrelated river image, while an 'experimental group' used a river sketch showing natural features and containing age-related vocabulary. Before and after teaching, the children were asked to draw a river and to locate photographs of river features at characteristic sites. These features were a delta, meander, canyon, waterfall, lake, stream, spring and mountain.

It was found that most children understood the model of a river from source to mouth, although most of those in the control group drew the river as a straight line, while most in the experimental group appreciated that it has a 'curvy' course and tributaries. Well over three-quarters of children recognised that rivers started in mountains, although some mentioned features like lakes and discharge into the sea. Nine-tenths of the experimental group referred to a river's mouth, although less than 50 per cent of the control group did. There was a greater use of geographical vocabulary by the former group. Well over three-quarters of the experimental group located key river features at appropriate sites, while only between half and three-quarters of the control group did.

The study broadly confirmed previous research – namely, that older primary children have a sound spatial sense of a river's course, but that this can be inhibited by a lack of experience of rivers, since children try to relate their classroom learning to what they already know. This reinforces Tapsell *et al.*'s (2001) findings that 9–11-year-old urban children have only marginal experiences of rivers. Through providing the children with experiences alongside a river, their research identified how children perceived the states and affordances of rivers, which included that they may be polluted and dangerous places, while also being natural places that offer relaxation and escape as well as being places to play and socialise. Rivers can be challenging, risky environments that children respond to positively, seeing them also as liminal (or in-between) zones, as marginal sites, their banks being 'edge' spaces between the water and the land. They noted that the attitudes of the majority of the children became more positive about rivers and that the visits raised their interest level in rivers. Many children wanted to spend time at accessible river sites. There was less impact on the small minority of children familiar with river sites.

Mackintosh (2005) has noted that a small minority of older primary children do not recognise that a river flows downhill, which teaching and site visits can help to tackle. Dove *et al.* (2000) identified that urban children tend to prefer images of rural rivers, since these seem to fit their stereotypical sense of a river. She noted (Dove, 1999) that children perceive the speed of flow of upland streams as being faster than in lowland rivers, perhaps because of their 'frothy' appearance in photographs. Children bring varying levels of knowledge and understanding of streams and rivers into school, including alternative conceptions derived from stories and seeing only a short length of a river or stream.

The water cycle

Investigating the water cycle involves helping children begin to understand the relationship between clouds, rain, water on the ground and its evaporation (Bowden and Copeland, 2017). Children can become familiar with the water cycle on a very local scale to start with by considering what happens to rain water when it falls on the surface of the playground, grass, or tree leaves and by observing what happens as it dries and by considering where the water goes. This introduces children to the scientific concepts of precipitation, evaporation, percolation, and condensation and their interrelationships. They might follow the 'journey of a water molecule' (or of a raindrop). They can experiment by pouring water on to different surfaces and by observing the after-effects of rainfall as the weather changes to see what occurs and to try to explain this. They can take photographs, make notes and look at the sequence they see. Diagrams can be used to help develop their understanding of the water cycle (Image 6.3). Children can begin to realise that it is a closed system with water neither lost nor gained; it is self-sustaining. They might consider also how water in the air creates humidity. It is important to link the water cycle with studies of weather and rivers.

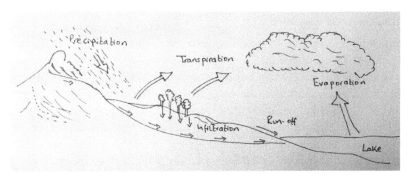

Image 6.3   The water cycle

Rocks and soils

Rocks and soils are the basis of land (Zalasiewicz, 2016) and fundamentally are of three types. Children can look in the school grounds and locally at the soils, stones and pebbles that make up their neighbourhood. In rural areas this can be straightforward to investigate, but it may be trickier in heavily built-up and concreted urban environments, but parks and gardens can be good sites to explore. A fieldwork visit to a quarry can be an insightful way to help children realise that rock forms the ground beneath our feet. They can find out about different types of soils and rocks, and about how they have been formed and why they appear where they do.

What does it mean?

Three types of rocks

Igneous rock: Rock formed from magma, molten material from within the Earth which reaches close to or appears at the Earth's surface. Granite is an igneous rock formed underground, while lava and ash deposits form surface rocks following a volcanic eruption.

Sedimentary rock: Rock formed when eroded materials like sand and decomposing materials such as sea creatures or plants are compressed over many thousands and millions of years. They can be formed in river-beds, lakes, seas and oceans. Sandstone and chalk are sedimentary rocks.

Metamorphic rock: Rock formed as a result of very high pressure and/or heating usually, but not always, on sedimentary rocks. Marble is metamorphosed limestone; slate is metamorphosed mudstone; and gneiss is metamorphosed granite.

Earthquakes and volcanoes

Plate tectonics is the study of the movement of the continental plates across the surface of the Earth (Molner, 2015). Where the continental plates overlap, through the process of subduction when one plate 'slides' below the other or at times alongside the other, they cause earthquakes and volcanic eruptions. This topic fascinates primary age children, particularly examining the processes that cause them, watching video clips of volcanic eruptions and the effects of earthquakes, finding out about how they have affected people's lives. This is an excellent topic through which to examine the idea of natural hazards (see Topics in environmental geography below).

Vegetation belts and biomes

The Earth's land surface is covered in many different types of vegetation (flora) and contains many different types of creatures (fauna). They create vegetation belts and ecosystems. One way to classify and group these is as biomes, of which there are many across the world. The box below provides a brief summary of information about biomes, vegetation belts, natural regions and ecosystems. While primary age children can investigate and begin to understand the idea of an ecosystem at a very immediate and local level, grasping the idea of a natural region, vegetation belt and biome is challenging. Older primary children can be introduced to these concepts through photographs of indicative plants and creatures and world maps of their locations (Image 6.4). One value in undertaking such studies is that children encounter the idea of a region as a large area of the Earth's land surface which has shared or common characteristics, but this is a complex idea that will only make greater sense with time and further study in secondary education (see Chapter 13). It should not be forgotten that the oceans cover 71 per cent of the Earth's surface and that they hold a myriad of plant and creature life, of which we know something but about which we continue to learn more as we explore the oceans (Stow, 2017). We still have much to learn about their biomes and ecosystems. Primary age children should be helped to recognise this.

It is useful to link investigations of vegetation belts and biomes with the world's climate zones, providing opportunities to develop and extend children's global mental maps and knowledge. Older primary children can be introduced to the different climate zones (see box below) and connections with biomes and vegetation belts can be explored (Collis, 2017).

What does it mean?

Biomes, vegetation belts, climate zones, natural regions and ecosystems

Biomes

A biome is a very large area of continental land in which the flora (plants) and fauna (animals, insects, etc.) have adapted to the particular environment influenced by the climate, soil type and relief or height of the land above sea level. A key facet of a biome is its flora or vegetation. It is larger than an ecosystem and may contain different ecosystems within it.

(Continued)

(Continued)

The five main types of biome are as follows.

Desert An environment that has extreme water shortage, with an arid climate. There are subtropical, temperate and cold deserts. Deserts may be rocky or sandy.

Grassland An environment dominated by grassland that includes tropical or savannah grassland and temperate grassland.

Forest An environment dominated by trees and woody plants. It includes tropical rain forests and temperate forests.

Tundra A treeless environment in arctic and sub-arctic regions with long freezing winters and brief summers.

Aquatic Environments where plants and creatures live and grow in or on water, such as along the shores of oceans, seas, major lakes and major rivers, and may include swamp lands.

Vegetation belts

Vegetation belts are also called vegetation regions and they have very distinctive types of plants, soil and weather patterns. There are five major types of vegetation belts. Their climate, soil type, water availability, and the height and slope of the land determine what types of plant grow on them.

Desert These are areas that have very little precipitation – less than 25cm rainfall a year – with the result that very little can grow. The temperatures are very high during the day and can be freezing at night. There is very little humidity due to the low precipitation rates. There are a surprising number of species that have adapted well to the conditions such as the cactus, which can take advantage of any moisture around. Deserts do not have to be hot and the Antarctic is itself a desert because it receives less than 25cm of precipitation a year. Deserts can also be rocky; they are not necessarily sandy and may not have dunes.

Grassland These areas are flat and covered in a wide variety of different types of grasses – they can be found on every continent, except Antarctica. Different grasslands can be found in different latitudes being dependent on the climate. There are two main types: tropical, also known as savannah, for example the Serengeti in Tanzania, Africa;

and temperate grasslands which have seasonal variety in the climate and are recognisable in the prairies of North America. Grasslands are where dairy cattle thrive and so are very important for humans as well.

Forest These grow in a variety of different places and can be of many different kinds, growing on flat land or steep slopes. They can be *deciduous*, in which case they lose their leaves each year like a maple tree, or are *evergreen* and the leaves stay green throughout the year – for example, the fir tree. Tropical forests, as their name suggests, are found around the tropics and contain up to half of all the world's plants and animal species. *Conifers* do not have leaves but they do have needles and cones, and boast the oldest, biggest and tallest trees in the world. Other forests are a mixture of different types of trees such as the eucalyptus forests of Australia.

Tundra This is sparse vegetation due to the cold temperatures and species find it hard to survive. There are two types – *arctic* and *alpine* tundra – arctic being in the northern hemisphere around the Arctic circle and where the surface land may be permanently frozen such as in the Russian steppes. Alpine tundra occurs on high mountains where it is cold as well as windy, making the environment very inhospitable.

Ice-sheet This is an unusual vegetation belt as there is almost no vegetation there at all. Ice-sheets are not the same as ice-shelves or glaciers, as they are much bigger and cover vast areas in Greenland and the Antarctic.

Climate zones

There are five main climate zones. They are indicated by the interrelationship between temperature and precipitation (the humidity, or water vapour, in the air, rainfall, and so forth). There are evident links between climate zones and vegetation belts, biomes, natural regions and ecosystems.

Equatorial climate This is found in the area on either side of the Equator and has a consistent climate characterised by high temperatures, high humidity and high rainfall. Tropical rainforests are found in areas of equatorial climate.

(Continued)

(Continued)

Tropical climate This lies between the Tropics of Cancer and Capricorn and is characterised by hot, very wet summers and very hot but dry winters. Savannah grasslands with sparse shrubs and trees are found in areas of tropical climate.

Hot desert climate This is found in the areas of the Tropics of Cancer (Northern Hemisphere) and Capricorn (Southern Hemisphere). They are areas of very little rain with daily temperatures that vary between very hot during sunlight and cold, even freezing, at night. It can be sandy or rocky. The Sahara Desert and the deserts of Australia are in the hot desert climate zones. Plants are rare but can thrive for a short period following a rainfall.

Temperate climate This is found to the north of the Tropic of Cancer and south of the Tropic of Capricorn. The climate has four seasons: spring, summer, autumn and winter. Humidity and rain are moderate and temperatures vary between hot in summer and cool to cold to freezing during winter. Towards the tropics it tends to be hotter and towards the polar circles it tends to be cooler, and there is likely to be snow, which can occur also on higher ground. Grassland and forest vegetation are abundant in this climate, but there are areas that receive very limited rain and form temperate deserts.

Polar climate This is concentrated around the poles, inside the Arctic Circle and the Antarctic Circle. While the ground may be frozen and covered in ice for much of the year, it is a comparatively dry area, with short, wet, cool summers and long periods of deep frost during autumn, winter and spring. Vegetation survives but has a short growing period. At the North and South Poles temperatures can be extremely cold.

Natural regions

These are geographic units based on their geography, geology and climate. They are often quite distinctive areas and are shaped by their physical geography. An example is the Burren in Ireland which is unique and known for its massive pavements of limestone rock criss-crossed with the distinctive features of limestone 'clints' and 'grikes'. This means that the land is very well drained and there is little evidence of any surface water as it sinks through the vertical fissures – the grikes – and travels underground through caves and subterranean channels. Although it sounds like a bleak environment, it has a wide variety of plant life, such as foxgloves and rock roses, and even has its very own species of butterfly unique to the area, the Burren Green. It has been inhabited since the Stone Age and there is much evidence of ancient human settlement in the form of stone forts and tombs, as well as churches and castles from later periods. It is the rock type forming the landscape that has created this unique environment and everything else is dependent on that – the geology, fauna and flora, and human activities creating the landshape and landscape (Dolan, 2019).

Ecosystem

An ecosystem (or ecological system) is a community of plants and creatures in a particular physical environment. An ecosystem can be very small, such as the flora and fauna community in a small pond, or cover a sizeable area. We sometimes use the word to describe the whole of life on planet Earth. Plants, animals, fungi and micro-organisms are linked together through the interactions of their living and non-living components. Examples of ecosystems include a lake, a forest, a river's drainage basin and a moorland.

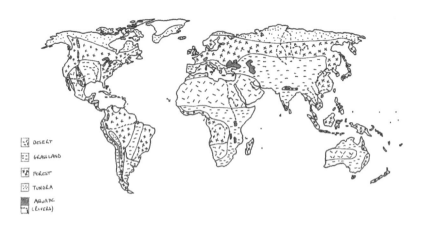

Image 6.4   The world's biomes

In the classroom

Investigating rocks and soils

Their teacher brought into class a collection of pebbles of different shapes and sizes that he had collected since his childhood because he was fascinated by their texture, colour, weight, shape, composition and look. Providing appropriate resources, he set the class of 9–10-year-olds the task of finding out what 'rock' each of the pebbles was composed of and how they might have come to look at they did. Some were smooth while others were jagged. The children considered how rough stones might become smooth. Their teacher brought in a stone tumbler to show them what happened when rough pebbles were knocked against each other to illustrate what would happen over a very long time to stones in flowing river water or the sea. The children examined the school's buildings to investigate weathering of materials, and to look at other ways in which stones, bricks, concrete and other materials could be eroded. Because they knew when the school was built, they could identify how long it had taken for the building materials to become weathered. They considered what the causes for such erosion were and looked around the school site to find places where there was more and less weathering.

During the project, the children explored the school grounds to find a variety of different stones and to investigate what types of rock they were. Some they found were natural rocks and others artificial, including pieces of concrete and brick. They recorded where they found them, whether in play area surface materials or in flowerbed soil or on the grassy field. This led to several children examining soils and undertaking some basic tests to find out more about them. They also experimented by growing cress seeds to see which were more helpful, and they related this to different soils for agriculture.

Practical task

Developing your subject knowledge

Physical geography is an area of the subject that many primary teachers feel less confident about teaching. This might be because it has received less coverage and focus in schools over the past decades when human or social elements of the subject were prioritised, especially topics such as distant place study and environmental issues (Ofsted, 2008a, 2011). Sources of effective subject knowledge development can be found at subject associations, such as the Geography Association (GA) and the RGS-IBG in the UK, the National Geographic Society and the National Council for Geographic Education (NCGE) in the USA and the Australian Geography Teachers' Association (AGTA). These organisations provide guidance, resources and development opportunities for teachers, and primary and elementary schools.

Subject-specific publications and journals can also help to develop subject knowledge such as the *Primary Geography* journal (Geographical Association) and *The Geography Teacher* journal (NCGE). Good information about physical geography topics and approaches to teaching can be found by using search terms on the Internet. For examples of sites see the end of this chapter.

Topics in human geography

Human geography is about people and how we construct the spaces around us and adapt the environment in which we live to support us in our everyday lives. It concerns what, how and why human activities and their outcomes are located and distributed across the surface of the Earth, and focuses on how we understand our uses of place and space. Like physical geography, it is not just the tangible outcomes that are investigated, but it is also the processes behind the physical manifestations of what we do, use and create in places to live as effectively as we can. It is, for example, not just about settlements or the layout of buildings and streets in a city but also about the town planning decisions (or the lack of them) that have led to where it is best to locate developments and the transport infrastructure that is provided to move goods and services from one place to another. Human geography allows us to recognise patterns, networks and processes created in the landscape by the actions of people in relation to each other. It helps us to understand their spatial patterns and what we can do, with understanding, to improve, hopefully sustainably, what we have now and want for the future.

Human geography covers very many aspects of global life. The topics outlined below are those that appropriately offer primary age children insight into various aspects of human geography.

Settlements

Studies of settlements examine what they are, their range of features, services and facilities, their physical setting, the reasons and decisions affecting the location of different places, how people make use of them, and the look of villages, towns and cities. Children can be explorers as settlers of their local area. For instance, they might consider where they live in the local neighbourhood and where else in the area they might imagine living, and why. They can investigate the facilities they use or would wish to add, then rank for 'likeability' or quality different parts of the locality, and examine food, water and energy supply as well as transport and access to other nearby and more distant places. They might explore the range of building uses, local play areas, and recreational and leisure facilities. They might examine how the neighbourhood has changed over time.

Children can be introduced to the idea of settlements at various scales, from hamlets and villages to towns and cities and suburbs, what these are, how people use them, what they contain, why people live in them, and how they relate to each other. Using maps and criteria about what a new village might need, teams of children can explore settling an unpeopled area, investigating and justifying what that area can offer, why their settlement would be where they place it, and what they would include in it. The can make a presentation to demonstrate their understanding about what settlements are.

Population

Children can investigate where people live in their region, nationally and across the Earth. Using national road atlases and atlas maps, they can look at the spatial distribution of places in which people live, why there are heavily and sparsely populated areas, how people live where they do, why there are increases or decreases in numbers, and how and why movement and migration occurs from one place to another and the impacts this has. Given that more than half the world's population now live in urban environments – towns and cities, some of many millions of people in size – children can investigate and consider why people do so, what they will need to have access to and the range of jobs that will need to be done. They might consider how such populations obtain food, where this comes from, what this means for transport systems and how family waste will be disposed of, considering the impact of large populations on places and people.

Cultural diversity

Our communities and countries are diverse places. We can consider the diversity of our local and national populations. Do people have the same interests and ways of living? Cultural diversity and what it offers is an aspect of every population. People's different interests and preferences relate to what they choose to eat, their leisure activities, religious beliefs and practices, and how they interrelate with others in their communities, nationally and internationally. Children can develop their awareness of different cultures, considering how these overlap, such as through sports and leisure interests, and what they have in common as well as what may be different from one culture to another. This can help them explore notions of belonging and identity as well as challenge notions of separation, prejudice and bias.

Transport

Transport examines the systems and processes of moving people, goods and services from one place to another. People's travel may be for work or for leisure and recreation. Children can explore the range of transport they use, which they use frequently and, perhaps, if there are forms of transport they have not yet used, and why. They can investigate the impacts of different forms of transport, from walking to bicycles, cars, trains, boats and planes, listing the benefits and problems of each in a range of circumstances, from going to a local shop to travelling to a different part of their country or going abroad. They can consider how the roads around their school may affect them, from the amount of traffic and resultant pollution to parking concerns (Dolan, 2019).

Children can also investigate the ways in which goods are moved locally, nationally and internationally, exploring questions such as: How do goods reach our shops? If they are produced or packaged elsewhere in our country, how do they reach our area? How are goods that are imported or exported transported? Are there different scales of transport, such as the size of lorries and ships? Do some goods need to be transported more speedily while others can be moved more slowly, and why is this? The importance of transportation to the ways we live, from food to clothes to much else, is fundamental in our daily lives.

Trade

Trade concerns how we obtain goods and services. It encompasses the production, commerce, employment and links that enable goods and services to be provided. Trade occurs at a range of scales from local exchange of services and consumable goods to global trading patterns, partnerships of nations individually and in groupings such as the European Union and the World Trade Organization. Buying goods in local shops is trade, the shopkeeper having already traded to obtain the goods the shop sells. Children can investigate what is available in shops locally and what they might know is available through online shopping, from food to household goods and books, and so much more. Considering how and why this happens leads to looking at why local, national and global trade occurs, in the varieties of resources and goods we want to access. Where resources and goods originate, why people in some places wish or need to have these from places elsewhere, nationally and internationally, and why some nations trade in the same types of goods, such as cars, with each other for people to buy can be investigated. Children can question why, for example, people buy a car made in another country when they could buy a car made in their own country: why do people do this, and what has it to do with costs and preferences? The reasons for trade, and the desires and values involved, can be explored, from the accessibility of goods from and to different people to 'just society' initiatives such as Fairtrade which link specific parts of the world together. Fairtrade (see box below and Chapter 8) is a stimulating topic to examine, one that children can look for on shopping trips with their families or carers, looking for the Fairtrade logo or Fairtrade labels.

What does it mean?

Fairtrade

Fairtrade is the idea that the producers of goods are paid a fair price for the work they do in growing or producing the goods they make and sell, be these flowers, chocolate, coffee, cotton, and many other resources and commodities.

Fairtrade developed from initiatives following the Second World War to improve the quality of and fairness in production and trade links between less economically developed and more economically developed countries for the benefit of less economically strong nations. Provision of decent livelihoods and social development made significant progress during the 1960s and 1970s, and have continued and extended significantly around the world. The Fairtrade Foundation has grown considerably since its introduction in 1992 to become a major trade association designed to help poorer farmers and industrial workers in some of the poorest parts of the world to provide them with opportunities to improve their working conditions and lifestyles. It encourages sustainable and self-sufficient practices and fair employment rights. Sustainability is examined in Chapter 7, and Fairtrade is considered further in Chapter 8. You can find out more about Fairtrade and the Fairtrade Foundation at www.fairtrade.org.uk/

Do you know what Fairtrade links your area has with other parts of the world? Where can you buy Fairtrade goods? What varieties of commodities are they?

In the classroom

Investigating trade and trading

Learning about trade patterns and processes between different countries is complex and potentially contentious. Examining it through interactive, engaging activities in which the children are encouraged to think about the issues from different perspectives and angles can help them gain a deeper and more realistic understanding. They become able to appreciate that there is much more to the situation and that there is no good/bad, right/wrong binary solution to the issues.

A teacher used this approach to help her class of 9–10-year-olds see that in order for us to be able to consume goods such as food and drinks on demand, buying whenever we want to, we need to purchase food from shops. The children considered how food items arrived in shops and where they came from. They looked at the sources of foods and found that some food items must be imported from different parts of the world and traded with us. They developed this understanding through investigating the packaging of different typical supermarket foods to recognise the diversity of places from which they originate. The children were asked to bring in the packaging of some typical food and drinks that they had consumed at home during one week, with their parents' or carers' agreement. Using national and world maps, they identified and located the places where they had been produced (and perhaps grown) and worked out how far they had travelled. Their teacher encouraged the children to use Google Earth and atlases to locate the countries and develop their mapwork skills in scale and proportion to calculate the distance that they had travelled. The sources of some locally grown, seasonal food items were also located.

To develop a deeper understanding of the complexity of trading, the children were encouraged to look at the website for the Fairtrade Foundation (www.fairtrade.org.uk/). They investigated the idea of 'fair trade' and what this involved, using examples from Kenya and Peru to help them understand the purpose of fair trading. They used opportunities out of school to spot Fairtrade goods and made comparisons with other producers. They discussed the benefits and limitations of a fair trade way of trading.

The teacher used questioning techniques to deepen their understanding of whether or not the food crops needed to be fresh, such as bananas or cut flowers, and if so, what the implications were in terms

(Continued)

(Continued)

of time taken to transport these goods, as well as encouraging discussion about the environmental impact. The children considered the energy that goes into transportation as well as refrigeration at all stages of the process.

Probing questions were asked about choice and the price that has to be paid for being able to choose exactly what we eat and when, about access to local and seasonal food, and about who produces the food, where and how they live, and the food that they eat if their livelihood is gained by producing food to sell to others rather than for themselves. The ideas of 'cash crops' and 'subsistence farming' were introduced and discussed.

The children, prompted to consider the livelihoods of others, started to consider what might happen to those who depend on other people's demand for 'their' food if farming it declined or stopped, perhaps because of drought, and the farm workers were no longer able to produce their 'cash crops' for others to consume.

Through this unit on trade, the teacher enabled the children to start thinking about many of the implications. She used discussion and debate and led rather than directed them to explore the facts and the issues. The children considered a variety of aspects of the nature and processes of trade from different perspectives and unpicked some of the issues, beginning to recognise some of the complexities of local and global trade systems and processes. They learnt more about where locally, nationally and globally food items they enjoyed came from, their production and how they reached them.

 Practical task

A variety of physical geography and human geography topics have been outlined briefly in the two subsections above. Consider your local, state or national geography curriculum for younger children. Are additional physical and human geography topics mentioned? Write a short paragraph about each of these to say what the focus in primary geography should be.

Topics in environmental geography

Environmental geography concerns how physical and human geographies – that is, natural and human processes, events and activities – interrelate and affect each other. Commonly, this interaction is perceived to be either positive or negative, but it can, of course, be balanced or *sustainable* (see Chapter 7). This means that humans can live in physical and natural environments without degrading them so that people and other species can live alongside each other now and into the future. Investigating topics in environmental geography involves teaching children about the complexity of the world around them and that answers to problems are not simple and binary, and that there is rarely a wholly right or wholly wrong response. Primary children's understanding can be most effectively developed through geographical enquiry and in discussion, debate and role play.

Environmental geography involves consideration of interconnected topics, and it is these that often prove to be the ones that most engage and fascinate children. Several environmental geography themes for primary children are outlined below.

Landshape and landscape

The Earth's story – its landshape – with our story superimposed upon it – the landscape – demonstrate well the interplay between physical and human features and environments, and the effects of each on the other. For example, over centuries the level of ground has risen in cities like London and Rome, which have long and complex histories of human habitation. Digging down several metres we discover the layers of human impact on the landscape over time, each generation having left evidence through their marks and stories. Other examples include landscaped mining slag-heaps and quarries filled with water or landfilled by rubbish to make lakes and reclaimed land for recreation and leisure, woodland or agriculture. Children investigating such examples can look at aspects of human and physical geography and consider the reasons for mining and quarrying originally as well as the changes made more recently. They can begin to see how past and present are interwoven to better understand what is seen in the landscape. This can be explored locally to recognise the historical geography of the area, which directly affects the children's lives. Digging into a local library's map and written archives rather than the soil can uncover stories about the people who used to lived there, what they did and their impact, helping children to see how the past has helped to shape the present and that change has always occurred.

Climate change

Building on children's investigations of local weather can lead effectively into an enquiry about what is happening to our climate now and over a longer period of time, what climate is and that climate changes (Maslin, 2013, 2014). It is important to help children recognise the difference between weather and climate. They need to understand that it is really a question of time and area: weather is about what is happening over a short period of time in places, be it sunny and calm or raining and windy; climate describes the patterns in the atmosphere and the cumulative and consistent behaviour of the weather over a long period of time and a large area such as our country or regions of our continent. Older primary children can examine summary local weather reports over a period of time to see changes over seasons and recent years to look for local patterns in the weather. They can then look at more generalised climate data and information in atlases or available on the Web to see what these patterns are nationally or in a wider continental area. They can investigate information about the debate about climate change to lead to discussion about why the climate appears to be changing and what it is that is happening to cause this. They can consider how a changing climate helps us to understand why changes in our weather seem to be happening (Baby Professor, 2017; Dolan, 2019).

Pollution/litter

Concern about littering and pollution more widely is a tangible issue which children see around them locally, such as discarded paper and packaging along their streets. It lends itself well to a class enquiry through which children can develop their understanding of why it is an issue, how it is caused, the problems that it creates and its implications for their neighbourhood, including how it is dealt with. This gives it relevance and encourages children to look at what might be done to improve the situation. Children can be encouraged to ask questions such as the following.

- Is there evidence of litter/pollution in our local area?
- What types of litter/pollution are there?
- Why is there litter/pollution along our streets?
- Why is it a problem that our local area has litter/pollution?
- What can be done to keep our local area clean and tidy?
- In which ways might we and everyone else help to achieve this?

Having investigated, and perhaps acted, locally, children can then consider other matters of waste and pollution, such as food waste, and look at these at a larger scale. They might ask 'where does our rubbish go?', which can lead to an investigation of landfill, recycling and reuse, connecting with the impact and sustainability of such practices. Using a problem-solving approach, children can examine how improvements might be made, while being realistic about the complexity of such situations. This might prompt an investigation of local air pollution through local authority studies and news reports about air quality in cities. It could examine a myriad of human practices on land, seas, waterways and oceans – for instance, about the 'plastic gyre' in the central Pacific Ocean and the sizeable scale of plastic pollution found on uninhabited Henderson Island, an atoll in the remote South Pacific (Lavers and Bond, 2017). Ocean plastic pollution is outlined in the box below. It is important children appreciate this (Hartley et al., 2015).

What does it mean?

Ocean plastic pollution

There have been consistent reports in national and international media, through television news documentary programmes and in online information media about the scale of plastic pollution in the oceans of the world and along beaches and coastlines for some years (Derraik, 2002). Four concerns are highlighted here. One is the scale of plastic pollution, in all the oceans and across the globe, in the Pacific, Indian and Atlantic Oceans and from the Arctic to the Southern Ocean. A second concern has been the variety of plastic goods that have been found in the oceans and along coasts, indicating how ubiquitous human use of plastic is, from packaging to pens, toys, cosmetic containers, seats and ropes, in scale from the flimsy and thin to thick and bulky objects, many of which do not break down or will only do so over very long periods of time. A third is that seabirds and fish, for example, eat plastic items that are small enough for them to swallow, perhaps attracted to them as possible food; they can also become entangled in items from fishing nets and lines to transparent wrappers and containers and other plastic waste. The fourth concern is that many plastics break down into microplastic particles and fibres, and are found in the sea and the stomachs of sea creatures; these microplastics have now been found in national tap-water supplies around the world, indicating that they are ingested by people (UNEP, 2016). Plastic is everywhere.

Plastic pollution of the oceans comes from several sources, including freight, passenger and fishing ships depositing waste overboard, people presumably assuming that this action is of no or little consequence. It

(Continued)

(Continued)

comes also from waste left on beaches and taken out by tides, as well as from waste discarded into rivers where it emerges from estuaries to be taken out to sea tidally and moved on by coastal water, sea and ocean currents. A further source is untreated sewage pumped raw into the sea with no concern for the manufactured plastic items it contains that have been flushed down toilets and carried through drains. Some 8–9 million tons of plastic waste is deposited in the world's oceans annually. Most plastic is not recycled but thrown away or casually discarded. It accounts for about 80 per cent of marine debris.

A survey of uninhabited and rarely visited Henderson Island in the South Pacific Ocean (Lavers and Bond, 2017) found that the island's beaches were covered in plastic items. It was estimated that almost 38 million items lay on the island, weighing some 17.6 tons. Two-thirds of the plastic was buried up to 10cm depth, indicating its accumulation over many years. The authors raised concerns about ocean-living creatures being affected, as well as amphibians and those living on land. This study provided insight into the amount of plastic debris that is discarded at sea, affecting just one small place, as well as the impact of currents in moving it around the ocean and of tides bringing it to land.

The issue of plastic debris is a prime example of the interrelationship between human activities and the natural environment. It does not take into account the plastic debris that does not reach the world's seas.

 Practical task

How much of what you buy is wrapped in plastic? What goods do you purchase that are in plastic containers? Note these and the other plastic items you have. Consider how fully plastic is a part of your everyday life.

What do you do with the plastic when you have used or finished with it? What happens to it once it leaves your care? Consider how you might develop this as a topic for an enquiry with a class to see how much plastic is a part of all our lives. For example, you might take the plastic cup often found in cafés and school canteens as a starting point: What is it for? Why is it used? What happens to it when it has been used? Do we need to use them and what are the alternatives? It should include the origins of plastic and how it is manufactured. In such a study, plan for a debate about the benefits and impacts of plastic materials and items, and consider what is to be done to mitigate damage on the environment.

Natural hazards

There is a wide range of natural hazards that arise from events such as river and coastal flooding, volcanic eruptions and earthquakes, cyclones and hurricanes, and mudslides in mountainous areas. These natural events have profound implications for human activities and decisions. They occur regularly across the world, from floods in Bangladesh and the UK, to forest and scrubland fires in the USA and Portugal, to earthquakes in Nepal and China, to cyclones in north-eastern Australia. Investigation of a local powerful storm with very heavy rainfall and/or winds, which caused flooding and/or damaged trees, buildings and communication and power lines can help children understand such events from their own experience, perspective and scale. Such events can be topical, so if it is not possible to investigate them at the time, it is useful to collect reports and images of them for later use. Teaching about such hazardous events is an important starting point that can lead to examining hazards and catastrophic events elsewhere in the world. When a significant natural disastrous event happens, it is important to explore where it occurred and why it happened, addressing local impacts on communities to help children appreciate what and why they have the impacts they do.

 In the classroom

Investigating natural hazards

A class of 8–9-year-olds were about to embark on a study of natural hazards, titled 'Catastrophes', starting with an examination of recent flooding in their local area which had caused damage to local houses and forced people to move out for some time. However, two days after they had begun their enquiry into this event and its consequences, there was a major earthquake which destroyed homes and other buildings in a country some of the children had been to on holiday. It was a major news item with print, video and online images and text updated daily. The children raised this as a catastrophe, with the result that their teacher decided to change tack in their study. Leaving the local flooding aside, to return to later in their 'Catastrophes' unit, he set up an enquiry into what had happened and was unfolding.

Because information was readily available, including a wide range of images and text, their teacher initially worked to select material from

(Continued)

(Continued)

the Web and other news sources for the children to use. However, he realised that they were accessing a much wider range of material at home. As a result, he decided to engage the children in developing their own questions in class teams and to pursue their investigations in class and at home. Through discussion, the children agreed to investigate when and how the earthquake had occurred and to look more widely at the causes of earthquakes. They would consider the consequences for the local people, including the levels of damage to buildings and the injuries and deaths, information about which changed daily for several days. They examined how the people affected were helped by their national government, hospitals and other survival and support organisations, including the provision of a tent community for temporary accommodation for those unable to move and stay elsewhere. As part of their study, they looked at how the news information changed over the days and first three weeks of the aftermath to consider how news is gathered and to remain quizzical about speedy and unconfirmed information and opinion reports. They examined some of the technical information about earthquake causes from television news reports and other media sources.

The outcome of this study was that the children provided an informed account of what happened from the initial earthquake through its aftershocks and of the damage it did to the physical environment, and how it affected people and its impact on their lives. They created drawings, models and maps of how earthquakes are caused and may happen, and discussed their understanding of how rolling news reporting provided both incorrect and accurate information. This led to both incorrect assumptions as well as clear information about the events and their aftermath which they learned to differentiate. The children provided a display for all the children in the school to see and they gave a presentation in a school assembly, which included a short role play, digital projection and a discussion asking their audience what they knew or thought they knew.

Regeneration

As some areas of our natural and agricultural landscapes are consumed by increasing urbanisation and development, governments turn their attention to regenerating areas such as past mining, quarrying, storage and industrial 'brownfield' sites where that land use has declined and died. This is done to conserve unurbanised natural areas, or 'greenfield' sites, that exist as far as possible. Such brownfield regeneration takes place in urban and rural settings. It may be government funded or private developers may be supported to bring 'new life' to these areas. The purpose is to reuse such land for housing, leisure facilities, nature conservation or high-tech and other service industrial estates. Through researching the local or a nearby area, children can examine such regeneration and be encouraged to think about why the original site had declined and find out what is happening to re-create it to support and redevelop the community. They can make tangible links to local history through past maps and archive documents, supported by the local history library, and begin to appreciate the need to continue to use available land for new and different purposes. They might look out for, or know, a derelict or declining site and might make proposals to regenerate its use.

Land reclamation

There is much land that has been identified as being unproductive for human use due to its particular physical conditions, such as that it is too wet, rocky or steep, the soil is infertile, or it is unusable for another reason. Examples of land that has been reclaimed include coastal and marshy areas that have been drained and put to agricultural use, such as the polder areas in Holland or the Fens in the UK. Land in dry climates or with seasonal rainfall has been irrigated. Infertile land has been made productive through the addition of fertilisers or rotational farm practices, and steep land has been terraced for such uses as rice growing in paddies in Vietnam. The Banaue rice terraces in the Philippines have been farmed for over 2,000 years and are a World Heritage Site, some claiming they are the 'eighth wonder of the world'. Investigating your local area might identify similar, albeit small-scale, reclamations. Children can consider areas that might be adapted or developed for human use, being mindful of the impact such initiatives would have on the physical and human geography of the area. They should consider whether these are always positive and beneficial – and who might gain and who might lose. By considering the pros and cons, children learn about the challenges in making decisions about changes that affect places and people's lives.

Energy and resource extraction

Resources such as coal, oil, water, wind and sunshine are natural or physical attributes of our planet. It is what we do with and to such resources to make them useful that places them in the context of environmental geography. By exploiting them, we have an impact on our environment, though not always in a positive way. There has been benefit in mining coal, but the effects of such extractive practices as open-cast or deep mining are considerable, as is the impact of burning coal as a fossil fuel adding carbon to the atmosphere. A current contentious issue is fracking to extract oil and gas from shale rocks; we have yet to appreciate properly the likely impacts of the fracking process, as well as the benefits in using the oil or gas provided in a world that is trying to reduce dependence on fossil fuels. Undertaking problem-solving enquiries, children might examine the benefits, limitations and dangers of resource extraction and use. They can look into how we might reduce the impact of pollution in schemes such as carbon capture and storage, using sustainable energy sources (such as solar, tidal and wind) and energy-efficient vehicles. Children can investigate how resources can be used in more efficient and, consequently, sustainable ways. These are contentious matters for some people and children should consider different points of view and arguments.

Deforestation/desertification

As forests recede to provide more agricultural land and as deserts expand, we can see a close relationship between human activity and changes to the natural environment. As more land is demanded for food and other resource production, so the natural environment is reduced, often with damaging results for flora and fauna. Removing the natural canopies and protection of the forest floor in areas of the Amazon basin, Madagascar and Indonesia means that the fragile and vulnerable soil in tropical rain-forest areas is laid bare to the elements. When heavy rain falls, soil is rapidly eroded, creating infertile and soon-to-be unproductive land. There is increasing awareness of the problems that short-term gain creates through long-term damage in many more parts of the world. Children might study one such issue, such as the encroachment of desert into areas of sub-Saharan Africa, where the scale of infertile and unproductive land is increasing; previously habitable areas can no longer be farmed, destroying livelihoods in fringe areas of deserts. This comes about through changes in the climate as well as through over-exploitation of the land. Such examples illustrate that people have in the past, as well as today, taken land out of productivity and damaged the natural environment. Children might enquire into what has happened or is occurring, and look at possible causes to understand why. They can consider what might be done in the future to prevent or reverse this trend and to regenerate natural habitats.

Tourism

With increasingly accessible transport around the world, people can get to places more easily and quickly than ever before. This has positive and negative consequences for the environment. As actual or potential tourists themselves, it is important that children begin to understand tourism's benefits and limitations, whether this is as day visitors or holidayers staying in other parts of their country or elsewhere in the world. Tourism is a stimulating topic and introduces children to complex issues. People travel to visit physical environments, such as the seaside or a mountain area, and human environments, such as cities and theme parks. What tourists do does have an impact on the environment. Travel by plane provides speedy transport but has a negative impact in terms of air pollution. Tourists bring money and employment to areas of the world that seem wealthy, as well as to countries that are impoverished where investment in their infrastructure is to the benefit of the local population. This can transform a place's local human geography by creating a more prosperous, even thriving economy, but it can be the multinational hotels and other companies that invest in the area that benefit rather than the local people who provide much of the workforce.

Using locally produced resources can ensure increased employment and expenditure in the local economy and can develop the cultural capital of such 'attractive' places – for example, through ecotourism. Children can identify the challenges of ecotourism by examining the potential drain on local resources that are produced only for visitors and not for the local population (a similar issue to the production of cash crops) and consider the benefit to the tourist of increased awareness of the importance and fragility of natural environments and ecosystems. Children can examine the possible dilution of local cultures by re-creating them for the tourists, possibly as caricatures of the local culture. The effect may well be one of stereotyping local people and their culture, as a commodity for the tourist market, indicating the impact of dominant Western or global cultures – the local culture becomes tokenistic and divorced from its origins. Children can investigate how this raises the question of exploitation, consider different cultures and explore what a culture means to whom.

Water in the environment

Water is a substantial theme and includes a myriad of topics, from people's leisure uses of coastal and river water features, to access to clean water and sanitation, and to human impact on the climate and the weather's effect on our lives. It includes matters of supply and the many ways in which we use water, as well as issues of flooding, drought, landslides and subsidence. There are many ways to initiate, approach and develop a water-based topic. One is to use a text, such as Brian Patten's poem, *The River's Story*, by involving children in exploring imaginatively their understanding from such a source by creating illustrations to interpret and depict what Patten intends to convey. This provides a useful link between geography, literacy and art, for example. Children might use a variety of pictorial and information sources to help them know more about the river, and rivers and streams. They might investigate the uses of rivers and draw on what they learn to write their own stories and poetry using the river theme. For some, it may involve how a river is used by people; for others, it may concern the pollution of a river, and for yet other children, it may concern change and conservation. A fieldtrip to a stream or river would be a further vital stimulus, as indicated in a research summary earlier in this chapter.

The River's Story

I remember when life was good.
I shilly-shallied across meadows,
Tumbled down mountains,
I laughed and gurgled through woods,
Stretched and yawned in a myriad of floods.
Insects, weightless as sunbeams,
Settled upon my skin to drink
I wore lily-pads like medals
Fish, lazy and battle scarred,
Gossiped beneath them.
The damselflies were my ballerinas,
The pike my ambassadors.
Kingfishers, disguised as rainbows,
Were my secret agents.
It was a sweet time, a gone-time,
A time before factories grew,
Brick by greedy brick,
And left me cowering
In monstrous shadows.
Like drunken giants
They vomited their poisons into me.
Tonight a scattering of vagrant bluebells,
Dwarfed by those same poisons,
Toll my ending.
Children, come and find me if you wish,
I am your inheritance.
Behind the derelict housing-estates
You will discover my remnants.
Clogged with garbage and junk,
To an open sewer I've shrunk.
I, who have flowed through history,

Who have seen hamlets become villages,

Villages become towns, towns become cities,

Am reduced to a trickle of filth

Beneath the still, burning stars.

Brian Patten

Image 6.5   Brian Patten's poem *The River's Story* represented as a sketch

In the classroom

'Follow that drop of water!'

A class of 7–8-year-olds explored different concepts of water in the environment in an interactive and participatory way using an enquiry approach. They talked about and investigated ideas about water and its presence in the local environment. They considered rainwater falling to the ground and staying there for a while in the form of puddles which they could splash in. They observed that water comes out of a tap and can be used to drink and wash with. They were made very aware that water is essential for life and that without it we would not survive for very long. They were encouraged to think about how it changed from one form to another, such as ice to fluid water.

(Continued)

(Continued)

They then moved on to a series of lessons which began with the question 'What happens to a water droplet?'

The children were encouraged to think about rain and to focus on one particular drop of rainwater. They were asked to create a story around this water droplet, giving it a name and personalising it so that its journey and adventure could be followed. Outside, different children imagined their individual water droplet falling on to different surfaces and they observed what happened to it.

The children were asked to think about questions such as:

- Does it stay on the surface or not? If so, where does it go?
- Does it disappear and go into the ground? If so, how does this happen and where does it go?
- What happens to it if it falls on to a leaf or a tree trunk?

They were encouraged to find answers to the questions by pouring water on to different surfaces and observing what happened. They were asked, for instance, Why? Why does it go straight into the sand but stay on top of the tarmac for a while?

A mini-plenary ensured that the children had understood that their water droplet does different things depending on the surface that it falls on to. Once they were confident with that and had an idea as to why that might happen, they were asked to think about what would happen to it when they went away and came back the next day: Where would it be then? What might have happened to it?

The children began to formulate explanations about what happens to water when it falls to the ground. Their teacher began to introduce some subject-specific vocabulary – absorption, evaporation, condensation – and involved the children in getting their tongues round them and talking about what the words meant.

These and other scenarios provided a range of adventures for the water droplet to go on, which some children wrote about, others related to their friends, and some created a song and a play about.

Once the children had understood some of these basic concepts, they were able to start thinking about the water cycle and what happens to the rain once it has been absorbed, where it goes to and what might happen to it. They were continuing to think about their personalised water droplet and developing their story about it. This included presenting their narrative in a variety of ways, through diary entries, cartoons, drama, collages and dance.

The children investigated rain falling on to the land surface using the sandpit and helped to create a small world with hills, model houses, animals and people. They explored a range of different scenarios, such as what might happen to the environment if there was a 'surplus' of water coming down the 'rivers', introducing them to the concept of flooding, what the effects of flooding were and how the impact of the flooding could be managed. They considered examples of where this happened in their local and regional area, making it real and relevant. They looked, too, at flooding in other parts of the world.

Through these lessons, the children came to a better understanding about the water around them and how it is present in many ways. They were able to begin to appreciate the processes that are at work, resulting in the landforms and various events that affect people's lives.

Reflective task

Using two or three examples of environmental geography, explain how physical and human geography are drawn together in environmental geography. Provide another one or two examples of environmental geography topics that you might teach with a primary age group. Say how they connect and interrelate physical and human geography.

Key points

This chapter has:

- introduced the notion of the Anthropocene as the geological epoch in which we are living and related it to Earth's geological timeline;
- considered what physical, human and environmental geography means and includes;
- noted that while we can study physical and human geography separately, they are fundamentally interdependent and are being brought together in environmental geography;
- presented a range of topics in physical, human and environmental geography which can be investigated in primary geography.

Moving on

Seek out and note further possible topics and creative opportunities and approaches to teach physical, human and environmental geography through interactive, hands-on activities inside and outside the classroom.

Further reading

Topics in and approaches to teaching about physical, human and environmental geography can be found in a number of publications.

Dolan A (2019) *Powerful Primary Geography: A toolkit for 21st century learning.* Abingdon: Routledge.

Martin, F (2006) *Teaching Geography in Primary Schools: Learning How to Live in the World.* Cambridge: Chris Kington.

Pickering, S (ed.) (2017) *Teaching Outdoors Creatively*. London: Routledge.

Pike, S (2016) *Learning Primary Geography: Ideas and inspirations from classrooms.* Abingdon: Routledge.

Scoffham, S (ed.) (2010) *Primary Geography Handbook.* Sheffield: Geographical Association.

Scoffham, S (ed.) (2017) *Teaching Geography Creatively* (2nd edn). Abingdon: Routledge.

Scoffham, S and Owens, P (2017) *Teaching Primary Geography*. London: Bloomsbury.

Useful websites

Australian Geography Teachers' Association (AGTA): www.agta.asn.au

Earth Learning Ideas: www.earthlearningidea.com/index.html

Geographical Association Physical Geography Special Interest Group: www.geography.org.uk/getinvolved/committeessigs/physicalgeographysig/

National Geographic: www.nationalgeographic.com

National Geographic for Kids: www.natgeokids.com/uk/

Oxfam Education: www.oxfam.org.uk/oxfam

Royal Geographical Society-with IBG: KS1&2 Resources: www.rgs.org/OurWork/Schools/Teaching+resources/Key+Stage+1-+resources/Key+Stage+1-2+resources.htm

CHAPTER 7

EXPLORING SUSTAINABILITY

Environmental impact, sustainability and sustainable schools

 Chapter objectives

This chapter enables you to:

- understand what is meant by environmental impact and sustainability;
- recognise that environmental impact and sustainability are inter-connected with, and take forward aspects of, environmental geography;
- know about approaches that promote sustainability for children and schools;
- recognise the importance of helping children develop their sense of environmental well-being and the potential value of learning about the futures dimension.

Introduction

This chapter examines environmental impact and sustainability. This is a core geographical concept because the quality and nature of the Earth's and humans' present and future depends on understanding the interactions in and between the natural or physical environment, and the human and social environment, which were introduced in Chapter 6. Environmental impact and sustainability are inextricably intertwined with environmental geography. In deepening their studies of places and physical and human geography, geographers examine the uses and misuses of resources and technologies in our environments, people's access to resources and outcomes of unequal distribution, the cultural and social values held about the environment, the decision-making and decisions that affect the environment, and the extent to which the ways in which we live and use resources and the environment are sustainable. Geographers try to explain and evaluate what is being done and to offer advice about what needs to be and could be done most helpfully. It is important that children learn about these aspects of the world during their primary schooling and that their schools can be, in themselves, sustainable environments, setting an appropriate example for living and acting sustainably (Clarke, 2012; Massey, 2012; Nolet, 2016).

For us, as teachers, to be able to teach sustainability effectively, it is essential that we have a good understanding and appreciation of what sustainability means and is concerned with, as we should of all the areas of geographical knowledge and understanding we teach (Tambyah, 2006; Hicks 2012; Dodds *et al.*, 2017). This requires more than knowledge of the physical environment and its processes; it is about our relationships with the environment and each other (de Leo, 2012; Wals and Corcoran, 2012). It concerns our approaches to teaching about sustainability (Taylor *et al.*, 2006; Kennelly and Taylor, 2007; Harrison and Purnell, 2012; Bourn *et al.*, 2016). While we tend to hold positive attitudes towards environmental matters and concerns, locally and globally, we need to develop, as early years and primary teachers, more clearly and fully our understanding and knowledge about the natural and social geographic environment, to ensure that we have a wide appreciation rather than focus only on that of which we have experience and prior learning. We need to be more robust in the ways we examine and analyse evidence and draw conclusions from it, not to be swayed by opinion and rhetoric. 'Fake' news and 'alternative facts' should not be received uncritically. Ensuring that we are well informed and knowledgeable about environmental impact and sustainability is essential to high-quality and effective teaching and learning.

There continues to be the challenge of recognising and appreciating that the 'environment' is more than the physical and ecological environment, and is not separate from us; it is not simply 'out there'. Rather, we need to understand the interconnected nature of 'environment' in a *relational* context, which involves seeing and valuing the interrelationship of natural and social knowledge with our mutual and personal responsibilities for the ways we interact with and in our environments and how we affect them, just as they influence us. In this sense, it is about how we live and develop now and for the future. The better informed we are, the better we consider environmental matters critically and the more we are engaged with environmental care, management and concerns, the more likely we are to hold positive attitudes towards our places, environments, other people and creatures, which means that social and cultural dimensions and living sustainably are equally involved. We are then better able to understand this relationship as mutually sustaining and essential to our futures. Such understanding often appears to be better appreciated by indigenous peoples, through their traditional relationships with the environment, which provide for strong opportunities to work with and in local communities (Webber and Robertson, 2012).

Education for environmental sustainability, sustainable living and sustainable development has been a key global focus for several decades, particularly since the Earth Summit of 1992 (United Nations, 1992). A revised Agenda of 17 Sustainable Development Goals to work towards by 2030 was set by the United Nations in 2015 (United Nations, 2015; Dodds *et al.*, 2017). These goals include:

- promoting sustainable agriculture and ending food poverty, providing sustainable consumption;
- sustainable management of water and sanitation globally;
- access to reliable and affordable energy for all;
- settlements at all levels to be inclusive, resilient, safe and sustainable;
- reducing inequalities in and among countries, and achieving gender equality and equality in education;
- urgent action to combat climate change and its effects;
- using sustainably and conserving the ocean's resources;
- protecting, restoring and using sustainably ecosystems, including forests, while tackling desertification, and halting and reversing land degradation and biodiversity loss;
- promoting sustainable development and living at all levels.

Education is key in promoting these and the other goals to the young, and geography is an essential subject in the primary curriculum for doing so. Around the world many nations have included sustainability within their curricula (see, for instance, Gorana and Kanaujia, 2016; Lee and Williams, 2009; Lotz-Sisitka *et al.*, 2017; Robertson, 2012; de Amorim Soares and Petarnella, 2011) and there has been an increasing emphasis on education for sustainability from the earliest years in countries such as Australia and the UK (de Leo, 2012; Davis, 2015; Boyd *et al.*, 2018).

Environmental impact

As discussed in Chapter 6, geography studies the physical or natural and human or social environment. Central to geographical studies are the processes that cause and create changes in physical and human environments and the impacts that the outcomes have on environments, people and places, matters of interest in environmental geography. Children encounter the phrases 'environmental change' and 'environmental impact', usually in the context of destruction and degradation. Natural 'hazards' are associated with, for example, the destructive impact of flooding, very high winds and earthquakes damaging homes and the local infrastructure. Settlement studies may focus on families who live in run-down areas of boarded-up and vandalised housing and closed amenities. Yet, we must recognise and appreciate that environmental change and impact can be positive – for example, the redevelopment schemes in urban and dockland areas regenerating communities, tramway systems being built to reduce car usage and improve access to public transport, and the creation of natural habitats on wasteland encouraging the return of endangered species.

Studying changes that result from spatial and environmental processes leads to examination of their impact on the environment, people and places. The core focus is on the ways in which environmental impact is managed and enabled. Central to this aspect of geography is recognition that the environment is a resource to be used well, not mismanaged, inadvertently or intentionally. Environmental change and impact can lead to real and vital improvements in or to the serious degradation of places and environments. For instance, the provision of car parks and tourist amenities along scenic coastal areas can lead to greater interest by more people in the beauty of the landscape, or conversely, overcrowding and damage by visitors who are unmindful of their effects on the place they are visiting, which can be offset by visitors and information centres. Geography studies, explains and may propose solutions to the management, use, replenishment and development of the environment. In particular, these studies concern the ways in which decisions are made about environmental use, who makes the decisions, why they are made and the impact they have in the short and long term for better or for worse. It can focus on local environments as much as on national and international contexts.

A key topic in geography is the use of resources. There are finite resources, such as oil and other fossil fuels, which in time will run out. There are renewable resources, such as water and wind, although there is increasing debate about how we use, manage and sustain the uses of these. There are regenerative resources, which include ocean fish stocks and the major areas of tropical and temperate forest, which, if exploited rather than being carefully managed and renewed through breeding and replenishment, will be irreversibly damaged. Geography examines the activities and resulting outcomes and issues that affect people and the Earth from the local to the global, including scarcity, misuse and exploitation, access, control and power, natural cycles and disasters, and environmental changes and impacts resulting from people's actions. For instance, geographers study climate change, its causes and effects, as they do the changes to city centres resulting from the building of large shopping malls, the impact of increased traffic in residential communities, and the spread and effect of genetically modified crops. In doing so, geographers ask questions such as the following.

- How do people use and misuse the natural and social environment – why and with what impact?
- Who makes the decisions that lead to effective use or misuse of physical and human environments and of their resources – why are they made and in whose interests?
- What can be done to create and ensure beneficial impacts from environmental changes, and reduce and minimise the negative effects of change – what and who benefits and how?
- As citizens, what role can we play and how in making decisions that affect the environment, people and places – what do we wish to gain in doing so?

Geographers' concern for environmental issues and their impact is important for primary children because they are the future and will be living in that future environment. Young children need to understand and consider how they might respond to and deal with environmental hazards and issues that will directly affect or impact upon their lives, be these local floods, urban change, wildfires or more low-key environmental degradation. With greater unpredictability in our natural and social worlds, it becomes essential that children benefit from hazards education (Smawfield, 2013; Pike, 2016) and from education for sustainability and risk (Clarke, 2012; Shaw and Oikawa, 2014; Bourn et al., 2016). If children are to act responsibly in their stewardship of the world for coming generations, they need to develop their understanding of how to live in harmony with the Earth and how to come to decisions that are beneficial to and balanced for people, both locally and globally (Dunne, 2016). Geography plays a vital role in developing children's environmental awareness, knowledge, understanding and values, so that they may act as thoughtful and responsible local and global citizens (Willy, 2017).

In the classroom

Exploring *The River's Story*

A class of 10–11-year-old children were introduced to Brian Patten's poem *The River's Story* (Patten, 2012; see Chapter 6) within a wider study of the nature of and people's engagement with rivers in the country and cities. This enticing and challenging poem is rich with images and unusual vocabulary. It depicts the life of a river and introduces issues about people's impact on it through industrialisation, buildings, agriculture and pollution. The poem brings the river's course to life. After reading and discussing the poem, the children worked in groups, using the text and artwork, to produce their own river 'viewpoint'. This provided the opportunity for consolidation of their work on rivers. A display was created to show the children's views, and they debated their different interpretations of people's impact on the river and its effect on people's lives.

Practical task

Find a poem or story about ways in which people affect a place or the environment (see Appendix 2 for examples). Use the headings, 'Features and processes' and 'Impact and response', to note the natural and human features and processes involved, and to identify how the people and environment were affected and what happened in response.

Sustainability

Sustainability is complex and contentious, and has various meanings in primary geography teaching and learning (Willy, 2017). Its everyday meaning describes the capacity to maintain ways of life and the usage of particular resources at current levels. The widely accepted definition provided by the Bruntland Commission (United Nations, 1987), which examined the use of the Earth's resources, stated that a 'sustainable' way of life is one that *meets the needs of the present without compromising the ability of future generations to meet their own needs*. A more recent restatement of this perspective has been:

The goal of sustainable development is to enable all people throughout the world to satisfy their basic needs and enjoy a better quality of life, without compromising the quality of life of future generations.

(Ofsted, 2008b)

The place of education for sustainability in the primary school curriculum varies from country to country. One example has been in Australia, where it has been and remains a high priority. It is seen as integral to the study of geography, where it is argued to be central to an *holistic understanding of human dependence on the environment* and to the investigation of *the attitudinal, demographic, social, economic and political influences on human use and management of the environment. It enables students to explore how world-views and belief systems influence these relationships and interactions with the environment* (ACARA, 2012a, pp. 15–16). Children should be encouraged to examine ways in which people's activities affect the local environment, such as its ecosystems and local wildlife, and how people's decisions, approaches and actions affect the environment and society. Children can consider what they might do to plan, advocate and act to create and have more sustainable futures. They might do this for their own place and look at what others consider in other places they study, bearing in mind that there will be a variety of different, even contradictory, arguments made about what people want to happen.

In the UK, sustainability was prominent in geography after 2000 (DfEE/QCA, 1999). However, its importance was reduced after 2010. Indeed, the word 'sustainability' was not mentioned at all in the revision of England's primary national curriculum at that time (DfE, 2013). That sustainability is missing in any country's curriculum guidance or requirements does not preclude or prevent it from being included by a school and taught. Sustainability emphasises using resources so that they are self-renewing or carefully replenished, and with working finite resources so as to manage a smooth transition from declining resources to new, hopefully renewable and regenerative resources. Sources for energy are an example, such as the move from coal and oil sources to solar, wind and tidal sources. How we use resources and live is a matter of future sustainability. This concerns the distribution of resources between and their use by people, with the goal of enabling all to live comfortably rather than a few to live very well while the majority live less well. As well as studying what is happening, geography reflects on the practical and ethical uses and misuses of the environment, and of people and their places and communities. Examining environmental impact and sustainability involves concern with social and environmental justice.

The term 'sustainable development' is frequently used and it can seem contradictory to talk about sustainability as maintaining the status quo while implying suggestions of expansion and advancement.

Commonly, we perceive development to mean economic and lifestyle progress and so mean economic development, and this has been manifest in developing technology to improve material possessions and using increasing amounts of energy and material resources to do so. However, we have come to understand development in much broader terms to include environmental development and social well-being. It is important to remember that sustainable development must involve environmental sustainability; it implies the need to steward renewable and regenerative resources such that when we use them they remain available in future, as well as to provide improving environments for people's lives. One point that the Brundtland Commission made in 1987 (United Nations, 1987) implied that we will develop alternative, renewable sources to replace finite resources. Yet, this perspective has been viewed as highly problematic and difficult to achieve. We need to explore and help children who will live in this future environment to perceive environmental sustainability and sustainable development in terms of improvement, not simply materially but for the benefit of our environment, societies and communities, *as environmentally friendly growth* (Huckle and Martin, 2001). Only then can we have real sustainability globally and understand that we are here for good and not just for the weekend (Patten, 2000). Martin and Owens state that sustainability is less a product than *a process: thinking about ourselves, thinking about others and using our knowledge to make responsible decisions and actions* (Martin and Owens, 2008, p. 6).

Following the 2015 publication of the 17 revised Sustainable Development Goals (United Nations, 2015) – in itself a positive recognition of the importance of sustainability issues when updating the previous 8 Millennium Development Goals (United Nations, 2000) – UNICEF spelt out ways they can be achieved for children (UNICEF, 2015a). The organisation used three phrases, stating that there should be *enough for all for ever, especially the most vulnerable*, that *prevention and preparedness are better than a cure*, and that we need to keep *building resilience, building back better* (UNICEF, 2015b). UNICEF's emphasis for children, therefore, is on the provision of essential services, such as nutrition, safe water, sanitation, energy and education; support to ensure preparation through knowledge and life-saving skills when disaster strikes, and by taking action to prevent problems, issues and damage; and being resilient and enabling communities through involving children to rebuild better places so as to return lives to normal and to be more sustainable for the future.

Sustainability challenges the way we live. Its focus is on developing solutions that can improve the environment in which we all live and, thus, people's and communities' lives. It encourages us to think about how we can improve public services and facilities and how we can reduce, reuse and recycle to preserve the precious resources we have and utilise them in more effective and economical ways. In doing so, it helps us to improve others' well-being and so develop their senses of social justice and equity. To help do so, young geographers can be encouraged to ask the following questions.

- What do sustainable lifestyles and environments look like?
- What creates, aids, damages or prevents the potential for sustainability?
- What options are there to enable a balanced, equitable and just use of the environment and its resources for a sustainable future, and how might the best options be identified and implemented?
- How can decision makers be encouraged to adopt environmentally, people-friendly and just strategies and actions to improve the lives of people across the world?

With an increasing focus in our societies globally on climate change, extreme weather and environmental degradation, we are seeing a shift in attitudes towards tackling issues around sustainability (Hicks, 2016). We must address this with children, for they will carry forward in time the initiatives decided upon to tackle environmental and social problems. Consequently, many government and non-governmental organisations have attempted to inject concepts of sustainability into the curriculum and the ethos of schools. The emphasis is to develop children's understanding of their carbon and ecological footprints, such as positive and negative waste disposal, for our actions affect the Earth's whole environment, its ecosystems, the built environment and the global community. This is about how we live sustainably.

Living sustainably is not something new to us and, until relatively recently in our history, it is how we have lived in and with our natural environment (Harari, 2014). Indeed, the indigenous communities of the world have the most important lessons for us to learn about living sustainably, now and into the future. Their experience in living in harmony with, respecting and valuing the land and its ecology provides an evident base to learn from. Because of their varied and multiple ways of relating to the landscape and ecosystems and to the life they sustain and which sustains them, learning about indigenous communities' relationships with the land can support children in developing their understanding of how to live with and from the land, how to sustain and manage our needs and lifestyles in relation to the resources available, and how to help to change and shape the landscape in a sustainable and positive way.

Opportunities to study such indigenous communities raise questions about what sustainability means for us, and enables us to explore some of the ethical matters, dilemmas and implications of disregarding and exploiting our environment rather than caring for and managing it, which we must ultimately do in order to live sustainably in the future.

Reflective task

Sustainable and ethical living is fraught with dilemmas. Consider where you stand on this dilemma. What would be your responses to children who asked you about it? What are their views?

We are constantly being made aware of the detrimental effects of food being transported across the world for us to eat whatever we like at any time of the year, irrespective of seasonality. Changing this is seen as positive and environmentally conscious. How do we square such change with the farmers in other parts of the world, perhaps in a Fairtrade business, who, to meet our insatiable demand, have developed their agriculture such that their survival depends on the production and sale of their cash crops to our market all year round? Which option do we choose: the reduction of food miles to support the planet, or supporting communities in other parts of the world reliant on us for their income? What other factors do we consider? Do we see this as good economics and supportive or as injurious and socially unjust?

Sustainable schools

A key concern that has developed in recent years has been the sustainability of schools. This has been raised in terms of their uses of resources, such as energy and water, as well as their impact on the physical and social environment of the local community (DEH, 2005; Nikolopoulou *et al.*, 2010; Marsh and Hart, 2011; Massey, 2012; Reynolds, 2014; Davis, 2015; Pike, 2016). While many teachers are keen to teach about sustainability, research shows that they often lack the confidence to do so (Green *et al.*, 2016). Some governments have taken this on board and developed policies for implementation in the curriculum and the school community. The Australian government, for example, established the Australian Sustainable Schools Initiative (AuSSI) to promote positive changes in schools towards better sustainability in the school grounds and buildings, and for the local community. It aimed to achieve the following goals.

- *Learning and teaching for sustainability as an integral component of school curricula.*
- *Schools actively engaging in a continuous cycle of planning, implementing and reviewing their approach to sustainability as part of their everyday operations.*
- *Schools using natural resources, including energy, water, waste and biodiversity, in more sustainable ways. Schools and school authorities reporting on changes towards sustainability.*

- *Schools working towards sustainability in partnership with their local communities.*

AuSSI (2010, pp. 1–2)

This set of intentions is potentially an admirable and broad brief for schools in every country and community. By adopting such an approach, primary schools, for instance, could demonstrate ways in which they are developing their children's experiences and learning of sustainable approaches for the future. For instance, a school's policy for education for sustainability would involve its children in shared ownership of sustainable initiatives and decision-making, encourage them to make their own sustainable decisions and choices, through which they promote a sustainability ethos and values across the school.

In the classroom

A school approach to sustainability

One primary school in England adopted as its core ethos education for sustainable development (Massey, 2012). Among its many actions it engaged children as leaders alongside the school's whole staff, embedded sustainable development education in the curriculum, engaged parents and the local community, and maintained a process of continuous evaluation and development, including risk-taking. It involved the children across the school in examining how best they learned, what mattered to them, what they wished to achieve and wanted from the school. Children across classes used a range of digital tools, from cameras to the Web, to investigate, debate, make cases for and propose real improvements for the school and their learning. They were constantly challenged and rigour was demanded of them in making cases and providing arguments, whether as eco-warriors or in tackling dilemmas posed to them.

It was not always straightforward and easy. Practical and financial constraints existed, but the attitude focused on how to address and overcome these, even if it took time. What the children gained through their involvement was deep learning about sustainability, the nature of and care for the environment in the widest sense, and how to critique, identify good evidence and argue for and against a proposition. The approach developed the children's language, mathematical, scientific, artistic and environmental and humanities knowledge, understanding and skills, and they appreciated why this mattered: it gave them a stake in their own

(Continued)

(Continued)

knowledge, learning, achievements, choices and decisions. The essential message to other primary schools from the headteacher was: think and go 'outside the box', take risks, not recklessly but with thought, trust the children and your staff, and believe in and promote what you do.

In the UK, the Sustainable Development Education Panel (Holland, 1998) argued that sustainability education develops the understanding, values and skills to enable us all to take up the challenge provided by the Brundtland definition of sustainability. The Brundtland Report had argued that decisions about resource use and stewardship, for instance, must be made for the long term not the short term, taking account of inter-generational equity. This perspective helped the UK's Sustainable Development Education Panel to identify seven key concepts for Education for Sustainable Development (ESD) (Table 7.1). They remain important. The ESD concepts reflect the ideas implicit and explicit in environmental geography, particularly in relation to environmental impact and sustainability. They have been variously interpreted and used widely in schools. It is evident that they are both geographically informed and inform geography teaching, as similar principles and areas have in Australia and other nations.

ESD concept	Developing the knowledge, understanding, values and skills
Interdependence	To understand the connections and interrelationships between people, places and environments at local and global levels, and that decisions taken in one place have an impact elsewhere.
Citizenship and stewardship	To realise our rights and responsibilities to participate in making decisions that affect people, places and environments, and that everyone is entitled to a say in what happens in the future.
Diversity	To understand and value the importance of diversity in our lives, culturally, socially, economically and biologically, and that we are impoverished without it.
Quality of life, equity and justice	To recognise that for any development to be sustainable, it must provide equitable benefit to people, improving their lives and welfare.

ESD concept	Developing the knowledge, understanding, values and skills
Sustainable change	To appreciate there are limits to the ways in which the world can develop, and understand that the consequences of unsustainable growth are increased poverty, hardship and environmental degradation, disadvantaging everyone.
Uncertainty and precaution in action	To realise, through our continuous learning about the Earth, to be cautious in our approach because our actions may have unforeseen consequences for people, places and environments.
Needs and rights of future generations	To learn to lead our lives considering the needs and rights of future generations, and recognise that what we do now has direct implications for what life will be like in the future.

Table 7.1   The key concepts of education for sustainable development (adapted from www.nc.uk.net/esd/index.html; Holland, 1998; Martin, 2006c; Martin and Owens, 2008)

A further approach that primary teachers can use is a framework based around what have been called the eight 'doorways' for exploring sustainability, particularly in relation to the local environment and community. These 'doorways' have the potential to promote children's understanding and appreciation of and commitment to sustainability (Table 7.2) through investigating aspects of their daily local lives and experience in their school, neighbourhood and community.

The doorways	Focus of interest
1. Food and drink	• access to and supply of food and drink; • sustainability of supply from local producers; • environmental impact of drink and food production and consumption.
2. Energy and water	• issues of increasing water and energy demand; • approaches to sustainable conservation and reduced use.
3. Travel and traffic	• examining journey and travel decisions and practices and traffic concerns; • creating sustainable travel and transport to schools, and reducing congestion and accidents.

(Continued)

Table 7.2   (Continued)

The doorways	Focus of interest
4. Purchases and waste	• evaluating the 'throw-away' culture, actions and impacts; • exploring sustainable resource purchase, use and practices; • examining recycling, reuse, repair and reduction.
5. Buildings and grounds	• appreciating how physical environments affect well-being; • reviewing the nature and use of built and natural spaces in school and locally to improve environmental quality and sustainability.
6. Inclusion and participation	• evaluating the inclusive nature of the school community; • creating places and actions that respect human rights, cultures, freedoms and creative expression; • enabling children to participate in place and environment decision-making and development.
7. Local well-being	• schools as centres for change and enhancement of the local community and environment; • understanding local issues and needs, with active engagement in school and locally.
8. Global dimension	• recognising and valuing local–global interconnections; • taking an international outlook and understanding the impact of personal and community values, choices and behaviours, as global citizens.

Table 7.2   Taking an 'eight doorways' focus in teaching children about sustainability (DfES, 2006a, 2006b)

The 'doorways' framework is founded in the context of the '4Cs' (Figure 7.1). The Child is at the core of the interlinked spheres of the school Campus, the Curriculum and the local Community, the three key elements involved in providing and enabling the study of sustainability (Owens, 2013). This programme involves embedding the doorways and the '4Cs' into the ethos of the school to create a holistic learning experience, in which geography has a central role to play (Catling, 2007; Chalkley *et al.*, 2009).

The 'eight doorways' and '4Cs' approaches can be augmented to include wider coverage of the issues around sustainability, by using them to encourage a focus in primary schools on the following aspects of the areas through which schools might become increasingly sustainable (DfE, 2012).

- Reduction of carbon in schools.
- Reduction of energy and water use in schools.
- Sustainable purchasing in schools.
- Reduction of waste in schools.
- Sustainable school travel.
- Sustainable school food and catering services.
- Engaging with biodiversity.
- Development of the global dimension in schools.

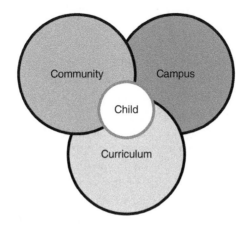

Figure 7.1   The '4Cs' (DfES, 2006b, p. 11)

Primary children are not necessarily well informed about such matters as energy resource use and concerns about it. For such reasons it is important to recognise the need to help develop their knowledge and understanding. This has led to the realisation that we need to encourage and facilitate children's increased interaction with and contribution to their environment and community. This is reflected in an increasing encouragement for schools to provide a focus for children's interaction with the local community (Boyd *et al.*, 2018). Through geographical studies of the local area, involvement in environmental schemes in school and locally in the community recycling, school garden initiatives, water conservation activities, introduction of solar power sources for energy, conserving local ecosystems, taking care of buildings and play areas features, encouraging reductions in travel journeys, and such like (AuSSI, 2010), children can be encouraged to connect again with and contribute to their community, both in and out of school. Likewise, the local community can become more fully involved in education for sustainability with classes and schools supporting curriculum and after-school initiatives and activities (Massey, 2012). This can lead to taking eco-school initiatives out into the community.

Research summary

Children's energy literacy

An investigation, using interviews and photo elicitation methods, of a group of 10–11-year-olds' energy literacy in New Zealand (Aguirre-Bielschowsky *et al.*, 2017) identified that while they were aware of the costs of electricity and that it was a finite resource, only half could name an energy source; their knowledge of energy production was weak. For many children, much of their learning was informal in source, disorganised and opportunistic, and discussions at home were rare, if at all, as they were at school. General awareness of environmental concerns was noted by children, but it was generally stimulated by media reports. A number of children learnt about energy through reading. The children were largely positive about energy saving, though many were not active in trying to promote this at home, indicating low agency, and were personally not particularly interested in conserving energy, most stating additionally that they were unsure how to do so. The authors concluded that introducing energy as a curriculum topic would help primary children to understand the connections between knowledge about energy production and use, approaches to energy conservation and how they could act to save energy. Teachers interviewed felt that primary children were capable of such understanding, and children and parents thought it should be a curriculum matter.

Creative and active approaches, using fieldwork, drama and role-play, and stories can be used to explore environmental and sustainability issues locally and with global topical and current events and concerns (Davis, 2015; Owens, 2017). Children might develop their own class (or even their school's) sustainability charter about how they use resources and behave in environmentally positive ways. Gardening provides a 'hands-on' approach to children engaging with natural resources, whether this is in an area of the nursery setting and/or school grounds or in a window planter (Woodhouse, 2017). There are many stories (see Appendix 2) that can be used to stimulate discussion of how we care for or mismanage, damage or enhance and develop local environments, from small areas of waste ground to local redevelopment projects. *Adam and Paradise Island* (Keeping, 1989) provides a stimulating tale about how inner urban children create a playground when theirs is blighted by a road development, while *Kenju's Forest* (Morimoto, 1990) examines the value of urban woodland. *The Little House by the Sea* (Blathwayt, 1992) considers how a derelict cottage can be reclaimed from its wildlife while respecting them, and Jeannie Baker's *Window* (2002) and *Belonging* (2008) show how environments change over time, and her *Where the Forest meets the Sea* (1989) helps us understand how we can look after environments.

Environmental well-being

Hayward (2012) argues that we seem often not to examine and take seriously children's views about what matters to them in and for the environment and that this can affect their sense of well-being. In part, this is the result of considering that education for sustainability is a 'good thing' and that often it seems to adopt a moralistic tone in schools, which is not without its critics (Standish, 2009, 2012; Selby and Kagawa, 2015). To an extent, this is because listening to children seriously is still emerging as we understand better that children are more informed and hold views that can be highly relevant to our teaching of geography, including at a young age, particularly where this relates to their perceptions and perspectives of the local environment, as well as in relation to global sustainability concerns (Catling and Martin, 2011; Boyd *et al.*, 2018). Geographical enquiry and philosophy for children offer approaches that engage children through the questions they ask and the methods of discussion and debate in response to these (see Chapter 4; Pickford *et al.*, 2013; Rowley and Lewis, 2003).

Environmental well-being (Catling, 2007; Collins and Foley, 2008; DfES, 2006a; Atkinson *et al.*, 2012) concerns our understanding of and state of happiness and contentment within our environment (Orr, 1991; Stone, 2009; Stone and Barlow, 2005; Goleman *et al.*, 2012), natural and built, and is underpinned by the concept of care (Noddings, 2005). Two criteria used to measure well-being are satisfaction with life and personal development (NEF, 2005). Many of the issues concerning environmental well-being lie in sustainability. For many people, the natural environment is a key factor in their contentment with life (Countryside Commission, 1997) and that engagement in it encourages better social ties and sense of community, improved physical and mental health, strengthened economic prospects, reduced crime rates, and enhanced children's play and learning.

This can, however, create the tension that the more we strive to search for and reconnect with nature, the greater our negative impact on the environment as we drive and fly to access it, holidaying often in modern facilities (NEF, 2005). We seem reluctant to reduce our choices and constrain our economic growth, although these do not seem to equate with well-being (Shah and Marks, 2004). Brown and Kasser (2005) noted that, when given the opportunity, children are keen to take greater responsibility ecologically and consciously, and show a more stable and contented state of mind when thinking that they are able to help and be effective. This is further reflected in the findings of an extensive review of England's primary education: *Where schools had started engaging children with global and local realities as aspects of their education they were noticeably more upbeat, and that the sense that 'we can do something about it' seemed to make all the difference* (Alexander and Hargreaves, 2007, p. 12).

It is undoubtedly our responsibility in this unsettled world to give children the opportunity to take ownership of their future and allow them to be active, effective citizens, with a role to play and a difference to make, not least to foster their sense of environmental well-being (Reynolds, 2014; Hayward, 2012). One approach to supporting children's well-being is the development of school and community gardens (Gaylie, 2011; Williams and Brown, 2012; Woodhouse, 2017; Bromley, 2017), where children co-operate not just in maintaining the nature and quality of a site with each other, but with older children and adults. As Hart (1997) notes, children value working with others; they do not simply want to take over, but to learn with and from others who are more informed and experienced. This way, they develop competence and independence, as well as becoming better informed and feeling that they are more in control. Undertaken through environmental activities, this fosters their self-esteem.

 In the classroom

Investigating waste

5–7-year-olds examined in their geography topic what happened to waste at home and in school. They identified the variety of types of waste produced at home and school, and surveyed classrooms and other parts of the school to see how much waste was produced over a week and what became of it. They considered what they found through the *4Rs*: *reduce, recycle, reuse, repair,* and added a *5th R*: *replace,* looking for more sustainable resources to use. They offered some ideas about changes that could be made in their own and other classes. They produced posters to encourage their ideas about the *5Rs,* which they placed around the school and used drama in an assembly to demonstrate changes in behaviour to support a sustainable environment.

Reflective task

There are many sustainability concerns and issues that we encounter on a daily basis, including refuse and waste disposal, access to clean water and to nutritious and sustaining food, providing shelter and hygiene, poverty and inequality, climate change and harsher weather, environmental degradation and rising demand for energy. Can you add to this list?

Choose one issue and use the Web to find out more about it. Try the Oxfam, ActionAid, Save the Children, Christian Aid, UNICEF, WWF or other aid agency websites. Consider what might be effective approaches to developing children's understanding and positive attitudes.

Practical task

In England, there has long been encouragement for walkers to consider how to act responsibly in the countryside. From the 1930s, there has been a Country Code in England. This is now called The Countryside Code (DEFRA, 2014). This states:

Respect – Protect – Enjoy

***Respect** other people*

- *Consider the local community and other people enjoying the outdoors*
- *Leave gates and property as you find them and follow paths unless wider access is available*

***Protect** the natural environment*

- *Leave no trace of your visit and take your litter home*
- *Keep dogs under effective control*

***Enjoy** the outdoors*

- *Plan ahead and be prepared*
- *Follow advice and local signs*

This is very helpful advice, which many walkers and others follow when in the country. It encourages a positive and thoughtful attitude and behaviour which is of benefit to everyone – those who live there and visitors.

(Continued)

(Continued)

Most people live and spend their time in urban environments, in their streets and buildings, as well as spending time in parks and perhaps playgrounds. But we do not seem to have an Urban Code for being outside or visiting places in urban areas.

Can you devise an Urban Code, or more helpfully involve a class of children in developing an Urban Code? What would be its key words and the most important matters for people to do? You might introduce children to The Countryside Code and discuss this as a prompt and pointer to what the children might consider including in their Urban Code. It will be a way to help them understand the term 'urban' as well as to think about attitudes and behaviour in our towns, cities and villages.

Sustainability, hope and the futures dimension

Children want to be involved in doing something to help improve life and the environment. Such an approach reflects a sense of the future and being a positive part of it. Huckle (1990) argued that:

> If we are not to overwhelm pupils with the world's problems, we should teach in a spirit of optimism. We should build environmental success stories into our curriculum and develop awareness of sources of hope in the world [.]

(Huckle, 1990, p. 159)

Hicks (2014) noted that the concepts of hope and optimism are often overlooked but echoed Huckle's sentiment. Children can be confronted with images, sounds, soundbites, videos, tweets, posts, messages, instagrams, news, fake news, alternative facts and much else frequently, but these messages are rarely steeped in hope or optimism – rather the opposite – and it can prove to be overwhelming. For every bad news story, we ought really to find good news to counterbalance it. We have a responsibility to the children we teach to show them how we can succeed in a sustainable way as stewards of our environment. Indeed, there are good news stories about where conditions and communities are improving and engaging with the natural world, which facilitate people's positive values and attitudes (Turner, 2008; HRH Prince of Wales et al., 2010; Willson, 2015; Hicks, 2016). It is this world that we can begin to shape through a 'Futures' dimension in sustainability teaching.

Education incorporating the futures dimension is beneficial. In an education where the majority of time and consideration is spent looking at and analysing the past and the present, it is increasingly pertinent to enable children to consider the future and begin to understand how they might plan for and shape it. Aside from science, where the future is often concerned with developments in technology, and science fiction, which is concerned with the fantastical, geography is the key subject that enables young people to engage with their future and consider how they might shape the world in which they would like to live. Hicks (2002) argues that the future is 'the missing dimension' in the curriculum, and that if we are to live sustainably, we must give children the opportunity to consider their future. Geography is ideally placed to provide this, using its enquiry-based learning and real-world problem-solving approaches.

Hicks (2002, p. xiii) identifies three different kind of futures:

- *The possible future:* what could happen, considering all eventualities.
- *The probable future:* what is most likely to happen.
- *The preferred future:* the one we would most like to happen, but that will take a conscious effort, through planning and vision.

Children should be encouraged to explore different environmental futures and be able to discuss them openly and safely. They often feel unsure about their future. Given the regular diet of despondency via the media, this is not surprising. Children think a great deal about the future, but are rarely given the chance to discuss or explore it and, even less often, the empowerment to feel that they might be able to do something to influence it. There are many ways to encourage children to consider the future and at different scales. They can be encouraged to think about how things are changing locally, nationally and globally for other people and themselves, and project their ideas into the future. Issues of environmental change and impact and of sustainability provide obvious focuses for this approach, about what could happen, might occur and they would prefer to happen.

It is important to emphasise that change is not just about what happens to us but is also about how we contribute to change, how we can affect change and what its impact might be. This can feed effectively into geography topics – for example, considering both the immediate impact of a new shopping development and the long-term implications locally, of continuing development at such scales and about how local people, including children, can make their voices heard. In investigating places near and far, we can consider how they can and might change in the future and of what value positive and helpful changes might be.

Reflective task

Consider ways in which geography in your class or school curriculum can help to develop children's well-being and encourage them to think about their future and how they want to live in their adult world. What do they value about the environment they live in? How can they help to manage and maintain or develop it as well as improve it for everyone to benefit from it? What type of classroom activity would you organise to help children investigate and discuss this?

In the classroom

Exploring sustainable futures

A class of 9–11-year-olds was given some graphic illustrations of possible future worlds from Hicks's (2012) book: *Sustainable School, Sustainable Futures*. These were drawn to show themes such as travel and transport, food and farming, energy and water, inclusion and participation, and so on in a possible future world. The children discussed these, the positive and negative aspects of them, and were asked what they would like and what would challenge them about living in such scenarios. They were encouraged to select a theme or consider a community and plan for how they would like it to be. They used a range of different media to portray these: some made models; others drew maps and plans, and annotated them to explain the scenario; and other groups made up a drama about what it might be like to live in such circumstances. Both the discussions and the outcomes helped the children to think deeply about their preferred futures in a realistic as well as optimistic way.

Key points

This chapter has:

- considered the key concepts of environmental impact and sustainability;
- noted how sustainability can be incorporated into the fabric of primary schools;

- identified examples for consideration in the classroom;
- noted the connections between environmental well-being and sustainability;
- introduced the role of a futures dimension.

Moving on

Develop your reading about sustainability and environmental change and its impact, and consider how you might develop this as part of your geography curriculum.

Further reading

The following books provide useful follow-up reading about the topics considered in this chapter.

Davis, J (ed.) (2015) *Young Children and the Environment.* (2nd edn) Port Melbourne, Victoria: Cambridge University Press.

Dolan A (2019) *Powerful Primary Geography: A toolkit for 21st century learning.* Abingdon: Routledge.

Grigg, R and Hughes, S (2013) *Teaching Primary Humanities.* Harlow: Pearson.

Halocha, J (2012) *The Primary Teacher's Guide to Geography.* Witney: Scholastic/ Book End.

Martin, F (2006) *Teaching Geography in Primary Schools: Learning How to Live in the World.* Cambridge: Chris Kington.

Martin, F and Owens, P (2008) *Caring for our World: A Practical Guide to ESD for Ages 4–8.* Sheffield: Geographical Association.

Nolet, V (2016) *Educating for Sustainability: Principles and Practices for Teachers.* New York: Routledge.

Pike, S (2016) *Learning Primary Geography: Ideas and Inspiration from Classrooms.* London: Routledge.

Reynolds, R (2014) *Teaching Humanities and Social Sciences in the Primary School.* (3rd edn) Melbourne: Oxford University Press.

Wals, A and Corcoran, P (eds) (2012) *Learning for Sustainability in Times of Accelerating Change.* Wageningen, the Netherlands: Wageningen Educational Publishers.

Useful websites

Australian Education for Sustainability Alliance: www.educationforsustainability.org. au/policy-resources/

Australian Sustainable Schools Initiative: www.environment.gov.au/education/aussi
Carbon Kids: www.csiro.au/resources/CarbonKids.html
EcoSchools: www.keepbritaintidy.org/ecoschools/
Geographical Association: www.geography.org.uk
Living Greener: www.livinggreener.gov.au
Oxfam Education: www.oxfam.org.uk/education/
UNICEF: www.unicef.org/agenda2030/
World Wide Fund for Nature: www.panda.org

CHAPTER 8

GEOGRAPHY AND SOCIAL JUSTICE

Citizenship, equity and controversial issues

  Chapter objectives

This chapter enables you to:

- understand the meaning of social justice and appreciate children's learning about it in primary school;
- recognise the connections and interrelationships between sustainability, citizenship, controversial issues and environmental geography;
- recognise that geography is an effective and appropriate subject for teaching about equity and social responsibility;
- realise that there are a variety of geography topics that explore matters of social justice and equity;
- appreciate that learning about matters of social justice involves examining controversial issues and dilemmas.

Introduction

Geography is not a detached study. Geography is ethically informed, concerned and focused. It relates at all times to what is happening in the lives of people and the places and environments around us and worldwide. This is important in geographical education in primary schools (Catling, 2003). Connections with social justice, equity and citizenship, and the controversial issues that tend to be raised when studying them are essential in geographical education to help children recognise and take greater responsibility for their places, the environment and the future. This involves considering matters of social justice and equity in the ways in which they impact through geographical contexts on people's lives. In itself, this is an area of controversy, and it needs to be taught sensitively and inclusively, allowing primary children a sense of ownership and participation in their school, community and environment, as well as developing their awareness of such concerns in the world and an understanding of why they happen.

Values are part of our cultural and social make-up (Edwards, 2016). Geography informs us about the world in which we live, locally, regionally and globally, and it helps shape our values about our living in the world, about how we use resources, and about how we consider and look after our planet. If we consider that we, our neighbours and other peoples should be treated fairly and well, it would seem incumbent on us to treat all others just as positively. This reflects our values. By values we mean the personal, social and cultural codes that influence the ways in which we live in our communities. These may be values such as fairness, thoughtfulness for others, respect for all people, care for our neighbourhood and other environments, and our sense of identity, be this regional, national or global. How we perceive ourselves and our relationships to others and the world – our concerns (or the lack of them) for people, places and the environment – affects how we act and how we are seen by others. Cox (2017) states that

> *from a socio-cultural perspective, children develop values as they live their lives in everyday settings and in schools, as they learn how to act and who to be [.] constructing meaning as they engage in the activities (imbued with values) of the social world around them [.].*

(pp. 375–6)

Through their geographical studies children are able to explore and develop their values concerning such aspects of their lives and places as their school and local area, as well as the other places they engage with. Such values are fostered through their interactions with their family, peers and familiar places, as well as their schooling. The values they take up underpin their development of citizenship.

The relationship between geography and citizenship is one way in which children are able to examine, consider and develop (or reject) values. Exploring matters of equity and social justice through geographical contexts provides another basis for considering their values and the values of others. These are considered before the significance of teaching about controversial issues in geography is explored.

Geography and citizenship

Geography's big idea of environmental impact and sustainability links directly with citizenship. Citizenship provides children with opportunities to examine, and possibly be involved in activities as a group member, through which they can examine social and environmental matters, issues and problems, enabling them to consider and identify likely outcomes of relevance to their own and others' lives. This serves to strengthen and enhance both geographical and citizenship learning (Boyle-Baise and Zevin, 2014), though it is not an uncontroversial area (Hartung, 2017).

In the classroom

Investigating a local community issue

A mid-western USA elementary school was committed to community enhancement and environmental stewardship. Selected groups of 8–9 and 9–10-year-olds in its classes investigated various matters pertinent to their community. One context and topic for both sets of children was the town's population decline. The 8–9-year-olds examined the local facilities and services and their built environment, using fieldwork and their mobile phones, to identify evidence of depopulation and emigration. They identified a core cause as being local poverty, which they outlined in a presentation to parents and community members. The 9–10-year-olds contacted a number of experts and obtained information from a wide range of sources, including a food bank, housing officials and youth networks, to understand better what was happening to their town. They interviewed the experts using prepared questions, taking digital notes. This led them to propose ways in which they thought local depopulation could be tackled in the community, about which they also made a presentation. The school's approach illustrates a way

(Continued)

(Continued)

in which a matter of concern for the local community can be investigated by primary children in the context of civic action, working through place-based education on a geography topic of local significance (Morris, 2017).

Citizenship or civics education, depending on the national term used, is important in many countries. As a curriculum subject, it can take a number of forms, including helping primary children understand what it is. For example, in Australia citizenship is described as *the legal relationship between an individual and a state*. Citizenship may well include *being a citizen of social, religious, political or community groups, locally, nationally and globally*. This implies that such group membership *carries with it a sense of belonging or identity that includes rights and responsibilities, duties and privileges [which] [.] are guided by the agreed values and mutual obligations required for active participation in the group*. It is underpinned by *social values and community involvement* and *participation and representation* (ACARA, 2012b, p. 2). Thus, citizenship is civic, social and political, all of which connect intimately with geography.

Not all countries include citizenship education in their primary curriculum. England, for instance, has no statutory requirement to teach citizenship in primary schools. This means that it has become increasingly important for geography, and subjects such as history, to adopt this vital role. This subject role reflects that primary schools around the world recognise the importance of including citizenship education, even where it is not a compulsory curriculum component. Many nations have similar interpretations of citizenship and what it should entail for younger children. This is illustrated by the 'wordle' in Figure 8.1, drawn from a range of national citizenship curricula (the size of the word represents the frequency with which it is mentioned in statements about citizenship education). Aspects pertinent in primary geography are involved, including social and community contexts, the neighbourhood and environment, responsibility, and global and development contexts, as well as experience, activity and justice.

In geography, citizenship is considered in local and global contexts. The focus is about helping primary children to become increasingly aware of and responsibly thoughtful in relation to people's lives, communities and the environment, wherever these are in the world (Young with Cummins, 2002). Geography and citizenship education together help develop younger children's knowledge and understanding, values, and attitudes and skills. There are various opportunities to develop children's awareness as citizens in their local and national communities (Osler and Starkey, 2005; Collins, 2008; Littledyke *et al.*, 2009; Hartung, 2017). The range of mutual interests

Figure 8.1   A 'wordle' representing citizenship content in primary schools around the world

between geography and citizenship enables children to consider the responsibilities that everyone, including themselves, has in every community (Boyle-Baise and Zevin, 2014; Martusewicz, *et al.*, 2015). Guidance for citizenship education in English primary schools (DfEE/QCA, 1999), when it was encouraged in the 2000s, noted several aspects to develop (see box below). These were set out in relation to:

- identifying likes and dislikes, fairness or unfairness, right and wrong;
- considering social, environmental and moral dilemmas;
- researching, discussing and debating issues, problems and events;
- sharing opinions and explaining views on issues, and making choices and decisions;
- resolving differences by looking for alternatives.

Mutual aspects of geography and citizenship

Geography and citizenship education working together help primary children to develop their awareness, appreciation and understanding about the following.

- Involvement in communities.
- The range of jobs carried out by people in places.

(Continued)

(Continued)

- What improves and harms the local natural and built environment.
- How resources can be allocated in different ways and how these choices affect individuals, the community and the sustainability of the environment.
- Knowledge of different people's needs and responsibilities, and that these can sometimes conflict with each other.
- Respect for differences and similarities between people, and the realisation that they arise from certain factors, including cultural, ethnic, racial and religious diversity, gender and (dis)ability.
- How the media present information selectively and create images (positively and critically) about people, places and environments.
- The role of voluntary, community and pressure groups.
- The decision-making process affecting local decisions.
- Topical environmental and place issues as they affect people.
- Different people's responses to environmental and place changes and issues, and their impact on them.
- Interdependence, the world as a global community, and challenges affecting the world.

 Reflective task

There are evident links that can be made between geography and citizenship education in relation to local area and geographical studies, in wider environmental geography, and with sustainability.

Consider and note what possibilities there are from your reading of Chapters 5, 6 and 7.

When you read Chapters 10, 11, 12 and 13, consider also the links between geography and citizenship education. For instance, geography, citizenship and the global dimension interplay through the concept of global citizenship, which is discussed in Chapter 13.

Equity, social justice and geography

The meaning of equity is to be fair and balanced. It implies impartiality in considering situations that appear inequitable, by drawing on principles of fairness when making judgements. It is allied with the concept of justice.

For example, the sense of social justice is undermined where there is a lack of equitable access to a resource such as education. Equity demands fairness and equal opportunity for all, fully supported by human rights and its concomitant responsibilities (Catling, 2003; Kenreich, 2013). The UN *Convention on the Rights of the Child* (UNICEF, 1989) states unequivocally several essentially geographical dimensions that directly affect children's lives. These include access to a home, to sanitation and clean water, to a healthy diet and an adequate standard of living, to good health and welfare, and to play and leisure. The *Convention* refers to access to education, to freedom of thought and expression, and to protection from exploitation and deprivation of liberty. It talks of giving children a voice and agency in matters that affect their lives (Catling, 2014a). Teaching children about equity and social justice issues is crucial if they are to begin to and develop their understanding of the many issues and complexities of global equity and human rights (Catling, 1993).

Learning about social justice in primary schools and geography education is pertinent in a number of aspects of geography, such as access to the facilities and services in a local area, the quality of environments and opportunities to use transport to make journeys to visit other places. Investigating such topics should not only consider what is provided and available, but also who has access and can make use of such provision. These are matters of equity and opportunity. They may relate to decisions made within the family or by local authorities or private companies, which are influenced by perceptions and information about people's needs, levels of wealth and attitudes. Differential access to services and facilities may be the result of discrimination, poverty and lack of power to argue for change and improvement. Social justice in geography teaching concerns helping children to begin to understand that the locality and the wider world are not necessarily equal or fair places, and to challenge the ways in which children see people and places – for instance, by enabling them to recognise and confront stereotyping and bias. Taking a broad rather than narrow approach, engaging with matters of social justice helps to develop children's understanding of the world around them and about elsewhere (Kenreich, 2013; Paren, 2005; Dolan, 2019).

This is not to say that social justice in geography is not without its critics and challenges (Standish, 2012; Kenreich, 2013). One concern is that the focus of teaching may be imbalanced, not especially developing children's knowledge and understanding of a topic because it focuses more on promoting their, often preferred, attitudes to particular societal and environmental issues. Another is that such topics have more to do with making geography 'relevant', or seemingly agreeable, to children rather than examining what children need to know to understand it. A third is that the emphasis may move to focusing on skills and critical thinking rather than on examining the topic thoroughly using these capabilities. While it can be that the social justice focus may be over-emphasised, these criticisms can mislead. Good geography teaching with primary age children ensures that to understand the topics they investigate and learn about, children engage with the knowledge and information relevant to the topic, that they use their enquiry skills to investigate the topic, and that they learn to use evidence critically to examine and justify views that they might come to and values that they may espouse. Misuse of the 'relevance' argument is certainly unhelpful, because geography is about the world today and about what affects people's lives, places, environments and the ways in which we construct and use spaces, and how space affects us. By definition, geography is a vitally relevant subject at every age.

To explore aspects of primary geography, social justice and equity, several topics are considered. These are mobility access for people, the nature and effects of migration, the purpose of Fairtrade and children's preparation to face natural hazards wherever they live.

Mobility access

One social justice focus for study in primary geography is the ease and difficulty of mobility access in the local environment for all who live there. This encompasses particularly being able to 'walk' the streets, enter buildings and use local services, such as buses, for those who find walking difficult or move around using wheelchairs. Built environments have evolved over many years and have been largely constructed for those who simply walked from place to place. Little thought was given to those who had difficulty walking or had to use a wheelchair. For those who pushed a child's buggy, or who used walking sticks or crutches in the short term, the inconvenience and difficulties of pavements and building entrances went unconsidered until recently. The curbs on pavements made crossing roads almost impossible for wheelchair users, as did getting on to buses in which there was no room for a wheelchair or pushchair to fit. Society was relatively unconcerned about such inequalities. Much has changed in recent years, with sloped bobble-surface crossing places on pavements that everyone can use, including those with sight limitations or loss. Public transport is largely readily accessible with buses that lower their entrances or have ramps to allow wheelchair and pushchair access, and with designated spaces on board for these. There can be difficulties accessing rail transport at some stations and on some trains. In many countries there is greater inclusivity of those making local non-car journeys. Indeed, for drivers with disabilities, parking spaces are provided for their use with space to get in and out of vehicles – although there are members of the public who do not have a disability badge who use these spaces because they find them convenient rather than necessary. Inequity in the locality can still arise through thoughtlessness or selfishness, something that primary age children notice. Children can discuss what they have seen in their neighbourhood and undertake field-work to examine the patterns of good and poor access to open places and buildings (Catling *et al.*, 2006; Kitchen and Freundschuh, 2000).

In Chapter 14, the Tables on pp. 435–40 provide an approach to planning a geographical investigation in the local area about this geographical issue. In initial class discussion, children can provide examples of places that are more or less accessible to those with mobility needs to initiate such a study. By undertaking fieldwork they can investigate where there is good practice locally and where improvements are needed. They might talk to residents of a care home locally, or to other residents they know or meet who walk slowly, are infirm or use wheelchairs about their mobility access in the local area, to gather their experiences and views to compare with their own. From their investigations children can consider how the local environment is inclusive for all its residents and visitors, and discuss the social justice concerns that might arise from what they find out.

Primary schools were built to be accessible to ordinarily 'able-bodied' children, but in very many schools this has improved greatly, particularly in newly built schools. The oldest schools can be the most problematic if there has not been investment so that they serve all younger children in their community, such as by installing lift provision to upper floors. While school grounds have usually been the most accessible places for everyone in a school site, there have been developments, such as adventure playgrounds or sunken areas only reached by steps, which may not be fully inclusive. Primary children can investigate their school grounds to assess and make judgements about the accessibility of their grounds and buildings for wheel-chair users or a child with a foot or leg in plaster, and they can suggest improvements (Catling, 2005d).

Migration

An alternative geography and social justice topic concerns the location and movements of people: migration. This may focus on in-country urban and rural movement, or concern the cross-national emigration or immigration of people. In this context, one equity issue concerns child migration, which is a continuing and considerable reality and concern, frequently caused by destructive war and insurgency, but also the result of natural and human-made disasters, such as earthquakes, floods, drought and wildfires, as well as by poverty and the lack of current and future opportunities for work (Adams and Kirova, 2006; Ensor and Gozdziak, 2010; Mapp, 2011; Minujin and Nandy, 2012; Swamfield, 2013; Veale and Donà, 2014; Hunner-Kreisel and Bohne, 2016; Dolan, 2019). Children are sent abroad by some families to escape such situations, especially when homes are lost and in the belief that they may have access to a better life. Even primary school-age children can find themselves travelling from one country to another either with their family, with minders or alone.

Migration affects many children, not only those who move from one country to another. Within nation, within region and within town, migration occurs for many families and children for a variety of reasons. These moves may be caused by parents changing jobs or the need or desire for new accommodation. As with international migration, perhaps as a refugee, it may be a challenging and difficult experience coming to a new place and getting to know new people and a new neighbourhood. One way to examine an issue such as migration with primary children is through stories (Dolan, 2014; Hope, 2017). Imaginative picture books – for example, *Azzi in Between* (Garland, 2012), *The Journey* (Sanna, 2016) and *My Name is not Refugee* (Milner, 2017), are one source about international migration to use. There are information books about migrants and refugees – for example, Roberts and Kai, 2016; Rosen and Young, 2016. However, true-story picture books such as *Hamid's Story* (Glynne and Senior, 2016) and *Ali's Story* (Maldonado and Glynne, 2015) provide for primary children's insights into real families' reasons for moving countries, means of travel and settling into a new place.

Arriving at and settling into a new nighbourhood and city can be a scary place when all is new, particularly when it involves encountering a new language and unfamiliar street signs, shops, people, school and home. This is well illustrated in one text-free story of learning to live in a new place, *Here I am* (Kim and Sanchez, 2014). It takes time for children, as anyone, to develop familiarity, and it is not always easy to do – nor is it straightforward for those who may always have lived in the area, as is described in *The Silence Seeker* (Morley and Pearce, 2009) when there are new arrivals living next door. It takes time for local residents to get to know and understand migrants to their area. These are important matters for primary age children to discuss, both to understand the situation of a new member of their class, school and neighbourhood, and to help that child (and family) feel welcomed and settle into the area.

 Research summary

'They're leaving home': a role-play study

James (2017) investigated the use of role play to introduce children to the issue of migration from war-torn Syria. She identified that teachers were apprehensive about teaching such topics. Working with her class of 7–8-year-olds, she 'storied' the background to the war and that a family wished to move but that not all family members could leave. Groups of children role-played members of the family to decide who should go and for which reasons; they showed their capacity to take up particular roles, such as mother, father and different children. To each other they had to justify and respond to questions and challenges about their rationales and arguments for their decisions. James noted the criticality in the children's discussions and quality of the arguments they made that showed their capability to relate to real-life circumstances and to have strong emotional empathy with family members, not least because they were family members themselves. Having to pack in just a few minutes focused the group 'families' on the urgency of the situation and the impact of enforced separation, including not knowing if or when they would meet again. She found that through role play young children were able to explore different and new perspectives that might not appear in group or class discussions, that the children developed a deeper understanding about this aspect of the world's geography, and that it focused their thinking about the ethics of respect and tolerance in the context of migration. She wrote that *Geography is crucial in this, because it helps pupils become well-rounded individuals with balanced opinions* (p. 11). She demonstrated to staff in the school that role play is a valuable approach to examining controversial issues in class.

In the classroom

Enquiring into migration

A class of 8–9-year-olds were introduced to a topic on migration through the children's novel, *A Bear Called Paddington* (Bond, 1958/2014). Taking the starting point of Paddington's curious arrival and his label saying 'Please look after this Bear. Thank you', children commented on what it might have been like for Paddington to have travelled from 'darkest Peru' to the UK and how he might have felt while sitting on his case at Paddington Station. This led to groups discussing how they felt when they visited somewhere new and led to disclosures by some children about their own moves into the locality. As

(Continued)

(Continued)

the story unfolded, many children shared their experiences of coming to a new place, about home, shops, roads, play areas, making new friends and the responses of local people. While Paddington, happily, talks fluent English, five children in the class told of their learning a new language while continuing out-of-school to use their native language. A few parents offered to and did tell of their own experiences in moving into the area, what they found good and difficult in moving and settling in.

The class used a variety of sources to investigate migration to begin to understand the range of reasons causing people to migrate and what it can be like to arrive and settle somewhere new, what might be familiar and what different. In doing this, the children considered what a family moving into their area would find helpful to know, and they produced information leaflets that the school could give to new families whose child or children joined the school. What they gained from this topic was awareness that many of them had moved from one place to another and could be called 'migrants', about reasons for migration, some information about where in the world migration was significant and why, that there was much to learn when coming to a new place, and that there was real value for a community to which new people came. They developed a strong sense that people should be welcomed, treated equitably and given time to settle.

Fairtrade

Another important geographical topic with an equity dimension is trade (see Chapter 6). A study of trade with primary children would focus on how countries, regions and local areas produce, sell and transport cultivated and manufactured goods within and between themselves. It concerns the commercial activities we engage in when we shop in order to eat regularly and for other items we need. However, trade and commerce need to be understood in their local and international contexts. In communities people have different incomes, as do people in different countries. Indeed, nations have very different levels of income and expenditure. Trade within a country and particularly with other nations generates a country's wealth, but this depends on the value and the amount of goods sold – that is, what others are prepared to pay for them. Very many types of goods are traded between nations, in particular food, clothes and other manufactured goods such as cars, computers and other technology products. Many services are also traded, such as financial and hotel services.

While there is wealth and poverty in all nations, it is not evenly distributed and where countries find it difficult to have high prices for many of their goods and services, their national income will be lower than in those nations that can command high prices. Gross National Product (GNP) is a country's overall income, effectively stating how rich a country is. Some nations have high levels of GNP, such as many in Western Europe, and are classed as More Economically Developed Countries (MEDCs). Other nations with lower GNP, such as many of the countries in the continent of Africa, are known as Less Economically Developed Countries (LEDCs). High numbers of people living in LEDCs with very low levels of GNP tend to have low incomes and may be more affected by poverty, even though the prices of everyday goods that people need, such as foodstuffs, in their country also may be relatively low. It has long been felt that many people around the world receive too low an income for the work they do and to meet their needs, and that this inequity needs to be addressed. One way to tackle this is through increasing the price of goods, but international competition for trade undermines this.

One initiative introduced to help change these circumstances has been the Fairtrade Foundation, which is aimed at aiding poor workers living in LEDCs – whose incomes are often barely enough to sustain even subsistence living – to receive a decent income on which they can live reasonably and to ensure that they have employment rights and are working in fair conditions. The purpose of Fairtrade is to create for workers in agricultural and other industries and businesses, situations in which they are treated equitably as a matter of social justice: a fair day's pay for a fair day's work in their national context.

Fairtrade is not simply about developing trade; it has an ethical purpose. It has developed for several reasons (Murray and Raynolds, 2007, p. 5), which are to:

- make consumers aware that they can have a positive impact on producers through buying Fairtrade goods and can help to discourage producers from exploitative practices;
- develop market access and better prices for their goods for producers, with stronger producer organisations and consistency and continuity in trading;
- foster partnerships in trade, encouraging transparency, respect and dialogue;
- support new opportunities for producers, especially indigenous peoples and women;
- give protection to children from exploitation by producers and others;
- encourage, through campaigns, improved international trade practices;
- promote greater economic security, improved environmental practices and social justice by protecting the human rights of those engaged in fair trade production.

In Chapter 6, in the boxes on pp.178–180, a summary of Fairtrade and a classroom example about investigating trade were provided. Fairtrade has developed strongly, to the extent that a wide range of Fairtrade goods can be found in very many shops, and it has attracted many consumers to look out for Fairtrade products, from chocolates to clothes, to flowers, to fruit. It has also encouraged some companies to ensure that they sell fairly traded goods, negotiated outside the Fairtrade Foundation remit. Fairtrade has had and continues to have challenges, including concerns about the scale of producers and the scale of trade needed to remain viable, competition in increasingly competitive markets because Fairtrade goods can be more expensive, the need to meet increasingly stringent food safety requirements in higher income nations, and the roles of Fairtrade producers in leading and creating their own organisations to promote Fairtrade, taking consumers with them.

A further challenge has arisen, which concerns the transportation of Fairtrade goods, a good number of which (as with other producers) need to reach markets speedily while travelling major distances by sea or air. This raises the concern about the impact of carbon footprints – that is, what it costs the Earth to transport goods (Berners-Lee, 2010). This is a concern that applies across the production of goods – in effect, to all trade, not only for Fairtrade products. It raises a dilemma about buying several Fairtrade goods, since those that need to reach markets quickly, such as flowers, are usually flown to destinations around the world. Air transport is increasing, driven by both goods transport and tourism, which raises carbon emissions in the atmosphere, and this looks likely to increase further. It is a conundrum to which there is no ready answer. If consumers are more thoughtful about the environmental impact of air flight, it may well have a negative effect on Fairtrade producers. How do you encourage one while discouraging the other when they appear to be mutually interdependent? Social justice issues are not necessarily straightforward or easy to resolve. They raise moral questions that we have to make decisions about. These are important in primary geography, as across the curriculum, and children can be involved in such debates, employing, for instance, a Philosophy for Children dialogic approach in debate (see Chapter 4).

     Reflective task

Many shops stock and sell Fairtrade goods, produced by farms and companies that have been certified by the Fairtrade Foundation (www.fairtrade.org.uk), and they can use its logo to show that they meet its criteria for fair trade. These producers own their products and the social premium these generate. They decide for themselves their priorities and ways to improve income and undertake further poverty reduction.

There have been moves by at least one UK national supermarket chain to introduce its own 'fairly traded' label which is run directly by the company and not by the local fair trade network. Concerns have been raised about the control the company might exert over priorities to tackle poverty and challenges in their supply chains. It has been contentious.

Information about this debate can be found at websites such as:

www.about.sainsburys.co.uk/discover-more/fairly-traded

www.fairtrade.org.uk/Media-Centre/News/May-2017/Statement-on-Fairtrade-withdrawal-from-Sainsbury's-partnership

www.telegraph.co.uk/news/2017/06/02/not-fair-trade-sainsburys-misleading-shoppers-replacing-fairtrade/

www.change.org/sainsbury-s-don-t-ditch-fairtrade/responses/39511

The Fairtrade Foundation has supported some commercial companies where it is evident that ethical and sustainable sourcing of a product meets its principles for producers, though these are not validated by the organisation.

Consider your own stance about products being labelled 'fair trade' and 'fairly traded'. What might the differences be between these two terms? Would you want to know that goods you buy have been certified by the Fairtrade Foundation and/or are identified as 'fairly traded' as stated by a particular producer? What would you expect happens in the trade relationship?

What activities would you plan to undertake with a class in the 7 to 11/12 age range to investigate and debate 'fair trade' and 'fairly traded' goods? What would be the matters about equity and social justice that you would want the children to become aware of and begin to grasp?

Preparing for natural hazards

We have noted that primary children can be introduced to circumstances in which social justice and equity are fundamental aspects of such human geography topics as mobility access, migration and fair trade. In the context of environmental geography, another topic is the impact of flooding and floods on a landscape and people's lives. Across the world floods occur frequently. In some cases they are predictable with the seasons, while in others unexpected and sudden. Tropical storms during rainy seasons take many forms, from the annual monsoon that affects areas in India and Bangladesh, to the cyclones affecting countries such as the Philippines and Australia, to the storms that develop into hurricanes as they cross the Atlantic Ocean into the Caribbean and affect the island states there as well as the coasts of Mexico and the USA. These bring wind and rain damage often alongside flooding. Floods occur in temperate parts of the world, such as Western Europe, where they may be localised due to a particularly torrential storm and for which the local area may be or may not be prepared. The social justice concern is how well supported the people who live in such places are when storms strike, whether they have several days' notice to prepare for a storm's arrival or none because of its suddenness. In whichever situation, there is the need for resources for rescue and shelter, and to help people rebuild their homes and lives (see Chapter 6, pp.185–186).

Those parts of the world that suffer the normality of or recognise the potential of such events – and of other hazards such as earthquakes, tsunamis and volcanic eruptions – have developed systems and resources to aid people in distress. At times, the impact of such natural events is truly devastating and these places can take years to recover, while in other situations it may only take months to rebuild infrastructure, homes, lives and communities. International organisations, such as the United Nations alongside many others, have worked with government ministries, national bodies and local leaders in countries and communities in regions where natural hazards are a constant threat in order to prepare responses (Shaw and Oikawa, 2014). Until relatively recently, children's voices were not an element in such considerations. Given their work in many of these areas, non-governmental organisations such as UNESCO and Save the Children have not only argued for the agency of children in preparing for hazardous events, but have sought their views about their knowledge of these situations and their potential roles (Catling, 2014a). This supports the cases made for children to be involved in home, school and community preparedness for such eventualities, however small the chance of a major natural incident might be; it involves their lives as much as those of adults.

From studies of children's perspectives in several parts of the world – for example, on the effects of climate change – it has become clear that both younger and older children want to be involved. These views are found among children around the world, recorded, for instance, in Western Europe, southern Asia and in the Pacific-rim nations (Catling, 2014a). They wish to contribute their ideas and agency, not least because they may well have experienced the effects of violent storms, flooding and other natural hazards. For instance, in Japan and the western USA schoolchildren regularly practise earthquake drills. Those children who live in areas of the world affected by such hazards develop some knowledge of what is happening and want to understand better these events through their schooling (Smawfield, 2013). Children living in areas that are affected at times by very strong winds and local floods wish to know more about the causes, impacts and consequences, in such countries as the UK and Australia. Through their experience and from news reports and social media, increasingly children know about what the emergency and other services do, but often they wish to be better informed about how they themselves might respond in such situations, not least by contributing to preparations, drills and responses. In other words, primary children desire to participate in becoming aware and in making themselves ready, rather than simply by being told and expected to respond (Catling, 2014a). Primary age children are making a social justice and equity argument for inclusion in understanding and dealing with hazardous events as well as in preparing contingencies, such as for clean water, sanitation, sustenance and actions to take and where to go – being treated as active and equal participants. The obvious place to focus such preparation is in the home, but this can best be initiated in primary school. This provides a real context for interrelating geography and citizenship education, and an approach socially and culturally through inclusion of all the people in a community. It is an evident aspect of geographical education for all school-age children.

In the classroom

Flood alert!

As a result of local flooding, following torrential rain across the town's river catchment area, a whole school topic was introduced by one primary school the following term to investigate the causes and consequences of the floods and of flood events in other parts of the world. The school itself escaped direct flooding, but floodwaters did reach its boundary and the school was closed for several days and used as a temporary shelter. As the culmination of their work, the six classes were tasked with drawing up plans for an evacuation of the school were such an event to occur which threatened to engulf the school. While the youngest children's classes examined what they should do, where they should go and how the school would contact their parents, classes of older children investigated the lie of the school's grounds to identify where and at what rate water would rise towards the building, put forward proposals about how this could be slowed and developed a

(Continued)

(Continued)

sequence of actions to be undertaken in the school, including contact details for emergency services, so that everybody could be evacuated safely. Each class made presentations to the school and its governors. The outcome was the development of a policy and action plan for flood protection and evacuation, to which the children contributed. The 'Flood Preparation Plan' included actions to preserve many of the school's resources from water damage. The children felt that they had direct involvement and were equal members of the school team in drawing up the procedures to help safeguard their school and all who studied and worked there.

When dealing with concepts such as equity, human rights, social duties and responsibilities, citizenship and related issues, it is inevitable that different opinions and beliefs, values and attitudes will be expressed by children. It can be difficult, given the complexity of global, national and local situations, to be entirely objective and impartial. The following section on teaching about controversial issues discusses such difficulties and suggests ways these may be tackled in the primary classroom.

Controversial issues

Woolley (2010, p.2) states that *a controversial issue is one that presents a challenge and stimulates debate; it involves no universally held or fixed point of view. Almost any issue can feel controversial when people hold different beliefs, views or values.* Roberts (2013, p. 114) notes that *a controversial issue is a matter about which individuals and groups disagree.* She identifies four kinds of controversial issue, noting (a) that controversy arises where evidence is not sufficient to support an agreed explanation, such as why parking may be considered a problem; (b) controversy can arise because there are different interpretations about a situation, such as about the need for more housing in an area; (c) different views and opinions about what should be done in a particular circumstance can lead to controversy – for example, locating a new shopping mall in a particular part of a city centre; and (d) when ethical or moral dilemmas suggested by a particular issue lead to controversy – for instance, an argument to build on farmland may be thought an unavoidable decision by some people, but seen as environmental destruction by others who see it costing long-term jobs and reducing agricultural production, even though small scale. Roberts argues that studying geographical topics that include aspects of controversy helps children to recognise that not all problems or challenges have straightforward solutions that everyone can agree on; that it is important to examine evidence carefully and to challenge arguments; that it is essential to recognise the values that underpin proposals and viewpoints, and to look critically at these to clarify what they are; and that investigating issues to understand why they are controversial engages children since they can see how such concerns might affect themselves and other people. Teaching about controversial issues challenges us, but it is vitally important to do.

Many geography, citizenship and social justice topics examine matters of controversy. There can be reluctance or concern to tackle controversial issues. It takes confidence in the children and yourself, but younger children are interested in issues and controversy (Claire and Holden, 2007; Cowan and Maitles, 2012). However, controversies rarely involve straightforward solutions. It is frequently difficult, if not impossible, to conclude whether something is 'right' or 'wrong'; the issues are complex and there may well be differing, valid perspectives and opinions (Oxfam, 2006b; Woolley, 2010; Zimmerman and Robertson, 2017; Mitchell, 2018). The importance lies in enabling different views to be heard and respected. This involves developing a number of skills, abilities and attitudes in children, including:

- listening to others;
- distinguishing between fact and opinion, and recognising 'fake' or 'alternative' (untrue) information (news);
- recognising and accepting other points of view;
- arguing a case;
- dealing with conflict;
- understanding and accepting that there may be alternative solutions.

Buchanan (2013) offers helpful advice for tackling matters and topics involving controversy with primary children. This includes:

- being as honest as you consider you can be with your children, making judicious choices but not distorting what you discuss with them;
- knowing your children to the extent that you are aware when a topic or question may be more personally relevant to them than usual;
- being aware if a child is or might be upset by a particular controversial topic and adjust appropriately;
- when children ask awkward questions, try to find out what they know already about the matter, so that you can give them a thoughtful and helpful response;
- you may not know 'the answer', so say that you need more time to find out, or turn it into a task for discussion or investigation by the children;

- at times, points of controversy may arise unexpectedly during a topic because a natural disaster has hit the headlines, so make use of these as 'teachable moments';
- as others have argued (Hicks, 2012), balance the reality of the issues in a topic with possible ways forward, so that there are positives that emerge for children alongside the critical concerns;
- if it seems sensible, inform colleagues and parents about what you are teaching so that they are aware, but know that you might need to revise what you are teaching or how you approach it if concerns are expressed by several people.

While Buchanan's advice can apply across the curriculum and in school in general, it is highly pertinent when engaging with controversial topics in geography teaching. By no means all controversial geography topics will have agreed views among your children. Nonetheless, develop their understanding and appreciation that different views and feelings – and what they value differently – are the stuff of daily life. Playground and home life examples can help them appreciate this, and learn to acknowledge and respect different views from their own – for example, when two groups of children wish to play in the same space or when shopping with parents, conflicting interests may arise and an equitable solution needs to be sought. A P4C approach to such challenges can be useful (see Chapter 4).

Teaching controversial issues

Controversial issues have a number of elements, concerning personal, social, environmental and/or political impacts that can arouse strong feelings, relate to genuine concerns, and deal with questions of values and belief. The box below lists several potentially controversial geography topics, which may be used as a stimulus for discussing and investigating controversial issues. Such issues can generate differing and contradictory opinions, some valid and others less so but in need of consideration and being weighed on merit. This should be facilitated when teaching about controversial issues in geography by adopting specific approaches with primary children. These include the following.

- Children are involved in establishing ground rules for and behaviours in discussion and debate.
- There is balance in the variety of perspectives considered, with children engaging with more than one set of issues.
- A balanced range of evidence and viewpoints is provided to children, using, where possible, information and claims from the different sides and interest groups involved.

- Views and arguments should not be ignored or discounted because they are challenging or minority perspectives.
- Children should offer other interpretations to those provided, including contradictory perspectives.
- Children should consider carefully what the evidence informs them about and be encouraged to distinguish fact from opinions, values and beliefs.
- Children are allowed to decide the extent to which they express their own opinions but be explicit when doing so.
- Children are aware that they are not the sole authority or arbiter on matters of opinion or information.
- Conclusions should take account of minority perspectives.
- Children are challenged when they present assertions as fact or without care or viewpoints too speedily arrived at.

Examples of controversial geographical topics

- Changes to traffic management – e.g. road humps, chicanes on roads.
- The impact of traffic – e.g. traffic congestion, parking charges, safe road crossing.
- Building on farmland – e.g. for housing, industry or commerce.
- The loss of essential local services – e.g. shop and service closure, reduction of buses.
- Littering – e.g. in local streets, dumping on farmland in the countryside.
- Failure to improve residential and industrial areas – e.g. derelict housing, closed factories.
- Pollution of water – e.g. effluent discharged into rivers.
- Atmospheric pollution – e.g. fossil fuel burning, ozone damage.
- Poverty and the unequal distribution of resources – e.g. clean water, food access.
- Destruction of the rainforests – e.g. illegal forest clearance in Amazonia and Indonesia.

A variety of teaching approaches and strategies can be used when geography teaching includes controversial issues, providing safe contexts through which to tackle the potential for bias and subjectivity.

- *Enquiry:* identifying the questions, deciding on the approach to inves-tigation, evaluating the initial findings, continuing the investigation, drawing conclusions.
- *Philosophy for children (P4C):* often also known as enquiry-based learn-ing, P4C encourages children's learning through enquiry and the explo-ration of ideas. Children learn to understand that their views and those of others are important and valued, and that it is not always about being right or wrong, one or the other, but that there are a range of different ideas and opinions, and that their view is one of many. It helps children to see things from different perspectives and to appreciate the com-plexity of the world around them, and how we all are interrelated and interdependent.
- *Conducting interviews:* arranging to interview a variety of people who have different perspectives on a particular issue.
- *Preparing a balance sheet:* listing and balancing against each viewpoint – the evidence, perspectives and conclusions.
- *Proposing a change:* putting forward proposals for change to an area, looking at the possibilities and alternatives, seeking advice and differ-ent viewpoints, balancing ideas and arguments, and making proposals based on evidence and argument.
- *Debate:* groups putting forward the cases for different sides in an issue.
- *Role play:* taking on the roles of different participants in the issue and arguing the case from the perspective of your 'character'.
- *Hot seating:* questioning individuals about the views of their 'character'.
- *Drama:* writing a play script and acting out with the variety of view-points examined through different 'characters'.
- *Conducting a 'public enquiry':* inviting the different sides arguing about an issue to present their cases and arguments to an adjudicator (perhaps their teacher, the head teacher or a governor).

These approaches can be stimulated in various ways. The box below highlights several approaches to topics in which two or more perspec-tives need to be considered and about which judgements need to be made (see also Chapter 4). These approaches are based on raising awareness of a problem or issue, considering ways in which it might be resolved and becoming involved in making it happen – itself a con-troversial approach, yet one in relation to environmental impact and sustainability that a good primary geography curriculum necessitates by encouraging children to consider what action they would take (Woolley, 2010). This helps to reinforce geography's important ethical dimension.

Nine examples of approaches to environmental impact and sustainability

Heightening awareness

- Use *poetry* about an environmental matter to stimulate debate about care for the environment.
- *Photograph* 'attractive' sites and sites of 'concern' in the local area; create a display and encourage children to write captions for the photographs to express their views and say why.
- Examine an environmental issue in the media and create a *radio, TV programme, video or blog* to describe and explain the causes and consequences of the issue.

Proposing ways forward

- Identify a local issue and *plan* a way to improve it.
- Use *role play* to identify possible solutions to an environmental issue.
- Develop an *exhibition* of drawings, text, maps, models, digital photographs, charts and labels to describe and explain how an area might look in the future.

Taking action

- *Design* and create a distinctive area in the school grounds, such as a wild area, a garden or a quiet area.
- Put into *practice* improved ways to reduce waste and increase recycling.
- Meet a local environmental action group and *join in* with their activities to improve the environment.

Values education

As is evident from the discussion in this chapter, geography, citizenship, social justice and equity involve values education. This places a clear responsibility on us all as teachers to ensure that we focus on helping children to encounter the different values that others hold and to seek to clarify their own values. This is a core part of helping primary children tackle controversial issues in geography. It means ensuring that values become explicit. As teachers, we have the responsibility to support positive values, such as respect for each other and ways to behave thoughtfully with others, but we need to consider seriously the types of values we wish to develop with children. For instance, we may well wish to foster their care for the environment, and their awareness and avoidance of stereotyping other peoples and places. We need to consider whether in encouraging these stances we approach our teaching through inculcating particular values or by helping children to develop their own moral reasoning and thus clarify their own values (see box below). Primary geography is not immune to encouraging a single point of view, perhaps implicitly, such as about appreciating the local park as a positive facility or believing that keeping our oceans free from non-degradable plastic waste are 'good' things, but we need to discuss and debate with children the values inherent in these positions rather than presume their 'rightness' and seemingly impose them. This may mean that through discussion children adopt or change particular values, but in doing so they will learn to be able to reason and justify their positions.

There are rarely clear-cut 'answers' to controversial issues. The teacher's role is to enable learning, including of knowledge and information, and of values. Many issues contain various dilemmas and possible outcomes.

Approaches to values education	
Values inculcation	Its objective is that children will adopt a predetermined set of values.
Values analysis	It employs structured discussion and analysis of evidence to investigate the values inherent in issues.
Moral reasoning	It provides opportunities to discuss reasons for a value position and choices, aiming to encourage children's growth in moral reasoning ability.
Values clarification	Its objective is to help children become aware of their own values in relation to their behaviour and thinking and that of others.
Action learning	It encourages children to see themselves as interacting members of social and environmental systems through analysing and clarifying values with the intention of enabling them to act in relation to social and environmental issues according to their value choices.

Table 8.1   Approaches to value education

Source: modified from Biddulph *et al.*, 2015, p. 282.

In the classroom

Geographical dilemmas

Groups of 9–11-year-olds were given access to a topical, current children's newspaper (see *First News* or *The Week Junior*) and asked to look through the issue to find stories that related to geography, of which there were several, including reports on sea pollution, climate change, refugee concerns and endangered species. Having done this, each group selected one report and discussed the information and issues that were raised in the article. Having identified the geography inherent in the story, debated the issues and agreed a summary of these, they were tasked with re-presenting the story through a different medium. Different groups created a play, a dance, a radio report, a video, a poem and a blog; one group asked to write a series of tweets. Next, the groups were encouraged to research the background to the topic they had focused on, and to clarify and explain what its geography was and what were the 'geographical dilemmas' it exposed and considered. They were asked to give reasons for their views about these 'dilemmas'. They presented their interpretations to their class. In the follow-up discussion their teacher used the term 'values' to help them identify, understand and appreciate what underpinned the views. This provided all the children with the sense that geography is not only topical but an important and significant dimension in theirs and everyone else's lives. The approach used in this topic demonstrated the children's clear understanding of the content and the complexity of the geographical matters reported, which they made accessible and engaging to their peers.

It is essential that we understand this complexity to overcome the tendency to oversimplify and look at issues in binary and clear-cut terms, stating, for example, that 'fair trade is good' or that 'driving is bad'. We must encourage children to question and consider, and to reflect critically and with balance, if not impartially. While it is difficult for any teacher to be neutral, it is important that we ensure balance when involving children in investigating geographical topics that involve matters of equity, social justice and controversy. This is a vital contribution that geography can bring to developing children as citizens (Mitchell, 2018).

Examining 'good causes', environmental or other, requires thoughtful teaching and being explicit about our own values and intentions, with our reasons for holding them. Organisations and initiatives such as Oxfam, Philosophy for Children, de Bono's six thinking hats and Open Spaces for Dialogue and Enquiry provide help to do this (see Useful websites).

 Reflective task

Read Oxfam's (2006b) advice on teaching about controversial issues (see the Oxfam website). What are the most important points made about the role of the teacher in this?

Consider values that may be promoted through geography teaching with primary children, such as about environmental concern, attachment to your home area or the significance of fair trade. Do you think they are important and, if so, why?

How have you come to hold the values you have? Have you changed your values at any point, and if you did, why?

Are there values in relation to people, places and environments that you would wish to encourage children to hold and why is this? How might you help primary children consider such values and which values education approach would you most prefer to employ?

 Key points

This chapter has:

- outlined the meaning of social justice and explained the importance of children learning about it in primary school;
- considered the place of values in geography education;
- summarised and exemplified the connections and interrelationships in geography between values, citizenship, equity, social justice and controversial issues;
- recognised that geography is an effective and appropriate subject for teaching about equity, social justice and responsibility;

- raised awareness that learning about matters of social justice may initiate controversial issues and dilemmas, and outlined strategies for teaching about them.

Moving on

Develop your reading about social justice, citizenship and equity, and the reasons why these important aspects of geography are often controversial.

Further reading

The following books provide useful follow-up reading about the topics considered in this chapter.

Bourn, D, Hunt, F, Blum, N and Lawson, H (2016) *Primary Education for Global Learning and Sustainability*. Cambridge Primary Review Trust Research Survey 5 (new series). York: Cambridge Primary Review Trust. Available at: http://cprtrust. org.uk/wp=content/uploads/2016/02/Bourn-report-160217-final.pdf.

Boyle-Baise, M and Zevin, J (2014) *Young Citizens of the World*. New York: Routledge.

Claire, H and Holden, C (eds) (2007) *The Challenge of Teaching Controversial Issues*. Stoke on Trent: Trentham Books.

Dolan A (2019) *Powerful Primary Geography: A toolkit for 21st century learning*. Abingdon: Routledge.

Grigg, R and Hughes, S (2013) *Teaching Primary Humanities*. Harlow: Pearson.

Martin, F (2006) *Teaching Geography in Primary Schools: Learning How to Live in the World*. Cambridge: Chris Kington.

Pike, S (2016) *Learning Primary Geography: Ideas and inspirations from classrooms*. Abingdon; Routledge.

Reynolds, R (2014) *Teaching Humanities and Social Studies in the Primary School*. Melbourne: Oxford University Press.

Young, M with Cummins, E (2002), *Global Citizenship: The Handbook for Primary Teaching*. Cambridge: Chris Kington.

Useful websites

Association for Citizenship Teaching: www.teachingcitizenship.org.uk/

Australian Sustainable Schools Initiative: www.environment.gov.au/education/aussi/

British Red Cross www.redcross.org/educationresources

Carbon Kids: www.csiro.au/resources/CarbonKids.html

Citizenship Education: www.citized.info

Council for Europe: http://pjp-eu.coe.int/en/web/charter-edc-hre-pilot-projects/ teaching-controversial-issues-developing-effective-training-for-teachers-and-school-leaders?desktop=true

de Bono: www.debonogroup.com/six_thinking_hats.php

Fairtrade Foundation: http://schools.fairtrade.org.uk/

First News: https://schools.firstnews.co.uk/

Geographical Association: www.geography.org.uk

GeogSpace (AGTA): www.agta.asn.au

Oxfam Education: www.oxfam.org.uk/education/resources/teaching-controversial-issues?cid=rdt_tools-and-guides-controversial-issues

Open Spaces for Dialogue and Enquiry: www.osdermethodology.org.uk

Philosophy for Children (P4C): www.sapere.org.uk

Teaching about controversial issues: www.teachingcitizenship.org.uk/sites/files/ downloads/FULL%20Prevent%20and%20controversial%20issues%20guidance.pdf

The Week Junior: http://theweekjunior.co.uk/schools

CHAPTER 9

EXPERIENCING AND VISUALISING GEOGRAPHY

Fieldwork, photographs, artefacts and maps

 Chapter objectives

This chapter enables you to:

- appreciate the importance of outdoor learning;
- recognise the significance of undertaking fieldwork with children of all ages;
- know how to manage fieldwork;
- understand the value and role of photographs and maps in geographical learning, and know some ways to develop children's understanding;
- appreciate that children learn through 'virtual' environments and can use appropriate technology.

Introduction

Geography is founded on investigation of the real world. It is, therefore, essential that children engage in learning outside the classroom and undertake fieldwork as a key element in their studies. We cannot always take children out, but it is possible to bring the outside world into the classroom, through the use of photographs, film, artefacts, maps and digital information technologies. These are key resources in geographical learning and they provide the potential for children to engage in active learning through their enquiries and field studies. This chapter introduces these aspects of primary geography.

Learning outside the classroom

Outdoor learning provides evident motivation for early years and primary children. There is a strong case that learning outside the classroom *helps to make subjects more vivid and interesting* for children and *enhance their understanding* (Ofsted, 2008c, p. 7). Out-of-classroom learning makes a significant contribution to children's personal, social and emotional development. Indeed, there is growing evidence that outdoor learning improves children's overall behaviour and interpersonal relations and well-being (Gill, 2011; Rockliff and Chinnery, 2016; Malone and Waite, 2016; Waite *et al.*, 2016).

Forest Schools

The increased and growing interest in many schools in outdoor learning, emanating from Northern European countries such as Sweden and Denmark, includes the highly efficacious Forest School movement (Knight, 2013a, 2016). The Forest School approach fosters early years and primary age children's interactions with the natural environment in risky-within-safe-bounds and supervised places, such as woodlands (see also Chapter 10). It has fostered good practice across early years and primary schooling beyond the Forest School approaches (Bilton and Crook, 2016). Its focus is on connecting with nature and learning what the natural world is like, whether on wet and muddy days or in sunny dry weather. It is about learning naturally in the outdoors (Knight, 2017). Originating in Wisconsin, USA, in the late 1920s, it was adopted and developed in Sweden and Denmark during the 1950s and has grown from there (Joyce, 2012). The aim of Forest Schools is to engage and inspire children using positive outdoor learning experiences through being in and connecting with nature. Children develop self-confidence through working with others in an outdoor natural context and learn skills inaccessible to them in a classroom context. The collaborative nature of the activities helps children to work effectively and creatively together to solve problems and tackle challenges.

The Forest School movement has been seen by some to contribute to tackling various concerns about children's lack of experience in and of nature, particularly evident in highly urbanised environments. It results in what Louv (2005, 2011) calls 'Nature Deficit Disorder'. Louv and others (Waller *et al.*, 2017) refer to children's increasing disconnection with nature and the concomitant problems that this causes, including disregard for the environment (natural and constructed), anti-social behaviour, obesity, depression and attention deficit disorders. Reconnection with nature and spending time constructively and positively outdoors is argued to help rebalance children's feelings and sense of self-esteem, to help build their confidence and to allow them to regain some of their natural childhood behaviours and living patterns.

The Forest School movement has helped to promote the focus on learning outside the classroom as something that should imbue the whole curriculum, although it is not new to good geography teaching with young children. Other natural allies of the Forest School are the Water School, which focuses on younger children's education through natural water environments, such as rivers, lakes and coasts (Horvath, 2016), and the Beach School, focused on coasts and beaches (Mackintosh, 2017). As with the Forest School, the Water School and Beach School provide early years children with an excellent introduction to aspects of the environment and a way into early geographical learning through children's natural engagement with water environments, features, water play and associated activities with mud, pebbles, sticks and natural forces. Naturally, a safe approach to risk is essential in each of these approaches.

Learning in and about the outdoors

Learning outside the classroom is not new to primary schools. Indeed, in good geography teaching the outdoors has always been used. It is an essential element for children's geographical experience. It is worth recalling the reasons for and value in taking learning out of the classroom. The essence of the case for learning outside is that the place where learning occurs is vitally important (Waite, 2017). For geography, this seems to be common sense, particularly through investigating the most obvious site and place children know, their school's grounds and their own neighbourhood, as well as accessible locations they visit further afield. What these outdoor places provide is the authenticity in learning that comes through engagement with the realities of the daily environment and life beyond the classroom and school. Children relate to these places because they are familiar and places in which they have a stake. Furthermore, working in places is frequently motivating and engaging, provides rich contexts for investigation and debate, acts as a resource for the development of appreciation, understanding and knowledge about the sites, and provides ways for children to observe the 'worlds around them'. Children can begin to understand how school subjects may provide insights into local and other places. Outdoor sites provide places in which to develop skills and habits of thinking (DfES, 2006c).

Sedgwick (2012) argues that what teaching and learning outside the classroom brings is the *vitality of learning*, which is not simply about its *surprise* element as a less used site for learning and teaching, but because it takes place outside, it brings to life what so often is only encountered at second hand in the classroom. Outdoor learning is often justified in terms of learning through experience and active learning, but these can occur well in an effective indoor classroom (Monk and Silman, 2011). What the outdoor classroom provides is places where learning makes sense because it has immediacy, connects with the places learnt in, and examines the 'objects' of learning in situation (Beames *et al.*, 2012; Broda, 2011; Bason, 2010; Waite *et al.*, 2016; Witt, 2017; Pickering, 2018). It is place-based learning.

Engaging in fieldwork

Discussing their views about their primary schooling, children contrasted their considerable classroom-based experience of learning revolving around paper, books, the computer and virtual environments with their limited experience of going outside to learn. They considered the latter to be of real value *because you're seeing things, feeling things, real things* (Alexander and Hargreaves, 2007, p. 13). Unknowingly, children were reiterating Confucius when he claimed in the 6th century BC that:

I hear and I forget

I see and I remember

I do and I understand

In England, the government's Education Department has argued for many years that *we believe that every young person should experience the world beyond their classroom as an essential part of learning and personal development, whatever their age, ability or circumstances* (DfES, 2006c, p.2). This is an important commitment to children that working outside the classroom is a key element in the school curriculum. Out-of-classroom work will include fieldwork in geography, as well as in other subjects, such as science, history and art. Fieldwork is required in England's primary geography curriculum (DfE, 2013).

The importance of fieldwork

The significance of fieldwork in younger children's learning is emphasised in curricula around the world. For instance, in Australia, Wales and Ireland, it is emphasised that in learning geography children must be ensured opportunities for fieldwork, because it is an essential aspect of understanding and appreciating the subject. In early years and primary geography *fieldwork is any study undertaken outside the classroom, and could be within the school grounds, around the neighbouring streets, or in more distant locations* (ACARA, 2012a, p. 16).

One of the enduring memories many people claim to have of geography at primary school is of field trips and visits they undertook (Image 9.1). Fieldwork brings subjects alive, involves children in investigating and exploring real places and environments, and develops their interpersonal skills (Pike, 2016). This approach to *out of the classroom learning* engages pupils' interest and provides a relevant, real-life stimulus for geographical questions, setting up a sequence of focus, investigating, collecting, recording, analysing, evaluating and presenting evidence in a geographical enquiry (Richardson, 2010a; Tanner and Whittle, 2015). In doing so, it provides opportunities to promote higher order thinking skills and is a useful vehicle for developing and applying decision-making skills based on real places and issues, while appreciating other people's values and attitudes. It contributes to children's social learning, to changes in their behaviour *for the positive* and to *their resilience to be able to respond to changing conditions in their environment* (Malone, 2009, p. 6).

It is not only invaluable, but also essential to include fieldwork in geographical studies for all early years and primary age children. While it is not always easy to organise, particularly beyond the school grounds, there is evident encouragement to provide a variety of outdoor learning and fieldwork experiences and activities for children as part of their geographical learning (Dolan, 2019; Porter, 2018).

Image 9.1 Children observing 'in the field'

In the classroom

Primary geography fieldwork

Ofsted England (2008a) has described many aspects of good practice in fieldwork studies. Two examples are summarised by Ofsted inspectors here.

Undertaking fieldwork children completed an audit of the school and grounds to ascertain their sustainability, embedding the work in the eco-school ethos. This work prepared the children for a visit to a landfill site where they considered both the potential hazards at the site and ways to reduce the carbon emissions and improve general recycling facilities in the area. Back in class, the children then used software to manipulate and analyse photographs that they had taken on the excursion and presented their findings to the rest of the school to improve safety on future visits. They produced a safety pamphlet which they presented to the landfill operators and which was subsequently used for other primary schools visiting the site. This gave real meaning and relevance to the trip that was stimulating, inspiring and productive.

(Ofsted, 2008a, pp. 35–6)

At the start of a topic investigating the pedestrianisation of the local main street children thought primarily of their own interests and attitudes to the idea. It was not until they engaged in meaningful, qualitative fieldwork, conducting surveys and interviews, that they recognised and understood that other people had vested interests in the proposals and began to value these viewpoints. Sketching and photographing the proposed site allowed the children to draw up detailed and annotated maps of the area which they used to argue their case, in different interest groups for and against the proposal. They devised their own risk assessment for their fieldwork by identifying and minimising potential hazards. This gave them a heightened sense of awareness and responsibility for their own well-being and safety. Further work involved them writing up the arguments for and against and submitting them for publication in a local newspaper, so developing their communication and persuasive writing skills.

(Ofsted, 2008a, pp. 36–7)

Reflective task

Reflect on the two classroom examples above. Consider the role of field-work in these topics. What are the elements of good practice in planning for and making use of fieldwork that are described? What was the role of the teacher in the planning? What was the role of the children? How might these be adapted for your own context?

Where to carry out fieldwork

Fieldwork can be undertaken in a wide variety of locations and sites. Figure 9.1 indicates the range of 'nested' distances from school where fieldwork might be organised. These cover many different sites that can be used for fieldwork. The box below provides examples of the variety of features and places that might be visited (Grigg and Lewis, 2016), which may vary in type and size as well as in their context and distance from school. It would be usual to include several different types of features within one site in one fieldwork visit. Sites might be chosen to stimulate an enquiry, with the fieldwork visit taking place early in the topic, perhaps as a stimulus to initiate awareness and interest for a study of a specific place or an aspect of physical, human or environmental

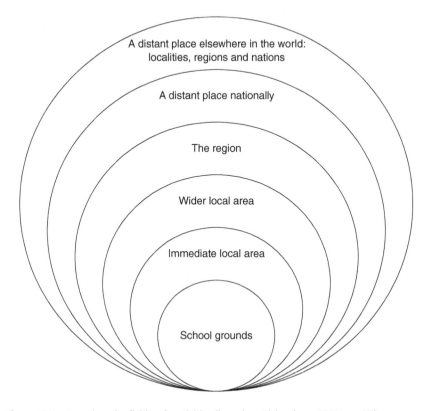

A distant place elsewhere in the world: localities, regions and nations

A distant place nationally

The region

Wider local area

Immediate local area

School grounds

Figure 9.1   Locations for fieldwork activities (based on Richardson, 2010a, p. 37)

geography, or to generate initial questions, and perhaps both. It may occur later in a geography unit, planned by the children, coming at an appropriate point to gather the data desired. It is possible that more than one visit takes place during a geographical enquiry, so that findings from a first visit can be followed up and developed on a later field trip. This is most likely when using the school grounds and the local area of the school.

Some possible sites and features for fieldwork	
• The school building and grounds	• Leisure centres
• Buildings, housing areas	• New developments
• Local improvement schemes	• Shopping arcades, streets and centres
• Shops, supermarkets, markets	• Business park, small businesses
• Leisure centre, library, sporting facilities	• Local services, fire station, police station, doctors' surgery
• Roads and pavements, railway station, bus depot, airport	• Water features, creek/river, pond/lake, reservoir
• Refuse depot, rubbish tip, recycling plant	• Coast, sea
• Sewage works	• City centres, suburbs, towns, villages
• Woodland, open spaces, footpaths	• Allotment, rural and city farms, livestock market
• Bridges	• Quarry, landfill site
• Park, playground, green spaces, wild places	

Usually, geographical fieldwork is pre-planned and well organised, for good reasons, but sometimes stimulating out-of-classroom learning can occur seemingly spontaneously. It can be as down to earth as taking children into the playground and asking them questions such as the following.

- What can you see?
- What can you hear?
- What does it feel like to be here?
- What do you think happened here yesterday and what might happen tomorrow?
- What changes would you like to see made here?

Fieldwork should be well focused and planned and, if going further afield, children need organised investigations, either teacher led or from child-generated questions and enquiries. Links can be made to other curriculum areas so that the children have a holistic experience of the site, and recognise and appreciate the interrelationships in the environment around them. Connections between geography and history are obvious ones to make (Catling, 2006c; Cooper, 2004, 2013; Martin, 2004; Bettany *et al.*, 2017).

Fieldwork should develop thinking and feeling, and discussion of attitudes and values (Pike, 2016). It should encourage children to take a fresh and creative look at their environment, and enable them to consider explanations for and resolutions to problems. This requires thorough and meaningful preparation, inclusive, creative, even innovative and participatory activities, and considered, significant follow-up work. It is most effective as part of an enquiry approach where the children have initiated and developed the questions and investigations. Ofsted England (2008c, 2011) reinforces the importance of preparatory work for successful fieldwork – for instance, when commending a well-focused lesson in which children analysed photographs and maps of the area that they were to visit, allowing them to draw on their prior geographical knowledge during their field visit. This enabled them to decide how they would collect and analyse the information on the field trip and to evaluate and draw conclusions from it on their return.

For the youngest children, fieldwork will use the nursery and school grounds and take them out into parts of the immediate area. It may involve walks such as those described in the box below that have been organised locally. During the primary school years the area will be extended and older children are likely to travel further distances. This might include for one or more year groups a school residential visit or excursion based in another locality for several days. It is important to give all children a variety of scales to study – for instance, taking younger children out to a farm. Similarly, 9 to 11/12-year-old children can study their own locality intensively or another nearby urban setting or rural community.

Mywalks (nuweb.northumbria.ac.uk/mywalks)

An excellent way to connect children with their local environment is through the use of Mywalks. This is a simple yet effective idea to engage all ages with their surroundings (Owens, 2008a, p. 25). Walks in the local area can become a real adventure with children stopping at various places to take photographs and record on a digital recorder or video what they see, feel and discover. They can then download the photographs and annotate them orally or with text from the evidence they recorded. The concept has invaluable learning and experiential possibilities, such as providing a focused approach to the local area where children concentrate in groups on different aspects of the locality, perhaps striking sites or buildings, information signs, noise in the environment, evidence of wildlife, noting cameras mounted on buildings and poles, the variety of shops, the ages of buildings in the street, the people who are using them, and much more.

Organising successful fieldwork

Organising fieldwork successfully means that you must take several things into account. Invaluable advice and guidance are provided in various places (e.g. Scoffham, 2010; Catling, 2014c; Tanner and Whittle, 2015; Pickering, 2018). A very thorough, informative and helpful website is that of the Council for Learning Outside the Classroom (www.lotc.org.uk). The following points are a guide to key considerations and decisions that you need to appreciate and make.

- Check the school's requirements for the adult/pupil ratio for taking children out of your classroom into the grounds and off the school site. Adult helpers who can accompany you are school support staff, parent helpers, school governors and councillors, and others the school's leadership agrees can do so.
- Be clear about your aims and objectives for the visit and your expected outcomes. Ensure that the work you prepare with and for the children can meet these. Fieldwork must be a meaningful and productive learning experience for the children.
- Organise the class into groups with an adult and ensure that each group and individual is allocated specific tasks, whether by themselves or by you. This is essential with younger children who need a higher ratio of adults, but its key purpose is to enable children to work together and focus on the tasks they undertake.
- You must undertake a thorough recce and check of the area that you visit even if it is local. You should carry out a risk assessment (see Table 9.1) to ensure you have considered all eventualities and taken appropriate precautions to minimise risks. Complete your school's risk assessment pro forma. There may already be one completed previously for your visit site and activities, but you must check and update it. If you go to a managed site or field centre, the staff there may well have partially completed risk assessment forms you can complete. Doing this, you must consider inclusion, particularly any children who might have difficulties accessing the areas that you visit and those who need particular supervision. You must state how you will provide for them. Involve children in making risk assessments by using photographs and maps alongside their knowledge and common sense. This approach is beneficial because it informs the children, gives them a focus and stimulates interest.

Risk assessment is essential in preparing to undertake a fieldwork visit. It should be undertaken even if you think you know the site or area you are taking your children to. There are four key matters to consider.

- The school's coordinator of out-of-school visits should advise, support and help you complete the necessary paperwork. You may need to

Location	Hazard/event	Risk	Action to be taken to reduce risk	Action to be taken in event of occurrence

Table 9.1　Example of risk assessment format

complete a school off-site visit checklist, such as that in Table 9.2, when you go off site.

- Ensure you have the resources you need to make the learning experience as effective as possible. As well as the educational resources, such as clipboards, pencils, paper, digital cameras, maps and photographs, you need to have contact numbers for the school, relevant medical information about your children, a list of your helpers, a first aid kit, and items such as bin liners, collecting boxes, tissues and spare waterproofs. Someone should be a first aider.
- Provide a thorough briefing to all the adults involved in the fieldwork: teaching staff, school support staff, parents and other helpers.
- After your visit, complete an evaluation to inform your teaching and planning, and to reflect on any lessons learnt and adaptations for future trips. Debriefing and thanking your accompanying adults is also essential.

Site visit preparation and evaluation form		
Date of visit:	Time of departure:	Return time:
Venue:	Telephone no.:	Mobile no. of group leader:
Year group:	No. of pupils:	Adult/pupil ratio:
Group leader:	Accompanying adults:	First aiders: First aid kit:
Transport booked:	Name of coach co.: Name of coach driver:	Risk assessment: Date completed: (copy attached)
Consent letter sent out on: (copy attached)	Consent forms: Medical information:	Cost per head: Money collected/given to office: Initial payments made:
Additional information:		
Post-visit evaluation		

Table 9.2　School off-site visit details

Bringing the outside in

We cannot go out all the time, but 'learning outside' opportunities can be provided in the classroom. We can introduce children to places and environments that they might not have the opportunity to experience through fieldwork. A story of a cancelled family visit to the seaside because it rained, *The Inside Outing* (Laird, 1994), illustrates imaginatively a way to have an 'outing' and an 'outdoor' adventure 'inside' with young children by being creative with some accessible resources. The children imaginatively create various environments they would have liked to have visited, drawing on their everyday geographies of elsewhere, 'creating' the beach, tropical islands, various sea creatures and adventurous travel using everyday home resources. Such explorations can be re-created in the early years and primary classroom using classroom furniture and objects, allowing children to experience and articulate through play places, activities and feelings that they would not otherwise encounter. It can be the basis for some imaginative role play, drawing on children's experiences.

Travel to a new place or environment can be simulated and re-created with, for example, the children buying tickets, showing their passports and boarding an 'aeroplane' – pairs of chairs lining either side of an aisle to 'fly' to a new 'destination'. This might present an opportunity to discuss the impact of flight, of carbon emissions and alternative forms of transport. Alternatively, an imitation train carriage or a coach could be arranged for an imagined journey. Once the children have reached their 'destination', there are many ways to bring it alive. Resources to use include photographs, photo packs, artefacts, maps, brochures, leaflets, simulated computer-based activities, Internet information sources, films, audio recordings, food and cooking, music and invited visitors familiar to the area. Of course, an area in the setting or classroom can be 'turned into' the place being visited.

     Reflective task

Think of somewhere you would like children to visit and experience. How might you create that environment in your classroom? What resources would you need? How would you arrange and organise them? What would children do to help create it? Older children might plan and manage this 'place play' creation for themselves or younger children, identifying the resources they need, where they can obtain them, how they will arrange them, and what they plan to do on arrival in the 'new environment'. To do so will require some research by the children to know what to plan.

Virtual fieldwork

Another approach, when it is not possible to experience somewhere directly, is to use virtual fieldwork. Increasingly, resorts, cities and national parks, for instance, have on their websites (as do many museums) virtual walks and other trips around parts of the whole site, including 360° views. Alternatively, you might prepare a series of digital photographs and film clips of an area, including specific features you would like the children to focus on, so as to bring another place to life. You can enhance this by encouraging children to superimpose themselves on to the photographs, using appropriate software, so that they begin to imagine what it might be like to be there, and what they would see, feel, hear and do in that particular place. They can examine details in the photographs, imagining what is happening, whether it is the powerful erosive force of river water flowing against the outside of the river bend, or the ways in which people might be buying and selling items in a market.

Undertaking a 'visit' and sequencing events can be experienced through the use of hyperlinks on a PowerPoint presentation as well as by creating an animation on one of the many software programs. Presenting sequential photographs of an environment and having 'stopping off' places to ask and answer questions can re-create the sense of discovery and exploration on a journey, and be highly motivating and engaging. Using one of the many backdrops of a green screen can stimulate reality and excitement, and take children to distant environments and places. Google Earth and Google's Street View, among many other sources, provide opportunities to access photographs to use to create such 'tours' and investigations (see the Mywalks box on p.255 and the Google street view box on p.267).

Progression in fieldwork

It is important that fieldwork is undertaken consistently during the year and across classes. Fieldwork skills are developed with experience. While with the youngest children in the early years observing their immediate school grounds and particular sites in the local area can occur frequently, with older primary children observing locally might be organised into particular topics that incorporate elements of the local area, be these about local services and amenities, a local issue or the nature of the natural environment or concerns about waste in the area. While Figure 9.1 notes the concentric relationships of places at different distances and scales from the school (and home), it does not indicate that this is the basis for a fieldwork approach. A group of 6–7-year-olds might be taken away overnight to a place not too far away, during which they do some geographical studies, and some 10–11/12-year-olds might be away on a school excursion or journey for four to five days at a field centre in another part of the country or even abroad.

Equally, children of all ages can undertake fieldwork locally. Fieldwork locations can be at varied distances for children of different ages.

In the same way, observational skills, mapping skills, taking photographs, data gathering and many other fieldwork techniques can be used at different ages throughout early years and primary schooling. A focus on identifying features and activities may be used with 4–5-year-olds, but observing and identifying features, especially new ones, will be important for 10–11/12-year-olds visiting an environment for the first time where there might be familiarity but also novel features. This means that it is not straightforward to set out fieldwork approaches or skills to use for particular age groups and ranges. Enabling children to make progress in their fieldwork skills and activities will relate to their age and experience, the focus of the fieldwork, the context in which it occurs, the children's confidence and developed skills, and the expectations and opportunities given to them. Undertaking fieldwork is about developing children's skills and techniques for gathering data and information of various sorts, and it is about applying what they can do so that they develop their skills and techniques further. Gathering information and data about a place includes obtaining quantitative data such as the number of shops or how many and what type of vehicles people park where, and qualitative data such as people's views about a feature, an area or an issue. In planning for fieldwork, the key questions to consider include the following.

- What is the purpose of the fieldwork element in a geography topic and why is it included?
- What type(s) of data are to be gathered and in what form (such as by counting, taking photographs or mapping)?
- Given the children's age, experience and knowledge, which skills and techniques will help them gather the data required, and which of these can they use and which will be new to them?
- How do the children build on what they can do already, and how will they develop and apply their new skills or techniques, such as before or during the fieldwork, with what support?

Children's fieldwork learning will progress and they will be increasingly able to lead the development of fieldwork enquiries through considering what they are intending to find out and why, what alternative ways to investigate there may be and deciding on which seem most appropriate to use, and in organising and putting these into practice through their fieldwork investigations. Focused on selected aspects of the school grounds 4–5-year-olds can be initiated into such an approach, while 9–10-year-olds can draw on their developed experience and understanding to decide how to undertake fieldwork studies in another part of their town or at a waste recycling centre. You need to have a good idea about what your children have done, involve them in planning the fieldwork and identify how you can extend their skills. This may mean that you plan to support children across the class who may have more or less confidence and capability in fieldwork situations and in using fieldwork skills. Table 9.3 presents an indicative sense of the development of fieldwork foci and skills and techniques across the early years and primary age range.

Using photographs

Fieldwork is evidently a visualising approach in learning. It involves children in observing in the real environment to see what places are like and what occurs there. Pictures and photographs are another form of visualisation.

The importance of photographs

Visualisation is a key skill for children to develop their understanding of places, environment, events and lifestyles which they have not seen with their own eyes. It allows them to use their imagination in order to build up their own picture of something or somewhere that they are not able to experience directly. Some children, for example, may never have been to the coast, so when we talk about cliffs, they may not have any visual image of them. We need to help children 'see' phenomena through photographs, diagrams, video, and so on to provide opportunities to observe, interpret and make meaning of what is portrayed in such images, developing their understanding of the world around them. Mackintosh (2010, 2011) notes that just as we interpret meaning from written words (literacy), spoken words (oracy) and numbers (numeracy), we make meaning through pictorial forms of spatial information (graphicacy). Graphicacy often receives less direct recognition and attention in primary schools, although it is a very potent, indeed essential and effective, skill to develop, particularly to enhance use and critical awareness of our increasingly visual forms of communication.

Graphicacy encompasses the range of visual images we see daily. These include not only pictures in story books and photographs of features and places, but also maps, drawings, sketches, art works and diagrams. Many road signs are graphic symbols that we readily recognise, as are company and shop logos. While many may be black line graphics, colour is an important element in graphic images. In geography, graphicacy skills are extremely important for reading and making such images, particularly photographs and maps. The focus in this section is on photographs.

Research indicates that rather than seeing pictures and photographs holistically, younger children perceive the different parts as apparently

Children 3/4–5/6 years old	Children 5/6–7/8 years old	Children 7/8–9/10 years old	Children 9/10–11/12 years old
Children:	Children:	Children:	Children:
observe their early years setting indoor area

and

observe and discuss their early years setting outdoor area and the grounds beyond it, perhaps exploring the school grounds (depending on the setting's site), noting weather and seasonal and other changes and suggesting improvements.

They make visits off the setting site, perhaps to a nearby play area or park and to a shop. They observe features along the route taken and at the site they visit.

In all settings they:

- name and talk about what they see;

- take digital photographs;

- begin to record features on pictogram charts; | examine and investigate their school's building, grounds, local streets and aspects of the local area and its natural, managed and built environment, including its weather.

They might visit another site or area further away, perhaps linked with a partner school.

They are introduced to a variety of techniques and skills during fieldwork, including:

- observing, naming and discussing selected aspects of the local environment;

- relating photographs to features and views;

- relating oblique and vertical aerial views to features and streets; | develop their physical, human and environmental geography investigations of the school's grounds and local area, including its weather, as well as make one or more visits to another area perhaps through links to another school or field study centre, possibly staying one or more nights.

They develop their use of a variety of techniques and skills during fieldwork, including:

- observation, identification and discussion of local features and scenes;

- relating photographs to views;

- relating oblique and vertical views to what they can see and sites beyond; | examine in detail, as appropriate, aspects of the school's grounds, and develop further their investigations in the physical, human and environmental geography of the local area, including its weather and climate, and of further afield, making specific visits and perhaps staying for one to several nights at a suitable site.

They extend their use of a variety of techniques and skills during fieldwork, including:

- observation, identification and discussion about aspects of the area;

- relating oblique and vertical views to where they are and the wider area;

- taking digital photographs and film and making sound recordings; |

Children 3/4–5/6 years old	Children 5/6–7/8 years old	Children 7/8–9/10 years old	Children 9/10–11/12 years old
• count different features	• taking digital photographs and film and making sound recordings;	• taking digital photographs and film and making sound recordings;	• making more sophisticated sketch maps;
• make drawings;	• making simple sketch plans and maps;	• making sketch maps;	• relating and orienting maps of different scales in the area;
• relate photographs of features to those they see.	• identifying features, streets, directions and routes on large-scale maps;	• locating themselves on a map, relating to the environment and orienting large-scale local maps to the area;	• recording investigated data on maps;
	• adding information to plans and maps;	• recording selected data on maps;	• annotating and making more detailed sketches of scenes;
	• annotating and making sketches of features;	• annotating and making sketches of features and scenes;	• collecting numerical data appropriate to their investigations;
	• collecting information about features;	• collecting numerical data relevant to their investigations;	• undertaking interviews and questionnaires;
	• asking prepared questions to local people;	• undertaking interviews with local people;	• make a transect locally;
	• making and recording views about features and streets.	• making and recording reasoned judgements about features and scenes;	• making and recording justified evaluations about scenes;
		• measuring information about the environment using instruments.	• measuring information using instruments and making estimates about aspects of the environment.

Table 9.3 Indicative progression in early years and primary geography fieldwork

disconnected details and need to learn how to see both the parts and the whole picture, as well as to 'read' and appreciate its scale and dimension to understand what it shows. There is progression in the interpretation of images from very young children who identify mainly the 'big' details to more sophisticated, merged and holistic understanding of the whole picture by children at the ages of 10 to 12 years old (Mackintosh, 2010).

Taking geographical photographs

Almost everyone and every school has access to various forms of digital camera – as cameras, on mobile phones and on iPads, for instance. Cameras are a very useful learning tool in geography, especially when children are given some simple guidance and suggestions for taking geographically focused photographs.

First, consider what you want to communicate with the photograph. Why would you take this particular view or image? Is it to show something particular, unique or contrasting, of special interest, or perhaps a changing environment? Is it about a particular feature, perhaps a building, or is it of a wider view, such as of a street, park or play area? Consider the scale of the view you will take and what you wish to convey by taking this photograph.

Second, consider how you might best take the photograph to achieve your purpose. Good photographs might be taken using one of these techniques.

- Frame the photograph, so that it clearly highlights what you want to show. Exclude anything that is extraneous to this purpose.
- Choose the position you take it from, particularly the height – looking up or down can give totally different impressions – but also the range of view you wish to include or limit.
- Choose carefully what is in the foreground and the background. Which do you want to emphasise?
- If you want to show change, consider taking two contrasting photographs of the same view in different seasons or from different directions.
- If you want to show contrasts, consider taking photographs of features that are next to one another (juxtaposed) but very different.
- Consider including people or some other familiar object, mainly for a sense of scale or to give a sense of perspective.

You and the children can use the readily available editing tools with digital photographs to reframe them, straighten them and change their dimensions. You and the children might annotate them to identify, highlight or explain particular features of the activities shown. Children can effectively insert and use digital photographs in their fieldwork notes, enquiry reports and presentations to the class to illustrate and evidence points that they want to make.

Using photographs

When children look at photographs they ask questions in order to understand more about what they see, what is going on, and why it looks the way it does. Photographs are a snapshot and need to be 'read' carefully to consider what might have happened before or could come after. Consequently, children ask questions to fill in the gaps. It may be that no specific answer can be given. It is the discussion and the asking of effective questions that allow the development of observational and interpretational skills (Bowles, n.d.). If there is clear information, then this should obviously be given to the children.

Many activities can be used with children to enable them to observe and interrogate photographs. An effective stimulus is to give children a photograph and encourage them to ask questions about it. To introduce this activity you might model some questions for them, as Image 9.2 illustrates. Encourage children to ask realistic, rather than fanciful, questions. Place a photograph on a larger sheet of paper and encourage the children to write their questions in speech bubbles around the photograph, after which they can seek information to identify possible answers. As the teacher, you can supplement their questions and add others to develop the challenge in examining the scene in the photograph.

The following four approaches to using photographs indicate further possibilities. Photographs for these activities can be ones you or the children have taken in the school grounds, the local environment or somewhere else that you have been. They can be selected from a pack of photographs produced for the study of a local, national or overseas locality or about an aspect of physical, human or environmental geography.

- *Ranking photographs.* Children can place a set of photographs in order. A vertical line sequence can be used, but agreement on order can be difficult. An alternative to use is a 'diamond 9' structure (using nine photographs) in which children place their most significant photograph at the top, their next two important photographs on the second line, followed by three on the third line, then two below these and the least important photograph at the bottom. This is a useful way to make decisions when working in a small group since not all of the children will give the same photographs the same importance. It helps them to resolve through discussion, agreement and acceptance (even reluctantly) what is decided by the group as a whole. Encourage the children to avoid simplistic criteria such as like/dislike, and use more sophisticated criteria such as damaged/improved environments with all ages. Always ask the children to explain their decisions and viewpoints.
- *Captioning photographs.* Children can match captions they are given to photographs, or they might create captions for photographs to capture

their essence and context, and demonstrate their understanding of what is shown. As an alternative or in addition, children might annotate the photograph.

- *Stimulate a story.* Give the children a scene and ask them to write about what happened before and what might happen next, weaving geographical vocabulary and understanding into their 'story', and keeping their tale as realistic as possible, based on what they can see in the photograph. They might focus on an individual they can see in the photograph and try to describe why that person is there, what they are doing and what they may do next.

- *Where is it?* Show photographs of views and scenes in one particular urban or rural environment and ask children to say where they think the place is located and justify their choice. They might locate the places they name on atlas maps. At the end of the activity, explain that the photographs show the same place, although there seem to be various different features, views and activities that the children associated, perhaps, with different places. A similar activity can be used with *GeoGuessr*, encouraging children to work out a range of different locations using clues in the landscape.

Image 9.2   Possible teacher-directed questions about an image of a market (source: T Willy)

Using film

Short, focused excerpts from films and videos can be effective ways to enhance children's virtual experience and allow them to visualise places and scenes that would otherwise remain limited to a still photograph or inaccessible film. TV programmes and Internet clips about journeys around or to distinctive areas of the world, about natural processes and spectacular events, or about particular places and environmental issues are excellent sources of high-quality visual geography. You might use programmes made to support children's geographical learning. An effective approach is to watch short, selected parts of a film or video, and then discuss and interpret what has been viewed. Film introduces dimensions and senses that still photographs do not, such as the sounds and dynamism of a place or the processes occurring during a river flood, the building of a shop or road, or the impact of an event or development on a place. Animations can be informative about processes such as river erosion and deposition, and of the sequence of events in an earthquake or volcanic eruption.

Google street view (maps.google.com.au)

This facility provides photographic views of an increasing number of world and national cities, towns and villages. Car-mounted cameras take the street views. It was launched in March 2009 amid some controversy since the photographs capture whatever was happening in the street at the time. These still photograph views may not be entirely up to date for an area you might access. If it is a place you can visit, you may be able to investigate changes that have taken place and look at the impact of change, as well as take up-to-date photographs to create an alternative 'street view'.

Photographs and films have their limitations, because they are chosen, edited media. We need to be wary that children do not assume or take away images that the whole of the continent of Africa, or even that one nation in the continent, for instance, is as depicted in the few photographs of a village or city that they have seen. Visual images can be powerful creators of negative stereotypes if what children see, via the television 'special' or Oxfam/ActionAid/Save the Children 'appeal', is a view of poverty, shanty settlements, arid lands or war-torn places. It is vital that children see a representative and versatile array of different photographs and types of footage, showing the considerable range and variety of life. This is essential to geographical accuracy and integrity.

In the classroom

Learning about a farm

A group of 4–5-year-old children discussed with their teaching assistant the different features, animals and activities shown in three photographs of a farmer feeding his cattle. Children used their awareness of 'farms' and what farmers do from stories that they had been read and seen, to describe what the farmer was doing in the photographs and to sequence the photographs in the correct order. In the discussion, the teaching assistant was able to provide the children with some more accurate information and to challenge a couple of stereotypical views about farms and where our food originates, which some children expressed.

Using artefacts

Using artefacts helps to bring places and people's lives alive. Geographical artefacts are the items that we can collect from places we visit everyday or on holiday and which are in daily use, such as local newspapers, sweet wrappers and paper bags. Commercial tourist items, such as postcards and maps are also artefacts.

There are various types of 'geographical' artefact, as Table 9.4 illustrates. Artefacts can be items we regard as ephemera, to be kept for a short while and then thrown away. We may display them on the sideboard, put them away in a box, or leave them, if photographs, on our phone or computer. Yet they are frequently resources that provide children with a 'human' insight into the lives of people in places, and tell us what we have seen, valued, used and brought home. They provide a sense of reality about places and people's activities and what is available to them, although, of course, they do not tell the 'whole story' about any place, but merely give us a glimpse. Artefacts are a valuable supplement to photographs of places and people's lives, especially if photographs have been taken showing them in the place and context in which they were obtained, such as postcards on a display stand, familiar sweet wrappers as snacks for sale on a stall or a menu on a restaurant table alongside food from that menu.

Using and interpreting artefacts is a popular and effective teaching strategy in historical enquiry (Hoodless, 2008; Cooper 2013). Similar approaches can be used in geography. Artefacts allow children to touch, feel and even smell things and so get a sense of what they are like, introducing a wider range of senses through which to learn. Asking questions about the artefact, discussing what its use is or might be, what it tells us about the activities in

Type of artefact	Geographical connection	Examples
Ephemera	Items of transitory use, usually discarded, because they are disposable. They identify and inform you about the place in some way – for instance, its features, goods sold, and events and activities you have seen, bought or undertaken.	Local and national newspapers, timetables, shop till and transport receipts, chocolate bar and other food wrappers, postcards, leaflets and cards, posters, plastic and paper bags, restaurant and take-away menus
Purchased goods	Items purchased for their usefulness or interest at the time or as mementoes of a particular place. They name or indicate what is available in the place or the wider local area.	Clothing, tea towels, mugs and bowls, sunglasses, food ingredients and samples made locally or commissioned for sale in the area
Local publications	Publications that provide information for future reading about or as mementoes about the place and wider area visited.	Tourist guides, locally and nationally available maps, books and booklets about the locality, walking guides, story and poetry books produced locally, parish and council or similar types of magazines, and local directories
Personal creations	Items that would not exist about the particular place or wider area had not the visitor created or taken them while on the visit.	Personally taken photographs, sketches, drawings and sketch maps
Natural collectable objects	Natural objects that might be possible to collect from the environment. (It is important to be considerate. Talk to the children about taking care of the environment and not disturbing living things.)	Small pebbles, rocks, soil and dead flowers (which in many places cannot be taken or picked), and naturally discarded items such as sheep's wool
Toys	Small-scale reproductions and models of features and objects that are about or relevant to places and activities in the environment, reproduced to be used in play activities by children.	Toy vehicles, planes, trains, urban buildings, street furniture, farm buildings, walls and fences, animals, people and larger scale model houses and their fixtures and furniture
Replicas	Faithful and not-so-faithful copies, usually at a much-reduced scale, or stylistic representations of features and objects in the place and its local environment, usually sold as mementoes.	Reproductions of well-known area-associated features, such as the Eiffel Tower or the Taj Mahal, or they may be porcelain copies of particular local buildings

Table 9.4   Types of geographical artefact (source: adapted from Catling, 2012a)

Photographs taken in the area	'Home' items, e.g. cooking utensils
Postcards	Clothes, e.g. T-shirts
Tourist brochures and guides	Local directories
Local newspapers	Advertising leaflets and posters
Local street, tourist and other maps	Local or council magazines
Google Earth maps and aerial photographs	Rock and soil samples
Bus and rail timetables	Local publications, factual, stories and poetry
Tea towels and other mementoes showing the area	Wrappers from small items, such as sweets, bought locally
Restaurant and take-away eatery menus	Other collectable items, such as sheep's wool from a walk in the country
Items made locally	
Paper and plastic bags provided by local shops	
Shop register receipts of purchase	
Food ingredients and samples	

Table 9.5 A checklist of 'geographical' artefacts to collect

Reflective task

Drawing on the points made about the value and role of photographs, make a list of reasons why 'geographical' artefacts are important resources for studying places and environments, and what children might learn about a place by using them.

a place, who does or might use it, how it got there, and so on are all important questions in the search to find out more about the place it came from, why it was there and about how it is or might be used. Artefacts are an invaluable component of the study of local and distant places, allowing children to engage with places, affording them a fuller, overall picture of what life is or might be like were you to live there (Catling, 2015c, p. 194, 2012a). A variety of artefacts to collect are listed in Table 9.5.

Using maps

The value of maps

Using and making maps and plans are fundamental components of good geography teaching and learning (Seldin, 2008; Edelson, 2014; Richardson and Richardson, 2016). The interpretation of maps is one of the essential skills that children should develop. Wiegand (n.d.) states: *whether conventional or digital they [maps and atlases] capture the essence of geography more than any other resource.* Maps allow children to record and pass on information about places that they know and to 'read' an environment they cannot visit. Maps are selective but still provide very considerable amounts of useful information remarkably concisely.

Essentially, maps show what is where. They provide information about the features or places they show, or the themes they portray, such as damage to environments. They show the spatial layout, distribution and pattern of these features. From maps we are used to, such as local and national road maps, we can see where places are and the road networks connecting them. We can find our way around, although increasingly this is something that SatNav devices (on mobile phones or used when driving) may help us with or do for us. But it is vital that we know how to read such maps and to be aware of their limitations.

We can develop, from a large-scale topographic map, an idea of what may be in a place, such as a hotel or a post office, whether it is a small or large place, and what type of place it might be – perhaps a coastal resort or an industrial area. As we learn to 'read' and interpret the map, we may be able to develop a sense of what a place may be like and plan what we might do there – for example, while on holiday. We can use maps to indicate how we might like somewhere to change and look in the future. They can help us make predictions of the impact of particular activities on places and the people who live there, such as the building of a new road or housing estate. Furthermore, we might buy several postcard maps to send to friends to show where we are, or as mementoes of places we have visited (Catling and Baker, 2011). Children can be encouraged to collect these and share them with each other to show aspects of places they have visited.

Map use and making enables children to learn how to describe where they are and to record information in an accessible way. Children can use maps to plan and record routes around the classroom, the school, or to and from school and elsewhere. As they develop these skills, children encounter maps from the globe and atlas maps to maps of their country and local area. Effective use of maps, whether creating or interpreting them, allows children to understand better the world around them, and develop their sense of place and relative location within it.

There are many different types of maps, such as those listed in Table 9.6. It is important to have in the classroom or school a good, wide-ranging collection of maps for children to see and refer to. One way to enable this is to encourage children to bring in maps that can be included in a table and wall display of maps. Over time, a class and school can build up a collection of many types of maps that have been collected during visits and holidays by school staff, and have been donated by parents and children. The variety of maps will show the many designs, styles and forms of maps, how ubiquitous they are, and what they portray of the geography of places. However, not all places that are visited have maps, or may have only a few, which in itself can be a matter to discuss: why would a resort or a country not provide many maps for its own people and for visitors?

In the classroom

A mental map memory game

A class of 7–8-year-olds used a large uncluttered picture map of a rural area to develop their awareness of maps and what they communicate. The children worked in groups of three, using large sheets of paper and a set of coloured pens. In each group they numbered themselves #1, # 2 and #3. First, the #1 from each group came out to look at the picture map, observing it carefully for a minute. They returned to their groups and described what they had seen, with #2 drawing what #1 described for two minutes. Next, #2 came out and repeated the observation for one minute looking at what was on the map that had not been mentioned. #2 returned to the group and gave #3 further information to draw for two minutes. Finally, #3 went out, repeating the process, with #1 drawing for one minute. The completed maps were displayed. The children discussed what they had done and how their maps looked, what they found easy and difficult, and so on. They discussed the features of the area, its spatial layout and what sort of place it was.

Practical task

Build up a collection of as many different types of maps as possible. Use the list in Table 9.6 as a guide, but extend it. Create a display of maps in class to discuss what maps are like, what they show, how they show places, information and feelings. This might be undertaken as a settling down or circle time activity, not necessarily part of a geography topic. It can be followed up by asking children to create maps that they would add to the collection.

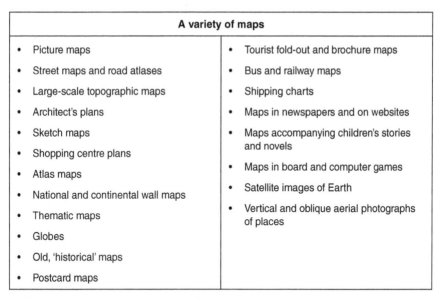

A variety of maps	
• Picture maps	• Tourist fold-out and brochure maps
• Street maps and road atlases	• Bus and railway maps
• Large-scale topographic maps	• Shipping charts
• Architect's plans	• Maps in newspapers and on websites
• Sketch maps	• Maps accompanying children's stories and novels
• Shopping centre plans	
• Atlas maps	• Maps in board and computer games
• National and continental wall maps	• Satellite images of Earth
• Thematic maps	• Vertical and oblique aerial photographs of places
• Globes	
• Old, 'historical' maps	
• Postcard maps	

Table 9.6   A variety of different types of maps

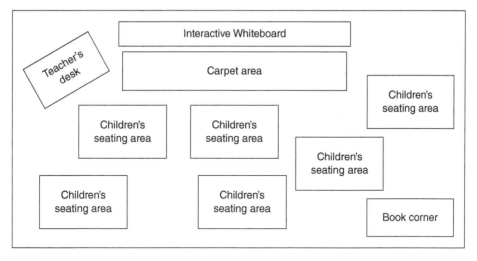

Figure 9.2 A classroom basic plan to orient and also add features and information

Map skills

There are a number of characteristics of maps that children need to be introduced to so that they can learn to use them effectively (Wiegand, 2006). In doing so, they develop various map skills, such as using a map key to interpret the symbols or using a grid reference to find a location. These skills need to be developed through active experience using plans and maps of their classroom (Figure 9.2) as well as outdoors, in place and environment-based tasks, alongside map annotation and map drawing activities.

There are a number of skills that children should develop across the primary years in order to read, understand and interpret maps. The four core skills require that they can understand the meaning of symbols, find the location of features, be able to find directions on and when using a map, and recognise what the scale of the map is.

Symbols: including shapes, lines and colours to show the variety of features and networks on maps. Symbols can help to avoid clutter on maps. Words and numbers – for example, street names and contour heights, can inform map readers of other information to augment symbols. Initially, pictorial symbols are best to use with young children, only later introducing plan shapes and more abstract symbols, as children come across these when using commercial maps. Children enjoy devising and using their own symbols when drawing their own maps. Remind them to make their symbols 'accessible' and intuitive for others to understand so that it is clear what is shown on the map. To help readers, children must be encouraged to provide 'keys' for their maps, which state what their symbols stand for.

Location: stating where features are on maps and finding your way around the map. Initially using phrases such as 'next to' or 'beside' provide relative locational information. Later, children can learn to use alphanumeric grids, development of which can be linked with understanding grids in mathematics, moving to increase complexity with four- and six-figure grid references used on topographic maps.

Direction: encompassing relative direction such as behind, in front, left, etc., and cardinal directions, such as north, southeast, etc. Children can be unsure of directions. As frequently as possible, refer to left, right, straight ahead, behind, to help young children become familiar with and use these relative directions themselves. It is a useful ice-breaker and reinforcement to have children go to different parts of the room or playground (north, south, east and west) according to their name or some other criterion to introduce and build awareness and knowledge of compass points. A support for them is to paint the words at each side of the playground. Continue to familiarise the children with the points of the compass using a compass and compass rose (perhaps drawn on the playground) to which they can refer, allowing them to construct an habitual sense of direction. Increase the complexity with age by using the 4, 8 and even 16 points of the compass. Always encourage the use of correct and accurate directional vocabulary to describe and locate directions and places.

Scale: a vital understanding allowing places to 'fit' on to the map as well as to give an accurate idea of the size of features and places, and their distance in relation to each other. Children should be encouraged to think about relative scale and relative size and distance to begin with, then move on to measurements and absolute scales. Freehand drawing of plans of the classroom and playground can be an introduction, aiming to draw relative lengths accurately and to include relatively accurately drawn features in plan form. This is a difficult concept for young children and needs to be built up gradually, with clear and obvious scales initially, becoming increasingly fine as children's skills develop. Useful links are effectively made with mathematics and in drawing items to scale before making scale drawings of shapes.

Table 9.7 provides a structured approach to progression in developing the wider range of map skills and understanding across the early years and primary age range. Other sources for guidance and advice on children's map progression include Owens (2016), Mohan and Moham (2013) and Wiegand (2006).

A wide variety and range of scales of maps can be used with all children at all ages. Children under 5 can be introduced to the globe and an outline world map where the focus is on the major shapes and areas, such as the continents and oceans, the names of which can be introduced. They can also use a simple picture-plan of their room spaces and walk around noting what is in the room, relating it to what is shown. Children at ages 6–7 can be introduced to plans (Figure 9.2) and begin to use these to identify and name features of their classroom, as well as look at local street maps to find where they live. With older primary children, plans, local and national road maps, atlases and globes may all feature. What develops over the period of their learning is a move from using relative directions to compass directions, from relative sizes and distances to measures and scales. It is the increasing complexity and demand that is made, alongside the use of greater awareness and knowledge of places and environments, for the children to be able to read and interpret more from maps and to make their own maps more appropriately relevant to their topics. Young children will identify and talk about features, while older primary children should be noticing patterns on maps, such as the network of streets in a suburb or the distribution of towns in the local region. Wiegand (2006) provides a detailed account of the development of younger children's map understanding and of approaches to teaching. The *GeogSpace* and *Digimaps* websites provide frameworks for recognising and using the stages of children's understanding of maps; these are applicable and helpful for all children everywhere.

Aerial photographs

The same approach is appropriate with children being introduced to and using aerial photographs. Both oblique aerial photographs (showing the view from above looking down at an angle) and vertical aerial photographs (looking down directly from overhead as in a map) can be introduced in the early years. Using these, children can identify features they see and

	Location	Representation	Distance/size	Perspective	Style	Map drawing	Map use	Map knowledge
Ages 3/4–5/6	Follow and give relative directions – e.g. up/down, left/ right, behind, in front.	Use own symbols on imaginary maps.	Use relative distance vocabulary – e.g. bigger/smaller, longer/shorter.	Look down on model layouts. Draw round objects to make a plan shape.	Extract information from and add to picture maps. Use land/sea globes and world playmap.	Draw picture maps of imaginary places and from stories.	Talk about own picture maps. Talk about features in the classroom, school grounds.	Consistent reference to continents, seas and place names on globe and large maps.
Ages 5/6–7/8	Talk about relative positions. Follow the 4 compass directions: North, South, East, West.	Use own and class agreed symbols on simple maps.	Spatial matching: begin to match the same area – e.g. a continent or country, on a larger or smaller scale map and to a globe.	Develop understanding of plan view: look down on objects to draw a plan. Look at features on oblique and vertical aerial photographs.	Name land/sea on globes and atlas maps. Compare a world map with a globe. Use modified plans and large-scale maps in school grounds and local area.	Draw maps using symbols of real and imaginary places and routes.	Identify and discuss features in the school grounds and local area. Follow a route. Use a plan. Use an appropriate atlas and globe to find oceans, continents and other features.	Locate and name on a national map, such as a desk-top or wall map, major features – e.g. seas, rivers, cities, home location, and use pictures to illustrate these.
Ages 7/8–9/10	Use letter/ number co-ordinates. Use the 4 compass points to locate features.	Introduce need for key and standard symbols.	Discuss distances and size of large and small areas on maps.	Draw shapes of features from vertical aerial photographs.	Identify features on oblique and vertical aerial photographs and on large-scale maps.	Draw a map of a short route with features in the correct order.	Use larger scale map outside. Use maps of other localities.	Continue to locate, name and illustrate features on your national map, and introduce locating features on continental and World maps.

	Location	Representation	Distance/size	Perspective	Style	Map drawing	Map use	Map knowledge
	Introduce the tropics and polar circles and equator.	Use symbols to identify information on different maps, including atlas maps.	Spatial matching: boundary matching (find same boundary on different scale maps).	Draw sketch map from high viewpoint.	Look at variety of types of maps: local to national and world maps.	Make a map using simple proportional scale drawing.	Discuss features on maps and how they are shown.	
Ages 9/10– 11/12	Use 4-figure co-ordinates to locate features on a map. Introduce 6-figure grid references. Use 8 and then 16 compass points. Introduce latitude and longitude on atlas maps to find places and time zones.	Draw a sketch map: use symbols and key. Develop awareness of symbols on large- and medium-scale national maps. Begin to use standard national mapping symbols. Develop use of atlas map symbols to find out information.	Measure straight-line distances on a map. Introduce scale drawing using measurements. Develop scale reading of non-linear distances. Compare map scales and what is included related to scale.	Develop use of plan view and symbols in mapping. Use models and photographs to introduce slope, shape and contour lines to identify relief features.	Use index and contents pages in atlases. Use medium-scale (e.g. 1:10,000, 1:25,000 and 1:50,000) national maps. Note distribution patterns on maps. Develop relational understanding of the globe and atlas map.	Draw a variety of thematic maps, based on own data – e.g. showing geographical patterns in the environment. Draw scale plans showing greater detail and accuracy, with a scale bar.	Compare large-scale maps and vertical aerial photographs. Select and justify map for a purpose. Discuss how maps are made and used. Follow routes on small-scale national maps and describe features seen.	Extend locating features and places on national, continental and World maps. Discuss, using illustrations, what places might be like. Consider the important places to know around the nation and the World.

Table 9.7 Progression in children's map understanding and skills across the early years and primary schooling

recognise, particularly if the aerial photograph shows their school and the area round about at a large scale. The widespread availability of Google Earth and Google Maps means that aerial photographs are now common-place. Large-scale aerial photographs should be used throughout the pri-mary school, with demands increasing on children to find features on both oblique and vertical photographs and relate the two to each other as well as to simple and, later, more complex topographic maps. Children can use aerial photographs alongside local and other maps to look at patterns and to identify information the map does not show, such as vehicles on the road and car park use. They can consider the time of year and look for changes shown by comparing the sources.

The use of maps and aerial photographs should always be linked with other aspects of study, such as an enquiry in the local area into a particular topic or concern, or into another locality (which might be found on Google Earth or Google Maps), or related to a particular environmental theme or issue. Children should use them alongside ground-level photographs and the other information that is available, so that by connecting photographs and information with what is shown on maps, they gain deeper insight into how a place is today, how it may have developed in the past, and what it might become like in the future.

Using maps with children

Introduce young children to 'plan view' by looking down on familiar objects in their classroom and playground, photographing and drawing these, full size and in reduced size. Such photographs or plans of features in class and around school can be given to children to find. Children might be asked to imagine what a feature they cannot look down on looks like from above, such as their playground (which they might be able to view from where they stand or an upper-floor window) or a school building, and to draw a plan of it. This might be compared with an aerial photograph or a map. These activities can be part of a topic on 'exploring how our school looks', as one of the 'angles' at which to look at the school. While using teacher-prepared and commercially available maps with children, it is equally important for them to create their own plans and maps whenever possible. This develops their mapping skills, helping them to recognise how maps work and how important they are in com-municating information that we want to get across. Starting with simple plans of the classroom and using them to navigate their way around helps to develop several map-work skills. Working in small groups, children can make their own plan and get each other to follow it, developing accuracy and clarity as it is used. Similarly, children can make their own maps from information about their own local area or another place they study.

Roberts (2013) argues that children should be encouraged to use *affective mapping*, recording their feelings about particular places and environments, alongside developing their practical map-making skills. Children could develop affective maps of their school grounds before doing so for their local area.

Trails are an excellent way to engage children and develop their orientation and map-work skills. These can be designed for any level and can include clues to be found in order to complete the trail. This approach is a particularly effective way of encouraging older children to work and learn with younger children as they support them in following the trail. Trail maps can be informative and also explore emotional responses (see also the box above, Mywalks on p.255).

Other kinds of mapping such as map lines and journey sticks provide a three-dimensional approach (Whittle, 2006). Map lines originate from the Native American Indian tradition of collecting memorable natural objects on a journey such as leaves from a specific tree, stones from a river bed and grasses from a meadow, and tying them on to a piece of string so that the journey can be remembered and retraced on the way back. It is an environmentally generated memory map. Children can go on a similar journey in the school grounds, their local area or further afield, collecting objects on the way to remind them of where they have been. It might be that these objects are less natural and include crisp packets, old rail tickets, and so on (although be careful how such items are collected in a safe way). For younger children, it is easier and more rewarding to use a piece of card with some sticky tape, on to which they can stick their memorable objects. As well as string, sticks can be used, with children encouraged to choose a dead stick that they find in a wooded area (not remove one from a tree) and stick their objects on to those – hence, a *journey stick* (Whittle, 2006). However, in all cases we need to take into account guidance about care for the environment and discouragement in particular places of scientific and scenic interest, and in relation to wild flowers, not to pick plants or collect items unless it is clear that this is allowed. Thoughtfulness about the environment is essential to take into account.

As children's map skills develop, they can begin to use increasingly complex maps with more detail and can be encouraged to use more sophisticated vocabulary, referring to the points of the compass, grid references and scale (Bridge, 2010; Catling, n.d.). This will give them increasing access to a wider range of different maps that they can use in conjunction with local area studies, understanding the locational context of places, patterns and processes in the environment, and of distant place and global themes. Linked to this is the potential for using digital maps and introducing primary children to geographical information systems (GIS).

In the classroom

Mapping in the school grounds and with stories

A class of 7–8-year-olds used maps to become more aware of their school grounds. Working in small teams, they were given three or four different photographs. In their classroom they discussed where they thought each photograph was taken. They were given a map and taken out to find the different locations/features shown on the photographs in the grounds, which used and developed their observational skills. On the map they marked where the photograph was taken, the direction of view, and anything that had changed since it was taken. They used a digital camera to take a similar photograph. Returning to class, they located their retaken photographs on a prepared map of the school grounds on the computer, noting its orientation and listing changes. Displaying the whole map on the interactive whiteboard, they discussed the changes they found as a class and identified similarities and patterns in their findings

In cross-curricular contexts, maps can be an excellent enhancement to stories (Bridge, n.d.). Drawing maps and plans, children can create an imagined world for their stories. Many storybooks have a map or a plan of the imagined world, and these can be read and shown to stimulate children's imagination. Classic examples include *Treasure Island, Winnie-the-Pooh* and Katie Morag's adventures on Struay. Children might draw maps for those stories that do not include a map, interpreting and describing the environment. Historical geography enquiries into how the local area has changed over time requires the use of old maps. The use of local large-scale maps and of older maps and earlier editions of current maps can be particularly effective here. Atlas maps can be used in studies of other times and places to find out where places that are mentioned are located and what that part of your country or the world is now.

Practical task

Create your own affective map of your local area using the information at the following website and consider how to adapt this for different ages of children.

www.geography.org.uk/projects/valuingplaces/cpdunits/think maps/#924

Introducing atlas maps

Primary children can be introduced to globes and world playmat and beginner atlas maps from their earliest school years. Indeed, it is valuable to have both a solid globe and an inflatable globe available for children in their pre-school and reception year settings. Here children can be introduced to the idea of the Earth as a globe (or sphere). They are able to become used to seeing a globe and to handling it, and can begin to learn that there is land and sea, how these may be shown by shapes and colours, and that we name the various large and small areas and places they can see. Scoffham (2018) notes that children entering primary school have some sense of the wider world, about which they have built up ideas from picture books, television cartoons and young children's films and digital media sources. It is important, then, that from their start in school, children continue to make use of globes and are introduced to atlas maps. A wall map of the world ought to be a staple of every classroom and setting. The use of globes and atlas maps will help children from their earliest years to develop their awareness of the world through reference to maps showing the world, continents and their home nation.

Children's understanding of the world and national, continental and world maps builds over time. They have to begin, even vaguely, to grasp the enormous areas that they look at, begin to appreciate that they are drawn at a very reduced scale and that the maps are highly selective, not least in atlas maps drawn to introduce young children to the outline of the world, continents, oceans and some major features of the Earth, such as rivers, mountains and deserts as well as cities. Later in their primary school they will meet and use maps showing, for instance, more detailed physical geography, and maps showing countries, cities and transport links, which are aspects of human geography. Older primary children are likely to be asked to find information from thematic atlas maps, showing such topics about the world as where various significant foods are grown, where key resources are found, the distribution of where people live, trade, weather and climate patterns, the distribution of volcanoes and earthquakes, places of conflict and areas where there are significant environmental concerns, to name just some.

Atlas maps involve language – as almost all maps do – which provide challenges for primary children of all ages, not least because of their developing reading skills, but also because of the unfamiliarity of names and that their pronunciation is not always ensured by their spelling. Various type sizes and fonts are used in atlas maps to denote the types and significance of names, an aspect of symbols with which they need to become familiar. Children need to learn the ways in which dots, lines, shapes and colours are used to represent areas and places through symbols. Scale will introduce them to 'big numbers', of which they may have a limited grasp, and the idea of representational scale (1cm shows 100km) takes quite a while to appreciate. Primary children also find it hard to go beyond the direct information on the page, tending to take it literally; if there are few places shown in a country, then there must be few there: but have them look at a map of your country and discuss the number of places they know about in their area and nearby which are not shown on the atlas map to help them recognise that not marking places does not mean they are not there. The use of small-scale maps at different scales can help their developing understanding – for example, use a national road atlas and look at atlases produced for secondary schools, which include more detailed national and other maps.

It is important that children use atlases throughout their primary schooling. When places are mentioned in the news or by children about family holidays and connections, look up these places, which might mean using Google Maps (see the box below) to search them out if they do not appear in a detailed high-quality atlas map which every primary school should have. A wall map of places encountered from these sources and through their studies across the curriculum, from stories, artists and history topics, as well as geographical studies, can be created over a year. Children might look at various points in the year at where the places that have been mapped are mentioned, and consider why some places seem to have few, if any, references (Catling, 2017a). This can help children realise that places we note relate to what we hear, see and study; our knowledge of the world is both selective and to an extent chosen for us. We might wonder what sort of understanding of the world children in other nations build up about the world. In these ways, teaching and learning with atlases helps children to develop their world awareness and knowledge, as much as it can help them understand that their knowing about the world is partial and that they should not jump to conclusions or make assumptions about places, but recognise their own lack of knowledge and reserve judgement.

Further advice on using atlas maps to help children find out about countries, continents and the world is given in Chapter 14.

Three world satellite photo and mapping websites

Google Earth (www.google.com/earth/)

The site provides detailed images of different places across the world and allows children to take 3D virtual tours to otherwise inaccessible spots. The technology continues to develop and becomes more sophisticated, offering more insights into our environment and its processes. Children can create maps and plans of their local and other areas, tagging places on the map with photographs and information. Google Earth can be used to help children learn to use satellite navigation and global positioning systems (GPS) to create their own hyperlinks on a virtual tour they create using images. By using the facility 'virtual tour' and choosing a place you want to visit, children can be encouraged to explore and investigate the images and features. Video footage can be particularly effective in re-creating scenes and bringing them to life. YouTube offers footage of many different environments.

Google Maps (https://maps.google.com/)

This is a mapping service provided via the Web. It includes area and street maps that show roads, rivers and streams and other water features, public buildings and other features, depending on the scale of map you use. It provides the capacity to plan travel routes by car, bicycle or on foot, and by public transport. A key feature is that you can zoom in and out of the map to see it at the scale you wish to, which can help children see at an enlarged scale the local area and move out by decreasing the scale to view the larger area around it, widening the area as the scale is decreased further to regional, national and continental scales. Children can undertake similar activities on Google Maps as on Google Earth images.

Worldmapper (www.worldmapper.org)

A highly visual and immediate Web-based project that presents a large number of world maps, each depicting how the world would look if each country was drawn not according to the area taken up by its land, but by some other variable (Pritchard, 2008, p. 30). Some maps depict the Western world hugely distorted in size using a wealth variable, while others distort other global regions considerably using a variable such as child labour. The maps raise many important and relevant issues. Links between geography and citizenship can be made. The website contains useful areas for ideas about using the maps in the classroom, including with older primary children.

Geographical Information Systems (GIS)

Learning through cartography and GIS

Maps motivate children's engagement and enhance their understanding of the world around them in a joined up and connected way. Using maps and other geographical information enables geographers to 'draw' the landscape in which we live, and allows us to identify and comprehend different environments and places and how they are interconnected. All maps are a key source of geographical information. They provide layers of information in a two-dimensional surface – for example, on a national landscape map you might look at the pattern of roads, the distribution of settlements, the relief form of the landscape and the layout of an urban area or rural field. This spatially based information is the basis of geographical information systems (usually referred to by the acronym GIS).

GIS refers to a system that manages geographical data spatially using digital computer hardware and software. The geographical data is the information that is included in the GIS system. For our purposes here, the geographical data must contain locational information (just as a global positioning system – GPS – data for finding your location and routes on maps does), which enables it to be saved, retrieved and presented in map format. GIS data includes such examples as the location of cameras in cities or where certain sorts of crimes are committed, where electricity, water, telecommunications cables or gas pipes run under streets, and where changes occur in crop growth patterns and woodland destruction or planting. Almost any environmental and place-based information you can identify is geographical information and can be included in a GIS database. Enabling primary children to learn to read and understand maps, including viewing them via the web and on map and atlas programmes, provides children with the basics for recognizing, understanding and working with GIS systems.

GIS uses digital computer programs to represent and analyse our natural and urban landscapes so that we can understand them more fully. GIS can enable us, for instance, to examine two-dimensional maps and plans in three dimensions, to navigate environments and to move between different scales, zooming in and out. GIS can also provide information and data about places and layer this information on to maps, helping us to 'see' what is there and to focus on selected aspects of the natural or human environment, and of environmental concerns and issues (Harder, 2015).

The importance of GIS is that it is now very much part of our lives, be it for locating a new distribution warehouse for a delivery company, managing traffic flows, informing planning debates about housing or city centre developments, or environmental monitoring (Milson et al., 2012). The value of GIS is that it not only provides geographical information, but that it enables the data to be interrogated in order to understand a particular situation, to consider solutions to problems and to find out new information by layering different environmental information about a place or area to see what it shows.

Introducing primary children to spatial technologies, such as through digital maps, is a starting point for their developing use of GIS during their secondary education (Biddulph et al., 2015; Fargher, 2017). Given the importance of digital technologies in our lives, and increasingly children's awareness and use of such technologies, they can be introduced to GIS. This needs to begin simply through the use of digital mapping resources. From the many recent developments that can be used in varied ways with primary children – and who seem to be able to manipulate them at an increasingly young age – the digital software noted in the box below can be used to encourage further and creative approaches to using and understanding mapping as an introduction to GIS.

Software to use in introducing primary children to GIS

ZeeMaps (www.zeemaps.com)

ZeeMaps is similar in concept to Google Earth and Google Maps. It encourages and enables children to create their own interactive maps of places of interest and mark them using images, videos and audio inputs. Older children can learn about different ways to create layers of information about places they can then retrieve, question and use to understand and explain a wide range of physical and human geographical phenomena. It is appropriate for use with older primary children.

ArcGIS (www.arcgis.com)

ArcGIS is better used with older primary children. It is a cloud-based mapping platform and a useful tool for accessing geographical data, enabling children to search for, load and import different data sets from the Web. It can also be used to import the user's own data, which can then be mapped and presented. ArcGIS is a good basis for primary children to begin to understand what GIS is about, but as with ZeeMaps and Google Maps, you will need to be familiar with how it works and competent in using it before introducing it to children.

Digimap for Schools (http://digimapforschools.edina.ac.uk)

Digimaps, which is provided by the UK's Ordnance Survey (OS) national map producer, has a wide range of geospatial data that can be accessed and manipulated, much of it for free with other elements available through a subscription. This resource includes maps at a variety of scales as well as historical layers for the 1890s and 1950s allowing local historical geography explorations and making effective links with local history studies. There is also aerial imagery layers with and without road views, as well as *Geograph for Schools*, with geotagged imagery that can be viewed on the OS map.

Data visualisation (http://earth.nullschool.net)

Data visualisations of geospatial data, such as representations of the wind systems blowing around the Earth, illustrates a different focus and scale of geographical information that can help children recognise and appreciate particular aspects of the Earth's systems.

An important aspect of developing GIS understanding involves children's burgeoning spatial skills. Decoding and following clues on trails and orienteering courses develops children's spatial awareness, reasoning skills and collaboration, and above all is engaging and highly interactive. It is a practical way to foster their geospatial reasoning.

- The use of QR codes to encrypt clues and position them in strategic places can prove to be highly efficacious, and children can be encouraged to make up their own trails and maps, and get their friends to try them out. See: www.qrstuff.com
- Geocaching has proved to be a similarly absorbing and educative activity. See: www.geocaching.com

A further area of daily geography to explore involves the use of digital technologies at personal and societal levels to record information and to enable communication, such as mobile phone photography and the use of geo-located images from iPhones, iPads and other digital cameras for quickly mapping fieldwork data or revisiting trails and then sharing that information – for example, through Twitter. This raises questions about not just using new technologies in geographical learning, but of investigating their impact as aspects of our geographical lives. This focus can extend the topics we might want to plan into our geography curriculum. One topic might be to what extent children communicate locally and globally using email and related systems, text messaging and social media such as Facebook, Instagram, Twitter, and so on (Moores, 2012). Another concerns the nature, purpose and ubiquity of surveillance in society provided through the use of visible and hidden cameras in shops and malls, on high streets and along roads across the nation. Do you and the children know where these cameras are and why they are there? It might be a topic for investigation.

Do you have locational information on your mobile phone on or off? As we know, we are able to locate individuals through the use of the mobile phone signal networks. Increasingly, parents are willing to provide their older primary children with mobile phones in order for their children to feel safe, to be able to contact their parents when they need to and have contact with friends who they arrange to meet. Such prized assets as mobile phones can also be used for surveillance by parents of their children covertly (Freeman and Tranter, 2011; de Souza e Silva and Frith, 2012), especially when linked with GPS mapping. With primary age children increasingly accessing mobile phones, using them to maintain contact with family and friends, and for other activities, there is a primary geography topic to link with local studies. Of course, this requires children's agreement to undertake, for ethical reasons.

Technologies are not only tools to use; they are used to respond to and shape our interests and lives as consumers – a point not lost on national supermarkets with their interconnected computer systems linking stores, warehouses and production companies, to ensure the goods that people 'want' are in the stores when they 'need' them, particularly in terms of 'next day' and 'just in time' deliveries – and to ensure that you are informed about these if they have your digital contact details. As a growing element in our everyday geographies, we can investigate their impact in primary geography as much as use them (Poore, 2013). Such topics as those outlined above can act as informative introductions to GIS is our lives and societies.

Be up to date with digital technologies in geography

Two areas that have benefited and continue to gain from the development of computer software and hardware are map work and fieldwork. The use of digital cameras, videos and other mobile technology, such as hand-held digital recorders and mobile phones, has created advances not only in the efficacy of the work, but also in the children's engagement and interaction with their own learning (France *et al.*, 2015). There is immediacy in using such resources since data gathered can be uploaded to class computers and whiteboards on return to school. This has allowed children to connect with what they are doing and become excited about doing it.

There have been and will continue to be considerable advances in the provision and range of digital technologies supporting geographical learning (Reynolds, 2014; Pickford, 2006; Russell, 2010). Increasingly, new technologies are available for children in primary schools to use, whether these are iPad cameras and data-recording devices for weather or information collected on fieldwork. It can prove difficult to keep up with the latest innovations and developments, but it is worth keeping abreast of the dissemination of innovative ideas on Twitter, for example. New technologies are soon superseded by even newer ones and keeping up with developments is challenging. Using what others have recommended is advisable. Ensure that you try out any new software, hardware and Web sources first. You can keep up to date with developments through the Australian Geography Teachers' apostrophe Association SpatialWorlds site and the websites of the Geographical Association, Royal Geographical Society and The National Geographic, as well as through the journal *Primary Geography*. There is a variety of good advice provided by Pickford (2006) and Russell (2010). Sources for applied contexts include Nielsen and Webb (2011) and Reynolds (2014).

Reflective task

Consider how advancing technology is enhancing children's geographical thinking. This link can help you get started: www.geography.org.uk/projects/gtip/orientationpieces/usingictl/#top

What might be one or more ways you can develop children's understanding of maps through using GIS?

 Key points

This chapter has:

- advocated the importance of outdoor learning and fieldwork in geography;
- outlined approaches to organising fieldwork, indicated a sense of progression, provided ideas for carrying out fieldwork and developing relevant skills outside and inside school;
- considered the importance of photographs, film and artefacts in geographical learning, and outlined some approaches;
- discussed the centrality of maps in geographical learning and provided a sense of progression in map and atlas learning skills and understanding;
- identified an approach to introducing children to geographical information systems (GIS);
- noted the need to keep up to date with developments in digital technologies.

Moving on

In school, find out how often children work outside the classroom, go out for fieldwork and use photographs and maps. Which geographical studies do they undertake fieldwork in? To what extent do they use maps and photographs outside the classroom as well as in class in geographical and other studies? When and how are artefacts used in geography teaching? What roles do digital technologies and ICT play in geographical teaching and learning?

Further reading

The following books provide further insight and ideas about fieldwork, map work
and the use of photographs and ICT.

Council for Learning Outside the Classroom (2008) *Out and About Guidance*. www.
lotc.org.uk

Dolan A (2019) *Powerful Primary Geography: A toolkit for 21st century learning*.
Abingdon: Routledge.

Hoodless, P, Bermingham, S, McCreery, E and Bowen, P (2009) *Teaching Humanities
in Primary Schools*. Exeter: Learning Matters.

Pickford, T (2006) *Learning ICT in the Humanities*. London: David Fulton.

Pike, S (2016) *Learning Primary Geography: Ideas and inspirations from classrooms*.
Abingdon; Routledge.

Scoffham, S (ed.) (2010) *Primary Geography Handbook*. Sheffield: Geographical
Association.

Waite S (ed.) (2017) *Children Learning Outside the Classroom* (2nd edn). London:
Sage.

Wiegand, P (2006) *Learning and Teaching with Maps*. London: Routledge.

Look for further teaching approaches in issues of *Primary Geographer*.

Useful websites

ACT Outdoor Education Association (ACTOEA): www.actoea.org.au

Bing maps: www/bing.com.maps

Council for Learning Outside the Classroom: www.lotc.org.uk

Digimaps for Schools: http://digimapforschools.edina.ac.uk/

Forest Schools: www.forestschools.com

Geographical Association: www.geography.org.uk

Geographical Association Photo Gallery: www.geographyphotos.com

Geographical Association special interest groups:

ICT: www.geography.org.uk/getinvolved/committeessigs/ictsig/

Fieldwork and outdoor learning: www.geography.org.uk/getinvolved/committeessigs/
fieldworksig

Geocaching: www,geocaching.com

GeogSpace (Australian Geography apostrophe Teachers' Association): www.geog
space.edu.au

GeoGuessr: https://geoguessr.com/

Google Earth: www.google.com/earth/

Map Creator: http://mapcreator.here.com

National Geographic – Map Skills for Elementary Students: www.nationalgeo
graphic.org/education/map-skills-elementary-students/

Quikmaps: www.quikmaps.com

QR Codes: www.qrstuff.com

Royal Geographical Society: www.rgs.org

Teaching Outside the Classroom: www.teachingoutsidetheclassroom.com

SpatialWorlds: www.spatialworlds.blogspot.com

PART 2

EXPLORING GEOGRAPHY TEACHING and CURRICULUM

CHAPTER 10

IN THE BEGINNING

Geographical learning in the early years

 Chapter objectives

This chapter enables you to:

- be aware of the geographical potential in children's pre-school and early years education for initiating and developing their knowledge of the world;
- have explored a variety of play approaches and activities that support young children's geographical learning;
- know of activities to use to develop young children's understanding of place and sustainability.

Introduction

Play and play environments are important for all children (Frost, 2010). This chapter explores opportunities available in pre-school and nursery environments and settings to enhance our youngest children's geographical experiences and understanding. Young children's early development is stimulated by their opportunities for observation and play in their own and other places (Louis, 2009). A key element of provision and practice in the early years is play, which lies at the heart of the learning environment inside and outside (Bilton, 2005, 2010; Bilton and Crook, 2016; Bruce, 2001, 2005; White, 2014; Else, 2009; Smith, 2010; Walsh *et al.*, 2017). The play environment, its space and resources, its accessibility and its planned use are central in developing early geographical learning. In several parts of the world geographical learning is initiated and supported with pre-school children in the context of early years learning initiatives, such as those that focus on children's awareness of, connections with and early understanding about the world from their local places to the wider environment – for instance, in the constituent countries of the UK and in Singapore, New Zealand and Australia (CCEA, 2006; Scottish Government, 2008; DEEWR, 2009; MOE, 2012; Curriculum for Wales, 2015; DfE, 2017; Ministry of Education, 2017).

The 'future' starts here

While the term 'environment' is used, the word geography unsurprisingly is never directly mentioned in national early years learning requirements, but the premise underpinning references to developing children's connections with and early understanding of their world is that the *child is a young geographer* (Owen and Ryan, 2001). A variety of evidence was outlined in Chapter 3 showing that young children develop their geographical and environmental awareness from their very earliest years, through their everyday geographies. They bring this developing and evolving background into their pre-school and nursery settings as 3/4 to 5/6 years old. Their early lives have been lived in places, and place lies very much *at the heart of children's geographical understanding* (Milner, 1996, p. 7). This provides a strong rationale for developing their environmental and geographical experience during their learning in their early years (Alcock, 2012; Conway *et al.*, 2008; Cooper, 2004a; Cooper *et al.*, 2010; Cutter-Mackenzie *et al.*, 2014; Heal and Cook, 1998; Martin, 1995; Martin and Owens, 2010; Milner, 1996, 1997; Palmer and Birch, 2004; Spink *et al.*, 2008). Several very good reasons underpin this.

- *Children's play experience:* Children's experiences of and in places, and of their features, is enhanced through providing a variety of play and other learning opportunities in the nursery setting indoor and outdoor areas. The nursery environment becomes a part of their everyday and personal geographies.

- *Children's observations in and of their immediate environments:* Involving children in close observation of natural aspects of their environment in their pre-school setting and nearby off-site and in using play resources on-site to engage their awareness of, interest in and fascination for the world immediately about them.
- *Children's direct experience:* Taking young children into the local area to walk interesting routes and visit particular places to discover more about them and make use of them develops their experience of real places, enhancing their personal geography.
- *Children's imaginations:* Reading a variety of story and other books to and with children, which introduce them to a wider range of places and environmental matters, develops their awareness of their own places and brings new places to them, particularly where stories focus on events and people's lives and activities.
- *Children's mental maps:* Children's play and exploration in the nursery, as well as through guided walks locally, supports the development of their awareness of places as the foundation of their 'mental maps'. This is vital for understanding how our world works, for ways of finding, and for understanding pictures, maps and artefacts.
- *Children's awareness of the 'wider world':* Young children's knowledge of the world about them and further afield, of people's lives in places and of environments will be partial, inaccurate, even perhaps stereotypical and biased. This is not unexpected, since their experience is very limited and evolving. Misunderstandings and prejudices can become embedded at an early age (Grigg and Hughes, 2013). Through play, activities and talk, children may exhibit their understandings and feelings, which can be responded to and tackled.
- *Children's curiosity and sense of wonder:* Young children are naturally curious about the world around them. We can encourage their asking of questions and provide opportunities and resources to respond to them. We should foster their fascination with the world, their sense of awe at the new places they encounter, at the variety and incredible nature of the natural world, as well at people, their lives and activities, landscapes, features and urban environments.
- *Children's awareness of how the environment is treated and used:* Young children are not unaware of how people make use of and care for, or not, the places where they live. They learn about this through family experiences and others they engage with and begin to understand that people can be tidy or untidy, drop litter or bin it or take it home, and keep places they play in well or do not care for them. They have favourite and disliked places. They notice dirt, smells and tastes in their places and places they pass through, and they see sites where damage is done.

We must recognise that children have feelings about this, as well as views on what they encounter and what should or could be done to improve matters – to 'make them better'.

- *Children's active participation:* Their experience of and engagement with the world at hand should be active, through helping to look after and put away the resources used daily. It can occur through discussion and choices about which place and environmental activities to undertake. It can involve suggesting ways to enhance activities in the nursery outdoor area. Children learn through active participation in contributing to decisions that affect their environment.

In the classroom

Enacting a place-based children's story

A group of 3- and 4-year-old children were read and shown the engaging picture story, *Rosie's Walk* (Hutchins, 1992) by their nursery assistant (QCA, 2005). They talked about the characters and the farmyard shown in the pictures. Several of the children had seen farmyards in other stories and on television. They were encouraged to recognise the locational language in the story. They went outside to enact the story. The assistant retold *Rosie's Walk*, encouraging the children to act out the different roles as they went around the outdoor area, pretending that the various features were different parts of the farmyard scene. This resulted in much merriment as the children tried to imitate Rosie's 'journey' and her encounters. When the re-enactment was completed, the assistant used a variety of relative positional and distance language to involve the children in looking around the outdoor area, so that they began to use terms such as 'beside', 'behind' and 'close to'.

Practical task

Find a suitable picture story book to read to 3/4 to 5/6-year-old children based on a place or an environment. There are many picture story books to select from, set all around the world. Select and read one of these or find a comparable one about a place and/or environment.

Where the Forest Meets the Sea (Baker, 1987); *We're Going on a Bear Hunt* (Rosen and Oxenbury, 1993); *The Lighthouse Keeper's Lunch*

(Armitage and Armitage, 1994); *The Snail and the Whale* (Donaldson and Scheffler, 2003); *The Boy on the Beach* (Daly, 1999); *Are We There Yet? A Journey Round Australia* (Lester, 2004); *Mia's Story* (Foreman, 2006); *Meerkat Mail* (Gravett, 2006); *Rattle and Rap* (Steggall, 2008); *Charlie and Lola: But Where Completely are We?* (Child, 2009); *One World Together* (Anholt and Anholt, 2013); *Kicking a Ball* (Ahlberg, 2014); *Grandad's Island* (Davies, 2015); *Amelie and the Great Outdoors* (Barker, 2016); *Lucy in the City* (Dillemuth, 2016).

For further 'geographical' stories, see Appendix 2.

See how you would use your chosen story to develop one or more activities for young children to encourage them to think about, imagine and 'look at' the place and/or environment. Which 'geographical' and 'environmental' language would you encourage the children to practise and understand through a play activity?

Young children connecting with and understanding their world

In their early years, young children learn about the world around them through exploration in safe environments, from their family and friends, through the media and places they visit, through what they see, hear, smell and touch, and through stories (Dolan, 2017). Early years provision in national education systems encompasses many of the basic aspects of environmental, geographical, cultural and social awareness and understanding, including respect for where they live and other places, concern for the environment, appreciation and valuing of diversity, a sense of belonging and identity, and an understanding of rights, responsibilities and fairness as prerequisites for community participation. There may also be links with basic aspects of scientific, technological, historical and social awareness and early understandings. It involves developing children's awareness, knowledge and understanding, as well as skills, values and attitudes associated with these areas. It encompasses ideas to do with places, the natural and social environment and communities. It helps to lay the foundations of young children's geographical learning. There are a number of geographical dimensions that underpin this early learning (DEEWR, 2009), particularly the following:

1. developing a sense of the local community, and in doing so of their neighbourhood – their place;
2. finding out about the diversity of culture, heritage, background and tradition, and developing awareness of the similarities, differences and connections between people, and valuing distinctiveness;

3. becoming aware of ways in which people are included or excluded from physical and social environments;
4. showing increasing knowledge of and respect for natural and constructed environments;
5. demonstrating a growing appreciation of and care for natural and constructed environments and places;
6. being able to explore, infer, predict and hypothesise in order to develop an increased understanding of the interdependence between land, people, plants and animals;
7. being observant of and responsive to changes in their setting, community and neighbourhood;
8. developing awareness of the impact of human activity on environments and the interdependence of living things.

In developing their experience, knowledge and understanding, our youngest children should:

- encounter accurate information about their immediate and the wider world, including about how people live, various ways of life, what affects these and how they affect others;
- undertake explorations and investigations to find out about their environment, their places and their wider world, and begin to apply the knowledge, understanding and skills they gain;
- learn to respect and value people, their communities and their places, and develop positive but critically aware views and attitudes about others, places and environments;
- find out about the world they inhabit, its varied environments, and the lives and activities of peoples and places similar to and different from their own;
- find out and talk about environmental concerns and ways to care for the environment.

These aspirations draw on children's 'world awareness', which emerges at an early age (Cooper, 2004a; Glauert *et al.*, 2003; Palmer and Birch, 2004) and support the exploration of cultural awareness and environmental feelings.

 Reflective task

Look back to Chapter 3 and the section on 'The youngest children pre-school'. Consider how your national early years guidelines on helping young children connect with, know about and make a contribution to their world reflect and build on 3/4–5/6-year-olds' emergent geographical understanding.

Now consider how such pre-school experience can lead into geographical learning where it is an aspect of the curriculum for 5–7-year-olds. Identify examples of the connections between pre-school children's geographical experience and their first years in school.

In Singapore, the early learning intentions state that by the age of 6 young children should:

- *show an interest in the world they live in;*
- *find out why things happen and how things work through simple investigations;*
- *develop a positive attitude towards the world around them.*

(MOE, 2012, p. 37)

These outcomes are founded on the premise that *children are naturally curious and their sense of wonder should be nurtured and sustained. They should be encouraged to observe, ask questions and make sense of the world around them* (MOE, 2012, p. 29). These interests are the basis of early geographical learning and are reflected in other nations' early learning expectations and goals.

Young children, play and geography

Learning through play is essential for children's effective early learning (e.g. Bilton and Crook, 2016; Bruce, 2001, 2005; Filer, 2008; Walsh *et al.*, 2017; Wood, 2013; Whitebread, 2012; Whitebread and Coltman, 2015; Cutter-Mackenzie *et al.*, 2014). While there are many approaches to take to play provision in the early years, it is suggested that three types of play approach can best facilitate early years environmental learning: open-ended play, modelled play and purposefully framed play (Edwards and Cutter-Mackenzie, 2013; Cutter-Mackenzie *et al.*, 2014). These are outlined in the box below. Purposefully framed play connects open-ended and modelled play with adult engagement with the children, providing guidance for the children towards the geographical, environmental or sustainability theme or concept. It is argued that combining these three approaches enables children's engagement with, growing awareness of and early knowledge about, and emergent positive attitudes to, the environment and its understanding and care. These play approaches offer children opportunities to develop their sense of their world, but there is a requirement for contexts within which children can *explore, develop and represent their learning experiences* (DCSF, 2008, p. 7). Physical and virtual places, such as those outlined in Table 10.1, can be such play contexts for young children, providing opportunities to play out aspects of their place and environmental experience.

Three approaches to play

Open-ended play

Children are provided with natural and other resources that indicate a sustainability, environmental and geographical theme or concept, but with which they can investigate, play and explore with minimal adult engagement or suggestion.

Modelled play

Adults in the setting show, outline and/or explain the potential of the available resources for an environmental, geographical or sustainability theme or concept before the children are able to interact, examine and play with them with minimal adult interaction.

Purposefully framed play

Materials are provided that suggest geographical, sustainability and environmental activities, and the adults give the children time to play open-endedly before providing modelled guidance about potential play and interact with the children to foster their engagement with the environmental, geographical or sustainability theme or concept.

Source: Edwards and Cutter-Mackenzie, 2013; Cutter-Mackenzie *et al.*, 2014

Play environments	Context of geographical play	Examples of environments
Real environments	Places that are part of the 'normal' or adult environment, used by people of many ages and not necessarily intended for children's play or use but which children may subvert or manipulate for play activities.	Rooms, gardens, playgrounds, parks, the beach, water/derelict land, overgrown areas, woodlands, paddocks, paths/alleys, streets, shopping centres, car parks, 'out-of- the-way' spaces in playgrounds and around buildings.

Play environments	Context of geographical play	Examples of environments
Miniature environments	Places designed for younger children to play in, adapted to younger children's sizes. Places created for play and games rather than for physical exercise.	Playgrounds, adventure play areas. Child-sized play buildings, forts, walkways and playground street markings. Small-scale furniture: tables, chairs, cookers, cupboards, beds and 'home' equipment such as cutlery, crockery, cooking utensils, model foods.
Toy environments	'Small world' play equipment. These can be realistic and replicate the world children see or can be fanciful. Their role is to enable children to create their own 'real' and imagined places.	Model buildings, furniture, equipment, people, animals. Place/environment play mats, road layouts, buildings, street furniture, vehicles, people, trees, fences, domesticated and farm animals, railway tracks, engines and carriages.
Virtual environments	'Places' created using computer software for children. These might be based on a TV or film animations or created to be explored, 'inhabited' or played within by children to which they may be able to add features from sets of icons.	Simulated 'real' places, fantasy 'worlds'. Pictograms to move and position in extant 'worlds' or to create new places and scenes.

Table 10.1   Environmental contexts for geographical play (adapted from Catling, 2006b, pp. 69–70)

In the classroom

Creating a habitat

The teacher of a class of 5–6-year-olds used the children's interest in animals to show them how animals fitted into a particular habitat. She used toy animals they played with that belonged to the children and the school. They made models of habitats from cardboard boxes. A cardboard box with one side removed became jungle, desert or savannah grassland by putting cut-out trees, grasses or bushes into it. A blue line across the bottom became a river, and a small blue piece of card became a waterhole. Green fibres became strangler vines and yellow paper became grass. The teacher then discussed with the children which animals they would see in which habitat. This enabled the development of their geographical learning. Some children went further and invented stories, several based on films and stories they knew, about the animals.

Children make sense of their place and environmental experiences through a variety of means. In their early learning, young children learn through sensory experience as much as through the journeys they make with their families, through their imitations of the adult activities they observe as much as through their physical exploration of the places within which they are allowed some freedom of movement, and through their own imaginative play with models as much as through sources such as stories and television programmes. Table 10.2 outlines five aspects of early years play that support geographical learning (Catling, 2006b).

Aspects of play	Opportunities to support young children's geographical learning	Geographical illustrations
Sensory play	Encounters in and examinations of the environment through the senses: sight, touch, sound, smell, taste, mobility.	• Feeling the texture of natural and built features. • Identifying different types of smell in the locality and their source. • Discriminating different sounds locally and their sources. • Eating/preparing different foods from various parts of the world. • Talking about favourite and disliked places locally, elsewhere and from stories and television programmes.
Exploratory play	Movement about the environment to develop spatial awareness. Investigating places to find out what is there, in familiar and new places.	• In the outdoor area, journeys around road layouts and obstacle courses. • Journeys to the local playground or park, to shops and other sites. • Talking about play areas, seeing what shops sell and asking why and to whom, buying resources for cooking. • Using a simple map to locate places in relation to each other in school grounds and other sites such as a playground.
Imitative play	Role play used to begin to grasp ways that adults act in and use places and what is in them.	• Use of free imaginative play in the 'home bay' set up as a type of place – e.g. a shop, room, etc. • Role-playing staff and customers in a layout for a bus, aeroplane, etc. • Being people debating what to do with waste items, the use of an empty shop, about cutting down trees, etc. • Pretend play as children/adults in their own and other communities locally and across the world. • Setting up a play building or tent for free-play activities.

Aspects of play	Opportunities to support young children's geographical learning	Geographical illustrations
Representational play	Model making, drawing and early writing involved in activities in places, to re-create them and to extend the play.	• Using play-map mats to make journeys and identify routes and activities. • Using pictures, maps and aerial photographs of familiar sites to find objects/features in and outside. • Making drawings of objects and features in and out of school. • Using toys, boxes and other materials to make models of places, locally and imaginatively, and to people them with activities.
Fantasy play	Creation of imagined places and environments, realistic or fantastical, which might be acted out, drawn, discussed or written about.	• Using play materials, boxes and toys to make buildings, sites, etc. for free play. • Using natural and artificial materials in the outdoor area to create features and places for imaginative play.

Table 10.2   Five aspects of place play that support young children's geographical learning (Catling, 2006b, p. 68)

Practical task

Use Tables 10.1 and 10.2 to plan a play-based activity for a group of 4/5 or 5/6-year-old children. How will you organise the activity? Which aspects of geographical learning are you introducing to children? What resources will you need?

The 'outdoor classroom'

The outdoor area is a vital learning environment for young children. The essence of a good outdoor area is the variety of environments for the children to use (Bilton, 2005, 2010; Bilton and Crook, 2016; Garrick, 2009; Rowe and Humphries, 2012; White, 2014), including:

• a creative area, for painting, rubbings, music making, craft activities and other such activities;
• a quiet area with seats and shelters, books and pictures;

- an environmental play area where there are a wide variety of resources including a sandpit and water tray; model vehicles and buildings, toy animals and people; path or road markings, mobile child-size buildings or building fronts painted on walls, wheeled vehicles, and similar play resources; ground to dig, and a garden area to grow plants in; an 'unkempt' area with natural objects to make things with;
- an open space area with equipment and small apparatus for activities such as off-the-ground climbing, balancing, swinging, sliding, etc.;
- a natural area, which, while planned and maintained, appears to be a 'wild' area with plants, shrubs, bushes, trees, mounds, open soil, rocks, grass and natural materials such as sticks, and has spaces for den building, shelter and sitting in the open, an area that allows for play in the 'wildscape'.

Outdoor areas such as these reflect the Reggio Emelia approach to young children's experience and learning in pre-school environments (Cadwell, 1997; Thornton and Brunton, 2007; MacQuarrie *et al.*, 2015). The message is that, as high-quality environments and places in themselves, much can and should be made of and developed in the outdoors within this secure and safe setting. These areas have much potential for geographical learning through investigations, exploring, making and building, using water, sand and earth, enacting and role playing, small toy play, the use of language and vocabulary, imagination, and much more. These activities are not exclusive to particular outdoor 'spaces'. Creativity can occur in any one of them through imaginative role play or the use of provided apparatus, which might as readily be the source for explorations and investigations as might the wild area, a street scene or a set of photographs.

The use of play implies that young children have both the right and opportunities to make choices about their activities outdoors (and inside). The resources available to children construct or constrain these choices – what is provided on the day and how it is set up. Permanent features, such as climbing frames and small-scale huts, can be used regularly for place and environmentally oriented play. When provided with a variety of 'environmental' toys, children have the chance to direct their own learning in relation to the event, place and environmental experiences they have had or imagine.

Forest Schools

The development of the Forest School movement in Europe (see Chapter 9) exemplifies providing young children (as well as older children) with opportunities for outdoor play and exploration in natural settings such as woodland, and in spaces in pre-school and nursery play areas provided with natural features and materials, including trees, bushes, water, sticks, pebbles, and suchlike (Bilton and Crook, 2016; Constable, 2012; Knight, 2011a, 2011b, 2013a, 2013b, 2016; Rowe and Humphries, 2012; Williams-Siegfredson, 2017; Wilson, 2012). Its approach can be adapted and applied readily in early years settings and primary schools. The focus is on enabling children to play with natural materials and in natural places – or places largely nature-alised – so that they can explore, handle, construct, investigate and imagine, in and with nature (Buchan, 2016; Houghton and Worroll, 2016). An enhancement of this approach is the development and use of gardens in pre-school settings and primary schools (Lockie, 2007; Gaylie, 2011; Williams and Brown, 2012; Woodhouse, 2017). Activities in Forest School sites may, of course, use manufactured or commercial resources: a drink may be brewed on a campfire in a billycan; there may be a hut to keep equipment, such as tarpaulins and ropes, pots and trowels, and magnifying glasses and twine.

The key features of the Forest School approach are a number of aspects that are or can be applied at times within the early years setting or on a school site, particularly if it has an area that young children are rarely allowed to use (Knight, 2011a, 2011b, 2013b). These include:

- the play setting is not the usual one, which may be rough ground, woodland or an area of a park – or if it is in the nursery or school grounds, it has been adapted in a way that creates a different look and feel to it, even temporarily;
- it is a safe environment – enclosed – that nonetheless facilitates children's risk taking;
- activities in the environment take place over time and have some regularity to them, perhaps across the school year even though once a week, so that children get to know the site;
- the children, and adults, are out in all weathers – there is no 'bad' weather – and in all seasons; it is about having and wearing appropriate clothing (even if this needs to be supplied at times);
- there is trust of the children by the adults, with the children allowed to explore freely, be on their own, engage with others as they choose to, but where there is a central place where young children can seek help or know that they can go to when they want to be in a 'home' place;
- activities and learning that are largely child-led and child-initiated;
- there is a time period with a clear start and finish;
- there is a gathering point and time when children can chat and share – or not – and, appropriately, have a drink and a snack;
- the adults involved have been trained.

Forest School activities use play to enable young children (and older primary children) to become involved with the natural environment, to get their hands dirty and encounter soils of different textures and states and make things with them, to build dens, look under decaying logs and stones, sit between branches, hear and listen to natural sounds and quiet, seek viewpoints and contemplate, take risks in climbing or moving logs or helping to make the 'home-base' fire, and engage quietly or actively with other children in investigating or playing.

The geographical and environmental aspects of the Forest School approach concern 'getting to know' a place over time, learning about the elements and coherence of the natural environment, being able to investigate a place and make use of it through play – even to modify it through place-making and den building – and creating 'worlds' for imaginary and games play, where the child is somewhere else as someone else, enacting lives and events, but always respecting the environment, taking care and being careful of the plants, creatures and insects that inhabit and use it. It is about building 'a sense of place', of positive interest in and attachment to the site, enabling the child to recognise what it affords them, in terms of play, exploration and investigation, alone and with others. It enables opportunities for children to engage with nature in a positive, safe and enhancing context. The variety a site provides for children – its affordance capacity – is essentially a matter for the children; they are remarkably good at spotting opportunities that adults might miss, which give enjoyment, confidence, wonder, excitement and enthusiasm, taking risks while being safe. A sizeable and varied 'big school' grounds may have one or more such areas that can be used for play and learning in this way.

What is invaluable to fostering early geographical experience and awareness is young children's opportunities through Forest School sites and activities to be in the outdoors, hopefully off-site from their pre-school setting. The safe environment allows 'getting to grips' with the real environment, through exploring and investigating, asking questions, making discoveries, perhaps getting dirty and wet, and being enticed by a place. Over several visits what is at first a novel place can become familiar, but for young children it retains its fascination because it changes through the seasons and will be different – and responded to variously – in different weathers, looking and feeling different. Hunting games, spotting tasks and other exploratory activities may be used to stimulate enquiries about different parts of the site, perhaps for different individuals or pairs of children who then share their observations and, perhaps, collections and even 'found' sites. This approach can be a precursor to related investigations within their own nursery setting or the school's grounds. Children learn about places, develop habits of looking and watching, interest in aspects of the environments (even where these may be largely familiar and in the pre-school setting), and appreciation of care for environments, leaving what they find for rediscovery and for others to engage with and enjoy. It can enable the discovery of the natural, nurture recognition of the wild, and facilitate awareness of the special nature of environments and places.

Outside the classroom

Being natural in a Forest School site

In the Forest School woodland site, two 3-year-olds spent their time looking between the gnarled exposed roots of two trees, fascinated by the decaying leaves, insects and spaces they found there. They used small sticks to poke about before placing some longer and thicker pieces of broken branch across several roots and 'driving' their acorn 'vehicles' back and forth across them. Another 3-year-old crouched beside the small stream that ran through the wood, piling twigs, leaves, pebbles and some earth to create a dam and watch the build-up of water behind it before it flowed over the top and began to wear down the dam.

Outside the classroom

Creating places in the sandpit

In the nursery sandpit two 4-year-olds used a variety of toy vehicles and buildings. They moulded the sand to create smoothed out 'roads'. One child used a bus to make journeys, stopping at points along the 'road' to pick up passengers. After a while both children began to put buildings alongside their 'roads'. The second child parked two cars and a van by the 'homes' he had placed. They both played close by each other and became so engrossed that they ran their vehicles along each other's 'roads', moving around each other to play in the larger area. This overlapping activity became a cooperative activity when they added new roads and buildings to join up and extend their 'town'. At different times they concentrated on each other's homes and cars for people to make journeys to go to the shops and the garage.

Reflective task

Consider the Forest School and sandpit activities in which these very young children were involved. These were initiated by them and not structured activities. Select one of these examples. How did their play in the site support their geographical learning? What was the role of the natural or provided resources in this play? If the pre-school staff had intervened, how might they have enhanced or inhibited the children's learning?

 Research summary

In the Czech Republic, research was undertaken to identify the effect of introducing an eco-school approach in a number of kindergartens for 4–6-year-olds (Cincera *et al.*, 2017). The study found that the kindergartens used the eco-school approach differently, some giving much greater democratic responsibility to the children, while others were much more directive of the children to ensure appropriate environmental outcomes. Teachers taking a more collaborative and power-sharing approach to involving the children commented that it enabled them to see higher level changes in their children for the benefit of the kindergarten. However, seemingly regardless of teachers' styles, the children were found to develop significantly more positive environmental attitudes as a result of eco-school experiences. Gender differences were negligible but age appeared to be important, with the youngest children showing the strongest development of pro-environmental attitudes and behaviours. One effect for a minority of teachers was their (unrequired) introduction of children's monitoring of other children's environmental behaviour across some primary schools, providing benefit to the children by taking responsibility and to the schools. Many kindergarten teachers who did not already hold positive environmental values had been wary of the approach, but nonetheless provided benefit for their young children and the pre-school setting, though they found the effort involved a challenge. The researchers felt that, while more research was needed, the eco-schools approach offered good encouragement for developing pro-environmental values and action among pre-school children.

Activities for early geographical learning

Providing opportunities for geographical learning in early years settings means allowing children to play freely in a designated area. It may include particular focuses for their play suggested, setting up areas with particular resources, inside or outside, organising particular activities in specific bays, choosing the focus of the story to be read with the children, and observing and spending time with particular children to encourage their learning in a specific direction. There is much advice and guidance on geographically and environmentally related activities to provide in the nursery and kindergarten setting (Alcock, 2012; Ashbridge, 2006; Bilton *et al.*, 2017; Boyd *et al.*, 2018; Conway *et al.*, 2008; Cooper, 2004a; Cooper *et al.*, 2010; Featherstone, 2010; Glauert *et al.*, 2003; Greenwood and Linklater, 2015; Heal and Cook, 1998; Jeffery, 2014; Martin and Owens, 2008, 2010; Milner, 1996, 1997; Owens, 2004a, 2004b; Salaman and Tutchell, 2005; Simco, 2003; Thwaites, 2008; Ward, 2009; Warden, 2015; White, 2011; Witt, 2017) and about organising outdoor spaces (Learning through Landscapes, 2014; Walsh, 2016). The examples below illustrate indoor and outside activities and a journey into the locality. The box below outlines other activities to use or adapt.

The view from the window

Inspired by Jeannie Baker's (1991, 2004) books *Window* and *Belonging*, create a large window frame on a wall or a display board. Use cut-out drawings to create a scene viewed through the window. Every day or two introduce a change to the scene – e.g. a building added or something removed. Children might make the new features. Continue until the view has changed very much. At different points in the 'development', discuss with the children what is happening. Take photographs of the changing window view. Use these to talk about the changes that have taken place, showing children the view changing over time. This approach helps young children to see what is changing in a place and how those changes have an impact. They can talk about why the changes are happening and what they feel about them. As the area develops, different children might become 'residents' in the new development, giving them a stake in their views on environmental change. Later, arrange a proposal to make another change that they must discuss and agree to before it can be made. What will their views be? Will they all agree? Why will they hold the views they do?

'In the den'

Children love dens and places they can make into their own 'bases' in bushes or woods, in alcoves or under stairwells in or outside buildings (Tovey, 2007; White, 2014; Witt, 2017). While the nursery area may not provide such opportunities, there may be a 'play hut', small-scale 'buildings' or tents that children can use as play spaces for imaginative games, or crates, boxes, frames and drapes which, with adults, they can use to create dens (Cooper, 2004b). These should be allowed to be the children's own 'secret places' (Dixon and Day, 2004). A variety of 'home' resources, such as furniture, cushions, crockery, cutlery and toys can be provided for the children to use in their play hut or den, but they must decide what to use. Children can be encouraged to talk about what they play, perhaps even to take digital photographs of their special place and activities, although they may be reluctant to let adults into their world. The adults responsible for supervision can provide prompts and ideas to extend the children's own 'den' play, to encourage photographing it across the year, talk about how to care for it and discuss ways the children might improve it. It can be a source for role play, for storytelling and modelling, to 'show me what it's like because I cannot go in there', or a context for talking about how it 'feels like home' and 'what I like about it', exploring ideas about a sense of place at a young child's scale.

Going to the park

Taking children out of the nursery and school area is always stimulating. Various possibilities can be pursued in local urban and rural environments (Conway *et al.*, 2008; Milner, 1996; Salaman and Tatchell, 2005; Simco, 2003; Thwaites, 2008). Walking to the local park or play area offers several possibilities for young children to observe and use appropriate vocabulary to name features and discuss what they see along the street and in the park or play area.

- Focus on the children's view of the 'world', at their eye level. Features can be noticed, including street names; service covers in the pavement; entrances to drives and gardens; fences and walls; seats; different surfaces; worn areas; pavement and road markings about parking, and where to cross the street safely.
- Looking up reveals street signs giving directions and warnings; street furniture, such as lamp posts and bus stops; home and shop fronts and entrances; and further up, the heights of buildings, roofs and chimneys.
- They pass people making journeys, shoppers and others working in the street.
- When visiting (or going to buy something in) a shop, look at the various goods on sale, where they are and what is near to or further away from them and why. Talk with the shop-keeper or assistants about what they do, how the goods get to the shop and from where (check when might be a quiet time to do this). Ask shoppers why they have come to the shop and what they buy.

- In the park, the children observe various features, including signs and seats, but also find pathways and natural elements, the grass, trees, plants and shrubs, and birds, animals and mini-beasts. A park-keeper might answer children's questions about the park, how it is looked after and who uses it, how and when.
- Young children associate parks with play activities. They should play in the open spaces or fenced off areas available. Encourage them to talk about what they like to play and when they might come.

Children can take digital photographs to record selected features and views that they see or to record their comments and thoughts for reflection and discussion back in the nursery. During their walk, they might talk about what they like or dislike, about favourite places or where and why people drop litter, use directional language when they turn corners or to indicate where features are in the park, and indicate features they would like to see added to or removed from the street, the park and play area.

Taking young children out of the nursery setting and school grounds requires good organisation and careful management, as outlined in Chapter 9. A visit should be introduced to them before going so they know the purpose of their outing (Salaman and Tatchell, 2005).

Caring for our place

Developing children's sense of care for the environment requires active engagement (Martin and Owens, 2008; Cutter-Mackenzie *et al.*, 2014). There are many opportunities to involve the children in maintaining and improving the quality of their indoor and outdoor nursery environments. Children can:

- take resources out and put them away carefully, discussing why this helps, what they learn about care and what others should do;
- be responsible with adults for looking after particular areas in the nursery to see that everything is in order and is being cared for;
- walk around the nursery outdoor area periodically to see what is there and to talk about how plants grow, the needs of mini-beasts, birds and other creatures, to check the fencing, to see that paths are looked after, to check for litter or fallen leaves;
- observe whether something seems 'shabby' and in need of repair or painting – they can discuss who would do this, and how to improve the look and use of the resources and area;
- observe and discuss how the weather affects the outdoor area, what areas are like when they are (very) wet or dry, and how some areas might be protected from rain or sun, which can benefit others.

Through such foci and activities, young children learn about environmental care and concern, using observation and discussion, appreciating who helps to keep places clean and tidy, and about using safe practices when doing so. They can record what they see and hear, and discuss what care for the environment is and why people think it is important. They can consider when it is important to tidy up, and when and why some things may be left untidy, such as a wild area in the grounds or if we leave off part-way through an activity to come back to it later. This focus and such activities help young children learn about sustainability and its value for us all (Boyd *et al.*, 2018).

Examples of activities to develop geographical awareness in the early years

Journeys

Hide and seek: Use outdoors or inside to play hide and seek. Talk about good and bad places to hide and why they are.

Along the street: Use child-size vehicles in the playground for play journeys along marked-up 'roads' in the playground (use playground chalk or have them permanently marked). Plan and make journeys to stops along the routes. Use large boxes or make large cut-outs of features, like shops, to stand along the route, for children to visit. Make road signs to be followed: one way, stop, no entry, etc. Involve pedestrians and drivers. Link this to road safety. Use location, direction and distance vocabulary. Children use the road to act out and talk about what happens there. Role-play shopkeepers and residents.

Places

Model playhouse: Provide a model house (preferably with a removable roof and floors) with model furniture and people. Encourage children to sort furniture into rooms and to create layouts. Look down on the floor and room layout. Talk about what is where, why furniture has been put in specific rooms, the spatial arrangement and the view from above. Take photographs from above of the layouts.

Changing places: Use a play mat showing a town or country area. Talk about what is shown on the 'map' and what the area is like. Propose that an area of the town, village or farm is to be changed and developed. Ask the children what they would like to put there and why. Using appropriately sized pieces of paper, involve the children in drawing or making models of the features they would build. Fix these to the 'play map'. Discuss the effect of the changes.

Shops and food

Shopping: Choose an item to buy that the children like, such as milk. Talk about where to buy it, types of food shops and supermarkets. Discuss where nearby shops are and how to get there. Encourage children to mention shops they are taken to. Visit a local shop to buy something. Observe and talk about other items sold there, why people buy them and what you can do with them.

On the farm: Use farm toys (buildings, fences, animals, vehicles) or make farm features. Use a farm play-mat or design and make the layout of the farm. Sort the animals and locate them on the farm. Talk about where different animals live and vehicles are kept. Discuss what farms are for and what farmers and farm workers do. Compare different areas around the farm and their uses: how the land is used and what happens at different times of year.

Environments

Creating new environments to explore: Make a variety of different environments in one or more nursery bays. Create a jungle with materials and imagine walking through it; think about how you would get there and what you would see, hear and smell. Use chairs to create a plane, bus or train. Decide where to go on your journeys, locally and around the world, and 'visit' them. Where are we going and for how long? What is it like there and what could we do?

Dressing up: Use clothes to talk about and enact what to wear for different activities: play, dirty work, clean work, etc., and where you would wear them. What are we going to do in them? Discuss what to wear to go out in dry or wet weather, when it is hot, cool or cold, to play in the mud or in a wild area, to wear on short or long journeys, or if you are expected to 'look smart'.

(Continued)

(Continued)

Mapping

A treasure hunt: Hide familiar toys outdoors or inside for children to find. Say 'hot', 'warm' and 'cold' as clues, or give instructions or other clues, such as pictures or pictorial symbols, for the children to follow. Alternatively, mark the locations on a large-scale aerial photograph or a simple plan or map of the outdoor area which children use to find them (Plester et al., 2006).

Earth from space: Use Google Earth, postcards or posters of views of the Earth from space (of the continents and oceans) and a globe. Create a spaceship for children to imagine they are astronauts orbiting the Earth. From time to time they must spot and identify the Google Earth or postcard views of the Earth by looking for them on the globe, which is placed outside the 'spaceship' window and rotated during the play to help simulate the spacecraft orbiting the Earth.

    Practical task

Select three of the activities outlined in the box above. Using Tables 10.1 and 10.2, identify the aspects of play and the contexts for play that are involved.

    Key points

This chapter has:

- provided a rationale for developing young children's geographical and environmental experience through play and emphasised its importance;
- described a variety of contexts for and aspects of place-based play to develop geographical learning and understanding;
- noted the role and value of the 'outdoor classroom' in the nursery and pre-school environment;
- provided various examples of activities to use with young children to foster experience of geographical ideas, skills, values and attitudes.

Moving on

You may have visited or have the opportunity to visit an early years setting in a nursery or primary school. Consider the approaches and opportunities the nursery teacher uses to develop young children's geographical and environmental experience and learning (they may not call it this). What does the outdoor area offer for children's geographical and environmental play? Note the variety of equipment and sites that are available to encourage place and environmental play, and that children might use and adapt to create environments of their own.

Further reading

There are many publications on early years school environments, but only a few that discuss the provision of geographical and environmental experiences through play and other approaches for learning.

Bilton, H (2010) *Outdoor Learning in the Early* Years (3rd edn). London: David Fulton.

Catling, S (2006) What do five year olds know of the world? Geographical understanding and play in young children's early learning. *Geography*, 91(1), 55–74.

Cooper, H (ed.) (2004) *Exploring Time and Place Through Play*. London: David Fulton.

Cooper, L, Johnston, J, Rotchell, E and Woolley, R (2010) *Knowledge and Understanding of the World*. London: Continuum.

Cutter-Mackenzie, A, Edwards, S, Moore, D and Boyd, W (2014) *Young Children's Play and Environmental Education in Early Childhood Education*. Dordrecht: Springer.

Greenwood, J and Linklater, H (2015) So what is long ago and where is far away? A sense of time and place. In D Whitebread and P Coltman (eds) *Teaching and Learning in the Early Years* (4th edn). London: Routledge, pp. 311–25.

Knight, S (2013b) *Forest School and Outdoor Learning in the Early Years* (2nd edn). London: Sage.

Louis, S (2009) *Knowledge and Understanding of the World in the Early Years Foundation Stage*. Abingdon; Routledge.

Palmer, J and Birch, J (2004) *Geography in the Early Years*. London: Routledge.

White, J (2014) *Playing and Learning Outdoors*. London: Routledge.

See relevant issues of *Primary Geographer.*

Useful websites

Early Years Geography: www.geography.org.uk/eyprimary
Early Years Teaching Ideas: www.teachingideas.co.uk/earlyyears/contents.htm
Forest Schools: www.forestschools.com
Learning Through Landscapes: www.ltl.org.uk
Playing with sand, water, etc.: www.communityplaythings.com

CHAPTER 11

INVESTIGATING THE SCHOOL AND ITS GROUNDS

 Chapter objectives

This chapter enables you to:

- recognise that the school building and its grounds are geographical sites of interest;
- appreciate and explain the value in using the school grounds for learning and teaching geography;
- recognise the geographical opportunities that the school site provides;
- plan for geographical topics and activities in the school grounds.

Introduction

The school is a key site in children's everyday geographies. It is the place they share as members of its community, users of its buildings and grounds, participants in its activities, routines and rules – its culture and place. They can describe and discuss what life there is like, how, where and why things happen, who does what, where they can and cannot go, what they think and feel about this, what they know and do not know around the school, and how they might like it to be in the future. The school provides a geographical site to explore. The children who investigate it are active participants in the social and physical environment they study. They can both observe it from the 'outside' as investigators and provide insight by being 'inside' members of the school (see Chapter 3). Exploring the school's geography creates opportunities to develop children's enquiry and research skills (Bucknall, 2012; Kellett, 2005, 2010).

A learnscape

We have noted already the value of the outdoor environment and local community for very young children's learning. The physical and social environments of the school and the neighbourhood affect children's lives directly throughout their primary years (Mayall, 2010; Wall et al., 2010; Pike, 2016). They are the landscapes they inhabit. The twenty-first century has seen the development of arguments for the importance of places in children's learning – that is, not only the study of places geographically, but the value of being in particular places as learners. This focus is on the local meaning of places as sites of living and learning (Wattchow and Brown, 2011; Sobel, 2013), where, for instance, local cultures, traditions, circumstances and sites offer possibilities and opportunities particular to that locality (Smith and Sobel, 2010). Studies of place-based and community-based pedagogies argue for the value of the local in children's education (Hutchinson, 2004; Callejo Pérez et al., 2004; Ellsworth, 2005; Gruenewald and Smith, 2008; Altman et al., 2015; Demarest, 2015; Getting Smart, 2017) in relation to the ways in which the places in which we live shape us, provide opportunities and may have limitations, and to which we contribute in the ways we make use of them and respond to them. This applies to everyone and provides for the local in an increasingly global world. The physical features, the natural aspects, the social dynamics and the communities that imbue places with their character, from their making, over several generations or many millennia, to living in them, for both their long-standing and most recent members, offer a myriad of possibilities for experience and study connecting children's lived worlds with geography and other subjects in school (Somerville et al., 2009; Evans and Savage, 2015). Such localities can become what have been termed 'learnscapes' (Skemp and Bergmann, 2006).

Learnscapes are sites where teachers and children can undertake investigations and activities designed to engage them in interacting with the environment (Skemp and Bergmann, 2006; Tyas-Tunggal, 1997). A school's grounds are probably the most accessible venue to use as a learnscape. Indeed, learnscapes can be any part of the school and its grounds or sites and areas off-site in the school's neighbourhood (or at times further afield). However, it is not the features in the school's grounds or in the local area, or the grounds or locality themselves, that are the learnscape; they are its context. Rather, a learnscape comprises the collaboration and interaction that occurs in creating, maintaining and using features and environmental activities – be these a wild area, a quiet garden or recycling – or the wider place itself that make it a landscape in which to learn, and a key location for in-place pedagogy. It is through involvement in learning that a site becomes a learnscape (Boylan and Wallace, 2009). Yet there is more to this than just examining the place.

A learnscape is a landscape with which we are or we can become involved as teachers and children; and engagement in learnscapes can include community members. Schools and their grounds can be learnscapes because children, particularly, and adults, consistently engage with them, making use of them, learning (often informally) in and about them, and subtly or intentionally changing them. Such change might be physical, as in children and adults creating a wild area, or by appreciating how play spaces are used, monitored and controlled and changing some aspects of these uses and controls. To be a learnscape a place needs to be acted on consciously. Skemp noted that some teachers do not always make use of a school's grounds, perhaps because they have concerns about managing children outdoors or because they lack the knowledge about the possibilities for geographical, scientific, musical and other investigations, but he noted that most teachers ensure they know the affordances that school grounds (and the locality) offer and are innovative in making use of them and in engaging the children in environmental encounters and learning, as well as in considering environmental attitudes and values (Skemp, 2009; Skemp and Bergmann, 2006).

Clearly school grounds already exist and may not readily be changed without appropriate approval. Nonetheless, we can apply the notion of learnscape in a broader context, for instance by being geographically and place thoughtful about the ways in which we interact with our whole school environment, not just some particular parts of it. We should think of the school's environment in human and physical terms, as a landscape and as a place of social interactions, behaviours and decisions and the interrelationships between them. The school and its grounds offer considerable possibilities for fostering geographical learning, as a learnscape and a broader place-pedagogy site. It is helpful, initially, to consider why we might investigate the school's grounds and, indeed, what they are. These are considered next as a prelude to exploring some affordances for geographical learning in school grounds learnscapes.

Why study the school building and grounds?

Studying the school's geography enables children to explore its buildings and landscape, how it works as a place, and to enquire into key aspects of its environment. Studies in the school and its grounds link geography with science, history and art (Hare *et al.*, 1996). A few schools use their school environment as the focus of their curriculum; it is their 'place of learning' and their 'learning environment' (Jeffrey and Woods, 2003; Rowe and Humphries, 2012; Hopwood-Stephens, 2013; Learning through Landscapes, 2014; Bilton and Crook, 2016). That it is a living place in which children are its *raison d'être* and prime participants is the core reason for using the school as a geographical focus for study. It provides a key context for active learning. Fieldwork is essential to exploring its current and future geographies from mapping what is where to identifying ways in which the school grounds could be landscaped to provide more varied environments for playtimes and for learning and teaching. These lead to the obvious reason – it's there. However, it is an important place for a more vital reason, which is that children strongly value their school and its grounds as a place in their lives for being, playing and learning (Pike, 2016).

Accessibility

The school building and grounds are readily accessible, the place to take children for out-of-classroom learning. There are few constraints on access around the school areas, except those parts 'out-of-bounds' and perhaps when there is heavy rain, strong winds or exceptional sun and heat. Children might investigate which areas of the school are accessible or not, when and why, whether accessibility changes during the day or across the year, and who decides about whose access.

Many school grounds have a good variety of features and facilities from tarmac or concrete and grassy areas to gardens, but some remain little more than asphalt yards with no apparent variety. It is important to recognise that even what appear to be rather barren school playgrounds may well have markers for various games, can have decorated walls, may well have plants somehow surviving in neglected spots, and will have worn, weathered or otherwise damaged ground and wall areas that can be investigated. School grounds have physical and human geographies. Children find a wide range of ways to use even the barest of sites for play, physical games and social activities. All playgrounds provide opportunities for use if we look for them, even if their affordances seem limited.

Immediacy

Apart from particular school requirements, it is relatively straightforward to arrange fieldwork in the school grounds, given the usual need to plan appropriately and to bear in mind that other classes may be working outside too. But you can also respond to spontaneity, take opportunities to use the school grounds and develop learning that was not planned for, but which you judge would benefit from work outside.

Children can also bring into class information about what occurs inside and outside the school buildings. They can share their knowledge of the activities children engage in and where they do so. They bring through their experience of the place and its spaces an immediacy in their experience, knowledge and feelings about the school and its grounds.

Motivation

There is ample evidence that investigations in the school's buildings and grounds stimulate children's interest and engagement (Catling *et al.*, 2007; HMI, 1989; Ofsted, 1999, 2008a, 2011), particularly when examining what their school is like, what happens in it, its features and layout, what people do and the uses made of it at different times and in different areas, as well as by examining energy use or dealing with waste and how to reduce these, and by looking into who does the classroom cleaning and site maintenance. Furthermore, children have views and ideas about how the school might be improved as a place for themselves and adults.

A site to apply key geographical ideas, concepts and content

The school site is an excellent environment for developing children's geographical understanding. It provides a space, a place and an environment for study at a manageable scale, enabling investigation of the sort of place it is, how space is designated and used, what changes occur and with what effect, and of the sustainability of practices around the school. Its external connections provide insights into where the school draws it pupils from, the sources of its resources and how they reach the school, and about its local impact. Physical and human processes, such as local weather patterns and how people respond to these, can be investigated. Through its school community, cultural awareness and diversity can be examined.

A context to use and develop geographical skills

Children can use enquiry and fieldwork approaches and skills – for instance, planning an investigation of the use of water in the school or the location of a new feature. They will use skills such as mapping, taking photographs, making sketches, and gathering, analysing, evaluating and presenting data, and using digital technologies in a variety of ways.

A site to introduce and follow up geographical topics

The school buildings and grounds provide opportunities to initiate new geographical ideas and topics. The different uses of a large space might be explored first by identifying and mapping land use around the school site, and then by observations and interviews about the various activities on the site. An environmental issue might be illustrated by looking at waste and its disposal in and from the school, while controversy might be explored through examining competing and conflicting uses of the playground spaces.

Creating an impact on the school site

Geography, as an ethical subject, leads to active involvement in finding ways to care for places and environments, and to make improvements. One way to achieve this is by identifying ways in which the school can be more sustainable – for instance, through energy reduction, by collecting rainwater to use in the school's garden area, through composting some of the food waste and in considering how food wrappers and plastic bottles brought into school can best be recycled or replaced, among other possibilities (AuSSI, 2010).

 Reflective task

The reasons given for using the school site referred mainly to the school's grounds. You can, as easily, undertake geographical studies of the school building(s) and in classrooms. Which indoor places, spaces and environments would you include? List reasons for using either the school building(s) or the classroom as sites for geographical study. Draw on the points mentioned about the school grounds to guide you.

What are the school and its grounds?

Schools contain three key physical and social spaces.

- The classroom and other rooms which have particular uses.
- The school buildings.
- The school grounds.

The classroom and other rooms

The classroom and other rooms and areas include not just the physical features of these spaces, fixed and movable, but also the people who work in them, full- and part-time. For example, a classroom's geography includes its layout, the variety of features, why it is laid out as it is, its 'routeways' around features like desks, access to it, how people use it regularly (as intended or otherwise), how and why its layout may be changed or used differently from time to time, and who creates or makes the decisions about the 'sense of place' that a classroom has.

Other rooms around the school can be considered similarly. There will be a variety of rooms, many or all of which will have specific and distinctive uses. These can include a hall that may have multiple uses, a kitchen and a dining area, a library, the headteacher's office, a school office, the staffroom, coat and changing areas, toilets, and perhaps a quiet room for use by a visiting nurse or a sick child. The entrance area and corridors are other such spaces. There may be a caretaker's room or even a boiler room. Some of these rooms may not be normally accessible to children without permission or for safety reasons, but they can all be worth investigating to see how they look, are laid out, what they contain and what uses are made of them. Almost all these spaces are likely to contain features such as cupboards, tables, chairs, shelves and other items for various uses. Where they are, what the layout of an area is like, how these features help make the space what it is used for and even how they might perhaps be an encumbrance can be examined. Children can draw on their own experiences of rooms such as the hall or library to describe their uses and features as key aspects of their geographies.

The school buildings

There may be more than one building on the school site, including other teaching blocks and outbuildings of different sizes and purposes. A building's geography includes its overall shape and size, the layout of the one or more floors, and their features and uses, the corridors and routes around the building(s) including stairs up and down, the range of activities that happen inside, how what occurs is affected by its layout, shape and community, which rooms are accessible to whom, the times of day when the building(s) or its parts are used, by whom and what for, the 'atmosphere' of the school provided through the decor and displays, the teaching and other activities, its rules and regulations, explicit and implicit, and how it feels as a place. It includes the exercise of control and order over spaces in the building, what is in or out of bounds, and who decides, for what purpose and with what effect. Its geography may also include whether there have been extensions built and other modifications made, including why and when, and if they are now used for what may have been their original intended purposes.

The school grounds

A school's grounds includes all the features that are within the territorial boundary of the site. Its geography covers its physical and natural features: the shape of the site, its boundary walls and/or fences as borders along its edges, the lie of the land, which may be flat or on a slope, its landscaping such as terracing, the nature and sites of its plant and animal/insect ecology, its weather, its entrances, its buildings, access roads, car park, internal paths and route ways, wild areas, perhaps particular features such as a stream, and what lies immediately adjacent to it such as roads, neighbouring buildings, a river or a railway together with their noise effects. For instance, if it is on the flightpath of an airport, it can include overhead flights and their impact.

Its social and cultural geography include the designation of the spaces in the school grounds, the roles and activities of the people there, the nature of its community, its regular and occasional visitors, whether parents, grounds maintenance staff or drama and other community groups who use it 'out of hours'. Its geography includes the quality of the site, what children consider it offers them – its affordances – the 'feel' of the place at playtimes and during lesson times, as well as in the evenings and during school holidays, the ways in which it is cared for and maintained, how people treat the site and its features from its users to the local authority or independent owner, and the sense of place that its users develop. Although perhaps speculative geography, this is how it seems when it is closed and in the dark, sensed essentially from the outside.

A sense of the school's geography

The 'everyday' environment and experience of the school is more than its physical environment. It is the community and social and cultural life in the school. Its geography concerns the social ethics of space and place, who can go where and do what in which parts of the school, why this is so, what differences there are between what children and adults can do where, how they subvert these positively and negatively, inside and outside the rules, who is consulted over the uses of spaces and the activities in them, and who decides on the regulations that organise space, set expectations of behaviour and allow activities. While we can break its geography into the component elements of the site and into different topics for investigation, to gain a deeper understanding of the geography of a school we need to consider these holistically to be able to sense it as a place. In many ways, a primary school is a microcosm of the neighbourhood and the community, with its variety of features and people, of relationships and activities, of possibilities and constraints.

A primary school, of course, is a place of learning; it is a place that children have to attend; and it is imbued with particular expectations, standards and social norms, encased in the meanings attached to the site and its buildings. It is time- and date-bound through its daily teaching timetable, when it is open, and its term times and vacations. Its geography includes these facets of schooling, as well as of the school site itself. It is this physical and human world, this place and environment that are the everyday geography of the school and its grounds, that make it the place it is, with the role that it has. It can seem isolated, but its geography is local, national and global.

Practical task

Recall a school site you know, from current or recent experience or from your own schooling. List the range of features of that site that you recall. Draw freehand or sketch maps of the school grounds and of a floor of the school building. Annotate your maps about the physical and social geography of the school. Consider how easy or challenging this has been and why. Identify how best you can become well acquainted with a school's geography, its buildings, grounds, and social and cultural life.

Core resources

Investigating school geography requires resources. While children will develop their own resources during investigations – such as sketch maps of their classroom or the school grounds, digital photographs, questionnaires and checklists – there are published or teacher-prepared resources to acquire or develop for use. Among those that are available are the following.

- School site plans and maps.
- A large-scale topographic plan/map (e.g. 1:1250 scale) of the school site.
- Access to Google Earth, NearMap or similar vertical aerial photography of the site.

- Prepared plans of the school building, floors and classrooms.
- Photographs of various features around the school.
- Old photographs and maps of the site.
- School rules, regulations and codes.
- Documents from the headteacher, school governing board and others, such as past plans for changes, records of meetings, reports and old school log books.
- Children's information books about schools and the people who work in them.
- Directional compasses, tape measures, trundle wheels, a clinometer and weather-recording instruments.

 In the classroom

Parking in school

A class of 8–9-year-olds became concerned about the overuse of the school car park area. Often visitors parked, blocking staff cars that might be needed in an emergency. They studied this problem by considering if the space could be reorganised so that more cars could park. When this proved impractical, they looked for car parking spaces in the streets outside and nearby. They identified and drew up plans for parking spaces for visitors to be marked on the road outside the school and noted alternative nearby parking areas. They outlined their plans to the school's headteacher and governors, and to a local councillor and a planning officer.

Investigating geography in school

Investigating the school and its site should use an enquiry approach, as advocated in Chapter 4. A problem-oriented enquiry is a useful focus for investigating matters on the school site. It goes beyond simply identifying information and presenting it; it focuses on a concern to understand better the place and possibly to follow through on any matters that emerge. Such an issue might be the car park study outlined above or the best locations for rubbish bins in the playground areas. A problem-oriented approach is not a problem-solving approach. Too often children can be given the impression that by undertaking a study and making recommendations, the problem they have studied will be resolved. Some problems can be tackled and changes made; others cannot be changed, perhaps for resource reasons, because there are competing interests, because regulations override the children's proposals or because the scale of the change is too demanding in the current school context. This is how the everyday world works. By engaging in problem-oriented enquiries children meet everyday problems and outcomes (or the lack of them) and learn to deal with such situations that they might encounter out of school as citizens in their local, national and global communities. In selecting with children geographical problems to investigate, ensure from the start that they realise that their geographical learning comes through the investigation and by making proposals, not necessarily through change actually happening.

Almost all school building and grounds investigations will involve fieldwork. This should be effectively planned and draw on the advice provided in other chapters. It can be included within a classroom-based lesson. Good quality learning is more likely to occur during well-organised fieldwork. Even in school, you should always undertake an informal risk assessment of the area(s) you intend to use. An example of a lesson plan is included in Chapter 14 in the box on pp.450–452. It outlines a fieldwork session in the school building and grounds undertaken during a lesson that also includes class-based work.

Practical task

Identify a particular aspect of your school's grounds and a concern or problem associated with it. Use the advice on organising an enquiry in Chapter 4 to plan, undertake and report on your geographical issue. Include how you could adapt it to use in school.

Topics to investigate

There are many possible geographical topics to investigate in school. The following are used quite often, investigated in their own right, or in an early lesson in a topic that focuses on the local area or somewhere further away, to familiarise children with the topic and ideas being studied, and enquiry approaches and methods to be used. They are by no means the only possibilities (Tanner, 2017; Witt, 2017).

- Roads, paths and routes, and finding your way around.
- Location and variety of features and activities, including natural and constructed features.
- Room, building and land uses.
- Signposts to and labels for rooms and other facilities.
- Access and movement, including for the able-bodied and wheelchair users.
- Feelings about and attitudes to the school community, building and grounds.

- How we identify with and belong to the school community and relate to its site: its importance to us.
- What is special to us about the school site.
- People's jobs and activities, and similarities and differences in their work.
- How people use and affect the site, including informal, deliberate and unintended activities, and their impacts by children and adults.
- What enables and inhibits uses of and activities on the school site.
- The 'natural' and ecological environment.
- The school's layout and spatial patterns.
- What is distinctive about our school, its site and community.
- What we can rearrange, and what we cannot, in classes and the site, and why and how this affects our use of spaces.
- Origins of and changes to the school buildings and site, and why, when and by whom these were made.
- Microclimate, weather and their impact.
- Water and weathering.
- Impact of rubbish and waste disposal.
- Damage on and to parts of the site.
- Energy and water distribution, location, consumption and conservation.
- Changes to the school's environment.
- Caring for, protecting, managing and improving the site.

The geographical topics, questions and activities outlined below cover five themes: the school as a place, its physical environment, patterns around the school, sustainability, and the school's wider world connections. The common feature is that they link into the everyday life of the school and the everyday geographies of the children and those who work there. They involve a problem or concern to investigate, are initiated by geographical questions, and require active fieldwork to be developed effectively. Two or three examples are given for each theme. Each of them can be adapted to different primary age year groups.

School as a place

There are many ways to study schools as places, from their location and features to the types of community they are. Two topics illustrate this: how the school site is used, exploring aspects of its community role; and what those in the school think and feel about it as a place, focusing on affective responses to places.

Topic: How our school is used

Suggested enquiry questions: Who uses our school, what for, when and why? What types of jobs and activities are done? Can changes and improvements be made?

Possible activities

- Monitor who uses the school buildings and grounds during the school day from observation and experience, and what they do.
- Interview the children and staff about the activities and jobs they do, where and when, or use questionnaires or focus groups.
- Investigate who uses the building and grounds for what activities outside school hours.
- Map the school areas used, for the activities undertaken, by whom and when.
- Create a timetable to show the use of the school across the day and week, in term times and holidays.
- Identify the benefits of the different uses and for users, and any limitations.
- Consider improvements and/or additions to the use of the school site.
- Report to the headteacher on the use of the school.

Topic: How we think and feel about our school

Suggested enquiry questions: What do we think of and feel about our school and its grounds? Why do we feel this way?

Possible activities

- Children develop criteria for evaluating the quality of the school buildings and grounds.
- Survey sites around the school using the criteria. Map the results.
- Involve children in other classes and staff to find out what they think of the school site and how they feel about the school as their place.
- Report your findings with proposals about what could be done to develop positive views and attitudes further, or to address negative feelings and views.

    In the classroom

Investigating feelings about the school grounds

A group of 5-year-old children discussed what they liked about their school. Top of their list were the people they worked with, adults and children. Second were the resources they could play with at playtimes. Third was the landscaped area where they could go to sit, talk or play quiet games with their friends. They liked to be able to run about from time to time, but they were concerned about the older children not always noticing and bumping into them. This raised a question about whether everyone in the school liked the same things. A sample investigation took place with small groups of children, working with their teaching assistant, asking five children in each other class what they liked or did not like about their school. They had a mixture of responses, with playtimes being popular with some but not with others, and most children liking the variety of places to play around the school. A general view was that their school was a nice place to come to.

The school environment

There are many aspects to the school's physical environment, including its built features and ecology. There are factors that impact on a school, though, that are not of its own making. The following topics illustrate these matters. One concerns the weather and its effect on people and life in school; the other considers the problem of damage to the school's fabric through human activities and natural forces. These topics link geography and science, through undertaking scientific investigations (Sharp *et al.*, 2017) for weather recording, and to observe and record erosion in the school grounds (Bowles, 2010).

Topic: How the weather affects us

Suggested enquiry questions: What is the weather like on our school site? How does it affect us? How do we respond?

Possible activities

- Observe different aspects of the weather.
- Discuss how the weather feels: cold, hot, warm, cool, etc., and why it feels like this, including at different times of the year.
- Observe and discuss how people respond to different types of weather: what they do and what they wear, as well as why they do similar or different activities and wear the clothes they do.
- Estimate, measure and record different aspects of the weather – e.g. rain type and amount, wind direction and speed, temperature, amount of cloud cover and sunshine.
- Make weather records for a period of time, for at least a week but perhaps for a month or the duration of the topic, to consider and review what has happened across that period. This could be done more than once in different seasons for comparisons.

- Find out about the processes that cause different weather conditions and their effects – e.g. rain, wind, heat, cloud.
- Create and present a daily weather report and forecast.
- Report patterns in weather and people's responses over time – e.g. a week, a month, a term.

Topic: Damage around the school

Suggested enquiry questions: Is there any damage to features around the school? What types of erosion occur to school buildings and in the grounds? What can be done to stop or limit such damage?

Possible activities

- Discuss the idea of damage to the environment – e.g. through graffiti, broken windows, broken plants/trees, and why this might happen.
- Find out and discuss what erosion means and includes.
- Consider how damage and erosion compare to temporary lack of care, such as littering, whether there is a difference and why this might be.
- Observe, describe and map areas where there is damage or erosion around the school – e.g. worn areas on grass or tarmac, damaged plants at the edge of the playground, graffiti and scratches on walls, and worn stairs, wall bricks or paintwork through human use or rain or wind action. Take photographs.
- Examine how and why damage and erosion has happened, and consider how serious it is and if it poses a safety problem.
- Identify ways to reduce and/or prevent damage to the buildings and grounds.
- Report on your findings and proposals.
- Investigate how weathering and erosion occur and ways damage can be caused.

 Reflective task

Consider how the topics outlined here support the development of children's geographical understanding of key concepts. For instance, 'Damage around the school' illustrates environmental impact and sustainability, and physical and human processes. Which key geographical concepts (Chapter 2) can be developed through the other topics?

Patterns around the school

Understanding how space is used within the school site means studying the distributions of features and activities and their resulting spatial patterns. The first topic examines the distribution of rubbish bins around the school site, inside and outdoors, focused on their location in appropriate places and whether their distribution is the result of considered thought, guess-work or whim. The second considers the ways rooms are designated and used, the distribution of these uses and the impact of this pattern. The third explores routes and journeys around the school and their impact.

Topic: Rubbish bins around the school

Suggested enquiry questions: Where are the rubbish bins? Why are they there? How much are they used? Are they in the right places? Can they be better located?

Possible activities

Discuss the use of rubbish bins and how well they are used in their present sites, inside and out.

- Map their location and discuss the reasons why they are located where they are.
- Observe and record littering and throwing away, and the use of rubbish bins. Is their use effective?
- Interview children and staff about attitudes to dealing with litter, the use of bins and their location.
- Make proposals, with plans, for locating rubbish bins more helpfully and explain why these changes are needed.
- Report on what has been found out and request that your proposals are implemented.
- Trial and evaluate relocating bins and make any amendments as necessary.

Topic: Room use in the school building(s)

Suggested enquiry questions: How is the use of rooms in the school best arranged? Are they used appropriately at present?

Possible activities

- Map the use of rooms in the school building and identify the patterns of use.
- Identify the relevant size and accessibility of different rooms – e.g. the library, from classrooms, and find out times of use and flows of movement.

- Note which rooms/services can be changed and which cannot – e.g. toilets or a music room.
- Consider whether there are more practical locations for particular services, related to use, need, room size, etc.
- Report on whether the best use is made of the rooms in the school and on your proposals for change.

Topic: Routes around school

Suggested enquiry questions: What are the main routes around school? Why are they used and what is the effect of using them at which times of day?

Possible activities

- Using maps of the school building(s) and of the grounds, mark the routes that children and adults use, and which are priorities for whom and when.
- Investigate at playtimes the density of use of a variety of routes. Check the use of these routes during class time.
- Consider the benefits and issues raised by the use of routes in school, inside and outdoors, and whether these are the same or different for different people.
- Confirm effective uses of routes and identify ways in which routes or times of use can be improved.
- Report your findings and proposals, and ask whether any changes can be trialled and evaluated.

 In the classroom

Making changes to playtime

Effecting changes within a school should involve children being able to raise concerns, but also being involved in or taking responsibility for providing solutions to their concerns. This example illustrates one way in which the children's voice was heard and led to their involvement in making justified proposals for changes in the use of playgrounds at playtime.

A group of 8–9-year-girls did not enjoy having to spend their time in the playground area designated for the older primary children because of the boisterous activities and games of the boys, which marginalised them. They asked to move to the playground set aside for the younger children. Before considering whether they could 'change places', they were asked to investigate and report on the problems they perceived and whether other children felt the same way or differently, and to include the older and younger children in their surveys. They reported that children across both playground areas were dissatisfied with the present designation of play areas by age and suggested that they should be redesignated according to the activities that children wished to participate in. As a result, one playground was reallocated for lively activities, such as running and ball games, while the other was set aside for quiet activities, such as sitting and chatting or reading, skipping, and so on. Children had to choose which playground to be on at the start of each playtime. The group of girls monitored the changes and reported after a month that they were effective, except that some children surreptitiously changed playgrounds to be with friends. The pre-playtime choice rule was scrapped and children could move freely. The change was a success.

A sustainable school

A sustainable school is the aim of many school communities. The key intention of sustainable school approaches is to ensure that children understand the concept and reality of sustainability, to foster their positive attitudes and values towards the environment, to involve children in working to ensure that their school becomes more sustainable through careful management of its resources, and to engage in dialogue and action for improved sustainability with the local community. It is about developing positive attitudes to sustainability and providing children with experience of living and working in a sustainable community.

One way to develop sustainable ways of working and attitudes is to use the 'eight doorways' approach outlined in Chapter 7. This offers rich and stimulating opportunities to involve children in investigating and acting to encourage and put in place a class and school approach to sustainability, as well as caring for and enhancing the school's social and physical environment. The topics in this section provide ways to connect sustainable schools' activities with geographical studies, focused on environmental impact and sustainability. Studying recycling in school can complement the rubbish bin study. The use of, and understanding access to, water in school is another 'doorway' topic.

Topic: Recycling in school

Suggested enquiry questions: Do you recycle? What and how? Why? Is it enough? What else could you do?

Possible activities

- Discuss and find out about the various types of waste produced in school.
- Undertake interviews to find out about waste produced in areas such as classrooms and the kitchen.
- Invite the school caretaker into class to talk about waste disposal.
- Within health and safety limits and using appropriate clothing such as gloves, observe, examine, categorise and weigh types of waste products found in school.
- Find out about recycling practices used in school.
- Invite someone from the waste-disposal company that serves the school to answer children's questions and tell them about waste recycling, how it is done, the benefits and the difficulties.
- Propose ways to extend, improve or initiate recycling waste to the headteacher.

Topic: Our water use in school

Suggested enquiry questions: Where does our water come from? Who uses it? Where, when and what for? How can we be more careful in its use?

Possible activities

- Consider why water is so important, how we use it and how much we use.
- Map the location of water access and disposal around the school.
- With the help of the caretaker, investigate where water comes into the school and how it is distributed around the school.
- Survey who uses water, what for, when and why during the school day.
- Investigate how much water is used through sample surveys of where it is used.
- Ask a representative from the local water board into class to talk and answer questions about water sources, provision and use. Prepare questions beforehand.
- Consider the necessity of the amount of water use and ways to reduce consumption.
- Make proposals for measuring and reducing water usage.

In the classroom

Energy use in school

A class of 9–10-year-olds proposed various geography topics to investigate. The class voted to explore energy issues. This topic developed from comments by children that lights and computers were often left on in classrooms when no one was there. This initiated a survey and linked with science to develop further their understanding about electricity, light and energy use. It led to proposals for classes to monitor their use of lights and to turn them off whenever possible. It examined the heating of the school, the class inviting local electricity and gas officials to talk to them about ways to make savings. With the caretaker's help, they learned about the electrical and heating systems of the school. The outcome was a poster campaign encouraging energy saving. Complementing their school site studies, the children examined their use of energy at home and noticed how energy was used in their local area. They became much more conscious of the role that energy plays in our everyday lives, how much we use and depend on it, and why efforts are made to encourage people to save energy.

Connections beyond school

Schools recognise their interconnections with their local community, not least through their pupils, and with the wider regional, national and global world. Geography provides an effective focus to explore such links. An obvious connection is children's travel to school, focused on the local links. Schools are connected with the wider world through such diverse forms as using the Internet, the origins and delivery of resources, and the variety of places children visit with their families and on school fieldwork and other activities.

Topic: Travel to school

Suggested enquiry questions: How do we travel to school? Are there travel-to-school improvements that can be made?

Possible activities

- Survey the ways in which children and adults travel to school and why.
- Map the catchment area of the school to see where people travel from and the routes they use. Link this to their modes of travel.

- Monitor and map the ways children travel to and arrive at the school entrance(s). Include home sites, modes of transport or travel – e.g. walk, car, bus – where children meet up – e.g. to join a walking bus or friends – and arrival points, use of particular entrances to the grounds and buildings, and times. Consider local travel risks, including road crossing.
- Examine the traffic on the roads outside and close to school to see how they help or hinder travel to school by walking or bicycle. Is there a need for a road crossing point outside or near school?
- Consider the positives and negatives of cycling to school and bike storage, school bus drop-off points and car parking at or near school.
- Create a display showing the variety of ways travelled to school, collection and drop-off points, and where and when people enter the school.
- Consider and propose ways to improve travel safety, reduce car journeys and ensure safe access into school.

Topic: Connected to the wider world

Suggested enquiry questions: Where are we connected to? How? Why there and with what effect?

Possible activities

- Investigate the links that people in school have and that the school has with other parts of the local region, country and wider world, including interpersonal connections, food and goods, and the ways in which they have these links.
- Select a variety of sources to survey – e.g. children's personal links, links through the Internet, where some of the goods and resources in school come or are delivered from, places visited on fieldwork and school journeys, holiday destinations. Map them.
- Explain why these links exist, such as in families, for meals, or as resources for school use, their value and benefit.
- Consider which links are most useful, whether others might be developed and which could be ended.
- Create a display to show the school's connections to the wider world.

Topic: Travelling into and out of our country

Suggested enquiry questions: From which countries have people in our school come? Which countries have people in our school visited or lived in for a short or long time?

Possible activities

- Survey children and staff in class and in other classes about their travel experiences and locations to and from other countries.
- Write the names of people on pin tags and locate the places they name on a wall map of the world.
- Make a list of countries of birth and with strong family connections and of countries visited.
- Allocate each country to a child or a group of children to investigate and find out several interesting points about it.
- Investigate how children have travelled to and/or moved countries and the reasons why they have done so.

Reflective task

Select one of the geography topics outlined here and consider how you might introduce it to a class. What would be the main geographical concepts and skills you would want to develop? How would you start your topic? What would you do next? What would be the focus for field-work in the school? Plan it as an enquiry.

Key points

This chapter has:

- introduced you to studying a school's geography and provided reasons why it is a good geographical site;
- outlined the various aspects of the school site and its geography;
- provided you with a number of possible topics to investigate using a problem-oriented enquiry approach.

Moving on

In your school look around to familiarise yourself with its geography. Walk the school's grounds and observe it from different angles. Use your phone or a camera to photograph various features of the buildings and

(Continued)

(Continued)

grounds, large and small. Walk around the school building(s) to see how inside spaces are used. Make a sketch map of the grounds and building(s). Annotate a copy of the map with what you see happening in the school. Take account of activities at different times of day. For example, map the variety of children's activities in the playground during one or two playtimes. Reflect on and note the aspects of geography you have encountered as you made your observations and maps. Think how you could use them to help children's learning in geography.

Further reading

Views and ideas about using the school grounds appear in several publications.

Halocha, J (2012) *The Primary Teacher's Guide to Geography*. Witney: Scholastic/ Book End.

Hare, R, Attenborough, C and Day, T (1996), *Geography in the School Grounds*. Exmouth: Southgate.

Pike, S (2016) *Learning Primary Geography: Ideas and inspirations from Classrooms*. Abingdon: Routledge.

Scoffham, S (ed.) (2010) *Primary Geography Handbook*. Sheffield: Geographical Association.

Titman, W (1994) *Special People, Special Places*. Winchester: Learning through Landscapes.

See issues of *Primary Geography*, published by The Geographical Association.

Useful websites

Campaign for school gardening: www.rhs.org.uk/schoolgardening/default.aspa
Council for Learning Outside the Classroom: www.lotc.org.uk
Eco-schools: www.keepbritaintidy.org/ecoschools/
Learning through Landscapes: www.ltl.org.uk
Let's Walk to School: www.livingstreets.org.uk/walk-with-us/walk-to-school
Making your School More Eco-friendly: www.youthcentral.vic.gov.au
Sustainable Learning: www.sustainablelearning.info
Sustainable Schools Alliance: www.sustainable-schools-alliance.org.uk
The Walking School Bus: www.travelsmart.gov.au/schools/schools2.html
WWF One Planet Schools: www.wwf.org.uk/oneplanetschools

CHAPTER 12

EXPLORING LOCALLY, REGIONALLY AND NATIONALLY

   Chapter objectives

This chapter enables you to:

- understand the meaning and importance of local area studies and the links to children's geographies;
- know and appreciate key aspects of the geography of a locality;
- recognise opportunities for children to investigate their local area;
- be aware of connections between local studies, sustainability, citizenship and local environmental participation;
- identify opportunities for local enquiries and fieldwork;
- know of the range of resources to use in locality studies;
- appreciate the role of studying your own and another national region;
- understand the reasons for and some approaches to studying your own country.

Introduction

The study of a local area provides opportunities for children to develop some understanding of a smaller scale place. The locality of the school is an excellent place to investigate, not least because it is most children's home area. This neighbourhood offers various possibilities, such as studies of physical and human processes in the environment, and of environmental impact and sustainability, as well as of their sense of place and as a particular familiar place. Study of the home locality has long been recognised as essential in primary geography teaching for younger and older primary children. It is a key element in many nations' primary geography curriculum because it is their place, and there is much geographical understanding that can be introduced and developed. This chapter examines several aspects of local area studies, looking particularly at the immediate locality, or neighbourhood, of the school, but noting that similar studies can be made of other similar or different localities, possibly using fieldwork, elsewhere in the wider region and nationally. The school locality offers the same opportunities for 'learnscapes' that were outlined at the start of Chapter 11. Given that localities are places within a wider region and country, this chapter also considers the teaching of national regions and about children's home nation.

Studying localities in primary geography

A key aspect of geographical study with early years children, from 5 to 7/8 years old, is the study of their own immediate local area – their own and/or their school's neighbourhood. Here they can investigate its features, its layout, what goes on there, how it is cared for and perhaps how aspects of it have changed. Children should consider how they feel about and relate to 'their' place.

Between the ages of 7/8 and 11/12 years old children should investigate their own locality further, examining how it compares with other places, looking at how their locality has developed in the way it has, considering how it might be improved, and investigating its connections with other places, its wider region, other areas of the country and, indeed, the world. They should become aware of and informed about where it is in their country, so building their mental maps from the local to the wider context.

Why study localities?

Studying their own locality helps children to know, understand and appreciate the place they live in. There are powerful reasons for studying local area geography. These draw on children's everyday geographies and arise because it is accessible for fieldwork.

Among the strong reasons for studying the local area are the following.

- Investigating the local area draws on children's curiosity, interest, experience and knowledge of their place, enabling them to share the awareness and understanding they bring from their homes in different but overlapping parts of the area.
- Its study develops children's knowledge, understanding and appreciation of their home area. It challenges misinformation and misconceptions they may have and helps them to become better informed locally.
- It encourages them to develop a sense of their place in the world, where they are in relation to other places, and their interconnectedness regionally and globally.
- The local environment provides an excellent 'laboratory' – a close-by site for investigations – to study geographical ideas and skills and to develop children's:

    o geographical knowledge, such as of features and activities, travel and transport, the local community, and local facilities and services;
    o geographical understanding – for instance, of what goes on where and why it happens, awareness of geographical patterns and processes, and of local interdependence with the wider world;
    o sense of place;
    o environmental change, impact and values/attitudes related to care for the environment, environmental management, damage and improvement, and feelings for and concerns about the area;
    o geographical enquiry and skills, including fieldwork and map work;
    o geographical language, and place and environmental vocabulary.

- Local area study builds on links to the local community, an important aspect of place and sustainability education, and offers opportunities to:

    o draw in and draw on local people;
    o use local facilities;
    o connect with local amenity groups;
    o look at local situations, needs and issues.

- Much of the local area is, potentially, readily accessible to the school. Studying it cries out for and facilitates fieldwork activities.
- Using the local area can build on and develop geographical studies undertaken initially in the school grounds.

Studying the local area is much more than identifying a range of features and activities, services, changes and connections. For primary children it is about developing their sense of neighbourhood and community, as well as their knowledge and appreciation of the nature of the area. In an increasingly mobile society with ever greater virtual connections locally, nationally and internationally, there is an important role for geography in helping to create more cohesive, resilient and safe communities. Fostering social and community cohesion has the benefit of creating more supportive, positive and enterprising neighbourhoods and communities where children, young people and adults feel comfortable and welcomed, where diverse identities and backgrounds are appreciated and valued, and where there is a sense for all of belonging (Cantle, 2008; Lanza, 2012). Schools are central to this. This links effectively with the development of sustainable schools in sustainable communities, where there is concern to improve the quality of school and local area environments and to value local involvement and a sense of place alongside global awareness and citizenship. Indeed, they connect strongly with an agenda emphasising improved personal and social well-being together with enabling children's voices to be listened to (Hayward, 2012).

There are strong justifications to develop in children their sense of local environmental well-being (Catling, 2007) through geographical studies of the local area. These link directly into a sense of neighbourhood and community, including:

- awareness and knowledge of one's own community;
- building a sense of belonging and identity locally;
- encouraging concern and respect for 'the local';
- fostering a sense of care for the community;
- becoming engaged with community groups;
- being neighbourly;
- observing and participating in sustainable practices;
- encouraging and empowering children's 'voice' and involvement;
- recognising local interdependence.

Not only does the focus on local geography encourage children to investigate and deepen their understanding of their own area as it is, but it enables them to explore its possible and their preferred futures, developing their sense of responsibility and potential for involvement and participation.

Attachment to place

Across the world their local place has considerable meaning for local people. While place meaning often is associated with rural and natural environments, urban places are just as important for those born and brought up in towns and cities (Chawla, 1992; Taylor, 2010; Manzo and Devine-Wright, 2014; Cresswell, 2015). Many people conceive of their identity in terms of connections, or attachment, to place (Malpas, 2018).

A useful way to consider attachment to place is through ways in which native peoples identify with places, such as Native Americans, the Aboriginal peoples of Australia, tribal groups in the Amazon rainforest and other native peoples in Asia and Africa. For example, Sarra (2011) identifies the origins and closeness of Aboriginal peoples to the land of Australia, their indigenous home, as centrally important to their lives. These senses of land and place are vitally important for and to them, and they are linked with such concepts as home, community and sustainability. They have deep respect for, appreciation of and commitment to the land. Pride in being Aboriginal, as with other native peoples, is very strongly to do with place, with attachment both to it and to the notion of 'country' as defined by a local people. This is equally important for people who regard their place and land in their country, whether in urban or rural areas, as their home, with which they have family associations for many years and, perhaps, generations. This sense of attachment and belonging to place is found in all societies across the world and can be very strong in migrant and displaced communities.

Places are very much part of our identity, which we often acknowledge when referring to which country or part of that country we come from. This is an important way into recognising and valuing our sense of ourselves and our locality, the connections with where we each live and go about our daily lives (Edmondson, 2008; Gerber, 2001). For the large majority of us, localities have been respected for generations because they provide such things as food and shelter, as well as social and even spiritual connections. Often we affirm this sense when we feel that our place is threatened, not least when we see change happening and familiar landmarks being demolished and replaced, affecting our connections with the past and the future in a place we value. We can feel a sense of dispossession physically and metaphorically. This means that it is important for us to consider how places are perceived, understood and valued, how local environments are respected and used, and what can be shared and learnt from each other.

This provides a strong case for including in local geographical enquiries a focus on how people locally perceive, feel about and value their local area. Such exploration might include:

- being aware of traditional formal and informal names for places locally;
- knowing local stories about the area that might tell us about its distinctiveness and the nature of local features;
- how people living locally identify with and give meaning to and take meaning from places;
- what people regard as the area in which they live – its boundary and boundedness – and about those who live there and their places within them;
- appreciation that there are local ways in each place and environment, and that people have concerns that these have been, are and can be sustained;
- ways in which local land has been, is and can be managed for the benefit of all;
- comparisons with the lives, ways of living and local issues faced by people in other places nationally and globally.

Reflective task

Recall or look back to the points made about children's personal geographies in Chapter 3. Make a list of reasons for studying local geography, drawing on children's experience of their neighbourhoods and communities. Consider how these reasons relate to those who feel a strong sense of attachment and belonging to a place – to their identity with place(s) and the importance of place and the land or urban environment to them – indeed, to us all.

Outside the classroom

Where is our neighbourhood?

As part of their local study, a class of 9–10-year-olds asked shoppers they interviewed to draw on a local street map a line around the area they felt to be their local area. They asked the adults they spoke to why they drew the line where they did and received a variety of answers, ranging from 'I should know, I'm the local postman', 'I think it includes the school, the shops on that road and all the homes round there', to 'I have no idea, I'm just visiting for today'. They recognised that different people had different ideas about the extent of the area and what was included. They used all the maps in class to construct a map that showed all the 'boundary' lines drawn by more than 40 adults and discussed whether the periphery of all of them was the range of the area or whether it should include just those areas that many or most people had drawn, deciding on the latter and rejecting some 'outliers'. They also identified the 'core' of the local area and that it included several key features, including most of the main shopping street close to the local station. This gave them a sense of the centre of the area and the extent which most people included and felt was local.

What is a locality?

The school's local area and neighbourhood

The local area is the area around the school, the area where the majority of the children live who go to the school; it is referred to as the school's catchment area. For schools with a very wide catchment area the local area might be limited to an area that stretches a kilometre or so in each direction. The 'size' of the local area needs to be differentiated thoughtfully for children at different ages and stages of their early years and primary education. The local area might be viewed as a series of concentric circles, although depending on features and barriers, such as major roads, it might be a rather rougher shape.

- *For 3/4 to 6/7-year-olds:* the setting and school grounds, the streets round about and a nearby park or play area in the school's immediate neighbourhood;
- *For 6/7 to 8/9-year-old children:* the school grounds and the close neighbourhood or nearby area around the school: its vicinity, perhaps including many children's homes;
- *From 8/9 to 11/12-year-olds:* the school grounds and the wider, extended neighbourhood of the school, possibly the school catchment area from within which almost all children travel to get to school. This should be reassessed if many children live far away, but it is a useful rule of thumb.

Progression in studying the local area can start with the school's immediate surroundings and then develop into a wider area as children become more familiar with their local area. It is important to remember that the local environment should be revisited continually through different geographical 'focal lenses' as the children develop and deepen their experience and knowledge of their surroundings, and consider increasingly complex aspects and issues as they move through their geographical studies.

 In the classroom

Discussing the local area

A class of 5–6-year-old children used photographs of local buildings and street scenes taken by their teacher to discuss the variety of features and shops they saw on their way between school and home, and when out with their families. The children commented on the variety of homes near where their friends lived, about shops they used, and on some local problems they encountered, such as litter and the time taken to cross roads. They drew their favourite places to visit and were helped to write about why they liked these places. They talked about where or what they did not like and what could be done to improve it or make it more pleasant. They were encouraged to suggest what they might like changed to make their locality more interesting for them.

Local area study elsewhere in our country

To be able to develop a coherent sense of the scale and variety of your home country, it is important to study more than one locality in the country. A locality elsewhere in your home region, the much wider part of the country in which you live, might be investigated alongside or before another in a different part of the country. This supports making comparisons with other places, which can be undertaken with primary children at any point in their primary years. A comparative locality enquiry involves the study of a place of an equivalent size as the local area of the school and should examine the nature of the neighbourhood and community. It provides the opportunity for children to examine some or many of the same aspects of their own locality, as well as contrasting aspects (Walker, 2010). Children might study an area that is different from their own and use a variety of secondary sources. Urban children might investigate a rural area, inland children a coastal place, or children living in a relatively flat place a mountainous area, and the converse for each of these examples. There might well be opportunities, through a school's residential visit for older primary children, for them to travel to another part of the country to undertake extended fieldwork.

Complementing the reasons for study of the school locality, the purposes of investigating another locality include:

- that some or many children in a class may already have experience of localities elsewhere nationally, through family visits to some places, even if of limited duration, or because they have moved from another part of the country to live where they do now. Such study builds on and extends their sense of 'elsewhere' and knowledge of other national places;
- their awareness of other places nationally through relatives, friends and the media, which may be very similar to or different from their own, and which they can contrast to their own lives in a rural or an urban environment;
- providing opportunities to identify and examine similarities and contrasts with their home locality;
- that there may be the possibility of making a visit to the locality if nearby or, if it is further afield, on a school journey over several days.

The most successful locality studies are of small, contained areas where real and meaningful comparisons to the children's lives can be made. Comparing places of very different scales, such as comparing a neighbourhood with a large town, a city or a region, is unhelpful, providing inappropriate and quite meaningless comparisons. It needs to be remembered that a locality is not simply a physical entity; its people, community and neighbourhood dimensions are central. An aspect of geographical studies of localities, which is important to and engages children, is the lives of those who live there. Comparing and contrasting lives, and the natural and constructed physical environments can be stimulating and enticing.

Outside the classroom

Investigating another locality on a residential visit

One primary school takes its 10–11-year-old primary children for a week's residential visit to a contrasting coastal locality from its inner city site to investigate the local geography of a seaside town as part of their studies. The school uses a field centre and works with the staff there. In several previous years it has been to a mountainous area to provide different contrasts. The residential field visit involves much prior planning and is very rewarding. The children focus on exploring the central area of this small town and its beachside to find out what is there and what happens locally. Their geographical investigations are the central but not the only aspect of their residential visit. During their visit they also investigate aspects of the history of the area and use their art and literacy skills creatively. In their geographical studies they explore the physical environment, make visits to key features such as the lighthouse and lifeboat station, find out about local shops and transport, note the types of businesses in the area and consider why they might be there, look at why the area attracts visitors (including themselves), and observe how the place has changed and changes they notice during the time of their fieldwork. Their enquiry is part of a curriculum unit of work initiated before the visit by examining maps, brochures and photographs of the town, developing enquiry questions and undertaking some risk assessments. On their return they examine and analyse their information and experiences. They evaluate what they have learnt and create a display and presentations for parents and other children in their school. The children are invariably very enthusiastic and there is much deep learning. In the past, some 9–10-year-olds, when places were available, returned the following year and helped to lead some investigations, acting as informed visitors and initiating new lines of enquiry that their previous year's experiences had generated.

In the classroom

Making a place comparison

A class of 10–11-year-olds used a variety of secondary sources to compare a town in the north of their country to their own place, which they located on their national map. They used websites, maps, brochures, Google Earth, photographs and connections to children of their own age in a school in the area. After a general introduction, groups in the class selected different areas of enquiry, and pursued these using questions to direct their investigations. They were able to establish the attractions of the town for tourists, the varieties of accommodation for visitors, concerns about and benefits from the key times of year of tourist visits, the impact of access to and parking in the town and the interesting features that attracted people. They each chose different methods to present their information to the class. Asked to say what they had learnt from their investigations, children referred to the variety of jobs, some of its features, the nature of the town, the importance of tourism to the area, that they could probably buy many things there that they could in their local supermarket, and how attractive a place it seemed to be. They wanted to visit the area.

Reflective task

What do you consider to be the most important learning that children should take from geographical studies of a locality? What are your reasons for this?

Aspects of local geography

There is much geography that can be studied in any local area. Very often the focus is on the physical features of the area, both the shape of its land – its physical geography – and its built environment, as well as on what facilities are available and what adults and children do there – elements of its human geography. These are important aspects of a local area and its community to investigate and are among those listed in the box below, which includes elements of environmental geography (Richardson, 2018a, 2018b).

Children will know from their daily experience whether the land slopes or is flat (and undulates even if it seems flat). Their walks to school provide a useful way in to develop children's sense of the local landshape and to consider how it has influenced the way in which the locality looks and the area has developed. The core area of a village, town or city is usually alongside or, more often, straddles a small or large river and a tributary or two. It is probably on an area of higher ground by the river so as to avoid flooding, but more recent developments may lie on the floodplain and be subject to occasional flooding. Alternatively, while a village or town may have grown up alongside a stream in a relatively shallow or a steep-sided valley, there are likely to be housing and other developments that stretch up the hillside with steep streets and 'contoured' level streets providing a road pattern lattice of access. There may or may not be more available space for the town or village to develop further.

Children will be aware of local facilities and services, such as a variety of shops, a garage, a hairdresser, some commercial and/or industrial premises, a library, religious buildings and other features, as well as of the roads, their street furniture, where people park cars, safe and unsafe road crossing points and other aspects of their locality. They may not notice or see some businesses if these are located on the upper floors of buildings, such as offices above shops, because they tend not to look at what is above the ground floor. Finding out about what we often do not notice in a neighbourhood provides an informative investigation that tells us more about what there is and what goes on locally.

Aspects of localities to study across early years and primary geography

Nature of places

- Local features and micro places – e.g. street furniture, buildings, fields, streets
- The physical landscape, its slopes, flat areas and river or stream
- Who lives in the area: long-term residents to those who have moved locally recently
- People's lives and use of the local area – e.g. where they shop and why
- Local activities and events
- Leisure activities, play areas/parks

(Continued)

(Continued)

- Land/building use: types and varieties of use
- Service/goods provision: shops/businesses
- Work: jobs people do, employment
- Access: ease of getting into places and about
- Travel: journeys, transport
- The patterns of streets and layout of locality
- Variety of types of housing along streets and in estates
- Local weather impact and microclimate
- Security surveillance: local camera monitoring of people, activities and places
- Relationship between features and activities

Character of places

- Focus of area – e.g. suburb, business/industrial park, farmland, shopping centre
- The type of settlement and its community
- The diversity within and cohesion of the community
- What localities are like, feel like, look like
- Areas and sites that appear prosperous and that seem to be neglected or run down

Sense of places

- Views and feelings about people, places and their environments
- Appreciation of places: likes and dislikes about features, activities and places
- Concerns and what is valued about places
- A sense of belonging and identity with the locality; what it means

Management and improvement of places

- Responsibility for local services – e.g. rubbish collection; how these are carried out
- Identifying local issues – e.g. traffic and parking, housing development
- Safeguarding the area and its inhabitants from local hazards, such as flooding

- How damage to and pollution of locality are tackled
- Care for the local environment
- What people might want places to be like

Changing places

- How localities have become the way they are
- How and why localities are changing
- Changes in land use, features and activities, on individual sites or large tracts of land
- Who makes decisions leading to change and why
- Conflicts over change
- The impact of changes on people, places and environments
- How localities may change and become in the future

Place locations and connections

- Where features and activities occur in the local area
- Links to other places locally, regionally and globally: transport, goods/services, virtually
- Localities in the wider geographical context, local to global: from locality to surrounding region to country to continent to world
- Ways in which places are interdependent, benefits and limitations

Comparing places

- How localities compare with other localities
- How and why localities are similar to and different from other places in the same country and elsewhere in the world
- The valuing of commonality and diversity within and between places

While the list in the box above provides a helpful checklist for possible topics locally, these topics need to be translated into an effective local study. The box below outlines one way to structure a local area topic using enquiry questions.

Aspects of localities to study across early years and primary geography

1. What do we know about our locality?

    - What is our area like?
    - What is special about it?

2. What are the main activities in the area?

    - What facilities and services are there?
    - What do people do for work and leisure?

3. How is the land used across the area?

    - What is the land used for if we look in each direction from school?
    - What can we find out about the land use around our homes?

4. Who lives in our locality?

    - What do people do and like to do locally?
    - Why do they live in our area?
    - What are their connections with other places?

5. How do we think and feel about our place?

    - What is important to people about our locality?
    - What sort of character does our locality have?

6. What is changing in our place?

    - What can we see that shows how our area has developed?
    - What is changing here now?
    - What is the impact of changes?

7. How do we look after our local area?

    - In what ways have people affected our locality?
    - What changes would we like to see in the future and why?

8.   What can we tell someone else about 'our place'?

- What would we show someone about our locality?
- What do I appreciate now about my area that I did not before?

 In the classroom

Creating local brochures

Undertaking a local study using a similar structure to that in the box above, a class of 7–8-year-olds concluded their project by making local brochures that they planned for families who would be new to the locality. As a part of their investigation, they asked at home what their families would like to know about the local area if they were new to it. Small teams produced their brochures and these were displayed and shown to three new sets of parents by the headteacher when they visited the school shortly after the project was completed.

There is value in having a clear focus in local area studies, particularly if the children at times provide such foci from their interests, experience and knowledge. Rather than undertaking shop or land use surveys of an area – which can be informative and useful in knowing and understanding what types of shops, facilities and services are available or the range of uses that local land has – it can be more stimulating and effective to focus on a particular concern or problem, using the problem-oriented enquiry approach outlined in Chapter 11. For example, the local shopping parade and wider area might be studied for its accessibility for everyone, including those who use wheelchairs, parents with single or double baby buggies, the elderly or infirm, the partially sighted and the hard of hearing. The emphasis might be on how challenging it is to get around the area, what signage helps or hinders, how easy or difficult it is to get into shops, and what can be done to improve matters (Catling, 2005d). An example of a plan for such a topic is provided in Chapter 14, Table 14.1. Inviting your children to suggest and select foci for local studies both identifies their interests and concerns, and motivates their engagement in investigations. The box below lists several topics to stimulate your ideas.

Twelve stimulating geographical topics to investigate locally

- *What a waste!* From local waste bins to refuse collection and disposal, how much is recycled?
- *Is there a parking problem?* What is parking like locally and what can be done about local concerns?
- *There's an empty shop.* Who would like the shop used for which service/business and why?
- *Who created the local play area?* How were decisions made about local play facilities? And what do children really want there?
- *Who uses public transport?* Exploring the use of bus services (or the lack of them) locally and the impact and value to different users.
- *Cars and vans and lorries.* What is the traffic like in the local area and why is there so much? Is it local traffic mainly or just passing through?
- *Introducing the local area.* Produce a leaflet about the locality for new parents and children. What should be put in and what left out?
- *The best and worst of places.* What is most and least attractive about the local area? Children's and adults' perspectives.
- *Out for a walk:* What is it like going for a walk in the locality? What do you see? Are there back alleys to use and green spaces, or can you walk only on streets?
- *What's available?* People's perspectives on what is available and what is not and where you have to go to get it.
- *Keeping an eye and ear open.* Look at the sites of surveillance cameras in the local area. Why there? What for? How useful?
- *Elsewhere here.* Identify and explain all those visible local connections to other places. What other national and international connections are there?

Place, environmental impact and sustainability: topics for local investigation

Localities are rich resources for engaging and creative enquiries. Being dynamic and constantly evolving, they provide good examples of real-life issues and give children the opportunity to ask questions about what is happening and to develop potential solutions. Much information about the local area, and what concerns people, can be gathered through local websites, newspapers, radio and television. Schools and children can access such information readily.

Local sources, which include the knowledge and perspectives that children bring from home and their own experience, provide the potential for a variety of topics and issues from which to select. Many local issues focus on changes to the environment, and the impact and sustainability of these changes. A concern in many urban environments around the world (Freeman and Tranter, 2011) is the safety of the streets and the opportunities for play in the local area (Lanza, 2012). A topic about this issue might examine where local play spaces are, to what extent the streets are safe places for walking or biking for children, the attitudes of adults to children playing out in groups, and how provision could be improved, perhaps not just for young children but for teenagers as well. Concerns and issues should be ones with meaning for the children and the local community. The following are examples of local problems to examine. You will be able to identify related types of issues from your own area.

- The changing provision of local facilities and services, such as the closure or relocation of a local post office or shop and the different impacts on local people.
- Different people's use of and requirements for services locally, such as leisure facilities, and provision for specific groups of people such as the young, the elderly and people with disabilities.
- Development projects that spark local people's opinions about change and improvements in the area, including the potentially conflicting views and needs of different groups of people.
- Examining local heritage to introduce children to their local cultural past, what it means to people, how it has affected the development of the locality, how it is changing and what its future might be.
- Valuing the local area and developing a sense of place, considering which areas the children have feelings for and about justifying their views alongside examining other groups of people's values and attitudes.
- Transport impact, the sufficiency of provision, and possible conflicting views on such issues as parking and plans for road widening or pedestrianisation.

Citizenship and local environmental participation

Examining a local change or problem, such as the closure or change in use of a shop, has clear links with citizenship education (Jackson, 2010). This is particularly strong in many of the issue-based topics investigated in primary geography. It is essential that the connections are made. In investigating a locality, primary children should engage in matters of concern and importance in their community. This provides opportunities to express and develop their values and attitudes about their place, and to think about their role as community members. It supports effectively the ethos of citizenship education and the aim of involving children as community participants. Developing such understanding at a local level enables children to learn about and take up informed, responsible and active roles as local citizens. It promotes their understanding of good neighbourhood relationships and respect for the different views of local people, as well as helping children to consider and contribute to local environmental sustainability, matters of social justice and economic resilience.

Such enquiries into important issues in the locality initiate and deepen children's understanding of the geographical processes at play in our neighbourhoods and communities, as well as more widely in our societies. Children can begin to explore the issues around local sustainability, what might happen to a place in the future and begin to develop a sense of the part they can play in determining whether that future is their preferred one. It helps them to appreciate the reasons for local decisions and changes, even though they may not agree with what has been decided and undertaken by others. Investigations may bring to their notice initiatives such as the transition town and plastic bottle, packaging and bag-free movements. These can empower children, as citizens, to recognise that they may be able to do something positive for change, now and in the future.

 In the classroom

Investigating a local issue

An enquiry undertaken by 10–11-year-old children was provoked by a headline in a local newspaper:

COMMUNITY MARKET TO CLOSE AS SHOPPERS FLOCK TO NEW SUPERSTORE

Using the report in the local newpaper and found on the Internet, the children built up an idea about what was happening. Their teacher recorded a local TV regional news bulletin from which the children learnt about the views of local people. They planned and organised with their teacher, who provided photographs for their own risk assessment, a field trip to undertake their own survey of the market and of both the stall-holders' and shoppers' views. They considered what the proposed changes would mean locally, the impact on other businesses such as the market suppliers, and other effects such as traffic increases. They invited into school the local councillor to explain the superstore side of the proposal, which the council supported. They debated their own perspectives, drawing on family views and their fieldwork investigation, and took a vote on whether they agreed with the store development and market closure. What clearly motivated the class was the reality of this local issue.

 ## Practical task

Buy a local newspaper, watch the regional TV news, or visit local area websites. Find out about a local issue that is attracting attention. It may concern a housing development, the dumping of rubbish and other waste or another pollution issue, a traffic problem or a road safety matter. Consider how you would encourage a class to identify the main problem to investigate. How would you help children to plan and undertake a geographical enquiry, and how might you conclude the project?

Local cross-curricular links

Studies in the local area, or of another locality through fieldwork, provide opportunities to make cross-curricular subject links. The strongest links for geography occur usually with history (Catling, 2006c; Martin, 2004; Rowley and Cooper, 2009; Grigg and Hughes, 2013; Barnes, 2015; Kerry, 2015; Barlow, 2017), but good links can be made with literacy, mathematics and science as well as with art, music and computer or Information Technology studies. Table 12.1 indicates some connections that can be made with other subjects in subject-led or cross-curricular enquiries.

Primary geography is a subject that can readily make cross-curricular links, but it is a subject that, like most other school subjects, is not simply tied within its subject. For instance, literacy is essential in geography. There is much information to draw on that is text-based, such as newspaper or Web sources. Information and text books are rich sources, and there are many other literary resources to draw upon. Reading and writing are integral in developing children's geographical understanding. This is just as much the case in relation to the use and appreciation of number, scale, space and shape. Not only are numbers essential in appreciating distance and in making measurements, but they are equally important to children appreciating scale. For older primary children, using and understanding numbers lies behind understanding contours and lines of latitude and longitude. Counting objects, looking at and comparing the shapes of features in the environment and on plans and maps are key to geographical learning, as are notions of relative and cardinal directions, grid systems. Geography's use of mathematics is fundamental in the subject.

Curriculum area	Links to local area study
History	To understand what the local area is like now, investigate the past and how the area has changed. Give children opportunities to look at old maps, photographs and newspaper articles about the area, and talk with people from the local community about how it has changed, such as what has gone and come to the area and what they think of such changes, be these shops, public transport, homes or businesses. Increasingly, databases can be accessed from the classroom in the search for relevant resources.
Literacy	Oracy skills are engaged and improved through listening and speaking in discussions and debates about issues. Reading development is supported when using primary and secondary written information sources to find out more about the local and other areas. Writing newspaper articles about a local issue, persuasive letters to the local council about possible changes, and empathic accounts about living in a different place, use and support the development of children's literacy skills. The preparation and 'publication' of written work can be supported with the use of word-processing technologies.
Mathematics	Collecting numerical data about the local area, analysing and presenting it, and using it as evidence to consider the future potential of a local area supports mathematical learning. Using databases, graphing and other computer software can help record, analyse, interpret and present data. Measuring, mapping and using other spatial mathematics during a geographical study can help children appreciate the value and role of mathematical knowledge and skills.
Science	Investigating natural habitats in the local area, environmental factors that determine local attributes, the quality of water supply and waste disposal and cleansing, and why certain building materials are used in the area can support studies of the variety and vitality of a locality. Weather and stream or river studies can make use of scientific techniques and skills, as well as enable children to begin to understand the natural environmental processes at work. Again, recording, analysis and presentation can be undertaken using digital technologies.

Curriculum area	Links to local area study
Art and music	Photography is a valuable way to examine the 'look' of a locality, not simply to record what is there, but to encourage children, for instance, to look at view lines along streets, the viewpoints in playgrounds and parks, and at the juxtaposition of buildings or across roofs, to see different aspects of the area through its composition, the effect of light and dark (days), shadows and shade, and the way that colour is used to draw the eye.
	Sketching, painting and making rubbings are other ways to examine textures and visual perspectives locally. Other sources to explore as local markers are graffiti graphics and why they are where they are, created by whom.
	Smells and sounds from different sites may provide a further palette of sensual experiences in the neighbourhood. Consider the ways in which local sounds, from traffic, people talking or music played, provides an insight into an area. These can be recorded and used to create a composition to reflect the area, as musical instruments and other sources of musical notes can be the means to compose a local tune. Indeed, are there songs and instrumentals which are heard or may have been composed locally for the children to consider how they represent the place where they live?

Table 12.1   Possible links between geography and other curriculum areas in local studies

Geography makes considerable use of visual, or graphic, sources and resources, particularly through maps and pictures, as well as in the environment itself linked with sketching and drawing. Geography helps children to learn about and appreciate the role of symbols and keys through the central use of plans and maps of a wide range of scales from a building to world maps and atlas maps. Pictorial and symbolic thinking requires being able to see places and environments through representations of them, such as in vertical aerial photographs and drawings of how places looked in the past. Children are enabled to begin to understand what photographs show about places, whether in scenes of parts of streets or looking across a wide area and at a landscape. Such visual skills have close links with art education but remain particular and distinctive in geographical learning. More might be said in relation to history and science, where cross-curricular links in terms of subject methods, especially in enquiries and investigations, and content interplay with geography.

Resources for locality studies

Useful and effective digital technologies and secondary information sources enhance successful investigations into the local area or localities further afield. Table 12.2 notes some of the appropriate and informative resources that support a local study. Relate these to the variety of artefacts that can

Resource	Use
Digital cameras (for younger children, DigiBlue and TuffCam), including those on iPads and similar tablet computers.	Essential resources in any investigation for recording a wide range of features, townscapes and landscapes, activities, etc. Many cameras also have a video facility, which can be invaluable – e.g. for sound. A wide range of data and information, including GPS, can be recorded, downloaded to interactive whiteboards and used immediately for analysis.
Hand-held digital recording devices.	Are very useful and beneficial for geographical investigations to record comments in the field, for environmental sound recordings.
Secondary information sources: • leaflets, pamphlets, etc., about localities; • local books and magazines, local maps; • recent local newspapers, local TV news, local websites outlining current and topical issues; • Internet access for relevant local websites.	Provide vital background information, as well as detail, for a locality study and can allow children a wider and deeper understanding of their environment.
People involved in the area, such as: • local residents; • shop-keepers and business people; • councillor; • planning department, library and other council officials.	Can provide a wealth of local perspectives on the local area, as well as provide access to information and comments to support locality studies and access to people to interview about particular matters of interest.

Table 12.2   Resources to use in a locality study

support locality studies (Chapter 9, Table 9.4) and the list of maps and photographs in the section 'Different types of maps' in Chapter 9, Table 9.6. The list in Table 12.2 is not exhaustive, and there will be other resources you can add to it.

In the classroom

A local geography and history study

To initiate a locality study linking geography and history, a class of 6–7-year-olds was given copies of two photographs of the same play area, one taken in the 1980s and another recently. They identified similarities and differences between the site shown, discussed their use of the play area and speculated what children would have done in the 1980s. Two parents who had regularly played there in the 1980s shared their memories, and the children discovered that there was much in common across childhoods. They visited the play area to see it used during the school day by pre-school children and parents. They considered what different people thought about the play area. In class, they each played the role of someone from a different age group, including grandparents, parents, teenagers and toddlers. In small groups they planned what they wanted to have there and shared their ideas, noticing common features and different proposals. Using a group approach to 'hot seating', the children questioned each other's groups about their plans. The council planning office was contacted and plans were shared with a local planner who visited the class.

In the classroom

Contributing to local regeneration

A class of 10–11-year-olds in an urban primary school in an area of major regeneration became involved in putting their ideas for redevelopment to the architects and planners. This arose because a number of the children's homes were to be demolished and the families relocated. The head teacher and staff felt that it was important that the children understood and appreciated what was being done. Early in their studies, children in different classes looked at the area in a number of different ways. Some took photographs to show features they liked and wanted to remember, and others of sites they wanted replaced. Other children made sound and 'scent/smell' maps of the area, to recall a different sense of the locality. Older children imagined how the area had looked 5,000 years ago and 100 years ago, and how it might look in 100 years' time, annotating their sketches of views from a high point locally. Others wrote about their feelings for the area and, following fieldwork during which they had listed words to record their feelings and views, wrote haiku poems that drew on their words. These activities and others enabled the children to decide and propose what they wanted to see emerge during the redesign and rebuilding of the area. In particular, children across the age ranges argued for retaining as much greenery as possible, for child-friendly side streets, safe crossing

(Continued)

(Continued)

points, accessible play areas, colour in the environment (not drab building exteriors), and accessible routes to key facilities. They presented
their ideas to the architects and planners, who were both surprised and
elated by the children's engagement and ideas, which they felt were
both realistic and useful. They acknowledged that the children 'knew
what they were talking about'.

Reflective task

Consider the two classroom examples above. How do they demonstrate
teaching that draws on children's geographies? In which ways do they
reflect cross-curricular aspects within geography?

Investigating our regions and our country

Localities, both our own and others nationally, are each specific places that
share much with the many other particular places where people live – from
neighbourhoods to villages, towns and cities, in rural and urban areas,
including isolated and widely spread out homes in wildscapes (moorland
and mountainous areas). Investigating another locality in our own country
helps us to begin to understand the variety and common aspects of our
nation. We can develop our understanding more fully through investigations of our own wider region – the part of the country in which we live –
other national regions and our country as a whole. Such geographical
studies with primary age children begin to develop their sense of the wider
context in which their home is, as well as help them start to understand the
idea of a country and what it means. It also helps them to begin to appreciate the relationships between their local scale place, the wider region at
a larger scale and the national scale of places (Claval, 1998; Edensor, 2002;
Cresswell, 2015), helping develop their sense of class inclusion (metaphorically, Russian dolls one inside another).

Teaching about national regions has a long history in geography education, including in primary geography (Bailey, 1974; Graves, 2001). It remains
an important aspect in geography curriculum guidelines in several countries, including the USA, Australia and England (Heffron and Downs, 2012;
DfE, 2013). But what is a region within a country and what might primary
children study about such a region? We have encountered natural regions

in Chapter 6 (see the box on pp.172–173) in a global context. National regions are at a smaller scale.

What is a region?

We would think that the concept of the 'region' would be straightforward to define, but it is not that simple. A region is a larger area than a locality, but there is no particular scale or size for a region. Regions may be very large or quite modest in area. Deciding on the size of a region depends on selected criteria, which can be very different and identify different regions. One way to identify a region is to delineate it through its physical geography, such as a river basin – that is, the area covered by the land a river and all its tributaries drain; formally, it is defined by a particular spatial characteristic. Another example is a linguistic region within which a particular subnational language is dominant. A different region can be the area covered by a supermarket distribution centre to its shops in the urban centres it serves, such as in the south of a country; or a region might be a political area such as a county 'local' authority or state government, both of which are delineated by the spatial function of the region (Gregory et al., 2009). Another functional region can be the area covered by a 'local' television or radio station; this will have a somewhat fuzzy spatial boundary related to where its transmissions can be received. This might be a large section of a country or part of a province or a whole state, such as in Canada and the USA. These examples indicate that there are many different ways to determine a region, from naturally defined regions to regions based on human activities (Scoffham and Owens, 2017). What they share is that all regions are spatial entities. It may be that a region according to one set of criteria overlaps closely with or is rather different in shape from a region defined by other criteria. The key to defining a region is that identifiable criteria delineate its area; there is something shared across the region. Regions are characterised for a purpose; they are not 'out there' but identified by people, be they physical geographers, politicians, commercial managers or many others (Allen et al., 1998).

In the spatial context, regions are 'territories', in that they identify a bounded area, be this clearly marked or fuzzy. Such territories may be described in terms of a river's catchment area or a 'bounded' landscape such as a national park; here terrain and landscape are used for identification. Regions may be characterised according to the population of an area, perhaps culturally or in terms of economic circumstances. Regions may refer to a vibrant industrialised area or one in decline, or to other ways that land is used such as for agriculture or significantly large habitation, as in a city. One approach to studying regions has been to compare separate regions to identify and differentiate their characters, an approach that focuses on how regions are different from each other. Another way to consider a region is to examine what they have in common and share.

A 'life-world' region

A further way to consider a region is as a 'life-world' (Claval, 1998). This means that a region is described more holistically in terms of people's lives, aspects of an area's history, the variety of activities in which people engage such as for work and pleasure, its population's age range, its economic and socio-cultural diversity and interrelationships, its transport networks, aspects of its physical geography and political delineation, and more. A life-world region has a sense of unity about it, although within this it may well be very varied across its urban streets or agricultural settlements and across people's lives. It intends to characterise a region as a whole. A life-world region can be considered as a region to which people relate and feel a sense of identity; it holds meaning for them whether they are inhabitants or perceive it from outside. This would seem to be an appropriate and useful sense of a region for primary children to investigate.

A focus on regions for primary children

For middle and older primary school children, studying a region can focus on one or several of its characteristics (DfE, 2013; Maude, 2014; Heffron and Downs, 2012), perhaps bringing them together to outline a life-world region. These include the following.

- Outlining the shape of the region in which you live, which might be simply an area of a country such as south-west Ireland or northern Vietnam, or it could be more formally delineated within a country physically, politically or commercially.
- Various physical or topographical features of the region, such as key rivers, coasts, hills, mountains, deserts, lakes and weather patterns.
- Various human features of a region, including cities, shopping centres, and types of land use such as agriculture, industry and commerce.
- What people do and how they live their lives, including work and leisure activities.
- Ways in which some aspects of a region have changed over time.

These are similar characteristics, or elements, you will have noted, as those that might be examined in a locality study. A helpful resource to use will be national and atlas maps of the country that show the various government or cartographer defined regions within it. Other sources about your own region or other national regions can be found through Web searches and may well provide maps that identify the area of the region and indicate some of its characteristics.

Introducing and developing understanding of the term 'region'

A useful way to introduce the idea of a region to primary children is to explore the idea initially at a much reduced scale, beginning by using the school's grounds as an analogy. Invite children to consider different areas within the school, perhaps using the term 'region', such as the playground 'region' or the built-up (school buildings) 'region'. Perhaps there is a field 'region' and an access and car park 'region' (Scoffham and Owens, 2017). We have encountered these ways to describe and delineate spaces in Chapter 11 about the school grounds, where they were referred to as different land uses. Next we might discuss with children the idea of the school as a whole as a 'region' – that is, a space and area with a variety of characteristics that together create their life-world region. A similar life-world region analogy might be their neighbourhood. Children could identify some other regions locally, either based on just one or two criteria, such as the shopping 'region' and a housing 'region', or taking a more holistic life-world region approach. The purpose is to help children begin to appreciate that a region is a territorial space, that it can be of different sizes, and that it can be quite particular in character or bring together a number of criteria to characterise it as a life-world.

We can expand from the local area into the wider city, town or rural area. We can find out which places further away can be visited, say, by car, bus or train and returned from within a day. Children can draw on family experience of other towns where they go shopping, for leisure pursuits or to see family and friends. They can talk about what they do and examine maps to see where these places are and how far away, as well as to identify that there are other places in that wider area that they do not know. It is likely that across a class, different children will know different parts of the wider region, for it is that which the children will be starting to develop awareness of and begin to investigate. They can be encouraged to notice that a region has a range of different elements and connections, although some might appear dominant such as farming or housing or roads, and they can discuss that a region is a combination of many elements, its life-world. Through investigation and discussion, children are being helped to develop the idea of a large area that can be described and given meaning as their region, the larger area of their country in which they live.

The home region

The point is that children's studies of their local area should not be curtailed at whatever might be thought to be its probably fuzzy edges. A local area lies within a larger region, evidenced through its road and other links to nearby places, as noted above and in the box above, on pp.349–351. This larger region within which their locality lies can be called the 'home region' of that locality. It will also be the home region for all the other localities within it.

A starting point for study of the home region is to explore the idea of the school's address, as a way to help children recognise that their school is within their neighbourhood, which is within their region, helping to foster their understanding of a nested hierarchy (Catling, 2017b; Scoffham and Owens, 2017). Children might be given a number of different-sized paper shapes with names on them such as the school's name, its street, the neighbourhood or locality, village or suburb, the town or city, the county, province or state and the country. They can be encouraged to place them one 'inside' (on top of) the other in order of area size to see the way that relationships are inclusive. They can be encouraged to show the relationship on a map of the country and to talk about 'my school in our street in our neighbourhood in our town and our country'. This is an approach that can be used more than once in the middle and upper years of primary school, helping children to appreciate their interrelationship within their region. They might examine other addresses from other parts of the country to describe the same relationships. These might be family addresses or of organisations and companies.

    Research summary

Understanding the nested hierarchy of places

Children in their earliest years, aged 3–5 years old, are often asked to learn their address (home number, block and/or street, district or town or city, county or state, and post or zip code). Although they are able to do this, they have little sense of the relationship of each of these places to the other (Harwood and McShane, 1998; Storey, 2004). While few children aged around 5–7 years old can recognise the spatial nesting of these elements in their address, it seems that many in their middle primary years from 7 to 8 years old are able to describe the interrelationship between, for example, 'home–Nuneaton–England–Britain' (Harwood and McShane, 1998). Earlier studies argued that this notion was challenging for many older primary children (Scoffham 2017a), who thought of each place as exclusive from each other and not nested one within the other. Harwood and McShane (1998) considered that perhaps increased travel by primary age children with their families helped them to develop this understanding more effectively, and that this relationship was understood by the large majority of children by the end of primary school. Another reason they noted was that improved teaching of geography helped primary children begin to recognise and understand the nested hierarchy of places, because they were finding out about places at a range of scales, and used various types and scales of maps from local plans to street maps, to regional and national atlas maps. This was argued to indicate that learning about places from their school and neighbourhood to the home region, to the national scale, and then in the context of their continent, enables children to become aware of and appreciate how places are interrelated.

There are a variety of approaches to finding out about the home region within which the children live and go to school. By combining several of these approaches, an idea of the home region as a life-world region can be developed. These ways to examine the home region include the following.

- Explore links to other nearby places from the local area. Signposts indicating road destinations, bus and railway timetables and destinations, what is known from visits to other places by car or public transport, family links and other connections provide a wealth of regional information, which can be mapped. Consider where people travel to, why they travel and what they do at their destinations. Illustrate the range of this region with photographs from the Internet.
- Ask adults in school and at home what is the region they live in. Perhaps invite them to mark it on a map of the country and ask them why they have marked that area (they may or may not have any idea about their home region). Ask about what they think makes it their home region, such as whether there are any particular things about the area that characterise it for them. Collect and collate the maps and reasons, and create a display about adults' ideas about the home region. Discuss what has been found out.
- Focus on one aspect of people's travel and visits to find out about the home region. For instance, collect information about which places are visited for leisure activities and days out, or for shopping trips away from the usual local shops. Map these to see what area is covered and explain how you might describe such a region. Create a photo-map of the region, showing the variety of similar places focused on, such as shopping malls and streets. Consider what you might name such a region.
- Look at maps in atlases or found on the Internet that show what is the region around your locality. Find a variety of maps from different sources and note what they are supposed to show and who created them, whether a local authority, central government, a company, a service provider (such as a bus company or hospital) or another source. Overlay these maps to see if there is a shared area across the regions, how much overlap they have and what the widest home region boundary might be. Try to explain why there are differences and overlaps, and what you might call the shared home region area.

- Using one or more home region maps, look at the range of features in the region, including hills and/or mountains, rivers, lakes, towns, villages, shopping centres, leisure areas and centres, well-known features such as historic homes, and so forth. Look at the road network connecting them. Create a photo-album and a map of the region and have the children write a description of what they regard the main characteristics of the home region to be. Consider whether there are particular types of land use in the region, such as agriculture, settlements, housing or industries and illustrate these.

- Obtain a guidebook or a range of visitor guides, including photographs, descriptions, information and maps, to find out how the home region is shown and characterised through what has been included in the guide. Consider how it characterises the region and what is prominent in it. Look at who the guidebook is for, whether for visitors or those who live in the region, and whether things that interest children are clearly identified, and what they are. Discuss whether the children agree. Children might make their own guidebook to their home region, following research about the area, perhaps a guide on the region for children.

- Using maps of the wider area, involve the children in identifying, defining and naming what they think their home region is. Investigate the region they have delineated to find out as much as they can about it in terms of what is there, what people do, which might be attractive or unattractive parts, how to get around the area, what they think of the area, and whether they might give it hard or fuzzy 'borders'. They might, drawing from the Internet, make a photo-collage of the region.

- Children might investigate the region looking at environmental concerns. Are there particularly contentious matters that are being discussed, such as housing or business developments, concerns about dumping waste on farmland or road congestion issues? Do they occur across the region or only in particular places, and why is this? Using local newspapers and Internet sites, children can examine the range of local concerns, what is happening, the variety of views expressed about these and what responses and actions about them are.

By investigating several or even all of these approaches to learning about your home region, it will be relevant to help children recognise that there may well not be a single delineation of their home region, nor will they find out everything about it. They will learn that people 'create' different boundaries for a region and that within a region they see the same area differently. This is important for them to realise. Geography is about more than one perspective or point of view about a place, however small or large that place is. Places are not often contained by a single boundary; indeed, such borders are imposed rather than inevitable and can be changed. Home regions are human constructs that are living places, life-worlds for those who inhabit them.

Other national regions

It is important that children recognise that their country is composed of a number of regions, however they are defined; theirs is not the only region. You might use a national map that shows the government's delineation of the country's regions, or you might use other sources, such as the counties in a country or a nation's provinces or states, national park areas, warehouse distribution areas for major retailers, rail, bus or coach franchise areas, and other sources. Select one region elsewhere nationally to investigate. For example, you might check what is provided on the Internet about this named region. There may be photographs and maps with descriptions of some aspects of the region, perhaps of its physical, human and environmental geography. You can adapt the ideas for investigating your own home region to explore another region. These would enable you to undertake the following.

- Find out whether children and their families have heard of other regions nationally, what these are and where they are. Perhaps some children have visited them or have relatives in the region, in which case it may be possible to find out from family experience about the region.
- Examine what is shown on wall and atlas maps of your country within the region.
- Consider whether the region is similar to or different in size and scale from your home region.
- Look at whether it is similar or different in terms of being an urban or rural region, perhaps a very large city region or a largely agricultural or moorland or mountainous area.
- Identify its main physical and human features, perhaps using a guidebook to the region as an aid, to find out about the range of people's lives there.
- Explore this region or parts of it as a visitor. National regions attract tourists and holidaymakers. Find out why this is: what attracts them to the region, where they stay, whether this happens at certain times of the year or all year round, how people travel there, what they might do and even whether there are souvenirs that they might buy to remind them of their time there. In this context, children can examine how these facilities, services and activities are provided by local people or those who work there seasonally.
- Investigate a region that is usually described as an area that has seen much change, such as the decline of mining or manufacturing industries, to look at what has changed and why, whether this has happened across the whole region, how it has changed, what has come into the region, whether there have been benefits, and what else might happen there.

The value for children in investigating some aspects of a second national region is that they have another area to compare with their own region, to find out about similarities, variations and differences. This can help them to begin to recognise that regions vary in their 'make up', but that there is much that is shared and common between places and people's lives around the country. It should be borne in mind that some children may have migrated from another part of the country to the area; they may well bring some experience and knowledge of another region that they can share.

It may be that children go on a school visit, for a day or overnight for several days, from their school and home region to a particular place, perhaps a field centre or a hotel, in a region elsewhere in their country. This provides an opportunity to make some prior and post-visit investigations about the region within which they stay and investigate while there. They may make local enquiries around the area where they stay, but they may also travel to some nearby sites, which helps to give them a sense of other places within the region. This will only ever be a snapshot, as their geographical investigations inevitably are, but it can provide access to finding out more about the region to which they have been and about what else they might find in the area.

Developing a sense of my country

The word 'country' can be confusing for children, as it was for the hedgehog Oggy when making his journey to find his 'family' (Lawrence, 1973; see Chapter 5). Young children may well confuse the idea of 'country' as countryside (a rural area) with the idea of 'a country', being another name for the territory of a nation. The word 'country' is used in many contexts, from country music to travelling across country (which can be through urban and rural areas) to living in a part of the nation colloquially named 'The West Country' or 'Brontë Country'. This is important to remember in order to ensure that when talking about a country such as China, South Africa or New Zealand, children realise that these are nations. Using place and environmental vocabulary is as much about meaning, nuance and context.

A country is an independent nation (at times also called a nation-state or state, not to be confused with the states in the USA and other countries), which has its own government, jurisdiction and borders delineating and marking its territory and distinguishing it from every other country. A country will have a capital, a flag, an anthem, and pride itself on its sense of identity. It may well have one, or perhaps more, national languages and may have a major ethnic and/or religious group, but be diverse ethnically, as well as culturally. There is likely to be a shared history, although this may be open to debate and revision. A country is a geopolitical entity. Physically, it may be a single land area, perhaps surrounded by others, such as

Switzerland, or it may be composed of many islands with or without a major island or continental area, such as the Solomon Islands in the Pacific Ocean. Countries may be very large, as is Russia, or very small, such as Andorra. They may be highly urban in character, such as Singapore or largely rural, as Botswana, or in a largely desert environment, like Mali.

There are some 195 identified countries or sovereign states, of which 193 are members of the United Nations (UN), but these numbers may grow as more territories achieve independence. They exist on six continents, Antarctica being the only continent that has no countries on its frozen land-mass. The continent of Africa has the most countries (54). There are many dependencies and territories that are governed by countries and not recognised as independent nations, and there are a few that call themselves countries but are not considered as such – for example, Taiwan, which is viewed by the UN as represented by China.

Since the world is divided into countries, it has been one of the aspects of the world that geographers, and others, have studied. It is important to help primary children begin to develop their understanding of what a country is, and where better to start than to help them gain a sense of their own country. From a young age, through their family, primary children begin to develop an idea that they live in a country and are members of that country. The question arises about what they should learn about their country during their primary education. Understanding the meaning of 'a country' is a challenging idea and takes some years for most children to appreciate.

Research summary

Children's country knowledge

Drawing on evidence from his own research and several other studies of children's ideas about their own country, Barrett (2005, 2007) identified a number of facets of pre-school and primary age children's geographical knowledge and understanding. He noted that children younger than 5 years old knew little about their own country, perhaps not even its name. By around 6 years of age, children may know their country's name but are uncertain what a country is. By 10/11 years old, children know in which country they live, and they tend to know of some features, parts, national landscapes or other aspects of their country rather than have a sense of the whole nation. Barrett noted that social and economic backgrounds have an impact on children's geographical knowledge about their own country, with those in higher socioeconomic

(Continued)

(Continued)

groups being more knowledgeable. Learning about their country, and other nations, in school appears to have a positive effect. From the age of 7, children appear to develop a preference for their own country over other nations. By the end of primary schooling, they are likely to know their nation's flag, currency, head of state, and perhaps some well-known places and features, and identify with their country, although whether there is a relationship between knowledge of one's country and attachment to it remains unclear.

Further discussion about national identity can be found in Chapter 3.

There are starting points in learning about countries that primary geography can initiate. It has been noted that children should investigate their local area and find out about their home region and another national region. These studies need to be provided within a national context in which they can be situated and developed. As children learn that they live in Australia or Tunisia or the United Kingdom, and are Australian, Tunisian or British, it helps that they pick up some information about their country. A key element in geography guidelines, such as in England (DfE, 2013), has been a focus on children learning locational knowledge about their country (see Chapter 5). During their primary schooling it is useful for children to build their knowledge of the following.

For 5/6 to 8/9-year-olds:

- The name and shape of their country.
- Its capital city.
- Countries or seas that border it.
- Its flag.
- Some of its nationally recognised features, such as monuments, buildings and resorts.
- Where in the world the country is located on a world map.

For 7/8 to 11/12-year-olds:

- Some of the major cities in their country.
- Some or all of the major regions, provinces and states of their country, and some of their characteristics.
- Some of its significant physical features, such as major rivers, hills, mountains and lakes.
- The significant ways in which land is used, such as urban areas, agriculture, industry, leisure and resorts, moorland and deserts.

- Further nationally recognised characteristics, such as national parks, major routes, main airports, leisure centres, national emblems and sports, and other aspects internationally recognized.
- Which continent the country is in, and which other countries border or are proximate to it, shown on continental and world maps.

To aid their investigations, children should use an atlas and wall maps of their country (see Chapters 9 and 13) and draw on photographic and textual information from the Internet and information books. For younger primary children, it makes sense to place their exploration of their local area in the context of their country. It will help older primary children to link their studies of the home and another national region to the location and context of these in their country, so that their enquiries are not undertaken compartmentally and discretely. However, care should be taken not to leave such studies as simply about locational knowledge; children need to develop a sense of what such places, even as large areas, are like for people to live in.

If primary children are to develop some sense of their country, they should examine some views about the country. One way to do so is to look at information provided to tourists from overseas through questions such as the following.

- What are the main pieces of information and images readily available about the country to tourists from overseas?
- Where are tourists recommended to visit and what are they encouraged to see, especially if they are visiting the country only for a few days?
- Do the children know about these places? Indeed, what and where are they?
- Why do the children think these sites and places have been selected for tourists to visit?
- If tourists want to buy a souvenir of their visit, what might they buy and why?
- By examining the sources they use, what ideas about their country do children think those who created these sources wanted to portray about it?
- What places would the children choose to encourage tourists to visit and why?
- What views of their country would children like tourists to take home with them?

Another approach is to ask adults, perhaps in school and at home, about what is important to know about their country and why this matters. Children might pursue questions such as the following.

- What do you think we should all know about our country?
- What are the most important things about our country to you?

- How do you know this information about our country?
- What do you enjoy and like and not like about our country?
- Where do you, or would you, most like to visit nationally?
- Which places nationally would you recommend a friend and a tourist to visit?
- What is important for you about being a member (a national) of our country?
- If you can only describe our country in 50 words, what would you write?

What children find out can be collated and presented through a display, in class or to the school.

Children might also undertake their own investigations, seeking sources and deciding what to use and what information and images to choose. They might do the following.

- Examine atlas maps of their country to identify what is included in them and consider why.
- Begin to create their own national map, adding information to and around it, selecting from the range of sources they use.
- Include any places they have visited nationally, with what they know about them.
- Be required to select up to ten pieces of information and up to ten images about their country, although they will need to search more widely to choose which information and images to include, the choices of which they must justify.
- Note the sources that are considered to have been the most helpful and the least useful, to find out national information.
- Discuss, following their individual or team investigations, what they have identified and, as a class, agree on a limited number of pieces of information and images about their nation.
- Debate how they feel about being a member of their country, to encourage them to think about their national identity.

It is important to bear in mind that a small minority of primary children may not identify with their country of residence. A few children may be at school because their family has moved countries for work, although they expect to return to their home nation. It might be that one or two are refugees who are being resettled temporarily or long term. Other migrant children may be permanently settled but have yet to change their sense of national identity or their nationality, while some children could hold dual nationality. These are matters that need to be borne in mind from your knowledge of the backgrounds of the children in your class. These children will benefit from investigating the country they live in now, and they can provide other perspectives from their family if it is thought helpful to do so and it is sensitively undertaken.

In the classroom

'This land is our land'

Their teacher asked her class of 9–10-year-olds what they knew about their country. They wrote their ideas individually, then shared them in groups of four to choose four items they agreed on. Next, they investigated each of the items to provide images and text to show and describe what they were and why they had selected them. They created a small display to share with one other group. This larger group then selected four of their eight items to share with the class. Each larger group had to explain why they made their choice. The group's selections included a map of their country and its continental location, its capital and major cities, and some well-known features that children had visited. These places were marked on a large wall map, and the children were asked 'What is in all the blank spaces on the map?' Taking different parts of the country, the children worked in pairs to provide information about their allotted region. They selected two images and wrote three sentences to add to the map display.

Once this work was completed, pairs were asked to consider what they thought was missing that should be added, and to write a paragraph about what the map and its images and text helped them think about their country. Finally, they were each asked to choose five aspects of their country that they would recommend to their family to visit. These statements were included in a new display. The children's families were invited to the classroom at the end of two school days to see and read what the children had found out and decided was important and helpful in appreciating their country. It surprised some children that their parents and some older siblings did not know about some of the things they had included. To follow this up, the class decided what it would help everyone to know about their country.

Practical task

Undertake one or both of these tasks. Record your responses to them.

My home region: Reread the section above again about regions and consider the following questions.

What is your home region? Why have you decided on this area? How do you think people use places in your region? How do they

(Continued)

(Continued)

travel around, where do they go, what do they do for work, shopping and leisure, and which places in the region are those most used? What do people like in your region? To help someone who has just come to your region, where would you recommend them to visit and why?

My country. Reread the section above about your country and consider the following questions.

What is important about your country that you would want children to know by the end of their primary schooling? Why have you selected these? What understanding of your country do these points give primary age children? If you were only able to select ten images – photos, drawings or video clips – to show children about your country, what would these images show and why did you choose them?

                            Key points

This chapter has:

- considered the meaning of locality studies and their importance in drawing on children's geographies and in engaging their interest;
- identified ways in which locality studies can encourage effective links between geography, citizenship and children's involvement in their local community and environment;
- indicated a number of ways to involve children in local investigations, using fieldwork, based on problem-oriented enquiries, providing examples of locality topics;
- noted some cross-curricular possibilities for local studies;
- explained about national regions, the home region and your country;
- provided several approaches to investigating and studying children's home regions, other regions and their country;
- identified a variety of resources to use in locality, regional and national studies.

Moving on

Think about a place you know well, perhaps your home locality or region. Your own experience of a place can be a powerful stimulant for children's learning about places, because you can talk from first-hand experience and show photographs you have taken and items or souvenirs you have collected from the place. What are the things that have made an impression on you about this place? Make a list of the types of resources that you could collect to use with children. What might be the focus for your home locality or region study? How might you use your resources to help children develop their understanding of what is there, the lives of people, how it feels to be there and a sense of place? If there is a different locality or national region you know well, such as a national park, you might undertake a similar activity.

Further reading

There is much advice available on using the local environment for geographical studies. The following offer some further development points.

Barlow, A (2017) Geography and history in the local area. In Scoffham, S (ed.) *Teaching Geography Creatively*. Abingdon: Routledge, pp. 118–30.

Grigg, R and Hughes, S (2013) *Teaching Primary Humanities*. Harlow: Pearson.

Halocha, J (2012) *The Primary Teacher's Guide to Geography*. Witney: Scholastic/Book End.

Macintosh, M (n.d.) *GTIP Think Piece: Human Geography*. Available at: www.geography.org.uk/projects/gtip/thinkpieces/ humangeography/

Martin, F (2006) *Teaching Geography in Primary Schools: Learning How to Live in the World*. Cambridge: Chris Kington.

Pike, S (2016) *Learning Primary Geography: Ideas and inspirations from classrooms*. Abingdon; Routledge.

Scoffham, S (ed.) (2010) *Primary Geography Handbook*. Sheffield: Geographical Association.

Scoffham, S (2017) *Teaching Geography Creatively*. Abingdon: Routledge.

There is much useful advice and many examples of local area and other locality projects and classroom activities published in *Primary Geography*.

Useful websites

The key websites you will need are those that provide information and resources about your local area and home region. You can also make use of websites for other regions and national websites.

You can use national mapping websites, photography websites and those of national organisations providing regional and national information.

Other websites might include the following.

Bing maps: www.bing.com/maps

Council for Learning Outside the Classroom: www.lotc.org.uk

Google Earth: www.google.com/earth

CHAPTER 13

EXPLORING GLOBAL DIMENSIONS AND PLACES ELSEWHERE IN THE WORLD

→ **Chapter objectives**

This chapter enables you to:

- appreciate the importance of children learning about the wider world through geographical study;
- develop an understanding of global learning, the global dimension and global citizenship;
- provide reasons for teaching about countries and regions in primary geography;
- understand about teaching distant locality studies through primary geography;
- know of approaches to teaching and learning about distant places in the wider world;
- know about a range of resources to use when teaching about the wider world;
- be aware of some of the challenges faced when teaching about the wider world.

Introduction

Children are fascinated by the world around them. This extends beyond their direct experiences. They hear about other parts of the world – different places and countries – through their family and friends, via the media, and possibly having travelled and been tourists. Children like to know more to satisfy their curiosity. This chapter considers the importance of studying the wider world, its places and environments, developing their awareness of the global dimension and as global citizens. Children's perceptions of other places may be partially informed, even stereotypical. It is vital to redress any imbalanced and misconceived ideas they may have.

Why teach about other places?

Reasons for studying places and the wider world include enabling children to develop a sense of what it is like to be or live somewhere outside their own country by developing awareness and knowledge of what such places are like. These aspects of geography develop their understanding about the world, encourage them to explore their feelings and values and develop their sense of empathy with others. Primary geography includes the study of localities in other parts of the world and of larger regions and countries. Through these studies children learn about the interconnectedness of the world in which they live, and by better understanding how others live, appreciate the impact that we have on each other globally (Mackintosh, n.d.). Even though curricula may not prescribe specific places to study, children are encouraged to investigate different places, localities and countries, and explore key geographical features, environments, lives within, and similarities and contrasts between places. You may refer to places overseas from which some children's families originate as well as investigate places that appear in the news, so making the geography topical and meaningful, and ensuring that it is engaging and real for the children.

Locational knowledge

> At seven years old, I had saved up my allowance for months to buy this atlas, and it became my most prized possession. I remember it sometimes lived at the head of my bed at night next to my pillow, where most kids would keep a beloved security blanket or teddy bear. Flipping through its pages, I could see that my atlas had been as well loved as any favourite plush toy: the gold type on the padded cover was worn, the corners were dented, and the binding was so shot that most of South America had fallen out and been shoved back in upside down.

(Jennings, 2012, p. 2)

A core aspect of geography that supports global understanding is that children know where places are in the world: what is termed 'locational knowledge' (Catling, 2002, 2017), a traditional aspect of geographical learning (see Chapter 5). It has always been associated with using atlases, but latterly, for instance, with Internet information through interactive news stories. Most primary curricula will include mention of the importance of developing locational knowledge through reference to children knowing the locations of key features in their own places and about their knowledge of their own country, the wider political and geographical region and across the world. Atlases, globes and digital maps are essential in facilitating this learning. Building our knowledge of where places are develops our mental maps of our locality, region, nation and the world.

One way in which children enjoy understanding about places and their nested hierarchy relationships at different scales (see Chapter 12) is through their address. Children like writing their address from their home street to 'The World'. Addresses are about rather more than where someone lives, as the box below illustrates. Our address connects us with where we are but, importantly, is concerned also with our sense of identity and belonging, and the connections we have with our region, our country and the wider world.

How does our address relate to us and to geography?

It is about our *where-ness*.

- Being at a particular site or spot on the Earth.
- States our presence.
- Puts us in a place that we may well call 'our place', even 'home'.

It relates to our sense of identity and belonging.

- Knowing where we are.
- Knowing how we fit in, personally and spatially.
- Our identity within the world in which we live.

It relates us geographically.

- To spatial location and distribution.
- To the idea of 'nested hierarchy' (Russian dolls).
- To a sense of scale and size compared to other places.
- To the interrelationship of places: local to global.
- To global interdependence.
- To being a member of the global community.

In the classroom

Finding where so many places are

To initiate a topic in which 8–9-year-old children developed their knowledge of where places are on their national map, and the world map and the globe, their teacher asked friends and contacts in various countries to send her a postcard, which also included their home addresses. This resulted in a number of postcards arriving over a few weeks for the class. Using wall maps of their country and the world, the children identified where to place pins that they linked to the postcards displayed around the maps. To do this, they searched a variety of atlases and the Internet and used globes to develop their research skills and learn about where the postcards had come from. Some children asked their own family and friends who lived in other places to send them postcards, along with the sender's address. This caught on and became very popular. The class made a sizeable collection of postcards from a wide variety of places nationally and globally. The children talked to children in the rest of the school about what they were doing. It continued alongside and linked in with other geographical studies the class undertook.

Discussions about what the pictures showed enabled the children to recognise and discuss the variety of environments, and urban and rural places there are globally. They went on to practise their locational map skills and ability to 'read' the environment using the interactive game 'geoguessr', an engaging and informative Internet game.

Using atlases and globes to explore places

Whenever pursuing global studies, it is vital to have an atlas and globe to hand. Atlases and globes fascinate younger children, since they 'open up' the world to children through incidental interest as well as by the organised seeking out of the places mentioned in topics and in the news. Keep several atlases in your classroom and always have an inflatable globe to hand – be careful, though, to check their accuracy as some of the cheaper globes may contain locational 'mistakes'. It is helpful and interesting to consider their place of manufacture and their price, and whether these have a bearing on their accuracy in showing and locating places. Children can always examine and check the quality of less reliable resources.

Children need opportunities to develop their awareness of the shapes of the continents – the fact that 71 per cent of the Earth is covered by ocean – and the various physical features and countries of our world, through regular exploration of globes and atlases. They will begin to develop their knowledge of the relationships between these features and to become aware of how they are represented (Wiegand, 2006) through exposure to and by making regular use of atlases and globes (see Chapter 9). They should encounter a variety of atlas maps and seek out the same places and features on the globe. Just as you would keep other reference books available, children should be able to access a range of atlases in class – and they will prove to make popular 'reading'.

Having wall maps permanently on display in the classroom enables children to make comparisons with globes and atlases, to begin to notice some of the consistencies and variations in place representations on maps, as well as to examine and discuss which features and places are included. They can compare different atlases and globes to see whether the same places are shown on each and consider why some places may be included on one map but not in another, even in the same atlas. They could go on to compare atlas maps to maps shown online, in news reports and topical stories. This way, they begin to develop a sense that what is included is related to the scale of what can be shown, as well as to decisions about what is regarded as important to include and what is omitted. Some atlas maps, aimed at older children, can appear as very crowded and difficult to 'read' for primary age children. Children can confuse which name goes with which city 'dot' and with which river's blue line, where many features close together are included. They will need to be helped to read and interpret these more demanding maps.

You can encourage and develop children's use and understanding of atlas maps and globes by:

- asking them to find the pages in an atlas showing particular continents or countries, through using the *contents* page;
- encouraging them to locate places and features they find on a wall map or in an atlas or have seen on the Internet on the globe (even if not actually marked and named), and to consider where these are in relation to their home and other places;
- using the atlas *index* to find specific places, from physical features to capital cities and countries;
- investigating how *lines* are used on maps and globes to show features such as rivers, railways, roads and borders/boundaries, as well as to show lines of longitude and latitude;
- looking for *shapes* on maps, such as the shapes of countries;
- noting that *points* (such as dots, squares and triangles) are used on maps to show such features as cities and mountain peaks;
- looking for the various ways in which *colours* are used to show countries and different environments;
- considering how colours show height on maps, and how shades of blue show depth in oceans;

- understanding the use of *symbols* (including lines, shapes, points and colours) to depict features and how their size might represent (and possibly exaggerate) the size of a settlement, for example;
- reading the *names* of features and places on atlas maps, such as for countries, cities, rivers and mountains, and noting the different fonts and font sizes used to denote the importance of these;
- using the *scale* bar to measure distances and to discuss just how far these large and very large distances are – developing a sense of distance takes quite some time and might usefully be discussed in terms of travel-time distance, which some children may have experience of through air travel, bearing in mind the form of transport;
- looking at how journeys might be made, including whether they can be in straight lines, what a 'great circle' is and why the shortest route shown on an atlas might be curved – here a globe is invaluable to compare 'length': use string or thread to help make measurements and show distances;
- noting the variety of routes that you can travel by vehicle, rail, ship and airplane – and comparing this with the instant communications provided by television, the Internet and mobile phones;
- reflecting on how atlases and globes are informative but also partial in the information they include, how they can be of use but also have limitations, and how they compare with the maps of continents, nations and regions which we can find on the Web, as well as with the satellite photographs and images we can access via Google Earth and other sites.

A good model is always to have an atlas to hand yourself and to refer to it when places are mentioned. It is surprising how often good habits catch on through the modelling of appropriate behaviours. Equally, share your awareness of the world with your children and be content to look up places you do not know the whereabouts of. Showing that you like to find out about places around the world, as much as anything else, gives children positive encouragement and the message that it is good practice to look things up.

Reasons for studying 'distant' places

Knowing where places are is one reason for including a global dimension in geography teaching, but there is more to it than this. There are very good reasons for children to study 'distant' localities and the wider world, as the box below sets out. Distant places provide an invaluable context for learning about the world and should be used to engage children in exploring the intricate links between places, people and the environment the world over.

Practical task

Which places do you think are significant enough for children to know and be able to locate on a national map and on a globe, a world wall map or in an atlas? If you did the Reflective task at the end of Chapter 5, which places from your listings would you include? If not, go back and try it – or create your own list now. Why should children learn to locate these places? What makes them significant to know?

In class, ask the children which places they think they should know the location of in their own country and in the world. Encourage a discussion about the places. Provide atlases, newspapers, news websites and information books for them to use; they might add their own sources as well. Have groups of children create their own lists and compare these. Give them a limit to the number of places and features they should include. Say to the children that they do not have to include any or all of those named in class or group discussions, but they do need to be able to justify and explain why they have included the places in their list: what is significant about them to be on their list, which criteria are they using to select them? They can name a wide variety of geographical features if they wish to: physical and human features, sites of significant events, large and small places, continents and countries, and so on.

Share your list with the children, as they share theirs with you and each other. What is similar and what is different? Why is this? Can the whole class (including you) create maps to show, say, the 20–30 places which everyone should know in your country and in the world, and be able to locate as a matter of general geographical information, as part of their national and global mental maps? Could you make this into a whole class map and use in a display?

Perhaps have a blank-map quiz at a later time to encourage children to be able to recall where the class's significant places are. Perhaps they could add their personal places too, to their individual maps.

For other activities, see Catling (2002, 2017).

Reasons for studying distant places

- Children hold images of places and peoples from an early age. It is important to recognise and develop their images of other places and people positively.
- Children's curiosity about distant places can be used to help them ask more effective questions and consider carefully the

information they find out about places and the world around them.

- It provides a context to explore geographical ideas of similarity and difference, spatial pattern, change and its impact and sustainability, and to use and develop their enquiry approaches and skills, including map reading and vocabulary.
- It extends children's knowledge and understanding about the variety of places, environments and cultures around the world.
- It offers contexts to foster awareness of the common needs of life, such as homes and clothing, food and water, and work and leisure, and to consider the differences in the resources and opportunities people have available to them and to consider why this might be. This helps children develop a sense of what life is like elsewhere for other people, enabling comparisons with their own lives.
- There are opportunities to examine and clarify children's existing awareness and understanding of places, which they have developed through engagement with a variety of sources, including television, films, websites, games, stories and family links.
- Through the study of people and places in contrasting parts of the world, it is possible to address children's ignorance, partiality and bias, which frequently are the basis for their misunderstandings, stereotypes and prejudices about people and places in other parts of the world.
- Children's spatial awareness is developed towards a global scale through exploring particular places and their regional, national and global settings.
- It enables children to recognise their interdependence with the rest of the world, appreciating that this is a two-way process and that our actions impact on others, as do theirs on us, but not always obviously or directly.
- It builds a global sense, extending children's local, regional national and international perspectives, as informed thinkers about and actors in the world around them.
- This helps children to be better informed and supports their understanding of the lives of others, why places are as they are, and what they might aspire to and become in the future, as well as how they think they will change.
- It encourages children to appreciate and value the diversity of people, places, environments and cultures around the world, and fosters understanding of others, building positive attitudes to other people both in their own country and around the world.

Source: Adapted from Catling, 1995; Weldon, 2010.

We noted in Chapter 3 aspects of children's understandings about places beyond their direct experience, that such places for children are 'distant places'. Scoffham (2007) argues that the study of 'distant' places and learning outside our own experience is challenging since it takes us beyond our direct and immediate knowledge and understanding into new realms, places, ways of life and more.

> *The requirement to study distant places is perhaps one of the most problematic areas of the primary school curriculum. It raises questions about stereotypes and prejudices, it taps into our historical perceptions and it challenges us [as teachers] to clarify our own attitudes and values.*

(Scoffham, 2007, p .5)

Reflective task

Consider why Scoffham argues above that teachers need to clarify their *own values and attitudes* in relation to studies of other, distant places and the wider world. Make a list of your own values and attitudes about studying other places and the wider world.

Challenge stereotyping and value difference

The basis of a stereotype is that it points to the core characteristics of something and appears to create an archetype that might infer that all examples are the same, as though one story or illustration is enough of a statement, be this about a place, a country or a people. In doing this, there is a potential danger that lies in highlighting matters simplistically and, quite possibly, negatively. A people or country might simply be described as though they are all the same, offering no sense of the diversity within those people or that nation. One example of how we think stereotypically and which is imbued historically is the often undifferentiated use of the name 'Africa' to refer to any country or people in that continent as though they are homogeneous and undifferentiated – all appearing to be the same. We seem to do this uncritically, as though, in Adichie's phrase, there is only a 'single story' to tell about the continent (Adichie, 2009). As a moment's thought reminds us, the continent of Africa is very diverse, containing 54 countries and a wide range of environments, from deserts to tropical rainforests, savannah, mountains and temperate highlands. It is a continent rich in resources, both mineral and agricultural, variously developed by its nations and peoples, who are resourceful and entrepreneurial, although it has been much exploited by others in the past – particularly European nations – which has helped to create national and international single stories. The continent has rich and varied cultures with long histories. It is the source continent of humankind. Its nations are varied and different. There is no 'single story' that encompasses the continent; indeed, there is so much variety and difference, as across the continents of the world, that to try to encapsulate Africa, as anywhere else of any scale, with a 'single story' is not simply to stereotype but intentionally to mislead and to reinforce prejudices, not challenge them. This can equally be the case in the ways in which we perceive migrants and refugees from wherever they have come, assuming that they all fall into the same category, move for the same reasons and have intentions we impose upon them. Using a lone image, such as a photograph, to depict a place is equally limiting and inhibiting since it paints also a single story (Griffiths and Allbut, 2011). It needs to be questioned and supplemented by much else to gain a fuller picture, although it will never depict a place fully. We need to become and remain aware of the limitations of our knowledge and understanding of places, be they distant and our own.

The difficulty is that we often pick up on difference – the difference of another place to our own – where difference implies that somewhere else is 'not like us' and separate. Martin (2012, 2013b) challenges this as the highlighting of difference as *object-based*, where she suggests that similarity is usually *the starting point for understanding difference* (p.118). She goes on to argue that similarity, in this context, is about dominant group power, where the 'different' are accommodated in relation to the dominant group's characteristics; 'we' are letting 'you' in and celebrating aspects of your places, environments, cultures and lives, but effectively continue to see 'you' as separate from 'us'. This approach through exploring similarities continues to stereotype and separate, 'othering' those not in the dominant group. What this fails to recognise, Martin argues, is the importance and vitality of difference, that it is a relational concept through which places, environments and people are understood only because of their variations and differences, and that a sense of 'sameness' between them cannot be recognised and appreciated without acknowledgement of difference. Thus, difference is vitally important, that *difference is the point from which determinations of sameness can be made, rather than the other way round* (p. 119).

Martin's perspective is that the world is complex and that by drawing on difference and sameness, because 'they just are', children can be enabled to develop a fuller and deeper understanding of *the differences within and between cultures through relating and dialogue* (Martin, 2012, p. 119). In effect, she argues that to help children understand *distant places* and to avoid falling into stereotypes and prejudices, we need to take children beyond the superficial and instant information to investigate more deeply, to respect and to value others, be these places, environments, cultures or peoples, not judging and choosing between them, but rather enjoying the diversity. This reflects the reality of our lives, in which we value the range of possibilities and opportunities we have. As Martin states, it is about 'and', not about 'either' or 'or'.

 Reflective task

Be aware of the references to Africa that appear in the press, television programmes and on social media. In what ways is the name Africa used? To whom does it apply? How do you respond to its use? What stereotypes do you hold about Africa? Where have you learnt these from and how limiting are they? How might you know and think otherwise about Africa and, indeed, about other places and peoples that seem often to be stereotyped?

The global dimension

The study of specific distant places is an aspect of the global dimension of the geography curriculum. The global dimension and global learning are increasingly associated with a wide range of topical and significant areas of study, with clear links to sustainability education and global citizenship (Bourn *et al.*, 2016). For some, the global dimension is controversial (Standish, 2012), while for others it is fundamental if challenging for all children's learning (Maguth and Hilburn, 2017; Peterson and Warwick, 2015; Martin, 2015; Demirci et al., 2018). Young (2010, p. 217) perceives the global dimension to be *in essence about social justice and living sustainably: how we choose to behave towards each other and towards Earth itself.*

The global dimension has particular significance and meaning within geography, since it is essentially about the wider world and global perspectives. The global dimension in primary geography not only focuses on learning about different places in the world and how people live in them, but also explores the bigger issues to do with moral, social, cultural and spiritual concerns affecting people, places and the environment. It encourages children's interest in living more sustainably and in adopting greater responsibility for their own actions through critical thinking and reflection, and it challenges their preconceived, partial and possibly biased and stereotypical views (Young, 2010; Martin, 2013b).

In England, for example, the global dimension was included and then removed from its curriculum requirements. Nonetheless, to sustain this aspect of the primary and secondary school curriculum, a cross-curricular programme was developed during the mid to late 2010s to encourage increased teaching and learning about a range of global issues, in which geography played a key role (GA, 2014a). The initiation and introduction of the Global Learning Programme (GLP) provided a clear message, supported by time-limited funding by the UK government's Department for International Development, subject associations and other non-governmental organisations, about the importance of teaching about global issues (https:// glp.globaldimension.org.uk/). It focused on opportunities for teachers to develop, share and disseminate their own knowledge and understanding of the global dimension and effective approaches to teaching and learning.

A key intention of the GLP was to introduce children to development education and to the idea of developing nations (Bourn, 2015), so as to promote the value of learning about the globe and the range of global interests and issues that affect people across the world (Maguth and Hilburn, 2015; Peterson and Warwick, 2015; Reynolds *et al.*, 2015). The aims of the geographical dimensions of the GLP (GA, 2014a) were to develop children's knowledge and understanding of developing countries, development and development issues, awareness of and some understanding about globalisation, knowledge of the importance of sustainability, increased familiarity with the idea and reality of global interdependence, and awareness of ways in which global poverty can be reduced. Working on the GLP involved exploring the different approaches and their merits in these areas of global learning. The project emphasised that these themes and topics should be approached through enquiry and critical thinking about global issues. The context for this has been that children need to be prepared throughout their schooling for life in a fast-changing world (Shin, 2012; Dolan, 2019).

Sargeant (2008) and Bourn *et al.* (2016) recognised that alongside local matters, global concerns are important to younger children. Among the themes emerging from Sargeant's study were that children had an evident sense of reality, albeit shaped to an extent by their personal experience; a clear sense of altruism – that is, feeling for and thinking of others – and awareness of and concern about environmental and global issues, troubles and unrest, informed through the news, for instance, which can be used as a teaching and learning source and focus (Pike and Kilcrann, 2015). Children find these topics and events disconcerting and troubling, but they seem to retain a sense of optimism for the future and a view that their families and communities support them. They are clear about their sense of justice for people elsewhere in the world, seeing migration, poverty and inequality as issues to address. This seems to lead to children valuing their *genuine place in the global community through their awareness and concern for people under threat of issues that they themselves do not experience* (Sargeant, 2008, p. 130). The global dimension is a core part of their lives. To an extent, already they go beyond national citizenship to be citizens of the world and think globally (Armitage, 2017).

Eight key ideas form the essence of the global dimension (DFID/DfEE, 2005), set out in Table 13.1. These resonate strongly with the key concepts of global citizenship (Table 13.2), education for sustainable development (see Table 7.1 in Chapter 7) and global learning. The key ideas of these four areas are set out alongside each other for comparison in Table 13.3. You will note that they interrelate with each other and are mutually supportive.

Young (2010, pp. 218–221) presents several vital reasons for incorporating a global dimension and global learning into the primary geography curriculum, seeing its inclusion as essential in any meaningful geography. She argues that it is essential because:

- we live in an interdependent world and we have responsibilities towards each other;
- there is the need to address the discrimination present in our society;
- we need to counter misinformation and stereotyped views about each other;
- there are so many inequalities in the world, which are caused by the way the world works;
- it is imperative that we live more sustainably;
- we can affect what happens in the future;

Key concepts	Description
Citizenship	Gaining the knowledge and understanding necessary to become informed, active, responsible global citizens.
Social justice	Understanding the importance of social justice as an element in both sustainable development and the improved welfare of all people.
Human rights	Knowing about human rights and understanding their breadth and universality.
Sustainable development	Understanding the need to maintain and improve the quality of life now without damaging the planet for the future.
Diversity	Understanding and respecting differences and relating these to our common humanity.
Values and perceptions	Developing a critical evaluation of images of the developing world and an appreciation of the effect these have on people's attitudes and values.
Interdependence	Understanding how people, places and environments are all inextricably interrelated and that events have repercussions on a global scale.
Conflict resolution	Understanding how conflicts are a barrier to development and why there is a need for their resolution and the promotion of harmony.

Table 13.1   The key concepts of the global dimension (DFID/DfEE, 2005, pp. 8–9)

- it encourages many schools to develop a link with another school;
- teaching approaches that incorporate the global dimension are of interest to pupils and can promote learning.

Global learning and the global dimension are not curriculum dimensions that are accepted uncritically. In particular, Standish (2009, 2012) has argued that the concept of the global dimension diminishes geographical learning about knowledge of the world because it emphasises values and attitudes that seem to place opinion and activism above understanding the world. He is critical of all three approaches to developing global understanding and citizenship, averring that *with global education, knowledge is rejected as a means to intellectual understanding and socialisation into society* (2012, p. 95). He goes on to state that as with history *any content will do*, since its role is simply to take forward the perspectives and issues argued for by proponents of the global dimension, global citizenship and education for sustainability. The counter-argument is that far from ignoring or rejecting knowledge and understanding, the global and sustainability cases rest essentially on a strong knowledge base of clearly researched and critically appraised information, well-made cases grounded in evidence, and aware of and able to counter alternative perspectives. In other words, they require the use of higher level thinking skills and knowing about the world and its physical and human processes and their effects, as the mechanism to foster and develop children's learning about their own and the wider world. Global learning is central to primary geography whether it is listed in national school curriculum requirements or not. Schools are able to take a whole school approach to teaching the global dimension and global learning, such as that illustrated in Figure 13.1.

In the classroom

Deepening geographical understanding and reflection

8–10-year-old children studying the Yangtze River Valley in China began by considering words they associated with the area. Their teacher wrote these on a board. As they found out more and more about the region, they added more words, but found that they had to remove several of the early words because their learning had shown them that their initial impressions were not always accurate. They looked at photographs and video clips about different parts of the Yangtze River, and from these recognised both the diversity and the speed of change in this region. They realised that they could not rely on impressions and stereotypes.

Key elements	Description
Knowledge and understanding	
Social justice and equity	Understanding of inequality and injustice within and between societies. Knowledge of basic human needs and rights, and of responsibilities as global citizens.
Diversity	Understanding of cultural and other diversity within societies and how the lives of others can enrich our own. Knowledge of the nature of prejudice towards diversity and how it can be combated.
Globalisation and interdependence	Knowledge about the world and its affairs; the links between countries, power relationships and different political systems. An understanding of the complexities of global issues.
Sustainable development	Knowledge of how to take care of things. Recognition that the earth's resources are finite, precious and unequally used. An understanding of the global imperative of sustainable development.
Peace and conflict	Understanding of historical and present-day conflicts and conflict mediation and prevention.
Skills	
Critical thinking	Ability to assess viewpoints and information in an open-minded and critical way and to be able to change one's own assumptions and make ethical judgements as a result.
Ability to argue effectively	Ability to find out information and to present an informed, persuasive argument.
Ability to challenge injustice and inequalities	Ability to recognise injustice and inequality in whatever form it is met and to select appropriate action.
Respect for people and things	Ability to take care of things – animate and inanimate – and respond to the needs of others. Ability to make choices and recognise the consequences of choices.
Cooperation and conflict resolution	Ability to share and work with others effectively, to analyse conflicts objectively and to find resolutions acceptable to all sides.
Values and attitudes	
Sense of identity and self-esteem	A feeling of one's own value and individuality.
Empathy and sense of common humanity	Sensitivity to the feelings, needs and lives of others in the world; a sense of common humanity, and common needs and rights. A capacity for compassion.
Commitment to social justice and equity	An interest in and concern about global issues; commitment to fairness and readiness to work for a more just world.
Value and respect for diversity	Appreciation that everyone is different but equal and that we can learn from each other.

Key elements	Description
Concern for the environment and commitment to sustainable development	Respect and concern for the environment and all life within it. A willingness to consider the needs of future generations and to act responsibly.
Belief that people can make a difference	A realisation that individuals can act to improve situations and a desire to participate and take action.

Table 13.2 The key elements of responsible global citizenship (Oxfam, 2006a, pp. 4–7; Young with Cummins, 2002, pp. 42–43)

The global dimension	Sustainable development education	Global citizenship	Global learning
			Developing countries Development and development issues
Citizenship	Citizenship and stewardship	Sense of identity	
Social justice		Commitment to social justice and equity Social justice and inequalitles Ability to challenge injustice and inequalities	Social justice (not charity) mentality
Human rights	Needs and rights of future generations Quality of life		Global poverty reduction
Sustainable development	Sustainable change	Sustainable development Concern for the environment and commitment to sustainable development	Sustainability
Diversity	Diversity	Diversity	
Values and perceptions		Value and respect for diversity Empathy	
Interdependence	Interdependence	Globalisation and independence	Globalisation Global interdependence
Conflict resolution		Co-operation and conflict resolution Peace and conflict	
	Uncertainty and precaution	Belief that people can make a difference Critical thinking Ability to argue effectively	Enquiry and critical thinking

Table 13.3 The key ideas of the global dimension, sustainable development education, global citizenship and global learning (DFID/DfEE, 2005; Holland, 1998; Oxfam, 2006a; GA, 2014a)

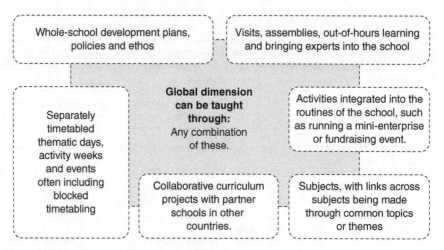

Figure 13.1   Teaching the global dimension (QCA, 2007, p. 3)

    Reflective task

Consider the reasons for learning about distant places and the global dimension outlined in this chapter.

What would be your core four or five reasons for ensuring that such global learning is part of each child's entitlement to geographical learning at primary school, or do you feel that it need not be and, if so, why?

Global citizenship

Chapter 8 introduced geography and citizenship, and we now consider this in relation to the global dimension. Tanner (2007, p. 52) argues that in primary geography *Global citizenship initiatives are [.] reflecting the reality that pupils must be prepared not only with knowledge, but also with the skills and values necessary to face and respond to the challenges for the twenty-first century.* She acknowledged that it is crucial to understand how everything in our world is bound together in a web of interconnections against the backdrop of living in a time of unprecedented change and challenge. It is the knowledge, understanding and skills acquired and the values developed that will underpin children's learning to live effectively and responsibly in our changing world (Table 13.4). Oxfam (2006a, p. 2) has stated that it is important for primary children to have *the opportunity to develop critical thinking about complex global issues in the safe space of the classroom.* Bourn *et al.* (2016) have emphasised the need to embed global citizenship into educational policy and practice in order to address the UN agenda for global education introduced in 2015 (UNESCO, 2015).

Young children encounter and are aware of controversial issues that affect the world (see Chapter 8). They need to be able to explore their own ideas and discuss and express their own views, rather than being given a set of prescribed answers to questions where there is no obvious right or wrong side or view (Oxfam, 2006b), indeed, there may be multiple perspectives. This requires participatory and exploratory teaching and learning methods, including discussion, debate, role play, communities of enquiry and open-ended problem-oriented enquiries (see Chapter 4). Such approaches help to develop children as global citizens (Oxfam, 2006a, p. 2), with the qualities of someone who:

- is aware of the wider world and has a sense of their own role as a world citizen;
- respects and values diversity;
- has an understanding of how the world works;
- is outraged by social injustice;
- participates in the community at a range of levels from the local to the global;
- is willing to act to make the world a more equitable and sustainable place;
- takes responsibility for their actions.

From these perspectives, it becomes clear that global citizenship is more than learning about the global dimension, which in turn is more than learning about distant places, as Table 13.4 shows. Global citizenship is about active participation and engagement, developing children's critical thinking skills, autonomy and capacity to take increasing personal responsibility (Allum *et al.*, 2008). Oxfam (2006a, p. 2) outlines a process through which this can be facilitated, which has close links with the enquiry approach in geography. Through it children:

- absorb new information;
- judge its bias and reliability;
- analyse it;
- synthesise it through a process of reflection on their own current views;
- draw their own conclusions;
- make informed decisions;
- take considered action.

Teaching about distant places, the global dimension and global citizenship is challenging but essential. Martin (2007) notes that teachers need to be well informed and to draw on appropriate subject knowledge, as well as remain positive about the problems that children investigate rather than overburdening them with worries and uncertainties, which they may take

Distant-place studies	
Focusing on describing, understanding, comparing and contrasting different places, environments and people. *The 'What is it like?' question.*	
The global dimension and learning	**Global citizenship**
Explaining the interrelationships and connectedness between people and places: *The 'Why is it like that?' question.*	The ability to analyse situations and injustice, to respect and value difference and sameness and to take responsibility. *The 'What can I do?' question.*

Table 13.4   Distinctions between distant place studies, the global dimension and global citizenship

to heart when not able to discuss them because of other priorities, a point reinforced strongly by Hicks (2012, 2014). Young with Cummins (2002) and Hirst (2006) assert that where the global dimension and learning and global citizenship are incorporated and embedded, children seem to be more motivated and enthused by what they are learning, something Alexander (2010) would endorse. It may be that this is fostered through inter-school links where the school's consistent engagement has enabled children to make real connections and develop deeper understandings (Disney, 2004; Disney and Mapperley, 2007).

Hicks (2007, 2014, 2016) advocates tackling global issues with children at all ages and stresses the importance of helping them understand that problems do not just occur 'elsewhere' – and are consequently less relevant – but that every issue has some local impact even if its form varies from place to place. He sees local and global issues as two sides of the same coin. Underlying much of the advice on teaching about these aspects (e.g. DFID/ DfEE, 2005; National Assembly for Wales, 2008; Scottish Executive, 2001) is the view that it is impossible to understand properly our own local environment and community without understanding what is happening in the wider global context, whether it is to do with, for example, food, transport, energy, music or culture, not least because of their digital connections. Thus, we must educate children to become global citizens, able to think and act locally and globally. This involves examining global impacts arising, for instance, from natural disasters, climate change and environmental pollution, and necessitates helping children to consider possible resolutions (Hicks, 1998, 2014). As Freire (1994, p. 9) argues, *One of the tasks of the progressive educator [.] is to unveil opportunities for hope, no matter what the obstacles might be.* Such an approach focuses not simply on the present and the issue, but looks to the future, encouraging children to consider possible, probable and preferable solutions for their future. Scoffham (2013) similarly espouses the importance of giving hope in children's learning.

Practical task

Find out more about the global dimension and global citizenship through a variety of websites: have a look at the ones at the end of the chapter and find some of your own useful ones. Choose a topic or project described there. How are the global dimension and global citizenship exemplified through it? What care needs to be taken when using such information from a website?

In the classroom

Fair Trade fortnight

Inspecting education for sustainability in primary schools, Ofsted (2008b, p.11) identified several examples of effective practice which can be adapted for other schools' contexts. Two examples are given here.

> One school's 'Fair Trade Fortnight' made very effective use of the expertise of a parent who worked for a fair-trade food company. He helped the pupils establish links with a school near one of the company's plantations in India. Through email exchanges and other correspondence, the pupils gained first-hand experience of the equity of fair trade and the ways in which it had improved the quality of life for the Indian children and their families.

> One primary school developed a very successful unit for year 5 students on 'micro-loans' to people in developing countries. The children learnt much about success stories in development, as well as about the difficulties that people in these countries face in their everyday lives. Because the loans are one of the only ways that women can set up businesses, it made the students particularly aware of the special problems faced by women in countries where levels of poverty are high.

Exploring countries and regions

Chapter 12 introduced the study of regions and countries through investigating your own nation and its regions. In essence, the same principles and approaches can be applied when investigating regions and countries elsewhere in the world, although these may well be at different scales. There are, of course, obvious differences, since other countries and regions in them and across nations in continents will not be directly accessible. But distance and scale should not preclude introducing other countries and regions to older primary age children. They will already be aware of other countries through news and social media, at least as names which they hear mentioned. That children are aware of places far away is not new and research into their ideas about other peoples and places has a strong background, as indicated in Chapter 3 (Barrett, 2007; Matthews, 1992; Wiegand, 1992, 1993).

    Research summary

Children's ideas about other countries

Pike and Clough (2005) investigated primary children's ideas about countries in rural and urban schools in Ireland. They used a mixed-methods approach to ascertain the children's knowledge and views; these included using open-ended questions in group interviews, class discussions and completion of a knowledge matrix. The purpose was to gather the children's perspectives. The children were positive about this aspect of geography since it opened their eyes to the wider world. In all, they named some 200 nations, with more economically developed nations in the high majority, and younger children tended to mention non-country places of which they were aware, usually towns. While common names such as 'America' for the USA were included, the misunderstanding that Africa is a country persisted. Their home nation received the most mentions. The children displayed some knowledge about countries, dominant among which were locational and landmark knowledge, which nonetheless was largely superficial, such as reference to a famous national landmark – for example. the Eiffel Tower in France. While these might seem stereotypical, it appeared that the children had some sense that what they knew was limited, that there is more to a nation than their current knowledge and that they had an imbalanced knowledge of the world, knowing little of and about less economically developed countries. Children's knowledge came from a variety of sources, particularly through family visits and links. Television, reading and school were other sources. Some had lived in other nations. Children enjoyed learning about other countries, cultures and people, and were interested in doing so themselves with help. While they wanted to know more about countries – and some felt they should know about every country – they felt that more depth of study of fewer countries would be beneficial. Pike and Clough noted that teaching about countries in the primary geography curriculum was influential, but could also be constraining, dependent on the teacher's interest and skill. Children wished to learn about places elsewhere and for this to be enjoyable. Many of them expressed interest in developing a wider base to their knowledge, since they were aware of the stereotyping of their own country and they wished to go beyond encountering only superficial information about countries.

Scoffham (2017a) draws together research about primary children's knowledge and understanding about countries, cultures and people, while recognising that it has been limited and spread across several decades. He avers that children's learning about nations is an important aspect of primary geography, but he notes that it is challenging to undertake, since it can provoke some 'awkward questions' – for instance, about inequality within and between countries. He notes, with Andreotti (2013), that country studies are complex, contingent and carry historical baggage, including why nations became as they are today. Nevertheless, he argues that Andreotti's view that it is essential to open up and develop primary children's perspectives, knowledge, understanding and attitudes, is a task that geography is best equipped to undertake.

Learning about other countries

The world comprises 195 recognised countries. Countries are geographical entities that are bounded, independent, governed states (see Chapter 12). Whether large or small, they contain physical and human features; these and their environmental geography can be investigated. It is important that primary children begin to develop some awareness of countries.

A significant way into investigating another country, in order to gain insight into people's lives and communities, is to undertake a locality study. Approaches to doing this are outlined in the next section. Localities do not exist in isolation; each is one of many in any nation. No locality can represent a country, although it might be a starting point for more extensive enquiries, which can include other places across the nation. You can only begin to build a sense of a country through exploring a variety of its aspects, to gain some ideas about its people, cultures, landscapes and activities. Inevitably, though, understanding what a country is challenges almost all primary children; what children begin to learn is just the start of a journey. Several approaches that initiate a country investigation were outlined in Chapter 12.

A helpful starting point is to ask children to list and then discuss what they know about a particular country: the current state of their knowledge. This may produce very little information across a class, or it might be that several or many children have ideas, feelings and views about it. It is likely that some countries may be better known than others, for a variety of reasons. For instance, close neighbour nations may be known about, and one or more children may have visited some of them, while others might be known through the media images that children have encountered, but such sources may provide partial and even distorted information and views of a nation. This starter activity should lead to groups of children and the class to consider what needs to be found out by posing questions to investigate. This in turn might lead to enquiries into the veracity of the information already known and to identifying specific lines of enquiry to follow through. Children can consider potential sources, from information books to the Web. Once individuals, pairs and/or groups have selected or been allocated topics to explore, they can develop their investigations, reporting back to each other on their progress periodically and making final presentations to the class.

Another starter activity might be stimulated through these questions: where is this country, which nations are its neighbours, and what can we find out about it from maps? Here children will need access to atlas maps, a globe and continental and world wall maps. This may involve an introduction to using the contents page and index of an atlas, as well as discussion about the symbols used on the maps and what they stand for. In looking at a country's map, at whatever scale, it will be important to consider just what is shown: why are there so few cities and are there others? Are there only a few main roads and railways? What does a border look like? When high or low land is shown, what does it look like? It will be essential to engage the children in examining photographs, perhaps using Google Images, to begin to gain an idea about what the lines, shapes, points and colours on atlases, wall maps and globes show. It will be very helpful for the children to have access, through the Web and in atlases, to national maps offering different levels of detail. Children are likely to begin by using a specifically produced primary atlas that will present limited and highly edited information. By looking at a secondary school or adult atlas, children will be able to see that atlases can contain much more information about cities, railway lines, roads and airport, for instance. It is important to help children recognise that atlas maps are highly selective; they can talk about how many villages, towns and roads there are near their home. Look at a national atlas and national maps to see which are shown and which are left off. If they have already used this approach to investigate their own country, they can apply the understanding they have developed to this new exploration. This can help children to realise the limitations of an atlas map and prompt them to enquire further and use other sources. At this point they can determine questions they wish to pursue and begin to seek the range of resources they will need for their investigations.

A third approach, illustrated in Chapter 12, is to begin as though they are a tourist wishing to plan a holiday. They might have access to one or more guides and other booklets published about a country and its key cities, leisure centres and landmarks for visitors. They can examine websites that provide tourist information about the country, as well as look at how they might travel to this nation and travel around it. This will involve them in considering how countries are marketed to attract tourists. They will learn that this is an important way in which nations encourage visitors to spend money in their country, so they should look also at what is advertised for tourists, such as places and hotels to stay in, souvenirs to buy, what they can eat where, and what it might cost to travel to and go into specific sites. Children can share and collate this information in order to establish a 'tourist perspective' about the country. They should then consider what might not be included by tourist companies, both in the country and external to it, and identify questions they can investigate in order to gain a more rounded picture of the country. Again, individuals, pairs and groups can make their enquiries and provide presentations. This could include inviting a travel agent and making contact through a national embassy with a visitor who can tell the class about the country.

A fourth approach might begin with one or more locality studies within a particular country. Here, groups of children may investigate different localities using a shared set of questions or themes they have identified with you. The localities should cover a spread of types of settlements and communities, including rural and urban areas. Using provided resources, children can find out about each of these places and report to each other about what the places they examined are like, where they are in the country, how one can travel between them, and so on. Children should then consider what ideas and questions about the rest of the country these places prompt. They cannot hope to find out all about the nation, but they can engage with gaining a fuller insight by looking further at what these places share and what their variety tells them about the country. There may be some key pieces of information they want to ensure they have included – for example, about the nation's significant features, its capital and other major places, and its borders and neighbours.

There are a variety of other approaches to country enquiries, including the following.

- Invite the children to ask their parents or carers what they know about a particular country. They might ask other adults in the school what they know. They can collate this information and consider what images are held about the country, what they think might not have been included and what they can investigate further.

- Ask the children each or in pairs or groups to find out about a particular country, with each of the children, pairs or groups investigating different countries. Before they begin, discuss and agree some criteria about what they should all try to find out and how they might provide what they learn. Allow them to extend their enquiry by following lines of interest they develop about the country. Each child, pair or group might be asked to create a poster to show what they consider the most important things they have learnt are, perhaps adding questions about what they could follow up if there was more time or they had the relevant resources.

- Children could focus on particular features of a country, such as investigating its physical features (rivers, mountains, surrounding seas, etc.) or its human aspects (settlements, what people do, population size and distribution, transport, well-known goods, etc.). They might investigate an aspect of its environmental geography, such as how it produces and provides electricity, the quality of its water and sanitation, the type and effect of its mining and manufacturing, pollution concerns on its beaches or collecting rubbish from homes.

- Building on Pike and Clough's (2005) research, children might investigate with another class what they know about a particular country or about countries in the world, asking children what they think a country is, naming countries, countries they have visited or have relatives and friends living in, some information about a country they choose, which country is their favourite and why, a country they know little or nothing about, and so on. The children can collate and analyse this information and report to the class they investigated.

Once children have undertaken a study of one or more countries, they might be asked to compare it with their own nation. This should be approached thoughtfully to avoid negative comparisons. For instance, children:

- can be asked to identify, say, three to five positive points about each country and to give their reasons for these;
- may say how the countries are different and add what the significance and value of these differences are;
- might consider what is the same about or similar between the countries and why this is informative;
- what they would like to know more about for each country.

At the end of any country study, whether linked with a locality study or in another context, it is important that the children reflect on their learning

about the country or countries. They can be asked to identify the most important things they have learnt, from confirmed and new information to views
about the country, to skills they have used and developed. They should consider how their own understanding and views about the country or countries
have developed. What is it that they appreciate at the end of their country
study that they did not recognise or appreciate when they started? To what
extent do they have an improved grasp of what a country is? What
approach(es) would they take when next undertaking a country study?

Learning about national and continental regions

All but one of the world's continents contain countries; they also contain
regions. There are regions within countries and there are regions that cut
across countries. The notion of a region within the home country has been
considered in Chapter 12. Similar approaches can be adapted and used to
investigate a region within a country elsewhere in the world; this might be
a designated and named political unit – for instance, a local government
region perhaps as large as an internal county, province or state, or it might
be a designated region of natural beauty such as a national park. In the
context of a locality or country study, a region within a country can be
explored to provide the wider context for a locality and/or to show that a
country has various types of region, be these politically designated, arising
from physical geography, or functional such as that of a bus company (see
Chapter 12). The importance for primary children is to enable them to
become aware that regions exist in other countries and for similar reasons
as in their home nation. This does not require any particular extent or depth
of study in the primary geography curriculum, but it should give children
the sense that any particular locality or place is within a larger area, which
is within a country, helping them to begin to grasp these relationships, as
those in the nested hierarchy of an address.

Investigating biomes and natural regions

We have already come across the idea of biomes and vegetation belts in
Chapter 6. These are examples of other types of region that usually cut
across countries. They are often large areas. One such region is the Sahara
Desert in North Africa, which stretches from the countries of Mauritania in
the west to Egypt and Sudan in the east, and from Algeria and Libya in the
north to Mali, Niger and Chad in the south. Another region is the Amazon
rainforest, named after the river in South America, whose extent includes
parts of the countries of Ecuador, Peru, Colombia, Venezuela, Guyana,
Surinam and Brazil. Other desert regions can be found, for instance, in
southern Africa, North and South America and Australia, and there are
tropical rainforest regions in central Africa, northern Australia and in

south-east Asia. There are temperate grassland regions in the world's Northern and Southern Hemispheres. Tundra and polar regions are found, for example, in Russia, Finland, Norway, Sweden, Canada and the USA (the state of Alaska). Further information can be found in Chapter 6.

Developing children's understanding of these large-scale natural regions is challenging. The purpose for primary children must be to initiate their awareness of such regions, through which they begin to appreciate that the world has very diverse environments. A useful approach to the idea of such regions is to investigate what a particular biome or vegetation belt might contain and where it is (Scoffham and Owens, 2017; Collis, 2017). This is a topic appropriate for children aged 9/10 to 11/12. A key resource will be a good primary atlas that includes maps showing biomes and vegetation belts. There are several activities that older children can undertake.

- Begin by asking children what they know about the region or type of region to be investigated and studied. What do children know about rainforests and deserts? Encourage children to question what their images are and to identify what they need to clarify and how they might find out and extend their knowledge.
- Use one or more atlas maps to identify different biome and natural vegetation regions, for example. Note where in the world particular regions are. Find and use photographs to help give the children images of these regions, so that they begin to construct a sense of what a type of natural region looks like. How does this change what they originally thought the region was like, and what questions does it raise that they wish to investigate?
- Use photographs and text to find out what is in a particular type of region. For instance, in a vegetation region, what types of plants grow and what sort of climate do they need to sustain them? Which creatures live in particular regions, and do some creatures only live in regions in particular parts of the world?
- Examine what the weather and climate is like in particular regions. Is the weather consistent day-to-day or does it vary from week-to-week or month-to-month and across the year? Are there variations in temperature during the day and night, and over the year? What is the sequence of seasons during the year?
- Explore what it is like for people who live and work in particular regions. Do many or few people live in particular regions and why might this be the case? What conditions exist for farming, and what can be grown there and what does not thrive? What daily patterns are there in people's work regimes and why is this?
- Create pictures and models, with explanatory text, about the region investigated. How will the children best depict an image of the region? What do they choose to include and to leave out? Why do they make

these choices? Children will need to consider what is most informative to show in their pictures and models and what is best explained in their text, perhaps as captions and explanatory notes to go with their images.

- Make a continental or world map to show the location of a particular region. Their maps should show the Equator, the tropics and the polar circles, as appropriate. Using atlas maps, they can mark the area and features of the region and colour it, providing a key. Children might include more than one region on their map. Discuss in which nations a continental region occurs, such as tropical forests or deserts. Ask them to show on their maps, by marking their borders, those countries that are included, wholly or partially, in the region.
- Different regions in the world are attractive to tourists, who may wish to holiday there because of the heat and sun or because of its attractive environment. Investigate what attracts people to visit different regions – for example, to go to a tropical area such as the Caribbean for a holiday or to travel into a polar region to look at the scenery. Use travel brochures and travel agents' websites to find out about places in a chosen type of biome, climate zone or vegetation area, for instance. Which places in a particular region are advertised as good to go to on holiday, and why? What is it they offer tourists? Which times of year do holiday-makers go to such places? What do they hope it will be like there?
- Across the world's biomes and vegetation belts there are concerns about environmental care and change. Children can investigate such issues as logging in the Indonesian rainforests or forest clearance for agriculture in the Amazon basin, and examine the gradual spread of deserts into surrounding areas. They can ask: why is this being done? What is the cleared land being used for or what useful land is being lost? Who works there, what do they do and how are they supported? What effect does this have on the biome and the people who live there? Who benefits and who loses out? Can the land that has been cleared regenerate or can it be reclaimed if it has become desert? What should we do about areas that are still pristine biomes? How might we sustain and care for them? Is there debate about this, and if so, what are the different views?
- Consider what has been learnt about a particular region. Working in pairs or groups, children should identify what the key characteristics, aspects and features are of the region(s) they have examined. How would they describe a particular biome or climate region, for instance, to those who do not know about it?

A multitude of regions to explore

Other types of cross-national or continental regions to explore include natural regions such as river catchment areas that can be investigated through using atlas maps to identify the catchment area of a major 'world' river, and climate regions that can help children to encounter and become aware of tropical, temperate and polar regions (in which there is some overlap with biomes and vegetation belts). There are human-created regions as well. Areas of farming for food production lie within but also cut across countries. Trade regions identify groups of neighbouring countries that trade with each other, as, for instance, within the European Union and in the trans-Pacific region, but trade also occurs globally. Another type of region is one that we might call a 'proximity' region, such as the group of islands collectively named the West Indies or Caribbean islands, or the set of countries in the Middle East, or the scattering of island nations in the western Pacific Ocean known as Micronesia. Geographical grouping by proximity and as neighbours, whether with land borders or separated by sea and ocean, has led, historically, to these regions being identified. Each of these types of regions can be investigated using the approaches outlined above.

A different type of region to investigate is a sea or oceanic region (not to be confused with aquatic regions that include freshwater lakes and rivers, coasts and estuaries, and some ocean biomes – for instance, tropical coral reefs like the Great Barrier Reef off eastern Australia). One way to explore this type of region is to take a named sea, such as the North Sea, the Coral Sea or the South China Sea, and to find out where it is in the world, name the countries and islands that surround and/or are in it, map the region, investigate its climate and life within the sea, identify some ways in which people use the sea for fishing and transport, and whether there are concerns about and issues in the way that humans treat its environment. This can provide a different focus about the idea of a region and helps children to be aware that geography studies the whole planet, not just what occurs on its land masses. Indeed, the oceans and seas, as the majority covering on the Earth's surface, should be an important concern in primary geography, though curricular around the world, for primary schools tend to overlook this fundamental dimension of our habitat.

Investigating time zones

When you drive from one place to another but do not necessarily know the route well, you might use an in-car GPS navigation system or that provided on your mobile phone. It will direct your route, show you where you are, and may give you enough information to have a sense of what is ahead of and behind you. Using GPS, you are relying on a navigation system that is based on the Earth's latitude and longitude, the means by which every place on Earth can be – and is – pinpointed. Lines of latitude and longitude are imagined horizontal and vertical lines, which you can most readily 'see' marked on maps of the world and globes. Lines of latitude run around the Earth laterally, such as the Equator, the Tropics of Cancer and Capricorn, and the Arctic and Antarctic Circles. Lines of longitude run from the North Pole to the South Pole.

It is the lines of longitude that are vital to understanding time zones. There are two key lines of longitude. One is the Greenwich Meridian, which runs north-south through London, from which the lines of longitude are measured in degrees. Go west and you move through 180°W; go east and you move through 180°E. On the opposite side of the Earth to Greenwich lies longitude 180°, which is the International Date Line: the agreed line of longitude where as you travel west across it one day becomes the next – or if you travel from the east across it, you move into the time of the day before.

When you travel from your home country to another, especially if you are travelling hundreds of miles, whether going east or west, and whether within your continent or to another, perhaps across an ocean, you are most likely to move into a different time zone. Indeed, you might cross several time zones. When you travel directly south or north, you will remain in the same time zone. When you move east or west around the world, you travel across lines of longitude. For each 15° of longitude you cross going east or west, you move forward or back one hour – at least in theory. Visiting places in other parts of the world to the east or west means thinking about the time there. You will adjust your watch from your home time to the time in your new time zone. Some people do this when they start an air flight, for example, while others wait until they arrive at their destination.

A time zone is a region of the world based on lines of longitude in which the countries, or parts of countries, observe the same time, essentially as a matter of convenience. This is helpful for social, commercial, transport and communication reasons in daily life. Furthermore, knowing about time zones helps in travel around the world for people and for trade, when times of arrival can be predicted and planned for. In reality, time zones do not follow neat straight, longitudinal lines, but are skewed because they follow the boundaries of countries or of subregions within countries. It may be that, as in parts of Europe, a number of countries agree to be in the same time zone. Several countries are so large, such as Canada, Russia and Australia, that they have several time zones within them, although other large nations, like China, have chosen to have the same time zone across their entire 'wide' country. Other nations use half-hour time divisions. Indeed, the International Date Line is not a straight line along the 180° East or West, since it 'bends' around the islands of particular Pacific Ocean nations.

Introducing time zones

Older primary children can be introduced to the reality of time zones. Indeed, it may well be that some or many children in class have experience of travelling across time zones and of staying in a place in a different time zone. The following are some approaches that can be used to help children begin to understand time zones.

- One way to introduce children to the idea of time zones is to use webcams in other parts of the world. A search of the Internet will identify many such webcams in central sites in major cities and coastal resorts, for example. Obviously, these should be checked before use. It is informative for children in, say, the UK to see in their early afternoon lessons what time of day or night it is in, for instance, Sydney, Australia, or in different parts of the USA, such as in the cities of Washington, Chicago or Los Angeles, or in a city in South America, Asia or Africa. Discuss what can be seen on the webcam view, and why. Find out the time difference to where you are.

- Use an atlas to identify lines of latitude east and west starting from the Greenwich Meridian (0°). Follow the numbers to the west and to the east, referring to them as 60°W and 120°E, and so on. Discuss the notion of time zones and that the hours move on or back by an hour for every 15°, depending on your movement west or east. Children work out what the time should be in named countries, based on the time of day where they are. To follow up, provide the names of 5–6 countries for the children to use the lines of longitude to work out what they estimate the time to be in that country. Use the Internet to check the accuracy of times.

- Give children the names of 5–10 countries across the world. They should use an atlas and globe to identify and name the capital city and one other city in each country. The children should use the Internet to find out the time in the two cities in each country and compare those times with the time in their own country. They might add such information to an outline map, or class wall map, which shows time zones round the world.

- Use a good quality primary atlas and a globe to look at the lines of longitude and latitude. On an outline map of the world children can mark and number the lines of longitude from 0°, at 15° or 30° intervals (or longitude lines may be pre-printed). Name the Greenwich Meridian and the 180° (east and west) lines of longitude. Then, by each line of longitude write the time of day (15° = 1 hour), counting west from the Greenwich Meridian, having set the time at 0° (it might be 12.00 noon or an earlier or later time – use the 24-hour clock times to aid counting forward and back). This can be done on an outline world map which shows countries or major physical features. Children can use an atlas and globe to identify and mark on the map the names of several different countries or features through which their numbered lines of longitude pass. They can estimate the time in those countries, and then use the Internet to help them find out how accurate they have been.

- When children come across somewhere in the world during their geography and other studies, they should discover in which time zone it is and work out how many hours ahead or behind their home country's time that time zone is.

Bringing distant places into the classroom

In today's world, digital technologies give our classrooms continuous and instant access to the outside world. As noted in Chapter 9, websites such as Google Earth, Zeemaps, NearMaps and Bing maps bring otherwise distant and far-off places directly to us, providing children with detailed, if pre-selected, images, photographs and maps. This access, supported by other primary and secondary sources such as visitors, books, photo packs, artefacts and stories, can help children construct more informed ideas about places. Studying a variety of places during their primary years and using diverse resources enables children to build a knowledge base about different places and environmental issues in the world.

Studies of distant localities should be of similar size places to the local area of the school (see Chapter 12). It is vitally important that studies of places, wherever they happen to be, are set in context. The range of geographical topics listed in the box in Chapter 12, pp.349–51, should form the basis for selecting topics for distant locality studies.

 In the classroom

Finding out about India

Early in their study of a village locality in southern India, a class of 7–8-year-old children used a globe, atlases and the Web to find out where the village is and about it. Using the travel experience of some children in the class, they discussed and looked at how they might travel to India. One child told them about a flight she had made to India, how long it took and what she did on the flight. Using a travel site, they found out flight routes, the airways that flew there and which airports they flew from and to. They identified which airport was the nearest to the village – which in fact was quite some distance away – and they discussed how to travel on to the village. They considered, discussed and selected the clothes they needed to pack if they went and found out about the various types of food they might eat. Through these activities, they became aware that they would travel far to India and about the idea of time distance for travel by aeroplane. They would also have a long journey by coach on arrival in India. They looked at atlas maps and the globe to see which countries their flight would take them over.

The focus for their geography topic was about visiting a number of places in northern India, arriving in Mumbai and travelling from there. They discussed the idea of holidays in other places and drew on their experiences

(Continued)

(Continued)

of daytrips, and on the national and international holidays some had made. They invited a local travel agent to bring them brochures and to discuss how to plan such a holiday. She returned voluntarily to help them decide where to visit, where to stay and how to travel around. They found pictures and films of places to visit and of hotels, trains and road travel, and arranged an itinerary for their 'visit'. The children were encouraged to include different aspects of life in India; they knew there are different 'sides' to their own country, and wanted to find out what life was like for different people and what different places were like. They listed a number of things they could do, such as shopping, particular sites to visit and meals they wished to eat; for this last element they arranged to try various foods and to do some cooking with a local restaurant as the culmination of their topic.

Following their study, they recognised that they had only seen a little of India. They had become aware of the size of the country and of some aspects of its diverse landscapes, places and peoples. They realised that it is an increasingly wealthy country that continues to have major issues of poverty to address. They reflected that they knew something but too little to generalise. They knew it is changing, but were unsure who was gaining from this and who was not yet doing so.

Activities to support learning through locality and global study

It is important, when beginning a place- or issue-based study, to elicit and probe children's pre-existing ideas and to consider some of the balances that need to be included. Your overall focus will be in your outline plan. While your distant locality topic will be planned, it is vital to remain flexible and to respond to children's needs when later you become aware of shortcomings, imbalances, misconceptions, stereotypes or prejudices that should be tackled. Table 13.5 provides some examples of activities to use to investigate so as to raise children's awareness in a locality global issue study (Garforth *et al.*, 2006, Council for Europe, 2015). These activities encourage the children to ask questions and discuss matters. They can be used at different points within a project and undertaken as class activities or by groups of children.

As in any locality study there are many activities that may be selected and used. The box below provides examples of a range of activities to adapt imaginatively and creatively. It will be a matter for you to decide how to apply them for an age group and when during a locality study you choose to use them. They complement the ideas in Table 13.5.

Activity description	Resources	Outcomes of activity
On an outline map of the country where your locality study is located, write the question: 'What do you know about [the country]?' Ask children to write down as many facts, feelings, etc., about that country as possible. Repeat this in relation to the locality, asking children to draw: 'What I would see if I went to [the locality].'	Large outline map of a specific country with the questions or activity title written at the top. Felt-tip pens, crayons, colouring pencils.	To find out what the children know or think they know about the country or locality of study. To assess the nature and accuracy of information they have and of views they express. To initiate discussion about a country, to consider how we know this 'information' and why we might need to find out more. Repeat the activities during or at the end of their study, and compare the images to assess development of their understanding as an idea harvest or audit.
Give out two or three photographs per group. Ask children to think about where the photograph was taken and to name the city (if appropriate), country and/or continent. Once they have decided, go through the photographs together. Ask each group for their response and to justify their location. At the end, tell them that the photographs in fact all show the same place.	A set of photographs (around 20) of varied views of the same city, country or continent, from your own collection or from a published photo pack or downloaded thoughtfully from Google Images, printed and laminated. Number the photographs so that they can be easily referred to in the lesson.	Children are surprised that all the photographs show the same place. This provokes discussions about the deceptiveness of appearances, and the issues in categorising and generalising about places. There are variations and differences wherever we are. Use this to challenge stereotypes and redress imbalances in what children believe to be true. Highlight and emphasise the similarities between places and people and be aware of differences within places, not just between them.
Use an assortment of photographs of different perspectives of a locality or a country. Ask children to diamond rank them according to which are the most and least representative of that locality or country.	Assorted images, all from the same locality or country, that show very different views and activities or places and events. Have some that are not apparently characteristic of the locality or country and others that are.	As above, in addressing preconceptions, children can consider where their ideas come from. Discuss the importance of being receptive and open-minded about the diversity of people, places and environments.
Identify a 'characteristic' child who lives in a particular distant locality. Provide a fact sheet about a typical day in her/his life. Ask children to produce a comparable fact sheet about themselves. They might make a poster about their locality. Consider providing a second and third child or adult and do the same task.	A poster showing where a particular child lives and a fact sheet showing a typical day in the life of a child, from the distant locality you are studying. Information and images about other children and adults in the same locality.	Encourage the children to look for similarities and differences in people's lives. Children will find much common ground between the basic activities that we all do across the world. It develops empathy for the commonality of people's lives, and encourages greater understanding and acceptance of people around us locally and globally.

(Continued)

Table 13.5 (Continued)

Activity description	Resources	Outcomes of activity
Use the interactive whiteboard or a large sheet of paper. Write: 'How can I make [this locality/the world] a better place?' Discuss what 'making it better' means, thinking about improvements and addressing issues. Ask children to write/illustrate their ideas about how the locality/world can be improved. (Remember that all places can be improved.)	The interactive whiteboard, or A1 or A2 size sheets of sugar or flip-chart paper, a large board, felt pens.	Provide the opportunity to discuss and express the concerns they want to see addressed, and how they would do so. These can be locality issues for the people there or significant global issues, hazards and events. Children should consider and discuss what is good and not so good in the locality/our world and what the word 'better' means to and for different people.

Table 13.5   Activities to raise levels of local and global awareness

Some possible teaching activities to use in a distant locality study

- Locate and mark the features and views in photographs on a map of the locality.
- From map and photograph information, create a model of the locality. As you find out more from other sources, add to or correct the layout of the model. Use it to trace journeys, see what happens where, and play out daily life and events.
- Find out why particular features are as they are, such as why the buildings are constructed as they are, why a road may or may not be in good repair, or where a stream or river has its source and flows through.
- Consider why particular goods are available, who might buy them and where they might come from.
- Examine where else people go shopping, for leisure activities or for work.
- Provide the children with a set of factual statements about the locality to read and discuss. Encourage them to group the statements and explain their categories.
- Provide a jumbled-up set of information about the daily life of a person in the community. The children must arrange the information into an appropriate (correct?) sequence and explain their order.
- Select aspects of daily life or a particular event and create an improvised drama to act through what occurs.

- Encourage children to find out about the life of a particular individual in the locality. Hot seat the character, who answers questions about their daily life, work, activities, leisure, and so on.
- Create the 'home corner' or a part of your classroom into a room in a home or shop. Use it to role play what happens there.
- Imagine you are going to visit this locality and plan a trip there. Find out about how you get there, how long it takes, and so on. Create an itinerary of what you would do there, who you would visit, what you might eat, what you would wear, etc. This might be enacted through spending a day travelling out, visiting and returning, with some children as visitors and others as community members.
- Create a 'balance sheet' of impressions of the locality. Identify what is liked and what is less appreciated. Individuals and groups share their views to identify what is common and what is less so. They should consider why this is and how what they know influences their views.
- Invite an external visitor or speaker to share their experiences and knowledge with the children and to answer their questions, which children should prepare beforehand. Visitors might be members of the local community who have travelled in the relevant country or people working with charity organisations who know the country or area. Ask them to bring in some personal possessions they acquired in the area that they can talk about to help the children envisage being there.
- Create a poster that shows the similarities and differences between life in your own locality and that being studied.
- If you have made a model of the settlement, once the children are reasonably well informed, have them take on the roles of local residents, find out more about their likely lives and share what they consider they do daily with their neighbours. You might create a change or event to see how the children respond in role to this.
- Encourage children to write a letter in which they evaluate what they have learnt about the locality.
- They should note what they have in common as well as how their places differ and diverge, which they should be encouraged to celebrate.

There are a number of important matters to bear in mind to provide primary children with the most valuable insights into other lives and places elsewhere in the world. Where possible, it is very helpful to have contact with children and adults living elsewhere to help bring such investigations alive for children. They do not involve international travel because this can be facilitated through virtual connections using Skype, FaceTime, tweets, blogs, and so on. Sahi and Willy (2016) have identified a number of perspectives and approaches to consider.

- Begin with the local and move to the global, thereby incorporating your own place within a broader global context and encourage children to value their own place.
- Study closely individual distant places in a country and then layer these by looking at a very different part of the country that provides a contrast – for example, a village, then a city, a coastal place and a mountainous place. This is a way into finding out about the country (but help your children recognise that they are only finding out about aspects of the country, not about the whole of it).
- Celebrate the differences and diversity within a country, different types of people, landscapes and economy, and recognise the similarities between us all as well.
- Focus on the different stories emerging from community to community or region to region, and explore the multiplicity of the country – and even locality – by not telling the single story.
- Ensure that your activities explore the issues in enough detail to appreciate the complexity of that place.
- Look at how that country has changed over time, encouraging children to explore development and change, and recognise that places are dynamic and made up of their past, helping children to understand what they see today, a point that Scoffham (2017a) reinforces. Consider, too, what it will be like to be in that country in 20 or 50 years' time, and contrast that to how the children's own place may be then also.
- Investigate the misconceptions held about the countries that you study as well as the standard perceptions (and stereotypes). What might children in the places you are looking at think, and what might they think about us? Be aware of others' perspectives.
- Explore reasons for different cultural, religious and political symbols such as flags, festivals, dress and food. Encourage children to consider what might represent us and how that varies from but has similarities with those in a different country. For instance, we all have flags, clothing, food and festivals.
- Examine the array of different media representations of a place. How true might these representations be, and how might it feel to be misrepresented? Consider what might cause these misrepresentations and who might benefit from and be undermined by them.
- Use a range of interesting, sensory and local artefacts, images, tastes, smells and sounds to weave together aspects of an image of a country that is as real as is possible. Children may think some of these are unusual, just as others elsewhere may think some of our things are unusual.
- Develop children's creativity and imagination. Ask them to hold an object in their hands, and imagine the world of the person who last

used it, then use it as a stimulus to write a story. Draw a map of the journey that the object might have been on to reach where you are, and weave in children's ideas about the places it has been to en route.

- Speak to people who have been to different places – children in the class, parents or people from the local community – interview them and share their experiences.
- Supplement teaching through using characters – for instance, a case study of a child living in a distant place. Write their possible diaries, draw what they might see and taste what they may eat.
- Refer to the distant place that you are studying as you teach across the curriculum to provide a richer experience.
- Explore the broader issues that the locality and its country may be facing – for example pollution, waste management, sustainability, conflict resolution or political change. Compare one or more of these with issues in your own country to help children to consider possible resolutions to challenging problems (but discourage them from thinking they have 'the answers').
- Make links with schools abroad if at all possible through organisations that connect schools and through other programmes. Depending on time zones and the timings of school days, you may be able to have direct contact through media such as Skype and FaceTime.

 In the classroom

Deciding on a local area pack contents

At the end of their study of a distant locality, a class of 9–10-year-old children spent a lesson identifying what they would include in a pack about their own local area to share with another school elsewhere in the world. They were limited to 15 photographs and 12 pages of information including maps and charts. They debated in groups and as a class what they would include and leave out, and why. Through this activity they began to appreciate the limitations of the resources they had used in their distant place study and became aware that their understanding was limited and partial. Several children commented about not assuming too much about the place they studied. They realised they had some understanding but that gaps remained in their knowledge. They recognised that they should remain conscious that they only had a limited appreciation and understanding of where they had studied.

Practical task

Plan a short topic looking at a global issue. Decide on your issue and identify six of the activities from Table 13.5 and the box on pp. 412–13, and from the guidance that Sahi and Willy (2016) provide, to adapt to use in teaching about the issue. Explain why you have selected those activities.

Some pitfalls to avoid

Studying distant places is not without its dangers. It is vital to maintain the focus on what children have learnt from the information they have. They should be encouraged always to distinguish facts from opinions. The statements they make and conclusions they draw should be evidence based, and they should acknowledge when they lack information and be open about a perception that they might attempt to justify (Weldon, 2010). There are other concerns to be aware of.

- When studying a locality, ensure that other parts of the country are encountered, whether urban environments when a rural locality or vice versa (Young, 2010; Young with Cummins, 2002). It is vital that children do not talk about pizza and think that it 'is' Italy. They must become aware of various attributes of a country, including its culture and the diversity of lives and places, so that they are aware the locality is not 'the country' – hence the need to investigate several places in any country. It is important to avoid sweeping generalisations about a country that can exacerbate stereotyping and paint an unbalanced view of life elsewhere.
- We are quick to identify and emphasise differences between others and ourselves as separations not as distinctions. As has been said, difference is important if thought of relationally, but it is vital also to focus on similarities, and sameness, to encourage children to see how their lives compare to those of children in a similarly sized locality, as well as with several others in the other nation. Through this focus, diversity and difference can be recognised and valued, while what is shared in common is valued, and the varied circumstances of lives are appreciated (Martin, 2012, 2013a).
- Learning through sympathy and charity – for instance, about people living in poverty, can lead to the problem of tokenism and undermine the sense of equality of people wherever they are. If an international week, where different classes study different countries, is planned and run superficially, it can lead to unbalanced views of those countries,

reinforcing stereotypes and perpetuating myths and perhaps prejudices. When focused on a variety of localities where children make comparisons to their own lives and experiences, locality studies and investigations into countries can prove to be rich, engaging and informative.

- Photographs may raise issues that children are keen to discuss. These may be challenging, with children asking – for example, during a study of a locality that may be based in a country in a different continent – why people's clothes look dirty, their houses are small and cramped, and they cook outside. Because this may be a very misleading impression gathered from the resources used, it is important that such questions are discussed together as a class and not avoided, although they may seem uncomfortable. Discussing such misconceptions or misinterpretations helps children develop positive values and attitudes based on reality and understanding. Where possible, they can be countered using other images of and information about people's lives in that locality and across the country.

In the classroom

Investigating a distant locality

A class of 7–8-year-olds were studying a village in Peru. While most of their resources were in English, this study linked appropriately with the primary language that the school had chosen, Spanish. During their studies, the children used resources written in Spanish that had been brought back by their teacher from a visit. They looked at information about Peru in Spanish on national and tourist websites. In learning Spanish, and alongside in their native English, their teacher ensured that they used relevant everyday geographical words and terms related to directions, streets and buildings, food and clothing, and the physical environment. They extended their vocabulary in English and Spanish because of their interest in their project. They also began to learn something of Spanish and Peruvian culture, and explored some of the history of Peru to understand why and how Spanish had become a language in the country, and they learned that Peruvians spoke other languages. This linked them into the wider context of international tourism as well as considering the idea of remoteness in finding out about the ancient ruined Inca city, Machu Picchu, which is a major tourist attraction. They examined the idea of conquest and its lasting impact, giving their project an historical awareness, a global dimension and involving global citizenship perspectives.

Resources for distant place and issues investigations

There is considerable and growing support, guidance and resource provision for teaching for global learning and global citizenship, as initiatives such as the Global Learning Programme in England attest (GA, 2014a). A wide variety of resources can be used for locality studies. Artefacts and the variety of resources noted in Tables 9.4 and 9.5 on p.269 and p.270 and in Table 12.2 on p.360 are invaluable aids. A further way into distant localities and some global environmental issues is through stories (see Appendix 2).

Many voluntary and non-governmental organisations (NGOs) have and continue to produce resources to support primary geography with distant locality, country and global dimension studies (Augustine, 2015). Some provide teaching materials, while others offer information and guidance useful for teaching. A number of NGOs are listed in the box below (Google them to see what is available on their websites). Such resources are produced from a particular context and for a reason, whether to support fundraising or to help change attitudes, challenge stereotypes and break down prejudices. Many have been produced by education officers and through curriculum projects involving practising teachers, and they are often developed with the help of the communities or countries portrayed in them.

> Some voluntary and non-governmental organisations providing resources and/or information helpful for distant place studies
>
> ActionAid
>
> CAΓOD
>
> Christian Aid
>
> Friends of the Earth
>
> Geographical Association
>
> Oxfam
>
> Muslim Aid
>
> Red Cross and Red Crescent Movement
>
> Save the Children
>
> UNICEF
>
> WorldVision
>
> World Wide Fund for Nature (WWF)

It is important to understand the context of locality and country packs and other materials before using them. When evaluating such resources, check that it is clear that they offer a balanced and inclusive approach. The materials often include factual information, and they do not avoid issues or problems, instead providing different points of view and debate to encourage gaining a fuller picture of a community and to see that a country has challenges to address alongside developments to build on. Such materials usually provide activities, including information and worksheets, role play about local concerns, and materials about the issues faced by communities. You should check the date of publication to ensure that you are not using dated resources, which will have been a year or more in preparation before publication. You should check the quality of the photographs and maps, the language level or levels, the variety of ways in which information is presented, and the usefulness of the activities suggested, and then be selective in the way in which you make good use of such resources, making use of the guidance provided above and in the notes about using the materials.

 Reflective task

One concern in studies of distant localities is using materials that are not up to date. What reasons can you identify that support this concern? How would you define an up-to-date resource for distant locality and country studies? When might you use older resources?

 Key points

This chapter has:

- considered what is meant by global learning and the global dimension in geography and advocated the importance of facilitating children's learning about the world;
- considered global citizenship in geography teaching and learning, and how this may raise children's awareness and a greater sense of responsibility and empowerment;
- made the case for studying localities in other countries in primary geography;

(Continued)

(Continued)

- introduced you to what might be considered appropriate to teach about countries and regions with older primary children, alongside some approaches to use;
- introduced you to approaches and activities for effective teaching of locality studies and the global dimension in the geography curriculum;
- noted some of the pitfalls to look out for when undertaking locality, national and global studies.

Moving on

Fair trade has been considered in Chapters 6 and 8. Tanner (2007) gives four reasons for introducing fair trade in practice and as a geographical topic in primary schools.

1. It allows children to make a connection between their everyday lives (buying and consuming a product) and the lives of people living and working in distant places.
2. It lends itself well to children's sense of justice and 'fairness', that people who work hard to make our food, clothes and goods should be paid a fair price.
3. It is an issue in which everyone has a role to play and can take part.
4. There are some excellent resources to support learning and teaching about the practice of fair trade in schools (see Dalrymple, n.d.).

Information and resources are available through the Fairtrade Foundation website, and through other sources such as Oxfam (see websites at the end of the chapter). Find out more about fair trade and the ways that it might support studies of a distant locality, the global dimension and global citizenship.

Further reading

There are many publications available to support learning about places beyond your own nation, a few of which are given here.

Bourn, D, Hunt, F, Blum, N and Lawson, H (2016) *Primary education for global learning and sustainability*. Cambridge Primary Review Trust Research Survey 5 (new series). York: Cambridge Primary Review Trust. Available at: http://cprtrust. org.uk/wp-content/uploads/2016/02/Bourn-report-160217-final.pdf.

Dolan A (2019) *Powerful Primary Geography: A toolkit for 21st century learning*. Abingdon: Routledge.

Garforth, H, Hopper, L, Lowe, B and Robinson L (2006) *Growing up Global*. Reading: RISC.

Grigg, R and Hughes, S (2013) *Teaching Primary Humanities*. Harlow: Pearson.

Hicks, D and Holden, C (2007) *Teaching the Global Dimension*. London: Routledge.

Johnson, S (2010) *Beginning Geography*. Monterey: Evan-Moor Educational Publishers.

Martin, F (2006) *Teaching Geography in Primary Schools*. Cambridge: Chris Kington.

Martin, F (2012) The geographies of difference. *Geography*, 97(3), pp. 116–22.

Pike, S (2016) *Learning Primary Geography: Ideas and inspirations from classrooms*. Abingdon; Routledge.

Scoffham, S (ed.) (2010) *Primary Geography Handbook*. Sheffield: Geographical Association.

Scoffham, S (2017) Young children's ideas of different peoples, nations and cultures: A research perspective. In S Catling (ed.) *Reflections on Primary Geography*, Sheffield: Register of Research in Primary Geography. pp.121–27.

Young, M with Cummins, E (2002) *Global Citizenship: The Handbook for Primary Teaching*. Cambridge: Chris Kington.

Useful websites

CAFOD: www.cafod.org.uk

Christian Aid: www.christianaid.org.uk/schools

Comic Relief: www.comicrelief.com

Council for Europe (Teacher controversial issues – pdf): http://pjp-eu.coe.int/en/ web/charter-edc-hre-pilot-projects/teaching-controversial-issues-developing-effective-training-for-teachers-and-school-leaders?desktop=true

Department for International Development (DfID): www.globaldimension.org.uk

Fair Trade Foundation: www.fairtrade.org.uk

Friends of the Earth: www.foe.co.uk

Geographical Association: www.geography.org.uk

Global Dimension https://globaldimension.org.uk/

Global Gateway: http://schoolsonline.britishcouncil.org

Global Learning Programme (GLP): http://glp.globaldimension.org.uk/

Geoguessr: https://geoguessr.com/

Oxfam Education: www.oxfam.org.uk/education

Red Cross: www.redcross.org.uk/What-we-do/Teaching-resources

Save the Children: www.savethechildren.org.uk

Think Global https://think-global.org.uk/resource/geography-the-global-dimension/

Sustainable Schools Alliance http://sustainable-schools-alliance.org.uk/doorway-resources/global-dimension/

UNICEF: www.unicef.org/education

World Vision: www.worldvision.com.au

WWF One Planet Schools: www.wwf.org.uk/oneplanetschools

CHAPTER 14

PLANNING PRIMARY GEOGRAPHY TEACHING

→ **Chapter objectives**

This chapter enables you to:

- understand that by planning effectively you are becoming a geography *curriculum maker;*
- appreciate the need for effective planning to enable successful learning outcomes in geography for the children you teach;
- recognise the need for short-, medium- and long-term planning for geography;
- appreciate the role of different types of plans and understand the importance of adapting these to suit your own needs as well as ensuring their suitability for your situation and circumstances;
- be aware of the need for progression and differentiation in your geography planning.

Introduction

This chapter considers the planning of your geography teaching. Planning is essential in order to give you a clear sense of direction, enabling you to make decisions as your teaching of a geography theme develops. Planning takes place at three levels: in the short, medium and long term. Each of these is considered in this chapter, although the focus is mainly on short- and medium-term planning – that is, lessons and units or topics of study.

Each primary school's geography policy and objectives will be particular to it and planning may be done in collaboration with your geography or humanities subject leader. Your planning will take account of the children you teach, their circumstances and needs, and the school's local context and connections to the wider world. You will need to consider the particular interests the school has in its geography policy and scheme, and what you bring to your geography teaching, whether in a single subject or within a cross-subject topic. You will have your own ideas and values about geography and the ways you wish to develop your teaching, something that is encouraged and lauded as you develop your expertise at being a curriculum maker. Combining these with the school's requirements and the curriculum that you follow is important in your planning process. Medium-term plans may already be in place and take into account the school's geography scheme. However, do not plan too tightly and rigidly, as this can constrain the children's involvement and contribution in enquiry-based teaching and you may miss important opportunities you can use by thinking flexibly and adaptively. You should be able to modify it as need be. It is *your* class's curriculum and you are the maker of that curriculum for your children. As you consider and evaluate your teaching, you should reassess regularly and modify appropriately what you have planned. Your plans are working documents to be annotated and adapted (Wyse *et al.*, 2012; Cox, 2011; Monk and Silman, 2011; Grigg and Hughes, 2013; Pike, 2016; Armitage, 2017).

Curriculum making

The Geographical Association discusses planning as being more than just a process of taking the requirements of a particular geography curriculum, sequencing them and providing a series of lessons for the children. It has termed the whole process of planning 'curriculum-making' and defined it as:

> *the creative act of interpreting a curriculum specification or scheme of work and turning it into a coherent, challenging, engaging and enjoyable sequence of teaching and learning. Curriculum making lies at the heart of good teaching.*

> (GA, n.d.).

Teachers are curriculum makers because they draw from their knowledge of its three essential elements. This was introduced in Chapter 1, referring to research in primary geography curriculum making. Curriculum making is based in and creates an appropriate balance between:

- the subject – geography – and what it is for;
- the children and how they learn geography;
- teaching approaches and specific teaching techniques, best enabling learning in and of geography.

At the heart of curriculum making lies the enquiry approach to learning in geography, the focus of Chapter 4. Geographical enquiry lends itself perfectly

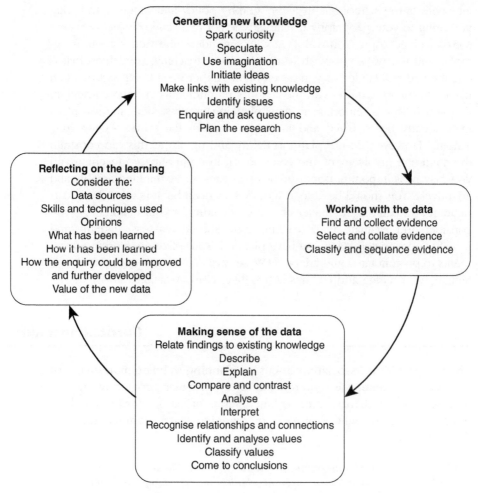

Figure 14.1   A process approach to geographical enquiry in the classroom (adapted from GA, n.d., and Roberts, 2003)

to the primary school environment with its tradition of exploration and discovery. Roberts (2013) reminds us that the enquiry approach has four central aspects: sparking children's curiosity and a 'need to know' with an engaging stimulus; collecting and using data; processing and making sense of that data and reflecting on learning that has taken place as a result and being able to apply it to future enquiries. Figure 14.1 presents these four elements as a process model that underpins an approach to curriculum making. These elements form a sound and robust framework for planning the curriculum and should be considered when embarking on planning in a primary geography context, especially, as Catling (2013c) notes, in relation to medium-term planning over an extended period of time (see also Chapter 1).

Curriculum making is not a new term or approach (Catling, 2013c; Biddulph, 2017). It has always been the case that teachers construct, create or make the curriculum and the lessons they teach, whether this is based in requirements structured within a school or in implementing curriculum requirements directed by a government. Teachers' making of a curriculum is based in their interpretation of any school or external requirements, their sense of the subject, their appreciation and knowledge of the children in their class, and their preferred approaches to teaching. The quality of primary classrooms is based in the types of relationships teachers have with all their children. Thus, interpersonal relationships, alongside their views about high-quality primary education and pedagogy, influence their making of a geography curriculum, just as much as they are influenced by their attitude to the subject and their confidence in their understanding of it (Alexander, 2010). Teachers are inevitably the drivers of the geography curriculum and of its teaching (Biddulph, 2017), but they are influenced by their school context and the three levels of curriculum planning appropriate for their classrooms: whole-school planning, unit or topic planning and lesson planning.

Whole-school planning

The purpose of a whole school's geography plan – sometimes termed its scheme of work – is to outline the cover, progression and development of geography across the school (Richardson, 2010b; Pike, 2016). It will ensure that from the early years through to the end of primary school, children are given the opportunity to meet the appropriate school, local or national statutory requirements for geography. The subject leader responsible for geography will regularly review, evaluate and adapt the geography scheme to ensure its clarity, thoroughness, topicality and balance, as well as its resource needs. It is important to seek advice from and work with your geography leader when planning your own class curriculum.

The school's geography scheme of work will have a number of features, drawn from the subject and any external curriculum requirements, the children's experience, prioritised approaches for its teaching and the school's context (Carter, 1998; Owen and Ryan, 2001; Richardson, 2010b; Scoffham, 2010; Reynolds, 2014; Pike, 2016). The features of an effective geography scheme will include the following.

- Recognition that children can contribute from their own geographies.
- Continuity and progression between year groups in the use of core geographical concepts and skills, as well as of the school grounds and local environment, and, possibly, sites further afield.
- Enquiry-based learning that encourages children to look for issues, and develop problem-solving and critical thinking skills.
- Integration of themes, methods, skills and real places to develop children's geographical experience, understanding, skills and values.
- A representative range of different places to study across the world, taking account of local connections related to the school's community and environment.
- Planned opportunities for learning outside the classroom, particularly through fieldwork.
- The integration of themes and appropriate cross-curricular links.
- Opportunities to investigate and discuss topical and controversial matters and issues that are deemed important, and/or that arise and are thought to be relevant and appropriate to examine.
- A wide range of resources, including maps and plans, photographs, artefacts, ICT hardware and software, and appropriate websites, books, resource packs, and much more.

Many schools approach the teaching of geography through topics or themes with an integrative or interdisciplinary learning approach (Pike, 2016). This cross-curricular approach can make children's learning engaging and meaningful, and it enables real-life leaning (Barnes, 2015; Kerry, 2015). When making plans, however, it is essential that the geography does not become 'lost'. The key to good planning for high-quality children's learning in cross-curricular topics and contexts is that the subject elements are clear and treated with integrity, that there is balance within the subject components, and that they link together. In that subjects or areas of learning tend to be the basis for a curriculum, it is essential that they are explicit at the minimum in the teacher's planning of a curriculum, but also important for at least older primary children to become aware of, so that they begin to understand that geography approaches the topic in its own way, history differently, and science and art with other lenses (see Chapter 12, pp. 357–59, and Chapter 14, pp. 446–49).

Planning is often presented as an integrated or cross-curricular scheme of work in an overall subject matrix. Figure 14.2 provides an example, outlined in the box below, with the focus for each year in a primary school. In this example, the school has developed and sequenced a number of geography questions and foci in its geography scheme of work. This supports teachers developing their own geography or cross-curricular units across the year for their class and children, to meet the intentions, content and sequence of the scheme.

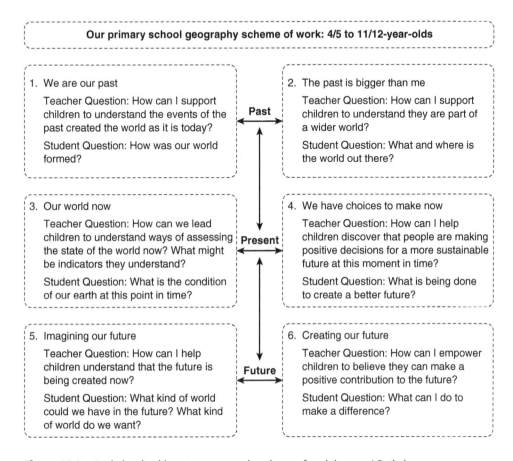

Figure 14.2   A whole-school long-term geography scheme of work (source: J Butler)

Sequence and progression in a geography scheme of work from pre-school to 11/12-year-olds

Past

1. **We are our past**

    Teacher question: How can I support children to understand that events of the past created the world as it is today?

    (Continued)

(Continued)

Child question: How was our world formed?

4/5–5/6 years: Observe how the landscape is changed by weather, seasons and people.

5/6–7/8 years: Become aware that the earth's resources were formed and are used in our daily lives. Living things have evolved and changed over time.

7/8–9/10 years: Natural and built environment and resources have been created. Land formations, mountains, valleys, plains, coasts, etc. Living things depend on each other to survive. Our settlements and way of life have been influenced by the landscape and people.

9/10–11/12 years: Geological events have formed the natural environment we have today.

2. **The past is bigger than me**

   Teacher question: How can I support children to understand they are part of a wider world?

   Child question: What and where is the world out there?

   4/5–5/6 years: We live on earth and there are other continents and countries. We can see these on a globe. We live in a country that is a part of a continent. There are other countries and continents out there.

   5/6–7/8 years: Study of places near and far expands to a larger variety of places and countries.

   7/8–9/10 years: Geographical reasons as to why people settle where they have around the world. Mapping and graphicacy skills to represent observable features in the environment.

   9/10–11/12 years: Where we can see evidence of geological events in the world – in our area, country and continent. Reference to other parts of the world.

Present

3. **Our world now**

   Teacher questions: How can we help children understand ways of assessing the state of the world now? What might be indicators they understand?

   Child question: What is the condition of our earth at this point in time?

4/5–5/6 years: Every creature has a home and is part of the environment.

5/6–7/8 years: People have caused changes in natural, built and social environments. Map and portray to show observable features in environments.

7/8–9/10 years: Living things adapt to their environment, some have life cycles. Use maps, graphs, texts, images and film to describe our world. Identify potential threats to our health and safety, and that of the environment.

9/10–11/12 years: Be aware that there are indicators that show the current state of the world. Groups that measure/assess the state of the world – Earth report card.

4. **We have choices to make now**

    Teacher question: How can I help children discover that people are making positive decisions for a more sustainable future at this moment in time?

    Child question: What is being done to create a better future?

    4/5–5/6 years: Discuss some problems that creatures, homes and environments might be facing.

    5/6–7/8 years: Understand that people's attitudes and values affect their interactions with natural features and cycles. Safety issues in homes, schools and the wider world need to be considered.

    7/8–9/10 years: There are threats to our resources. What factors are affecting the environment and what can we do to create more sustainable futures? Consider plans we might put into place to protect ourselves and our communities.

    9/10–11/12yrs: Identify some of the big issues at local, national and global scales that are currently creating discussion and actions.

Future

5. **Imagining our future**

    Teacher question: How can I help children understand that the future is being created now and that what we do now affects what will happen in the future?

(Continued)

(Continued)

Child questions: What kind of world could we have in the future? What kind of world do we want?

4/5–5/6 years: Talk about what I want my future to look like. Discuss how I can keep safe in the future.

5/6–7/8 years: Become aware of some potential dangers to world health and food availability.

7/8–9/10 years: Consider how we can overcome some of the threats to our resources and environment – ways we can improve things in the environment.

9/10–11/12 years: Debate and justify your vision of an ideal future for the earth.

6. **Creating our future**

Teacher question: How can I empower children to believe they can make a positive contribution to the future?

Child question: What can I do to make a difference?

4/5–5/6 years: Consider what I can do to look after our environment and help get the future I want.

5/6–7/8 years: Discuss what my ideal world might look like and what I can do to help make it happen.

7/8–9/10 years: Identify what I can do to make a difference – personal action plan, pledge, commitment.

9/10–11/12 years: Examine what I am going to do to make a better future for me and those around me. Protecting our future through safe decisions.

Considering progression

Two key elements that inform whole-school planning are progression and consistency (Pickford *et al.*, 2013). Consistency occurs through regular geography teaching in and across each school year. Progression is enabled as the children are engaged in greater depth and breadth with their studies as well as through tackling issues in greater detail and with more complexity, described by Bruner's term *the spiral curriculum* (Pike 2016; Bruner,

1960) to develop their understanding of the key ideas and approaches of geography. The aim is to evolve children's awareness and understanding of their own expanding and deepening knowledge, and their thoughtful and critical awareness of other people's values and attitudes about places and issues (Richardson, 2010b; Solem *et al.*, 2014; Solari *et al.*, 2017). Progression is supported through the following elements (Owen and Ryan, 2001).

- Development of more abstract ideas through the key geographical concepts.
- Increasing complexity and range of topics and issues studied.
- Development of fuller and more rigorously applied knowledge, values and skills.
- Increasing breadth of geographical knowledge.
- Increasing depth of geographical understanding.
- Extending the scale and nature of the areas studied.

In planning a geography scheme of work, the geography subject leader might consider how particular opportunities can be taken to develop progression and provide for the initiation, reinforcement and deepening of geographical learning (Pickford *et al.*, 2013), although Ofsted in England (2008a, 2011) has noted that it is not usual for schools to consider their whole-school planning of geography in this way. One approach to achieve this is through the use of key learning environments, such as the school grounds and local area at increasing levels of complexity. The box below outlines a sequence of learning opportunities that might form the basis for using a school's grounds progressively across a geography scheme for children from the early years to the end of primary school.

Planning for development in geographical studies of the school grounds

Early years: 3/4–5/6 years: Encountering the geography of the outdoor area.

- Observe and name features around the outdoor area, including the weather.
- Children talk about how they make use of the outdoor area and what adults do.
- Make journeys around the indoor and outdoor areas and school, using relative directions (e.g. left, right, forward, back).
- Notice changes to activities and resources and where they are.

(Continued)

(Continued)

5/6–7/8 years: Developing geographical awareness on the school site.

- Describe features and relative locations and directions around the grounds and school.
- Consider people who work in school: where and what they do, and why.
- Observe and make weather records: observation, leading to recording temperatures, windiness, sun/cloud, etc.
- Consider how weather and seasons affect 'me and you', and how school grounds are used in different weathers and different times of year.
- Places 'we' like and dislike, why and how we would change them.

7/8–9/10 years: Engaging children in geographical studies of the school.

- Examine room and space use in the school building, and land use around the school site.
- Notice and map patterns of features and activities.
- Look at changes around the school: older and newer features, dating features and building(s), considering changes in use of parts of the school inside and outside, development of the school site, and discuss changes that might improve the school.
- Caring for our school: energy watch, litter watch.
- Weathering and erosion around the school.

9/10–11/12 years: Becoming involved in developing the geography of the school.

- Study water in the school grounds: soaking in, puddles and run-off, evaporation; how to store and make use of rainwater in school.
- Consider the school as a settlement and community: features, people and groupings, services, uses, access and change.
- Look at reasons for patterns on the site, how these might change and why, with links to ways to improve the use of the school site.
- Ideas for a 'school of the future' on the site: what it is like, what happens there, who works and goes there, and much more.
- Plan a school guide for future parents and children.

It is vital also to take into account children's developing awareness and learning. The box below summarises, in broad terms, expectations for children's developing understanding of the global dimension as an example of progression. The geography subject leader's knowledge and application of appropriate and challenging expectations in children's geographical, social and cultural understanding should inform the way in which a geography scheme of work is planned effectively through a primary school.

Expected progression in understanding the global dimension

3/4–5/6-year-olds are offered a variety of experiences that encourage and support them to begin to make connections between different parts of their life. They become aware of their relationships to others and of the different communities that they are part of – for example, family and school. They begin to develop awareness of the diversity of peoples, places, cultures, languages and religions. They begin to understand fairness, the need for care for other people and the environment, and to be sensitive to the needs and views of others.

5/6–8/9-year-olds begin to develop a sense of their own worth and the worth of others. They develop a sense of themselves as a part of the wider world and gain awareness of a range of cultures and places. They learn that all humanity shares the same basic needs, but that there are differences in how and to what extent these needs are met.

8/9–11/12-year-olds develop their understanding beyond their own experience and build up their knowledge of the wider world and of diverse societies and cultures. They learn about the similarities and differences between people and places around the world, and about disparities in the world. They develop their sense of social justice and moral responsibility, and begin to understand that their own choices can affect global issues as well as local ones.

Source: DfID/DfES, 2005, p. 5

Practical task

Using the information about children's personal geographies provided in Chapter 3 and the ideas about place and local area studies in Chapters 5, 12 and 13, write a summary of expectations for local area study along the lines of those in the box above.

Medium-term planning

Medium-term planning is the planning of a geography unit of work or topic for your class (Monk and Silman, 2011; Grigg and Hughes, 2013; Pollard *et al.*, 2014; Pike, 2016). It may last just a few weeks, a half term or a full term, with one or up to two hours teaching a week. A unit of work is focused on a geography topic or theme, and it identifies clear learning objectives and expectations for the children's geographical learning (Richardson, 2010b; Scoffham and Owens, 2017). Some geography units or topics might be continuous units, which are dipped into and out of during a term or across the school year, such as about weather and seasons. These might relate to topical events, several being picked up across the year linked through a focus on, for instance, natural hazards or places and communities in the news. There are often a number of cross-curricular links, but it is important always to ensure that the geographical learning objectives and success criteria, or expected outcomes, are clear and explicit.

Many primary schools have planned and structured medium-term plans or units of work in place. They may provide a broad outline or be set out in some detail, stating the key enquiry questions, the sequence for study, the activities and the resources to use. These should be thought of as valued guides rather than as pre-structured units that have to be followed whether or not they are appropriate. As a geography curriculum maker, you should maintain your focus on drawing on, selecting from and adapting a provided unit whether developed within the school or take from an external source.

Tables 14.1 and 14.2 provide a fully developed and worked example of a primary geography teaching unit, designed for a class of 8–9-year-old children. Table 14.1 explains the purpose of the geography unit, its links with geography's key curriculum concepts, the children's learning and expectations of them, vocabulary opportunities, resource needs and cross-curricular links. Table 14.2 sets out the sequence of study using a series of geographical questions to organise and structure progression in the unit. This is a very detailed plan that has been provided to show the range of matters that need to be considered. In this sense, it is a 'thinking' document about planning your geography teaching, not necessarily what you would provide in such detail for your geography unit planning, which will be guided by your school's practices, and your own and your class's needs. Nevertheless, it may provide a useful approach to apply initially to help you plan your geography teaching, but be careful. It is important to remain flexible and be adaptable when teaching the topic day-to-day and week-to-week, so modify and change it and make it right for your children as appropriate.

Unit title: Getting about – exploring mobility and access in the local area

Age group: A fully planned unit to adapt as appropriate for 8–9-year-olds.

About the unit

This medium-term unit focuses on movement about the local environment for those who find mobility less straightforward, such as wheelchair users, those with hearing or sight impairments, the infirm, older people, parents/carers with pushchairs. It explores the accessibility of routes and places, and identifies good, moderate and poor examples of access, which help or hinder mobility for local people and visitors to the area. It enables children to examine the locality around their school, to consider local needs and concerns, and to propose solutions to difficulties that they find.

The key questions for the topic of this unit (which is issue-based) are as follows.

- Why is mobility access an issue?
- What are the local issues about mobility access?
- Who is affected and why?
- Where is mobility most and least a problem?
- What do people locally think about this issue?
- What do the children think?
- How can the problems locally be overcome?

You should add here questions that the children might have, to which they are interested in finding out the answers.

Curriculum connections

This unit offers links with the key subjects, language and mathematics, as well as to developing enquiry skills. It has links with citizenship, equal opportunities and inclusion. Connections can be made with local history, design, technology and environmental education.

Make connections with citizenship education and with personal, social, cultural and health education, helping to prepare children to play an active role as citizens.

Links to primary geography's key concepts	
Place and space • The school locality • What places are like • Locations of features and road networks	**Scale** • Distances between key features locally • Lengths of journeys people make
Interconnections • Mapping location distributions and patterns	**Cultural awareness and diversity** • The age profile of the local community • The variety of mobility needs among people
The environment: physical and human geography • Identifying human processes • The impact of the physical environment	**Environmental impact and sustainability** • Why people may want to improve the local area • Examine how decisions affect people's lives locally

(Continued)

Table 14.1   (Continued)

Unit title: Getting about – exploring mobility and access in the local area

	<ul><li>Identify ways to improve the local environment</li><li>Proposing how changes may be made</li><li>Opportunities for children's own involvement</li></ul>

Geographical enquiry and skills

- Asking questions
- Collecting, recording and analysing evidence
- Examining people's different viewpoints
- Using maps
- Undertaking fieldwork
- Drawing conclusions and making proposals
- Using decision-making skills

Vocabulary

In the unit, children are likely to use these words:

access, accessibility, benefit, council, facilities, features, improvements, limitations, mobility, planning, practice, proposals, routes, services, shops, transport and travel.

They may also use other more specific terms associated with the issue linked to disability, features in the local environment and aspects of equal opportunities and citizenship activity.

Resources

- Range of local maps, including large-scale adapted map, street maps
- Contemporary photographs
- Council planning department website address
- Local community action groups and relevant websites, blogs and other forms of media
- Local people and professionals, including residents, shopkeepers, planning access officer, local councillor
- Examples of interview questions and rating scales
- Information on any local reports in newspapers and on the Internet on accessibility issues

Prior learning

It is helpful for the children to have:

- studied aspects of their own locality;
- used maps and photographs;
- developed some fieldwork experience and skills;
- undertaken geographical enquiries;
- been introduced to environmental changes and their impacts.

Unit title: Getting about – exploring mobility and access in the local area
Expectations for the children's geographical learning
At the end of the unit, most children will: • be able to identify an issue affecting people's lives in their local area and how people may be able to manage and improve it; • be able to justify their own views and take account of those of others; • be able to use evidence to show the situation found through an enquiry. Some children will not have made so much progress and will: • develop their experience in using photographs and maps and in observing in the local environment; • state their own views and the views of others about an issue. Some children will have progressed further and will: • be able to put forward evidenced and reasoned arguments for proposals for change; • recognise and describe ways in which people can tackle a local matter of concern linked to equal opportunities and citizenship.
Future learning
Children build on their learning in this unit by undertaking a further issue-based enquiry in a subsequent year at school on a topic in which they will largely use information from secondary sources. They might consider other issues affecting people's lives and human rights in other studies with an equal opportunities and citizenship focus, perhaps on education for sustainability and/or about an environmental issue linked to a geographical theme, such as the climate, studied at a range of scales.

Table 14.1   The focus and rationale for a geography medium-term plan on local mobility and access

A locally based topic on the accessibility of the local environment to everyone, be they readily able to move around or in need of time, appliances or a supportive environment, is an excellent topic to investigate, since it provides opportunities for fieldwork as well as classroom-based study. Its importance as a pertinent geography topic has been noted in Chapter 8 relating geography with citizenship and social justice. As a geography topic, it requires that the children become knowledgeable about their locality and about an issue that affects people in the local area. Through the use of key geographical concepts it develops children's geographical understanding. Table 14.2 provides an outline of the teaching sequence of this topic on local mobility needs and concerns, identifying the intentions of the key questions around which it is constructed, a variety of possible teaching activities to use and what it is planned that the children will learn as outcomes from the topic.

Points to consider when writing medium-term geography plans

When asked to write a medium-term plan, you may be provided with only a brief outline of the theme or topic you are to teach. You will need to plan

Learning intentions	Possible teaching activities	Learning outcomes	Points to note
How do people get about in our locality?			
Children learn: • that people move about locally in various ways; • that people visit a range of different facilities locally; • to obtain information from photographs and maps.	Children: • discuss how, where and why people move; • use local photographs to identify and illustrate the variety and forms of transport; • use local maps to note the various routes that can be used; • prepare a poster or website in groups about travel in the local area.	Children: • know that people use different forms of transport; • know that there are a variety of different features and places that people travel to.	**Graphical skills:** encourage the children to look for evidence to support their observations from the photographs and maps.
What makes a place accessible for everyone?			
Children learn: • that people have different travel and access needs; • that streets should be accessible to everyone; • that local facilities and services should intend to be accessible to everyone; • to ask questions and develop their enquiry skills; • to select appropriate information.	Children: • undertake fieldwork in the school building and grounds to identify how easy or difficult it is to move around; • use a wheelchair, or move about a cumbersome object, to identify good and poor accessible routes, and inaccessible sites and routes, and create a map of the school to show this; • talk to the local authority access representative about access and what should be in place; • photograph and display sites on a map of good and poor access around school and in the neighbourhood.	Children: • understand that while able-bodied people can access routes and places, usually easily, it is often more difficult for those with mobility difficulties; • know that there are legal requirements for many facilities to be accessible to all people.	**Fieldwork:** use the school, its grounds and the immediate local area to explore questions, needs and issues about access and mobility. **Inclusion:** encourage the children to consider how all people move about. **Speaking and listening:** enable children to come up with effective questions to ask the local authority representative in response to what they have told the children. **Thinking skills:** focus the children on using evidence to justify comments and draw conclusions. **Action:** encourage children to consider possible solutions to problems of access and how they might be overcome.

Learning intentions	Possible teaching activities	Learning outcomes	Points to note
How are people affected by access to places locally?			
Children learn: • to collect meaningful data in the locality; • to use maps at a variety of scales; • to identify where people are helped and hindered in accessing facilities and services in the local area; • to undertake an interview.	Children: • create and use a checklist to assess the accessibility of various places in the local area; • develop and use a short questionnaire to interview people about their experience of and views about the accessibility of places, and log relevant data on appropriate data-handling software; • plan and carry out fieldwork to assess accessibility in the local area; • take photos of examples of good and poor access.	Children: • appreciate the value of investigating the local environment to understand an issue; • refer in an informed way to the provision of local facilities; • identify appropriate questions from which data can be recorded and ask suitable questions to interrogate the data collected.	**Enquiry:** involve the children in developing the checklist and interview questions by modelling examples of such approaches for different topics or issues. **Safety:** ensure the off-site visits are organised to meet the local authority and school visit guidelines. **Inclusion:** encourage the children to consider how all people move about. **ICT:** have the children consider which data-handling software is the most appropriate to use in relation to their map-making and data-handling.
What are the mobility access issues in the local area?			
Children learn: • to access data and identify key information; • to make a map to show specific information; • to understand that people hold different views about issues.	Children: • make maps to show where access is rated good or poor; • use a database to record and show categories and the balance of good, moderate and poor access; • categorise local people's views on access; • analyse the data to draw conclusions and prepare a report of their findings in groups.	Children: • summarise, organise and present their information and findings; • identify good and poor practices in the provision of access for all; • recognise that people hold different views.	**Thinking skills:** encourage children to justify their conclusions. **ICT:** use suitable software to support children in their mapping and data-handling activities. **Action and problem-solving:** encourage children to consider possible solutions to local residents' access difficulties.

(Continued)

Table 14.2 (Continued)

Learning intentions	Possible teaching activities	Learning outcomes	Points to note
Who is involved in trying to improve mobility access?			
Children learn: • how and why people are trying to improve the local area; • who is involved in making decisions that affect the local area.	Children: • reconsider the points about access locally made by the planning access officer to evaluate these points against the findings of fieldwork; • invite a local shopkeeper, a local resident who has mobility needs and a local councillor into school to discuss the problems and possibilities of making improvements and how these are decided.	Children: • understand who will benefit from improvements; • appreciate some of the costs of and problems in making improvements; • become aware of who makes decisions that affect the local area and what impact these decisions might have.	**Inclusion:** take the opportunity to explore the values and attitudes involved in trying to ensure access to all the streets, buildings and other places, and to services. **Citizenship:** use the opportunity to help children begin to understand how decisions are made locally.
How can access for everyone be improved locally?			
Children: • identify alternative ways in which improvements can be made; • understand that resources are needed to make improvements; • there may be limits to making changes; • present a case and use persuasive argument.	Children: • draw up a balance sheet to show the arguments for and against making local improvements, using the information and evidence gathered; • identify a number of ways in which improvements could be made locally to improve access for everyone; • create a role-play public meeting about improving accessibility, with children taking the roles of different people in the community, to put the range of arguments for and against improvements; • write an illustrated newspaper report of the debate, outlining the issues; • write to the local council presenting the case for improvements and making proposals.	Children: • suggest ways in which mobility access can be improved; • use role play to debate the issues of improving accessibility; • express and justify their own views and proposals.	**ESD/Environmental Education:** this provides the opportunity for children to see how they can contribute to making improvements to the environment. **Literacy:** apply reporting, analytic and persuasive oral and writing skills.

Table 14.2 The sequence of a medium-term plan about an enquiry into local mobility and access issues

it more fully, possibly approaching the extent and in a form similar to the examples provided in Tables 14.1 and 14.2. In such plans, individual children's ideas and needs may not be strongly present, because their involvement is not fully planned for, though it can be. There is likely to be more opportunity to do this in your short-term, or lesson, plans.

There is no necessary sequence for the study of a locality or an environmental or global issue, but there are points of guidance that can help you consider how you might best develop your geography topic and bring children's contributions more evidently into the study. The following questions provide a guide to how you might go about your medium-term planning. They refer to locality or global dimension topics, but can be adapted for any geography planning, such as a region or an aspect of physical or human geography.

- What is the focus of your study and its purpose? Is it focused on the locality as a place or has it more global interests and does it illustrate an environmental issue and explore sustainability, or both?

  An important initial decision is the purpose and context of the study. You might develop several geographical questions to guide your plan. You should be clear about what you want the children to understand by the end of the work.

- What do you and the children know of the locality and its country context or about the issue that is the focus of your topic?

  An elicitation activity can be a useful starting point to find out what information or general conceptions the children have.

- Where in the world is the locality or issue and where, on the globe, and in relation to your own place, is it located?

  This provides a sense of 'global where-ness', using atlases and globes. To locate a locality or issue, national, continental and world maps will be needed, augmented by up-to-date Internet searches on appropriate sites as well as resource packs if you have them.

- What do we want to investigate about this place or issue?

  This is where the children contribute to the development of the study through generating, selecting, refining and structuring their enquiry questions, perhaps using photographs, video, their initial ideas or other information to stimulate these. For younger children, these might be within a broad structure that you have set out or which is provided through the school's scheme of work for geography. With older children, the children's questions might provide the structure for much of the enquiry (see Chapter 4).

- How are we going to research the locality or issue? What resources are available?

For a strongly structured study, you may well provide all the resources. For a more child-structured enquiry it is useful for the children to use the resources provided as well as finding out about others and trying to obtain them, possibly via the Internet, visiting an appropriate venue or by inviting a visitor in. However, this may not always work and they need to remain realistic about their aspirations.

- How are we going to organise our study?

It will be important to decide how to work on the various questions, individually and/or in groups, as well as which aspects might be considered as a whole class. This is also the point at which to indicate the range of outcomes that might be worked towards: posters, a report, a role play, drama, a blog, and so on.

- What are we learning from the sources we have? What do we know now, or know something more about, this place or issue? What are we finding difficult or impossible to find out, and so where are our gaps in knowledge and understanding going to be?

Rather than only at the end of a study, it is useful to have 'checkpoints' along the way, for children to take stock and perhaps refocus their particular area of study. This might be because more stimulating questions have emerged or because there is a problem with resources. It may be helpful to agree that it is worth continuing or better to close a line of enquiry and move to another.

- What conclusions can we draw from our study?

Towards the end of the study children need to be focused on what the information and ideas they have gathered tell them about the locality or issue and their focus on it. The children's conclusions need to be reasoned and evidence based, but they might also include their own perspectives and speculations, inspiring debate and discussion.

- What have we learnt about finding out about other places or our issue? What should we apply in future studies?

Evaluation helps children realise and learn from what they have done in terms of what they now understand that they did not know initially, how their own views and preconceptions have changed, and what they have learnt about the process of study they can use in new contexts. Evaluations should also help them consider what they know about geography – what they consider the subject to be about – so that they might apply this understanding in their next topic.

- How has our study of this locality or issue provided us with a lens to re-examine our own locality and lives? How does it compare? What might we not know about our own place or context?

A key value in undertaking a locality or issue-based study is to enable comparison with other places and contexts, particularly with our own place and local issues. Children will have learnt that they can make comparisons, but they must recognise there are gaps that limit making too many assumptions. Can they identify the similarities and differences between their own and the other locality or context? Through this, they might appreciate that they do not know everything about their own area and local lives and issues, and consider what they can do to find out more.

Take an open-ended approach to your geography curriculum making

A further aspect of medium-term planning is to set out the aims and learning objectives for the geography topic without including the detailed lesson-to-lesson planning. This can be achieved through one of two approaches and does require some confidence and experience in planning, as well as a good sense of the geography about which the children are to learn.

The first approach involves developing your planning as the theme progresses from lesson to lesson, so that you plan for the first lesson and evaluate how this has gone, before moving on to plan the second lesson, which you might modify or change completely from your initial outline plans. This is an open-ended approach to planning that involves consistent reflection on the children's learning, but also requires you to keep clearly in mind the aims and learning objectives as well as the children's needs. The approach can be rewarding through the evolution and development of the geography theme (Monk and Silman, 2011), but less predictable than predetermined and closely structured planning.

The second approach is much more child-focused (Cox, 2011). In this case, you identify the geography theme, which might be determined by the school's geography scheme, and you set out the aims and learning objectives, as above. However, your first lesson is focused on bringing the children's ideas into the topic very directly. This requires careful planning of the first lesson so that the children understand what the focus of the theme is and what you want them to learn. You need to provide carefully chosen initial activities to foster their awareness of the theme and then to give them signposts to involve them in identifying possible topics and lines of investigation and enquiry.

From this you move to planning with the children the starting points for the study and a possible sequence for the work involved. Indeed, achieving this may require some deliberation by the children and yourself and take you into a second lesson. It is likely that you will have secondary themes that individual and small groups of children want to pursue. You need to keep bringing the children, and yourself, back to the learning objectives to use these as criteria for deciding what to take forward and what not to pursue (perhaps have them displayed prominently in the classroom). This is a riskier approach than the first option and very distinctly different from a detailed medium-term geography topic plan, but it can be highly motivating and engaging for the children. The lessons that develop may well be more child-focused and investigative with children taking their learning forward independently to a greater extent than may be the case in some other teaching and learning, but this is not to preclude that you may at times provide relevant direct teaching and guidance for them, individually, in groups or as a class.

However, this should not be allowed to develop unchecked. It is important that the children reflect on and evaluate as a matter of course the lines of their enquiry and what they are learning, and that they share what they are learning with each other periodically, not least because new ideas or lines of investigation can then be suggested by other children in the class. Important throughout is that your role as teacher is to challenge and question the children in their studies, as well as to praise or inform and, as necessary, redirect them from time to time. Your role as teacher remains extremely important in ensuring high-quality learning and in keeping the children on track and on task. It will also be important that you make and retain good records of your curriculum making, perhaps through:

1. an outline plan of where you expect the topic to lead, stating the overall topic's geography aims and outcomes (learning objectives) you intend;
2. developing a collection of the lessons you plan, indicating the links from one to the next, and with a brief indication of where you expect the next lesson(s) to go, which should include any specific teaching you decide is essential or relevant to include to support the children's geographical learning;
3. a journal record of the development of the children's engagement and of their geographical learning during the topic.

Whichever approach you take to your curriculum making or planning of your geography topic, you might use the following questions, building on Owen and Ryan (2001, p. 55), as a checklist to ensure you have covered the main elements.

- Are two or more aspects of geography included, linking place and physical, human and environmental geography matters and issues?
- Do your learning objectives draw on the curriculum and are they linked to the expectations and assessed outcomes?
- Have you involved children to a lesser or greater extent in asking geographical questions and planning the structure, sequence and progression of your enquiry?
- Are there opportunities for outdoor area or fieldwork, linked with indoor or class work?
- Have you planned to introduce new ideas and skills the children will need to use and for development of their understanding and skills?
- Have you planned for a variety of approaches to teaching and learning, and of activities and resources, differentiation and a variety in assessment strategies?
- Are there opportunities to support the key curriculum subjects and to make links with other subjects and so encourage cross-curricular elements?

What this stresses is that in your geography planning you remain fully responsible for the children's learning and for ensuring that when they need to encounter new content and ideas, as well as new skills for their enquiries, you provide these. This may be for individuals, groups or the whole class, and it may involve direct teaching as much as providing focused guidance or directing children to particular sources. As a curriculum maker you are involved in ensuring that children's geographical learning through their topic or unit of work, in a subject or cross-curricular context, is valid for the subject, correct in terms of information learned, rigorous in expectations. and fosters appropriate and positive values and attitudes.

 Reflective task

Find a medium-term plan for a geographical study of a locality or an issue on a suitable website (for example, the Geographical Association's website where there are a number of primary and early years examples). Examine the plan and consider to what extent the advice given in this section applies to it. Which aspects are used and which are not? Consider why this might be the case. How might you amend the plan to involve children's questions and ideas more fully?

Cross-curricular connections

In the early years of primary school – for example, in England – where geography is extensively or only taught with other subjects in an integrated approach (DfE, 2017), it will probably not be immediately obvious that you are planning specifically for geography; yet you should be, even if the geography has direct links and overlaps with other subjects. It is essential that when including in the curriculum and teaching a specific subject, such as geography, that the content and skills are explicit in the planning (Barnes, 2015; Kerry, 2015) and that there is a balance between subject knowledge content and its application to understand places, environments, and wider issues and themes. You, as their teacher, need to know what the geography is that is included in a class's cross-curricular topic. This ensures that children have the opportunity to develop their geographical knowledge, understanding and skills in a clear and explicit way. It has been advocated that making children aware of the nature of the subjects they are using and learning (metacognition) enables more effective understanding and subsequent achievement (Knight, 1993).

Geography is linked inherently to other subjects (Rowley and Cooper 2009; Grigg and Hughes, 2013). Links need to be specific and significant, not tenuous for the sake of a cross-curricular element. Learning about a distant locality can be considerably enhanced by, for example, links to music, art, dance and food technology. Making these links affords a wider understanding of the character of that place and area of the world. Carrying out a local enquiry on an environmental issue can encourage successful links with science and citizenship. If children undertake an audit of energy use, providing a rich and meaningful purpose for developing their mathematical skills, they can relate it to their personal use and investigate energy sources. They could look at the wider context of energy usage within school and home, and consider possible efficiency savings or introducing alternative types of energy, necessitating quite a sophisticated analysis of data. In addition, work on map skills is greatly enhanced through the effective development with mathematics of children's familiarity with scale, and coordinates and grids. This supports progression in both subject areas, providing an engaging context and relevance for geographical *and* mathematical learning, as it does with other subject connections. Local cross-curricular links were referred to in Chapter 12.

Cross-curricular learning can be organised in a number of different ways (Barnes, 2015; Kerry, 2015), all of which can be helpful and informative for geography teaching.

- *Hierarchical* approaches focus on one subject discipline, such as a geography topic, but which use aspects of another subject to foster and augment learning and support children's learning progress in the major subject. For instance, where a geography local area topic investigates aspects of past lives and how the locality has changed, it uses historical perspectives, understanding and enquiry to support the geographical learning.

- *Double-focus* planning and teaching involves promoting learning in two subjects equally within a topic. For example, in investigating the local environment to understand its nature, ecology and use, the focus might be balanced between geography and science, with the intention of fostering children's knowledge and understanding in both subjects together and equally.
- *Multidisciplinary* studies interrelate more than two subjects in a theme. A culturally focused enquiry might develop understanding in music, geography, art and dance. This might not be a consistently equal part-nership, since one or more of the subjects might be the main focus of study at any one time. Developing understanding of the relationships between music and dance may well involve developing geographical awareness and knowledge of the links to the land, leisure activities and resources, as well as relate to different cultural contexts nationally and in other parts of the world. It might be that similar connections are drawn out in relation to art.
- *Inter-disciplinary* approaches develop this in a different way, where they identify from a number of subjects the key concepts, ideas, knowl-edge, skills and values which all seem central to a particular theme for enquiry. Hence, aspects of the different subjects are used to develop the enquiry and nurture understanding of the theme involved. Barnes (2015) refers to 'fusing' a variety of aspects or elements from different subjects. At its heart, he argues, is a creative approach, and it requires a certain level of confidence in the teacher to be effective. An approach might involve the combining of film and website development to pro-vide information about and offer insight into the local community to new families moving into the area. From geography might be drawn mapping skills and the understanding of local features, facilities, ser-vices and location, layout and access, while other subjects might con-tribute through ideas such as change, community activities in societies and social groups, personal interests in art and sport, and links with literature, archaeology and music.
- *Opportunistic* cross-curricular teaching can be understood in two ways. One focus can arise through topicality, whether from something brought into class or in the news locally, nationally or globally. There may be opportunities here to look at aspects of the past and the present, such as with an artefact – not just what it is and what it might have been used for, but where it has come from and why it is of interest today – or to consider how a particular current event is being portrayed in news and social media, the language used, what facts and figures tell us and the

role of various images that are used. Here geography may link with other subjects. The other focus that can be called opportunistic relates to child-led, even initiated, cross-curricular teaching and learning. Such opportunities may be ideas brought in by children that stimulate a new topic or theme to pursue in parallel or in due course. This may involve exploring a place or weather events, which again might link geography, science and art, or concern an issue that arises for children, such as unexpected or unexplained changes to the local play area or affecting a farm or local shops, when geography and citizenship subject aspects may be involved.

Cross-curricular teaching is not unproblematic or uncritically accepted (Grigg and Hughes, 2012; Kerry, 2015). There are fierce debates about the importance and explicitness of subjects and the links made between subjects and key ideas from different subjects. Subjects like geography are a significant way in which we have constructed our knowledge and understanding about the world. Inevitably, they overlap and interrelate, as geography does with science, art, history, citizenship and others. But they are useful ways to categorise and help us appreciate particular aspects of the world. In one sense, we should recognise that all subjects are themselves 'cross-curricular' rather than isolated, separate, distinct, discrete and inviolable. Whether we have organised to teach using a subject focus or by linking two or more subjects, we should appreciate that for children there will be learning that cuts across subjects and we should always take opportunities to note or identify links, even if we do not pursue them at that point. This is important in younger children's geographical and wider learning. The key points we might draw from this are as follows.

- Subjects are constructs of interrelated ideas, concepts, skills and values, such as place, space, environment, sustainability and environmental location in geography (see Chapter 2).
- Children's learning can be aided by subject content knowledge, but it can also be compartmentalised and constrained if this is rigidly held to and enforced, such as that sustainability draws on much that is included in geography and science, but we can too easily put it simply in one subject rather than the other and overlook the contributions of both.
- There are themes – for example, change and communication – which benefit from a cross-curricular approach, just as more informational topics, such as the Great Barrier Reef, plastic detritus in the ocean or life in the desert, might benefit from it.
- We should make evident links between subjects when this is informative and aids learning in one or more subjects, such as with the idea of change in geography, history and science, for example.
- We should ensure that those aspects of subjects that are highly pertinent to the subject are linked explicitly with the subject, such that when we

are considering how our locality looks and is used today we state that these are geographical aspects we are investigating.

- Children are motivated and engaged through both subject and cross-curricular ways of enquiring and that this approach may have beneficial effects for different children in different ways, such as through children's enthusiasm and curiosity both in one of the subjects and related to linked aspects across subjects.

Short-term or lesson planning

Short-term planning focuses on the individual geography lessons that you teach. It turns the intentions in the topic plan into lessons and the activities therein, but it can also cover a sequence of two or three linked lessons, such as leading into, undertaking and following up fieldwork. This is the day-to-day planning of teaching (Butt, 2008; Grigg and Hughes, 2013; Lockyer, 2016; Pike 2016). Your planning needs to be adequately detailed to identify what is being taught, your learning objectives, the time available, how you will teach, how children are expected to learn, the assessment strategies you will use and the resources you need (Hattie, 2012; Cremin and Burnett, 2018). It is evidently dependent on your continuing lesson evaluations and formal or informal assessments of children's learning. Owen and Ryan (2001) and Butt (2008) identify a number of features to include when making lesson plans, such as:

- clear and specific objectives for teaching and learning and on which to assess the children, with clear criteria;
- key teaching points and questions;
- how the children will be organised, groupings, etc.;
- engaging activities and resources, which will be matched to the children's ability and experience and informed by previous assessment;
- differentiation, as appropriate;
- appropriate resources, including ICT, to enable and enhance the learning;
- feedback opportunities;
- clear sequence and progression, including an introduction and conclusion.

For all teaching in the primary school, planning needs to be focused and dynamic, open to adaptation and change according to children's progress and development through regular observations and assessment (Cooper *et al.*, 2010; Hattie, 2012; Pollard *et al.*, 2014; Coe *et al.*, 2014; Arnold, 2015; DfE, 2017). This is pertinent to the specific needs of the children and how these can be most effectively met. Clearly, such planning includes consideration of the resources needed on a daily basis – for example, in setting up a supermarket in the role-play area and the timing, space or room arrangements needed for such an activity. In the primary years key questions and related concepts help to focus the lesson plan and ensure that its essential elements of learning are covered.

The box below presents a full and detailed lesson plan derived from the medium-term plan outlined in Table 14.2, in order to indicate the range of matters that normally are considered when planning a lesson. It employs key questions, includes a variety of appropriate activities and is clear about the outcomes expected from the lesson. It is a class-based lesson, but it includes a fieldwork activity in the school grounds as part of the lesson. Further planning information is contained in a *SuperSchemes* teaching unit (Catling, 2005d), one series of teaching resources that provide many good examples of medium-term and lesson plans (GA, 2005–7 and 2014 plus) published by the Geographical Association. Such resources are available from other geography teacher associations, such as the Australian Geography Teachers' apostrophe Association, the National Geographic Society and the National Council for Geographic Education (see the websites listed at the end of this chapter).

Lesson plan for 8–9-year-olds incorporating fieldwork in investigating accessibility to the school

What relevant children's experience is being used?

- Mapping experience
- Use and knowledge of the school grounds
- Awareness that some people, including children, have mobility problems getting around

Which aspect of the topic does the activity contribute to?

- Study of school/local mobility access
- Inclusion and social justice issues
- Extending mapping skills and use
- Focus and experience prior to local area fieldwork

What is the focus of the activity?

- Making a route access map of the school grounds

How long is the session?

- 75 minutes

What do I want the children to learn?

- To understand that access is important for everyone

- To be able to record accurately routes into and around the building and grounds on a base map

Key geographical questions

- Where is access good or problematic in the school building and grounds for someone with mobility difficulties?
- Which places can only certain people go?
- Are all publicly available spaces accessible?
- Why are some places accessible and others not?
- What solutions to access problems might be proposed?

Which resources are needed?

- Base plans of the school grounds: copy per child
- Picture map of the school grounds: copy per pair of children
- Clipboards
- Pencils
- Plain paper
- Plan of school grounds on interactive whiteboard to use for class discussions
- iPad or similar for taking photographs

What will the children do?

Introduction to the session

- Discuss what is known of the school grounds and what they are used for – e.g. playground, wild area and pond, field, etc.
- Discuss how we move around the school, which routes and entrance ways are used
- Encourage questions about whether everywhere can be accessed by everyone, including those with various mobility difficulties, and what may help or hinder accessibility (check understanding)
- Show base plan of school grounds; recap on what the plan shows; refer to it as a base plan, one that we can write on: annotate
- Explain the fieldwork activity: check routes and access around the building and grounds and record these on the base plan
- Identify and check the fieldwork activities the children will do; children in pairs; who works with whom
- Pair to mark on base plan during the fieldwork whether they consider the access is good or a problem on route ways or entrances and to note why

(Continued)

(Continued)

- Each pair to check their resources – base plan, clipboard, pencil – and ensure they have them

Pairs go out as a class but work independently in time limit of 20 minutes, with an adult on hand for help, guidance and monitoring

On return to class

- Discuss access along route ways and at entrances; compare base plans to pool information
- Remind all about the use of map key, to show routes, access points and access problems
- Pairs to use second base plan to complete a neat map showing good and poor access points in building and school grounds
- Pairs who finish before end of lesson to make notes on these questions:

  o Why do some access points and routes have good access?
  o Why do others have poor access and who do they affect?

How am I ensuring appropriate differentiation?

- Four pairs to receive teacher/teacher assistant support when checking location of parts of school on plans and to ensure annotation correct as appropriate
- Three of these pairs will use a picture map as appropriate

How did it go?

- Note how effectively the mapping task was completed
- Consider whether I needed to differentiate more carefully
- Check that all the children have a grasp of the idea of access for everyone

Source: From the medium-term plan outlined in Table 14.2.

Differentiation

A key element in short-term or lesson planning is consideration of differentiation, to create more focused and personalised learning for children. Owen and Ryan (2001) recommend three key considerations to use when planning. These are:

Practical task

Select a focus for a geography lesson that you are interested to teach. You might draw on several of the topics referred to in preceding chapters or from one of the appropriate websites. Select an age group of children with whom you wish to teach the topic. Using the guidance on the previous pages, plan a geography lesson. Alternatively, you might wish to plan geography-oriented activities for the outdoor and indoor areas of the nursery.

- different approaches and strategies to engage the differing learners in the class;
- a range and variety of resources that will appeal to the children and engage them with the work through different media;
- a variety of assessment methods to gain a more holistic sense of children's success and to identify where there might be gaps or misunderstandings to tackle.

As Pike (2016) adds, differentiation must focus on the child, considering each of them individually, in small groups and as a part of the whole class. Planning for differentiation has to be inextricably bound up with assessment, thus triangulating the whole process of teaching, planning and assessment. Halocha (1998) and Johnston *et al.* (2007) noted the need to appreciate children's prior learning and their level of understanding in order to plan successfully for their further progress.

Differentiation can be provided through a variety of approaches.

- *By differentiated task.* The class is organised into different groups, each with a task to complete. For instance, a class, working in groups, is following a local trail, with one group of children using fairly simple directional language while others have more complex challenges and resources using maps, record sheets, a compass, and so on.
- *By learning outcome.* The class carries out similar tasks with the expectation that different children finish with different results. For example, producing a leaflet on the benefits of recycling can be completed according to the capabilities of the children. This is the most common form of differentiation and can be overused or used without due care or preparation. The expectations, often through individualised success criteria for different children, must be made clear to them so that tasks are adequately challenging and inclusive.

- *By scaffolding and sequencing.* The class starts with the same set of tasks that become progressively more challenging, with the highest attaining children being expected to complete all or the majority of them. For instance, this may be a sequence of activities using photographs about an environmental issue where all children start on the same task and work through the remaining activities at their own speed, not all of them completing the tasks.
- *By adult support.* Individuals or groups of children are given adult support for particular tasks. An example is one group of children being read a story about an environmental issue or being guided and helped in undertaking fieldwork observations, which other children undertake and complete on their own.
- *By recording.* Using a variety of methods to record observations, findings, viewpoints or feelings, not only using the written word but through photographs, video, drama, blogs, graphs, and so on, guided by their teacher or self-selected.

In practice, the last two approaches may well be used alongside other approaches, so that it is rarely a matter of supporting children by a single means alone.

The need for assessment in, for and of children's geographical learning has been noted in relation to planning. It is considered in Chapter 15.

     Key points

This chapter has:

- introduced you to the idea of being a curriculum maker when planning geography for your class;
- considered long-, medium- and short-term planning of geography teaching and learning;
- provided detailed examples of planning from schemes of work to individual lesson plans, and indicated criteria to support your planning at these three levels;
- discussed progression and consistency in children's geographical learning through rigorous and well-thought-out planning;
- noted the value in making effective cross-curricular links in planning;
- noted a range of approaches to differentiation.

Moving on

At a primary school you know or visit, ask to see the plans for geography. Consider how geography is organised across the classes and the type of whole-school planning that is available to teachers. You might ask, and then consider, one or more examples of geography units of work.

Further reading

The following books provide useful overviews of and advice about planning geography teaching.

Hoodless, P, Bermingham, S, McCreery, E and Bowen, P (2009) *Teaching Humanities in Primary Schools*. Exeter: Learning Matters.

Martin, F (2006) *Teaching Geography in Primary Schools*. Cambridge: Chris Kington.

Monk, J and Silman, C (2011) *Active Learning in Primary Classrooms: A Case Study Approach*. Harlow: Pearson.

Pickford, T, Garner, W and Jackson, E (2013) *Primary Humanities: Learning through Enquiry*. London: Sage.

Pike, S (2016) *Learning Primary Geography: Ideas and inspirations from classrooms*. Abingdon: Routledge.

Scoffham, S (ed.) (2010) *Primary Geography Handbook*. Sheffield: Geographical Association.

Scoffham, S and Owens, P (2017) *Teaching Primary Geography*, London: Bloomsbury.

Issues of *Primary Geography* include discussions of planning at different levels, particularly in relation to medium- and short-term planning. The planning for lessons can often be discerned from the articles on classroom and fieldwork teaching.

Useful websites

Australian Geography Teachers' apostrophe Association (Geogspace): www.agta.org.au

Education World – Lesson Plans: www.educationworld.com/a_lesson/archives/soc_sci.shtml

Geographical Association – resources: www.geography.org.uk/Teachingresources

Geographical Association SuperSchemes: www.geography.org.uk/eyprimary/superschemes/

Geography for kids: www.kidsgeo.com/geography-for-kids

National Geographic Society: www.nationalgeographic.com

National Council for Geographic Education: www.ncge.org

Royal Geographical Society with IBG: www.rgs.org/OurWork/Schools/Teaching+resources/Key+Stage+1-2+resources/Key+Stage+1-2+resources.htm

CHAPTER 15

ASSESSING GEOGRAPHICAL LEARNING

→   **Chapter objectives**

This chapter enables you to:

- understand the value and role of assessment for and of learning in geography;
- distinguish between formal and informal assessment and formative and summative assessment;
- become aware of a benchmark framework for primary geography;
- appreciate the importance of using a variety of approaches to assessment in geography and of linking this to your planning and teaching;
- understand the purposes of questioning, feedback and feed*forward* to support children's progression in learning geography;

- appreciate the value of self- and peer assessment, and how they can help children take greater responsibility for their own learning;
- appreciate the role of success criteria and benchmarks for progression;
- understand the value of monitoring and recording children's geographical learning.

Introduction

Assessment is central to teaching and learning. As Broadfoot (1996, p. 21) states:

> *Assessment is arguably the most powerful policy tool in education. Not only can it be used to identify strengths and weaknesses of individuals, institutions and indeed whole systems of education, it can also be used as a powerful leverage to bring about change.*

A teacher might formally conclude a geography topic with a task that has been designed to elicit children's understanding of a particular local issue they have investigated and ascertain the progress they have made in their understanding. A child might seek help during a geography task if they do not fully understand what is required; she might be encouraged first to self-assess so as to resolve the problem herself, or be encouraged to ask another member of her group for support. Alternatively, she may seek and receive feedback and help from her teacher. In these cases, the teacher and the child are fully involved in the assessment process that is being used to develop the child's understanding in order to enable progression in their geographical learning. In Chapter 14 you encountered reference to assessment when planning and teaching. This chapter considers the role of assessment and a variety of the ways it can be applied in geographical learning.

What is assessment?

The importance of effective assessment cannot be overstated.

> *Assessment has a profound influence on learning. It does not just measure or find out what a student has learnt, it also affects what is learnt, how pupils view themselves as learners, their attitude to school and possibly their whole future.*

> (Pollard *et al.*, 2014, p. 352)

Harlen *et al.* (1992) noted that the term 'assessment' covers a wide range of activities, including monitoring, assessment tasks and outcomes, recording, reporting and accountability. For primary school teachers and children, this remains the focus in many parts of the world (Carr, 2001; Reynolds, 2014; Hayward and Hayward, 2016; Sherrington, 2017), and the approaches to assessment have been restated much more in terms of support for and enabling children's learning, particularly based in ongoing observations (Grigg and Hughes, 2013; Faragher, 2014). The Department for Education in England recognises the importance of assessment.

> *Assessment plays an important part in helping parents, carers and practition-ers to recognise children's progress, understand their needs, and to plan activi-ties and support. Ongoing assessment (also known as formative assessment) is an integral part of the learning and development process. It involves practition-ers observing children to understand their level of achievement, interests and learning styles, and to then shape learning experiences for each child reflect-ing those observations. In their interactions with children, practitioners should respond to their own day-to-day observations about children's progress and observations that parents and carers share.*

(DfE, 2017, p. 13)

Indeed, the emphasis on assessment for younger children has shifted towards enabling children *to know what to do next to enhance their learn-ing* (Eaude, 2011, p. 145). Eaude's argument is that children should be actively involved in considering and deciding on the next steps in their learning. This involves them in monitoring and evaluating their own and each other's learning, being clear about what they have learnt, what they have found challenging and need to work further on understanding and become more skilled at, and what they identify and discuss with their teacher as their next steps or targets for achievement. This supports the principle that *effective pedagogy needs assessment to be congruent with learning* (James and Pollard, 2012, p. 4). The point of assessment is that it helps to take children's learning forward, both the process of learning and the goals and outcomes that have been set personally, with their teacher or externally (Pickford *et al.*, 2013; Pollard *et al.*, 2014; Peacock, 2016).

Among others, two sources of assessment are vital. Teacher assessment is the source of feedback from teachers to children, while self-assessment provides feedback from children to teachers. These are used to plan, adapt and modify the direction, nature and focus of activities that children are given to do subsequently (Black and Wiliam, 1998b; Faragher, 2014; Pollard *et al.* 2014; Peacock, 2016). Assessment occurs informally or formally during lessons, across the weeks of geography teaching, at the end of topics and the year's work, and in preparation for transition between different age groups and, at times, schools. There will be continuous informal assess-ment, part of day-to-day practice, as well as periodic planned or formal assessment, including formative and summative assessments (Briggs *et al.*, 2008), used to provide understanding about a child's geographical learning, achievements and needs.

Benchmark expectations for primary geography

There are different contexts in which assessments are set. The tendency for primary children is not to set annual expectations or to give lengthy and detailed assessment tasks in most subjects, including geography. However, in England for literacy and mathematics, while there are no statutory levels to be reached annually, there do exist standards or 'expectations' which are set out in the detailed curriculum for English and mathematics, as well as in science. In these subjects children are expected to achieve the developing termly standards set for them (described as 'benchmark' expectations), although it is recognised that some children will achieve in excess of the standard while others will not yet meet them. This has led to an approach to judgements about individual children to be made on a 'rolling' basis, which is set out as three descriptors to best identify a child's performance at any time. These descriptors are being applied across all subjects to indicate how a child is progressing:

- working towards the expected standard;
- working at the expected standard;
- working at a greater depth within the expected standard.

Assessment is one aspect of the learning environment and needs to build on the nature and purpose of a subject's curriculum, where the focus and expectations are set out. Table 15.1 outlines what you should take into account when developing your approach to effective assessment. You need to begin by being clear about what you intend to achieve through your geography curriculum. This provides the basis for your expectations for the children's learning and acts as the benchmark which you can work towards in your teaching and against which you can make judgements about the children's achievements and needs. In your planning you will need to build in opportunities for assessment and feedback in which you involve the children co-operatively, using a range of approaches for assessment. Much of this will be formative, even informal, and may include end of unit summative assessments. Recording the children's outcomes enables you to build a picture of their learning, progress and needs. At the end of each year or age phase, and at the end of primary schooling, you can draw on your own and colleagues' records to provide a summative statement against your school benchmarks to show children's achievements, progress and needs.

Curriculum purpose	Expectations	Planning for assessment	Assessing	Reporting
Vision: You need to establish clearly what geography the children are expected to learn and to achieve, and an understanding of progression in geography. **Aims and content:** You should have a clear understanding of any curriculum intentions and requirements for geography, or you will need to develop your own set of intentions for geography teaching and learning. **Assessment:** You must have a clear professional understanding of assessment and how it relates to planning, teaching and identifying children's needs and achievements.	**Benchmark expectations:** You should use subject or area of learning benchmark expectations for primary geography, however these are set out, to help your planning of engaging and challenging geography content and teaching across the primary age range to providing opportunities for children to make progress.	**Building in assessment:** You should build into your geography curriculum plans opportunities for assessment. Do this by using the benchmark standard statements to inform and set expectations for children's learning and achievements. **Assessment criteria:** Create criteria for your assessments for the geography units or topics that you teach.	**Day-to-day assessment:** Share your formative outcomes for their learning in geography with the children. Use peer and self-assessment, immediate feedback and next steps for the children to undertake. **Periodic assessment:** Use formative and summative assessments to give yourself and the children a broader view of their progress in geography. Use this to help to improve your curriculum planning. Assess children below/ at/above what is expected. Create a portfolio of children's work using the expectations for a geography unit as the basis for your marking and feedback.	**Transitional assessment:** You can make these essentially summative judgements using age phase benchmark statements for geography, supported by a portfolio of work. **Reporting:** Report to colleagues who will next be teaching geography with the children in your class (and to secondary geography teachers at school transition), as well as to parents/carers.

Table 15.1   The sequence and structure for primary geography assessment (adapted from GA, 2014b)

In one example of an approach to stating expectations for geography, the Geographical Association (GA) has provided benchmarks in their geographical learning for children of 5–7, 7–11 and 11–14 years old in England. These are useful to consider. They refer to three key aspects of geography. To state them in as straightforward a way as possible, the GA identified the three key areas of geographical learning as:

- knowing contextual world knowledge of locations, places and geographical features;
- understanding the conditions, processes and interactions that explain features and distributions, patterns and changes over time and space;
- competence in geographical enquiry, the application of skills in observing, collecting, analysing, mapping and communicating geographical information.

These set the key areas for benchmarks of expectations for primary age children (GA, 2014b). The benchmarks were set out at two-year intervals: ages 5–7, 7–9 and 9–11, based on England's primary school age range.

Table 15.2 provides a framework of benchmark expectations for assessment and progression in primary geography (Catling, 2015a), drawn directly from the frameworks drafted by the GA (2014b) and the Global Learning Programme (GLP, 2014). This framework enables you to make judgements about children's achievements in their geographical learning throughout the primary school age phase.

A benchmark framework for progression and assessment		
Aspect of achievement: Contextual World Knowledge of locations, places and geographical features. **Dimension of progress:** Children demonstrate increased fluency of knowledge of the world, drawing on growing breadth and depth of contexts and content.		
By age 7 children have begun to find out about people and places locally, and to develop some sense of themselves within the wider world. They become aware of and gain basic knowledge of other places, environments and cultures. They demonstrate some basic locational knowledge about individual places and environments, especially in their local area, but also in their home country and the wider world.	**By age 9** children have developed some increased awareness and knowledge of the wider world. They have begun to develop a framework of world locational knowledge, including knowledge of places in their local area, their home country and the wider world. They know of some globally significant physical and human features.	**By age 11/12** children have developed a more detailed and extensive framework of knowledge of the world, which includes globally significant physical and human features and places in the news. They know about life in their own country and in a locality or region of another country.
Aspect of achievement: Understanding the conditions, processes and interactions that explain geographical features, distribution patterns, and changes over time and space. **Dimensions of progress:** Children extend their knowledge and understanding from the familiar and concrete to the unfamiliar and abstract; they make greater sense of the world by organising and connecting information and ideas about people, places, processes and environments; they begin to work with more complex information about the world, including the relevance of people's attitudes, values and beliefs.		
By age 7 children show their understanding by describing the places and features they investigate using simple geographical vocabulary, identifying some similarities and differences, and basic patterns in the environment.	**By age 9** children demonstrate their knowledge and understanding of their local area and the wider world. They investigate places beyond their immediate surroundings.	**By age 11/12** children understand in some detail what a number of places are like, how and why they are similar and different, and how and why they are changing.

(Continued)

Table 15.2   (Continued)

A benchmark framework for progression and assessment		
They become aware that people share the same basic needs. They begin to recognise ways in which they are connected to other people, sometimes far away. They begin to recognise changes to and understand the need to care for familiar environments.	They know about some human and physical features and patterns and how places change. They begin to explore how people and environments are connected and ways in which they might be cared for. They become more adept at comparing places, and understanding some of the reasons for similarities and differences. They know that people share the same needs, and they can give some examples of how people have improved their lives. They are aware of how they are linked with people in the wider world.	They are able to make comparisons with their own place. They know about some spatial patterns in physical and human geography, some of the conditions that influence those patterns, and some of the processes that lead to change. They show some understanding of the links between places, people and environments. They know there are patterns of wealth and poverty in the world, some examples of how people have improved their lives in different places, and why people sometimes need support. They begin to develop their understanding of people's and places' interdependence. They begin to think about how the choices people make in their everyday lives affect people and places in other parts of the world. They begin to explore how people and environments interact and how environments might be cared for or improved in the future.
Aspect of achievement: Competence in **geographical enquiry** and application of **skills** in observing, collecting, analysing and evaluating geographical information. **Dimension of progress:** Children show an increasing range and accuracy in their investigative skills, developing their ability to select and apply these with increasing independence to geographical enquiry.		
By age 7 children are able to investigate places and environments by asking and answering questions, making observations and using sources such as basic maps, atlases, globes, images and aerial photos.	**By age 9** children are able to investigate places and environments by asking and responding to geographical questions, making observations and using sources such as maps, atlases, globes, images and aerial photos. They can express their own opinions and recognise that others may think differently.	**By age 11/12** children are able to carry out investigations using a range of geographical questions, skills and sources of information including some data and a variety of maps, graphs and images, to understand places, environments and issues, and to make judgements and draw conclusions. They can express and explain their opinions and recognise why others may hold different points of view.

Table 15.2   A benchmark framework for assessment and progression in primary geography (modified from Catling, 2015, which drew with acknowledgement on GA, 2014b and GLP, 2014)

To assess children's geographical learning and development, it is antici-
pated that you would use a wide variety of timings and types of assessment
to measure children's levels of achievement, such as those indicated in
Table 15.3. These provide the focus and some effective approaches that can
be used to assess children's geographical understanding and learning.
Children's learning can be assessed against the benchmarks by using the
approaches you select as most helpful or by preparing your own tasks,
bearing in mind the purpose(s) you have in mind.

Scale/focus	Practice	Progress and standards
Short term Day-to-day	**For example:** **Assessment for learning** classroom practice – e.g. questioning, formative feedback/response, etc.	Evident in teaching and learning in children's ongoing work, responses to feedback, etc.
Frequent Basic knowledge/skills	Short test, identified piece of homework More in-depth marking	Progress check (confidence vs. concern or need) to give you a sense of children's understanding/achievement/ development
Half-/termly Conceptual Procedural Knowledge	Short-term task, problem-solving exercise, etc. Access to work at particular standards, e.g. through display Peer and self-assessment	Criterion marking and feedback linked to age phase expectations
Long term Yearly/end of age phase Substantial Conceptual Developmental	A major piece of work – e.g. enquiry, decision-making exercise, extended writing End of year/final geography unit: perhaps synoptic, drawing learning together	As above, plus an opportunity to develop portfolio of geography work exemplifying and sharing standards and illustrating progress

Table 15.3   Monitoring progress at different time scales (modified slightly from GA, 2014b)

Why assess in geography?

Formative assessment is essential for a teacher to understand how much
learning has occurred, but it needs focus and development to be effective
(Spendlove, 2009). Assessment's role is to provide feedback constructively
to children on their geographical knowledge, understanding and skills. This
should also be the case when children provide feedback to each other. To
aid learning it is vital that informative and accurate feedback occurs through
informal day-to-day assessment as part of good practice in teaching and
learning.

Assessment, as Butt (n.d.) has argued, referring specifically to geography, is vital to:

- enhance students' learning;
- measure (or possibly raise) standards;
- check teaching objectives against learning outcomes;
- recognise and plan for students' learning needs;
- place students against different descriptors of achievement;
- motivate teachers and students;
- evaluate teacher effectiveness and performance;
- help students to devise personal targets;
- help plan future learning objectives;
- discover what students know, understand and can do.

To these reasons we might add and emphasise that assessment is for children to:

- understand and evaluate their own learning;
- become more fully involved in identifying their own progress, achievements and needs;
- plan their next areas of focus for learning (linked to personal target setting);
- identify how they will recognise they have achieved their targets.

An elicitation activity, as a formative assessment, might form the starting point to initiate a geography topic. When providing their responses children might note, using a traffic lights system, their confidence in their knowledge and understanding about the topic. The teacher can use the outcomes to revise the initial planning of her geography topic, taking account not only of how she views the children's responses but involving the children's self-evaluation (Weeden and Lambert, 2006). This can help children and teachers focus on the topic and be a stimulus and motivation for geographical learning.

During a geography topic, children might be asked to identify where they consider they are mistaking or misunderstanding the ideas, content or skills they are studying (Weeden, n.d.). Common problems can be highlighted and teaching adjusted, perhaps through some group or whole-class teaching, or by providing time for children who understand the work to support those in need.

These examples of formative assessment approaches underpin the essence of Assessment for Learning (AfL). *Assessment for learning is fundamental to the development of independent learners [.] (and) encourages pupils to take ownership of their learning* (AAIA, n.d.). One of the most influential publications espousing AfL was Black and Wiliam's seminal series of pamphlets, *Inside the Black Box* (Black and Wiliam, 1998a, 1998b, 2003). AfL has developed significantly since then and has been interpreted and used in many ways. The use of AfL in some schools has been

In the classroom

Using a starter activity as formative assessment to adjust geography planning

To initiate the study of a locality in Brazil, a teacher gave each of six groups of her 7–8-year-old children a large cut-out letter from the word BRAZIL. She asked the groups to write or draw what they knew about Brazil. This was a 20-minute activity, which she followed up by asking the children to list questions that they wanted to ask in their enquiry. After the lesson she reviewed the children's ideas about Brazil and examined the questions they had listed. From this first activity, she became aware of misconceptions, misunderstandings and misinformation she felt needed to be addressed. She adjusted her plan to engage the children in identifying some core information about Brazil before returning to the questions, which she then wanted the children to reconsider and revise, group and organise into priorities for their enquiry.

questioned by the original authors, feeling that the term 'assessment' has been misunderstood and misappropriated by many who think that it is all about testing and grading. Wiliam (2012) has written that a key error was to say that such activities were 'assessment'. His view is that when the term 'assessment' is used it is interpreted as about tests and examinations, when AfL, he contends, is about improving the quality of teaching.

At the heart of AfL lies the principle that all children are able to improve their learning, supported by the following core features (Johnston *et al.*, 2007; Keynon, 2010; Eaude, 2011; Wiliam, 2012; Barnes, 2015; Armitage, 2017).

- Learning intentions are explicit, clearly stated and shared with children.
- Children understand and appreciate the targets, expectations and standards they are aiming for.
- Feedback identifies clearly for children what they need to do to improve.
- Supported by their teacher, children evaluate their performance and develop their self- and peer-assessment skills, using the feedback from their teachers to help them to feedforward and think about next steps in their learning.
- Children can peer tutor and help each other, acting as mutual resources for each other in the feedforward process, thus taking some ownership of their learning.
- Children can judge their progress and know when they have succeeded.

Reflective task

Why is it important for both teachers and children to be involved in assessment for geographical learning? Can you think of an example of when this has helped a child to make significant progress? Why might that have been the case?

Approaches to assessing geographical learning

A number of approaches can be used in AfL to support and develop children's learning. Four are considered here, while others might include the following (Briggs *et al.*, 2008; Spendlove, 2009; Barnes, 2015):

- observation and listening;
- concept mapping;
- labelling;
- quizzes;
- undertaking a performance;
- making a presentation;
- critically reviewing a website;
- creating a series of tweets or using other social media or digital sources;
- a P4C discussion;
- an issue-based debate;
- a written and illustrated text;
- testing.

Many of these can be linked with each other to provide insights into learning within a geography topic. They are not mutually exclusive but can be enabling and supportive in understanding and appreciating children's learning.

Sharing learning intentions

The value in sharing the purpose of what children will be learning in a geography topic or lesson is to focus their interest during their studies, for them to be aware of the learning goals and to motivate them. This is not to share the plan of activities for the topic or lesson, but to help children understand the expectations and progress they are being challenged to achieve. It is about involving the children in their own learning, ensuring that they participate in their own development and progression. To support the children, it is important to let them know the success criteria for the work, so that at the end of a geography lesson or project, for example, they can see whether they have achieved the learning intention set. It is also important for children to be told how the purpose of the lesson relates to the subject they are doing (Clarke, 2001), affording it meaning and relevance.

In the classroom

Initiating a local study lesson

The focus for a class of 5–6-year-olds' geography lesson was on the children's awareness of their local area. The teacher's intention was to draw out from the children what their knowledge and views were about their neighbourhood. She saw this as the basis for children sharing their knowledge and opinions and for widening their awareness of the vicinity of the school.

On the whiteboard she shared the following with the children.

Learning intention: We are going to find out what we know about our neighbourhood, and we are going to say what we think about it.

Success criteria: We listed different features or places we know and have written a sentence saying why we like or do not like them.

She also said to the children that knowing about and sharing our knowledge of features and places in the neighbourhood helped in understanding what places are like, as part of geography.

Effective questioning

At the core of the enquiry process in geography is questioning, not least children's capacity to generate a variety of questions that provide an effective and invigorating focus for their investigations. Questioning is an equally vital aspect of assessment, whether the informal questions asked of children about the particular work they are engaged in or in the context of a summative assessment activity. Questioning and discussion inform teachers about children's knowledge, understanding, skill use and values. They can expose misconceptions and misunderstandings. Children can use questions of each other as well as their teacher to find out information, to see who can help them, and in relation to peer assessment.

While questioning can inform us about children's knowledge, it can also be used to probe the thinking underpinning that understanding. Children can be asked to give examples or explain the meaning of particular geographical terms. The wording of questions is important and open questions tend to be far more revealing and informative than closed questions. Closed questions might be those concerned directly with particular information, such as 'What is the capital of India?' but they may also seek knowledge of a particular system, for instance 'What are the main elements of the water cycle?' The question, 'Is there equal access to clean, safe drinking water in the world?' will lead to a straightforward 'No'. This question might be rephrased as an open question, in the form of, 'Why is there not equal access to clean and safe drinking water in the world?', where the given situation is the basis for the question, not the question itself. Such an open question should lead to discussion about a range of possible reasons, some of the issues involved and avenues to explore further. Levels of questions can be used and related to Bloom's Taxonomy and the concept of higher order questioning. In this context, children are encouraged not just to apply their knowledge but to analyse and synthesise it as they apply it thoughtfully and creatively to new situations and contexts through teachers' use of increasingly probing questions (Bloom *et al.*, 1956; Pike, 2016).

Focus on open-ended questioning

Questioning offers many opportunities. It is important to be clear about the reasons for questioning. Too often questions are asked of the same sort, only to particular children, using too demanding language, without providing children with time to think and without building on their response (Brown and Wragg, 1993). During a lesson a teacher will use a variety of questions, some of which will seek information and be closed, while others encourage thinking and probing, seeking to engage children in understanding their own developing knowledge and insights. Such open questions might take the following forms, which could all be applied to geographical contexts.

- How can we be sure that (local people do not want housing on the wasteland)?
- What is the same and what is different (between our neighbourhood and the district of the nearest city that we investigated)?
- Why is it sometimes/always true/false that (people move from the country to the city to find work)?
- How do you know (what children would most like to change in the playground)?
- How would you explain (the amount of litter we found on the beach)?
- What does that tell us about (how and where we use energy in school)?

- What is right/wrong with (saying that fair trade is always a good thing)?
- What reasons can you give for (people parking where they should not)?
- Why did you (choose the questions about access to water that you did)?
- How might you (find out what people would like to see replace the empty shop)?
- Why have you proposed that (the pedestrian area needs to be less cluttered for people with mobility difficulties)?
- Why do you think (it will be better if the shanty town is rebuilt)?

While closed questions usually seek succinct responses and may not be followed up, open questions require children to think before replying and may usefully be discussed with others first. An effective approach for facilitating this is through discussion or dialogue partners (Clarke, 2005a; Alexander, 2008; Phillipson and Wegerif, 2017) where children are encouraged to talk about the question and their response with their neighbour so that the response does not always have to be shared with a whole class. It is important to allow time for open-ended questions to be replied to. They may also have more than one type of response, so children need to listen to each other's answers, which may lead to discussion, with links to P4C-type sharing of different perspectives and views. Questioning is an important teaching strategy, while also providing assessment information. Weeden (n.d.) has suggested that it might be used in the following ways.

- *Discussion partners*: Pairs of children discuss the answer to a question and give feedback to the rest of the class.
- *Snowballing*: Groups of children explain their answers to each other and then to other groups.
- *Explaining*:The emphasis for explaining answers is encouraged by asking prompt questions such as 'Why?', 'Tell me more' [.] 'Go on'.
- *Phone a friend*: Children nominate someone to help them answer a question.

A dialogic approach

Phillipson and Wegerif (2017) argue that a dialogic approach to learning fosters questioning and reasoning and enables children to construct knowledge and understanding. We might add that it helps them to clarify and justify their views and values. Drawing on P4C approaches they identify four elements in their approach.

- *Caring dialogue for thinking* – for example, listening, showing sensitivity, taking others' views seriously and only talking one at a time.
- *Collaborative dialogue for thinking*, such as a willingness to participate, responding to what is said, accepting others' perspectives, helping others express themselves, and seeking agreement.

- *Critical dialogue for thinking*, including questioning, seeking clarification, identifying manageable elements of problems, seeking or giving evidence or reasons, noting differences and similarities, testing ideas, coming to conclusions, and reconsidering personal perspectives and opinions.
- *Creative dialogue for thinking* – for instance, offering hypotheses, proposing alternative ideas, finding good examples and making helpful comparisons, and connecting ideas.

Their concern is to ensure more rigorous and clearer thinking, which comes in questioning through dialogic engagement (Alexander, 2008). This is evidently a useful approach to teaching and helping children learn, but it is also a valuable way through which children can help their partner(s) think through what they wish to express and to enable them to see to what extent and in which ways they know and understand the learning they are engaged in. In other words, questioning dialogue provides formative assessment and feedback in an informal setting, which in itself helps develop children's learning. In geographical teaching and learning such conversations might explore aspects of knowledge such as what the children know about the flow of rivers, a local traffic concern or information an atlas shows about another country. Children might question, discuss and debate resolutions to the traffic concern, their views about buying locally produced foodstuffs and nationally manufactured goods rather than from further afield, or how another place they have studied is similar to and different from their own locality or country.

 Practical task

It is helpful to have in mind a number of open and probing questions to use during a lesson. Use a geography lesson you have taught or the one outlined in the box on pp. 450–2 in Chapter 14. Devise a number of open questions that you might use to help probe and encourage children's thinking about the topic.

Marking work and providing feedback and feed*forward*

It is essential when giving feedback on children's work to make it relevant and directly related to the learning intention and specific assessment criteria. For instance, when assessing a child's ability to locate a point on a map using four-figure grid references, their skill in giving the correct references is the focus. If an intention is met, feedback should celebrate this; if it is not met, it should show

how the child could meet it. Feedback should be used to scaffold children's learning and help them use their knowledge and skills to develop their own conclusions and solutions. This will encourage them to work through problems and situations on their own or with peers, and to become more self-reliant and responsible for their own learning and progression. Feedback can be written on the work and, thus, marked, but it is discussion of their assessment with individual children that is more effective and enduring than written feedback. Such dialogue encourages children to be more confident in asking questions to aid their own learning and seeking progress (Owen and Ryan, 2001; Johnston *et al.*, 2007; Eaude, 2011). The purpose of feedback is to help children identify their strengths and areas to develop by setting future targets. This approach moves the feedback into feeding *forwards* for the next learning steps.

Feeding back reflects on the work that has been done by the child. Consequent feeding *forward* looks ahead to the next piece of work and gives constructive guidance on how to develop any gaps, needs or ways of working identified and consider ways in which the work can be improved. Combining both feedback and feed*forward* helps a child to reflect on their work and understand for themselves what it is that they need to do in order to improve and progress. In this context the child as well as the teacher is involved in their learning and able to contribute to their own development. This empowers the child and allows them to take greater responsibility for their own learning, a useful skill to take through their education.

Marking provides a record for the child to refer to. It should provide positive and rewarding comments on the work and the child's attainment (feedback) and build in guidance by stating specific targets and actions for improvement (feed*forward*). When giving feedback about a piece of work in geography, you need to ensure that it is subject and topic specific, although you might comment on the quality of the language, graphics or other form of presentation where this is pertinent to effective communication of the geographical information and understanding. The geographical focus is vital for children to identify and recognise clearly their achievements in geography and to give them targets for what to do to progress further.

In the classroom

Providing feedback and feed*forward*

Talking to 10-year-old Lucy about her summary of the problems associated with the lack of ready access to water for many people, her teacher commented that 'You have explained very clearly several of the causes

(Continued)

(Continued)

and impacts of the lack of water access. You have given examples of ways to tackle these. Can you think of other situations where people are faced with similar problems in daily life that they have to deal with and how these affect them? You have used geographical vocabulary well, included the sources you used and presented your work attractively. Think about how you can use what you know and add to this in your next geography topic.'

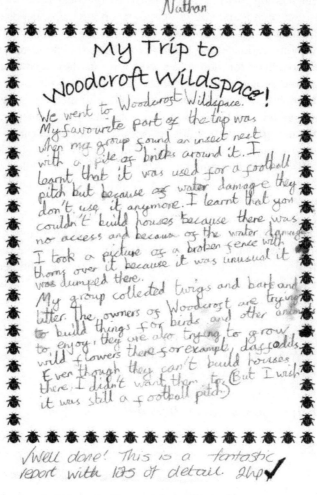

Figure 15.1 A marked piece of written work from a 9-year-old

Reflective task

Look at the extract in Figure 15.1 from a 9-year-old child's report on findings from fieldwork related to a local development issue. It includes references relevant to geography and science. Consider whether the comments by the teacher at the bottom are specific enough to highlight the geographical learning. How might the feedback be written to reflect more clearly the child's geographical learning? Try to assess formatively so that the child knows what they should do in order to move on. How can you feed*forward*, not only feedback?

Self- and peer assessment

Self-assessment involves children understanding the learning intentions and realising what they need to do to achieve them. It is best introduced to children with the support of their teacher (Image 15.1). When practised, setting their own targets from feedback and feed*forward* in this way can be a highly effective form of assessment and enable children to be much more involved in their own learning (Kelly, 2007; Grigg and Hughes, 2013). Children who carry out self-assessment become more reflective and realistic about their work, gaining the confidence to admit when they do not understand something and seeking help to address this, either from their teacher or increasingly, as they get better at it, their peers or in using resources themselves. They begin to recognise possible gaps and weaknesses, and consider effective means to address these (Clarke, 2005b).

For the youngest children, self-assessment is likely to be best fostered where they use a simple symbol, such as smiley or frowning faces, to indicate where they feel they have done well or think they need more help. For older children, it can be appropriate to invite them to discuss what they feel they have learnt in a one-to-one teacher and child conference, and encourage them to identify which areas could be strengthened and how.

A further approach to use, perhaps at the end of a geography topic, is a summative self-assessment approach in which the child responds to 'I can [.]' statements that include not just the skills and knowledge acquired but also the understanding of the key geographical ideas learnt about. Where the children are not able to provide any or accurate responses, these can be noted as targets for subsequent work. The example in Table 15.4 below links self-assessment to attainment expectations, using the idea of working below/ at/beyond the expected standard noted earlier.

Image 15.1   Children assessing their own work with the support of their teacher
(*source:* J Halocha)

Other ways to support children's self-assessment include adapting the approaches mentioned above. You can also use the following two approaches.

- Encourage children to look through a piece of their own work and indicate how specific statements or observations could be improved by annotating it with improvement comments. This can then feed into further work.
- Take photographs of children working and encourage them to annotate the photographs with comments about what they were learning, what they understood at that time and what they have learnt since then. They can then consider how to take their learning on to the next stage.

Peer assessment, through discussion between children, encourages them to recognise the learning intentions and the reason why they are learning. This approach clarifies their understanding and helps them to analyse, evaluate and assess the work of their classmates. Children who are well-practised discussion partners are able to peer assess more readily and more effectively because they have learnt the benefit of dialogue with their peers.

Peer assessment is most supportive when children are not sure whose work it is that they are commenting on, but, if this is not possible, it is wise to ensure that they mark different children's work each time, avoiding the

Should you go to St Lucia	Working towards the expected standard	Working at the expected standard	Working at greater depth within the expected standard
Describe the physical and human features of the island country of St Lucia	I can recognise and describe some features of St Lucia and tell the difference between human and physical features.	I can show a good understanding of the main physical and human features of St Lucia and know how they are different.	I can show a good understanding about the differences between physical and human features in St Lucia, and I can give reasons for some of them.
Analyse evidence and draw conclusions about whether to visit St Lucia	I can use some evidence that I have collected to give reasons why people visit St Lucia.	I can use the evidence that I have collected to give a variety of different reasons for and against visiting St Lucia.	I can use evidence I have collected to give several reasons for and against visiting St Lucia. I can explain the reasons why I believe that people should or should not visit St Lucia and why I might or might not go.
Understand the difference between sustainable and unsustainable tourism and how it affects people, places and environments	I can give some examples of how people are affecting and trying to look after the environment of St Lucia.	I understand a number of ways in which tourism can damage the environment in St Lucia. I can describe some ways used to care for and improve the island's environment.	I understand the difference between sustainable and unsustainable tourism. I can give some examples of how and why St Lucia is trying to be more sustainable and the difficulties that they have in doing so. I understand why it is important to have sustainable tourism to bring benefits to the people and environment of St Lucia.

Table 15.4 Self-assessment criteria for a place study by 8–9-year-olds (adapted from Owens, 2008b)

temptation to be competitive. An approach such as giving 'two stars and a wish' (two areas where the assessed child has done particularly well and an area for development) can be an effective and accessible one. They should relate the work to the success criteria for that geography assessment and comment on how the child has done. Peer assessment provides opportunities to engage children in discussion about success and future learning intentions. It involves children actively in each other's learning. Peer assessment has been shown to have a positive impact on the children's geographical learning and understanding as well as their collaborative and social skills.

In the classroom

Peer geography assessment

In one school, pupils assessed each other's work against clear descriptions of levels and grades. This helped them to understand the quality of their own work better; good diagnostic marking also contributed to this. Pupils recorded their results on a progress chart and indicated with an arrow whether they had improved, remained the same or fallen. They also noted specific targets. All pupils were very clear about the process and how to achieve their geography focused targets.

(Ofsted, 2008a, p. 23)

Linking teaching and assessment

One way to ensure assessment opportunities during the teaching of a geography topic is to plan activities into your teaching that provide insight into children's understanding as well as being stimulating learning tasks. A number of the activities mentioned in earlier chapters can be used in this way. Table 15.5 provides further examples of activities that serve both learning and assessment roles and can be adapted for different age groups. This is not to say that assessment of geographical learning is easy, as Ofsted have noted in England:

> *There can be a tendency in primary schools to focus on geographical vocabulary and skills such as map work, particularly because the outcomes are easier to identify. Geographical understanding is harder to measure and assessment therefore remains underdeveloped. As a result, the analysis of achievement and attainment does not always present a sufficiently accurate picture of what pupils have learnt.*

(Ofsted, 2008a, p.13)

There are several considerations that can help you move beyond a focus on more easily measurable skills and knowledge to support planning for assessment to ensure that it is meaningful and engaging (Owen and Ryan, 2001, p. 145). To be able to include good assessments in our teaching we need to be clear about:

- which aspects of geography are to be assessed: knowledge, understanding and/or skills;
- our criteria for assessing the geography we are focusing on;

- suitable activities and questions that allow children to show what they know and understand or can do;
- providing attainable learning intentions and tasks, appropriate for the children, so that they have opportunities to show what they can do and to succeed;
- how we will monitor and record the evidence of children's learning;
- some sense of the types of responses expected from the children, to be able to match and judge their outputs against;
- ways in which the assessment outcomes are to be recorded and used.

Geographical focus	Teaching and assessment context
Sort 4–8 photographs into sets to show likes and dislikes related to a locality or environmental matter.	To be able to give and explain criteria for their decisions about what they see.
Make a postcard to show what a particular place or site is like.	To use information to create an appropriate image or view of a place studied or self-chosen.
Write a story that is based on a map, either provided or self-made, of a place where the action occurs.	To be able to use a mapped environment, demonstrating the use of map skills and understanding of activities.
Create a map or mapped trail to show the way around the classroom, school or neighbourhood.	To select features and use mapping skills (at various levels) to communicate a route effectively.
Select maps, atlases and globes to use in different contexts – e.g. visiting a new town, showing visitors round the school, or showing the location of asked for global features.	To be able to identify, select and justify the appropriate resource for a range of activities and people's needs.
Write and illustrate a report on a topical item in the news about an event to show how it has a geographical dimension.	To identify and explain the aspects of geography that appear in or underpin an event.
Find out information about a particular country or physical features such as mountains and rivers.	To use a variety of sources and resources to gather and select relevant information, sort it and demonstrate factual knowledge of the topic.
Prepare a personal or class glossary of geographical terms built up during a unit – e.g. lake, canal, watermill, in a 'Rivers' topic.	To show understanding and ability to explain accurately key geographical words and phrases.
Use role play to explore the issues concerning development in a particular locality by taking on a character's role and arguing a case in a 'public debate'.	To develop and demonstrate knowledge and understanding of a local issue, to be able to take account of different arguments and to argue persuasively.
Make a short radio or video programme about a particular environmental issue.	To organise and communicate to an audience what has been learnt, including information, explanation and a personal viewpoint.

Table 15.5   Examples of geographical activities enabling teaching and assessment

Reflective task

Go through the previous chapters, particularly Chapters 5–13, and identify 8–10 activities that could provide both teaching and assessment opportunities. Note the activities, which aspect of learning they might support, and how they may be assessed using approaches such as those shown in Table 15.5.

Mastery and learning at greater depth

There has been a steady development in approaches to assessment, following recognition that inflexible linear attainment of content approaches can be inhibiting of and undermine confidence in children's learning. This has led to consideration of alternative assessment strategies, a number of which have been noted in this chapter. One of the criticisms of a structured and multi-stepped ladder of grades or levels of attainment approach has been that such steps have tended to discourage children's progress to greater depth in their learning; rather, this 'attainment' approach has tended simply to move children from one set of content to the next (Davies, n.d.), since essentially it is based on a sequenced content list.

An approach that has been recognised as helping children to make significant progress in their learning has been the concept of 'Mastery' in learning (Drury, 2015). This has been developed particularly in mathematics teaching and learning in Singapore and China. Mastery learning describes how successfully a child can use and apply their learning to different contexts and problems with increasing depth of understanding and application. Mastery is not only about knowing facts (content information), but is about using such knowledge in increasingly complex contexts (application). Davies (n.d.) explains that the pedagogy succeeds based on the argument that all learners will, with adequate effort, be able to reach the stated expectations. Key to this is excellent teaching based on formative assessment, in particular effective questioning and knowing each individual child's possible learning gaps and how to help them address these. The idea of Mastery is not an end-point but a process that leads children to work at 'even greater depth', to ensure that the learning endures, and that each child is able to recall and apply it to different circumstances and build on it further.

Davies (n.d.) identifies four levels of learning, in which 'shallow learning' can be developed through Mastery learning to 'working at greater depth'. In relation to benchmark expectations for geography, the Mastery approach can be applied with children at all stages in their learning. It can be related to the expected levels of working noted earlier in this chapter. The levels of learning and links with expectations are outlined in Table 15.6. Children developing Mastery can be assessed on their ability to demonstrate the characteristics of Mastery learning and for some, how they go on to show greater depth in understanding, as indicated in Table 15.7.

State of learning	Description	Expectations of working
Shallow learning	Surface learning, temporary, often lost	Working towards the expectation standard
Meeting expectations	With support, being able to meet the objectives of the curriculum	Working at the expected standard
Mastery	Obtaining a greater level of understanding and being able to apply learning in a different context	Working at a greater depth within the expected standard
Working at greater depth	Learning can be transferred and applied in different contexts and children can explain their understanding to others	

Table 15.6   Mastery and greater depth (developed from Davies, n.d.)

Characteristics of Mastery learning	Description
Independence	Apply the skill or knowledge without recourse to the teacher
Fluency	Apply the skill and knowledge with a high level of confidence and show good resilience when the task seems demanding
Application	Apply the skill and knowledge to a range of different contexts, including other areas of the curriculum
Consistency	Consistently use skills, knowledge and understanding
Synthesise	Organise ideas to make connections with other areas of learning and with new areas
Revisit	Return to the aspect of learning after a break and still feel confident that able to work on the knowledge and skill without difficulty
Explain it	Be able to explain to others their understanding, and perhaps be a learning buddy to others

Table 15.7   The characteristics of Mastery and greater depth (Davies, n.d.)

Practical task

Consider a geography topic – for example, a river or settlement study, or some other focus that you are studying with the children currently. Use the descriptors and characteristics in Table 15.7 when you assess your children's success in their geography learning and expectations at the end of the topic. Think about next steps for the children and how this will help you to plan for further work.

Like all effective teaching, Mastery requires understanding and careful planning and assessment in order to be used to best advantage. The Education Endowment Fund (EEF, n.d.) have found it to be particularly effective when children work together in groups and take responsibility for their own and each other's learning, a common approach when teaching geography. It has been found to be particularly effective with lower achieving children, and has been successful in narrowing the gap between them and the highest achievers. Evidence suggests that it is an approach best used for specific pieces of work – a new and challenging concept perhaps, or a complex enquiry – which makes it relevant and appropriate for an interactive, participatory subject such as geography.

Recording and reporting geographical learning

There should be a record of children's work and achievement in geography. Such a record should show children's progress in geography as they move through their early years and primary schooling. It should contain brief written comments, which might refer to particular learning, interests and/or misconceptions, and the achievements related to the geography benchmark expectations. These might be recorded at the end of each geography topic or at the end of the year. Brief, ongoing marking records such as that shown for five children in Table 15.8 can also be a helpful method for noting and monitoring progress, which helps inform your planning for those children. The key indicates the meaning of the shapes and letters, which provide alternative recording methods to use.

Records of learning provide information to be passed to the next teacher and across year groups and at transfer from primary to secondary school. They also enable reporting to parents. Reports should focus on the positive outcomes of children's geographical learning, particularly highlighting achievements in geography, and should indicate areas for development that should be picked up in later geography topics. Learning targets that have

Learning target	Child	Child	Child	Child	Child
	AB	CD	EF	GH	IJ
Can use accurately a 4-figure grid to locate a symbol on a map	/	∧	/	Δ	Δ
Knows the names of the 7 world's continents and where they are located	r	a	r	g	g
Understands and gives reasons why parking is allowed in some places locally but not others	E	D	E	S	S

Key: Geographical learning which is:
    Emerging /, r (red), E
    Developing ∧, a (amber), D
    Secure Δ, g (green), S					

Table 15.8 Alternative coding for use to record a range of assessment descriptors for five children

been agreed by the child and teacher might identify areas for development. An additional record perhaps should be the child's self-evaluation of her/ his geographical learning, completed at the end of each topic or the year.

Developing records of a child's achievement can be used to provide a summative account of that child's geographical learning across the year and the years. Summative assessment is quite often used as a 'one-off' approach providing a snapshot of a child's achievement at a particular point. The record is not infrequently closed, and what the child has achieved and needs support in remain simply 'on the record'. What summative assessment needs to provide is helpful feedback for the child about their learning and their next steps for development, so that it is enabling of their progress. It should be used by teachers to help their planning, but tends to be undertaken more for accountability.

A valuable way forward is to develop a cumulative geography record for each child, which is added to year to year, following them through school and passed on with them. With accompanying formative feedback it can helpfully guide the child in their next steps alongside self-assessment, becoming an effective assessment instrument. Taking a formative approach to appraising and recording children's geographical learning, which involves the children and takes account of both their and their teacher's understanding of what has been achieved and needs to happen next, provides a more rounded picture of the child's learning as well as insights into their particular geographical interests and their sense of what they can build on and need to revisit. This can be fruitful passed year to year from one teacher to the next and then passed to the secondary school geography staff, as a cumulative record. It is personal and enabling. Where the child is involved in creating their continuous record, they are more likely to be motivated and pursue their own development. Indeed, their personal cumulative geography record might be 'owned' by each child.

Practical task

Ask in school about the records that are kept for geography. What is the school policy? How are they informed by the geography expectations for each year and overall? Who keeps them? When and how are they used? Are they reviewed and revised regularly?

Key points

This chapter has:

- explained the purpose, role and types of assessment in geography;
- outlined practices associated with assessment for learning and detailed a number of different methods for implementing it;
- provided an outline of a benchmark approach, and identified a framework for assessment and progression in primary geography;
- stressed the importance of including assessment opportunities in planning for children's geographical learning and indicated ways in which this might be done;
- explained the role of self- and peer assessment and recommended ways to implement and develop them;
- considered the importance of feedback and feeding forward in helping children identify their own future learning and progression;
- introduced the 'Mastery' and 'even greater depth' approach in relation to children's geographical learning and progression;
- noted that children's geographical learning and achievements should be recorded, passed from teacher to teacher, and be available to children and parents.

Moving on

When you next plan a geography lesson or topic, consider carefully your core learning intentions and expectations so that you are able to state clearly the criteria against which to assess the children's learning. Be able to phrase these so that the children can understand and use them for self-assessment, as 'child- friendly success criteria', enabling them to understand their learning targets.

Further reading

The following publications provide further insight into assessment practices in early years and primary geography.

Hoodless, P, Bermingham, S, McCreery, E and Bowen, P (2009) *Teaching Humanities in Primary Schools*. Exeter: Learning Matters.

Martin, F (2006) *Teaching Geography in Primary Schools*. Cambridge: Chris Kington.

Pike, S (2016) *Learning Primary Geography: Ideas and inspirations from classrooms*. Abingdon: Routledge.

Scoffham, S (ed.) (2010) *Primary Geography Handbook*. Sheffield: Geographical Association.

Useful websites

Association for Achievement and Improvement through Assessment: www.aaia.org.uk/afl/

Australian Geography Teachers' Association (Geogspace): www.agta.org.au

Education Endowment Foundation (EEF): https://educationendowmentfoundation.org.uk/school-themes/feedback-monitoring-pupil-progress/

Geographical Association: Assessment Benchmarks: www.geography.org.uk/news/2014nationalcurriculum/assessment/#top

National Geographic Society: www.nationalgeographic.com

National Council for Geographic Education: www.ncge.org

Staffordshire Learning Net Geography: www.sln.org.uk/geography/afl.htm

CHAPTER 16

DEVELOPING LEARNING IN PRIMARY GEOGRAPHY EDUCATION

 Chapter objectives

This chapter enables you to:

- become aware of the value of developing children's geographical understanding;
- consider children's geographical outcomes by the end of primary school;
- encounter one approach to sequencing geography across primary schooling;
- be aware of the possibilities for research in primary geography;
- identify several ways in which you can investigate children's geographical learning in your classroom.

Introduction

This chapter begins by emphasising the significance of developing children's geographical understanding during their early years and primary schooling. It sets out expectations for the outcomes of primary geography education and outlines a suggested sequence for geography through the primary years. As a primary teacher you are expected to review and develop your practice. One approach to this is to consider how you might investigate what happens in your classroom to learn more about your geography teaching and the geographical understanding and learning of the children you teach. We conclude by restating the inherent nature of geography in all our lives and its importance in young children's education.

Developing primary children's geography

The emphasis in this book has been that the basis for geography in the primary curriculum must build on children's everyday geographies, and that their geographies are not confined to the local or familiar but have many national and global connections. The role of geography teaching is to enable children to develop their understanding so that they may deepen and extend their geographical knowledge, values and skills. This involves helping children consider and understand their personal geographies, alongside providing for them experiences and insights into areas of geographical study beyond their direct experience. Here we summarise the basis for teaching geography through five elements in geographical learning: the five geographical Es: exploring, engraving, embedding, enabling and engaging geographical learning and understanding (Catling, 2001a) and refer to the notion of being a *geocitizen*.

Exploring geographically

Children's desire to explore the world is intense. As outlined in Chapter 3, children are very curious but their experience initially is episodic in their home and local world, and through their family, friends and peer group, stories and the media with the wider world. Through this experience they construct an informed though partial awareness of places, the wider environment and environmental concerns. Their understanding gains increasing coherence as they mature. Children bring to their earliest years and into school an excitement about their experiences, which must be drawn upon to extend their knowledge and understanding of the world. They bring growing skills in observing and noticing, in enacting what they have seen about them through play, in their making sense of their images and perceptions, and through their evolving appreciation and understanding of the world. This experience supports children's geographical learning in pre-school and across their schooling, enabling them to become increasingly better informed and more insightful about their local and the wider world. Essential in this development is that children from the earliest age and throughout their primary schooling explore and investigate the school grounds, the local area and the wider world through first-hand and indirect experience and sources.

Engraving geographical learning

Children's exploration – their active learning about the world, about people, places and environmental matters – engraves their awareness, knowledge, understanding and appreciation of their world into their self-identity and affects their sense of themselves. Children's learning and self-esteem can be constrained by the limitations of their experience and by the inconsistency, partiality and stereotyping that they encounter as they learn, circumstances that cannot go unchallenged. A teacher's responsibility is to ensure that children not only become well informed about the world around them, but also reflect critically on their understanding. In developing children's place and environmental knowledge and understanding, and in tackling misunderstandings and prejudices about their own and the wider world, geography very clearly matters.

Embedding geographical perspectives and understanding

Teaching geography involves embedding for children awareness and, gradually, a range of skills, understandings and values, to develop their capacity for critical reflection on their perceptions, knowledge and ideas about places and environmental matters. Essential to this development is children's involvement in geographical enquiry, built around questions, interests and problems, encompassing description, analysis, evaluation and clarification of their own viewpoints, alongside their awareness and understanding of those of others. The process of embedding learning necessarily involves challenging children to explain what they have found and to justify their conclusions, to have considered the different perspectives in problems and debates, particularly where controversy and preferences are involved. Developing competence in undertaking enquiries fosters an ingrained inquisitiveness alongside a healthy criticality, where the limits of their geographical awareness, understanding and speculation are recognised by themselves and personal perspectives are developed with due thought. Vital in this embedding of geographical learning for early years and primary age children is constant and consistent use of geographical concepts and vocabulary in their studies. This enables children to investigate further and communicate their understanding of how and why places and environments have developed to be as they are. It helps them begin to realise and appreciate what might happen or develop next, consider alternative possible, preferable and probable futures, and reflect on how such decisions might be made and their impact on a sustainable future. Through these experiences children examine values and attitudes, their own as well as those of others. This learning combines to enable them to think geographically.

Enabling the use of geographical skills

Growing competence in using a variety of geographical skills lies at the heart of enabling children to undertake useful and informative enquiries about places and environmental matters. Literacy, oracy and numeracy skills provide access to much core information and data about the world, particularly beyond direct personal experience. Children need to be introduced to and develop their capability in using graphicacy skills, a wide range of paper and digital maps, pictures, artefacts, and equipment to investigate the real environment and secondary sources about the world. For young children, learning outdoors through fieldwork is an essential source and inspiration for geographical learning. Based in children's fascination in exploring outside and absorbing primary and secondary sources about the world, geography's skills in observation and investigation, and their growing knowledge and understanding for responding to and valuing places, landscapes and people's lives, provide access to the realities of the world. Primary children begin to understand and appreciate geography's 'big ideas' or key concepts and develop their own values and attitudes through being enabled by using the subject's skills and resources.

Engaging in geographical commitment

Emerging through their developing experience, understanding, capability and values, children construct a 'geographical citizenship'. Such a citizenship enables children to learn to take responsibility personally and alongside others locally, and in and for the global community. Through engaging in their learning about the world, its places, peoples and environments, and in becoming increasingly aware of their personal perceptions, knowledge, images, values and ideas about how they would like the world to be, children develop and clarify their personal ethic about their world, as *geociti-zens*. By considering place and environmental issues, problems and matters in inequality, they develop and extend their sense of social justice. It is the children of the present who will carry the responsibility for the future of their communities, country and the world as their generation matures.

They will pass this responsibility to their children in time. They recognise this. Fundamentally, then, primary teachers must ensure that younger children begin to understand and take on board the values inherent in environmental sustainability, to do with the equitable distribution and use of resources and social justice in access to a good quality of life peaceably across the world for everyone. Engagement with the local and global community necessarily requires that through their geographical education, primary children develop their analytic perspectives and become clearer about their personal values for their community and the wider world. This is contentious (Standish, 2009, 2012), since it involves fostering in younger children the values of care for and improvement of the world, its people, places and environments. It involves thinking and acting geographically and responsibly. Such geographical engagement moves beyond explanation to involvement; it requires commitment alongside study and it shifts from evaluation to action (Hart, 1997; Palmer and Birch, 2004).

Taking primary geography forward

The inclusion of geography as a named subject in some nations' curricula – for example, in England – and as a subject within social studies curricula in other countries, as in Singapore and the USA, enables opportunities to develop and enhance younger children's geographical learning, building on their implicit personal geographies. Geography curriculum requirements are set out normally as the content to be covered during primary schooling, and aspects of geography may be included in the curricula for pre-school and early years children, although the subject is rarely mentioned by name but is implicit if looked for. In whichever context and format, and however directly or indirectly it is stated, the inclusion of geography content provides an evident basis for planning for progression across the primary years and for understanding and appreciating what is to be provided in geography topics and learning activities. This has been referred to in Chapters 14 and 15 and indicated in earlier chapters, such as about enquiry, fieldwork and mapping skills in Chapters 4 and 9. Such a focus supports children's geographical learning and development and employs approaches like the use of benchmarks to elucidate what children might learn in and about the subject. It enables consideration of what the outcomes in geographical learning might be for and during children's primary schooling.

Primary geography outcomes

While geography has a long tradition of description, analysis and explanation, it is not a neutral discipline and its role in the primary curriculum is value based, to promote geographical understanding. It scrutinises its knowledge and values through the careful and balanced study of places, people, environments and related issues and concerns (Martin, 2006c). This provides a basis for developing geographical understanding through consistent geographical learning from 3/4 to 11/12 years old. Such consistency provides benefits through continuous learning, in examining experiences, by developing new knowledge and understanding and skills, and reflecting on, even changing, values and attitudes (Leeder, 2006). The box below presents a set of possible outcomes by the end of primary schooling for geographical education, drawn from the aspects of geography explored in earlier chapters. If such outcomes for geographical learning were even partially achieved, there would be a good basis for progress for children into their secondary school geography education.

Key geographical outcomes for early years and primary children by the age of 11/12 years old

Children should:

- know about places, environments and people in different parts of the world;
- know of and give reasons for some natural, physical and social characteristics of communities, places and environments, and explain some of the commonalities shared and the differences and diversity between them;
- be able to locate important places in the news and in relation to their own experience and interests on maps from the world to local scales;
- have some awareness and understanding of the links that connect places and people and create interdependence locally, nationally and globally;
- show some understanding of the role of location, and of the distributions and patterns formed by natural, physical, economic and social features;
- be able to describe and explain how some natural, physical, economic and social processes and activities can cause changes to places, environments and people's lives;
- be able to express their sense of wonder at some of what they see of the world and their concern over other aspects of the world that they encounter;

(Continued)

(Continued)

- describe and explain how people, including themselves, may have planned or unintended impacts on places and the environment, near and far, and that people may hold different views about ways places and environments do and might change;
- begin to recognise, appreciate and express some of the concerns associated with resource distribution, the quality of life and environmental and social justice, from local to global scales;
- be able to act on their understanding of how to live increasingly sustainably and explain why this is important for their own future and that of others;
- consider and develop informed views about places and the environment, and why and how they might commit to taking actions to influence the present and future;
- raise interests, questions, problems and issues to investigate using geographical enquiry, draw on a variety of skills and resources, and communicate their findings and viewpoints;
- make use of digital and other technologies, including the Web, social media, mobile phones, GPS and GIS, to find out about, make sense and use of, and communicate about their own and others' worlds, near and far;
- be able to use maps to find their way around, know the relationship between globes and atlases and how to use these to locate and find out about places, and create maps of their own at a range of scales.

A sequence for progression in primary geography

One way to express the development of the geography curriculum to achieve its outcomes across the early years and primary schooling is to consider the focus for learning progressively across age phases. This might be thought of in terms of two-year or so age phases to avoid too rigid a structure from year to year, particularly where children may be in mixed-age classes in small primary schools. In this way it is possible to identify progression broadly in the development of children's geographical learning (Catling, 2005a, 2010; GA, 2014b; ACARA, 2012a), while allowing opportunities for schools to create their own geography curriculum based in their priorities for geography teaching and their knowledge of the children from the community they serve. The box below offers an example of the development of such a geography curriculum. It can be read alongside Table 15.2 in Chapter 15.

Possible core elements for the early years and primary geography curriculum

Through their early years and primary geography curriculum, children should have sustained opportunities to do the following.

Between ages 3/4 to 5/6, encounter geography through acquainting themselves with people, places and environments:

- observe and find out about features in the nursery/school and local streets through outdoor learning;
- build up their vocabulary about the everyday world about them, of features, events, directions and space using photographs and outdoor learning;
- talk about what they like and dislike about their immediate and local environment and other places and consider how to care for places;
- talk about the lives of people in their own and other places using photographs and descriptions;
- play with environmental toys, playmat maps and listen to stories about people in places.

Between ages 5/6 to 7/8 in primary school, develop geographical awareness through exploring local and more distant places:

- investigate features and activities, changes that have taken place, and people's lives in their local area, involving the use of fieldwork;
- examine places elsewhere, what they are like, ways people live and activities that happen there, and make some reasoned comparisons;
- through reference to globes and atlas maps begin to become familiar with the Earth, its continents and oceans and their own nation and, possibly, others, and with a world map;
- use questions, fieldwork, photographs, maps and other resources, and extend their vocabulary, to investigate, describe and comment on places near and far;
- through stories and play, explore lives and activities in places and environments;
- find out about a local issue, be aware of other views and express their own, and participate in activities about improvements locally;
- recognise roles that people can and do play in affecting, caring for and sustaining environments.

(Continued)

(Continued)

Between ages 7/8 to 9/10 in primary school, engage with geography through investigating places and environments:

- contribute to planning geographical enquiries and how they can be carried out, including using fieldwork, and begin to evaluate how informative they have been;
- begin to use more geographically appropriate vocabulary to describe and express findings and views about places and the environment;
- use world, national and other atlas maps to find out and know where significant places and environments are that they hear about;
- examine the location of features and patterns that particular features make, using maps as an aid to investigation and for communicating their findings;
- consider how some changes they have identified in places and environments are caused and have an impact, and offer views on the effect of these changes;
- look at variations in people's lives in different places and their impact on these places and other people, exploring more than one place in detail, and make comparisons, recognising and valuing similarities and differences;
- begin to recognise and appreciate the connections between and the interdependence of people and places;
- consider how people interact with their environment, can improve it, what 'improve' might mean for whom, and how to act sustainably.

Between ages 9/10 to 11/12 in primary school, become involved geographically through explaining places and investigating the world:

- plan, undertake and share geographical enquiries using a variety of resources, including fieldwork, maps, photographs, numerical and literary sources;
- use, accurately, geographical terms and skills to describe, explain, communicate and evaluate their investigations;
- know where significant places are, and be able to use appropriate globes, atlases and maps to find places, including those new to them;
- describe ways in which human and natural processes create and shape places and aspects of the environment, such as rivers or towns, and affect locations and spatial patterns;

- examine and begin to explain the importance of the interdependence of places and people;
- compare what places are like, appreciating their similarities, differences and diversity, and recognise how they are changing, giving reasons for their comparisons and the changes they note;
- examine how places and environments can be cared for sustainably, what this means, and why it is vital for the present and the future;
- consider how decisions affect places and environmental issues, and begin to appreciate why different people's views have different impacts on decisions and events;
- identify and justify actions in which they can be involved in managing, improving and sustaining environments.

Source: revised and developed from Catling, 2004a, p. 83.

 Reflective task

What for you are the most important aspects of geography to include in the geography curriculum for early years and primary children? How do your ideas relate to children's geographies? What is your justification for your choice? What has influenced your views and selection?

Self-evaluation of geographical learning

It can be helpful at the age of 11/12 for children to complete a self-evaluation of their competence and confidence in their geographical understanding, as their personal reflection on their geographical learning during their primary school years. They might take this personal record to share with their secondary school geography teacher following school transfer. Indeed, it might form part of a portfolio of their work with their last primary teacher's and their own earlier geography unit evaluations. Such a self-evaluation might be a piece of directed or free writing, or it can be completed using a pro forma provided by their primary school, such as that in Table 16.1. It is an informative way for children to express their sense of confidence and competence about their geographical learning, and for their future teachers to note this to help the children's continuing learning most effectively.

My geographical understanding I am confident that I can:	My level of competence		
	High	Medium	Low
1. show you where my country and several other countries and features are on a globe and map of the world;			
2. talk about the main features, activities and events in my locality and community, explain why they are important, and draw you a map of the area;			
3. tell you about one or more other localities, explain what it is like to live there and why, and compare them to my own local area;			
4. use examples to describe some natural and human processes and how they can change features and places;			
5. explain why it is important to know where places are, using examples from the news or other sources;			
6. say how changes in places and environments have helpful or damaging impacts on people's lives;			
7. give examples of one or more geographical (spatial) distributions and patterns in the environment;			
8. give examples of ways that people damage and improve the environment and why this happens;			
9. think of some useful geographical questions and say why they are useful;			
10. explain how to undertake a geographical enquiry, and say which skills will help me investigate a problem or an issue, and how to share what I find out with other people;			
11. say clearly what I think about a particular event or issue, give reasons for my point of view and what actions I think should be taken, and I can recognise that other people may have different views and say why they might hold them;			
12. give examples of geographical words and terms, and use them correctly;			
13. select and use a suitable map to find my way around an area and choose appropriate maps and atlases to find out about other places;			

My geographical understanding I am confident that I can:	My level of competence		
	High	Medium	Low
14. say how useful photographs, pictures, drawings, charts and graphs are in informing us about places and environments, and explain why they might be of limited help when used without other information;			
15. use the Web and other sources to find out information about places, environments and issues, and be able to check their accuracy and usefulness.			
In my geographical learning I have really enjoyed:			
In geography I would like to learn more about:			

Table 16.1   An example of a primary school geography self-evaluation form for secondary school transfer.

Practical task

Use the outcomes of geographical learning listed in the box on pp. 489–90 and see how they are expressed in Table 16.1. How confident do you feel about your geographical knowledge, understanding and skills in the statements included in Table 16.1?

Researching geographical learning and teaching

Developing understanding of children's geographical learning in your class is not always achieved by marking the children's work or observing an activity they are doing. It requires more careful investigation with a purpose. Interest in and commitment to developing your classroom research skills is important because it is concerned with improving your practice in and outside the classroom for the benefit of children's learning. You might examine children's learning in a particular sequence of geography lessons over a short period. You may, over a longer period, perhaps a year, investigate how children's understanding has developed through two or three geography topics.

Research related to primary geography is mixed. There is much research into children's geographies, their experience in their environments, their spatial awareness and, to a lesser extent, their sense of the wider world, as illustrated in Chapter 3. Other than in learning about maps (Wiegand, 2006), the research around the world into children's geographical learning in school and into teaching geography in primary classrooms is sparse and small scale (Catling, 1999a, 1999b, 2000, 2005b, 2013b, 2013d, 2015b; Catling and Martin, 2004a; Halvorsen, 2017; Segall and Helfenbein, 2008), even as it is in global education and environmental education (Maguth, 2012; Stevenson *et al.*, 2013). Few publications have focused on primary geography research (Bowles, 2000, 2004c; Catling and Martin, 2004b; Schmeinck, 2006; Schmeinck *et al.*, 2010; Catling, 2015b). Nonetheless, these have been drawn on in texts on teaching primary geography over many years to show what teachers and children can do, achieve and mis-understand (Wiegand, 1993; Owens and Ryan, 2001; Palmer and Birch, 2004; Scoffham, 2010; Pike, 2016). Research is helpful even where it might be constrained.

Five elements in primary geography are central to and critical foci for primary geography research: children's geographies, children's geographi-cal learning, approaches to teaching geography, the geography curriculum and policy, and historical perspectives. Chapter 3 covers the range of aspects of children's geographies research. The box below illustrates the need and opportunities that exist to investigate and develop our under-standing of primary school and classroom practice, and of younger chil-dren's learning in geography (Catling and Martin, 2004a; Martin and Catling, 2004; Catling 2013a; Pike, 2016). This list provides a variety of possible

Some areas in need of classroom research in primary geography

1. Early years and primary children's learning in geography

    - Ways in which children's personal geographies affect their learning in and of geography.
    - How children's environmental experience and perceptions can be built on and enhanced in their geographical learn-ing.
    - The understanding that children have of specific geographical concepts and vocabulary, such as village/town, transport/travel, holiday/leisure, land use/development, etc.
    - The nature of children's geographical misconceptions and misunderstandings.
    - Ways in which children undertake and respond to geographical investigations and enquiries, perhaps compared with their ways of working in science and history.

- Ways in which children read and understand 'geographical' photographs.
- How children's geographical learning has an impact on the ways they understand and appreciate the 'world' around them.

2. Approaches to teaching early years and primary geography

- Teachers' expectations of children in geography.
- How teachers approach, plan and see through geographical enquiries and investigations.
- The role of questioning in geography lessons to promote higher-order thinking skills.
- The uses of ICT to promote geographical analysis, evaluation and the communication of the findings of topics.
- How teachers identify and address children's misconceptions in geography teaching and devise strategies to tackle these.
- Ways in which teachers plan and teach for differentiated needs in geography.
- The effect of different strategies used in teaching geography on children's learning – e.g. fieldwork, role-play, modeling, mapping, etc.
- How and with what impact teachers intervene to support and extend children's geographical learning.
- Ways in which resources are used effectively in geography teaching, from stories, the school grounds, photo packs, maps and atlases, and more to digital technology applications.
- How teachers assess and take forward children's geographical understanding during topics.

3. The early years and primary geography curriculum

- Teachers' understanding of geographical concepts and skills they (will) teach.
- Teachers' attitudes to and valuing of geography and children's geographical learning.
- What teachers select to teach and how they plan to teach in geography.
- Ways in which teachers' geographical understanding affects their teaching.
- Schools' approaches to planning for geography throughout a school and of progression in geographical experience and learning.
- How and why teachers select and use resources in their geography teaching.

areas to investigate in your own teaching.

To the topics for early years and primary geography research outlined in the box above can be added a further set (Catling, 2013a), which concern the significance given to teaching and learning geography with younger children by governments and other educational organisations. This focus on policy and purpose for early years and primary geography education includes such topics as the following.

- The purposes and value for early years and primary children of geographical education.
- The status of geography in national education agendas and in schools, reflecting perspectives on its status and standing.
- Who constructs geography curricula for younger children and on what grounds.
- Ways in which government initiatives and policies promote or inhibit primary geography and why.
- Support nationally, locally and by subject associations for teacher development to teach geography in early years settings and primary schools.
- How early years and primary geography has changed over time and why this has happened.
- Cross-national comparisons of geography curricula and expectations for primary children.

The limitations of and the need for increased research in geography education broadly was recognised towards the end of the twentieth century (Downs, 1994) and this concern was reiterated in the USA twenty years later (Bednarz *et al.*, 2013). The report on research directions for twenty-first century geography education (Bednarz *et al.*, 2013), which drew on international studies and reviews, identified that geography education research generally was limited and, indeed, in a fragile state. This was underlined by the International Geographical Union Commission of Geographical Education's international declaration on research in geography education (IGU-CGE, 2015), which identified many aspects of geographical teaching and learning in need of research. What was evident from the report is that research into geography in early years and primary education is not strong, because little is undertaken. There is, therefore, a real need to engage with primary geography research, which you, as a classroom teacher, can do.

Approaching classroom research

As an essential element of your teaching praxis you investigate and evaluate aspects of your own teaching and its impact on children's learning, essentially by using reflective approaches (Pollard *et al.*, 2014). Alternatively, you undertake research to investigate systematically and rigorously an aspect of children's learning or of your own teaching over several lessons in a geography topic.

Much advice is available about research approaches to investigate children's learning and the nature and impact of your teaching. This includes advice about research philosophies and methods (Denscombe, 2014; Newby, 2014; Cohen *et al.*, 2017; Thomas, 2017; Coe *et al.*, 2017), insights into particular research topics, and reasons for using specific methods and the benefits and limitations of such research. Some advice focuses on researching alongside children (McLeod, 2008; Harcourt *et al.*, 2011). Kellett, Kim and others (Kellett, 2005, 2010; Kim *et al.*, 2017) argue for engaging children as researchers. However, there has been comparatively limited support in geographical, social studies and environmental education about research methodologies and methods (Bowles, 2000, 2004c; Catling and Martin, 2004a; Manfra and Bolick, 2017; Reid and Scott, 2008; Stevenson *et al.*, 2013; Williams, 1996), even in terms of understanding place-based approaches to researching school and the local area (Thomson and Hall, 2017). Some relevant research, including how the research was carried out, has been published particularly in the journals *International Research in Geographical and Environmental Education* (IRGEE) and *Environmental Education Research*, but little relates to the teaching and learning of geography in primary schools. Occasional research summaries appear in *Primary Geography*, and research reports may be published very occasionally in the range of education research journals to be found in university libraries.

It is important to consult the literature on research philosophies and methods when initiating and developing a research project. You may need to use more than one method to gather your data so as to have confidence in it. Table 16.2 outlines five methods you might use to research your primary geography teaching, but these need appropriate and thoughtful use, not unprepared application. Indeed, there is a wide range of research foci and approaches you might apply in your research. The examples that follow illustrate some of these.

Method	Brief description	Geography research example
Field notes	A descriptive, contemporaneous account of what happened, was observed and was heard. Brief, note form, from summary to direct quotations. Can include reflections made at the time. Essential that a clear focus, possibly with criteria, is used to direct your observations. Can include the incidental and unexpected.	Notes/describes the sequence of teaching events during a geography lesson; identifies who did or said what in various activities and tasks; notes the engagement of children, impact of the tasks; notes responses to the resources used, ways in which children adapted/developed tasks and learning.

(Continued)

Table 16.2   (Continued)

Method	Brief description	Geography research example
Interviews	A face-to-face interview can be structured or semi-structured, using closed or open (or a mixture of these) questions with children to explore their understanding, ideas, views, feelings, etc. Careful planning must be given to the questions.	To find out what children have thought about the geography topic they have studied, devise a number of semi-structured open questions to gather their views about the way they studied the topic, what was helpful/unhelpful, what they consider they learnt, etc.
Episode analysis	Focus on a 'typical' episode in a lesson, such as a dialogue between two or three children during a group task. Record and transcribe the discussion. Analyse the nature of the discourse involved, the type of dialogue, the vocabulary, meanings intended, etc.	Record a discussion between a group of children (perhaps led/stimulated by yourself) about a geography concept or topic – e.g. river flow, traffic issues locally. Examine the nature of the understanding shown and the thinking skills involved.
Problem-solving activity	Set up a problem for a group to tackle, perhaps one with no specific solution but various possibilities. Observe who leads, who needs support, how they understand the problem, what they identify the key concerns to be, ways they tackle the problem, how they agree on the outcome(s).	A group of five or six children is given a set of resources about an environmental issue and asked to develop a presentation for the rest of the class to help theme understand what the specific issues are and possible solutions might be. Observe the ways members of the group work and their thinking about the topic they have been given.
Assessment task	Develop an assessment activity for the children to undertake during or at the end of a topic, requiring them to work at different levels: description, explanation, evaluation, synthesis. Be clear about the focus: what the children know, can do, understand, value.	Provide individual children with information and two or three photographs about a particular place or theme – e.g. benefits and concerns associated with water. Set them questions or tasks requiring them to describe the place/theme, explain key points, offer their own views, etc.

Table 16.2   Five research methods to use in geographical education research

 Research summary

Researching young children's environmental values

Owens (2004b) researched 4–7-year-olds' environmental values and the connection with their vocabulary use and development in expressing their values. One technique she used was concept drawings, which involved children drawing and talking about things that were special to them in the school grounds. It required annotating the children's drawings as they talked. Field notes were made of the reasons children gave for their valuing of features. Owens found that:

- children valued features they used more than once;
- their first-hand experience of using features enhanced their vocabulary acquisition;
- there was a strong link to playtime activities;
- involvement in outdoor learning activities could have long-lasting effects;
- the use of rules about care for the environment had a positive impact.

She describes the value and effect of free activity play, the role of rule learning and the impact of teacher–learner engagement on the development and application of children's environmental values.

Children's feelings about geography

Children may be aware that they have been studying geography topics. Certainly, older primary children have ideas and views about school geography (see Chapter 3). You might investigate what children understand geography to be about, whether they like their studies or what they think the main aspects of their learning in geography have been or should be. You might ask the children to write about their ideas and views, or to prepare a poster or other visual image of 'geography'. Analyse their writing and images to identify common, major and minority ideas, understandings and themes that run through their 'statements'. Which aspects of their geographical learning appear consistently or less often? You might interview a sample of children about what they wrote or drew, asking them for reasons or more detail. You might consider how this relates to your teaching of geography and to the geography curriculum of the school.

How you plan your geography teaching

Keep a journal of field notes whenever you plan your geography teaching, recording, for example, what you have chosen to include and why, your reasons for starting the topic where you have, why you have sequenced a lesson or lessons in a particular order, how you came to use specific resources, what the constraints or opportunities in your planning have been, how you plan to and have taken account of the children's questions, experience and learning, what children think of the resources they use and their tasks in class and outside, and so on. Maintain this record throughout your teaching, noting how you develop, amend or utterly change your initial plan, always noting the reasons why to explain what happens. This will help you to analyse how you went about your planning and to understand what has been helpful and what might have inhibited your teaching and the children's learning. By reviewing your planning you learn about your planning process and can consider how you might adapt it for future topics.

Exploring children's geographical learning

Focusing on a particular aspect of children's geographical learning helps you become clearer about how their learning might be influenced by your teaching. In a topic, select a particular geographical concept or skill, such as land use or understanding the use of symbols on maps. Ensure that you plan your teaching of your focus explicitly and provide a variety of opportunities for children to use the ideas or skills. Plan activities through which the children show you their understanding or capability. You might start a topic by eliciting their initial understanding, check how this is developing through the topic using specific activities and tasks, and include a summative assessment of their learning. You could compare the children's responses from the different timings to see how their understanding has evolved. You might keep field notes during your research on learning events that you consider might have influenced the nature of the children's understanding at that point. Using your notes, evidence of the children's evolving understanding and your reflections on your teaching and the children's engagement in activities, consider what the main influences might have been on their geographical learning.

Research summary

Researching group work activity in geographical learning

Thurston (2006) investigated the effects of collaborative group work on the attainment of 8–9-year-old children in their geography topics. Curriculum materials were designed for topics on water and (linked with science) Earth in space. An experimental approach was used in which small groups investigated the topics, with listening, discussion and communication central. Pre- and post-attainment tests were used with the children, who followed a structured programme that involved a child-oriented enquiry approach. Observation of the children's discourses employed video and discussion transcripts. The discourse was analysed and evaluated, and used to help explain attainment outcomes and developments. Evidence emerged of increased attainment in geographical learning resulting from the discourse interactions of the children in small groups where the tasks required in-group activity rather than individual contributions.

Investigating your school and locality

Frequently used sites for teaching geography are the school's grounds and the neighbourhood or locality of the school. But how well do you know both of these? Do you know the school building(s) and grounds fully? If you live in the school's catchment, you may know the area; there again, you may not, if you live further away. What opportunities do these sites offer for children's geographical learning? How well do the children know them and make use of them? These sorts of questions can be the stimulus to research into what the school grounds offer and about how children make use of their grounds and for which reasons. You might use a geographical study focused on the school grounds or take opportunities in a broader-based topic in which you make use of the grounds for particular research. This might focus with the children as co-researchers investigating the variety of outdoor spaces children spend time in or avoid and the reasons why they do so. It may go on to enquire what they would like to improve and develop in their school grounds. Such studies may involve not only your own class, but observations by the children and yourself of other children of different ages, to see what you all learn about the range of ways in which school outdoor spaces are used, at what times, in what circumstances and influenced by what other factors, such as playtime supervision. Investigating the local area around the school again might be the focus of a geography (and history) study, during which children find out about each other's experiences of the area, when and how these happen, the extent of the area they know in common and differently, who enables or constrains their knowledge development in and of the locality, their feelings about specific sites, and so on. Sharing and comparing their knowledge and views, perhaps inviting them to create a 'learning map' for you to get to know the area better as a research approach, will provide you with insights into both the children's place understanding and give you raw material to develop your geography teaching in and using the locality. Engaging children as participants in such research will enhance your awareness of what they can do, how they consider their places and spaces, and develop your knowledge of local geography.

            Research summary

Researching children's first memories of the place that is school

Fleet and Britt (2017) investigated children's memories of their early years in school, working with pairs of children who were in their last primary school year, having always been at the school. They wished to

(Continued)

(Continued)

find out what influenced the children's understanding of the space and place of the school when they arrived age 5 years old on school entry. The studies in two primary schools involved photography and mapping. In particular, the researchers were interested to listen to the children talking about their experiences. What did the children recall about how they made sense of their new environments? A key feature of their findings concerned the sense of place the children developed, especially in terms of how the children 'inhabited' the space of school. The children's learning to be in the space of school was constructed through their use of functional sites and features, the affordance the sites offered. Imaginatively, they adapted these to their own concerns – for instance, by creating 'secret' places. This indicated the importance of the children's agency in their making use of space, of creating places they identified as specific sites they felt to be 'theirs', both indoors and outside. These were places with which they engaged intensively because these sites facilitated opportunities to do things, such as a wall to climb or as a place to sit or to be used as a shelter from weather, whereas the supervising adults might simply regard the wall as no more than a boundary to a play area. What was really important for the children in 'shaping' place was their early friendships. The children were not loners, for relationships were important to them, about who they played with and how the friendships helped them to construct particular places and their senses of place. Older primary children, recalling how in their first years in school they took on the place they were required to be in daily during term times, identified that school grounds are not simply spaces in which children play but are given meaning from a very young age, influenced by personal interests and relationships interplaying with the affordances of the spaces.

     Reflective task

Select one of the examples of research from the references, read the paper, book or chapter, and follow it up by finding out about the research method used. Consider why the researcher used that particular method and reflect on whether you might use that method in a study of your own.

Concluding remarks

Geographical awareness and understanding are fundamental to all our lives. We use geographical ideas and skills regularly. Our everyday geographies are underpinned by an experiential and internalised sense of the world. Through being taught geography, and from reading and visual and social media children extend and deepen their geographical knowledge, skills and values, some of which is rarely recognised by adults. Primary geography has a lengthy history in countries and schools around the world, but it remains contested and contentious as governments periodically modify or dramatically change the focus and direction of their nation's geography education. There continues to be debate about the quality of geography teaching, the time available in younger children's education for it, the range of ways in which and how effectively children learn geography, the depth of teachers' knowledge and understanding of the subject, and exactly what its curriculum should be. Nonetheless, teaching geography provides a real opportunity to draw on children's experience and developing understanding to enable them to deepen and extend their geographical learning from their earliest years throughout their primary schooling.

Children's changing lives, still strongly influenced by their families and peers, are increasingly supplemented and extended by a range of technologies that are changing our connections with people and places around the world. These include: digital phones, increasingly accessed and owned by an ever younger age range of primary age children; their access to the world provided by the Internet, email and similar systems, various social media and other digital networks; and the variety of forms of representation of places, lives and events through television, films, computer games, news from various sources and advertising which children watch and with which they engage. It is essential that younger children develop a critical awareness of their involvement in their real, cyber and imaginary environments – the 'stuff' of their daily geographies. These are not the only geographies influencing and affecting children. The topical issues of today – climate change, poverty/development issues, migration, access to key resources such as water and food, war, transport, urban development, conservation and care for the environment – will continue to be real concerns for the future. Children know of these and enquire about them at increasingly younger ages. None of this will stand still, which makes it more rather than less important that geography's role and responsibility in the primary curriculum is recognised, revitalised and enhanced.

In this book we have aimed to provide you with a background understanding of geography, particularly focusing on place, physical and human geography, and on environmental impact and sustainability. We have considered geography teaching in the context of social justice and its role in relation to citizenship. We have emphasised the nature of children's geographical experience and the impacts on children of various geographies of others, essentially by adults. We have explored a number of ways in and through which primary geography is and can be taught to be insightful, to challenge, to foster understanding and provide skills, to be sensitive, to motivate and to engage. Geographical studies examine the challenges but also focus on the positive, enjoyable and valuable in our lives, communities, places, environments and the wider world. Geography looks, too, at ways in which the 'future world' matters and can be improved, and at children's responsible, positive and active involvement in this.

In concluding, we have three 'hopes' for you. We hope to have developed your understanding of geography, and to have provoked and stimulated some real, even deep, interest on your part in geography, its essential value, and its teaching and learning. We hope that you find its teaching motivating and joyous, and that you will see the engagement and excitement that children glean and take with them from being taught geography very well. We hope, as a result, that you and your children will become and be 'happy geographers', keen to want more.

 Key points

This chapter has:

- reflected on the importance of geography in children's development;
- identified a set of geographical outcomes for primary children;
- offered a basis for structuring the primary geography curriculum, with a suggested progression sequence for children from ages 3/4 to 11/12 years old;
- noted the value of and some of the needs in research in primary geography;
- provided you with some examples and approaches to research in primary geography.

Moving on

In this book you have read about children's geographical backgrounds, the nature of geography, its focus for primary children, key aspects of and approaches to teaching geography, its planning and assessment, and points about research in primary geography. From the range of material covered in this book, which area(s) have most interested you? Consider how you might follow these up by reading and reflecting using a selection of the references.

Further reading

Inevitably, there is much that you might read. The following are offered as stimulating texts.

Catling, S (ed.) (2015) *Research and Debate in Primary Geography*. Abingdon: Routledge.

Cooper, H, Rowley, C and Asquith, S (eds) (2006) *Geography 3–11: A Guide for Teachers*. London: David Fulton.

Gersmehl, P (2014) *Teaching Geography* (3rd edn). New York: The Guildford Press.

Griggs, R and Hughes, S (2013) *Teaching Primary Humanities*. Harlow: Pearson.

Martin, F (2006) *Teaching Geography in Primary Schools*. Cambridge: Chris Kington.

Pickford, T, Garner, W and Jackson, E (2013) *Primary Humanities: Learning through Enquiry*. London: Sage.

Roberts, M (2013) *Geography through Enquiry*. Sheffield: Geographical Association.

Scoffham, S (ed.) (2010) *Primary Geography Handbook*. Sheffield: Geographical Association.

Scoffham, S and Owens, P (2018) *Teaching Primary Geography*. London: Bloomsbury.

Key geography education research journals

Children's Geographies, Taylor & Francis: www.tandfonline.com/loi/cchg20

Children, Youth and Environments, University of Cincinnati: http://cech.uc.edu/centres/arlitt/children-youth-and-environment.html

Environmental Education Research, Taylor & Francis: www.tandfonline.com/toc/ceer20

EuroGeo, European Geography Association newsletter and journal: www.eurogeography.eu

Geographical Education, Australian Geography Teachers' Association: www.agta.asn.au/htm_files/journal/index.htm

International Research in Geographical and Environmental Education, Taylor & Francis: www.tandfonline.com/toc/rgee20

Journal of Geography, National Council for Geographic Education: www.ncg.org/journal-of-geography

Research in Geographic Education, Gilbert Grosvenor Center, Texas State University: www.rge.grosvenor.txstate.edu

Review of International Research in Geographical Education Online (RIGEO) (an open access journal): www.rigeo.org

Occasionally, research and review articles appear in:

Geography, Geographical Association, www.geography.org.uk/journals/geography

Primary Geography, Geographical Association: www.geography.org.uk/primarygeography

The Geography Teacher, National Council for Geographic Education: www.myncge.
bravesites.com/the-geography-teacher

Useful websites

Australian Geography Teachers' Association (AGTA): www.agta.asn.au
Geographical Association: www.geography.org.uk
National Council for Geographic Education: www.ncge.org
National Council for Social Studies: www.socialstudies.org
National Geographic Society: www.nationalgeographic.com
Royal Geographical Society (with IBG): www.rgs.org

APPENDIX I

Examples of Primary Geography Curriculum Requirements and Guidance Internationally

This Appendix lists curriculum websites for a sample of countries around the world to enable you to access their primary school geography curriculum or social studies or social sciences curriculum, where geography might be included by name or you may need to search for the 'geography' because it is incorporated only as topics within a broader curriculum area. (Primary/elementary school normally refers to Grades K or 1 to 5 or 6.)

England (United Kingdom)

The National Curriculum in England – Primary Curriculum (Geography):
www.gov.uk/government/publications/national-curriculum-in-england-
   primary-curriculum

Statutory framework for the early years foundation stage (Understanding the world): www.gov.uk/government/publications/early-years-foundation-stage-framework-2

Scotland (United Kingdom)

Curriculum for Excellence: Social Studies – Experience and Outcomes (Social Studies: People, Place and Environment, incorporating geography):
https://education.gov.scot/scottish-education-system/policy-for-scottish-education/policy-drivers/cfe-(building-from-the-statement-appendix-incl-btc1-5)/Experiences%20and%20outcomes#soc

Wales (United Kingdom)

New school curriculum for Wales [from 2021] (Humanities, including Geography): http://gov.wales/docs/dcells/publications/170707-new-curriculum-for-wales
Foundation phase framework [to 2021] (Knowledge and Understanding of the World Area of Learning):
gov.wales/topics/educationandskills/foundation-phase/?lang=en
Welsh curriculum Key Stages 2–4 [to 2021] (Geography):
http://learning.gov.wales/resources/collections/key-stages-2-4?lang=en

Northern Ireland (United Kingdom)

The Northern Ireland Curriculum (The World Around Us, incorporating-geography):
http://ccea.org.uk/sites/default/files/docs/curriculum/area_of_learning/fs_northern_ireland_curriculum_primary.pdf

Ireland

Social, Environmental and Scientific Education (including Geography):
www.curriculumonline.ie/Primary/Curriculum-Areas/Social-Environmental-and-Scientific-Education/Geography

Australia

Humanities and Social Sciences curriculum F-6/7 (including Geography):
www.australiancurriculum.edu.au/Search/?q=F-Year%202%20Humanities%20and%20social%20sciences%20curriculum
Early Years Framework: Belonging, Being, Becoming:
https://docs.education.gov.au/system/files/doc/other/belonging_being_and_becoming_the_early_years_learning_framework_for_australia.pdf

New Zealand

The New Zealand Curriculum: Social Sciences (incorporating geography):
http://nzcurriculum.tki.org.nz/The-New-Zealand-Curriculum/Social-sciences

Te Whariki Early childhood curriculum:
https://education.govt.nz/assets/Documents/Early-Childhood/ELS-
Te-Whariki-Early-Childhood-Curriculum-ENG-Web.pdf

Singapore

Primary Social Studies Syllabus (incorporating geography):
www.moe.gov.sg/docs/defaulsource/document/education/syllabuses/
humanities/files/social-studies-syllabus-2012-110615.pdf
Nurturing Early Learners (Discovery of the World):
www.moe.gov.sg/education/preschool/resources-for-pre-school-
educators

South Africa

Life Skills Foundation Phases Grades R-3 (incorporating geography):
www.acsi.co.za/wp-content/uploads/2015/10/23.1.2012.FP-_-LS-_-English-_-
Gr-R-3-_-Web1734.pdf
Social Sciences Intermediate Phase Grades 4–6 (including Geography):
www.sahistory.org.za/archive/caps-curriculum-and-assessment-policy-state
ment-2011-grades-4-6-social-sciences

Hong Kong

Personal, Social and Humanities Education (incorporating geography):
www.edb.gov.hk/attachment/en/curriculum-development/kla/pshe/
PSHE%20KLA%20Guide%20Eng.pdf

Canada

Social Studies (incorporating geography) [only available by province]
e.g. Ontario: Social Studies (incorporating geography):
www.edu.gov.on.ca/eng/curriculum/elementary/sshg18curr2013.pdf
e.g. British Columbia: Social Studies (incorporating geography):
https://curriculum.gov.bc.ca/curriculum/social-studies/3

Pakistan

National Curriculum for Social Studies Grades IV-V (involving Geography):
http://bisep.com.pk/downloads/curriculum/Grades-IV-V/SOCIAL%20
STUDIES%20IV-V.pdf

USA

Geography for Life: National Geography Standards and Skills (2nd edn)
[Geography Education National Implementation Project, a non-
governmental group of geography societies. This is guidance for the
States to work from, if they choose to do so.]:
www.nationalgeographic.org/education/national-geography-standards/

Go to the website for each state's education department to find their specific Social Studies curriculum guidelines and requirements (including or incorporating geography).

Ethiopia

Environmental Science Grades 1–4 (incorporating geography):
http://info.moe.gov.et/curdocs/environment1-4.pdf
Social Studies Grades 5–8 (incorporating geography):
http://info.moe.gov.et/curdocs/socint5-8.pdf

Guyana

Social Studies Grades 1–6 (incorporating geography)
Grade 1:
https://education.gov.gy/web/index.php/component/docman/doc_details/279-curriculum-guides-grade-1?Itemid=642
Grade 2:
https://education.gov.gy/web/index.php/component/docman/doc_details/284-curriculum-guide-social-studies-level-2?Itemid=642
Grade 3:
https://education.gov.gy/web/index.php/component/docman/doc_details/287-curriculum-guide-level-3?Itemid=642
Grade 4:
https://education.gov.gy/web/index.php/component/docman/doc_details/293-curriculum-guide-social-studies-grade-4-contd?Itemid=642
Grade 5:
https://education.gov.gy/web/index.php/component/docman/doc_details/299-social-studies-curriculum-guide-5-2004?Itemid=642
Grade 6:
https://education.gov.gy/web/index.php/component/docman/doc_details/302-social-studies-curriculum-guide-level-six-6-2004?Itemid=642

Notes

Almost all nations provide online information about their primary school or basic level curriculum, although many of these are only available in the one or more national languages, and not in English. It is a matter of searching in the Ministry or Department of Education website in a particular country for its school curriculum documents, although they are not always readily accessible or easily found.

Be aware that national government websites that show the current curriculum may be revised from time to time, as governments make minor or significant curriculum changes.

An important document to be aware of is the *International Charter on Geographical Education*, which is available at the website below. It provides an outline of geography as a school subject, guidance on the subject and encouragement to countries to include geography in their school curriculum.

International Charter on Geographical Education: www.igu-cge.org/Charters-pdf/2016/IGU_2016_def.pdf

APPENDIX 2

Examples of geographically-informed children's picture story books

This Appendix lists a sample of picture story books for primary age children. Some are suitable for children in the early years of primary school, while others are appropriate for older primary children. They have been selected for their relevance to geography topics covered in this book. Some, but not all, are referred to in the text.

Places

Angelou, M (1994) *My Painted House, My Friendly Chicken, and Me*. London: Bodley Head.
Baker, J (1987) *Where the Forest Meets the Sea*. London: Walker Books.
Baker, J (1992) *Window*, London: Red Fox.
Baker, J (2010) *Mirror*. London: Walker Books.
Bancroft, B (2010) *Why I Love Australia*. Sydney: Little Hare.

Binch, C (1994) *Gregory Cool*. London: Frances Lincoln.

Birch, B and Chidley, A (1995) *The Village in the Forest by the Sea*. London: Bodley Head.

Child, L (2009) *Charlie and Lola: But Where Completely Are We?* London: Puffin Books.

Daly, N (1999) *The Boy on the Beach*. London: Bloomsbury Publishing.

Dillemuth, J (2016) *Lucy in the City*. Washington, DC: Magination Press.

Donaldson, J and Scheffler, A (2004) *The Gruffalo's Child*. London: Macmillan Children's Books.

Donaldson, J and Scheffler, A (2008) *Stick Man*. London: Alison Green Books.

Gravett, E (2006) *Meerkat Mail*. London: Macmillan Children's Books.

Hedderwick, M (1984) *Katie Morag Delivers the Mail*. London: Bodley Head.

Hedderwick, M (1999) *The Katie Morag Collection*. London: Bodley Head.

Jansson, T (2010) *The Dangerous Journey*. London: Sort of Books.

Knapman, T and Warburton, S (2012) *My Adventure Island*. London: Scholastic Children's Books.

Lester, A (2004) *Are We There Yet? A Journey Round Australia*. Camberwell: Penguin Viking.

Lucas, D (2005) *Walking with the Seasons in Kakadu*. Melbourne: Allen & Unwin.

McLerran, A and Cooney, B (1991) *Roxaboxen*. New York: Harpertrophy.

McMenemy, S (2011) *London/New York/Paris*. London: Walker Books.

Moore, I (2010) *Six Dinner Sid: A Highland Adventure*. Sydney: Hodder Children's Books.

Oakley, G (2000) *The Church Mice Take a Break*. London: Hodder Children's Books.

Oakley, G (2011) *The Church Mice Adrift*. Dorking: Templar Publishing.

Patton Walsh, J (1992) *Babylon*. London: Red Fox.

Provensen, A and Provensen, M (1993) *Shaker Lane*. London: Walker Books.

Russell, E (2005) *The Shack that Dad Built*. Sydney: Little Hare.

Schwartz, J and Smith, S (2018) *Town is by the sea*. London: Walker Books.

Sickler, J (2011) *Old MacDonald Has a Farm (in Bolivia)*. New York: Workman.

Steggall, S (2008) *Rattle and Rap*. London: Frances Lincoln.

Wheatley, N and Rawlins, D (1988) *My Place*. North Blackburn: Dollins Dove.

The global dimension

Arnholt, C and Arnholt, L (2013) *One World Together*. London: Frances Lincoln.

Ahlberg, A (2014) *Kicking a Ball*. London: Penguin Books.

de Beer, H (1987) *The Little Polar Bear*. New York: North South Books.

de Brunhoff, L (2005) *Babar's World Tour*. New York: Harry N Abrams.

Donaldson, J and Scheffler, A (2003) *The Snail and the Whale*. London: Macmillan Children's Books.

Foreman, M (2009) *A Child's Garden*. London: Walker Books.

Garland, S (2012) *Azzi in Between*. London: Frances Lincoln Books.

Glynne, A and Senior, T (2016) *Hamid's Story: A real-life account of his journey from Eritrea*. London: Wayland.

Heide, F and Gilliland, J (1997) *The Day of Ahmed's Secret*. London: Puffin Books.

Hollyer, B (2002) *Wake Up World*. London: Frances Lincoln.

Kim, P and Sanchez, S (2014) *Here I Am*. London: Curious Fox.

KIoll, V and Carpenter, N (1994) *Masai and I*. London: Puffin Books.

Maldonado, S and Glynne, A (2015) *Ali's Story: A real-life account of his journey from Afghanistan*. London: Wayland.

Milner, K (2017) *My Name is not Refugee*. Edinburgh: The Bucket List.

Morley, B and Pearce, C (2009) *The Silence Seeker*. London: Tamarind Books.

Parr, T (2009) *The Peace Book*. New York: Little, Brown & Co.

Petty, K (2007) *Home (Around the World)*. London: Frances Lincoln.

Readman, J and Roberts, L (2002) *The World Came to my Place Today*. London: Eden Project Books.

Readman, J and Honor Roberts, L (2006) *George Saves the World by Lunchtime*. London: Random House Children's Books.

Roberts, C and Kai, H (2016) *Refugees and Migrants*. London: Wayland.

Rose, D L and Saflund, B (1990) *The People who Hugged the Trees*. New York: Roberts Rinehart.

Ross, T and Willis, J (2006) *Daft Bat*. London: Andersen Press.

Rosen, M and Young, A (2016) *Who are Refugees and Migrants?* London: Wayland.

Sanna, F (2016) *The Journey*. London: Flying Eye Books.

Sheldon, D and Hurt Newton, T (1994) *Love, Your Bear Pete*. London: Walker Books.

Smith, D and Armstrong, S (2003) *If the World Were a Village*. London: A & C Black.

Sutton, E (1978) *My Cat Likes to Live in Boxes*. London: Puffin Books.

Wainwright, J, Moran, P, Wiltshire, S and Ecob, S (2011) *Where's the Meerkat?* London: Michael O'Mara Books.

Walsh, M (2004) *My World, Your World*. London: Picture Corgi Books.

Williams, K and Stock, C (1991) *Galimoto*. New York: Mulberry Books.

Environmental and sustainability themes

Anholt, L (1997) *The Forgotten Forest*. London: Frances Lincoln.

Atkins, J and Pinto, V (1995) *Aani and the Tree Huggers*. New York: Lee and Low Books.

Baker, J (1992) *Window*. London: Red Fox.

Baker, J (2004) *Belonging* (also published as *Home*). London: Walker Books.

Barker, F (2016) *Amelie and the Great Outdoors*. Kibworth Beauchamp: Matador.

Blathwayt, B (1992) *The Little House by the Sea*. London: Red Fox.

Brown, R (1991) *The World that Jack Built*. London: Red Fox.

Browne, A (1998) *Voices in the Park*. London: Picture Corgi Books.

Browne, A (2004) *Into the Forest*. London: Walker Books.

Buckingham, A (2011) *Turning Trash into Treasure for Young Children*. Auckland: Adam Buckingham.

Carle, E (2005) *10 Little Rubber Ducks*. London: HarperCollins.

Daly, N (1987) *Not So Fast Songololo*. Harmondsworth: Puffin.

Davies, B (2015) *Grandad's Island*. London: Simon & Schuster.

Foreman, M (1972) *Dinosaurs and All That Rubbish*. London: Puffin Penguin.

Foreman, M (2006) *Mia's Story*. London: Walker Books.

Grindley, S and Foreman, M (1995) *Peter's Place*. London: Andersen Press.

Gurry, C (2009) *Nicky's World*. Adelaide: Global Education Centre.

Hedderwick, M (1993) *Katie Morag and the New Pier*. London: Bodley Head.

Hughes, S and Poulin, S (2005) *Earth to Audrey*. Toronto: Kids Can Press.

Keeping, C (1989) *Adam and Paradise Island*. Oxford: Oxford University Press.

Mørch, R (2007) *Who Will Save Us?* Newton Abbot: Rebecca Mørch Publishing.

Morimoto, J (1990), *Kenju's Forest*. London: HarperCollins.

Orr, K (1990) *My Grandpa and the Sea*. Minneapolis: Carolrhoda Books.

Readman, J and Roberts L (2006) *George Saves the World by Lunchtime*. London: Eden Project Books.

Seuss, Dr (1971) *The Lorax*. New York: Harper Collins.

Solway, A (2009) *Graphing the Environment*. New York: Heinemann.

Strauss, R and Woods, R (2007) *One Well*. London: A & C Black.

For ideas about how various books might be used with children of all ages, consult the book reviews written for and presented by the Geographical Association at:

www.geography.org.uk/eyprimary/geographysubjectleaders/inspireme/bookreviews/#top

There are various publications about children's literature and story books relevant to geographical education, including:

Cutter-Mackenzie, A, Payne, P and Reid, A (eds) (2011) *Experiencing Environment and Place through Children's Literature*. Abingdon: Routledge.

Dolan, A (2014) *You, Me and Diversity*. London: Trentham Books/Institute of Education.

Goga, N and Kummerling-Meibauer, B (eds) (2017) *Maps and Mapping in Children's Literature: Landscapes, seascapes and cityscapes*. Amsterdam: John Benjamins Publishing Company.

Hope, J (2017) *Children's Literature about Refugees*. London: UCL-Institute of Education Press.

REFERENCES

AAIA (Association for Achievement and Improvement through Assessment) (n.d.) *Achievement for Learning*. Available at: www.aaia.org.uk/afl/

ACARA (Australian Curriculum, Assessment and Reporting Authority) (2011) *Shape of the Australian Curriculum: Geography*. Available at: http://docs.acara.edu.au/resources/Shape_of_the_Australian_Curriculum_Geography.pdf

ACARA (2012a) *Revised Draft Foundation to Year 12 Australian Curriculum: Geography*. Available at: http://docs.acara.edu.au/resources/Draft_F-12_Australian_Curriculum_Geography_Validation_Version_29082012.pdf.

ACARA (2012b) *The Shape of the Australian Curriculum: Civics and Citizenship*. http://docs.acara.edu.au/resources/Shape_of_the_Australian_Curriculum_Civics_and_Citizenship_251012.pdf

Adams, E and Ingham, S (1998) *Changing Places*. London: The Children's Society.

Adams, J (ed.) (2012) *Why Geography is Important*. San Marcos, TX: Texas State University Gilbert M Grosvenor Centre for Geographic Education.

Adams, L and Kirova, A (eds) (2006) *Global Migration and Education: Schools, children and families*. New York: Routledge.

Adichie, C (2009) *The dangers of a single story*. Talk given at TEDGlobal, July. Available at: www.ted.com/talks/chimamanda_adichie_the_danger_of_a_single_story.html

Aguirre-Bielschowsky, I, Lawson, R, Stephenson, J and Todd, S (2017) Energy literacy and agency of New Zealand children. *Environmental Education Research*, 23(6), pp. 832–54.

Ahlberg, A (2014) *Kicking a Ball*. London: Penguin Books.

Ahmadi, E (2011) *Children's Perception of their Neighbourhood Environment*. Saarbrücken: Lambert Academic Publishing.

Aitken, S (2001) *Geographies of Young People*. London: Routledge.

AITSL (Australian Institute for Teaching and School Leadership) (2012) *National Professional Standards for Teachers*. Available at: www.teacherstandards.aitsl.edu.au

Alabed, B (2017) *Dear World: A Syrian girl's story of war and plea for peace*. New York: Simon & Schuster.

Alcock, K (2012) *Our World*. London: HarperCollins.

Alexander, R (2008) *Towards Dialogic Teaching: Rethinking classroom talk* (4th edn). York: Dialogos.

Alexander, R (ed.) (2010) *Children, their World, their Education: Final report and recommendations of the Cambridge Primary Review*. Abingdon: Routledge.

Alexander, R and Hargreaves, L (2007) *The Primary Review Interim Reports: Community soundings*. Cambridge: University of Cambridge: The Primary Review. Available at: www.primaryreview.org.uk

Allen, J, Massey, D and Cochrane, A (1998) *Rethinking the Region*. Abingdon: Routledge.

Allum, L, Lowe, B and Robinson, L (2008) *How Do We Know It's Working?* Reading: Reading International Solidarity Centre.

Al-Nofli, M (2010) Students' perceptions about geography: A study of basic education school students in Oman. *European Journal of Social Sciences*, 16(1), pp. 11–20.

Al-Nofli, M (2013) The state of geography in basic education schools in Muscat, Oman. *International Research in Geographical and Environmental Education*, 22(2), pp. 109–19.

Altman, R, Stires, S and Weseen, S (eds) (2015) *Claiming the Promise of Place-Based Education*. New York: Bank Street College of Education.

Amedeo, D, Golledge, R and Stimson, R (2009) *Person Environment Behaviour Research*. New York: Guilford Press.

Anderson, B (ed.) (2016) *Philosophy for Children: Theories and praxis in teacher education*. Abingdon: Routledge.

Anderson, J (2010) *Understanding Cultural Geography*. Abingdon: Routledge.

Anderson, D, Goudie, A and Parker, A (2007) *Global Environments through the Quarternary: Exploring environmental change*. Oxford: Oxford University Press.

Andreotti, V (2013) Taking minds to other places. *Primary Geography*, 80, Spring, pp. 12–13.

Änggård, E (2016) How matter comes to matter in children's nature play: Posthumanist approaches and children's geographies. *Children's Geographies*, 14(1), pp. 77–90.

Anholt, C and Anholt, L (2013) *One World Together*. London: Frances Lincoln.

Ansell, N (2017) *Children, Youth and Development* (2nd edn). London: Routledge.

Ansell, N and Klocker, N (eds) (2016) *Geographies of Global Issues: Change and Threat*. Dordrecht: Springer.

Archambault, J (2012) It can be good there too: Home and continuity in refugee children's narratives of settlement. *Children's Geographies*, 10(1), pp. 35–48.

ARDT Consultants (2010) *Evaluation of the Operational Effectiveness of the Australian Sustainable Schools Initiative (AuSSI): Final report.* Available at: www.environment.gov.au/education/aussi/publications/operational-effectiveness.html

Armitage, S (2017) *Approaches to Learning and Teaching Geography: A toolkit for international teachers.* Cambridge: Cambridge University Press.

Armitage, R and Armitage, D (1994) *The Lighthouse Keeper's Lunch.* Leamington Spa: Scholastic.

Arnold, A (2015) When the chicks hatch, a man will come and bring them yolk to eat: Assessment in the early years. In Whitebread, D and Coltman, P, *Teaching and Learning in the Early Years* (4th edn). Abingdon: Routledge, pp. 77–92.

Ashbridge, J (2006) Is geography suitable for the Foundation Stage? In Cooper, H, Rowley, C and Asquith, S (eds) *Geography 3–11: A Guide for Teachers.* London: David Fulton, pp. 115–27.

Ataöv, A and Haider, J (2006) From participation to empowerment: Critical reflections on a participatory action research project with street children in Turkey. *Children, Youth and Environments,* 16(2), pp. 127–52.

Atkinson, S, Fuller, S and Painter, J (eds) (2012) *Wellbeing and Place.* Farnham: Ashgate.

Augustine, T, Harshman, J and Merryfield, M (2015) *Research in Global Citizenship Education.* Charlotte, NC: Information Age Press.

AuSSI (Australian Sustainable Schools Initiative) (2010) *Case Studies.* Available at: www.environment.gov.uk/education/aussi/case-studies.index.html

Austin, C, Knowles, Z, Richards, K, McCree, M, Sayers, J and Ridgers, N (2016) Play and learning outdoors: Engaging with the natural world using Forest School in the UK. In Nairn, K and Kraftl, P (eds) (2016) *Space, Place and Environment.* Dordrecht: Springer, pp. 116–36.

Australian Curriculum (2015) *Australian Curriculum: Humanities and social sciences.* Available at: www.australiancurriculum.edu.au/humanities-and-social-sciences

Avriel-Avni, N, Spektor-Levy, O, Zion, M and Levi, N (2010) Children's sense of place in desert towns: A phenomenographic enquiry. *International Research in Geographical and Environmental Education,* 19(3), pp. 241–59.

Ba, H (2009) *Children's Place Exploration.* Saarbrücken: Verlag Dr Müller.

Baby Professor (2017) *What Every Child Should Know About Climate Change.* Newark, DE: Speedy Publishing.

Bailey, P (1974) *Teaching Geography.* Newton Abbot: David & Charles.

Bakan, J (2011) *Childhood Under Siege.* London: Bodley Head.

Baker, J (1987) *Where the Forest Meets the Sea.* London: Walker Books.

Baker, J (1991) *Window.* London: McRae Books.

Baker, J (2004) *Belonging.* London: Walker Books.

Baker, J (2010) *Mirror.* London: Walker Books.

Balchin, W and Coleman, A (1965) Graphicacy should be the fourth ace in the pack. Reprinted in Bale, J, Graves, N and Walford, R (eds) (1973) *Perspectives in Geographical Education.* Edinburgh: Oliver & Boyd, pp. 78–86.

Barker, F (2016) *Amelie and the Great Outdoors.* Kibworth Beauchamp: Matador.

Barlow, A (2017) Geography and history in the local area. In Scoffham, S (ed.) *Teaching Geography Creatively* (2nd edn). Abingdon: Routledge, pp.118–30.

Barnes, J (2015) *Cross-curricular learning 3–14* (3rd edn). London: Sage.

Barrett, M (2005) Children's understanding of, and feelings about, countries and national groups. In Barrett, M and Buchanan-Barrow, E (eds) *Children's Understanding of Society*. Hove: Psychology Press, pp. 251–86.

Barrett, M (2007) *Children's Knowledge, Beliefs and Feelings About Nations and National Groups*. Hove: Psychology Press.

Barrett, M and Buchanan-Barrow, E (eds) (2005) *Children's Understanding of Society*. Hove: Psychology Press.

Barrett, M, Lyons, E and Bourchier Sutton, A (2006) Children's knowledge of countries. In Spencer, C and Blades, M (eds) *Children and their Environments*. Cambridge: Cambridge University Press, pp. 57–75.

Bartlett, L and Cox, B (1982) *Learning to Teach Geography: Practical workshops in geographical education*. Brisbane: Wiley.

Bason, S (2010) *Learning Outside the Primary Classroom*. London: Optimus Education.

Battersby, S, Mohan, A, Cooper, C, Curtis, M, Lane, J, Tabor, L and Wessell, J (2013) What supports or promotes the development of geographic knowledge, skills and practices? Pedagogy and research priorities to improve geography teaching and learning at the K-12 level. *Research in Geographic Education*, 15(2), pp. 29–43.

Baylina, M, Ortiz, A and Prats Ferret, M (2016) Nature in urban children's daily life in Catalonia. In Murnaghan, A-M and Shillington, L (eds) (2016) *Children, Nature, Cities*. Abingdon: Routledge, pp. 153–69.

Beames, S, Higgins, P and Nicol, R (2012) *Learning Outside the Classroom: Theory and guidelines for practice*. London: Routledge.

Beder, S (2009) *The Little Kiddy went to Market: The corporate capture of childhood*. London: Pluto Press.

Bednarz, S, Heffron, S and Huynh, N (2013) A road map for 21st century geography education: Geography education research. Available at: http://natgeoed.org/roadmap

Bednarz, S, Heffron, S and Solem, M (2014) Geography standards in the United States: Past influences and future prospects. *International Research in Geographical and Environmental Education*, 23(1), pp. 79–89.

Bell, D (2005) The value and importance of geography. *Primary Geographer*, 56, pp. 4–5.

Bell, S (2006) Scale in children's experience with the environment. In Spencer, C and Blades, M (eds) *Children and their Environments*. Cambridge: Cambridge University Press, pp. 13–25.

Bellamy, C (2003) *The State of the World's Children 2003: Children's participation*. New York: UNICEF.

Bellamy, C (2004) *The State of the World's Children 2005: Childhood under threat*. New York: UNICEF.

Bent, G, Bakx, A and den Brok, P (2017) Primary education teachers' self-efficacy beliefs for teaching geography lessons. *International Research in Geographical and Environmental Education*, 26(2), pp. 150–65.

Berners-Lee, M (2010) *How Bad Are Bananas?* London: Profile Books.

Bettany, J, Cutting, R and Kelly, O (2017) Understanding places and people through history and geography outside the classroom. In Waite, S (ed.) *Children Learning Outside the Classroom* (2nd edn). London: Sage, pp.172–82.

Beunderman, J, Hannon, C and Bradwell, P (2007) *Seen and Heard: Reclaiming the public realm with children and young people*. London: Demos.

Bhabha, J (2014) *Child Migration and Human Rights in a Global Age*. Princeton, NJ: Princeton University Press.

Bhandari, R (2014) *Disaster Education and Management: A joyride for students, teachers and disaster managers*. New Delhi: Springer.

Biddulph, M (2017) Curriculum enactment. In Jones, M and Lambert, D (eds) *Debates in Geography Education* (2nd edn). Abingdon: Routledge, pp.156–70.

Biddulph, M, Lambert, D and Balderstone, D (2015) *Learning to Teach Geography in the Secondary School* (3rd edn). Abingdon: Routledge.

Bilton, H (2005) *Learning Outdoors: Improving the Quality of Children's Play Outdoors*. London: David Fulton.

Bilton, H (2010) *Outdoor Learning in the Early Years*. London: David Fulton.

Bilton, H, Bento, G and Dias, G (2017) *Taking the First Steps Outside: Under threes learning and developing in the natural environment*. Abingdon: Routledge.

Bilton, H and Crook, A (2016) *Exploring Outdoors Ages 3–11: A guide for schools*. Abingdon: Routledge.

Binch, C (1994) *Gregory Cool*. London: Frances Lincoln.

Black, P and Wiliam, D (1998a) *Inside the Black Box: Raising standards through classroom assessment*. London: King's College.

Black, P and Wiliam, D (1998b) *Inside the Black Box*. Slough: NFER Nelson.

Black, P and Wiliam, D (2003) *Working Inside the Black Box: Assessment for learning in the classroom*. London: Nelson.

Blatchford, P (1998) *Social Life in School*. London: Falmer Press.

Blathwayt, B (1992) *The Little House by the Sea*. London: Red Fox.

Bloom, B, Engelhart, M, Furst, E, Hill, W, Krathwohl, D (eds) (1956) *Taxonomy of Educational Objectives, Handbook I: The cognitive domain*. New York: David McKay.

Blundell, D (2016) *Rethinking Children's Spaces and Places*. London: Bloomsbury.

Bond, M (1958/2014) *A Bear Called Paddington*. London: Collins/HarperCollins.

Bonnett, A (2008) *What is Geography?* London: Sage.

Bonnett, A (2013) Geography: The world's big idea. *Primary Geography*, 82, pp. 7–8.

Bonneuil, C and Fressoz, J-B (2017) *The Shock of the Anthropocene*. London: Verso.

Bourke, J (2017) Children's experiences of their everyday walks through a complex urban landscape of belonging. *Children's Geographies*, 15(1), pp. 93–106.

Bourn, D (2015) *The Theory and Practice of Development Education: A pedagogy for global social science*. Abingdon: Routledge.

Bourn, D, Hunt, F, Blum, N and Lawson, H (2016) *Primary education for global learning and sustainability*, Cambridge Primary Review Trust Research Survey 5 (new series). York: Cambridge Primary Review Trust. Available at: http://cprtrust. org.uk/wp-content/uploads/2016/02/Bourn-report-160217-final.pdf

Bowden, D and Copeland, P (2017) *Investigating Water*. Sheffield: Geographical Asssociation.

Bowles, R (ed.) (2000) *Occasional Paper No. 1: Raising achievement in geography*. London: Register of Research in Primary Geography.

Bowles, R (2004a) Children's understanding of locality. In Catling, S and Martin, F (eds) *Researching Primary Geography*. London: Register of Research in Primary Geography, pp. 29–42.

Bowles, R (2004b) Comparing children's and adults' understanding of locality. In Catling, S and Martin, F (eds) *Researching Primary Geography*. London: Register of Research in Primary Geography, pp. 211–24.

Bowles, R (ed.) (2004c) *Occasional Paper No. 4: Space and place*. London: Register of Research in Primary Geography.

Bowles, R (2010) Weather and climate. In Scoffham, S (ed.) *Primary Geography Handbook*. Sheffield: Geographical Association, pp. 230–45.

Bowles, R (n.d.) GTIP orientation piece: Using ICT (Primary). Available at: www.geography.org.uk/projects/gtip/orientationpieces/usingictl/#top

Boyd, D, Hirst, N and Siraj-Blatchford, J (eds) (2018) *Understanding Sustainability in Early Childhood Education: Case studies and approaches from across the UK*. Abingdon: Routledge.

Boylan, C and Wallace, A (2009) Engaging with Learnscapes: Connecting community and school. *The Australian Journal of Indigenous Education*, 38(Supplement), pp.94–102.

Boyle-Baise, M and Zevin, J (2014) *Young Citizens of the World: Teaching elementary social studies through civic engagement*. New York: Routledge.

Bradshaw, J and Mayhew, E (eds) (2003) *The Wellbeing of Children in the UK*. London: Save the Children.

Bridge, C (2010) Mapwork skills. In Scoffham, S (ed.) *The Primary Geography Handbook*. Sheffield: Geographical Association.

Bridge, C (n.d.) Project: Primary geography handbook extension project: Maps and stories (8–11). www.geography.org.uk/Primary-Geography-Handbook-Extension-Project--Maps-and-Stories-811

Briggs, M, Woodfield, A, Martin, C and Swatton, P (2008) *Assessment for Learning and Teaching*. Exeter: Learning Matters.

Broadfoot, P (1996) Assessment and learning: Power or partnership. In Goldstein, H and Lewis, T (eds) *Assessment: Problems, Developments and Statistical Issues*. Chichester: Wiley, pp. 21–40.

Brocklehurst, H (2006) *Who's Afraid of Children?* Guildford: Ashgate.

Broda, H (2011) *Moving the Classroom Outdoors: Schoolyard enhanced learning in action*. Portland, ME: Stenhouse Publishing.

Bromley, B (2017) Power to the pupils. *Primary Geography*, 93, pp. 14–15.

Brooks, C (2017) International differences in thinking geographically, and why 'the local' matters. In Brooks, C, Butt G and Fargher, M (eds) *The Power of Geographical Thinking*, pp. 169–79. Dordrecht: Springer.

Brooks, C, Butt, G and Fargher, M (eds) (2017) *The Power of Geographical Thinking*. Dordrecht: Springer.

Brophy, J, Alleman, J and Halvorsen, A-L (2013) *Powerful Social Studies for Elementary Students* (3rd edn). Belmont, CA: Wadsworth Cengage Learning.

Brown, F and Patte, M (2013) *Rethinking Children's Play*. London: Bloomsbury.

Brown, G and Wragg, E (1993) *Questioning*. London: Routledge.

Brown, K and Kasser, T (2005) Are psychological and ecological wellbeing compatible? (unpublished paper).

Bruce, T (2001) *Learning Through Play: Babies, Toddlers and the Foundation Stage*. London: Hodder Arnold.

Bruce, T (2005) *Early Childhood Education*. London: Hodder Arnold.

Bruner, J (1960) *The Process of Education*. Cambridge, MA: Harvard University Press.

Buchan, N (2016) *A Practical Guide to Nature-Based Practice*. London: Featherstone.

Buchanan, J (2013) *History, Geography and Civics: Teaching and learning in the primary years*. Port Melbourne: Cambridge University Press.

Bucknall, S (2012) *Children as Researchers in Primary Schools*. London: David Fulton.

Bullock, J, Haddow, G and Coppola, D (2011) *Managing Children in Disasters*. Boca Raton, FL: CRC Press.

Burke, A and Marsh, J (eds) (2013) *Children's Virtual Play Worlds: Culture, learning and participation*. New York: Peter Lang.

Butt, G (2008) *Lesson Planning*. London: Continuum.

Butt, G (2017) Debating the place of knowledge within geography education: Reinstatement, reclamation or recovery? In Brooks, C, Butt, G and Fargher, M (eds) *The Power of Geographical Thinking*. Dordrecht: Springer, pp. 13–26.

Butt, G (n.d.) GTIP orientation piece: Assessment. Available at: www.geography.org. uk/projects/gtip/orientationpieces/assessmentl#top

Cadwell, L (1997) *Bringing Reggio Emilia Home*. New York: Teachers College Press.

Caiman, C and Lundegård, I (2014) Pre-school children's agency in learning for sustainable development. *Environmental Education Research*, 20(4), pp. 437–59.

Callejo Pérez, D, Fain, S and Slater, J (2004) *Pedagogy of Place*. New York: Peter Lang.

Cantle, T (2008) *Community Cohesion: A New Framework for Race and Diversity*. Basingstoke: Palgrave Macmillan.

Carr, M (2001) *Assessment in Early Childhood Settings: Learning Stories*. London: Paul Chapman.

Carr, N (2011) *Children's and Families' Holiday Experiences*. London: Routledge.

Carrington, V (2013) An argument for assemblage theory: Integrated spaces, mobility and polycentricity. In Burke, A and Marsh, J (eds) *Children's Virtual Play Worlds: Culture, Learning and Participation*. New York: Peter Lang, pp. 200–16.

Carroll, J (2011) *Landscape in Children's Literature*. Abingdon: Routledge.

Carroll, P, Witten, K, Kearns, R and Donovan, P (2012) Kids in the city: Children's use and experiences of urban neighbourhoods in Auckland, New Zealand. *Journal of Urban Design*, 20(4), pp. 417–36.

Carter, R (ed.) (1998) *Handbook of Primary Geography*. Sheffield: Geographical Association.

Carver, A, Timperio, A and Crawford, D (2008) Playing it safe: The influence of neighbourhood safety on children's physical activity – A review. *Health and Place*, 14, pp. 217–27.

Carver, A, Watson, B, Shaw, B and Hillman, M (2013) A comparison study of children's independent mobility in England and Australia. *Children's Geographies*, 11(4), pp. 461–75.

Castree, N, Demeritt, D, Liverman, D and Rhoads, B (eds) (2009) *A Companion to Environmental Geography*. Chichester: Wiley-Blackwell.

Catling, S (1993) The whole world in our hands. *Geography*, 78(4), pp. 340–58.

Catling, S (1995) Wider horizons: The children's charter. *Primary Geographer*, 20, pp. 4–6.

Catling, S (1999a) Issues for research in UK primary geography. *Research in Geographical and Environmental Education*, 8(1), pp. 60–5.

Catling, S (1999b) Developing research in primary geography. *Primary Geographer*, 38, pp.15–17.

Catling, S (2000) The Importance of classroom research in primary geography. In Bowles, R (ed.) *Occasional Paper No. 1: Raising achievement in geography*. London: Register of Research in Primary Geography, pp. 29–38.

Catling, S (2001a) Primary geography matters! The geography curriculum: Principles, practice and evaluation. In Houtsonen, L and Tammilehto, M (eds) *Innovative Practices in Geographical Education*. Proceedings of the Helsinki Symposium of the IGU Commission on Geographical Education. Helsinki: Department of Geography, University of Helsinki, pp. 8–17.

Catling, S (2001b) English primary schoolchildren's definitions of geography. *International Research in Geographical and Environmental Education*, 10(4), pp. 363–78.

Catling, S (2002) *Placing Places*. Sheffield: Geographical Association.

Catling, S (2003) Curriculum contested: Primary geography and social justice. *Geography*, 88(3), pp. 164–210.

Catling, S (2004a) On close inspection. *Primary Geographer*, 55, pp. 34–6.

Catling, S (2004b) An understanding of geography: The perspectives of English primary trainee teachers. *Geojournal*, 60, pp. 149–58.

Catling, S (2005a) Children, place and environment. *Lecture Plus, Geographical Association Annual Conference, University of Derby*. Available at: www.geography.org.uk/download/Evcatling1.doc

Catling, S (2005b) Seeking younger children's 'voices' in geographical education research. *Research in Geographical and Environmental Education*, 14(4), pp. 297–304.

Catling, S (2005c) Children's personal geographies and the English primary school geography curriculum. *Children's Geographies*, 3(3), pp. 325–44.

Catling, S (2005d) *Improving the environment: Access for all – SuperSchemes Unit 8*. Sheffield: Geographical Association.

Catling, S (2006a) Young children's geographical worlds and primary geography. In Schmeinck, D (ed.) *Research on Learning and Teaching in Primary Geography*. Karlsruhe: Padagogischen Hochschule Karlsruhe, pp. 9–35.

Catling, S (2006b) What do 5-year-olds know of the world? Geographical understanding and play in young children's early learning. *Geography*, 91(1), pp. 55–74.

Catling, S (2006c) Geography and history: Exploring the local connection. *Primary History*, 42, Spring, pp. 14–16.

Catling, S (2007) ECM 6 = environmental wellbeing? *Primary Geographer*, 63, Summer, pp. 5–8.

Catling, S (2008) Children's geographies and new technologies. *Primary Geographer*, 67, Autumn, pp. 7–10.

Catling, S (2009a) The happiness of everyday geographies. *Primary Geographer*, 68, Spring, pp. 12–14.

Catling, S (2009b) 'Thinking of Britain' in children's geographies. *Primary Geographer*, 69, Summer, pp. 16–19.

Catling, S (2010) Understanding and developing primary geography. In Scoffham, S (ed.) *Primary Geography Handbook*. Sheffield: Geographical Association, pp. 75–91.

Catling, S (2011) Children's geographies in the primary school. In Butt, G (ed.) *Geography, Education and the Future*. London: Continuum, pp.15–29.

Catling, S (2012a) The place of artefacts in geography? *Primary Geography*, 78, p. 30.

Catling, S (2012b) The difference geography makes. *Primary Geography*, 79, pp. 26–7.

Catling, S (2013a) Introducing national curriculum geography to Australia's primary schools: Lessons from England's experience. *Geographical Education*, 26, pp. 29–41.

Catling, S (2013b) Editorial: The need to develop research into primary children's and schools' geography. *International Research in Geographical and Environmental Education*, 22(3), pp. 177–82.

Catling, S (2013c) Teachers' perspectives on curriculum making in primary geography in England. *The Curriculum Journal*, 24(3), pp. 427–53.

Catling, S (2013d) Editorial: Optimism for a revised primary geography curriculum. *Education 3–13*, 41(4), pp. 361–67.

Catling, S (2014a) Giving younger children voice in primary geography: Empowering pedagogy – a personal perspective. *International Research in Geographical and Environmental Education*, 23(4), pp. 350–72.

Catling, S (2014b) Pre-service primary teachers' knowledge and understanding of geography and its teaching: A review. *Review of International Geography Education Online*, 4(3), pp. 235–60.

Catling, S (2014c) Valuing, organising and managing learning outside the classroom. In Arthur, J and Grainger, T (eds) *Learning to Teach in the Primary School* (3rd edn). London: Routledge, pp. 231–49.

Catling, S (2015a) Introduction: Thinking about primary geography. In Catling, S (ed.) *Research and Debate in Primary Geography*. Abingdon: Routledge, pp.1–20.

Catling, S (ed.) (2015b) *Research and Debate in Primary Geography*. Abingdon: Routledge.

Catling, S (2015c) Creative primary geography. In Wilson, A. (ed.) *Creativity in Primary Education* (3rd edn). London: Sage, pp.188–204.

Catling, S (2017a) High quality in primary humanities: Insights from the UK's school inspectorates. *Education 3–13*, 45(3), pp. 354–64.

Catling, S (2017b) Not nearly enough geography! University provision for England's pre-service primary teachers. *Journal of Geography in Higher Education*, 43(3), pp. 434–58.

Catling, S (2017c) Mental maps: Learning about places around the word. In Scoffham, S (ed.) *Teaching Geography Creatively* (2nd edn). Abingdon: Routledge, pp. 58–75.

Catling, S (n.d.) GTIP think piece: Making and using maps. Available at: www.geography.org.uk/projects/gtip/thinkpieces/makingmaps/#top

Catling, S and Baker, P (2011) Wish you were where? Exploring postcard maps. *Primary Geography*, 75, pp. 12–13.

Catling, S and Martin, F (2004a) The state of research in primary geography. In Catling, S and Martin, F (eds) *Researching Primary Geography*. London: Register of Research in Primary Geography, pp.15–25.

Catling, S and Martin, F (eds) (2004b) *Researching Primary Geography*. London: Register of Research in Primary Geography.

Catling, S and Martin, F (2011) Contesting powerful knowledge: The primary geography curriculum as an articulation between academic and children's (ethno-) geographies. *The Curriculum Journal*, 22(3), pp. 317–36.

Catling, S and Morley, E (2013) Enquiring into primary teachers' geographical knowledge. *Education 3–13*, 41(4), pp. 425–42.

Catling, S and Taylor, E (2006) Children thinking about geographical significance. *Primary Geographer*, 60, pp. 35–7.

Catling, S, Willy, T and Butler, J (2013) *Teaching Primary Geography for Australian Schools*. Moorabbin: Hawker Brownlow.

Catling, S, Bendall, G, Cook, N, Elgie, S and Hammond, S (2006) Access denied? *Primary Geographer*, 59, Spring, pp. 35–7.

Catling, S, Bowles, R, Halocha, J, Martin, F and Rawlinson, S (2007) The state of geography in English primary schools. *Geography*, 92(2), pp.118–36.

CCEA (Council for the Curriculum, Examinations and Assessment) (Northern Ireland) (2006) *Curricular Guidance for pre-School Education*. Available at: www. education-ni.gov.uk/sites/default/files/publications/de/curricular-guidance-for-pre-school-education.pdf

CCEA (2007) *The Northern Ireland curriculum: Primary*. Belfast: CCEA.

Cele, S (2006) *Communicating Place: Methods for understanding children's experience of place*. Stockholm: Stockholm University.

Chalkley, B, Haigh, M and Higgitt, D (eds) (2009) *Education for Sustainable Development: Papers in honour of the United Nations decade of education for sustainable development (2005–2014)*. London: Routledge.

Chancellor, B (2013) Primary school playgrounds: Features and management in Victoria, Australia. *International Journal of Play*, 2(2), pp. 63–75.

Chang, C-H (2014) Is Singapore's school geography becoming too responsive to the changing needs of society? *International Research in Geographical and Environmental Education*, 23(1), pp. 25–39.

Chawla, L (1992) Childhood place attachments. In Altman, I and Low, S (eds) *Human Behaviour and Environment, Vol. 12: Place Attachment*. London: Plenum, pp. 63–86.

Chawla, L (ed.) (2002) *Growing Up in an Urbanising World*. London: UNESCO/Earthscan.

Chawla, L and Malone, K (2003) Neighbourhood Quality in Children's Eyes. In Christensen, P and O'Brien, M (eds) *Children in the City*. London: RoutledgeFalmer, pp.118–41.

Chew Hung, C (2014) *Climate Change Education: Knowing, doing and being*. Abingdon: Routledge.

Child, L (2009) *Charlie and Lola: But where completely are we?* London: Puffin Books.

Christensen, P and O'Brien, M (eds) (2003) *Children in the City*. London: RoutledgeFalmer.

Christensen, P and James, A (Eds.) (2000) *Research with Children: Perspectives and practices*. London: RoutledgeFalmer.

Christensen, P, Myrgind, L and Bentsen, P (2015) Conceptions of place: Approaching space, children and physical activity. *Children's Geographies*, 13(5), pp. 589–603.

Christensen, P, Hadfield-Hill, S, Horton, J and Kraftl, P (2018) *Children Living in Sustainable Built Environments: New urbanisms, new citizens*. Abingdon: Routledge.

Cincera, J, Kroufek, R, Simonova, P, Broukalova, L, Broukal, V and Skalik, J (2017) Eco-school in kindergartens: The effects, interpretations, and implementations of a pilot programme. *Environmental Education Research*, 23(7), pp. 919–36.

Claire, H and Holden, C (eds) (2007) *The Challenge of Teaching Controversial Issues*. Stoke on Trent: Trentham Books.

Clarke, P (2012) *Education for Sustainability*. London: Routledge.

Clarke, S (2001) *Unlocking Formative Assessment*. London: Hodder & Stoughton.

Clarke, S (2005a) *Formative Assessment in Action: Weaving the elements together*. London: Hodder Murray.

Clarke, S (2005b) *Formative Assessment in the Secondary Classroom*. London: Hodder & Stoughton.

Claval, P (1998) *An Introduction to Regional Geography*. Oxford: Blackwell.

Cloke, P, Crang, P and Goodwin, M (eds) (2014) *Introducing Human Geographies* (3rd edn). Abingdon: Routledge.

Çoban, G, Akpinar, E, Küçükankurtaran, E, Yildiz, E and Ergin, O (2011) Elementary school students' water awareness. *International Research in Geographical and Environmental Education*, 20(1), pp. 65–83.

Coe, R, Aloisi, C, Higgins, S and Major, L (2014) What makes great teaching? Review of the underpinning research. *The Sutton Trust*. Available at: www.suttontrust.com/wp-content/uploads/2014/10/What-Makes-Great-Teaching-Report.pdf

Coe, R, Waring, M, Hedges, L and Arthur, J (eds) (2017) *Research Methods and Methodologies in Education* (2nd edn). London: Sage.

Cohen, D and MacKeith, S (1991) *The Development of Imagination*. London: Routledge.

Cohen, L, Manion, L and Morrison, K (2017) *Research Methods in Education* (8th edn). London: Routledge.

Collado, S, Íñiguez-Rueda, L and Corraliza, J (2016) Experiencing nature and children's conceptualizations of the natural world. *Children's Geographies*, 14(6), pp. 716–30.

Collins, J and Foley, P (eds) (2008) *Promoting Children's Wellbeing: Policy and practice*. Bristol: Policy Press.

Collis, M (2008) *Global Citizenship for Young Children*. London: Sage.

Collis, S (2017) *Investigating Climate and Biomes*. Sheffield: Geographical Association.

Comber, B (2016) *Literacy, Place and Pedagogies of Possibility*. Abingdon: Routledge.

Conway, D, Pointon, P and Greenwood, J (2008) If the world is round, how come the piece I'm standing on is flat? Early years geography. In Whitebread, D and Coltman, P (eds) *Teaching and Learning in the Early Years* (3rd edn). London: Routledge, pp. 377–98.

Constable, K (2012) *The Outdoor Classroom Ages 3–7*. London: David Fulton.

Cooper, H (2004a) *Exploring Time and Place through Play Foundation Stage, Key Stage One*. Abingdon: Routledge.

Cooper, H (2004b) We're going camping. In Cooper, H (ed.) *Exploring Time and Place through Play*. London: David Fulton, pp. 117–30.

Cooper, H (2013) *Teaching History Creatively*. Abingdon: Routledge.

Cooper, H and Rowley, C (2009) *Cross-curricular Approaches to Teaching and Learning*. London: SAGE.

Cooper, H, Rowley, C and Asquith, S (eds) (2006) *Geography 3–11: A Guide for Teachers*. London: David Fulton, pp. 115–27.

Cooper, L, Johnston, J, Rotchell, E and Woolley, R (2010) *Knowledge and Understanding of the World*. London: Continuum.

Core Writing Team, Pachauri, R and Meyer, L (eds) (2015) Climate change 2014: Synthesis report. Available at: www.ipcc.ch/pdf/assessment-report/ar5/syr/SYR_AR5_FINAL_full_wcover.pdf

Council for Europe (2015) *Teaching Controversial Issues*. Strasbourg: Council for Europe.

Council for Learning Outside the Classroom (2008) Out and about guidance. Available at: www.lotc.org.uk/out-and-about-guidance

Countryside Commission (1997) *Public Attitudes to the Countryside*. Northampton: Countryside Commission.

Cowan, P and Maitles, H (eds) (2012) *Teaching Controversial Issues in the Classroom: Key issues and debates*. London: Continuum.

Cox, S (2011) *New Perspectives in Primary Education*. Maidenhead: Open University Press.

Cox, S (2017) Developing values in primary classrooms and the place of the humanities. *Education 3–13*, 45(3), pp. 375–85.

Cox, S, Dyer, C, Robinson-Pont, A and Scheisfurth, M (2010) *Children as Decision Makers in Education*. London: Continuum.

Cregan, K and Cuthbert, D (2014) *Global Childhoods: Issues and debates*. London: Sage.

Cremin, T and Burnett, C (eds) (2018) *Learning to Teach in the Primary School* (4th Edition). Abingdon: Routledge.

Cresswell, T (2015) *Place: An introduction* (2nd edn). Chichester: Wiley-Blackwell.

Crutzen, P J and Stoermer, EF (2000) The Anthropocene. *IGBP Newsletter*, 41(17), pp.17–18.

Cullingford, C (1999) *The Human Experience: The early years*. Guildford: Ashgate.

Cullingford, C (2000) *Prejudice*. London: Kogan Page.

Cullingford, C (2007) *Childhood: The inside story*. Newcastle: Cambridge Scholars Publishing.

Curriculum for Wales (2015) Foundation phase framework. Available at: http://learning.gov.wales/docs/learningwales/publications/150803-fp-framework-en.pdf

Cutter-Mackenzie, A, Edwards, S, Moore, D and Boyd, W (2014) *Young Children's Play and Environmental Education in Early Childhood Education*. Dordrecht: Springer.

Cutter-Mackenzie, A, Payne, G and Reid, A (eds) (2011) *Experiencing Environment and Place through Children's Literature*. Abingdon: Routledge.

Dalrymple, H (n.d.) *Fair Trade School Handbook: A small but useful guide to help you become a fair trade school*. Leeds: Leeds Development Education Centre.

Daly, N (1987) *Not So Fast, Songololo*. Hamondsworth: Puffin.

Daly, N (1999) *The Boy on the Beach*. London: Bloomsbury Publishing.

Danby, S, Davidson, C, Ekberg, S, Breathnach, H and Thorpe, K (2016) Let's see if you can see me: Making connections with Google Earth in a preschool classroom. *Children's Geographies*, 14(3), pp. 141–57.

Davies, B (2015) *Grandad's Island*. London: Simon & Schuster.

Davies, C (n.d.) Weaving mastery and greater depth in the national curriculum. *Blog: Focus education*. Available at: www.focus-education.co.uk/blog/weaving-mastery-and-greater-depth-in-the-national-curriculum/

Davis, J (ed.) (2015) *Young Children and the Environment: Early education for sustainability* (2nd edn). Port Melbourne: Cambridge University Press.

Day, C (2007) *Environment and Children*. London: Elsevier/Architectural Press.

DBE (Department of Basic Education) (2011) *The Curriculum and Assessment Statement (CAPS) for Social Sciences, Intermediate Phase (Grades 4 to 6)*. Pretoria: Department of Basic Education.

DCSF (2008) *Practice Guidance for the Early Years Foundation Stage: Setting the standards for learning, development and care for children from birth to five*. Annesley: DCSF Publications. Available at: www.routledge.com/textbooks/9780415485586/data/EarlyYearsFoundationStage-PracticeGuidance.pdf

de Amorim Soares, M and Petarnella, L (eds) (2011) *Schooling for Sustainable Development in South America*. Dordrecht: Springer.

de Blij, H (2009) *The Power of Place*. Oxford: Oxford University Press.

de Blij, H (2012) *Why Geography Matters More Than Ever*. Oxford: Oxford University Press.

de Block, L and Buckingham, D (2007) *Global Children, Global Media*. Basingstoke: Palgrave Macmillan.

de Bono, E (1977) *Lateral Thinking: A textbook of creativity*. London: Penguin.

de Bono, E (1982) *de Bono's Thinking Course*. London: Penguin.

de Bono, E (1985) *Six Thinking Hats*. London: Penguin.

de Leo, J (2012) *Quality Education for Sustainable Development*. Adelaide: UNESCO APNIEVE.

de Souza e Silva, A and Frith, J (2012) *Mobile Interfaces in Public Spaces*. London: Routledge.

DEEWR (Department of Education, Employment and Workplace Relations) (2009) The early years framework for Australia: Belonging, being, becoming. Available at: https://docs.education.gov.au/system/files/doc/other/belonging_being_and_becoming_the_early_years_learning_framework_for_australia.pdf

DEEWR (2010) Educators belonging, being, becoming: Educators' guide to the early years learning framework for Australia. Available at: www.deewr.gov.au/Earlychildhood/Policy_Agenda/Quality/

DEFRA (Department for Environment, Food and Rural Affairs) (2014) The countryside code. Available at: www.gov.uk/government/publications/the-countryside-code

DEH (2005) Education for a sustainable future. Available at: www.environment.gov.au/education/publications/pubs/sustainable-future.pdf

Demarest, A (2015) *Place-based Curriculum Design: Exceeding standards through local investigations*. New York: Routledge.

Demirci, A, de Miguel Gonzalez, R and Bednarz, S (eds.) *Geography Education for Global Understanding*. Cham: Springer Nature.

Denscombe, M (2014) *The Good Research Guide* (5th edn). Maidenhead: Open University Press.

Derraiki, J (2002) The pollution of the marine environment by plastic debris: A review. *Marine Pollution Bulletin*, 44(9), pp. 842-852.

DES/NCCA (Department of Education and Science/National Council for Curriculum and Assessment) (1999) *Primary School Curriculum: Geography*. Dublin: Government Publications Office.

Devine, D (2003) *Children, Power and Schooling*. Stoke on Trent: Trentham Books.

DEWHA (2009) Living sustainably. Available at: www.environment.gov.au/education/nap/index.html

DEWHA (2010) Sustainability curriculum framework: A guide for curriculum developers and policy makers. Available at: www.environment.gov.au/education/publications/curriculum-framework.html

DfE (Department for Education) (1995) *Geography in the national curriculum (England)*. London: DfE.

DfE (2012) Top tips for sustainability in schools. Available at: www.education.gov.uk

DfE (2013) The National Curriculum in England: Framework document. Available at: www.gov.uk/dfe/nationalcurriculum.

DfE (2017) Statutory framework for the early years foundation stage. Available at: www.gov.uk/government/uploads/system/uploads/attachment_data/file/596629/EYFS_STATUTORY_FRAMEWORK_2017.pdf

DfEE (1998) *Health and safety of pupils on educational visits*. London: DfEE.

DfEE/QCA (Department for Education & Employment/Qualifications and Curriculum Authority) (1999) The national curriculum handbook for primary teachers in England. Available at: www.educationengland.org.uk/documents/pdfs/1999-nc-primary-handbook.pdf

DfES (2003) *Excellence and enjoyment: A strategy for primary schools*. London: DfES.

DfES (2006a) Sustainable schools for pupils, communities and the environment: Consultation paper. London: DfES. Available at: www.webarchive.national archives.gov. uk/*/http://www.teachernet.gov.uk/sustainableschools

DfES (2006b) Sustainable schools for pupils, communities and the environment: Government response to the consultation on the sustainable schools strategy. London: DfES. Available at: www.webarchive.nationalarchives.gov.uk/*/http://www.teachernet.gov.uk/sustainableschools

DfES (2006c) *Manifesto for learning outside the classroom*. London: DfES.

DfID/DfEE (2005) *Developing a global dimension in the school curriculum*. London: DfID.

Dillemuth, J (2016) *Lucy in the City*. Washington, DC: Magination Press.

Dinkele, G (2010) Enquiries and Investigations. In Scoffham, S (ed.) *Primary Geography Handbook*. Sheffield: Geographical Association, pp. 95–103.

Dinsman, T and Rees, G (2014) Children's worlds international survey of children's well-being (ISCWeB): Findings from the first wave of data collection. Available at: www.isciweb.org/_Uploads/dbsAttachedFiles/FirstWaveReportFINAL(2).pdf

Disney, A (2004) Children's developing images and representation of the school link environment. In Catling, S and Martin, F (eds) *Researching Primary Geography*. London: Research Register in Primary Geography, pp.139–47.

Disney, A and Mapperley, J (2007) Sustaining a school link. *Primary Geographer*, 62, pp. 16–18.

Dixon, J and Day, S (2004) Secret places: You're too big to come in here. In Cooper, H (ed.) *Exploring Time and Place through Play*. London: David Fulton, pp. 92–108.

Dodds, F, Donoghue, D and Roesch, J (2017) *Negotiating the Sustainable Development Goals: A transformational agenda for an insecure world*. London: Routledge/Earthscan.

Dolan, A (2013) Critically 'reading the world' through picture-books. In O'Riorden, J, Horgan, D and Martin, S (eds) *Early Childhoods in the Global South*. Bern: Peter Lang, pp. 272–87.

Dolan, A (2014) *You, Me and Diversity*. London: Trentham Books/UCL Institute of Education.

Dolan, A (2017) Engaging with the world through picture books. In Scoffham, S (ed.) *Teaching Geography Creatively*. Abingdon: Routledge, pp. 30–43.

Dolan, A (2019) *Powerful Primary Geography: A toolkit for 21st century learning.* Abingdon: Routledge.

Donaldson, G (2015) Successful Futures: Independent review of curriculum and assessment arrangements in Wales. Cardiff: Council for Curriculum, Examinations and Assessment. Available at: http://gov.wales/topics/educationandskills/school-shome/curriculuminwales/curriculum-for-wales/?lang-en

Donaldson, J and Scheffler, A (2003) *The Snail and the Whale.* London: Macmillan Children's Books.

Dooley, M (ed.) (2010) *Their Hopes, Fears and Reality: Working with children and youth for the future.* Oxford: Peter Lang.

Dorling, D and Lee, C (2016) *Ideas in Profile: Geography.* London: Profile Books.

Dove, J (1999) *Theory into Practice: Immaculate Misconceptions.* Sheffield: Geographical Association.

Dove, J, Everett, L and Preece, P (2000) The urban child's conception of a river. *Education 3–13*, 28(1), pp. 52–6.

Dovey, K (2010) *Becoming Places.* London: Routledge.

Dower, N and Williams, J (2002) *Global Citizenship: A critical introduction.* London: Routledge.

Downs, R (1994) The need for research in geography education: It would be nice to have some data. *Journal of Geography*, 93(1), pp. 57–60.

Downs, R and Stea, D (1977) *Maps in Minds.* New York: Harper & Row.

Drury, H (2015) *Mastering Mathematics: Teaching to transform achievement.* Oxford: Oxford University Press.

Dudek, M (ed.) (2005) *Children's Spaces.* London: Architectural Press.

Dunlop, S (2017) *Weather: A Very Short Introduction.* Oxford: Oxford University Press.

Dunne, R (2016) Principles of Harmony. *Primary Geography*, 90, pp. 12–13.

Eaude, T (2011) *Thinking Through Pedagogy for Primary and Early Years.* Exeter: Learning Matters.

Eaude, T (2018) *Developing the Expertise of Primary and Elementary Classroom Teachers.* London: Bloomsbury.

Edelson, DC (2014) The importance of teaching children to read maps. *Esri ArcNews.* Available at: www.esri.com/esri-news/arcnews/fall14articles/the-importance-of-teaching-children-to-read-maps

Edensor, T (2002) *National Identity, Popular Culture and Everyday Life.* Oxford: Berg.

Edmondson, I (2008) A view from the ground: Life-world experiences for four Aboriginal children in a Western Australian desert community. In Gerber, R and Robertson, M (eds) *Children's Lifeworlds: Locating indigenous voices.* New York: Nova Science Publishers, pp. 33–56.

EEF (Education Endowment Foundation) (n.d.) Mastery learning. Available at: https://educationendowmentfoundation.org.uk/resources/teaching-learning-toolkit/mastery-learning/

Education Scotland (2009) Curriculum for excellence: Social studies – Experiences and outcomes. Available at: www.educationscotland.gov.uk/learningandteaching/curriculumareas/socialstudies/index.asp

Education Scotland (2013) Social studies 3–18: Transforming lives through learning. Available at: www.educationscotland.gov.uk/resources/0to9/genericresource_tcm4-826574.pdf

Edwards, J (2016) *Socially-critical Environmental Education in Primary Classrooms.* Dordrecht: Springer.

Edwards, S and Cutter-Mackenzie, A (2013) Pedagogical play types: What do they suggest for learning about sustainability in early childhood education *International Journal of Early Childhood*, 45(3), pp.327–346.

Ellesworth, E (2005) *Places of Learning.* London: RoutledgeFalmer.

Ellis, E (2018) Anthropocene: *A very short introduction.* Oxford: Oxford University Press.

Else, P (2009) *The Value of Play.* London: Continuum.

Ensor, M and Gozdziak, E (eds) (2010) *Children and Migration: At the crossroads of resiliency and vulnerability.* Basingstoke: Palgrave Macmillan.

Erebus International (2008) A study into the teaching of geography in years 3–10. Canberra: Department of Education, Employment and Workplace Relations. Available at: www.acara.edu.au

ETI (Education and Training Inspectorate) (2014) An evaluation of the implementation of the world around us in primary schools. Available at: www.etini.gov.uk/index/surveys-evaluations/surveys-evaluations-primary/surveys-evaluations-primary-2015/an-evalaution-of-the-implementation-of-the-world-around-us.pdf

Evans, W and Savage, J (2015) *Developing a Local Curriculum: Using your locality to inspire teaching and learning.* Abingdon: Routledge.

Faber Taylor, A and Kuo, E (2006) Is contact with nature important for healthy child development? State of the evidence. In Spencer, C and Blades, M (eds) *Children and their Environments.* Cambridge: Cambridge University Press, pp. 124–40.

Faragher, M (2017) GIS and other geospatial technologies. In Jones, M (ed.) *The Handbook of Secondary Geography.* Sheffield: Geographical Association, pp. 244–59.

Faragher, S (2014) *Understanding Assessment in Primary Education.* London: Sage.

Farmer, D (2017) Children and youth's mobile journeys: Making sense and connections within global contexts. In Ní Laoire, C and White, A (eds) *Movement, Mobilities, and Journeys.* Dordrecht: Springer, pp. 245–69.

Featherstone, S (2010) *The Little Book of Explorations.* London: A & C Black.

Filer, J (2008) *Healthy, Outside and Active: Running an Outdoors Programme in the Early Years.* London: David Fulton.

Firth, R (2011) Making geography visible as an object of study in the secondary curriculum. *The Curriculum Journal*, 22(3), pp. 289–316.

Firth, R (2012) Disordering the coalition government's 'new' approach to curriculum design and knowledge: The matter of the discipline. *Geography*, 97(2), pp. 86–94.

Firth, R (2018) Recontextualising geography as a school subject. In Jones, M and Lambert, D (eds) *Debates in Geography Education* (2nd edn). Abingdon: Routledge, pp. 275–86.

Fleet, A and Britt, C (2011) Seeing spaces, inhabiting places. In Harcourt, D, Perry, B and Waller, T (eds) *Researching Young Children's Perspectives.* Abingdon: Routledge, pp. 143–62.

Fog Olwig, K and Gulløv, E (eds) (2004) *Children's Places.* London: Routledge.

Foley, P and Leverett, S (eds) (2011) *Children and Young People's Spaces.* Basingstoke: Palgrave Macmillan.

Foreman, M (2006) *Mia's Story.* London: Walker Books.

Fox, M (2016) *Home: A very short introduction.* Oxford: Oxford University Press.

France, D, Whalley, W, Mauchline, A, Powell, V, Welsh, K, Lerczak, A, Park, J and Bednarz, R (2015) *Enhancing Fieldwork Learning Using Mobile Technologies.* New York: Springer.

Fraser, S, Lewis, V, Ding, S, Kellett, M and Robinson, C (eds) (2004) *Doing Research with Children and Young People*. London: Sage.

Freeman, C and Tranter, P (2011) *Children and their Urban Environment: Changing Worlds*. London: Earthscan.

Freeman, C, Nairn, K and Gollop, M (2015) Disaster impact and recovery: What children and young people can tell us. *Kōtuitui: New Zealand Journal of Social Studies Online*, 10(2), pp. 103–15.

Freeman, C, van Heezik, Y, Stein, A and Hand, K (2015) *Natural neighbourhoods for city children: Report of research findings*. Dunedin: University of Otago Department of Geography.

Freeman, C, van Heezik, Y, Stein, A and Hand, K (2016) Technical inroads into understanding city children's natural life-worlds. *Children's Geographies*, 14(2), pp. 158–74.

Freire, P (1994) *A Pedagogy of Hope*. London: Continuum.

Frost, J (2010) *A History of Children's Play and Play Environments*. New York: Routledge.

GA (Geographical Association) (2005–7) *SuperSchemes Geography at Key Stages 1 and 2*. Sheffield: Geographical Association.

GA (2009) A different view: A manifesto from the Geographical Association. Sheffield: Geographical Association. Available at: www.geography.org.uk/adifferentview

GA (2012) Thinking geographically. Available at: www.geography.org.uk/write/MediaUploads/Support%20and%20guidance/GA_GINCConsultation_ThinkingGeographically_NC_2012.pdf

GA (2014a) Global learning special. GA, Autumn. Sheffield: Geographical Association. Available at: www.geography.org.uk/GLP%20Schools%2012pp%20mailing_LO-RES%20final%20(2).pdf

GA (2014b) An assessment and progression framework for geography. Sheffield: Geographical Association. Available at: www.geography.org.uk/curriculum2014/assessment

GA (n.d.) Curriculum making introduced. Available at: www.geography.org.uk/cpdevents/curriculum/curriculummaking/

Galani, A and Rokka, A (2014) An investigation into hand-drawn representations of rivers by fifth-grade students in Greek elementary schools. *ISRN Education*, 14. Available at: http://dx.doi.org/10.1155/2014/548365

Gamble, N (2013) *Exploring Children's Literature: Reading with pleasure and purpose* (3rd edn). London: Sage.

Garland, S (2012) *Azzi in Between*. London: Frances Lincoln.

Garforth, H, Hopper, L, Lowe, B and Robinson, L (2006) *Growing Up Global*. Reading: RISC.

Garrick, R (2009) *Playing Outdoors in the Early Years* (2nd edn). London: Continuum.

Gaut, B and Gaut, M (2012) *Philosophy for Young Children*. London: Routledge.

Gaylie, V (2009) *The Learning Garden: Ecology, teaching and transformation*. New York: Peter Lang.

Gaylie, V (2011) *Roots and Research in Urban School Gardens*. New York: Peter Lang.

GEG [Geography Expert Group] (2013) *Thinking Geographically*. Available at: https://geognc.files.wordpress.com/2013/08/thinking_geographically.pdf

Gerber, R (2001) Developing a sense of community and place in different cultural settings and environments. In Robertson, M and Gerber, R (eds) *Children's Ways of Knowing*. Melbourne: ACER Press, pp. 62–78.

Gerber, R and Robertson, M (eds) (2008) *Children's Lifeworlds: Locating Indigenous Voices*. New York: Nova Science Publishers.

Getting Smart (2017) What is place-based education and why does it matter? Available at: www.gettingsmart.com/wp-content/uploads/2017/02/What-is—Place-Based-Education-and-Why-Does-it-Matter-3.pdf

Gibson, S and Haynes, J (eds) (2009) *Perspectives on Participation and Inclusion: Engaging Education*. London: Continuum.

Gilbert, R and Hoepper, B (eds) (2011) *Teaching Society and Environment* (4th edn). South Melbourne: Cengage Learning.

Gill, T (2007) *No Fear: Growing Up in a Risk-averse Society*. London: Calouste Gulbenkian Foundation.

Gill, T (2011) Children and nature: A quasi-systematic review of the empirical evidence. London: London Sustainable Development Commission. Available at: www.londonsdc.org.uk/documents/Children%20and%20Nature%20-%20Literature%20Review.pdf.

Giuseppina, M, Giovannelli, I and Spaccatina, F (2017) Children's independent mobility: Antecedents and consequences at macro- and micro-levels. In Ni Laoire and White (eds) *Movement, Mobilities, and Journeys*. Dordrecht: Springer, pp. 308–27.

Glaser, M (2007) Virtual worlds for kids entwined with real world. Available at: www.pbs.org/mediashift/2007/06/your_take_roundupvirtual_world.html

Glauert, E, Heal, C, and Cook, J (2003) Knowledge and understanding of the world. In Riley, J (ed.) *Learning in the Early Years: A Guide for Teachers of Children 3–7*. London: Paul Chapman, pp. 125–55.

GLP (Global Learning Programme) (2014) Progression in global learning through geography. Available at: www.globaldimension.org.uk/glp/page/11043

Glynne, A and Senior, T (2016) *Hamid's Story: A real-life account of his journey from Eritrea*. London: Wayland.

Goleman, D, Bennett, L and Barlow, Z (2012) *Ecoliterate: How educators are cultivating emotional, social, and ecological intelligence*. San Francisco, CA: Jossey Bass.

Gorana. R and Kanaujia, P (eds) (2016) *Reorienting Educational Efforts for Sustainable Development: Experiences from South Asia*. Dordrecht: Springer.

Gordon, N, Farberow, N and Maida, C (1999) *Children and Disasters*. Philadelphia, PA: Brunner/Mazel.

Goudie, A (2013) *The Human Impact on the Natural Environment: Past, present and future* (7th edn). Chichester: Wiley-Blackwell.

Goudie, A and Viles, H (2016) *Geomorphology in the Anthropocene*. Cambridge: Cambridge University Press.

Grainger, T and Arthur, J (2014) *Learning to Teach in the Primary School* (3rd edn). London: Routledge.

Grant, S, Swan, K and Lee, J (2017) *Inquiry-based Practice in Social Studies Education*. New York: Routledge.

Graves, N (2001) *School Textbook Research: The case of geography 1800–2000*. London: Institute of Education.

Gravett, E (2006) *Meerkat Mail*. London: Macmillan Children's Books.

Green, C, Kalvaitis, D and Worster, A (2016) Recontextualizing pychosocial development in young children: A model of environmental identity development. *Environmental Education Research*, 22(7), pp. 1025–48.

Green, M and Somerville, M (2015) Sustainability education: Researching Practice in Primary Schools. *Environmental Education Research*, 21(6), pp. 832–45.

Greene, S and Hogan, D (Eds.) (2005) *Researching Children's Experience: Approaches and methods.* London: Sage.

Greenwood, J and Linklater, H (2015) So what is long ago and where is far away? A sense of time and place. In Whitebread, D and Coltman, P (eds) *Teaching and Learning in the Early Years* (4th edn). Abingdon: Routledge, pp. 311–25.

Greenwood, R (2013) Subject-based and cross-curricular approaches within the revised primary curriculum in Northern Ireland: Teachers' concerns and preferred approaches. *Education 3–13*, 41(4), pp. 443–58.

Greenwood, R (2017) Playful learning in natural outdoor environment. In Walsh, G, McMillan, D and McGuiness, C (eds) *Playful Teaching and Learning.* London: Sage, pp. 116–32.

Gregory, D, Johnston, R, Pratt, G, Watts, M and Whatmore, S (eds) (2009) *The Dictionary of Human Geography* (5th edn). Chichester: Wiley-Blackwell.

Gregory, M, Haynes, J and Murris, K (eds) (2017) *The Routledge International Handbook of Philosophy for Children.* Abingdon: Routledge.

Griffiths, A and Allbut, G (2011) The danger of a single image. *Primary Geography*, 75, Summer, pp. 16–17.

Griffiths, J (2013) *Kith: The Riddle of the Childscape.* London: Hamish Hamilton.

Grigg, R and Hughes, S (2013) *Teaching Primary Humanities.* Harlow: Pearson.

Grigg, R and Lewis, H (2016) *A to Z of Learning Outside the Classroom.* London: Bloomsbury.

Gruenewald, D and Smith, G (eds) (2008) *Place-Based Education in the Global Age: Local diversity.* New York: Lawrence Erlbaum Associates.

Guldberg, H (2009) *Reclaiming Childhood: Freedom and play in an age of fear.* London: Routledge.

Gunter, B and Furnham, A (1998) *Children as Consumers.* London: Routledge.

Hackett, A, Proctor, L and Seymour, J (eds) (2015) *Children's Spatialities: Embodiment, emotion and agency.* Basingstoke: Palgrave Macmillan.

Hallett, C and Prout, A (eds) (2003) *Hearing the Voices of Children.* London: Routledge.

Halocha, J (1998) *Coordinating Geography Across the Primary School.* Lewes: Falmer Press.

Halocha, J (2007) Developing investigative work/inquiry. In Johnston, J, Halocha, J and Chater (eds) *Developing Teaching Skills in the Primary School.* Maidenhead: Open University Press, pp. 154–73.

Halocha, J (2012) *The Primary Teacher's Guide to Geography.* Witney: Scholastic/Book End.

Halvorsen, A-L (2013) *A History of Elementary Social Studies: Romance and Reality.* New York: Peter Lang.

Halvorsen, A-L (2017) Children's learning and understanding of their social world. In Manfra, M and Bolick, C (eds) *The Wiley Handbook of Social Studies Research.* Chichester: Wiley Blackwell, pp. 385–413.

Hamilton, C, Bonneuil, C and Gemenne, F (eds) (2015) *The Anthropocene and the Global Environmental Crisis.* Abingdon: Routledge.

Harari, Y (2014) *Sapiens: A Brief History of Humankind.* Vintage Books: London.

Harcourt, D, Perry, B and Waller, T (eds) (2011) *Researching Young Children's Perspectives*. Abingdon: Routledge.

Harder, C (ed.) (2015) *The ARCGIS Book: 10 Big Ideas about Applying Geography to Your World*. Redlands, CA: Esri Press.

Hare, R, Attenborough, C and Day, T (1996) *Geography in the School Grounds*. Bristol: Southgate.

Harker, C and Hörschelmann, K (eds) (2017) *Conflict, Violence and Peace*. Dordrecht: Springer.

Harlen, W, Gipps, C, Broadfoot, P and Nuttall, D (1992) Assessment and the Improvement of Education. *The Curriculum Journal*, 3(3), pp. 215–30.

Harrington, T (2016) Mental maps and a community-based sense of place: A case study among Kansas third graders. *Research in Geographic Education*, 18(2), pp. 86–111.

Harris, J (2001) *Blackberry Wine*. London: Black Swan Books.

Harris, M (2018) *Becoming an Outstanding Geography Teacher*. Abingdon: Routledge.

Harrison, A and Purnell, K (2012) Sustainability education in classrooms: Developing teacher expertise. In Robertson, M (ed.) *Schooling for Sustainable Development: A focus on Australia, New Zealand and the Oceanic region*. Melbourne: Springer, pp.15–31.

Hart, R (1997) *Children's Participation*. London: Earthscan.

Hartley, B, Thompson, R and Pahl, S (2015) Marine litter education boosts children's understanding and self-reported action. *Marine Pollution Bulletin*, 90 (January), pp. 209-217.

Hartung, C (2017) *Conditional Citizens: Rethinking Children and Young People's Participation*. Singapore: Springer.

Harwood, D and McShane, J (1998) Young children's understanding of nested hierarchies of place relationships. *International Research in Geographical and Environmental Education*, 5(1), pp. 3–29.

Hattie, J (2012) *Visible Learning for Teachers: Maximising impact on learning*. Abingdon: Routledge.

Hawkins, C (ed.) (2017) *Rethinking Children as Consumers: The changing status of childhood and young adulthood*. Abingdon: Routledge.

Hawkins, H (2017) *Key Ideas in Geography: Creativity*. Abingdon: Routledge.

Haynes, J (2008) *Children as Philosophers: Learning Through Enquiry and Dialogue in the Primary Classroom* (2nd edn). Abingdon: Routledge.

Hayward, L and Hayward, S (2016) Assessment and learning. In Wyse, D and Rogers, S (eds) *A Guide to Early Years and Primary Teaching*. London: Sage, pp.165–83.

Hayward, S (2012) *Children, Citizenship and Environment*. London: Routledge.

Head, K, Simmons, J, Wilson, J, Nockolds, K, Colliver, A, Hunt, P, O'Sullivan, P and Harris, D (1996) *Geography for Primary Schools*. Booragoon: Australian Geography Teachers Association.

Heal, C and Cook, J (1998) Humanities: Developing a sense of place and time in the early years. In Siraj Blatchford, I (ed.) *A Curriculum Development Handbook for Early Childhood Educators*. Stoke on Trent: Trentham Books, pp.121–36.

Hedefalk, M, Almqvist, J and Ostman, L (2015) Education for sustainable development in early childhood education: A review of the research literature. *Environmental Education Research*, 21(7), pp. 975–90.

Hedegaard, M, Aronsson, K, Højholt, C and Skjær Ulvik, O (2012) *Children, Childhood and Everyday Life: Children's perspectives*. Charlotte, NC: Information Age Publishing.

Heffron, S and Downs, R (eds) (2012) *Geography for Life: National geography standards* (2nd edn). Washington, DC: Association of American Geographers and National Council for Geographic Education.

Heide, F and Gilliland, J (1997) *The Day of Ahmed's Secret*. London: Puffin Books.

Hemmer, I, Hemmer, M, Kruschel, K, Neidhardt, E, Obermaier, G and Uphues, R (2013) Which children can find a way through a strange town using a street map? – Results of an empirical study on children's orientation competence. *International Research in Geographical and Environmental Education*. 22(1), pp. 23–40.

Hennerdal, P (2016) Changes in place location knowledge: A follow-up study in Arvika, Sweden, 1968 and 2013. *International Research in Geographical and Environmental Education*, 25(4), pp. 309–27.

Henshall, A and Lacey, L (2007) *Word on the street: Children and young people's views on using the street for play and informal recreation*. London: National Children's Bureau.

Hergan, I (2018) Children's perception of surroundings in an unfamiliar environment, *Journal of Geography*, 117(1), pp. 64-74.

Hergan, I and Umek, M (2017) Comparison of children's wayfinding, using paper map and mobile navigation. *International Research in Geographical and Environmental Education*, 26(2), pp. 91–106.

Herod, A (2011) *Key Ideas in Geography: Scale*. Abingdon: Routledge.

Hicks, D (1998) Stories of hope: A response to the 'psychology of despair'. *Environmental Education Research*, 4(2), pp.165–76.

Hicks, D (2002) *Lessons for the Future*. London: Routledge.

Hicks, D (2007) Responding to the world. In Hicks, D and Holden, C (eds) *Teaching the Global Dimension*. London: Routledge, pp. 3–13.

Hicks, D (2012) Sustainable schools, Sustainable futures: A resource for teachers. *Worldwide Fund for Nature*. Available at: http://assets.wwf.org.uk/downloads/sf_full_version.pdf

Hicks, D (2014) *Educating for Hope in Troubled Times*. London: Trentham Books/Institute of Education Press.

Hicks, D (2016) *A Climate Companion for Family, School and Community*. Bath: Teaching4abetterworld.

Hicks, D and Holden, C (eds) (2007) *Teaching the Global Dimension*. London: Routledge.

Higgins, N and Freeman, C (eds) (2013) *Childhoods: Growing up in Aotearoa New Zealand*. Otago: Otago University Press.

Hillman, M and Adams, J (1992) Children's freedom and safety. *Children's Environments*, 9(2), pp. 12–33.

Hirst, B (2006) *The impact of global dimension teaching on children's achievement*. Manchester: North West Global Education Network, Manchester Development Education Project.

HMI (Her Majesty's Inspectorate) (1986) *Curriculum matters 7: Geography from 5 to 16*. London: Her Majesty's Stationery Office.

HMI (1989) *Aspects of Primary Education: The Teaching and Learning of History and Geography*. London; HMSO.

Holden, J (2011) *Physical Geography: The basics*. Abingdon: Routledge.

Holden, J (2012) *An Introduction to Physical Geography and the Environment*. Harlow: Pearson.

Holden, K (2004) Educating for Europe: The knowledge and understanding of British children. *Education 3–13*, 32(1), pp. 39–44.

Holland, G (1998) A report to DIEE/QCA on education for sustainable development in the schools sector from the Panel for Education for Sustainable Development. Available at: www.defra.gov.uk/environmentlsustainable/educpanel/1998ar/ann4.htm

Holloway, L and Hubbard, P (2001) *People and Place: The Extraordinary Geographies of Everyday Life*. London: Prentice Hall.

Holloway, S and Valentine, G (2003) *Cyberkids: Children in the Information Age*. London: RoutledgeFalmer.

Holmes, R and Procaccino, J (2009) Preschool children's outdoor play area preferences. *Early Child Development and Care*, 179(8), pp.1103–12.

Holt, L (2007) Children's sociospatial (re)production of disability within primary school playgrounds. *Environment and Planning D: Society and Space*, 25(6), pp. 783–802.

Holt, L (ed.) (2011) *Geographies of Children, Youth and Families: An international perspective*. Abingdon: Routledge.

Holt-Jensen, A (2018) *Geography: History and Concepts* (5th edition). London: Sage.

Hoodless, P (2008) *Teaching History in Primary Schools*. Exeter: Learning Matters.

Hoodless, P, Bermingham, S, McCreery, E and Bowen, P (2009) *Teaching Humanities in Primary Schools*. Exeter: Learning Matters.

Hope, J (2017) *Children's Literature about Refugees*. London: UCL-Institute of Education Press.

Hopwood-Stephens, I (2013) *Learning on Your Doorstep: Stimulating writing through creative play outdoors for ages 5–9*. Abingdon: Routledge.

Hordyk, S, Dulude, M and Shem, M (2015) Where nature nurtures children: Nature as a containing and holding space. *Children's Geographies*, 13(5), pp. 571–88.

Hörschelmann, K and van Blerk, L (2012) *Children, Youth and the City*. London: Routledge.

Horton, J and Kraftl, P (2014) *Cultural Geographies: An Introduction*. Abingdon: Routledge.

Horvath, J (2016) *Educating Young Children through Natural Water*. Abingdon: Routledge.

Houghton, P and Worroll, J (2016) *Play the Forest School Way*. London: Watkins.

HRH The Prince of Wales, Juniper, T and Skelly, I (2010) *Harmony: A new way of looking at the world*. London: HarperCollins.

Hsiao, C-Y and Shih, P-Y (2016) Exploring the effectiveness of picture books for teaching young children the concepts of environmental protection. *International Research in Geographical and Environmental Education*, 25(1), pp. 36–49.

Huckle, J (1990) Environmental education: Teaching for a sustainable future. In Dufour, D (ed.) *The New Social Curriculum*. Cambridge: Cambridge University Press.

Huckle, J and Martin, A (2001) *Environments in a Changing World*. Harlow: Prentice Hall.

Huggett, R (2003) *Fundamentals of Geomorphology*. London: Routledge.

Huggett, R (2010) *Physical Geography: The key concepts*. Abingdon: Routledge.

Huggett, R, Lindley, S, Gavin, H and Richardson, K (2004) *Physical Geography: A human perspective*. London: Arnold.

Huijsmans, R (2017) Children and young people in migration: A relational approach. In Ní Laoire, C and White, A (eds) *Movement, Mobilities, and Journeys*. Dordrecht: Springer, pp. 45–66.

Hume, C, Salmon, J and Ball, K (2004) Children's perceptions of their home and neighbourhood environments, and their association with objectively measured physical activity: a qualitative and quantitative study. *Health Education Research: Theory and Practice*, 20(1), pp.1-13.

Hunner-Kreisel, C and Bohne, S (eds.) (2016) *Childhood, Youth and Migration: Connecting global and local perspectives*, Dordrecht: Springer.

Hutchins, P (1992) *Rosie's Walk*. London: Puffin.

Hutchinson, D (2004) *A Natural History of Place in Education*. New York: Teachers College Press.

ICS (International Commission on Stratigraphy) (2016) *International Chronostratigraphic Chart*. Available at: www.stratigraphy.org/cschart/ChronostratChart2016-12.pdf.

IGU-CGE (International Geographic Union Commission on Geographic Education) (2015) The International Declaration on Research in Geography Education. Available at: www.igu-cge.org/charters.htm

IGU-CGE (2016) 2016 International Charter on Geographical Education. Available at: www.igu-cge.org/Charters.pdf/2016/IGU_2016_def.pdf

Incekara, S (2010) What did the new social studies program change in upper primary school level social studies in Turkish schools? An assessment from teachers' perspectives. *International Research in Geographical and Environmental Education*, 19(4), pp. 351–64.

IPCC (Intergovernmental Panel on Climate Change) (2015) *Climate Change 2014: Synthesis Report*. Geneva: IPCC.

Iwaskov, L (2004) Escape this primary trough. *Times Educational Supplement*, November.

Iwaskow, L (2013) Inspiring curiosity and fascination. *Primary Geography*, 82, pp. 24–5.

Jackson, E (2010) Citizenship and primary geography. In Scoffham, S (ed.) *Primary Geography Handbook*. Sheffield: Geographical Association, pp. 288–99.

Jackson, L (2013) Learning from adventure rock. In Merchant, G, Gillen, J, Marsh, J and Davies, J (eds) *Virtual Literacies: Interactive Spaces for Children and Young People*. Abingdon: Routledge, pp. 208–25.

Jackson, L, Gauntlett, D and Steemers, J (2008) *Children in Virtual Worlds: Adventure rock users and producers study*. London: BBC. Available at: www.art-lab.org.uk/ahrc-bbc-project.htm

Jackson, P (2006) Thinking geographically. *Geography*, 91(3), pp.116–122.

Jacobs Foundation (2015) Children's views on their lives and well-being in 15 countries: A report on the Children's Worlds survey, 2013–14. Available at: www.isciweb.org/_Uploads/dbsAttachedFiles/ChildrensWorlds2015-FullReport-Final.pdf

Jacobs Foundation (2016) Children's views on their lives and well-being in 16 countries: A report on the Children's Worlds survey, 2013–15. Available at: www.isciweb.org/_Uploads/dbsAttachedFiles/8yearsoldreport.pdf

James, M and Pollard, A (2012) Introduction. In James, M and Pollard, A (eds) *Principles for Effective Pedagogy*. London: Routledge, pp.1–5.

James, S (2017) Pack your bag, we're moving. *Primary Geography*, 94, Autumn, pp.10–11.

Jan Bent, G, Bakx, A and den Brok (2014) Pupils' perceptions of geography in Dutch primary schools: Goals, outcomes, classroom environments and teacher knowledge and performance. *Journal of Geography*, 113(1), pp. 20–34.

Jeffrey, B and Woods, P (2003) *The Creative School*. London: RoutledgeFalmer.

Jeffery, J (2014) *Outdoor Wonderland: The kids' guide to being outside*. Lewes: Ivy Press.

Jennings, K (2012) *Maphead – Charting the Wide, Weird World of Geography Wonks*. New York: Scribner.

Johansson, M (2006) Environmental and parental factors as determinants of mode for children's leisure travel. *Journal of Environmental Psychology*, 26(2), pp. 156–69.

Johnson, P (2013) Schoolyard geographies: The influence of object-play and place-making on relationships. *Review of International Geography Education Online*, 3(1), pp. 77–92.

Johnson, S (2010) *Beginning Geography*. Monterey: Evan-Moor Educational Publishers.

Johnston, J, Halocha, J and Chater, M (2007) *Developing Teaching Skills in the Primary School*. Maidenhead: Open University Press.

Jones, A (2011) *Human Geography: The basics*. Abingdon: Routledge.

Jones, M (ed.) (2017) *The Handbook of Secondary Geography*. Sheffield: Geographical Association.

Jones, M and Lambert, D (eds) (2018) *Debates in Geography Education* (2nd edn). Abingdon: Routledge.

Jones, P (2009) *Rethinking Childhood: Attitudes in contemporary society*. London: Continuum.

Jonsson, G, Sarri, C and Alerby, E (2012) 'Too Hot for the Reindeer' – Voicing Sámi children's visions of the future. *International Research in Geographical and Environmental Education*, 21(2), pp. 95–107.

Jørgensen, K-A (2016) Bringing the jellyfish home: Environmental consciousness and 'sense of wonder' in young children's encounters with natural landscapes and places. *Environmental Education Research*, 22(8), pp. 1139–157.

Joubert, I (2009) *'South Africa is my Best World': The Voices of Child Citizens in a Democratic South Africa*. Bern: Peter Lang.

Joyce, R (2012) *Outdoor Learning: Past and present*. Maidenhead: Open University Press.

Kagawa, F and Selby, D (eds) (2010) *Education and Climate Change: Living and learning in interesting times*. Abingdon: Routledge.

Kahn, P (1999) *The Human Relationship with Nature*. Cambridge, MA: MIT Press.

Kahn, P and Kellert, S (eds) (2002) *Children and Nature*. Cambridge, MA: MIT Press.

Kaplan, R (2012) *The Revenge of Geography*. New York: Random House.

Kastens, K and Liben, S (2010) Children's strategies and difficulties while using a map to record locations in an outdoor environment. *International Research in Geographical and Environmental Education*, 19(4), pp. 315–40.

Katsenou, C, Flogaitis, E and Lairakou, G (2013) Exploring pupil participation within a sustainable school. *Cambridge Journal of Education*, 43(2), pp. 243–58.

Katz, C (2004) *Growing Up Global*. Minneapolis, MN: University of Minnesota Press.

Katz, C (2005) The terrors of hypervigilance: Security and the compromised spaces of contemporary childhood. In Qvortrup, J (ed.) *Studies in Modern Childhood*. Basingstoke: Palgrave Macmillan, pp. 99–114.

Keeping, C (1989) *Adam and Paradise Island*. Oxford: Oxford University Press.

Kellett, M (2005) *How to Develop Children as Researchers*. London: Paul Chapman.

Kellett, M (2010) *Rethinking Children and Research*. London: Continuum.

Kelly, P (2007) The joy of involving pupils in their own assessment. In Hayes, D (ed.) *Joyful Teaching and Learning in the Primary School*. Exeter: Learning Matters, pp. 130–35.

Kennelly, J and Taylor N (2007) Education for sustainability for the K–6 curriculum: A unit of work for pre-service primary teachers in NSW. *Australian Journal of Environmental Education*, 23, pp. 3–12.

Kenreich, T (2013) Introduction. In Kenreich, T (ed.) *Geography and Social Justice in the Classroom*. New York: Routledge. pp. 1-8

Kenway, J and Bullen, E (2001) *Consuming Children*. Buckingham: Open University Press.

Kenyon, J (2010) Assessment for learning. In Scoffham, S (ed.) *Primary Geography Handbook*. Sheffield: Geographical Association, pp. 312–20.

Kerry, T (ed.) (2015) *Cross-curricular Teaching in the Primary School: Planning and facilitating imaginative lessons* (2nd edn). Abingdon: Routledge.

Kidman, G (2012) Geographical inquiry in Australian schools: A retrospective analysis. *International Research in Geographical and Environmental Education*, 21(4), pp. 311–19.

Kidman, G and Casinader, N (2017) *Inquiry-Based Teaching and Learning Across Disciplines: Comparative theory and practice in schools*. Basingstoke: Palgrave Macmillan.

Kim, C, Sheehy, K and Kerawalla, L (2017) *Developing Children as Researchers*. Abingdon: Routledge.

Kim, M, Bednarz, R and Kim, J (2012) The ability of young Korean children to use spatial representations. *International Research in Geographical and Environmental Education*, 21(3), pp. 261–77.

Kim, P and Sanchez, S (2014) *Here I Am*. London: Curious Fox.

Kindersley B and A (1995) *Children Just Like Me*. London: Dorling Kindersley.

King, T and Tarrant, R (2013) Children's knowledge, cognitions and emotions surrounding natural disasters: An investigation of year 5 students, Wellington, New Zealand. *Australian Journal of Disaster and Trauma Studies*, 2013(1), pp. 17–26.

Kitchen, R (2013) Student perceptions of geographical knowledge and the role of the teacher. *Geography*, 98(3), pp. 112–22.

Kitchen, R and Freundschuh, S (eds) (2000) *Cognitive Mapping*. London: Routledge.

Klonari, A (2013) Primary school pupils' ability to use aerial photographs and maps in the subject of geography. *European Journal of Geography*, 3(2), pp. 42–53.

Knight, P (1993) *Primary Geography, Primary History*. London: David Fulton.

Knight, S (ed.) (2011a) *Forest School for All*. London: Sage.

Knight, S (2011b) *Risk and Adventure in Early Years Outdoor Play: Learning from Forest Schools*. London: Sage.

Knight, S (ed.) (2013a) *International Perspectives on Forest School: Natural spaces to play and learn*. London: Sage.

Knight, S (2013b) *Forest School and Outdoor Learning in the Early Years* (2nd edn). London: Sage.

Knight, S (2016) *Forest School in Practice for all Ages*. London: Sage.

Knight, S (2017) Forest School for the early years in England. In Waller, T, Ärlemalm-Hagsér, E, Hansen Sandseter, E, Lee-Hammond, L, Lekies, K and Wyver, S (eds) *The Sage Handbook of Outdoor Play and Learning*. London: Sage, pp. 97–110.

Kraftl, P, Horton, J and Tucker, F (eds) (2012) *Critical Geographies of Childhood and Youth*. Bristol: The Policy Press.

Kress, W and Stine, J (eds) (2017) *Living in the Anthropcene: Earth in the Age of Humans*. Washington, DC: Smithsonian Books.

Kreutz, A (2015) *Children and the Environment in an Australian Indigenous Community: A psychological approach*. Abingdon: Routledge.

Kytta, M (2004) *Children in outdoor contexts*. Ph.D. dissertation. Department of Architecture, University of Helsinki.

Kyttä, M (2006) Environmental child friendliness in the light of the Bulerby model. In Spencer, C and Blades, M (eds) *Children and their Environments*. Cambridge: Cambridge University Press, pp. 41–158.

La Greca, A, Silverman, W, Vernberg, E and Roberts, M (eds) (2002) *Helping Children Cope With Disasters and Terrorism*. Washington, DC: American Psychological Association.

Laird, E (1994) *The Inside Outing*. London: Diamond Books.

Lake, A (2016) *The State of the World's Children 2016: A Fair Chance for Every Child*. New York: United Nations Children's Fund.

Lambert, D (2014) Reviewing the case for geography, and the 'knowledge turn' in the English national curriculum. *The Curriculum Journal*, 22(2), pp. 243–64.

Lambert, D (2017) Thinking geographically. In Jones, M (ed.) *The Handbook of Secondary Geography*. Sheffield: Geographical Association, pp. 20–9.

Lambert, D (2018) The road to Future 3: The case for geography. In Guile, D, Lambert, D and Reiss, M (eds.) *Sociology, Curriculum Studies and Professional Knowledge*. Abingdon: Routledge, pp. 132-145.

Lambert, D and Hopkin, J (2014) A possibilist analysis of the geography national curriculum in England. *International Research in Geographical and Environmental Education*, 23(1), pp. 64–78.

Lambert, D and Morgan, J (2010) *Teaching Geography 11–18*. Maidenhead: Open University Press.

Lane, R (2015) Primary geography in Australia: Pre-service primary teachers' understandings of weather and climate. *Review of International Geographical Education Online*, 5(2), pp. 199–217.

Lanza, M (2012) *Playborhood: Turn your neighbourhood into a place for play*. Menlo Park: Free Play Press.

Lastória, A and Papadimitriou, F (2012) Geographical education in Brazil: Past and present in 'the country of the future'. *International Research in Geographical and Environmental Education*, 21(4), pp. 327–35.

Lavers, J and Bond, A (2017) Exceptional and rapid accumulation of anthropogenic debris on one of the world's most remote and pristine islands. *Proceedings of the National Academy of Sciences*. doi: 10.1073/pnas.1619818114.

Lawrence, A (1973) *The Travels of Oggy*. London: Pan Books.

Layard, R and Dunn, J (2009) *A Good Childhood: Searching for Values in a Competitive Age*. London: Penguin.

Learning through Landscapes (2014) *Learn and Play Out: How to develop your primary school's outside space*. Abingdon: Routledge.

Lee, D-m (2018) A typological analysis of South Korean primary teachers' awareness of primary geography education, *Journal of Geography*, 117(2), pp. 75-87.

Lee, J and Butt, G (2014) The reform of national geography standards – trends, challenges and responses. *International Research in Geographical and Environmental Education*, 23(1), pp. 13–24.

Lee, J and Williams, M (eds) (2009) *Schooling for Sustainable Development in Chinese Communities: Experience with younger children*. Dordrecht: Springer.

Lee, N (2013) *Childhood and Biopolitics: Climate change, life processes and human futures*. Basingstoke: Palgrave Macmillan.

Leeder, A (2006) *100 Ideas for Teaching Geography*. London: Continuum.

Lehman-Frisch, S, Authier, J-Y and Dufaux, F (2012) Draw me your neighbourhood: A gentrified Paris neighbourhood through its children's eyes. *Children's Geographies*, 10(1), pp. 17–34.

Lenton, T (2016) *Earth System Science: A very short introduction*. Oxford: Oxford University Press.

Lester, A (2004) *Are We There Yet? A journey round Australia*. Camberwell: Penguin Viking.

Lewis, V, Kellett, M, Robinson, C, Fraser, S and Ding, S (eds) (2004) *The Reality of Research with Children and Young People*. London: Sage.

Liebel, M (2004) *A Will of Their Own*. London: Zed Books.

Lim, S and Clark, L (2010) Virtual worlds as a site of convergence for children's play. *Journal of Virtual Worlds Research*, 3(2), pp. 3–19.

Lindors, J (1999) *Children's Inquiry: Using language to make sense of the world*. New York: Teachers College Press.

Lipman, M (2003) *Thinking in Education*. Cambridge: Cambridge University Press.

Little, H (2015) Mothers' beliefs about risk and risk-taking in children's outdoor play. *Journal of Adventure Education and Outdoor Learning*, 13(1), pp. 24–39.

Little, H and Wyver, S (2010) Individual differences in children's risk perception and appraisals in outdoor play environments. *International Journal of Early Years Education*, 18(4), pp. 297–313.

Littledyke, M (2002) Primary children's views on science and environmental issues: Examples of environmental cognitive and moral development. Paper presented at the European Conference on Educational Research. Lisbon: University of Lisbon, Portugal. Available at: www.leeds.ac.uk/aducol/documents/00002338.htm

Littledyke, M, Taylor, N and Eames, C (2009) *Education for Sustainability in the Primary Curriculum*. South Yarra, Victoria: Palgrave Macmillan.

Ljung-Djärf, A, Åberg-Bengtsson, L, Ottosson, T and Beach, D (2015) Making sense of iconic symbols: A study of preschool children conducting a refuse-sorting task. *Environmental Education Research*, 21(2), pp. 256–74.

Lockie, B (2007) *Gardening with Young Children*. Stroud: Hawthorn Press.

Lockyer, S (2016) *Lesson Planning for Primary School Teachers*. London: Bloomsbury.

Loebach, J and Gilliland, J (2016) Neighbourhood play on the endangered list: Examining patterns in children's local activity and mobility using GPS monitoring and qualitative GIS. *Children's Geographies*, 14(5), pp. 573–89.

Lolichen, P (2007) Children in the Driver's Seat: Children Conducting A Study of Their Transport and Mobility Problems. *Children, Youth and Environments*, 17(1), pp. 238–56.

Lotz-Sisitka, H, Shumba, O, Lupele, J and Wilmot, D (eds) (2017) *Schooling for Sustainable Development in Africa*. Dordrecht: Springer.

Louis, S (2009) *Knowledge and Understanding of the World in the Early Years Foundation Stage*. London: David Fulton.

Louv, R (2005) *Last Child in the Woods: Saving our children from nature-deficit disorder*. Chapel Hill, NC: Algonquin Books.

Louv, R (2011) *The Nature Principle: Human restoration and the end of nature-deficit disorder*. New York: Alonquin Books.

Lowes, S (2008) Mapping the world: Freehand mapping and children's understanding of geographical concepts. *Research in Geographic Education*, 10(2), pp. 1–37.

Lucas, A and Dyment, J (2010) Where do children choose to play on the school ground? The influence of green design. *Education 3–13*, 38(2), pp. 177–89.

Luchs, A and Fikus, M (2013) A comparative study of active play on differently designed playgrounds. *Journal of Adventure Education and Outdoor Learning*, 13(4), pp. 206–22.

MacDougall, C, Schiller, W and Darbyshire, P (2009) What are our boundaries and where can we play? Perspectives from eight- to ten-year-old Australian metropolitan and rural children. *Early Child Development and Care*, 179(2),pp. 189–204.

Mackett, R, Banister, D, Batty, M, Einon, D, Brown, B, Gong, Y, Kitazawa, K, Marshall, S and Paskins, J (2007) Final report on children's activities, perceptions and behaviour in the local environment (capable). Available at: www.cts.ucl.ac.uk/research/chcaruse/

Mackintosh, M (2005) Children's understanding of rivers. *International Research in Geographical and Environmental Education*, 14(4), pp. 316–22.

Mackintosh, M (2007) The joy of teaching and learning geography. In Hayes, D (ed.) *Joyful Teaching and Learning in the Primary School*. Exeter: Learning Matters.

Mackintosh, M (2010) Images in geography: Using photographs, sketches and diagrams. In Scoffham, S (ed.) *The Primary Geography Handbook*. Sheffield: Geographical Association, pp. 120–33.

Mackintosh, M (2011) Graphicacy for life. *Primary Geography*, 75, pp. 6–8.

Mackintosh, M (2017) Beach Schools. In Pickering. S (ed.) *Teaching Outdoors Creatively*. Abingdon: Routledge, pp. 81–96.

Mackintosh, M (n.d.) GTIP think piece: Human geography primary. *GA website*. Available at: www.geography.org.uk/projects/gtip/thinkpieces/humangeography/

MacQuarrie, S, Nugent, C and Warden, C (2015) Learning with nature and learning from others: Nature as setting and resource for early childhood education. *Journal of Adventure Education and Outdoor Learning*, 15(1), pp.1–23.

Madge, N (2006) *Children These Days*. Bristol: Policy Press.

Madge, N and Barker, J (2007) Risk and childhood. London: RSA. Available at: www.thersa.org

Maguth, B (2012) *New Directions in Social Education Research: The influence of technology and globalization on the lives of students*, Charlotte, NC: Information Age Publishing.

Maguth, B and Hilburn, J (eds) (2017) *The State of Global Education: Learning with the world and its people*. Abingdon: Routledge.

Malandrakis, G and Chatzakis, S (2014) Environmental attitudes, knowledge and alternative conceptions of primary school children in Greece. *Applied Environmental Education and Communication*, 13, pp. 15–27.

Maldonado, S and Glynne, A (2015) *Ali's Story: A real-life account of his journey from Afghanistan*, London: Wayland.

Malone, K (2009) Every experience matters: An evidence based report on the role of learning outside the classroom for children's whole development from birth to eighteen years. *Farming and Countryside Education*. Available at: www.face-online.org.uk/index

Malone, K (2016a) Posthumanist approaches to theorizing children's human-nature relations. In Nairn, K and Kraftl, P (eds) (2016) *Space, Place and Environment*. Dordrecht: Springer, pp. 186–206.

Malone, K (2016b) Reconsidering children's encounters with nature and place using posthumanism. *Australian Journal of Environmental Education*. doi 10.101/aee.2015.48.

Malone, K and Waite, S (2016) Student outcomes and natural schooling: Pathways from evidence to impact report 2016. Available at: www.plymouth.ac.uk/uploads/production/document/path/6/6811/Student_outcomes_and__natural_schooling_pathways_to_impact_2016.pdf

Malpas, J (2018) *Place and Experience: A philosophical topography* (2nd ed.). Abingdon; Routledge.

Manfra, M and Bolick, C (eds) (2017) *The Wiley Handbook of Social Studies Research*. Chichester: Wiley Blackwell.

Manzo, L and Devine-Wright, P (eds) (2014) *Place Attachment: Advances in theory, methods and applications*. Abingdon: Routledge.

Mapp, S (2011) *Global Child Welfare and Well-Being*. Oxford: Oxford University Press.

Marsh, C and Hart, C (2011) *Teaching the Social Sciences and Humanities in an Australian Curriculum* (6th edn). Frenchs Forest: Pearson.

Marsh, J (2010) Young children's play in online virtual worlds. *Journal of Early Childhood Research*, 8(1), pp. 23–39.

Marsh, J, Plowman, L, Yamada-Rice, D, Bishop, J and Scott, F (2016) Digital play: A new classification. *Early Years*, 36(3), pp. 242–53.

Marshall, D (ed.) (2010) *Understanding Children as Consumers*. London: Sage.

Martin, F (1995) *Teaching Early Years Geography*. Cambridge: Chris Kington.

Martin, F (2004) Primary historians and geographers learning from each other. *Primary History*, 32, Autumn, pp. 18–21.

Martin, F (2005) North-south linking as a controversial issue. *Prospero*, 14(4), pp. 47–54.

Martin, F (2006a) Everyday geography. *Primary Geographer*, 61, pp. 4–7.

Martin, F (2006b) Knowledge bases for effective teaching: Beginning teachers' development as teachers of primary geography. In Schmeinck, D (ed.) *Research on Learning and Teaching in Primary Geography*. Karlsruhe: Padagogische Hochschule Karlsruhe, pp. 149–84.

Martin, F (2006c) *Teaching Geography in Primary Schools: Learning how to live in the world*. Cambridge: Chris Kington.

Martin, F (2007) The wider world in the primary school. In Hicks, D and Holden, C (eds) *Teaching the Global Dimension*. London: Routledge, pp. 163–75.

Martin, F (2008) Ethnogeography: Towards liberatory geography education. *Children's Geographies*, 6(4), pp. 437–50.

Martin, F (2012) The geographies of difference. *Geography* 97(3), pp. 116–22.

Martin, F (2013a) The place of knowledge in the new curriculum. *Primary Geography*, 82, 9–11.

Martin, F (2013b) Same old story: The problem of object-based thinking as a basis for teaching distant places. *Education 3–13*, 41(4), pp. 410–24.

Martin, F and Catling, S (2004) Future directions and developments for primary geography research. In Catling, S and Martin, F (eds) *Researching Primary Geography*. London: Register of Research in Primary Geography, pp. 301–11.

Martin, F and Owens, P (2008) *Caring for our world: A practical guide to ESD for ages 4–8*. Sheffield: Geographical Association.

Martin, F and Owens, P (2010) Young children making sense of their place in the world. In Scoffham, S (ed.) *Primary Geography Handbook*. Sheffield: Geographical Association, pp. 62–73.

Martin, G (2005) *All Possible Worlds: A history of geographical ideas*. Oxford: Oxford University Press.

Martusewicz, R, Edmundson, J and Lupinacci, J (2015) *Ecojustice Education* (2nd edn). New York: Routledge.

Maslin, M (2013) *Climate: A very short introduction*. Oxford: Oxford University Press.

Maslin, M (2014) *Climate Change: A very short introduction* (3rd edn). Oxford: Oxford University Press.

Massey, D (2005) *For Space*. London: Sage.

Massey, D (2012) *Leading the Sustainable School*. London: Continuum.

Matthews, H (1992) *Making Sense of Place*. Hemel Hempstead: Harvester/Wheatsheaf.

Matthews, H (1995) Culture, environmental experience and environmental awareness: Making sense of young Kenyan children's views of place. *The Geographical Journal*, 161(3), pp. 285–95.

Matthews, H, Taylor, M, Sherwood, K, Tucker, F and Limb, M (2000) Growing-up in the countryside: Children and the rural idyll. *Journal of Rural Studies*, 16, pp. 141–53.

Matthews, J and Herbert, D (eds) (2004) *Unifying Geography*. Abingdon: Routledge.

Matthews, J and Herbert, D (2008) *Geography: A Very Short Introduction*. Oxford: Oxford University Press.

Maude, A (2014) Developing national curriculum geography in Australia. *International Research in Geographical and Environmental Education*, 23(1), pp. 40–52.

Maude, A (2016) What might powerful knowledge look like? *Geography*, 101(2), pp. 70–6.

Maude, A (2017) Applying the concept of powerful knowledge to school geography. In Brooks, C, Butt. G and Fargher, M (eds) *The Power of Geographical Thinking*. Dordrecht: Springer, pp. 27–40.

Maude, A (2018) Geography and powerful knowledge: A contribution to the debate. *International Research in Geographical and Environmental Education*, 27(2), pp. 179-190.

Maxim, G (2006) *Dynamic Social Studies for Constructivist Classrooms: Inspiring tomorrow's social scientists* (8th edn). Upper Saddle River, NJ: Pearson.

Mayall, B (2008) Children's lives outside school and their educational impact. In Alexander, R with Doddington, C, Gray, J, Hargreaves, L and Kershner, R (eds) *The Cambridge Primary Review Research Surveys*. London: Routledge, pp. 49–82.

MCEETYA (Ministerial Council on Education, Employment, Training and Youth Affairs) (2008) Melbourne Declaration on Educational Goals for Young Australians. Available at: www.curriculum.edu.au/verve/_resources/National_Declaration_on_the_Educational_Goals_for_Young_Australians.pdf

Mcguire, B (2012) *Waking the Giant: How a changing climate triggers earthquakes, tsunamis and volcanoes*. Oxford: Oxford University Press.

Mcinerney, M, Berg, K, Hutchinson, N, Maude, A and Sorensen (2009) Towards a national geography curriculum for Australia. Milton: Australian Geography Teachers Association, Institute of Australian Geographers and the Royal Geographical Society of Queensland. Available at: www.ncg.org.au/report/index.htm

Mckendrick, J, Bradford, M and Fielder, A (2000) Time for a party!: Making sense of the commercialization of leisure space for children. In Holloway, S and Valentine, G (eds) *Children's Geographies*. London: Routledge, pp. 100–16.

Mcleod, A (2008) *Listening to Children*. London: Jessica Kingsley.

McLerran, A and Cooney, B (1991) *Roxaboxen*. New York: HarperTrophy.

McNeill, J and Engelke, P (2014) *The Great Acceleration: An environmental history of the Anthropocene since 1945*. Cambridge, MA: Belknap Press.

Merchant, G (2016) Virtual worlds and online videogames for children and young people: Promises and challenges. In Guzzetti, B and Lelsey, M (eds) *Handbook of Research on the Societal Impact of Digital Media*. Hershey, PA: Information Science Reference, pp. 291–316.

Merchant, G, Gillen, J, Marsh, J and Davies, J (eds) (2013) *Virtual Literacies: Interactive spaces for children and young people*. Abingdon: Routledge.

Meyer, J, Kamens, D and Benavot, A (1992) *School Knowledge for the Masses*. Lewes: Falmer Press.

Middleton, N (2012) *Rivers: A very short introduction*. Oxford: Oxford University Press.

Milner, A (1996) *Geography starts here! Practical approaches with nursery and reception children*. Sheffield: Geographical Association.

Milner, A (1997) *Geography through play: Structured play at Key Stage 1*. Sheffield: Geographical Association.

Milner, K (2017) *My Name is not Refugee*. Edinburgh: The Bucket List.

Milson, A, Kerski, J and Demirci, A (2012) The world at their fingertips: A new age for spatial thinking. In Milson, A, Demirci, A and Kerski, J (eds) *International Perspectives on Teaching and Learning with GIS in Secondary School*. Dordrecht: Springer, pp. 1–11.

Min, B and Lee, J (2006) Children's neighbourhood place as a psychological and behavioral domain. *Journal of Environmental Psychology*, 26(1), pp. 51–71.

Ministry of Education (New Zealand) (2017) *Te Whāriki Early Childhood Curriculum*. Available at: http://education.govt.nz/assets/Documents/Early-Childhood/Te-Whariki-Early-Childhood-Curriculum.pdf

Minujin, A and Nandy, S (eds) (2012) *Global Child Poverty and Well-Being: Measurement, concepts, policy and action*. Bristol: Policy Press.

MischiefPR (2006) *One in Five Brit Kids can't find UK on a Map*. London: MischiefPR.

Mitchell, C and Reid Walsh, J (2002) *Researching Children's Popular Culture*. London: Routledge.

Mitchell, D (ed.) (2009) *Living Geography: Exciting futures for teachers and students*. London: Chris Kington.

Mitchell, D (2018) Handling controversial issues in geography. In Jones, M and Lambert, D (eds) *Debates in Geography Education* (2nd edn). Abingdon: Routledge.

MOE (Ministry of Education, Singapore) (2012) Nurturing Early Learners: A curriculum framework for kindergartens in Singapore – A guide for parents. Available at:

www.moe.gov.sg/docs/default-source/document/education/preschool/files/kindergarten-curriculum-framework-guide-for-parents.pdf

Moghtaderi, F, Burke, M, Tranter, P and Armit, C (2013) Understanding Australian parents' attitudes about their children's travel behaviour: Results from the Catch and iMatch projects. *Paper given at the SOA Conference, Sydney.* Available at: www.coaconference.com.au/wp-content/uploads/3013/12/Moghtaderi-Movement.pdf

Mohan, A and Mohan, L (2013) Spatial Thinking About Maps: Development of Concepts and Skills Across the Early Years. Washington: National Geographic Society. Available at: https://media.nationalgeographic.org/assets/file/SpatialThinkingK-5FullReport.pdf

Molner, P (2015) *Plate Tectonics: A very short introduction.* Oxford: Oxford University Press.

Monk, J and Silman, C (2011) *Active Learning in Primary Classrooms: A case study approach.* Harlow: Pearson.

Montello, D, Grossner, K and Janelle, D (eds) (2014) *Space in Mind: Concepts for spatial learning and education.* Cambridge, MA: MIT Press.

Moran, J (2008) *Queuing for Beginners: The story of daily life from breakfast to bedtime.* London: Profile Books.

Morimoto, J (1992) *Kenju's Forest.* London: HarperCollins.

Morley, B and Pearce, C (2009) *The Silence Seeker.* London: Tamarind Books.

Moore, D (2015) The teacher doesn't know what it is but she knows where we are: Young children's secret places in early childhood outdoor environments. *International Journal of Play*, 4(1), pp. 20–31.

Moores, S (2012) *Media, Place and Mobility.* Basingstoke: Palgrave Macmillan.

Morris, G (n.d.) Teaching materials and resources (unpublished).

Morgan, J (2013) What do we mean by thinking *geographically?* In Lambert, D and Jones, M (eds) *Debates in Geography Education.* Abingdon: Routledge, pp. 273–81.

Morgan, J (2014a) Fortunate inhabitants? Challenges for school geography in New Zealand. *International Research in Geographical and Environmental Education*, 23(1), pp.53–63.

Morgan, J (2014b) Neither existence nor future: The social realist challenge to school geography. In Barrett, B and Rata, E (eds) *Knowledge and the Future of the Curriculum: International Studies in Social Realism.* Basingstoke: Palgrave Macmillan, pp. 136–52.

Morris, R (2017) Place-based learning for elementary civic action. In Hickey, M and Clabough, J (eds) *Digging Deeper: Activities for enriching and expanding social studies instruction K-12.* Charlotte, NC: Information Age Publishing, pp. 73–85.

Moseley, W, Perramond, E, Hapke, H and Laris, P (2014) *An Introduction to Human-Environment Geography.* Chichester: Wiley-Blackwell.

Moss, P and Petrie, P (2002) *From Children's Services to Children's Spaces.* London: RoutledgeFalmer.

Murayama, T (2015) Geography education as part of social studies education in Japan. In Ida, Y, Yuda, M, Shimura, T, Ike, S, Ohnishi, K and Oshima, H (eds) *Geography Education in Japan.* Dordrecht: Springer, pp. 197–208.

Murnaghan, A-M and Shillington, L (eds) (2016) *Children, Nature, Cities.* Abingdon: Routledge.

Murray, D and Raynolds, L (2007) Globalization and its antinomies: Negotiating a fair trade agreement. In Raynolds, L, Murray, D and Wilkinson, J (eds) *Fair Trade: The challenges of transforming globalization*. Abingdon: Routledge, pp. 3–14.

Nabhan, G and Trimble, S (1994) *The Geography of Childhood: Why children need wild places*. Boston, MA: Beacon Press.

Nairn, K and Kraftl, P (eds) (2016) *Space, Place and Environment*. Dordrecht: Springer.

Naish, M. Rawling, E and Hart, R (1987) *Geography 16–19: The contribution of a curriculum project to 16–19 Education*. Harlow: Longman.

Nam, Y, Karahan, E and Roehrig, G (2016) Native American students' understanding of geologic time scale: 4th–8th grade Ojibwe students' understanding of Earth's geologic history. *International Journal of Environmental and Science Education*, 11(4), pp. 485–503.

National Assembly for Wales (2008) *Education for Sustainable Development and Global Citizenship*. Cardiff: ESDGC. Available at: www.assemblywales.org

National Research Council (2006) *Learning to Think Spatially*. Washington, DC: The National Academies Press.

Natural England (2016) Monitor of engagement with the natural environment: A pilot to develop an indicator of visits to the natural environment by children. Available at: www.gov.uk/government/uploads/system/uploads/attachment_data/file/498944/mene-childrens-report-years-1-2.pdf

NCC (National Curriculum Council) (1993) *An introduction to teaching geography at Key Stages 1 and 2*. York: NCC.

NCSS (National Council for the Social Studies) (2010) *National curriculum standards for social studies: A framework for teaching, learning and assessment*. Silver Springs, MD: National Council for the Social Studies.

NEF (National Economic Foundation) (2005) *Wellbeing and the environment*. London: NEF.

Ness, D, Farenga, S, and Garofalo, S (2017) *Spatial Intelligence: Why it matters from birth through the lifespan*. New York: Routledge.

Newby, P (2014) *Research Methods for Education* (2nd edn). Harlow: Pearson Education.

Newcombe, N and Huttenlocher, J (2000) *Making Space: The development of spatial representation and reasoning*. Cambridge, MA: Massachusetts Institute of Technology.

Nielsen, L and Webb, W (2011) *Teaching Generation Text*. San Francisco, CA: Jossey-Bass.

Nieuwenhuys, O (2003) Growing up between places of work and non-places of childhood: The uneasy relationship. In Fog Olwig, K and Gulløv, E (eds) *Children's Places*. London: Routledge, pp. 99–118.

Nikolopoulou, A, Abraham, T and Mirbagheri, F (eds) (2010) *Education for Sustainable Development: Challenges, strategies and practices in a globalising world*. New Delhi: Sage.

Ní Laoire, C and White, A (eds) (2017) *Movement, Mobilities, and Journeys*. Dordrecht: Springer.

Ní Laoire, C, Carpena-Méndez, F, Tyrrell, N and White, A (2011) *Childhood and Migration in Europe*. Farnham: Ashgate.

Noddings, N (2005) *The Challenge to Care in Schools*. New York: Teachers' College Press.

Nolet, V (2016) *Educating for Sustainability: Principles and practices for teachers*. New York: Routledge.

Norman, D (2017) *Dinosaurs: A very short introduction* (2nd edn). Oxford: Oxford University Press.

North, W (2008) Everyday geographies: Planning with big ideas (or key concepts). Available at: www.primarygeogblog.blogspot.com/2008/01/planning-with-big-ideas.html

NZC (New Zealand Curriculum) (2014) The New Zealand curriculum online: Social sciences. Available at: http://nzcurriculum.tki.org.nz/The-New-Zealand-Curriculum/Social-sciences/Learning-area-structure

O'Brien, M (2003) Regenerating children's neighbourhoods: What do children want? In Christensen, P and O'Brien, M (eds) *Children in the City*. London: RoutledgeFalmer, pp. 142–61.

Ofsted (1999) *Primary Education 1994–1998: A review of primary schools in England*. London: The Stationary Office.

Ofsted (2004) *Ofsted Subject Reports 2002/03: Geography in primary schools*. London: Ofsted.

Ofsted (2005) *Ofsted Subject Reports 2003/04: Geography in primary schools*. London: Ofsted.

Ofsted (2008a) *Geography in schools: Changing practice*. London: Ofsted. Available at: www.ofsted.gov.uk/publications/

Ofsted (2008b) *Schools and sustainability: A climate for change*. London: Ofsted. Available at: www.ofsted.gov.uk/publications/

Ofsted (2008c) *Learning outside the classroom*. London: Ofsted. Available at: www.ofsted.gov.uk/publications/

Ofsted (2011) *Geography: Learning to make a world of difference*. Available at: www.ofsted.gov.uk/publications/geography/

Olle, H (2002) *Young Europe*. London: National Children's Bureau.

Örbring, D (2017) Geographical and spatial thinking in the Swedish curriculum. In Brooks, C, Butt, G and Fargher, M (eds) *The Power of Geographical Thinking*. Dordrecht: Springer, pp. 137–50.

Orr, D (1991) *Ecological Literacy: Education and the transition to a postmodern world*. New York: State University of New York Press.

Osler, A and Starkey, H (2005) *Changing Citizenship: Democracy and inclusion in education*. Maidenhead: Open University Press.

Owen, D and Ryan, A (2001) *Teaching Geography 3–11*. London: Continuum.

Owens, P (2004a) Can you get to grandma's safely? In De Boo, M (ed.) (2004) *The Early Years Handbook*. Sheffield: The Curriculum Partnership, pp. 38–43.

Owens, P (2004b) Researching the development of children's environmental values in the early school years. In Catling, S and Martin, F (eds) *Researching Primary Geography*. London: Register of Research in Primary Geography, pp. 67–76.

Owens, P (2008a) Mywalks: Walks on the child side. *Primary Geographer*, 67, pp. 25–8.

Owens, P (2008b) Level-headed geography: Planning achievement. *Primary Geographer*, 66, pp. 15–18.

Owens, P (2011) *Little Blue Planet: Investigating Spaceship Earth*. Sheffield: Geographical Association.

Owens, P (2013) More than just core knowledge? A framework for effective and high quality primary geography. *Education 3–13*, 41(4), pp. 382–97.

Owens, P (2016) Progression in mapping. Available at: http://digimapforschools.edina.ac.uk/schools/Resources/Primary/progression_in_mapping.pdf

Owens, P (2017) Geography and sustainability education. In Scoffham, S (ed.) *Teaching Geography Creatively* (2nd edn). London: Routledge, pp. 177–91.

Owens, P and North, W (2008) *Young Geographers: A living geography project for primary schools*. Geographical Association. Available at: www.geography.org.uk/projects/younggeographers

Oxfam (2006a) *Education for Global Citizenship: A guide for schools*. Oxford: Oxfam.

Oxfam (2006b) *Teaching Controversial Issues*. Oxford: Oxfam.

Palmer, J and Birch, J (2004) *Geography in the Early Years*. London: RoutledgeFalmer.

Palmer, J and Suggate, J (2004) The development of children's understanding of distant places and environmental issues: Report of a UK longitudinal study of the development of ideas between the ages of four and ten years. *Research Papers in Education*. 19(2), pp. 205–37.

Palmer, J, Suggate, J and Matthews, J (1996) Environmental cognition: Early ideas and misconceptions at the ages of four and six. *Environmental Education Research*, 2(3), pp. 301–30.

Panter, J, Jones, A, van Sluijs, E and Griffin, S (2010) Attitudes, social support and environmental perceptions as predictors of active community behaviour in school children. *Journal of Epidemiol Community Health*, 64(1), pp. 41–8.

Papageorgiou, N, Galini, A and Mavrikaki, E (2016) Junior primary Greek school pupils' perceptions of the city's public open spaces and especially the urban square: A case study. *Review of International Geographical Education Online*, 6(1), pp. 49–66.

Paren, L (2005) *Teaching Primary Environmental and Social Studies*. Macmillan Education.

Paton Walsh, J (1992), *Babylon*. London: Red Fox.

Patten, B (1990) *The River's Story*. In Patten, B (ed.) *Thawing Frozen Frogs*. London: Penguin, pp. 110–11. Available at: www.genese.com.np/forwardartfoundations/poetry/the-rivers-story/

Patten, C (2000) *BBC Reith Lectures: 1. Governance*. London: BBC.

Peacock, A (2016) *Assessment for Learning without Limits*. London: Open University Press.

Percy-Smith, B and Thomas, N (eds) (2010) *A Handbook of Children and Young People's Participation*. London: Routledge.

Perkins, H and Thorns, D (2012) *Place, Identity and Everyday Life in a Globalizing World*. Basingstoke: Palgrave Macmillan.

Peterson, A and Warwick, P (2015) *Global Learning and Education: Key concepts and effective practice*. Abingdon: Routledge.

Phillipson, N and Wegerif, R (2017) *Dialogic Education: Mastering core concepts through thinking together*. Abingdon: Routledge.

Pickering, S (ed.) (2017) *Teaching Outdoors Creatively*. Abingdon: Routledge.

Pickering, S (2018) Valuing outdoor learning, in Cremin, T and Boulter, H (eds.) *Learning to Teach in the Primary School* (4th Edition). Abingdon: Routledge. pp.216–228.

Pickford, T (2006) *Learning ICT in the Humanities*. London: David Fulton.

Pickford, T, Garner, W and Jackson, E (2013) *Primary Humanities: Learning Through Inquiry*. London: Sage.

Pike, S (2006) Irish primary school children's definitions of 'geography'. *Irish Educational Studies*, 25(1), pp. 75–92.

Pike, S (2008) *Children and Their Environments in Ireland*. Ed. D. thesis. Belfast: Queens University.

Pike, S (2011) If you went out it would stick: Irish children's learning in their local environments. *International Research in Geographical and Environmental Education*, 20(2), pp. 139–59.

Pike, S (2013) It's about the things we don't notice everyday: 10 years of children's definitions of geography. Paper presented at the Charney Manor Primary Geography Conference, Researching and Developing the Primary Geography Curriculum, Oxfordshire.

Pike, S (2015) Primary geography in the Republic of Ireland: Practices, issues and possible futures. *Review of International Geographical Education Online*, 5(2), pp. 185–98.

Pike, S (2016) *Learning Primary Geography: Ideas and inspiration from classrooms.* Abingdon: Routledge.

Pike, S (2017) Creative approaches to learning about the physical world. In Scoffham, S (ed.) *Teaching Geography Creatively* (2nd edn). Abingdon: Routledge, pp. 104–17.

Pike, S and Clough, P (2005) Children's voices on learning about countries in geography. *International Research in Geographical and Environmental Education*, 14(4), pp. 356–63.

Pike, S and Kilcrann, M (2015) Global news and views. *Primary Geography*, 87, Summer, pp. 18–19.

Plester, B, Blades, M and Spencer, C (2006) Children's understanding of environmental representations: Aerial photographs and model towns. In Spencer, C and Blades, M (eds) *Children and Their Environments*. Cambridge: Cambridge University Press, pp. 42–56.

Plumert, J and Spencer, J (eds) (2007) *The Emerging Spatial Mind*. New York: Oxford University Press.

Pollard, A, with Black-Hawkins, K, Cliff Hodges, G, Dudley, P, James, M, Linklater, H, Swaffield, S, Swann, S, Turner, F, Warwick, P, Winterbottom, M and Wolpert, M (2014). *Reflective Teaching in Schools* (4th edn). London: Bloomsbury Publishing.

Poore, M (2013) *Using Social Media in the Classroom*. London: Sage.

Porter, H (2018) *Educating Outside: Curriculum-linked outdoor learning ideas for primary teachers*. London: Bloomsbury.

Powell, M (2007) The hidden curriculum of recess. *Children, Youth and Environment*, 17(4), pp. 86–106.

Prezza, M (2007) Children's independent mobility: A review of the recent Italian literature. *Children, Youth and Environment*, 17(4), pp. 293–318.

Pritchard, J (2008) Worldmapper. *Primary Geographer*, 67, Autumn, pp. 30–3.

Pyyry, N (2017) Thinking with broken glass: Making pedagogical spaces of enchantment in the city. *Environmental Education Research*, 23(10), pp. 1391–401.

QCA (Qualifications and Curriculum Authority) (2005) *Seeing Steps in Children's Learning: Foundation Stage*. London: QCA.

QCA (2007) *The global dimension in action*. London: QCA

Readman, J and Roberts, L (2002) *The World Came to My Place Today*. London: Transworld Publishers/Eden Project Books.

Redfern, M (2003) *The Earth: A very short introduction*. Oxford: Oxford University Press.

Reid, A and Scott, W (eds) (2008) *Researching Education and the Environment: Retrospect and prospect*. Abingdon: Routledge.

Reid, A, Bruun Jensen, B, Nikel, J and Simovska, V (eds) (2008) *Participation and Learning*. New York: Springer.

Reynolds, R (2014) *Teaching Humanities and Social Sciences in the Primary School* (3rd edn). South Melbourne: Oxford University Press.

Reynolds, R, Bradbery, D, Brown, J, Carroll, K, Donnelly, D, Ferguson-Patrick, K and Macqueen, S (eds) (2015) *Contesting and Constructing International Perspectives in Global Education*. Rotterdam: Sense Publishers.

Reynolds, R and Vinterek, M (2016) Geographical locational knowledge as an indicator of children's views of the world: Research from Sweden and Australia. *International Research in Geographical and Environmental Education*, 25(1), pp. 68–83.

Richardson, P (2010a) Fieldwork and outdoor learning. In Scoffham, S (ed.) *The Primary Geography Handbook*. Sheffield: Geographical Association, pp. 134–47.

Richardson, P (2010b) Planning the curriculum. In Scoffham, S (ed.) *The Primary Geography Handbook*. Sheffield: Geographical Association, pp. 302–11.

Richardson, P (2018a) *Local fieldwork: Investigating our Street*. Sheffield: Geographical Association.

Richardson, P (2018b) *Local fieldwork: Investigating our Town*. Sheffield: Geographical Association.

Richardson, P and Richardson, T (2016) *The Everyday Guide to Primary Geography: Maps*. Sheffield: Geographical Association.

Rios, C and Menezes, I (2017) I saw a magical garden with flowers that people could not damage: Children's visions of nature and of learning about nature in and out of school. *Environmental Education Research*, 23(10), pp. 1402–13.

Rissotto, A and Giuliani, M (2006) Learning neighbourhood environments: The loss of experience in a modern world. In Spencer, C and Blades, M (eds) *Children and Their Environments*. Cambridge: Cambridge University Press, pp. 75–90.

Roberts, C and Kai, H (2016) *Children in our World: Refugees and Migrants*. London: Wayland.

Roberts, M (2003) *Learning Through Enquiry*. Sheffield: Geographical Association.

Roberts, M (2013) *Geography through Enquiry: Approaches to Teaching and Learning in the Secondary School*. Sheffield, Geographical Association.

Robertson, M (ed.) (2012) *Schooling for Sustainable Development: A Focus on Australia, New Zealand and the Oceanic Region*. Melbourne: Springer.

Robertson, M (2017) *Sustainability: Principles and practice* (2nd edn). Abingdon: Routledge/Earthscan.

Robinson, C and Fielding, M (2007) *The Primary Review Interim Reports: Children and their primary schools: Pupils' voices*. Cambridge: University of Cambridge: The Primary Review.

Rockliff, S and Chinnery, P (2016) *Using Outdoor Learning to Improve Behaviour for All*. Abingdon: Routledge.

Rodriguez, M, Kohen, R and Delval, J (2015) Children's and adolescents' thoughts on pollution: Cognitive abilities required to understand environmental systems. *Environmental Education Research*, 21(1), pp. 76–91.

Rogers, S and Wyse, D (2016) *A Guide to Early Years and Primary Teaching*. London: Sage.

Ronan, K and Johnston, D (2005) *Promoting Community Resilience in Disasters: The role of schools, youth and families*. New York: Springer.

Ronan, K and Towers, B (2014) Systems education for a sustainable planet: Preparing children for natural disasters. *Systems*, 2, pp. 1–23.

Rosen, M and Oxenbury, H (1989) *We're Going on a Bear Hunt*. London: Walker Books.

Rosen, M and Young, A (2016) *Who Are Refugees and Migrants? What Makes Them Leave Their Homes? And Other Big Questions*. London: Wayland.

Rowe, S and Humphries, S (2012) *The Coombes Approach: Learning through an experiential and outdoor curriculum*. London: Continuum.

Rowley, C (2006) Are there different types of geographical inquiry? In Cooper, H, Rowley, C and Asquith, S (eds) *Geography 3–11: A Guide for Teachers*. London: David Fulton, pp. 17–32.

Rowley, C and Cooper, H (eds) (2009) *Cross-Curricular Approaches to Teaching and Learning*. London: Sage.

Rowley, C and Lewis, L (2003) *Thinking on the Edge*. London: Living Earth.

Ruckenstein, M (2013) Spatial extensions of childhood: From toy worlds to online communities. *Children's Geographies*, 11(4), pp. 476–89.

Rupprecht, C, Byrne, J and Lo, A (2016) Memories of vacant lots: How and why residents used informal urban green space as children and teenagers in Brisbane, Australia, and Sapporo, Japan. *Children's Geographies*, 14(3), pp. 340–55.

Russell, K (2010) Geography and ICT. In Scoffham, S (ed.) *Primary Geography Handbook*. Sheffield: Geographical Association.

Sahi, I and Willy, T (2016) The value of personal international connections. *Primary Geographical Journal*, 91, Autumn, pp. 32–4.

Salaman, A and Tutchell, S (2005) *Planning Educational Visits for the Early Years*. London: Paul Chapman.

Salinas-Silva, V, Perez-Gallardo, P and Arenas-Martija, A (2015) Defining primary geography from teachers' expertise: What Chilean teachers mean by geography. *Review of International Geographical Education Online*, 5(2), pp. 166–84.

Salisbury, M and Styles, M (2012) *Children's Picturebooks: The art of visual storytelling*. London: Laurence King Publishing.

Sanna, F (2016) *The Journey*. London: Flying Eye Books.

Sargeant, J (2008) Australian children: Locally secure, globally afraid? In Gerber, R and Robertson, M (eds) *Children's Lifeworlds: Locating indigenous voices*. New York: Nova Science Publishers, pp. 119–33.

Sarra, C (2011) *Strong and Smart – Towards a Pedagogy for Emancipation: Education for first peoples*. London: Routledge.

Saylor, C (ed.) (2010) *Children and Disasters*. New York: Plenum Press.

Selby, D and Kagawa, F (eds) (2015) *Sustainability Frontiers: Critical and Transformative Voices from the Borderlands of Sustainability Education*. Berlin: Barbara Budrich Publishers.

Schänzel, H, Yeoman, I and Backer, E (eds) (2012) *Family Tourism: Multidisciplinary perspectives*. Bristol: Channel View Publications.

Schmeinck, D (2006) Images of the world or do travel experiences and the presence of the media influence children's perceptions of the world? In Schmeinck, D (ed.) *Research on Learning and Teaching in Primary Geography*. Karlsruhe: Padagogische Hochschule Karlsruhe, pp. 37–59.

Schmeinck, D (2013) They are like us – teaching about Europe through the eyes of children. *Education 3–13*, 41(4), pp. 398–409.

Schmeinck, D (2017) Overcome borders – an integrated subject approach for teaching science and social science in primary school. In Catling, S (ed.) *Reflections on Primary Geography*. Sheffield: The Register of Research in Primary Geography, pp.128–31.

Schmeinck, D, Knecht, P, Kosack, W, Lambinos, N, Musumeci, M and Gatt, S (2010) *Through the Eyes of Children: The implementation of a European dimension by peer learning in primary school*. Berlin: MBVBerlin.

Schoeppe, S, Duncan, M, Badland, H, Rebar, A and Vendelanotte, C (2016) Too far from home? Adult attitudes on children's independent mobility range. *Children's Geographies*, 14(4), pp. 482–89.

Schwägerl, C (2014) *The Anthropocene: The Human Era and how it shapes our planet*. Santa Fe: Synergetic Press.

Scoffham, S (2007) Please miss, why are they so poor? *Primary Geographer*, 62, pp. 5–7.

Scoffham, S (ed.) (2010) *Primary Geography Handbook*. Sheffield: Geographical Association.

Scoffham, S (2011) Core knowledge in the revised curriculum. *Geography*, 96(3), pp. 124–30.

Scoffham, S (2013) Geography and creativity: Developing joyful and imaginative learners. *Education 3–13*, 41(4), pp. 368–81.

Scoffham, S (2017a) Young children's ideas of different nations, peoples and cultures: A research perspective, in Catling, S (ed.) *Reflections on Primary Geography*. Sheffield: Register of Research in Primary Geography, pp. 121–7.

Scoffham, S (ed.) (2017b) *Teaching Geography Creatively* (2nd edn). Abingdon: Routledge.

Scoffham, S (2018) Maps and atlases for schools. In Kent, A and Vujakovic, P (eds) *The Routledge Handbook of Mapping and Cartography*. Abingdon: Routledge, pp. 388–98.

Scoffham, S and Owens, P (2017) *Teaching Primary Geography*. London: Bloomsbury.

Scoffham, S and Thomas, S (1997) *A World of Ideas*. Cheltenham: Stanley Thornes.

Scottish Executive (2001) *The global dimension in the curriculum*. Dundee: Learning and Teaching in Scotland.

Scottish Government (2008) A curriculum framework for children 3 to 5. Available at: www.gov.scot/Topics/Education/Schools/curriculum/present curriculum/3to5

Scourfield, J, Dicks, B, Drakeford, M and Davies, A (2006) *Children, Place and Identity: Nation and locality in middle childhood*. Abingdon: Routledge.

Sedgwick, F (2012) *Learning Outside in the Primary Classroom*. London: David Fulton.

Segall, A and Helfenbein, R (2008) Research on K-12 geography education. In Levstick, L and Tyson, C (eds) *Handbook of Research in Social Studies Education*. New York: Routledge, pp. 259–83.

Seldin, T (2008) *The World in the Palm of Her Hand: Introducing history and geography to the young child*. Terra Ceia: The Montessori Foundation.

Senyurt, S (2014) Turkish primary students' perceptions of geography. *Journal of Geography*, 113(3), pp. 160–70.

Shah, H and Marks, N (2004) A *Wellbeing Manifesto for a Flourishing Society*. London: NEF.

Sharp, J, Peacock, G, Johnsey, R, Simon, S, Smith, R, Cross, A and Harris, D (2017) *Primary Science: Teaching theory and practice* (8th edn). London: Sage.

Shaw, R and Oikawa, Y (eds) (2014) *Education for Sustainable Development and Disaster Risk Reduction*. Tokyo: Springer.

Shepardson, D, Roychoudhury, A and Hirsch, A (eds) (2017) *Teaching and Learning about Climate Change*. Abingdon: Routledge.

Sheppard, E and McMaster, R (eds) (2004) *Scale and Geographic Enquiry*. Oxford: Blackwell.

Sherrington, T (2017) *The Learning Rainforest: Great teaching in real classrooms*. Woodbridge: John Catt Educational.

Shimura, T (2015) Primary geography education in Japan: Curriculum as social studies, practices and teachers' expertise. *Review of International Geographical Education Online*, 5(2), 151–65.

Shin, E-k (2012) Fostering global citizenship from a spatial perspective with geospatial technology. In Maguth, B (ed) *New Directions in Social Education* Research. Charlotte, NC: Information Age Publishing, pp. 81-95.

Simco, N (2003) Developing a geographical perspective within an integrated theme. In Cooper, H and Sixsmith, C (eds) *Teaching Across the Early Years 3–7*. London: Routledge, pp. 168–80.

Sime, D (2017) Migrant children in cities: The spatial constructions of their everyday lives. In Ní Laoire, C and White, A (eds) *Movement, Mobilities, and Journeys*. Dordrecht: Springer, pp. 271–88.

Singapore Ministry of Education (2012) *Primary Social Studies Syllabus 2012*. Available at: www.gov.sg/docs/default-source/document/education/syllabuses/humanities/files/social-studies-syllabus-2012-110615.pdf

Singer, P (2006) *Children at War*. Berkeley, CA: University of California Press.

Skamp, K (2009) Understanding teachers' 'levels of use' of learnscapes. *Environmental Education Research*, 15(1), pp.93–110.

Skamp, K and Bergmann, I (2006) Teachers' perceptions of the value and impact of learnscapes: Implications for practice. Lismore, Australia: Southern Cross University. Available at: http://web.archive.org/web/20060904061030/http://www.mesa.edu.au/aaee_conf/Skamp-Bergmann.PDF

Smawfield, D (ed.) (2013) *Education and Natural Disasters: Education as a humanitarian response*. London: Bloomsbury.

Smith, F (1995) Children's voices and the construction of children's spaces: The example of playcare centres in the United Kingdom. *Children's Environments*, 12(3), pp. 177–90.

Smith, G and Sobel, D (2010) *Place- and Community-Based Education in Schools*. New York: Routledge.

Smith, P (2010) *Children and Play*. Chichester: Wiley-Blackwell.

Sobel, D (2008) *Childhood and Nature*. Portland: Stenhouse Publishers.

Sobel, D (2011) *Wild Play*. San Francisco, CA: Sierra Club Books.

Sobel, D (2013) *Place-Based Education: Connecting Classrooms and Communities* (2nd edn). Great Barrington, MA: Orion Society.

Solari, O, Solem, M and Boehm, R (eds.) (2017) *Learning Progressions in Geography Education*: International Perspectives. Dordrecht: Springer.

Solem, M, Huynh, N and Boehm (eds.) (2014) GeoProgressions – *Learning Progressions for Maps, Geospatial Technology and Spatial Thinking: A Research Handbook*. Washington DC: Association of American Geographers.

Somerville, M and Green, M (2015) *Children, Place and Sustainability*. New York: Palgrave Macmillan.

Somerville, M, Power, K and de Carteret, P (eds) (2009) *Landscapes and Learning: Place studies for a global world*. Rotterdam: Sense Publishers.

Spencer, C and Blades, M (eds) (2006) *Children and their Environments*. Cambridge: Cambridge University Press.

Spencer, C, Blades, M and Morsley, K (1989) *The Child in the Physical Environment*. Chichester: Wiley.

Spendlove, D (2009) *Putting Assessment for Learning Into Practice*. London: Continuum.

Spink, E, Keogh, B and Naylor, S (2008) Knowledge and understanding of the world. In Basford, J and Hodson, E (eds) *Teaching Early Years Foundation Stage*. Exeter: Learning Matters, pp. 85–97.

Spyrou, S and Christou, M (eds) (2014) *Children and Borders*. Basingstoke: Palgrave Macmillan.

Standish, A (2009) *Global Perspectives in the Geography Curriculum: Reviewing the moral case for geography*. Abingdon: Routledge.

Standish, A (2012) *The False Promise of Global Learning: Why education needs boundaries*. London: Continuum.

Stanley, F, Richardson, S and Prior, M (2005) *Children of the Lucky Country*. Sydney: Pan Macmillan.

Stea, D, Pinon, M, Middlebrook, N, Eckert, V and Blaut, J (2001) Place and space learning: The 'play pen' of young children. In Robertson, M and Gerber, R (eds) *Children's Ways of Knowing*. Melbourne: Australian Council for Educational Research, pp. 164–78.

Steggall, S (2008) *Rattle and Rap*. London: Frances Lincoln.

Steinberg, S and Kincheloe, J (eds) (2004) *Kinderculture: The corporate construction of childhood*. Cambridge: Westview Press.

Stephens, L, Spalding, K, Aslam, H, Scott, H, Ruddick, S, Young, N and McKeever, P (2017) Inaccessible childhoods: Evaluating accessibility in homes, schools and neighbourhoods with disabled children. *Children's Geographies*, 15(5), pp. 583–99.

Steuer, N, Thompson, S and Marks, N (2006) Review of the environmental dimension of children and young people's wellbeing. London: Sustainable Development Commission. Available at: www.sd-commission.org.uk

Stevenson, R, Brody, M, Dillon, J and Wals, A (eds) (2013) *International Handbook of Research on Environmental Education*. New York: Routledge.

Stewart, I (2018) *Plate Tectonics (Expert Books)*. London: Ladybird Books Ltd

Stoltman, J (1990) *Geography Education for Citizenship*. Bloomington, IN: Indiana University.

Stone, M (2009) *Smart by Nature: Schooling for sustainability*. Healdsburg, CA: Watershed Media.

Stone, M and Barlow, Z (eds) (2005) *Ecological Literacy: Educating our children for a sustainable world*. San Francisco, CA: Sierra Club.

Storey, C (2004) Teaching place: Developing early understanding of 'nested hierarchies'. In Catling, S and Martin, F (eds) *Researching Primary Geography*. London: Register of Research in Primary Geography, pp. 43–54.

Storm, M (1989) The five basic questions for primary geography. *Primary Geographer*, 2, pp. 4–5.

Stow, D (2017) *Oceans: A Very Short Introduction*, Oxford: Oxford University Press.

Tambyah, M (2006) Teaching geographical issues in context and developing a professional identity: The challenge facing primary school teachers. In Purnell, K, Lidstone, J and Hodgson, S (eds) *Proceedings of the International Geographical Union Commission On Geographical Education Symposium*. Brisbane: QUT/IGU-CGE, pp. 430–35. Available at: www.eprints.qut.edu.au

Tani, S (2014) Geography in the Finnish school curriculum: Part of the 'success story'. *International Research in Geographical and Environmental Education*, 23(1), pp. 90–101.

Tanner, J (2007) Global citizenship. In Hicks, D and Holden, C (eds) *Teaching the Global Dimension*. London: Routledge, pp. 150–60.

Tanner, J (2009) Special Places: Place Attachment and Children's Happiness. *Primary Geographer*, 68, Spring, pp. 5–8.

Tanner, J (2010) Geography and the emotions. In Scoffham, S (ed.) *Primary Geography Handbook*. Sheffield: Geographical Association, pp. 34–47.

Tanner, J (2017) Taking the learning outdoors at KS1: Extending early years practice for 5 to 7 year olds. In Pickering, S (ed.) *Teaching Outdoors Creatively*. Abingdon: Routledge, pp. 12–25.

Tanner, J and Whittle, J (2015) *The Everyday Guide to Primary Geography: Local Fieldwork*. Sheffield: Geographical Association.

Tapsell, S, Tunstall, S, House, M, Whomsley, J and Macnaghten, P (2001) Growing up with rivers? Rivers in London children's worlds. *Area*, 33(2), pp. 177–89.

Taylor, E and Catling, S (2006) Geographical significance: A useful concept? *Teaching Geography*, 31(3), pp. 122–5.

Taylor, N, Kennelly, J, Jenkins, K and Callingham, R (2006) The impact of an education for sustainability unit on the knowledge and attitudes of pre-service primary teachers at an Australian university. *Geographical Education*, 19, pp. 46–59.

Taylor, S (2010) *Narratives of Identity and Place*. Abingdon: Routledge.

Taylor, T, Fahey, C, Kriewaldt, J and Boon, D (2012) *Place and Time: Explorations in teaching geography and history*. Frenchs Forest: Pearson.

Thomas, D and Goudie, A (eds) (2000) *The Dictionary of Physical Geography*. Oxford: Blackwell.

Thomas, G (2017) *How to Do Your Research Project* (2nd edn). London: Sage.

Thomas, G and Thompson, G (2004) *A Child's Place: Why environment matters to children*. London: Demos.

Thommen, E, Avelar, S, Sapin, V, Perrenoud, S and Malatesta, D (2010) Mapping the journey home from school: A study on children's representation of space. *International Research in Geographical and Environmental Education*, 19(3), pp. 191–205.

Thomson, K (2005) *Fossils: A Very Short Introduction*, Oxford: Oxford University Press.

Thomson, P and Hall, C (2017) *Place-based Methods for Researching Schools*. London: Bloomsbury.

Thornton, L and Brunton, P (2007) *Bringing the Reggio Approach to Your Early Years Practice*. London: David Fulton.

Throssell, K (2015) *Child and Nation: A study of political socialisation and banal nationalism in France and England*. Brussels: Peter Lang.

Thurston, A (2006) Effects of group work on attainment in primary school geography. In Schmeinck, D (ed.) *Research On Learning and Teaching in Primary Geography*. Karlsruhe: Padagogischen Hochschule Karlsruhe, pp. 61–92.

Thwaites, A (2008) *100 Ideas for Teaching Knowledge and Understanding of the World*. London: Continuum.

Timperio, A, Crawford, D, Telford, A and Salmon, J (2004) Perceptions about the local neighbourhood and walking and cycling among children. *Preventive Medicine*, 38, pp. 39–47.

Titman, W (1994) *Special People, Special Places*. Winchester: Learning Through Landscapes.

Todd, R (2009) Recognizing geographic and spatial learning in children's drawings. *Research in Geographic Education*, 11(1), pp. 58–75.

Tovey, H (2007) *Playing Outdoors: Spaces, Places, Risk and Challenge*. Maidenhead: Open University Press.

Tranter, P and Malone, K (2004) Geographies of environmental learning: An exploration of children's use of school grounds. *Children's Geographies*, 2(1), pp.131–55.

Trend, R (1998) An investigation into understanding of geological time among 10- and 11-year-old children. *International Journal of Science Education*, 20(8), pp. 973–88.

Trend, R (2001) Deep time framework: A preliminary study of U.K. primary teachers' conceptions of geological time and perceptions of geoscience. *Journal of Research in Science Teaching*, 38(2), pp. 191–221.

Trend, R (2009) The power of deep time in geoscience education: Linking 'interest', 'threshold concepts' and 'self-determination theory'. *Studia Universitatis Babeş-Bolyai, Geologia*, 54(1), pp. 7–12.

Tudge, J (2008) *The Everyday Lives of Young Children: Culture, Class, and Child Rearing in Diverse Societies*. Cambridge: Cambridge University Press.

Turner, C (2008) *The Geography of Hope: A tour of the world we need*. London: Vintage Books.

Tyas-Tunggal, H (1997) Hands on Landscapes. Paper presented at the Learning through Landscapes *Grounds for Celebration* Conference, September. Winchester, UK.

Tyrrell, N and Kallis, G (2017) Children in transnational family migration. In Ní Laoire, C and White, A (eds) *Movement, Mobilities, and Journeys*. Dordrecht: Springer, pp. 329–46.

Uhlenwinkel, A (2017) Geographical thinking: Is it a limitation or powerful thinking? In Brooks, C, Butt, G and Fargher, M (eds) *The Power of Geographical Thinking*. Dordrecht: Springer, pp. 41–53.

UNEP (United Nations Environment Programme) (2016) Marine plastic debris and microplastics: Global lessons and research to inspire action and guide policy change. Available at: http://wedocs.unep.org/rest/bitstreams/11700/retrieve

UNESCO (United Nations Education, Scientific and Cultural Organisation) (2015) Education 2030: Incheon declaration and framework for action for the implementation of sustainable development goal 4. Paris: UNESCO. Available at; http://unesdoc.unesco.org/images/0024/002456/245656E.pdf

UNICEF (United Nations International Children's Emergency Fund) (1989) Convention on the rights of the child. Available at: www.unicef.org/crc/index_30166.html

UNICEF (2002) *A Life Like Mine – How Children Live Around the World*. London: Dorling Kindersley.

UNICEF (2005) *The state of the world's children 2006: Excluded and invisible.* New York: UNICEF.

UNICEF (2015a) The 2030 agenda for sustainable development. Available at: www.unicef.org/agenda2030/69525.html

UNICEF (2015b) What does sustainability mean for children? Available at: www.unicef.org.uk/define-sustainability-children/

UNICEF (2016) Uprooted: The growing crisis for refugee and migrant children. New York: UNICEF. Available at: http//:weshare.unicef.org/Package/2AMZIFQPSK8

United Nations (1987) Report of the World Commission on Environment and Development. New York: United Nations Department of Economic and Social Affairs (DESA). Available at: www.un.org/documents/ga/res/42/ares42-187.htm

United Nations (1992) Agenda 21. Available at: www.un.org/esa/sustdev/documents/agenda21/english/agenda21toc.htm

United Nations (2000) The millennium development goals. Available at: www.un.org/millenniumgoals/

United Nations (2015) Transforming our world: The 2030 agenda for sustainable development. Available at: https://sustainabledevelopment.un.org/post2015/transformingourworld.

Uttal, D and Tan, L (2000) Cognitive mapping in childhood. In Kitchen, R and Freundschuh, S (eds) *Cognitive Mapping: Past, present and future.* London: Routledge, pp. 147–65.

Valentine, G (2004) *Public Space and the Culture of Childhood.* Guildford: Ashgate.

Van Andel, J (1990) Places children like, dislike, and fear. *Children's Environments Quarterly*, 7(4), pp. 24–31.

Veale, A and Donà, G (eds) (2014) *Children and Youth Migration: Mobility-in-migration in an era of globalization.* Basingstoke: Palgrave Macmillan.

Veitch, J, Bagley, S, Ball, K and Salmon, J (2006) Where do children usually play? A qualitative study of parents' perceptions of influences on children's active free-play. *Health and Place*, 12, pp. 383–93.

Villanueva, K, Giles-Corti, B, Bulsara, M, Trapp, G, Timperio, A, McCormack, G and Van Niel, K (2014) Does the walkability of neighbourhoods affect children's independent mobility, independent of parental, socio-cultural and individual factors? *Children's Geographies*, 12(4), pp. 393–411.

Vleminckx, K and Smeeding, T (eds) (2001) *Child Wellbeing, Child Poverty and Child Policy in Modern Nations.* Bristol: Policy Press.

Vygotsky, L (1962) *Thought and Language.* Cambridge, MA: MIT Press.

Walford, R (2001) *Geography in British Schools 1850–2000: Making a World of Difference.* London: Woburn Press.

Waite, S (ed.) (2017) *Children Learning Outside the Classroom.* (2nd edn) London: Sage.

Waite, S, Passy, R, Gilchrist, M, Hunt, A and Blackwell, I (2016) Natural connections demonstrations project, 2012–2016: Final report. Worcester: Natural England. Available at: http://publications.naturalengland.org.uk/publications.66366 51036540928

Walker, E (ed.) (2012) *Children, Recovery and Disasters: Preparedness, response and recovery.* New York: Nova.

Walker, G (2010) Contrasting localities. In Scoffham, S (ed.) *Primary Geography Handbook.* Sheffield: Geographical Association, pp. 94–203.

Walker, M, Whittle, R, Medd, W, Burningham, K, Moran-Ellis, J and Tapsell, S (2012) It came up to here: Learning from children's flood narratives. *Children's Geographies*, 10(2), pp.135–50.

Wall, K, Dockrell, J and Peacey, N (2008) Primary schools: The built environment. In Alexander, R with Doddington, C, Gray, J, Hargreaves, L and Kershner, R (eds) *The Cambridge Primary Review Research Surveys*. London: Routledge, pp. 589–622.

Waller, T (2006) Don't come too close to my octopus tree: Recording and evaluating young children's perspectives on outdoor learning. *Children, Youth and Environment*, 16(2), pp. 75–104.

Waller, T, Ärlemalm-Hagsér, E, Hansen Sandseter, E, Lee-Hammond, L, Lekies, K and Wyver, S (2017) Introduction. In Waller, T, Ärlemalm-Hagsér, E, Hansen Sandseter, E, Lee-Hammond, L, Lekies, K, and Wyver, S (eds) *The Sage Handbook of Outdoor Play and Learning*. London: Sage, pp. 1–21.

Wals, A and Corcoran, P (2012) *Learning for Sustainability in Times of Accelerating Change*. Wageningen, The Netherlands: Wageningen Academic Publishers.

Walsh, G, McMillan, D and McGuiness, C (eds) (2017) *Playful Teaching and Learning*. London: Sage.

Walsh, P (2016) *Early Childhood Playgrounds*. Abingdon: Routledge.

Ward, S (2009) *The Little Book of Small World Play*. London: A & C Black.

Warden, C (2015) *Learning with Nature: Embedding outdoor practice*. London: Sage.

Wassermann, J (ed.) (2017) *Teaching Social Sciences: Intermediate and senior phases*. Cape Town: Oxford University Press.

Waters, J (2008) *Education, Migration, and Cultural Capital in the Chinese Diaspora: Transnational students between Hong Kong and Canada*. New York: Cambria Press.

Wattchow, B and Brown, M (2011) *A Pedagogy of Place*. Clayton: Monash University Publishing.

Webber, J and Robertson, M (2012) Indigenous perspectives on sustainable development: Children's views from the 'top end'. In Robertson, M (ed.) *Schooling for Sustainable Development: A focus on Australia, New Zealand and the Oceanic region*. Melbourne: Springer, pp. 125–39.

Webber, S and Dixon, S (eds) (2007) *Growing Up Online: Young people and digital technologies*. Basingstoke: Palgrave Macmillan.

Webley, P (2005) Children's understanding of economics. In Barrett, M and Buchanan-Barrow, E (eds) *Children's Understanding of Society*. Hove: Psychology Press, pp. 43–67.

Webster, A, Beveridge, M and Reed, M (1996) *Managing the Literacy Curriculum*. London: Routledge.

Weeden, P (n.d.) *GTIP Think Piece: Assessment for Learning*. Available at: www.geography.org.uk/projects/gtip/thinkpieces/assessmentforlearning/#top

Weeden, P and Lambert, D (2006) *Geography Inside the Black Box: Assessment for learning in the geography classroom*. London: NFER Nelson.

Weir, L, Etelson, D and Brand, D (2006) Parents' perceptions of neighbourhood safety and children's physical activity. *Preventive Medicine*, 43, pp. 212–17.

Weldon, M (2010) The wider world. In Scoffham, S (ed.) *Primary Geography Handbook*. Sheffield: Geographical Association, pp. 204–15.

Welsh Government (2015) *Curriculum for Wales: Foundation phase framework*. Available at: http://gov.wales/docs/dcells/publications/150803-fp-framework-en.pdf

West, A (2007) Power relationships and adult resistance to children's participation. *Children, Youth and Environment*, 17(1), pp.123–35.

Weston, B (ed.) (2005) *Child Labor and Human Rights: Making children matter*. London: Lynne Rienner.

Wheatley, N and Rawlins, D (2008) *My Place*. Newtown, Australia: Walker Books.

White, J (2014) *Playing and Learning Outdoors* (2nd edn). London: Routledge.

White, J (ed.) (2011) *Outdoor Provision in the Early Years*. London: Sage.

Whitebread, D (2012) *Developmental Psychology and Early Childhood Education*. London: Sage.

Whitebread, D and Coltman, P (eds) (2015) *Teaching and Learning in the Early Years* (4th edn). Abingdon: Routledge.

Whitehead, M (2014) *Environmental Transformations*. Abingdon: Routledge.

Whitley, D (2012) *The Idea of Nature in Disney Animation*. Guildford: Ashgate.

Whittle, J (2006) Journey sticks and affective mapping. *Primary Geographer*, 59, Spring, pp. 11–13.

Wiegand, P (1991) Does travel broaden the mind? *Education*, 3(13), pp. 54–8.

Wiegand, P (1992) *Places in the Primary School*. Lewes: Falmer.

Wiegand, P (1993) *Children and Primary Geography*. London: Cassell.

Wiegand, P (2006) *Learning and Teaching with Maps*. London: Routledge.

Wiegand P (n.d.) *GTIP Think Piece – Using Maps and Atlases*. Available at: www.geography.org.uk/projects/gtip/thinkpieces/usingmapsatlases/#top

Wiliam, D (2012) Think you've implemented assessment for learning? *Times Educational Supplement*, 13 June.

Willett, R (2017) Domesticating online games for preteens – discursive fields, everyday gaming and family life. *Children's Geographies*, 15(2), pp. 146–59.

Willy, T (2017) Sustaining primary geography. *Primary Geography*, 93, pp. 6–7.

Williams, D and Brown, J (2012) *Learning Gardens and Sustainability Education: Bringing life to schools and schools to life*. New York: Routledge.

Williams, M (1996) *Understanding Geographical and Environmental Education: The role of research*. London: Cassell.

Williams-Siegfredsen, J (2017) *Understanding the Danish Forest School Approach* (2nd edn). London: David Fulton.

Willson, A (2015) Educating for hope in troubled times: Climate change and the transition to a post-carbon future. *Teaching Geography*, 40(2), p. 82.

Wilmot, D and Irwin, P (2015) South African teachers' perceptions of the primary geography curriculum: An exploratory study. *Review of International Geographical Education Online*, 5(2), pp.137–50.

Wilson, N (2009) *Tunisia: Pocket guide*. Singapore: Berlitz Publishing/ Apa Publications.

Wilson, R (2012) *Nature and Young Children*. Abingdon: Routledge.

Winkler, E (2012) *Learning Race, Learning Place*. New Brunswick, NJ: Rutgers University Press.

Winter, C (2011) Curriculum knowledge and justice: Content, competency and concept. *The Curriculum Journal*, 22(3), pp. 337–64.

Witt, S (2017) Playful approaches to learning out of doors. In Scoffham, S (ed.) *Teaching Geography Creatively* (2nd edn). Abingdon: Routledge, pp. 44–57.

Witten, K and Carroll, P (2016) Children's neighbourhoods: Places of play or spaces of fear. In Nairn, K and Kraftl, P (eds) *Space, Place and Environment*. Dordrecht: Springer, pp. 331–50.

Wood, D, Bruner, J and Ross, G (1976) The role of tutoring in problem solving. *Journal of Child Psychology and Psychiatry*, 17(2), pp. 89–100.

Wood, E (2013) *Play, Learning and the Early Childhood Curriculum* (3rd edn). London: Sage.

Woodhouse, S (2003) *Assessing Progress*. Available at: www.qca.org.uk/geography/innovating/examples/assessing_progress.pdf

Woodhouse, S (2017) Sustaining school gardens. *Primary Geography*, 93, Summer, pp.16–17.

Woodward, J (2014) *The Ice Age: A Very Short Introduction*. Oxford: Oxford University Press.

Woolley, R (2010) *Tackling Controversial Issues in the Primary School*. London: Routledge.

World Commission On Environment and Development (The Brundtland Report) (1987) *Our Common Future: Report of the World Commission On Environment and Development*. New York: United Nations.

Wormald, D (2017) Deep time: A public engagement literature review. London: Natural History Museum. Available at: www.nhm.ac.uk/content/dam/nhmwww/about-us/visitor-research/Deep%20Time%20Lit%20review.pdf

Wyse, D, Baumfield, V, Egan, D, Gallagher, C, Hayward, L, Hulme, M, Leitch, R, Livingston, K, Menter, I and Lingard, B (2012) *Creating the Curriculum*. London: Routledge.

Xuan, X, Duan, Y and Sun, Y (2015) Primary geography education in China: Past, current and future. *Review of International Geographical Education Online*, 5(2), pp. 111–36.

Yarwood, R and Tyrrell, N (2012) Why children's geographies? *Geography*, 97(3), pp. 123–8.

Yoshida, K (2015) Problems and perspectives of geography education in Japanese elementary schools. In Ida, Y, Yuda, M, Shimura, T, Ike, S, Ohnishi, K and Oshima, H (eds) *Geography Education in Japan*. Dordrecht: Springer, pp. 19–24.

Yoshida, K (2017) Characteristics of primary geography in Japan. In Catling, S (ed.) *Reflections on Primary Geography*. Sheffield: The Register of Research in Primary Geography, pp. 82–4.

Young, M (Mary) (2008) *Bringing Knowledge Back In: From social constructivism to social realism in the sociology of education*. Abingdon: Routledge.

Young, M (Mary) with Cummins, E (2002) *Global Citizenship: A handbook for primary teaching*. Cambridge: Chris Kington.

Young, M (Michael) (2010) The global dimension. In Scoffham, S (ed.) *The Primary Geography Handbook*. Sheffield: Geographical Association, pp. 216–27.

Young, M (Michael) and Muller, J (2016) *Curriculum and the Specialization of Knowledge: Studies in the sociology of education*. Abingdon: Routledge.

Young, M (Michael), Lambert, D, with Roberts, C and Roberts, M (2014) *Knowledge and the future school*. London: Bloomsbury.

Zalasiewicz, J (2016) *Rocks: A Very Short Introduction*. Oxford: Oxford University Press.

Zhang, N (2015) Home divided, home reconstructed: Children in rural–urban migration in contemporary China. *Children's Geographies*, 13(4), pp. 381–97.

Zimmerman, J and Robertson, E (2017) *The Case for Contention: Teaching controversial issues in American schools*, Chicago: University of Chicago Press.

Zubenko, W and Capozzoli, J (eds) (2002) *Children and Disasters: A practical guide to healing and recovery*. Oxford: Oxford 4.

INDEX

Added to a page number 'f' denotes a figure and 't' denotes a table.

Aboriginal peoples 342–3
accessibility 62–3, 68, 71, 76,
    226–7, 319–20, 353
active engagement with the world 10
active and informed citizens 19–20
active learning 7, 16, 19, 105, 250, 486
activities
    enabling teaching and assessment 477t
    geographical learning 309–14
    local areas studies 410–15
Adam and Paradise Island 210
addresses 366, 380
Adichie, C. 386
adult supervision 58, 75, 310
adult support
    differentiation 454
    see also scaffolding
Adventure Rock 92–3
advertising 89
aerial photographs 59, 74, 275–8, 359
affective mapping 279

affordances 5, 58, 62, 65, 68, 69, 71, 166,
    306, 318, 319, 320, 323, 504
Africa 86, 371, 386–7, 388
agency (child) 60, 73, 90, 210, 234, 504
agency (teacher) 10
air transport 232
Al-Nofli, M. 99
Alexander, R. 97, 396
Ali's Story 228
'along the street' activity 312
alphanumeric grids 274
alpine tundra 171
alternative facts 196
Amazon rainforest 403
Andreotti, V. 399
animated films 92, 267
Anthropocene 149–50, 151t, 152–4
applied knowledge 21
aquatic environments 170
ArcGIS 285
arctic tundra 171

argument (effective) 392t
artefacts 268–70, 359–60, 447
assessment 456–83
    approaches to 466–76
    benchmark expectations 459–63
    centrality in teaching and learning 457
    defining 457–9
    importance 457, 458
    linking teaching and 476–82
    and planning 453, 459, 464, 465
    reasons for 463–6
    as under-played 14
    see also formative assessment; peer
        assessment; self-assessment;
        summative assessments
assessment activity (research) 500t
Assessment for Learning (AfL) 464–5
atlas maps 281–2, 367, 373, 374, 381–3, 400,
        404, 405, 408
attachment to place 68–9, 82, 83, 342–3
attitudes 110, 391
    challenging 386
    of curriculum makers 10
    in primary geography 48, 255
    sources informing 78
    towards sustainability 203
    see also moral attitudes; positive attitudes
Australia 407
    citizenship education 222
    early geographical learning 294
    education for sustainability 201
    primary geography 12
        curriculum 6, 20, 362, 510
        goal setting 19–21
        importance of fieldwork 251
        outdoor education 26–7
        quality of teaching 6
    values in pre-school education 25
Australian children
    global knowledge 79
    sense of national identity 82
Australian Sustainable Schools
        Initiative (AuSSI) 204–5
authenticity in learning 249
awareness
    of adult supervision 58
    of common needs in life 385
    of inclusion/exclusion 298
    relational 40
    see also cultural awareness; environmental
        awareness; geographical
        awareness; global awareness;
        spatial awareness
Azzi in Between 228

Baker, J. 211, 309
balance sheets 240, 413
Barnes, J. 447
Barrett, M. 371

Beach School 249
A Bear Called Paddington 229–30
'being for' the environment 97
belonging 36, 68, 73, 86, 135, 177, 222, 380
Belonging 211, 309
benchmark expectations 459–63
Bent, J. 99
bias(es) 45, 104, 137, 177, 225,
        239, 295, 385
Bing maps 409
biomes 169–70, 403–5
Black, P. 464
Blackberry Wine 127–8
Bloom's Taxonomy 468
Bonnett, A. 4, 34
Bono, E. de 118–19, 244
bordering/barrier crossing 86
boundaries 368
bounded landscapes 363
Bourn, D. 389, 394
Britt, C. 503–4
Broadfoot, P. 457
Brown, K. 211
brownfield regeneration 186–7
Brundtland Commission 200, 202, 206
Bruner, J. 430
Buchanan, J. 237
buildings and grounds 208t
built environments 226
Burren (Ireland) 172–3
Butt, G. 449, 464

Calman, C. 60
Canada 407, 511
capabilities, developing 27, 116, 487
car park problem, studying
        (example) 325
carbon footprints 203, 232
care for the environment 211, 279, 298,
        311–12, 321
caring dialogue for thinking 469
Catling, S. 98, 384
Cele, S. 69
Cenozoic era 150, 151t
challenge, geographical enquiry and 120
change(s)
    controversial issues and
        proposals for 240
    in the Earth's processes 153–4
    investigating regional 369
    in places and localities 133–4, 351
    sustainable 207t
    through assessment 457
    see also environmental change
changing places (activity) 312–13
child migrants 70–1, 86, 227–8, 374
child refugees 85–6, 228
child-focused planning 443–4
child-initiated approaches 115, 305, 448

childhood places 127
children
    ability to improve learning 465
    feelings about geography 501
    as geographers 294
    ideas about geography 97–100
    involvement
        and belonging 68
        in curriculum making 11
        in environmental
            improvement 96–7, 321
        and geographical understanding 48
        in learning 120, 458, 466, 475
        in practical projects 15
        in risk assessments 256
        see also engagement; participation
    listening to 60, 76, 96, 211, 342
    as researchers 499, 503
    see also disabled children; pre-school
        children; rural children; urban
        children
children's geographies 55–97
    active involvement 96–7
    environment see environment
    images of the world 80–2
    imaginary realism 91–2
    imagined geographies 90–1, 135
    impact of economic geographies 89–90
    independent mobility 72–3
    locational knowledge 66–8, 80
    migration 85–7
    national identity 82–3
    natural hazards 87–8
    perspectives on school grounds 61–4
    place see place(s)
    representations 59
    studies of 56
    visits abroad 89
    wider world
        awareness of 77–8
        impact of 84–5
    youngest/pre-school 56–7
China 6, 371, 407, 478
Christensen, P. 65
citizenship 342
    active and informed 19–20
    enquiry and 120, 396
    geography and 26, 221–4
    local environmental participation 355–6
    sustainability 206t
    see also geographical citizenship; global
        citizenship
civilisation 150
classroom research
    approaching 498–9
    areas in need of 496–7
classrooms
    bringing the outside in 258
    defined 322

climate change 39, 87, 88, 149–50, 182, 188,
    203, 234, 396
climate regions 406
climate zones 169, 171–2
clints (limestone) 173
closed enquiry 114, 115t
closed questions 468, 469
Clough, P. 398, 399, 402
Club Penguin 93
co-researchers 503
coasts 164–5
cognitive mapping see mental mapping
collaboration 249, 286
collaborative dialogue for thinking 469
colour, on maps 382
commodification 58, 75
common humanity 392t
commonality 40
communities of enquiry 117, 395
comparisons 40, 348, 351, 382, 402
complex maps 279
concern/taking action 110t, 111t
confidence (child) 19, 70, 248, 473
confidence (teacher) 14, 77
conflict resolution 390t, 392t, 393t
Confucius 250
conifers 171
connectedness 120, 297–9
consistency, planning for 430
consumerism, technologies and 287
consumers, children as 90, 94
contents pages (atlases) 382, 400
continental regions 403–6
controversial issues 112, 236–44, 395
cooperation 10, 60, 392t
Council for Learning Outside the Classroom 256
country(ies)
    developing a sense of 370–5
    exploring 138, 397–406
    geographical knowledge 371–2, 389, 398–9
Countryside Code 213–14
Cox, S. 220
creative dialogue for thinking 470
creative discipline, geography as a 34
creative individuals 19
creative planning 447
creativity 26, 304, 414
Cregan, K. 83
critical dialogue for thinking 470
critical friend 115
critical mentors 124
critical thinking 105, 225, 388, 389, 392t,
    394, 395
cross-curricular links 13
    in fieldwork 254
    global dimension 388–9
    local area studies 187, 357–9
        example 360–1
    maps and 280

in planning 426, 446–9
studying school buildings and grounds 319
Crutzen, P.J. 153
cultural awareness 40, 51, 177, 297, 298, 320
cultural diversity 40, 51, 176–7, 297, 320,
    364, 385
cultural influences 154
Cummins, E. 396
cumulative records 481
curiosity 4, 9, 16, 22, 44, 50, 60, 104, 105,
    107, 109, 112, 124, 137, 295, 341, 384,
    425, 449
curriculum see early years curriculum;
    primary geography curriculum
curriculum making see planning
    geography teaching
Cuthbert, T. 83
cyber-geographies 81
cyclones 234

damage (school), investigating 330
Data Visualisation 285
Davies, C. 478
Day, C. 65
Day, S. 58
debate 106, 240, 374, 395
deciduous forests 171
decisions 46, 135
decoding 286
deep time 154–5, 156
deforestation 149, 158, 188
Denmark 248
dens 58, 68, 309–10
Department for Education (DfE) 250, 458
desertification 188
deserts 170, 172, 403
development education 389
dialogic approach 469–70
difference(s) 5, 26, 40, 370, 387, 414, 416
A Different View 24
differentiation 452–4
Digimaps 275, 285
digital cameras 264, 287
digital communication 5, 37, 81, 286
    see also geographical information sys-
        tems; Internet; social media
digital maps/mapping 37, 279, 284, 409
digital photographs 8, 259, 264, 286, 310,
    311, 324
digital technologies 15, 19, 52, 86, 284, 286,
    287, 321, 359, 409
Dinkele, G. 121
dinosaurs, exploring (example) 155–6
direction, on maps 274
disabled children 62–3
disaster-relief efforts 87
discussion partners 469
discussions 106, 374
Disney films 92

distance 73, 383
distant places, studying
    in the classroom 409–10, 417
    distinction between global dimension,
        global citizenship and 396t
    pitfalls to avoid 416–17
    reasons for 383–8
    resources 418–19
distributions 4, 36, 37, 49
diversity 26, 137, 138, 206t, 390t, 392t,
    393t, 414, 416
    see also cultural diversity
Dixon, J. 58
Dolan, A. 60
double focus planning 447
Dove, J. 167
drama 8, 136, 210, 240
drawing(s) 59, 67, 74, 275, 280
'dressing up' activity 313
Dust Bowl (USA) 158
dynamic aspects
    of geography 34, 36, 150, 153, 157
    see also change(s)

early geographical learning 25, 51, 52, 293–315
    activities for 309–14
    connecting with and understanding
        the world 297–9
    outdoor environments 303–8
    play and 294–5, 299–303, 304
    rationale for 294–6
    see also pre-school children
early years curriculum 491
'earth from space' (activity) 314
earth sciences 156
earthquakes 168, 234
Earth's rotation, exploring (example) 144–5
Eaude, T. 458
eco-school approach 308
eco-tourism 189
ecological footprints 48, 203
ecological responsibility 211–12
economic geographies 89–90
ecosystems 169, 173
education
    children's views on 88
    citizenship 26, 222
    importance and significance of
        geography 4–5
    for sustainability 25–6, 96, 197, 199, 201,
        203, 204–11, 215, 341, 390
    see also teaching primary geography
Education Endowment Fund 480
Education for Sustainable Development
    (ESD) 206–7t
effective pedagogy 458
'eight doorways' approach 207–9, 333
embedding learning 486–7
emergent environmentalism 57–8, 60

empathy 83, 229, 392t
empowering enquiry 112t, 117, 121
empowerment 215, 471
enabling enquiry 112t, 121
enabling learning 487
enchantment 69
energy 207t
    and resource extraction 187–8
    sources 201
    use 209
        studying (example) 335
energy literacy 210
engagement 10, 11, 43, 109, 296, 320, 487–8
England
    citizenship education 222, 223
    Countryside Code 213–14
    environmental education and
        well-being 212
    pre-school education 25
    primary geography 12
        children's ideas about 98
        curriculum 6, 20, 23, 362, 488, 509–10
        debate about knowledge 21
        geographical enquiry 107–8
        global dimension 388
        importance and purpose of 49–50
        inspectors' perspectives on
            stimulating 8–9
        outdoor learning 250
        quality mark awards 11
        quality of teaching 7
English children
    images of the world 81
    understanding of nation 83
    visits to natural places 70
engraving learning 486
enhancing enquiry 112t, 117, 121
enjoying teaching and learning 15, 16–17
enquiry see geographical enquiry;
        problem-oriented enquiry
environment(s) 148–94
    active involvement 96–7
    awareness of involvement in 505
    care for the 211, 279, 298, 311–12, 321
    children's views of 95–6
    constraints on exploring 75–6
    human activity(ies) and 36, 149–50, 153,
        184, 188, 201
    new creations to explore (activity) 313
    physical and human processes 38, 51
    recognising interconnected/relational
        context 196–7
    spatial understanding 73–4
    and well-being 211–12
    see also local environment; natural
        environment(s); safe environments;
        school environment
environmental awareness 57–8, 91, 199, 210,
    241, 294, 295–6, 297, 298

environmental change 38, 198,
    211, 215, 341
    see also climate change
environmental concerns 59–60
    global citizenship 393t
    investigating 368, 405
    and participation 94–6
environmental degradation 158, 203
Environmental Education Research 499
environmental experiences 61, 62, 74, 75,
    81, 89, 300, 302, 304
environmental geography 149,
    157–60, 402
    environmental impact
        and sustainability 196
    sequencing learning in 160, 161–2t
    teaching and learning
        (example) 159–60
    topics in 157, 181–93, 233–4
environmental identity 97
environmental impact 39, 198–200
    natural hazards 133–4, 198
    studying 396
    and sustainability 39–40, 51, 112, 196,
        241, 354–5
environmental interests 93, 113
environmental justice 39–40, 201
environmental knowledge 95
environmental quality, sense of 94–6
environmental values 40, 48, 59–60,
    333, 500–1
environmentally friendly growth 202
ephemera 268, 269t
episode analysis, in research 500t
equatorial climate 171–2
equity 203, 206, 224–36, 392t
essential knowledge 21
Ethiopia 512
ethnic segregation 86
ethno-geographies 32, 33, 64
European children, dual identity 82
evergreen forests 171
everyday geographies 13, 31–3, 43, 46, 48,
    66, 127, 137, 317, 505
    see also children's geographies
exclusion 62, 298
exhibitions 241
experience, learning through 250, 294–5
explaining 469
exploration
    constraints on 75–6
    and geographical learning 65–6,
        298, 485–6
    in natural environments 70–1
exploratory play 302t

Facebook 286
factual knowledge 21–2
Fair Trade fortnight 397

Fairtrade 178, 179, 230–3, 420
Fairtrade Foundation 231, 233, 420
fake news 196
fantasy play 303t
farm activity 313
farming 158, 405, 406
feature representations 59
feedback 459, 463, 465, 470–2, 481
feedforward 465, 471–2
feelings (children's)
    about geography, researching 501
    about school grounds, investigating 328–9
field notes 499t, 501–2
fieldwork 7, 15, 27, 41, 98, 250
    adult/pupil ratios 256
    aims and objectives 256
    behavioural change 251
    briefing 257
    digital technology 287
    education for sustainability 210
    evaluation 257
    good practice in 252–3
    in groups 256
    importance of 251
    lesson plan for 7-8 year olds 450–2
    limited opportunities for 14
    organising successful 256–7
    planning for 260
    preparatory work 255
    progression in 259–61, 262–3t
    resources 257
    studying school grounds 319
    to identify local issues (example) 139
    virtual 259
    where to carry out 253–5
films 78, 91–2, 267
finite resources 198, 201
5Rs 212
Fleet, A. 503–4
flooding 233–4
    studying (example) 235–6
food activities 313
food and drink 207t
forest schools 71, 75–6, 248–9, 304–7
forests 170, 171
formal assessment 458
formative assessment 16, 458, 459, 463, 464,
    465, 470, 478
formative feedback 481
4Cs 208–9
4Rs 212
fracking 188
framed enquiry 114, 115t
France 83
freedom of movement 66
Freire, P. 396
friendships 85, 504
functional regions 363

'fusing' subjects 447
futures dimension 214–16

Galani, A. 166
gardens/gardening 71, 210, 212, 305
generalisations 21, 37, 416
geo-located images 286
geocaching 286
geocitizens 487
geographers 5, 41, 120, 133, 134, 196, 199
Geographical Association (GA) 11, 24, 423,
    450, 460, 461
geographical awareness 42, 43, 505
    activities to develop 312–14
    early years provision and 297
    enquiry and 110t, 111t, 120
    mobility and 73
    of place 136, 137
    virtual games and 93
    of the wider world 57–8, 77–8, 295
geographical citizenship 487
geographical dilemmas 243
geographical enquiry 7, 9–10, 41,
    51, 103–24
    children's awareness of 98
    controversial issues 240
    de Bono's techniques 118–19
    defined 105–7
    developing 108–12
    in England 107–8
    and environmental well-being 211
    expanding children's horizons 119–20
    focused, framed and facilitated 115–16
    global citizenship 396
    global dimension 389
    lack of 13
    local areas 341, 343
    Philosophy for Children 116–17
    process approach to 424f, 425
    progression in developing 120–4
    skills development 112–16
    'three Es' approach 112–15
geographical information
    systems (GIS) 279, 283–7
geographical investigation 4, 7, 20, 41–2
    early geographical learning 298
    geographical enquiry and 110t, 111t, 121
    lack of 13
    of the school and its site 316–37
geographical knowledge
    constructive feedback 463
    of countries 371–2, 389, 398–9
    debating the nature and
        importance of 20–3
    deepening 505
    of global places 78–9
    goal fulfilment and quality of life 24
    local area studies 341

locational 52, 66–8, 80, 139–45, 379–80
the power in 42
geographical learning
    about national and
        continental regions 403–6
    about other countries 399–403
    assessing *see* assessment
    contexts for 18–20
    embedding 486–7
    enabling 487
    engaging 487–8
    engraving 486
    enjoying 16–17
    enquiry approach 9–10
    exploring 485–6
    focus for 51–2
    importance 5
    key areas 460–1
    outcomes 488–90
    recording and reporting 480–2
    relational understanding and 5
    researching 495–504
    self-directed 8–9
    self-evaluation 493, 494–5t
    see also early geographical learning;
        global learning; outdoor learning
geographical significance 45–6
geographical skills 41–2, 51–2
    enabling the use of 487
    see also map skills; skills development
geographical thinking 42, 104, 114, 488
geographical topics 14, 16
    approaches to 7, 162–3
    controversial 237–8, 239
    for enquiry 112
    in environmental geography 157, 181–93,
        233–4
    in human geography 175–80
    local area studies 354–7
    in physical geography 163–75
    to investigate in school 326–37
    using school grounds
        for introducing 321
geographical understanding 4, 505
    deepening (example) 391
    enquiry and development of
        104, 116, 320
    environmental spatial 73–4
    geographical thinking and 42
    knowledge and 21–2
    lack of development in 14
    of local areas 69, 341
    place and 294
    topicality and evaluation of 44–5
    visualisation and 261
geography
    children's ideas about 97–100
    defining 33–4

importance and significance 4–5
key concepts (big ideas) 21, 35–40, 42, 52
pre-school *see* early geographical learning
primary *see* primary geography
role of 43–7
see also children's geographies; everyday
    geographies; personal geographies
geography teacher associations 175, 450
GeogSpace 275
GeoGuessr 266
geological epochs 149–56
geological eras 150–4
geological periods 150
geological time 150, 151–2t, 154–5, 156
global awareness 26, 298, 342, 389
global citizenship 388, 390, 391, 392–3t,
    394–6, 418
global dimension 208t, 388–97, 433
    see also distant places
global knowledge 78–80
global learning 388, 390, 391, 393t, 396, 418
Global Learning Programme (GLP) 389, 461
global perspective 137
global positioning systems (GPS) 37, 133,
    282, 406
globalisation 389, 392t
globes
    as contexts of locational knowledge
        142–3t
    introducing young
        children to 141, 275, 281
    using to explore places 381–2
    using to explore time zones 408
goals
    knowledge and fulfilment of 24
    in the primary curriculum 19–20
good causes, examining 244
Google Earth 8, 59, 133, 278, 282–3, 409
Google Images 400
Google Maps 133, 278, 282, 283
Google Street views 267
graphicacy 41, 261, 487
grasslands 170–1, 172, 404
green spaces 70, 71
Greenwich Meridian 407, 408
grikes (limestone) 173
Gross National Product (GNP) 231
group teaching 99
group work
    mastery learning 480
    researching 502–3
guidebooks 129, 368
guided play 61
Guyana 512

habitat, creating a (example) 301–2
Halocha, J. 106, 453
Hamid's Story 228

hard science 156
Hargreaves, L. 97
Harlen, W. 458
Harris, J. 127–8
Harwood, D. 366
Hayward, S. 76, 211
health 19, 70, 211
Henderson Island 184
Here I Am 228
Hicks, D. 214, 215, 216, 396
hide and seek (activity) 312
hierarchical cross-curricular teaching 446–7
high income localities 76
higher order questioning 468
higher order thinking 251, 391
Hirst, B. 396
historical geography 181, 280, 285
history 98–9, 187, 254, 358t, 359, 360–1
holidays 89
Holocene epoch 150, 151t, 153
Holt, L. 62
home region 365–8
Hong Kong 511
hope 214, 396
hot desert climate 172
hot seating 240, 361, 413
Huckle, J. 214
human activities, and the environment 36,
    149–50, 153, 184, 188, 201
human geography 41, 149, 156–7
    sequencing learning in 160, 161–2t
    topics in 175–80
    see also environmental geography
human processes 38, 51, 135, 320
human rights 390t, 393t
hurricanes 234
hypothesising 298

ice-sheets 171
identity
    cultural awareness and 40, 177
    global citizenship 392t
    group membership and 222
    place and 135, 343, 380
    regional 364
    see also environmental identity;
        national identity; personal identity
igneous rock 168
images of the world 80–2
imaginary realism 91–2
imagination 60–1, 91, 135, 295, 414–15
imaginative play 304
imagined geographies 90–1, 135
imitative play 302t
immediacy 44, 250, 287, 320
imperfect world 87
impotence, sense of 76
inclusion 208t, 256, 298

inclusivity 227
income 230, 231
independent mobility 72–3
independent working 19
indexes (atlas), using 382, 400
India, studying (example) 409–10
indigenous communities 203, 342–3
inductive enquiry 109
inequality 389, 392t, 399, 487
inequity 60, 226–7, 231
inert knowledge 21
infertile land 187, 188
informal assessment 458
information
    from globes and atlases 383
    from maps 271
    geographical 283–4
    locational 133, 284, 286
    studying tourist 129, 368, 373, 401, 405
information gathering 260
injustice 392t
Inside the Black Box 464
The Inside Outing 258
Instagram 286
integration 87
inter-disciplinary approaches 447
interconnectedness 37, 38, 51, 287, 335–7,
    341, 379, 394
intercultural understanding 40
interdependence 37, 51, 137, 206t, 298, 385,
    389, 390t, 392t, 393t
*International Charter on Geographical
    Education* (IGU-CGE) 4–5
International Date Line 407
International Geographical Union Commis-
    sion of Geographical Education (IGU-
    CGE) 4–5, 498
International Geological
    Congress (IGC) 152
*International Research in Geographical and
    Environmental Education* (IRGEE) 499
Internet 5, 367, 369, 373, 408
interviews 240, 500t
investigation *see* geographical investigation;
    issues investigation
Ireland 6, 11, 172–3, 251, 398, 510
issue investigation
    examples 221–2, 356–7
    fieldwork for identifying 139
    resources for 418–19
    sustainability education 241

James, S. 228–9
Japan 6, 234
Johnston, J. 453
The Journey 228
journey activities 312
journey sticks 279

journeys 383
justice
    and sustainability 206t
    see also environmental justice; social justice

Kasser, T. 211
Katie Morag stories 280
Kenju's Forest 210
Kitchen, R. 98, 99
knowledge *see* geographical knowledge;
    teacher knowledge
knowledge turn 21

land reclamation 187
landshape/landscape 181, 349, 363
language, in maps 281
lateral thinking 118
latitude 133, 406–7, 408
Lawrence, A. 140–1
learning
    children's ability to improve 465
    levels of 478–9
    see also active learning; geographical
        learning; global learning; mastery
        learning; social learning
learning intentions 465, 466–7, 473
learnscapes 317–19
Lehman-Frisch, S. 67
Less Economically Developed Countries
    (LEDCs) 231
lesson planning 449–54
liberated approach, curriculum making 10
life-world regions 364, 365, 367
limestone rock (Burren) 172–3
Lindfors, J. 105, 106
lines, on maps 382
linguistic regions 363
listening to children 60, 76, 96, 211, 342
literacy 357, 358t
literary documents 41
litter 182–4
The Little House by the Sea 210–11
living geographies 43–4, 46, 48
living sustainably 197, 203, 204, 388
local area(s)
    children's understanding of 69
    classroom discussion (example) 345
    as contexts of locational
        knowledge 142–3t
    defined 344–5
    early geographical learning 295
    exploring 138
    researching 503
    sustainability education 209
    teacher knowledge 76–7
local area studies
    activities 410–15
    aspects of geography 348–57

attachment to place 342–3
cross-curricular links 187, 357–9
deciding on pack
    contexts (example) 415
elsewhere 346–8
geographical enquiry 341, 343
    (example) 113–14
of other countries 399, 401
progression 345
reasons for 340–2
resources 359–60, 411–12t
understanding of place 340
local brochures, creating (example) 353
local community
    developing a sense of 297
    interconnections with 335
    involvement in sustainability
        education 209
    issue investigation (examples)
        221–2, 356–7
    local area studies and links to 341
local culture, tourism and 189
local environment
    children's awareness of 57–8
    connecting children with 255
    research into use of 34
    as a site for investigation 341
    studying impact of
        human activity on 201
local publications 269t
location(s) 132–3
    finding, from photographs 266
    on maps 274
    spatial 36
location theory 135
locational information 133, 284, 286
locational knowledge 52, 66–8, 80, 139–45,
    379–80
longitude 133, 406, 407, 408
Louv, R. 70, 249
low- to middle-income areas 76
lower achieving children 480
Lowes, S. 79
Lundegård, I. 60

Mackintosh, M. 167, 261
McShane, J. 366
making sense of the world 19, 21, 48, 106
map learning 74
map lines 279
map skills 273–8
    cross-curricular links 446
    trails and 279
maps
    activity for geographical awareness 314
    digital technology and 287
    drawing/creating 74, 274,
        280, 282, 374, 405

interpretation of 270–1
and locational knowledge 139
studying regions and countries 366, 367,
    368, 369, 373, 374, 400, 404
using with children 278–80
value of 270–2
varieties of 273t
see also affective mapping; atlas maps;
    digital maps/mapping; mental maps/
    mapping; wall maps; world maps
marginalisation 62
marking 470–2
Martin, F. 32–3, 40, 105, 202, 387, 388, 395
mastery learning 478–80
mathematics 357–8
Maude, A. 22
meaning, of places 134–5
media influence 79
media representations 89, 414
medium-term planning 434–49
memories of school,
    researching children's 503–4
mental map memory game 272
mental maps/mapping 34, 73, 78, 81, 93,
    139, 141, 145, 295
metamorphic rock 168
migration 84, 85–7, 227–30, 389
Minecraft 93
miniature environments 301t
misconceptions 81, 341, 410, 414, 417, 467,
    480, 496
misunderstandings 13, 78, 104, 295, 385,
    398, 453, 464, 467, 486, 496
mobile phones 286
mobile technology 287
mobility
    and accessibility 226–7
    for place exploration 72–3
    and place learning 66
model playhouse (activity) 312
modelled play 299, 300
modern humans 150
MOE 299
monsoons 234
moral attitudes 94
More Economically Developed Countries
    (MEDCs) 231
motivation 7, 99, 106, 120, 248,
    320, 396, 464
moving home 85
multiculturalism 81
multidisciplinary studies 447
My Name is not Refugee 228
Mywalks 255

Nam, Y. 154
names, of features and places 383
nation, understanding of 83

National Council for Social Studies (USA) 24
national frameworks 23–4
national identity 82–3, 86, 374
national politics 83
national regions 138, 362,
    363, 369–70, 403–6
natural collectable objects 269t, 279
natural environment(s)
    animated films and perceptions of 92
    children in 70–1
    consciousness about 60
    and contentment with life 211
    demonstrating an appreciation for 298
    interconnections in 37
    learning about through play 305–6
    resources 157
natural hazards 87–8, 168, 185, 396
    environmental impact 133–4, 198
    preparing for 233–6
    studying (example) 185–6
natural play areas/spaces 58, 63, 71
natural regions 172–3, 403–5
nature
    disconnectedness from 249
    reconnection with 211, 249
    understanding of 88
nature deficit disorder 249
Neanderthals 150
NearMaps 409
needs and rights 207t, 393t
negotiated enquiry 114, 115t
neighbourhood see local area(s)
nested hierarchies 79, 82, 366–7, 380
Netherlands 99
new technologies 39, 49,
    78, 89, 286, 287, 505
New Zealand 6, 76, 294, 510–11
non-governmental organizations, resource
    provision 418
Northern Ireland 6, 12, 510
numbers 357–8

observation 295, 298
ocean plastic pollution 183–4
oceanic regions 406
Ofsted 8, 9, 201, 252, 255, 397, 431, 476
Oman 6, 99
'on the farm' activity 313
ongoing assessment see formative assessment
Open Spaces for Dialogue
    and Enquiry 118, 244
open-ended enquiry 110, 114–15, 116
open-ended planning 443–5
open-ended play 61, 299, 300
open-ended questions 468–9
opportunistic cross-curricular
    teaching 447–8
optimism 95, 214, 389

orientation 74, 279
others/othering 40, 62, 86, 387
outcome differentiation 453
outcomes
  geographical learning 488–90
  pre-school education 25
outdoor learning 15, 26–7, 487
  case for 249–50
  in early years geography 303–8
  and environmental engagement 58
  fieldwork *see* fieldwork
  forest schools 75–6, 248–9
  limited opportunities for 14
  local area study (example) 347
Owen, D. 445, 449, 452
Owens, P. 202, 275, 500
ownership
  of the future 212
  involvement and sense of 97
  of learning 109, 465
Oxfam 244, 394, 420

Pakistan 511
Palmer 57–8
parental concerns 72–3, 75
parental surveillance 286
park activity 310–11
participation 208t
  environmental 94–6, 355–6
  and learning 296
Patten, B. 189, 200
patterns and processes 4, 21, 36, 37, 49, 51,
    106, 135, 136, 179, 279, 331–2, 341
peace and conflict 392t
pedagogy 11, 106, 458, 478
peer assessment 465, 474–6
peer tutoring 465
people 360t, 393t
perceptions (adult) 72, 127, 225
perceptions (children's) 36, 40, 44–5, 51, 67,
    71, 75, 78, 81, 89, 90, 91, 135, 137, 211,
    379, 386, 390t, 393t, 416, 487
personal creations 269t
personal experiences 36, 88, 91, 131, 136,
    137, 389, 487
personal geographies 5, 13, 33, 90, 91, 295
  see also children's geographies
personal identity 68
personal values 19
personalised sites 68
perspectives
  exploring multiple 395
  geographical 4
  global 26, 137, 385
Philippines 87, 187
Phillipson, N. 469
Philosophy for Children (P4C) 113, 116–18,
    144, 211, 232, 238, 240, 244

phone a friend 469
photographs
  artefacts as supplements to 268
  captioning 265–6
  in early geographical
      learning 309, 310, 311
  importance of 261–4
  limitations 267
  ranking 265
  in self-assessment 474
  in studying countries and regions 369,
      373, 400, 404
  in sustainability education 241
  taking 264, 286
  using 265–8
  virtual fieldwork 259
  see also aerial photographs; digital
      photographs
physical geography 41, 149, 156–7
  children's awareness of 98
  regions 363
  sequencing learning in 160, 161–2t
  subject knowledge 174–5
  topics in 163–75
  see also environmental geography
physical processes 38, 51, 135, 320
Pickford, T. 115, 124
picture stories
  and awareness 91, 136
  early geographical learning 296–7
  examining migration through 228
  exploration of place (example) 131
  learning about the environment 60
pictures, and exploration of place 129
Pike, S. 98, 99, 116, 398, 399, 402, 453
place(s) 35–6, 51, 126–46
  attachment 68–9, 82, 83, 342–3
  caring for (activity) 311–12
  changing (activity) 312–13
  character of 350
  comparisons 348, 351, 382, 402
  evolving direct experience of 64
  exploring 129–32
  in films 91–2
  and geographical understanding 294
  imagined 91, 135
  imagining being in 60–1
  learning about 65–6
  location and connections
      132–3, 351
  locational knowledge 139–45
  management and
      improvement of 350–1
  meaning of 134–5
  nature of 133–4, 349–50
  space 135–6
  studying schools as 327–9
  teaching about 136–9, 379–88

using globes and atlases
    to explore 381–2
valued 68, 75
in virtual games 92–4
see also distant places; sense of place
place representations 59, 382
place views 134
place-based children's story,
    enacting (example) 296
place-based research 499
plan views 74, 278
planning geography teaching 15, 422–55
    assessment 453, 459, 464, 465
    curriculum making 10–11,
        423–5, 443–5
    enquiry sequence for 111t
    fieldwork 260
    keeping field notes 501–2
    liberated approach to 10
    medium-term 434–49
    short-term 449–54
    whole-school 425–33
plans, introducing children to 275
plastic pollution 183–4
plate tectonics 135, 168
play
    early geographical learning 294–5,
        299–303, 304
    environmental engagement and learning
        58, 60–1
    feature and place representation 59
    forest schools 305–6
    in natural environments 70–1
    and personal geographies 294–5
    recreation of experiences 61
    in school grounds 61–2, 63
    see also role play
play environments 300–1t
play spaces
    commodification 75
    natural 58, 63, 71
    preferences for 65
    studying local 355
playgrounds 61, 62, 63, 69, 70
playtime, making changes
    to (example) 332–3
Pliocene epoch 150, 151t
'PMI' technique 118
poetry 241
points, on maps 382
polar climate 172
Pollard, A. 457
pollution 95, 149, 182–4, 188, 396
popular nations 81
populations 176
positive attitudes 95, 137, 196, 197, 299,
    308, 333
possible futures 215, 216

postcard maps 271
poverty 84, 85, 231, 389
powerful knowledge 21, 22
pre-school children
    emergent environmentalism 57–8
    feature and place representation 59
    fieldwork with 255
    personal/everyday geographies 56–7
    play space preferences 58
    see also early geographical learning
precaution(s) 207t, 256, 393t
predictions 135–6, 271, 298
preferred futures 107,
    117, 215, 216, 342, 487
prejudices 45, 104, 137, 177, 295, 385, 386,
    387, 410, 418, 486
primary geography 47–50
    children's development in 47–8
    citizenship in 26, 222–3
    enquiry see geographical enquiry
    key concepts in 48
    learning see geographical learning
    local area studies 348–57
    purpose 48–50
    social justice 224–36
    sustainability in see sustainability
    teaching see teaching primary geography
    thematic see environmental geography;
        human geography; physical geog-
        raphy
    topics see geographical topics
Primary Geography 499
primary geography curriculum 6–7
    debating knowledge for 20–3
    national requirements 23–4,
        488, 509–12
    possible core elements 491–3
    see also cross-curricular links; planning
        primary geography
private worlds 91
probable futures 134, 215, 487
probing questions 468
problem-oriented enquiry 9, 188, 325–6,
    353, 395
problem-solving 15, 74, 108, 183
problem-solving activity, in research 500t
professional development 11, 15
progress
    assessment and recognition of 458
    children's judgment of 465
progression
    benchmark framework for 461–2t
    in fieldwork 259–61, 262–3t
    in geographical enquiry 120–4
    lack of 14
    in local area studies 345
    in map skills 276–7t
    in planning 426, 427–31, 433

sequence for 490–3
see also skills development
proximity regions 406
public enquiry approach, controversial is-
    sues 240
purchase and waste 208t
purchased goods 269t
purposeful teaching 9
purposefully framed play 299, 300

QR codes 286
quality of life 24, 201,
    206t, 393t, 397, 488, 490
quality mark awards 11
Quarternary period 150, 151t
questions/questioning
    in assessment 16
    child-generated 116, 254
    in considering
        geographical significance 46t
    critical 15, 48
    for curriculum making 445
    effective 119–20, 467–70, 478
    in geographical prediction 135–6
    in learning about countries 373–4

rainforests 171, 403–4
real play environments 300t
reality, sense of 389
reasoning skills 286
records/recording
    of assessment outcomes 459
    of curriculum making 444
    for differentiation 454
    of geographical learning 480–2
    in planning 501–2
recycling in school 333, 334
reflection 117, 388, 391
reflective approaches 498
regeneration
    contributing to local (example) 361–2
    studying 186–7
regenerative resources 198–9
Reggio Emilia approach 304
regions
    defined 363–4
    exploring elsewhere in the world 397–406
    studying 362–3, 364–8
    see also continental regions; national
        regions; natural regions
relational awareness 40
relational understanding 5, 40
relationships 21, 37, 134,
    135, 136, 196, 380, 382
renewable resources 198
replicas 269t
reporting learning 480–2
representational play 303t

representations 59, 66, 74, 89,
    359, 382, 414
research
    into learning and teaching 495–504
    into use of the local environment 34
residential environments 75
resilience 251
resistances (children's) 58
resource extraction 149, 187–8
resources 10, 16
    for fieldwork 257
    as a geographical topic 198–9
    in lesson planning 449–50
    for local area studies 359–60, 411–12t
    natural 157
    published/teacher-prepared 324–5
    reliance on published 14
    for studying distant places 418–19
    sustainability and use of 201
    for travel simulations 258
    using appropriate 17
respect 229, 298, 392t
responsibility
    ecological 211–12
    in and for the global community 487–8
    for learning 471, 480
Reynolds, R. 79
risk assessments 256–7
risk concerns 63, 75
risky environments 166
rivers 164–5, 405
    studying (example) 166–7
The River's Story 189–91, 200
road safety 75
Roberts, M. 106, 114, 236, 237, 279, 425
rocks 168
    studying (example) 174
Rokka, A. 166
role play 395, 413
    controversial issues 240
    early geographical learning
        302t, 304, 310
    investigation of migration 228–9
    in sustainability education 210, 241
room use, school buildings 331–2
Rosie's Walk 296
routes 383
    around schools 332
Rowley, C. 108, 109
Roxaboxen 91
rubbish bins, around the school 331
rural children 71, 75, 76
Russia 407
Ryan, A. 445, 449, 452

safe environments 297, 305, 306
safe places 62, 95, 355
Sahara Desert 172, 403

Sahi, I. 414
sameness 387, 416
sandpit activities (forest school) 307
Sargeant, J. 389
Sarra, C. 343
satellite-sourced websites 133, 282–3
satisfaction, with localities 65
Save the Children 234
scaffolding 106, 155, 454, 471
scale(s) 37, 51
    and contexts of locational knowledge
        142–3t
    exploration of places 137–9
    as a geographical topic 176
    and insights into place 134
    on maps 274–5, 281
    numbers and appreciation of 357–8
    using too measure distance 383
schemes of work 425–33
school buildings
    defined 322–3
    exploring 138
    room use 331–2
school and community gardens 212
school environment 329–30
school garden movement 71
school grounds
    children's perspectives on 61–4
    as contexts of locational
        knowledge 142–3t
    exploring 138
    geography of 323
    investigating feelings
        about (example) 328–9
    as learnscapes 318
    mapping with stories (example) 280
    planning for development
        in studies of 431–3
    reasons for studying 319–21
    for understanding regions 365
school inspection reports 12, 13
schools
    accessibility 227
    catchment areas 344–5
    and everyday geographies 317
    investigating geography of 316–37
    as learnscapes 317–19
    physical and social spaces 322–5
    researching 503
    researching children's
        memories of 503–4
    and socialisation 86
science 358t, 359
Scoffham, S. 281, 386, 396, 399, 414
Scotland 6, 12, 510
seasons 164
secondary information sources 359, 360t
secret places 58, 310, 504

Sedgwick, F. 250
sedimentary rock 168
self-assessment 458, 465, 473–4, 481
self-directed learning 8–9
self-esteem 68, 212, 249, 392t, 486
self-evaluation 493, 494–5t
sense of place 36, 40, 51, 58, 62, 64, 68–9,
        73, 127, 134, 306, 342, 350, 504
sensory play 70, 302t
sequencing 454
settlements 176
shallow learning 478, 479t
shapes, on maps 382
sharing learning intentions 466–7
shopping activity 313
shopping area,
        problem-oriented enquiry 353
shopping environments 93–4
short-term planning 449–54
The Silence Seeker 228
similarity(ies) 5, 40, 370, 387, 416
Singapore 6, 294, 299, 478, 488, 511
Six Thinking Hats 118, 244
Skamp, K. 318
skills development 27
    controversial issues and 237
    fieldwork 259–61
    geographical enquiry 112–16
    local area investigations and 341
    school grounds as a context for 321
    spatial 63, 72, 286
    see also geographical skills
snowballing 469
social constructivism 106, 117
social distancing 76
social justice 39, 60, 201, 203, 224–36, 388,
        389, 390t, 392t, 393t, 487
social learning 251
social media 81, 286
social sciences curricula 6, 23–4, 157
socialisation, schools and 86
socio-economic background 76, 80, 83, 371
soils 168
    studying (example) 174
South Africa 6, 20, 511
space 36, 51
    place and 135–6
    understanding of uses of 58
spatial awareness 17, 49, 66, 93, 137, 141,
        286, 385, 495
spatial dimension 34
spatial relationships 135, 136
spatial representation 59, 66, 74
spatial skills 64, 72, 286
spatial technologies 284
spatial understanding 73–4
spiral curriculum 430
Standish, A. 391

statutory frameworks, UK pre-school
    education 25
Stephens, L. 62
stereotypes/stereotyping 13, 81, 82, 104,
    137, 189, 267, 385, 386–8, 388, 410,
    414, 416
stewardship 39, 199, 202, 206
stigmatisation 62
stories
    and encounters with the wider world 5
    examining migration through
        228, 229–30
    learning about the environment 61
    in local and global studies 414
    mapping in the school grounds with
        (example) 280
    stimulating through photographs 266
    sustainability education 210–11
    see also picture stories
storybooks, with maps/plans 280
structured enquiry 109
subject knowledge 11, 20, 174–5, 395
success criteria, sharing 466
successful learners 19
summative assessments 16, 459,
    467, 473, 481, 502
SuperSchemes 450
surveillance 75, 286, 350, 354
sustainability 39, 181, 200–4
    education for 25–6, 96, 197, 199,
        201, 203, 204–11, 215, 341, 390
    environmental impact and 39–40, 51, 112,
        196, 241, 354–5
    hope and the futures
        dimension 214–15
sustainability charters 210
sustainable development 201–2,
    205–6, 390t, 392t, 393t
Sustainable Development
    Education Panel 206
Sustainable Development
    Goals (UN) 197, 202
Sustainable School,
    Sustainable Futures 216
sustainable schools 204–11,
    321, 333–5, 342
Sweden 79, 80, 248
symbols 74, 274, 359, 383, 414, 473

Taiwan 371
Tan, L. 81
Tanner, J. 394, 420
Tapsell, S. 166
task differentiation 453
teacher agency 10
teacher assessment 458
teacher knowledge
    geographical 11, 12–13

of the school's locality 76–7
    see also subject knowledge
teachers
    conception of geological time 155
    curriculum making 10–11, 424, 425
    and high quality learning 444
    lack of in-service education 14
    professional development 11, 15
teaching primary geography
    about place 136–9
    characteristics of good quality 7–12
    choice of activities in 98
    controversial issues 238–41
    enjoying 16–17
    global dimension 394, 395–6
    influences relevant to 18–27
    limitations and opportunities 12–16
    linking assessment and 476–82
    planning see planning
        geography teaching
    quality of 6–7, 505
    researching 495–504
    role of 485
technological skills 41–2
technology see digital technologies; new
        technologies; spatial technologies
television 5, 41, 78, 89, 90, 91, 92, 398
temperate climate 172
temperate grasslands 171, 404
territories 363
texts, exploration of place 129
thematic atlas maps 281
thematic geography see environmental
        geography; human geography; physical
        geography
thinking
    dialogic approach 469–70
    pictorial and symbolic 359
    sustainability as a process of 202
    see also critical thinking; geographical
        thinking; higher order thinking;
        lateral thinking
'three Es' approach 112–15
Throssell, K. 83
Thurston, A. 502
time
    for teaching 15
    see also geological time
time zones 154, 406–8
Titman, W. 61
togetherness 87
tokenism 416
tolerance 229
topicality 44–5, 46, 447–8
tourism 188–9, 369, 373, 401, 405
toy environments 301t
toy play 61
toys 269t

trade 177–8
  investigating (example) 179–80
  see also Fairtrade
trade regions 406
traditional geographical enquiry 107
traffic 207t
trails 279, 286
transgression (children's) 58
transport 177, 232
travel 207t
  bordering/barrier crossing 86
  encounters and awareness of the wider
    world 5, 78
  independent mobility 72–3
  into and out of the country 336–7
  and locational knowledge 80
  simulating in the classroom 258
  studying regions 367, 369
  time zones 407
  to school 335–6
  and tourism 188–9, 369
  visits abroad 89
The Travels of Oggy 140–1
'treasure hunt' activity 314
Treasure Island 280
Trend, R. 154, 155
tropical climate 172
tropical forests 171
tropical grassland 170–1
tropical rainforests 171, 403–4
tropical storms 234
trust 305
tsunamis 234
tundra 170, 171, 404
Turkey 6, 98
Twitter 286, 287
'two stars and a wish' approach 475

UN Convention on the Rights of the
  Child 225
uncertainty(ies) 207t, 393t, 395–6
understanding *see* geographical understanding; intercultural understanding
UNESCO 234
UNICEF 86, 202
United Kingdom
  children's global knowledge 79
  early geographical learning 294
  education for sustainability 201, 206
  national identity 82
  outdoor education 26–7
  see also England; Northern Ireland; Scot-
    land; Wales
United Nations 234, 371
United States
  Dust Bowl 158
  natural hazards 87, 234–5
  primary geography 12

curriculum 6, 20, 24, 362,
  488, 511–12
  outdoor education 26–7
  quality of teaching 6
units of work 434–49
unpopular nations 81
unsafe places 65, 95–6
urban children 70, 71, 75, 166,
  167, 210, 346
Urban Code 214
use/users, of school sites 327–8
Utall, D. 81
values 25, 78, 110, 220, 255,
  386, 390t, 391, 393t
  see also environmental values;
    personal values
values education 241–4
vegetation belts 169–71, 403–5
verbal representations 59
Vinterek, M. 79
virtual communication 413–14
virtual environments 93, 301t
virtual fieldwork 259
virtual games 80, 92–4
visual skills 41, 359
vitality of learning 250
vocabulary 59, 71, 137, 274, 341, 487
volcanoes 168, 234
vulnerable children 86
Wales 6, 11, 25, 251, 510
wall maps 281, 282, 373, 381,
  382, 400, 408
waste, investigating (example) 212
waste ground 69, 75
water 190–3, 207t
water cycle 167
Water School 249
water use 334
wealth 230, 231
weather 37, 136, 164, 305, 329–30, 404
  see also climate change; climate regions;
    climate zones
web sources 133, 282–3, 287, 357
webcams 408
Weeden, P. 469
Wegerif, R. 469
well-being 70, 75, 84, 135, 202, 203, 208(t),
  211–12, 216, 342
We're Going on a Bear Hunt 17, 61
Western Europe 234
Where the Forest meets the Sea 211
whereness 78, 380
Whitley, D. 92
whole-school planning 425–33
Why Geography is Important 24
wider world
  awareness of 57–8, 77–8, 295
  connections to 336

exploration and encounters with 5
impact of 84–5
social justice, geography teaching and
    understanding of 225
young children's sense of 281
Wiegand, P. 60, 78, 79, 271, 275
wild areas 75
Wiliam, D. 464, 465
Willy, T. 414
Window 211, 309
window view (activity) 309
Winnie-the-Pooh 280
wonder, sense of 16, 48, 60,
109, 134, 295, 299
Woolley, R. 236
working at great depth 478, 479t
world

active engagement with 10
children's images of 80–2
conceptions of the 65
concerns about *see* environmental con-
    cerns
connectedness with 297–9
exploring in primary geography 138–9
knowledge of 20, 78–9
see also making sense of the world; wider
    world
The World Came to my Place Today 61
world maps 78, 79, 139, 141, 169, 179, 275,
    281, 359, 381, 405, 408, 441
Worldmapper 283
Young, M. 388, 396
ZeeMaps 285, 409
zone of proximal development (ZPD) 106